The Illustrated Encyclopedia
of
Hinduism

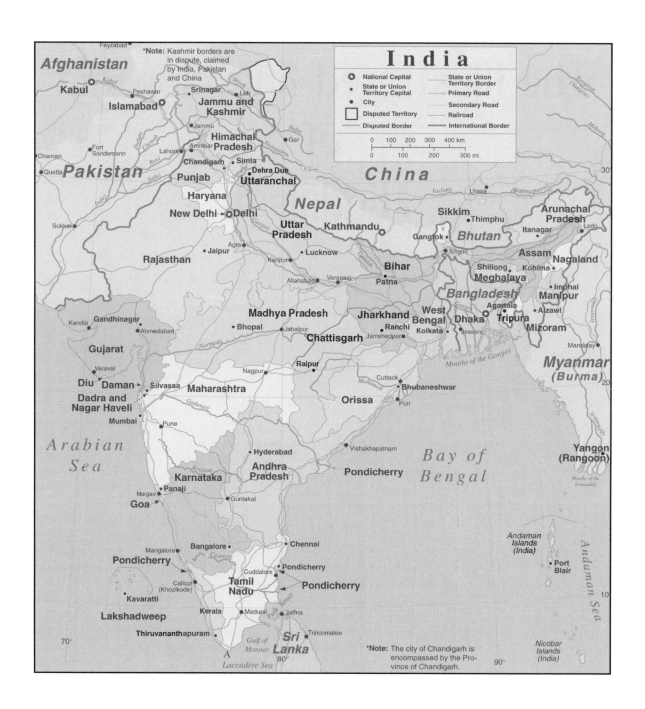

The Illustrated Encyclopedia
of
Hinduism

James G. Lochtefeld, Ph.D.

The Rosen Publishing Group, Inc.
New York

Published in 2002 by The Rosen Publishing Group, Inc.
29 East 21st Street, New York, NY 10010

Copyright © 2002 by James G. Lochtefeld

First Edition

Library of Congress Cataloging-in-Publication Data

Lochtefeld, James G., 1957–
The illustrated encyclopedia of Hinduism/James G. Lochtefeld.
   p. cm.
   Includes bibliographical references and index.
   ISBN 0-8239-2287-1 (set)
   ISBN 0-8239-3179-X (volume 1)
   ISBN 0-8239-3180-3 (volume 2)
   1. Hinduism Encyclopedias. I. Title
BL1105.L63 2002
294.5'03—dc21   99-27747
                                                      CIP

Manufactured in the United States of America

N

Nabhadas

(c. 1600) Author of the *Bhaktamal* ("Garland of Devotees"). In this hagiographic text, he gives short (six line) accounts of the lives of more than two hundred contemporary **bhakti** (devotional) figures, some from personal experience. Although Nabhadas identifies himself as a **Ramanandi**—a devotee (**bhakta**) of the god **Rama**—his work includes devotees of all sectarian persuasions. The text is notably free of marvelous and miraculous events, and Nabhadas emphasizes the devotee's personal qualities, to serve as a model of devotion for others. In many cases the *Bhaktamal* gives the earliest reliable account for these figures, making it an important source for northern Indian literary and religious history. Despite its importance the text cannot be definitively dated, although internal evidence suggests that it was completed early in the seventeenth century.

Nacciyar Tirumoli

One of two collections of poetry composed by the poet-saint **Andal** (9th c.), the other being the *Tirruppavai*. Andal was the only woman among the **Alvars**, a group of twelve poet-saints who lived in southern India between the seventh and tenth centuries. All the Alvars were devotees (**bhakta**) of the god **Vishnu**. Their emphasis on passionate devotion (**bhakti**) to a personal god, conveyed through hymns sung in the **Tamil language**, transformed and revitalized Hindu religious life. Andal's chosen **deity** was **Ranganatha**, the form of Vishnu presiding at the temple of **Shrirangam**. Yet both collections of her poetry are dedicated to **Krishna**, a different form of Vishnu. This seeming divergence may reflect her conviction that all manifestations of Vishnu are ultimately the same or indicate the difference between personal devotion and literary expression.

The thirty poems in the *Nacciyar Tirumoli* are told by a group of unmarried girls, who have taken a vow to bathe in the river at dawn during the coldest month of the year. This vow has a long history in southern India, where young girls would take the oath to gain a good husband and a happy married life. In the poem, the girls have taken the vow to gain Krishna as their husband. The poems in the cycle describe various features of the natural world at dawn, the girls' hopes in performing the vow, and their return to Krishna's house to awaken him and beg for his **grace**. The final poem in the series describes the benefits gained by one who chants the text.

Nachiketas

A primary character in the **Kathka Upanishad**, a speculative philosophical text considered one of the later **upanishads**. In the text, the boy Nachiketas is the seeker of ultimate wisdom. In a fit of anger his father curses him to be given to Death; Nachiketas obediently goes to the house of Death to give himself up. He waits for three days at Death's door, but receives none of the hospitality due to a **brahmin** guest. When Death returns he is disturbed to discover that his guest has been neglected. To atone for the lapse, Death offers Nachiketas three boons. With his first two, Nachiketas wishes to return to his father and to understand the meaning of a particular sacrificial ritual. With the final boon he asks what happens to a person after the death of the body. Death first tries to evade the question, then tries to bribe Nachiketas with other gifts. When the boy holds firm in his resolve, Death begins to reveal his secrets. This discourse makes up the bulk of the text. Death's secrets focus mainly on the reality of the Self (**atman**), its eternal and indestructible nature, and the difficulties in truly knowing it. The Self is portrayed as the ultimate truth, and to know it is to know the only thing that really matters.

Nadi

("tube") In general, the word *nadi* may be applied to any pipe or tube, whether in plumbing or the human circulatory system. A nadi has a more specialized meaning with regard to the Hindu conception of the **subtle body**. The subtle body is an alternate physiological system, existing on a different plane than gross matter, but corresponding to the material body. It consists of six psychic centers (**chakras**), visualized as multipetaled lotus flowers running roughly along the spine, connected by three vertical channels known as nadis. Of these, the **ida nadi** is on the left side, the **pingala nadi** on the right, and the **sushumna** in the center.

Naga

("naked") The general term for any fighting or militant **ascetic**. Ascetic orders traditionally chartered companies of fighting ascetics to protect the members and their resources. The Naga orders of the **Dashanami Sanyasis** were devotees (**bhakta**) of the god **Shiva**, whereas the **Bairagi** orders were devotees of the god **Vishnu**. In northern India during the eighteenth century these Naga ascetics developed into dynamic military and mercantile powerhouses. In several instances, Naga ascetics managed to carve out petty kingdoms of their own. In many other instances, they had significant influence in the northern Indian economy and politics, whether in their own right or as mercenary soldiers in the service of a reigning monarch. Their name was a literal description of their practices, since many of these ascetics would go into battle bearing only their weapons. Their ash-smeared bodies and flying matted hair presented a fearsome sight. As Indian social and political circumstances have changed, their military importance has faded. However, these organizations (**akhara**) of Naga ascetics still exist, although they are most important now in determining the order for bathing (**snana**) at the **Kumbha Mela**. The accounts of the ascetics themselves are full of tales of strife along sectarian lines (**Shaivas** versus **Vaishnavas**); a good indication that the Shaivas gained superiority is that they have priority in the bathing at the Kumbha Melas. For further information see Jadunath Sarkar, *A History of the Dasanami Naga Sanyasis*, 1958; David Lorenzen, "Warrior Ascetics in Indian History," in *Journal of the American Oriental Society*, Vol. 98, No. 1, 1978; and James G. Lochtefeld, "The Vishva Hindu Parishad and the Roots of Hindu Militancy," in *Journal of the American Academy of Religion*, Vol. LXII, No. 2, 1994.

Naga

(2) In Hindu mythology, the Nagas are a class of minor divinities who have the form of serpents. Their king is **Vasuki**. In popular Hinduism, Nagas are often considered to be the gods of a specific place. Often associated with fertility and fecundity, Nagas are usually believed to live in springs, ponds, and other small bodies of **water**. In Buddhist and Jain iconography the Nagas often play the role of minor protective **deities**. It is common to see a seated figure shadowed by an "umbrella" of Nagas. Although this is unusual in Hindu iconography, there may be remnants of this in the iconography of the god **Shiva**, who is often depicted wearing snakes for both his ornaments and his **sacred thread**.

Nagara

One of the three developed styles in medieval Hindu temple **architecture**, along with the **Dravida** and the **Veshara**.

Built in the Nagara style, the Triloknath Temple in Mandi consists of a series of towers, the largest of which contains an image of the presiding deity.

The Nagara style is found throughout northern and eastern India. One of its prominent features is a **shikhara** or tower. The shikhara is often surrounded by smaller towers that lead the eye up to the highest point, which is directly over the image of the temple's primary **deity**. Within this general pattern there are two variants, exemplified by the temples at **Khajuraho** and **Orissa**.

In Khajuraho the series of shikharas are connected, forming a continuous rising swell that draws the eye upward, similar to a series of hills leading to a distant peak. This verticality is accentuated through the use of turrets (**urushringas**) on the sides of the towers, which replicate the shape of the final peak. The entire temple is set on a raised base (**adhishthana**). Within the temple there are usually several different zones: an entrance porch (**ardhamandapa**), a hall (**mandapa**), an intermediate area (**antarala**), and a central shrine (**garbhagrha**) surrounded by a processional path (**pradakshina**). Despite their different parts, temples built in the Khajuraho style convey the artistic impression of an integrated, unified whole.

The Orissan style emphasizes the contrast between the temple's constituent parts. The two central components are the entrance hall (**jagamohan**) and the beehive-shaped temple tower (**deul**). The tower is often three or four times taller than the entrance hall, a difference that tends to heighten the contrast between the two. Other sections include a dance-hall (**natamandira**), traditionally used for performances, and a "food pavilion" (**bhogamandapa**), where the **prasad** was cooked. These architectural elements are connected like beads on a string, as seemingly separable parts lined up with one another. The most important temples in the Orissan style are the **Lingaraja Temple** in **Bhubaneshvar**, the **Jagannath** temple in **Puri**, and the **Sun Temple** at **Konarak**.

Nageshvar

Temple and sacred site (**tirtha**) about fifteen miles northeast of the holy city of **Dwaraka**, in the eastern state of **Gujarat**. The temple is named after its presiding **deity**, the god **Shiva** in his manifestation as the "Lord of Serpents." Shiva is present at Nageshvar in the form of a **linga**, a pillar-shaped image. The Nageshvar linga is one of the twelve **jyotirlingas**, a network of sites at which Shiva is uniquely present. Nageshvar's charter myth is based on the story of the demon Daruk and his wife Daruka. Daruka is a fervent devotee (**bhakta**) of Shiva's wife **Parvati**; through Parvati's **grace** Daruka gains protection for all the other **demons**. The demons use this power to oppress the righteous. As the demons are about to kill one of Shiva's devotees, Shiva appears and slays them. Parvati has come along with Shiva to protect Daruka, her devotee. Daruka persuades Shiva and Parvati to remain in Nageshvar as a sign of their **grace**. Since the city of Dwaraka is also connected with the god **Krishna**, some scholars believe the Nageshvar linga may have been promoted to maintain a Shaivite presence in an important **Vaishnava** area.

Nag Panchami

Festival falling on the fifth day (panchami) of the bright, waxing half of the **lunar month** of **Shravan** (July–August). This day is devoted to the **worship** of serpents, whether as **Nagas**—the minor **deities** who take the form of snakes—or actual cobras and other snakes. On this day the images of the Naga deities are bathed and given **offerings**. Offerings are also made to real serpents. On this day people refrain from digging in the earth, since snakes live there.

This rite occurs on the fifth day because in astrology (**jyotisha**), the guardian deity for this day is **Shesha**, the god **Vishnu's** serpent couch. This festival falls at the beginning of the rainy **season**, when the rising waters caused by the **monsoon** rains often drive snakes out of their dens, and at times into peoples' homes and gardens. The rainy season is also the time for growing crops; snakes pose a real danger for people working in the fields. According to one estimate, 10,000 Indians die from snakebites every year. According to popular belief, observing this rite will protect one from snakebites for the entire year. This observance is a protective ritual, marking the advent of a dangerous time for many villagers.

Nagpur

City in the eastern state of **Maharashtra**. Nagpur is the birthplace of the Hindu nationalist organization known as the **Rashtriya Svayamsevak Sangh**. The organization was formed in 1925 by **Dr. K. B. Hedgewar** and still maintains its headquarters in Nagpur.

Nahusha

In Hindu mythology, a king of the lunar dynasty, and a paradigm for a person afflicted with self-pride. Through amassing religious merits, Nahusha succeeds to the throne of **Indra**, the king of the gods, who has gone into hiding because of an evil deed. Nahusha is filled with lust for Indra's wife, **Indrani**. He tries to act on it despite the obvious improprieties of approaching another man's wife and a mortal making a claim on a goddess. Nahusha sets off for Indrani's palace in a **palanquin**. In his impatience, he whips the palanquin bearers, saying "Sarpa, sarpa" ("Move! Move!"). Unfortunately for Nahusha, one of the bearers is **Agastya**, the sage. For Nahusha's lust and disrespect, Agastya curses him to become a snake (sarpa). Nahusha remains a serpent for many years but is released from the **curse** by the sight of the **Pandava** brothers.

Nai

Traditional Indian society was modeled as a collection of **endogamous**, or inter-married, subgroups known as **jatis** ("birth"). Jatis were organized (and their social status determined) by the group's hereditary occupation, over which the group held a monopoly. The Nai jati's occupation was barbering, a low status job because it required continual contact with cut human hair, considered a source of impurity (ashaucha). In many instances the Nais also served as messengers.

Naimisha

City and sacred site (**tirtha**) in the state of **Uttar Pradesh**, about fifty miles northwest of the city of Lucknow. In the later sectarian literature known as the **puranas**, Naimisha is described as a forest. Today the city's major attraction is a spring-fed bathing (**snana**) pool named Chakra Tirtha. According to tradition, this bathing pool contains **water** from all the holy places of India, and thus is the best place for pious Hindus to take a holy bath.

Naimittika Karma

("occasional [ritual] action") One of three general types of ritual action, the others being **nitya karma** and **kamya karma**. Naimittika karma rites follow a particular cause (naimittika); when particular circumstances arise, one is required to perform the ritual. For example, when a child is born, certain rites must be performed. However, the ritual is not required unless a birth has taken place.

Naina Devi

Presiding **deity** of the Naina Devi temple in the **Shiwalik Hills** in the state of **Himachal Pradesh**, and one of the nine **Shiwalik goddesses**. Naina Devi's temple is located on a mountaintop close to the border of **Punjab**. It is nine miles from Anandpur Sahib, a famous Sikh place of pilgrimage, and about one mile from Nangal village. The greatest pilgrimage traffic occurs during festivals held on the eighth day in each half of the **lunar month** of **Shravan**, and also during the first nine days of the month of **Ashvin**, when the **Navaratri** festival takes place.

According to the temple's charter myth, Naina Devi is one of the **Shakti Pithas**, a network of sites sacred to the **Goddess** which spreads throughout the subcontinent. Each Shakti Pitha marks the site where a body part of the dismembered goddess **Sati** fell to earth, taking form there as a different goddess; **Naina Devi** was Sati's eyes (naina). As with many of the other Shiwalik goddesses, the images in Naina Devi's temple are self-manifested (**svayambhu** images) outcrops of stone. In a different version of the myth, the images were discovered by a herdsman named Naina, who heeded the command of the Goddess to build a temple for her. For further information see Kathleen Erndl, *Victory to the Mother*, 1993. See also **pitha**.

Naisthika

("fixed") A person who takes a vow to remain a perpetual religious student (**brahmacharin**), keeping lifelong vows of **celibacy**, austerity, study, and service to his or her religious preceptor (**guru**).

Naivedya

("to be presented") The thirteenth of the sixteen traditional **upacharas** ("offerings") given to a **deity** as part of **worship**. To treat the deity as an honored guest, a person may offer food. The food is often returned to the worshipers as **prasad**, the sanctified food bearing the deity's **grace**. The offering may be done in various ways, but the underlying motive for all the upacharas is to show one's love for the deity and attend to the deity's needs.

Naiyayika

Term for a follower of the **Nyaya** and **Vaisheshika** philosophical schools, two of the **six schools** in Hindu **philosophy**. After the early centuries of the common era, the Nyaya and Vaisheshika schools merged, as did the **Samkhya** and **Yoga schools** and the **Mimamsa** and **Vedanta schools**. The term Naiyayika is used to denote a follower of the combined Nyaya-Vaisheshika school of philosophy.

Nakshatra

In Indian astrology (**jyotisha**), a nakshatra is one of the twenty-seven signs in the lunar **zodiac**. In a single **lunar month** the **moon** moves through each of the twenty-seven lunar houses. The territory for these lunar houses is divided equally throughout the solar zodiac—with 2.25 lunar houses for each of the twelve solar signs. The nakshatras are important in Indian astrology, partly because they change quite rapidly, but also because the character and qualities associated with each nakshatra are believed to color the time period in which they fall. One group of five nakshatras, the **Panchak Nakshatra**, is considered extremely **inauspicious**; many activities will be curtailed until this period has passed. Certain nakshatras are judged to be incompatible with certain everyday activities, which should be avoided during that time. Hindus who pay attention to astrology are keenly aware of the passage of time and the quality of each moment.

Nakula

In the *Mahabharata*, the later of the two great Hindu epics, Nakula is the fourth of the five **Pandava** brothers, the epic's antagonists. Nakula's mother, **Madri**, is the younger wife of King **Pandu**. None of the Pandava brothers are actually Pandu's sons, since he has been cursed to die the moment he holds his wife in amorous embrace. Instead, they are magically created through the effect of a **mantra** given to Madri's co-wife, **Kunti**, by the sage **Durvasas**. The mantra gives the woman who recites it the power to call down any of the gods to conceive a son who will be as powerful as the god himself. With Pandu's blessing Kunti teaches the mantra to Madri. She meditates on the **Ashvins**, the divine twins who are the physicians of the gods. Thus, she bears twins. As the sons of the physicians of the gods, both Nakula and **Sahadeva** are skilled healers of **animals** and human beings. Although Nakula and Sahadeva are among the five Pandava brothers, they are less important to the *Mahabharata* than their three elder siblings.

Nala

In Hindu mythology, the King of Nishadas and the husband of **Damayanti**. The story of Nala and **Damayanti** appears as a story within the *Mahabharata*, the later of the two great Hindu epics. It is recounted to the five **Pandava** brothers, the epic's protagonists, during their twelve year exile in the forest, as a way to keep up their spirits by telling how others have transcended misfortune.

When Damayanti is old enough to marry, her father sends invitations to the kings of the earth, announcing her **svayamvara**, a rite in which Damayanti will choose her husband. The kings of the earth come to the svayamvara to seek her hand, as do the gods (**devas**) themselves. Yet Damayanti has already decided to choose Nala after being advised by a swan who praises him. The gods try to foil this by taking on the physical appearance of Nala, so that Damayanti will not be able to tell the difference between them. As a last resort, Damayanti makes an **act of truth**, a ritual action whose efficacy is based on the power of truth. In her act of truth, Damayanti declares that she has never loved anyone but Nala. To prove that this statement is true, she directs the gods to resume their true forms. Compelled by the power of truth, the gods immediately do as she commands. Nala and Damayanti are married, and as a reward for her fidelity, the gods give Nala various divine gifts. Hearing of the marriage, two of the rejected suitors curse Nala to lose his kingdom. Because of the **curse**, Nala and Damayanti are separated and suffer long tribulations, which include Nala having his body magically changed so that no one is able to recognize him. In the end Damayanti recognizes him by his divine powers, which cannot be hidden, and the lovers are happily reunited. See also **truth, power of**.

Naladiyar

One of the most important pieces of early Tamil literature, along with its predecessor, the *Tirukkural*. The Naladiyar is a collection of four hundred verses that date from the fifth or sixth century. Mainly concerned with moral and ethical life, the verses were written by a group of Jain monks who found shelter with a pious king in time of famine. In gratitude each monk wrote one verse. Despite the *Naladiyar*'s sectarian origin, it has become the cultural property of Tamils from all religious communities; many of the verses have come into the language as proverbial sayings.

Nalayira Divyaprabandham

("The Four Thousand Divine Compositions") Title for the collected

Namakarana samskara being performed on an infant, who in this photo is wrapped in cloth for protection from the evil eye.

hymns of the **Alvars**, compiled in the tenth century by **Nathamuni**. The Alvars were a group of twelve poet-saints who lived in southern India between the seventh and tenth centuries. All the Alvars were devotees (**bhakta**) of the god **Vishnu** and emphasized passionate devotion (**bhakti**) to a personal god, conveyed through hymns sung in the **Tamil language**. Their collected hymns were popularly known as the "Tamil Veda." They carry Vedic authority for many southern Indian Vaishnavas, particularly the **Shrivaishnava** school, which applied more developed philosophical articulation to these devotional ideas. See also **Veda**.

Namakarana ("name-giving") Samskara

The fifth of the traditional life-cycle ceremonies (**samskaras**), during which the newborn child is given a name. Although some commentators believe that this rite should be done on the day of **birth**, many others insist that it should be on the tenth day, indicating a difference between birth and the social ritual of name-giving. Some believe that the child's name should begin with the first letter of the **nakshatra** (sign in the lunar **zodiac**) in which the child is born; this practice is still widespread in northern India. Although the classical form of this rite has largely fallen into disuse, naming ceremonies are still an important part of the birth of a child.

Namarupa

Literally, this word means "name [and physical] form," two of the most identifiable and enduring aspects of a person. In philosophical discourse, the term *namarupa* is often used pejoratively to designate all aspects of personality that are ultimately ephemeral but help reinforce the illusion of a diverse world and a Self with an independent identity. These notions of independence are thought to be ultimately false since one's name and form will be different in one's next **birth**. In this context, namarupa designates all that is provisionally real.

Namaskara

("reverential salutation") Both a phrase and a **gesture** used to greet another person respectfully. The gesture is done by joining both palms, pointing the fingers up, with the base of the thumbs touching the chest. Namaskara is the fourteenth of sixteen traditional **upacharas** ("**offerings**") given to a **deity** as part of **worship**, treating the deity as an honored guest. In this action, the deity is given a gesture of respect, which can take a variety of forms: joining the palms with the fingers pointing upward (**anjali hasta**), kneeling and touching one's head to the floor, or a full prostration (**dandavat pranam**). The underlying motive for all the upacharas is to show one's respect and love for the deity by ministering to the deity's needs.

Nambudiri

Southern Indian **brahmin** community, which is a sub-division of the **Dravida** brahmins, one of five southern Indian brahmin communities (**Pancha Dravida**). The Nambudiris' traditional homeland is in the region that is now the modern state of **Kerala**. The Nambudiris are noted throughout India for their learning and piety. According to tradition, the great philosopher **Shankaracharya** was a Nambudiri brahmin. In his desire to revitalize Hindu religion, Shankaracharya reportedly chose one Hindu sacred center in each corner of the subcontinent, and at each established a **Dashanami Sanyasi** monastic center (**math**) to train learned monks. One of these sacred centers was at **Badrinath** in the **Himalayas**. According to the Badrinath temple records, for several hundred years the temple **worship** was performed by the **Dandi Sanyasis**, who were also Nambudiri brahmins. When the last of these died without a successor in 1776, the local king, who served as the protector of the shrine, invited a non-**ascetic** Nambudiri brahmin to serve as the temple's priest. This priest was given the title **rawal** ("deputy"), and his extended family has maintained the shrine since then. The rawal was the only person allowed to touch the image of the presiding **deity**. As a consequence he was required to remain a bachelor, lest the ritual impurity arising from the **birth** of a child (**sutakashaucha**) render him unable to attend to his duties. For a long time the rawals had sole rights to the **offerings** given at the shrine, but since 1939 the temple has been managed by a committee, and the rawal has been restricted to ritual duties.

Namdev

(1270–1350?) Poet-saint who is one of the great figures in the **Varkari Panth**, a religious community centered around the **worship** of the Hindu god **Vithoba**, at his temple in **Pandharpur** in the modern state of **Maharashtra**. According to tradition, Namdev was a cotton-printer, considered a low-status occupation, but the strength of his devotion rendered his worldly status irrelevant. He is said to have been an associate of **Jnaneshvar** and **Chokamela**, two other Varkari poet-saints. His songs have been preserved in several different collections, including the **Adigranth** (compiled by the Sikh community) and the **Panchvani** (a collection of songs by five poets compiled by the **Dadupanth**). For traditional information about his life, see G. A. Deleury, *The Cult of Vithoba*, 1960; and Justin E. Abbott and Narhar R. Godbole (trans.), *Stories of Indian Saints*, 1982. For a more critical look at his Hindu songs and the difficulties using them as biographical sources, see Winand Callewaert and Mukund Lath, *The Hindi Padavali of Namdev*, 1989.

Nammalvar

(10th c.) The most prolific composer of all the **Alvars**, a group of twelve poet-saints who lived in southern India between the seventh and tenth centuries. All the Alvars were devotees (**bhakta**) of the god **Vishnu**. They emphasized passionate devotion (**bhakti**) to a personal god, conveyed through hymns sung in the **Tamil language**, which transformed and revitalized Hindu religious life. According to tradition, Nammalvar was born into a princely family, but was completely disinterested with life in the world. His distraught parents eventually abandoned him. Nammalvar crawled into the hollow of a giant tamarind tree, where he sat in silent meditation. He remained there until the arrival of his disciple **Mathurakavi**, who managed to rouse him by posing a question on the nature of the Self. Nammalvar immediately poured

forth more than one thousand hymns to Vishnu, each beginning with the last word of the previous hymn. These hymns are known as the *Tiruvaymoli* ("holy words"). This collection of 1,102 stanzas is the concluding section of the *Nalayira Divyaprabandham*, the collected hymns of the Alvars. For further information see Kamil Zvelebil, *Tamil Literature*, 1975; John Stirling Morley Hooper, *Hymns of the Alvars*, 1929; A. Shrinivasa Raghavan, *Nammalvar*, 1975; and A. K. Ramanujan, *Hymns for the Drowning*, 1981.

Nanak Jayanti

Celebration falling on the **full moon** in the **lunar month** of **Kartik** (October–November). This day is celebrated as the birthday of the first Sikh **guru**, Guru Nanak, and is celebrated largely by members of the Sikh community.

Nanda

In Hindu mythology, the god **Krishna's** foster father, who cares for Krishna as his own child after Krishna is placed in his care. Nanda is described as the headman of the village. Under his care Krishna lives a comfortable, if simple, life. In Krishna's mythology, Nanda is a less important figure than Krishna's foster mother, **Yashoda**.

Nanda Devi

Nanda Devi is the name for one of the tallest mountains in India, rising over 25,000 feet, in the Kumaon region of the **Himalayas**. Nanda Devi is also a form of the **Goddess** who is identified with that mountain. With Nanda Devi, as for many of the other **goddesses** of India, divinity and the natural landscape are inextricably connected. Nanda Devi is a local Himalayan goddess who presides over the **Garhwal** and Kumaon regions. People in the region consider her to be a "daughter" of the region, who had to change her residence when she married the god **Shiva**. Nanda Devi's songs and rites show strong connections with the

Statue of Nandi, the bull who is the god
Shiva's vehicle.

life-cycle journeys of Himalayan **women**. Songs associated with Nanda Devi describe the difficulty of going from her natal home to her marital home, a reality for many Himalayan women. In the same way, Nanda Devi's pilgrimages, which emphasize journeys through the hills surrounding the mountain, imitate the women's periodic journeys back to their own natal villages. A major part of Nanda Devi's mythology is the adoption of an abandoned buffalo calf, which is later discovered to be a **demon** in buffalo form. The buffalo demon grows large and troublesome, and is eventually slain by Nanda Devi. This myth parallels the narrative in the ***Devimahatmya***, the earliest and most important source for the mythology of the Goddess; this is the most influential text used in Nanda Devi's **worship**. For further information on Nanda Devi, her rites, and her connection with Himalayan society, see William Sax, *Mountain Goddess*, 1991.

Nanddas

(late 16th c.) One of the **ashtachap**, a group of eight northern Indian **bhakti** (devotional) poets. The compositions of these eight poets were used for liturgical purposes by the **Pushti Marg**, a religious community whose members are devotees (**bhakta**) of **Krishna**. In the Pushti Marg's sectarian literature, all eight are also named as members of the community, and as associates of either the community's founder, **Vallabhacharya**, or his successor, **Vitthalnath**. Very little is known about his life, but he is mentioned in the ***Bhaktamal***, a collection of lives of the saints written by **Nabhadas** in the seventeenth century. Like all the poetry associated with the Pushti Marg, Nanddas's poetry focused on devotion to Krishna. His two most important works, written in elegant poetry, are extended poems on the **ras lila** and **Uddhava's** message. Both of these themes date back to the ***Bhagavata Purana*** (10th c.?), the most important text for Krishna devotionalism. These have been translated by R. S. McGregor, *The Round Dance of Krishna and Uddhav's Message*, 1973.

Nandi

("joy," "delight") Epithet of the animal vehicle of the god **Shiva**, which takes the form of a **bull**. Like all of the animal vehicles, it symbolizes the **deity**. Nandi is not only Shiva's vehicle, but his devotee (**bhakta**). Statues of Nandi are often sculpted outside Shiva temples (usually facing the image) as a way of marking the site as sacred to Shiva. He appears in many places in Shiva's mythology, but usually as a devoted underling advancing Shiva's purposes, rather than an independent agent with a purpose and ends of his own.

Nandigrama

In the ***Ramayana***, the earlier of the two great Hindu epics, Nandigrama is a village outside the city of **Ayodhya**, where Prince **Bharata** sets up the royal court during his brother **Rama's** absence. Bharata's mother **Kaikeyi** uses her influence to banish Rama for fourteen years, putting Bharata on the throne in his place. At Rama's command, Bharata agrees to act as the temporary king, but with two symbolic adjustments. The first is that Bharata moves the royal court from the capital city of Ayodhya to the village of Nandigrama, as a symbol of Rama's exile; the second is that throughout his regency, Bharata sits at the foot of the royal throne, upon which is placed a pair of Rama's sandals, symbolizing that Rama is the rightful ruler. Thus, Nandigrama is a symbol of Bharata's righteousness.

Narada

A famous sage in Hindu mythology, equally renowned for his qualities as a musician and as a gossip. Narada plays a stringed instrument known as the **vina**, serving as the bard to the gods. His ambition as a musician apparently exceeds his actual skill, since several of his mythic stories describe him being humbled. In his capacity as wandering musician, he also conveys news and gossip. In many cases Narada's newsbearing is the vehicle advancing the plot in a story. According to one famous story, he requests that **Vishnu** give a demonstration of his **magic** (**maya**). Vishnu sends him to a nearby farmhouse for some water, where Narada meets an enchantingly beautiful woman. Forgetting all about his errand, the two fall in love, are married, and have several children. After several years of wedded bliss, severe floods wash away his home and drown his family. As he mourns his loss, he finds himself back on the side of road with Vishnu, who is still asking him to go to the farmhouse to get some water.

Narada Smrti

One of the **smrtis** or "remembered" texts, a class of literature deemed important, but less authoritative than the other textual category, the **shrutis** or "heard" texts. This smrti is ascribed to the sage **Narada**, and is an example of one of the **Dharma Shastras**, which were manuals prescribing rules for correct human behavior and ideal social life. Unlike the **Dharma Sutras**, which are ascribed to recognizable individuals, the Dharma Shastras are usually ascribed to mythic sages, a strategy used to reinforce the authority of these texts. The *Narada Smrti* exists in several versions, one of which is much longer than the others. All of the versions were written later than the **Manu Smrti** (1st c. B.C.E.?), since this text is mentioned in the preface. Narada's text deals exclusively with the administration of justice (vyavahara), and treats this in exhaustive detail, with a strong emphasis on clarity and precision.

Narak Chaturdashi

Religious observance falling on the fourteenth day (chaturdashi) of the dark, waning half of the **lunar month** of **Kartik** (October–November). People who observe this day **worship** and make **offerings** to the god **Yama**. In the evening they light a lamp in his name. Yama is the lord of the underworld and the judge of the dead; he reviews the deeds of the dead and inflicts punishment upon people for their misdeeds. Those who faithfully observe Narak Chaturdashi are believed to be spared from the torments of **hell**.

Nara-Narayana

In Hindu mythology, two of the **sons** of the god **Dharma**; through their **ascetic** practices (**tapas**) these two boys became sages. The place where they performed their **asceticism** is believed to have been in the region of **Badrinath**. The duo are still associated with the charter myths for that place.

Narasimha ("Man-Lion") Avatar

Fourth **avatar** or incarnation of the god **Vishnu**, in which he appears as a figure with the head and shoulders of a **lion**, but the torso and lower body of a man. As with all of Vishnu's avatars, this appearance comes at a moment when the cosmos is in crisis, and decisive divine action is needed to restore cosmic equilibrium. See **Man-Lion avatar**.

Narasimha Jayanti

Religious observance falling on the fourteenth day of the bright, waxing half of the **lunar month** of Baisakh (April–May). This day is celebrated as the birthday of **Vishnu's** fourth **avatar**, Narasimha, although his birthday is different from those of Vishnu's human avatars. Narasimha is not human, but a creature with the head and shoulders of a **lion**, and the torso and lower body of a man. He is not born in the usual sense, but bursts forth fully formed from a pillar, to destroy the **demon Hiranyakashipu** and to protect his devotee (**bhakta**) **Prahlada**. See also **Man-Lion avatar**.

Narasimhavarman I

(r. 630–668) **Pallava dynasty** ruler during its most vibrant era, when it was a stronghold of Tamil culture. Narasimhavarman succeeded his father **Mahendravarman**, who had been killed in a battle with the forces of the **Chalukya** king **Pulakeshin II**. Narasimhavarman avenged his father's death by conquering the Chalukya kingdom and killing Pulakeshin II in battle, but the two kingdoms were so evenly matched that neither could retain control over the other. Like his father, Narasimhavarman was a great patron of the arts. It was during his reign that construction commenced on the great sculptures at **Mahabalipuram** in the state of **Tamil Nadu**. The most famous of these is a rock-cut **sculpture** depicting the myth of the Descent of the **Ganges**, in which a natural vertical fissure is used to lay out the river's path.

Narasimhavarman II

(r. 700–728) **Pallava dynasty** ruler during the dynasty's most vibrant era, when it was a stronghold of Tamil culture. Like all the great Pallava monarchs, Narasimhavarman II was a great patron of the arts. During his reign there was continued construction of the monuments at **Mahabalipuram** in the state of **Tamil Nadu**.

Narayana

Epithet of the god **Vishnu**. The name is traditionally interpreted as meaning "resting on the waters," based on the claim that the word *nara*, which usually means "man," in this case means "waters." Narayana is the image of Vishnu in the time of cosmic dissolution (**pralaya**). He is reclining on his serpent couch, **Shesha**, in the midst of the cosmic sea, with his wife, **Lakshmi**, seated at his feet, and his vehicle, **Garuda**, standing by. Vishnu is the sole remaining agent in the cosmos, as its beginning and end. When the time for a new creation arrives, a lotus sprouts forth from Narayana's navel, which opens to reveal the creator-god **Brahma**. The cycle of creation begins anew.

Narayana Bhatta

(1513–1570?) The most celebrated scholar and commentator on the **dharma literature** of his time, and the patriarch of a scholarly family. **Narayana's** father had migrated from the city of **Paithan**, in central India, to **Benares**, a center of **Sanskrit** learning. Narayana's work fell mainly in the class of commentarial literature known as **nibandhas** ("collections"), which were compilations of Hindu lore. Nibandha compilers collected references on a particular theme from the **Vedas**, dharma literature, **puranas**, and other authoritative religious texts, and then compiled these excerpts into a single volume. Aside from his unparalleled command of these traditional texts, Narayana was also noted for his learned interpretation and commentary; to these texts, he applied the rules that the **Purva Mimamsa** philosophical school had originally developed to interpret the Vedas, the oldest Hindu religious texts. According to tradition, he was a man whose personal holiness was equal to his great learning. He is reported to have performed a miracle by causing rain to fall out of **season**, convincing the Muslim officials ruling Benares to allow the **Vishvanath** temple to be rebuilt.

Narmada River

Central Indian river that has its source at the sacred site (**tirtha**) of **Amarkantak** in the state of **Madhya Pradesh**, and flows almost directly west through the state of **Gujarat**, then to the Arabian Sea. The Narmada is one of the few central Indian rivers flowing from east to west; rivers further south are channeled east by the upthrust of the highlands known as the Western Ghats. It is traditionally considered one of the seven sacred rivers of India, along with the **Ganges**, **Yamuna**, **Godavari**, **Saraswati**, **Indus**, and **Cauvery**. An important site on the Narmada is **Omkareshvar**, one of the twelve **jyotirlingas**, a network of sites sacred to the god **Shiva**. During the 1990s the Narmada has become a rallying point for environmentalists who have opposed construction of several massive dams, on the grounds that these dams have displaced too many people and destroyed too much prime farmland. Although work on these dams has continued, the pace has slowed. In 1997 a minor earthquake in the Narmada basin prompted the call for further consideration of this project's environmental dangers.

Narsi Mehta

(16th c.) **Gujarati** poet-saint who was a well-known figure in northern Indian devotional life. Narsi was a devotee (**bhakta**) of the god **Krishna**. His poetry describes the love affair between Krishna and his consort **Radha**.

According to tradition, Narsi's poetry was rooted in a vision of Krishna's **ras lila**, or great circle **dance**, in which Narsi was privileged to stand as attendant holding a torch to light the **lila**. Narsi is one of the devotees profiled in the **Bhaktamal**, a text that gives short biographical profiles of more than 200 devotional (**bhakti**) saints; in the text Narsi is portrayed as a paradigm of generosity, an earthly imitation of Krishna himself. For further information see John Stratton Hawley, "Morality Beyond Morality in the Lives of Three Hindu Saints," in John Stratton Hawley (ed.), *Saints and Virtues*, 1987.

Nasik

City and sacred site (**tirtha**) near the headwaters of the **Godavari** River in the state of **Maharashtra**, about 100 miles northeast of Bombay. Nasik is one of the four sites for the **Kumbha Mela**, a religious bathing (**snana**) festival. Nasik hosts this festival every twelve years. Nasik is an important bathing place and is a center of pilgrimage, piety, and learning. According to tradition the god-king **Rama**, his wife, **Sita**, and his brother, **Lakshmana** lived during much of their twelve years in exile in the nearby village of **Panchavati**. Rama, Sita, and Lakshmana are central characters in the *Ramayana*, the earlier of the two great Hindu epics. Although claims of them living near Nasik are impossible to prove or disprove, the legend adds one more layer of sanctity to the site.

Nasik Mela

The Nasik Mela is the celebration of the **Kumbha Mela** at Nasik. The Kumbha Mela is a religious festival celebrated in four different locations: **Haridwar**, **Allahabad**, **Ujjain**, and **Nasik**. The festival's focus is bathing (**snana**) in the sacred rivers during particularly holy moments. The Kumbha Mela's primary participants are **ascetics**, who come from all over southern Asia to bathe in the sacred waters. According to tradition, the Kumbha Mela was organized by the great philosopher **Shankaracharya** to promote regular gatherings of learned and holy men, as a means to strengthen, sustain, and spread the Hindu religion. The timing for each of these festivals is determined by the position of the **sun** and the **planet Jupiter**; the twelve years between these festivals correspond to Jupiter's orbit. The Nasik Mela is celebrated during the **lunar month** of **Shravan** (July–August), when the planet Jupiter is in the sign of Leo. This is the least important of all four Kumbha Melas, attended mostly by ascetics.

Nastika

("nihilists") In Hindu philosophical discourse, this was a pejorative term to denigrate certain other religious and philosophical schools. The name *Nastika* was applied to groups who denied the three most basic principles of religion: the authority of the **Vedas** as religious texts, the eternal existence of the soul (**atman**), and the value of religious life in general. In context this term could be applied to the Jains (who denied the first of these three) to the Buddhists (who denied the first and the second) or to the **materialist** philosophical school (which denied all three).

Natal Horoscope

In Indian culture, a person's natal horoscope or janampatrika ("birth-paper") is believed to reveal a great deal about a person. One's previous **karma** is thought to determine the moment when one is born. Thus, a natal horoscope provides a karmic "itinerary," indicating where one has been and what he or she might expect in the future. Natal horoscopes still play a role in decision-making, particularly in arranging marriages. Natal horoscopes are exchanged before fixing an engagement in order to determine the couple's compatibility. Sometimes this process takes place merely because the claim that the horoscopes are incompatible can provide an acceptable excuse to refuse an inappropriate or unacceptable match. Natal horoscopes are believed to reveal important things about a person's future. A person whose horoscope indicates an early death—or the early death of a spouse—may find it difficult to marry unless he or she performs certain rituals to remove these problems.

Natamandira

In the temple **architecture** of **Orissa**, one of the major forms of the northern Indian **Nagara** style. The natamandira is the section of the temple found between the **bhogamandapa** ("food-pavilion") and the **jagamohan**, or entrance hall leading to the main image. Natamandira literally means "**dance**-house." In many Orissan temples the natamandira was used for performance, in particular for the **Orissi** dance style that was developed and sustained in these temples. The performances were partly for the aesthetic appreciation of the spectators, but mainly as an **offering** of entertainment to the **deity** himself. Although dances are still performed at the natamandiras as a part of **worship**, they are primarily staged for entertainment.

Nataraja

Form of the god **Shiva** as the "Lord of the **Dance**." The most famous Nataraja image is in the temple-town of **Chidambaram** in the state of **Tamil Nadu**. The temple was erected during the reign of Vira Raja (927–997 C.E.), with Nataraja as its primary **deity**. However, the image of Nataraja is well known, particularly from the southern Indian **bronzes** of the **Chola dynasty** (9th–13th c).

As a divinity, one of Shiva's most important characteristics is that he transcends all duality; the Nataraja image symbolizes this concept. Shiva dances within a circle of fire, symbolizing birth and death, but remains untouched by these forces. As Shiva dances, his matted locks swing wildly, showing the force of

The god Shiva, in the form of Nataraja (the "Lord of the Dance"),
dances within a circle of fire that symbolizes the cycle of birth and death.

his activity, yet his face stays impassive and unmoved. One of his four hands holds the drum that beats the rhythm of creation, while a second hand holds the fire of destruction. His third hand is held palm upward in a **gesture** meaning "fear not." The fourth points to his upraised foot, the symbol of refuge and divine mercy for the devotee (**bhakta**). His other foot crushes a **demon**, displaying his power to destroy the wicked. The image is a well-developed theological statement, able to be "read" by those who can interpret it.

In Nataraja's charter myth, Shiva and **Kali**, the **goddess**, decide to settle their competition with a dance contest. Shiva finally bests Kali by manifesting as Nataraja and doing an athletic (**tandava**) dance style that Kali's feminine modesty prevents her from copying. Mythic roots aside, the Nataraja temple at Chidambaram has been an important center for classical Indian dance for well over a thousand years. The temple's eastern wall bears relief carvings of the 108 basic dance positions (**karanas**). These positions are central to classical Indian dance, particularly in the **Bharatanatyam** school, which is the major dance tradition in **Tamil Nadu**.

Nath

("lord") Epithet of the god **Shiva**, based on his power as the ultimate lord. Among the **Nathpanthis**, a renunciant **ascetic** community whose members are devotees (**bhakta**) of Shiva, "Nath" is added to the end of one's name after final ascetic **initiation** as a symbol of membership. This practice apparently dates from the Nathpanthis' earliest days, since according to tradition they were founded by the sage **Gorakhnath**.

Nathamuni

(10th c.) Compiler of the *Nalayira Divyaprabandham*, the collected hymns of the **Alvars** that are popularly known as the "Tamil Veda." Nathamuni is also a pivotal figure in the later development of the **Shrivaishnava** religious community, in which the passionate devotion in the Alvar hymns found more systematic philosophical articulation. According to tradition, Nathamuni's grandson was **Yamunacharya**, the teacher of **Ramanuja**, the greatest Shrivaishnava figure. See also **Veda**.

Nathdwara

City and sacred site (**tirtha**) about twenty-five miles north of the city of Udaipur in the south-central region of the state of **Rajasthan**. Nathdwara has a temple housing an image of the god **Krishna** in his form as **Shrinathji**. According to tradition, the image was originally hidden on the top of Mount Govardhan, a mountain in the **Braj** region where Krishna is said to have lived. The location of the image was revealed in a **dream** to **Vallabhacharya**, the founder of the religious community known as the **Pushti Marg**. Vallabhacharya built a temple to house it on Mount Govardhan, and his descendants have remained the image's hereditary servants since that time. The image was moved to the state of Rajasthan in 1669, prompted by fears that it would be destroyed by the Moghul emperor **Aurangzeb**. According to tradition Shrinathji revealed his wish to stay in Nathdwara by sinking his wagon's wheels deep into the **earth**, so that it could not go further. Nathdwara is a fairly remote location, making it a safe place to keep the image. See also **Moghul dynasty**.

Nathpanthi

Renunciant **ascetic** community founded by the sage **Gorakhnath**. The Nathpanthis are also known by many names: as **jogis** (from their emphasis on the practice of **yoga**), Gorakhnathis (from the name of their founder), **Kanphatas** (meaning "split-ear" by virtue of the signature earrings placed in the split cartilage of both ears), **Gosains** ("master of the senses"), and simply as **Naths** ("lord") from the characteristic suffix taken as part of their names upon ascetic **initiation**. The Nathpanthis are a very old organization and have a long tradition in northern India, but their historical record is relatively faint. The organization has no single organizing body; their emphasis on yoga has meant that their practice has been internalized, rather than focused on temples or other material objects. Although the Nathpanthis are usually described as devotees (**bhakta**) of **Shiva**, they are distinct from the **Shaiva Sanyasis**.

The spiritual practice of the Naths has traditionally focused on the mastery of the **subtle body** as the means to final liberation of the soul. The Naths believe that liberation is physical immortality, rather than escape from the cycle of transmigration, which is more commonly accepted. The subtle body is an alternate physiological system, believed to exist on a different plane than gross matter, but corresponding to the material body. It is visualized as a set of six psychic centers (**chakras**) running roughly along the spine; above and below these centers reside two divine principles, Shiva (awareness) and **Shakti** (power). The aspirant aims to join these two principles at the crown of the head, thus transforming the perishable elements in the gross body into immortality.

Among the Nathpanthis, the dominant metaphor for talking about this process is the union of **sun** and **moon**. The sun, identified with Shakti, stands for the processes of change and destruction, whereas the moon, identified with Shiva, symbolizes stability and immortality. In some cases this union of sun and moon is described in very abstract terms; for example, in the definition of **hatha yoga** "ha" refers to the sun and "tha" refers to the moon. Other abstract descriptions of this process speak of gaining equilibrium of the **vital winds** (**prana**), or yogic union in the subtle body. In other cases this union is symbolized in concrete ways, as in the practice of **vajroli mudra**. This sexual practice uses urethral suction or the "fountain-pen technique," by which a man, having ejaculated into his female partner, draws his **semen** back into his body. The semen has been refined through contact with the woman's uterine blood.

The Nathpanthis have been important both as an ascetic community in their own right, and as an influence on many of the northern Indian **bhakti** poet-saints, particularly **Kabir**. Their religious practice has consistently stressed internal religion, in which individual realization has been deemed far more important than performing social duties or established **worship**. The most complete source on Gorakhnath and his followers is George Weston Briggs, *Gorakhnath and the Kanphata Yogis*, 1973.

Natya

The word *natya* refers to the genre in classical Indian **dance** in which the dancer's movements convey a story to the audience. Natya is one of the two most basic dance genres. The other genre, **nrtya**, is "pure" dance, in which the dance conveys nothing more than the dancer's skill.

Natyashastra

Prescriptive manual (**shastra**) for the performing arts written during the second century, whose authorship is ascribed to the mythical sage **Bharata**. The text is divided into thirty-seven sections, detailing every aspect of the three major performance forms: music, drama, and **dance** (which combines both music and drama). Some sections of the text are devoted to aesthetics and poetics, helping to create and convey the correct atmosphere for the appreciation of the arts. Other parts of the text discuss concrete, practical issues, such as the construction of the stage. The text is still an authority for these three performing arts, but it is particularly important for dance. Many of the positions and gestures found in Indian dance were first codified in this text; the *Natyashastra* remains the ultimate authority for any dance form that claims to be "classical" dance, rather than "folk" dance.

Navadurga

("Nine Durgas") Collective name for nine differing forms of **Durga**, a powerful and dangerous form of the **Goddess**. One of the "nine Durgas" is worshiped each of the nine nights during the **festival** of **Navaratri**, which usually falls in October or November. Each goddess has her own identity, yet at the same time is a form of Durga. This fluidity is

Worshipers celebrating the Navaratri festival carry an image of the Goddess in the form of Durga.

characteristic of the Goddess; all female divinities are ultimately seen as manifestations of some single great Goddess. The nine Durgas, in the order in which they are worshiped, are **Mahalakshmi**, **Mahasaraswati**, **Yogmaya**, **Raktadantika**, **Shakumbhari Devi**, Durga, **Bhramari**, and **Chandika**.

Navadvip

City and sacred site (**tirtha**) on the Hugli River, about sixty-five miles north of the city of Calcutta. Navadvip is traditionally regarded as the birthplace of the Bengali saint **Chaitanya** (1486–1533), although in the twentieth century, the same claim

has been made for the city of **Mayapur**, on the other side of the river. For extensive information about Navadvip, see E. Alan Morinis, *Pilgrimage in the Hindu Tradition*, 1984.

Navaratri

("nine nights") Festival dedicated to the **Goddess** celebrated twice during the **year**. The spring Navaratri occurs during the bright, waxing half of the **lunar month** of **Chaitra** (March–April), and the fall Navaratri falls during the bright half of the lunar month of **Ashvin** (September–October). Each Navaratri celebration lasts for the first nine nights of these lunar months and concludes with a festival dedicated to the god **Rama**: **Ram Navami** in Chaitra and **Dussehra** in Ashvin. Of the two, the fall Navaratri is far more important. The fall Navaratri is celebrated with fervor in the Bengal region, where the Goddess is the dominant regional **deity**. The Bengali Navaratri is characterized by large processions featuring elaborately decorated clay images of the Goddess. These images are commissioned by individuals, businesses, trade unions, and neighborhood associations. Having the best image is a sign of great status. During the weeks around Navaratri, Bengali children get a holiday from school, state workers get paid vacation from their jobs, and the electricity supply in Calcutta runs without interruptions—a phenomenon dubbed the Navaratri "miracle," since during the rest of the year shortages and blackouts are common.

These Navaratri festivals are performed to gain the favor of the Mother Goddess, particularly in her powerful forms such as **Durga**. During these nine nights devotees (**bhakta**) perform a variety of different rites. Some fast (**upavasa**) and **worship** in their homes, often consecrating temporary images of the Goddess for use during this festival. Devotees may also worship young girls as manifestations of the Goddess, or sponsor readings of the *Devimahatmya*, the earliest and most important text for the mythology of the Goddess. They may also worship the Goddess in her form as **Navadurga**, paying homage to a different form on each of the nine nights.

Another common practice is to harvest shoots of barley, which are sometimes worn on the final day of the festival. This practice hints at the festival's purpose since, among other things, the Goddess represents the female power of fertility and procreation. In northern India, the spring festival comes before the crops are planted. Wearing sprouting grain is an attempt to please the Goddess so the crop may flourish. The fall Navaratri comes after the harvest, when this promise of fruition has been fulfilled, and is seen as a time of thanksgiving for blessings received. The Goddess also represents the triumph of good over evil; the readings of the *Devimahatmya* on these occasions remind the listeners of the Goddess' wondrous deeds and assure them of her continued protection.

Navyanyaya

("new **Nyaya**") A later branch of the Nyaya philosophical school. The Nyaya school was one of the **six schools** in traditional Hindu **philosophy**, which flourished in the early centuries of the first millennium, but then lost its influence. The Navyanyaya school developed in late medieval times (15th–17th c.), in an attempt to reinvigorate the school and to resolve some of the problems with the earlier Nyaya notion of **inherence** (**samavaya**). The earlier Nyayas perceived inherence as a weak relational force that connected objects and their qualities—for example, connecting the color red with a particular ball and thus making the ball red. It also connected material objects—the force that held a clay pot together once the two halves had been pressed against each other. Finally, inherence connected selves and their qualities—one became happy when inherence connected happiness to one's self, and unhappy when unhappiness was connected.

This notion of inherence explained many things in the perceivable world. However, objections were raised against the Nyayas' insistence that inherence was a single, universal property at work in different places. According to this criticism, a universal and eternal inherence could link an object with *any* property, including ones that contradict—the color brown with the moon or the appearance of a cow with a dog. Other attacks questioned whether inherence continued to exist after one of the things it had been connecting was destroyed. If it did not, opponents claimed, then inherence was clearly nothing to begin with, whereas if it did, then the remaining connecting power would exist unconnected to anything, which was clearly absurd. Finally, some attacked the need for inherence at all—which was cited as an example of "needless complexity" (**gaurava**).

The Navyanyaya school attempted to sidestep these problems by positing a new class of relationship, that of "self-linking connectors." These connectors were seen as an integral part of all things, by their very nature, and since they were self-linking, this eliminated the need for a separate inherence to connect things together. In this understanding, the relationship and the related objects are one and the same. This notion allowed the Navyanyayas to retain their fundamental assumptions that there are real objects in the world and they are connected to one another. For further information see Karl H. Potter and Sibajiban Bhattacharyya (eds.), *Indian Philosophical Analysis*, 1992.

Nayachandra Suri

(14th c.) The author of the *Hammira-mahakavya*, a **Sanskrit** drama that chronicles the defeat and death of the **Rajput** king Hammira by the Delhi sultan Alauddin Khilji in 1301. Aside from its historical value, this play is notable because Nayachandra Suri was a Jain monk. Although Jain monks are subject to a strict religious lifestyle that would seem to cut them off from the world, they have a long history of deep involvement with intellectual and literary culture. See also **mahakavya**.

Nayak Dynasty

Southern Indian dynasty whose capital was in the city of **Madurai** in the state of **Tamil Nadu**. The Nayaks came to power in the political vacuum created by the destruction of the **Vijayanagar dynasty** late in the sixteenth century. The Nayaks ruled the southernmost part of the subcontinent for about the next hundred years. The dynasty's greatest ruler was **Tirumalai Nayak** (r. 1623–1659), who constructed large sections of the **Minakshi** temple, dedicated to Madurai's patron **goddess**, Minakshi.

Nayanar

Group of sixty-three **Shaiva** poet-saints, who lived in southern India between the seventh and ninth centuries. In concert with their **Vaishnava** counterparts the **Alvars**, the Nayanars spearheaded the revitalization of Hindu religion vis-à-vis the Buddhists and the Jains. Both the Nayanars and the Alvars stressed passionate devotion (**bhakti**) to a personal god—**Shiva** for the Nayanars, **Vishnu** for the Alvars—and conveyed this devotion through hymns sung in the **Tamil language**. The Nayanars tended to be more overtly hostile to the Jains. According to legend the Nayanar **Sambandar** was instrumental in the **impalement** of eight thousand Jain monks in the city of **Madurai**. The hymns of the three most important Nayanars—**Appar**, Sambandar, and **Sundaramurtti**—comprise the *Devaram*, the most sacred of the Tamil Shaivite texts. An important later source is the *Periya Puranam* by **Cekkilar**, which gives hagiographic accounts for all the Nayanars.

Nayar

The Nayars are a Hindu **jati** who traditionally were the primary landholding community in traditional **Kerala**. Jatis are **endogamous** subgroups of traditional Indian society whose social status is determined by the group's hereditary occupation. The Nayars were one of the few groups in India to practice **matrilinear succession**, in which both descent and **inheritance** were passed on through the mother's line.

Nazar

("glance") The literal meaning of the word *nazar* is an unobstructed line of sight to a person or a thing. The word *nazar* is also the term most commonly used to denote the "evil eye," a malefic influence that is put on people through sight, particularly eye-to-eye contact. The existence of the evil eye is widely accepted among traditional Hindus. It is warded off either by avoiding this sort of gaze, or by performing **rites of protection**. For further consideration see David F. Pocock, "The Evil Eye," in T. N. Madan (ed.), *Religion in India*, 1991.

Nepal

A small Himalayan nation on the northern border of India that is deemed the world's only Hindu kingdom. One basis for this claim is that almost 90 percent of Nepal's inhabitants identify themselves as Hindu; the other is that since 1769 Nepal's ruling house has been a Hindu dynasty, the Shah dynasty. The present monarch, Birendra Bir Bikram Shah (b. 1945), was an uncontested absolute monarch until April 1990, when popular discontent led to a movement seeking the restoration of democracy in Nepal. The king was forced to accede to democratic reforms, and since May 1991 has governed as a constitutional monarch, with the Nepali Parliament wielding the real power.

Although Nepal is a small country, it has great geographical diversity. Its three major geographical regions are the submontane lowlands, the Himalayan foothills, and the high mountains. The country's uneven topography further subdivides each of these regions. This rugged geography has a marked effect on the country's economy, rendering agriculture impossible at anything more than a subsistence level. However, it provides the attraction for tourism, which is Nepal's greatest source of foreign exchange.

Such great geographical diversity promotes similar human diversity. The people of Nepal are an amalgam of many different groups, including people whose historical roots lie in India and indigenous hill tribes associated with particular parts of the country. Most Nepalese live in the fertile valleys of the foothills. These are the most habitable regions, as the climate in the mountains is far too harsh for permanent habitation, while the lowland regions are rife with disease, particularly malaria. In general, Nepali culture shows many similarities with the adjoining areas of India, and thus from a cultural perspective is firmly fixed in the Indian cultural orbit. Nepal is also the home to several important Hindu pilgrimage places (**tirtha**), notably **Pashupatinath** in the Kathmandu Valley, and **Muktinath**, at the headwaters of the Kali Gandaki River.

New Moon

(amavasya) In northern India, the new **moon** usually marks the midpoint of the **lunar month**, whereas in southern India it often identifies the end. Unlike the **full moon**, whose associations with fullness and completion make it always **auspicious**, the new moon's associations with darkness and emptiness make it a more ambiguous time. One of the most important festivals in the Hindu religious **year**, Diwali, falls on the new moon in **Kartik** (October–November). The new moon can also be highly auspicious on certain other occasions, such as a **Somavati Amavasya**, a new moon falling on a **Monday**. In general, however, the new moon is less clearly auspicious than the full moon. Not only are there fewer celebrations during the new moon, but there is also a proportionately greater number of holidays falling in the light, waxing half of the lunar month. The new moon and the dark, waning half are not in themselves **inauspicious**, they are simply deemed less auspicious than the light half and the full moon.

Nibandha

("collection") Genre of thematic commentarial literature that became prominent in medieval northern India. The nibandhas were compendia of Hindu lore, in which the compilers culled

Leader of a Toda tribe in the Nilgiri Hills.

excerpts on a particular theme from the **Vedas**, **dharma literature**, **puranas**, and other authoritative religious texts, and then compiled them into a single organized text. Excerpts from these same authoritative texts on a different theme would be compiled into a different volume, and so on. The compilers would often have to reconcile conflicting texts, or judge which passage was preferable to another. Such judgments were generally done using rules for textual interpretation developed by the **Purva Mimamsa** philosophical school, one of the **six schools** of traditional Hindu **philosophy**. The Purva Mimamsa school had originally developed these rules for interpreting the Vedas, the oldest and most authoritative Hindu religious texts. In many cases the nibandhas had between fifteen and twenty volumes, attempting to provide an exhaustive investigation of Hindu religious life. Among the most influential nibandhas are the *Kalpataru*, compiled by **Lakshmidhara** in twelfth century, and the *Viramitrodaya*, compiled by **Mitra Mishra** early in the seventeenth century.

Nigantha Nataputta

In early Indian **philosophy**, a figure whose views are mentioned in the Buddhist scriptures. Nigantha advocated a four-fold self-restraint, although these sources give no further indication of his doctrines. It is generally accepted that Nigantha was the same person as Mahavira. Mahavira is believed to have been the last of the Jain tirthankaras, the founding figures in the Jain religious tradition.

Night, Goddess of

In the **Vedas**, the earliest and most authoritative Hindu religious texts, the gods and goddesses are associated with phenomena in the natural world. In the Vedas the **goddess** Ratri (Night) is mentioned both as a goddess and as the night itself. At times she is seen as life-giving, allowing people the opportunity to refresh and renew themselves. At other times she is associated with the dangers of the night, such as wild animals and thieves. Ratri is considered a sister to **Ushas**, the dawn. As night and day alternate, the two goddesses mark out the regular passage of time that characterizes the cosmic order (**rta**). For further information on Night and all the goddesses of Hinduism, see David R. Kinsley, *Hindu Goddesses*, 1986.

Nilachal Hill

Sacred site (**tirtha**) overlooking the Brahmaputra River, about six miles outside the city of Guwahati in the modern state of **Assam**. Nilachal Hill is known for its temple to the **goddess Kamakhya**, one of the most powerful goddess temples in India. This site is one of the **Shakti Pithas**, a network of sites sacred to the Goddess which spreads throughout the subcontinent. Each Shakti Pitha marks the site where a body part of the dismembered goddess **Sati** fell to **earth**, taking form there as a different goddess. The Kamakhya temple is where Sati's vulva is said to have fallen to earth; the image of the goddess is a natural cleft in the rock around which the temple has been built. Since Kamakhya sprang from the most sexually charged part of the female body, the site is extremely powerful. See also **pitha**.

Nilakanth

("blue-throated") Epithet of the god **Shiva**; also the name of a manifestation of Shiva who is enshrined at the Nilakanth Mahadev temple outside the city of **Rishikesh** in the state of **Uttar Pradesh**. Shiva is present at Nilakanth in the form of a **linga**, the pillar-shaped object that is his symbolic form. The mythic charter for this epithet (and for the establishment of the temple as well) is drawn from the tale of Churning the Ocean of Milk. The gods and **demons** churn the ocean to produce **amrta**, the nectar of immortality thought to be the finest essence of the ocean. Yet their action produces not only the amrta, but also its antithesis, the **halahala** poison. This is an event of great peril; the poison is so powerful that if left unchecked, it can destroy the earth. When this poison appears, the gods and demons are unable to figure out a way to contain it. Shiva takes care of the poison by holding it in his throat, but the force of the poison is so great that it turns his throat blue. See also **Tortoise avatar** and **ocean, churning of the**.

Nilgiri Hills

Range of hills formed by the conjunction of the Western and Eastern Ghats, located at the junction of three southern Indian states—**Tamil Nadu**, **Kerala**, and **Karnataka**. In earlier times the hills were occupied by a tribal people known as the Todas, although only a few thousand Todas are left today. This region is important for its hill stations, such as Ootacamund and Kodaikanal, which are popular spots for vacations, honeymoons, and movie filming.

Nimbarka

(12th c.?) **Ascetic**, philosopher, devotee (**bhakta**) of the god **Vishnu**, and attributed as the founder of the **Sanaka Sampraday**, one of the four **Vaishnava** ascetic orders. According to tradition, Nimbarka was a Telegu (southern Indian) **brahmin** who was born in the city of **Paithan** in central India, but lived much of his life in the northern Indian **Braj** region, where the god **Krishna** is supposed to have lived. Nimbarka's philosophical position is described as dualism-nondualism (dvaitadvaita), a concept in which God and human beings are both identical and different. While earlier Vaishnavas worshiped **Vishnu** and **Lakshmi** as the divine couple, Nimbarka used the same concept, but changed the focus to Krishna and **Radha**.

Nimbarki

Name for the religious group founded by the **Vaishnava** figure **Nimbarka**. It is also used as a variant name for the **Sanaka Sampraday**, an **ascetic** community that traces its spiritual lineage to Nimbarka, as a way to reinforce their religious authority.

Nirakara

("without form") Epithet of the divine reality in its ultimate aspect. According to many Hindu traditions, God is ultimately without form, transcending all particularity and superior to any particular image. This belief is first phrased in the **Upanishads**, the speculative religious texts that are the most recent part of the **Vedas**, and is advocated by the philosophical traditions based on the Upanishads, such as **Advaita Vedanta**. This concept is opposed by certain Hindu theistic traditions, such as the **Gaudiya Vaishnava** religious community, in which a particular **deity**—in this case, **Krishna**—is conceived as the Ultimate Reality.

Niranjani Akhara

The name of a subgroup of the **Naga** class of **Dashanami Sanyasis**; a particular type of renunciant **ascetic**. The Dashanami Sanyasis are devotees (**bhakta**) of the god **Shiva**, organized into different **akharas** or regiments on the model of an army. Until the beginning of the nineteenth century the Dashanami Sanyasis' primary occupation was as mercenary soldiers, although they also had substantial trading interests; both of these have largely disappeared in contemporary times. The Niranjani Akhara is one of the seven main Dashanami Sanyasi akharas and along with the **Mahanirvani Akhara** is one of the most powerful. This power is clearly shown by their respective positions in the bathing (**snana**) processions at the **Kumbha Mela** festivals: in **Haridwar** the Niranjani Akhara goes first, followed by the Mahanirvani; at **Allahabad** the order is reversed. In 1962 the **Juna Akhara** acquired the status of a separate procession, rather than as a subsidiary of the Niranjani Akhara. According to the terms of the 1962 agreement, at Haridwar the Juna Akhara would lead the Sanyasi processions for the bathing on the festival of **Shivaratri**, followed by the Niranjani and Mahanirvani Akharas. The Niranjanis would be first for the other two major bathing days, followed by the Juna and Mahanirvani Akharas. The Niranjani Akhara's ability to command the premier position is based primarily on their local strength: the Niranjani Akhara was quite powerful in Haridwar, where it still owns significant property. The Mahanirvani Akhara, however, was based in Allahabad. Another sign of the Niranjani Akhara's status is that it has as a subsidiary group, the **Ananda Akhara**.

All of the akharas have particular features that define their organizational identity, especially specific tutelary **deities**. The Niranjani Akhara's tutelary deity is **Skanda**, the son of the deities Shiva and **Parvati**, and the celestial general commanding Shiva's supernatural army. Aside from serving as an identifying marker, the choice of a celestial warrior reflects the akhara's influence and former military strength.

Nirguna

("without qualities") Epithet of the divine reality in its ultimate aspect. According to many Hindu traditions, God is ultimately without qualities or attributes, transcending all particularity and superior to any qualified form. This conception is first phrased in the **Upanishads**, the speculative religious texts that are the most recent part of the **Vedas**, and in the philosophical traditions based on the Upanishads such as **Advaita Vedanta**. This belief is opposed by certain Hindu theistic traditions, such as the **Gaudiya Vaishnava** religious community, in which a particular **deity**—in this case, **Krishna**—is conceived as the Ultimate Reality.

Nirikari

Minor **Vaishnava** sect founded in the late 1700s, by a **Ramanandi ascetic** named **Baba** Sarjudasa. The name comes from their greeting, *Sat Nirikara* ("Truth Is Formless"). Their major areas of influence and operation are in **Punjab**, **Haryana**, and northwestern **Uttar Pradesh**.

At the Kumbha Mela festival in Haridwar the Niranjani Akhara proceeds first, followed by the Mahanirvani.

Nirjala Ekadashi

Religious observance on the eleventh day (**ekadashi**) in the bright, waxing half of the **lunar month** of **Jyeshth** (May–June). As for all the eleventh-day observances, this is dedicated to the **worship** of the god **Vishnu**. Most Hindu festivals have certain prescribed rites, which usually involve fasting (**upavasa**) and worship, and often promise specific benefits for faithful performance. The regulations for this ekadashi are more strict than all the others. Not only is all food forbidden, but the person performing this rite must not drink **water**, hence the name *nirjala* meaning "waterless." The fast must last from dawn till dusk. This is no easy task, since this ekadashi occurs during the hottest part of the **year**. The rewards are great: Those who fulfill the vow for this single ekadashi receive the religious merit for all twenty-four ekadashis during the year, whether or not they have done the rites for the others. Carrying out the vow for this ekadashi is also believed to bring one a long life and liberation of the soul after death.

Nirmala

("free from defilement") With the **Udasis**, one of the two Hindu **ascetic** communities tracing its origins to the Sikh community. According to one tradition, the Nirmala sect was established by the tenth Sikh **guru**, Gobind Singh. On the whole, the Sikh tradition has not endorsed **asceticism**, but rather an active life in the world. The Nirmalas have a large ascetic center in the northern Indian sacred city of **Haridwar**, where they run a primary school. As a community, the Nirmalas are known far more for learning and study than asceticism or **yoga**. At the **Kumbha Melas**, the Nirmalas bathe last of all, after the **Sanyasis**, **Bairagis**, and Udasis.

Nirmala Devi

(b. 1923) Modern Hindu teacher who claims to be an **avatar** of the primordial **Goddess**, and the founder of **Vishva Nirmala Dharam**, an organization dedicated to spreading her message. Nirmala Devi's teaching is based on traditional ideas of **hatha yoga** and the **subtle body**. The subtle body is an alternate physiological system, existing on a different plane than gross matter, but corresponding to the material body. It is visualized as a set of six psychic centers (**chakras**) running roughly along the spine; two divine principles, **Shiva** (awareness) and **Shakti** (power), reside above and below these centers. In practicing this yoga, the aspirant aims to awaken the latent spiritual energy of Shakti known as **kundalini**, move it into union with the Shiva principle at the crown of the head, and transform the perishable elements in the gross body to become immortal.

Nirmala Devi claims to be able to arouse a devotee's (**bhakta**) kundalini through an infusion of her own spiritual power, thus dramatically speeding up the path to liberation. Her Indian devotees are mainly middle-class, but she also claims to have a substantial following in Europe, North America, and Australia. For a skeptical account of an encounter with Nirmala Devi, see Sudhir Kakar, "Cooling Breezes," in *Shamans, Mystics, and Doctors*, 1991.

Nirmohi ("free from illusion") Ani

Among the **Bairagi Nagas**, renunciant **ascetics** who are devotees of **Vishnu**, the Nirmohis are one of the three Naga **anis** ("armies"). The others are the **Digambaras** and **Nirvanis**. In earlier times these anis were actual fighting units who made their living as traders and mercenary soldiers, but in modern times they are mainly important for determining the order in the bathing processions at the **Kumbha Mela**. Of the three Naga anis, the Digambaras are by far the most important and take precedence at the Kumbha Mela.

Nirriti

("decay, destruction") In the **Vedas**, the oldest and most authoritative Hindu religious texts, Nirriti is a **goddess** personifying all the negative aspects associated with life. Nirriti's personality is not well-defined, for she is rarely mentioned; the hymns mentioning her usually express the hope that she will stay away and allow the speakers to be free from misfortune. For further information on Nirriti and all the goddesses of Hinduism, see David R. Kinsley, *Hindu Goddesses*, 1986.

Nirukta

("explanation") One of the six **Vedangas**. These were the auxiliary branches of knowledge associated with the use of the **Vedas**, the oldest Hindu religious texts. Nirukta is concerned with the etymological explanations of archaic words. This was apparently a serious problem, since almost one-quarter of the words in the Veda occur only once, and with the passage of time their precise meanings became either unclear or unknown. The most famous nirukta text—known simply as the *Nirukta*—was written by **Yaska** the grammarian, in about the fifth century B.C.E. His work was immeasurably helpful to later readers, but it is clear that even in Yaska's time the meanings for many of these words had become uncertain and unclear. Aside from nirukta, the other Vedangas are **vyakarana** (**Sanskrit** grammar), **chandas** (Sanskrit prosody), **kalpa** (ritual instructions), **shiksha** (correct pronunciation), and **jyotisha** (**auspicious** times for sacrifices).

Nirvani ("liberated") Ani

Among the **Bairagi Nagas**, renunciant **ascetics** who are devotees (**bhakta**) of **Vishnu**, the Nirvanis are one of the three Naga **anis** ("armies"). The others are the **Nirmohis** and **Digambaras**. In earlier times these anis were actual fighting units who made their living as traders and mercenary soldiers, but in modern times they are mainly important for determining the order at the bathing (**snana**) processions at the **Kumbha Mela**. Of the three Naga anis, the Digambaras are the most important and take precedence at the Kumbha Mela.

Nirvikalpaka

In certain schools of Indian **philosophy**—among them certain Buddhists, the **Nyayas**, and the **Prabhakara** school of **Mimamsa**—nirvikalpaka is the name for a sort of simple non-conceptual awareness, produced solely by the operation of the senses. According to these schools, if the senses producing this awareness have no defect, such an awareness is believed to be true. However, it can be confused or misinterpreted through the action of the mind. This belief had important ramifications for **theories of error**, which seek to explain how erroneous judgments are possible. The schools that believed in this theory attributed error to the action of the mind.

Nishkramana ("going-out") Samskara

The sixth traditional life-cycle ceremony (**samskara**), in which the infant is taken for his or her first trip outside the house. Although the traditional texts consider this a minor rite and the traditional textual procedures are seldom performed, a young child's first outing is often still carefully planned. On a symbolic level, it represents the child's first encounter with the larger world, and thus the child's expanding sphere of possibilities. It also shows the continuing importance of **rites of protection**. Even in modern India many people believe in the power of the evil eye (**nazar**), and young children are considered particularly susceptible. Thus, a child's first encounter with the chaotic outside world must be carefully structured and carefully supervised.

Nishumbha

In Hindu mythology the name of a **demon** killed by the **goddess Kali** in the *Devimahatmya*, the earliest and most important text for the mythology of the Goddess. Together with his brother **Shumbha**, Nishumbha is one of the generals in the army of a demon named **Mahishasura**. Due to a divine boon given to Mahishasura, Shumbha and Nishumbha are able to vanquish the gods and assume control of **heaven**. However, they are devoured by Kali, who emerges as a manifestation of the Goddess's anger.

Niti Shastra

("instructions on diplomacy") General name for a genre of instruction that taught politically astute behaviors, such as making friends and allegiances, intimidating one's enemies, and knowing who can be trusted. This was a recognized branch of learning in the traditional Hindu sciences, and was taught to influential and royal families, for whom knowing the real workings of the world was considered essential to fulfilling their social functions. The fables of the *Panchatantra* convey these hard-edged lessons on self-interest and caution through the use of animal characters.

Nitya Karma

("perpetual [ritual] action") One of the three broad types of ritual action, the others being **naimittika karma** and **kamya karma**. Nitya karma is ritual action that is prescribed at regular fixed intervals, often on a daily basis; one gains no religious merit from performing them, but omitting them is considered a religious demerit. One example of a nitya karma is the **Gayatri Mantra**, which must be recited at morning and evening **worship** (**sandhya**) by every "twice-born" man who has received the adolescent religious **initiation** known as the "second birth." Another nitya karma is the Five Great Sacrifices (**panchamahayajna**), which are daily religious duties for a "twice-born" householder; they are rarely performed today.

Nityasamsarin

One of the three classes of beings in the **Dvaita Vedanta** philosophical school, founded by the philosopher **Madhva**

(1197–1276). Madhva's fundamental belief was that God was utterly transcendent, above and beyond the world and human beings. The strength of this conviction led him to stress the importance of **grace** as the sole means of salvation, since human beings were unable to save themselves. Given this dire view of human capacities, Madhva divided the beings of the world into three classes: The **muktiyogas** were destined for final liberation, the nityasamsarins were destined for eternal rebirth, and the **tamoyogas** were predestined for eternal damnation.

Nivedita, Sister

(b. Margaret Noble, 1867–1911) Irish disciple of the modern Hindu teacher **Swami Vivekananda**. Nivedita devoted much of her life to the service of the **Ramakrishna Mission**, particularly the education of Indian **women**. Nivedita was born in Ireland and taught in London, where she met Vivekananda. She accepted him as her spiritual master (**guru**) and came to India with him, where she founded the Nivedita Girls School in Calcutta. Nivedita was part of the first generation of Europeans who came to India searching for answers to life's ultimate questions.

Nivrttinath

(1268–1294?) Elder brother of **Jnaneshvar**, the first great poet-saint of the **Varkari Panth**, a religious community centered around the **worship** of the Hindu god **Vithoba** at his temple at **Pandharpur** in the modern state of **Maharashtra**. Nivrttinath is traditionally named as Jnaneshvar's religious teacher (**guru**), although his younger brother became more influential. According to tradition, Nivrttinath's guru, Gainanath, was a direct disciple of **Gorakhnath**, the celebrated **ascetic**. This relationship is indicated in the *Jnaneshvari*, in which Jnaneshvar describes himself as a pupil in Gorakhnath's line. For further information see George Weston

Briggs, *Gorakhnath and the Kanphata Yogis*, 1973.

Niyama

("observance") In the **ashtanga yoga** taught by **Patanjali**, the second of the eight constituent elements of yoga practice. While the first element lists five injurious actions and dispositions to avoid, Niyama gives five positive instructions, shifting the focus from abstinence to active cultivation. The five observances are: **purity**, contentment, **asceticism**, study, and making the lord the motive of all action.

Niyati

("destiny") Niyati was the central philosophical assumption for the **Ajivikas**, an ancient and extinct philosophical school. The Ajivikas were fatalists, who believed that niyati inexorably predetermined all things. Human beings can do nothing to influence destiny, since they can only do what has been preordained. The Ajivikas compared the process of reincarnation (**samsara**) to a ball of string, which would unroll until it was done, and then go no further. The word niyati still carries this sense of "fate" or "destiny," but with one important difference: While the Ajivikas conceived niyati as an impersonal and uncontrollable force, in modern times one's fate is believed to result from past **karma**.

Niyoga

("appointment") Practice by which a childless **widow** could have intercourse with her dead husband's brother, or some other "appointed" male, in order to bear a **son**. The child is considered the son of the dead man and preserves his lineage. There is significant disagreement about the propriety of this practice in the **dharma literature**. Some of these texts permit it, although hedged with numerous conditions, but others unconditionally condemn it. Niyoga is one of the practices judged to be

The two most basic genres of Indian classical dance are natya and nrtya. This dancer, performing in the natya genre, uses dance to tell a story. In the nrtya genre the dance conveys only the dancer's skill.

Kalivarjya, or "forbidden in the **Kali** [Age]." Kalivarjya, which first appeared in the twelfth century, was a legal strategy used to forbid certain religious practices that were prescribed in the sacred literature, but were no longer acceptable in contemporary times.

Nrtya

In classical Indian **dance**, the word *nrtya* refers to the genre of "pure" dance, in which the dance conveys nothing more than the dancer's skill. Nrtya is one of the two most basic dance genres. The other genre, **natya**, is an acting dance, in which the dancer's expressions, movements, and gestures convey a story to the audience.

Nryajana

("**sacrifice** to human beings") One of the Five Great Sacrifices (**panchamahayajna**) that is prescribed in the **dharma literature**, which describes religious duty. These Five Great Sacrifices are daily religious observances prescribed for a **twice-born** householder. This is a person who has been born into one of the three twice-born groups in Indian society—**brahmin**, **kshatriya**, or **vaishya**—

and who has received the adolescent religious **initiation** known as the "second birth." Each of the five sacrifices (**yajna**) is directed toward a different class of beings—from the Ultimate Reality of **Brahman** down to **animals**—and is satisfied by different actions. The nryajana is directed toward fellow human beings, and is satisfied by showing hospitality to one's guests. Although Hindu religious life has undergone significant changes and some of the other rites have fallen into oblivion, this rite is still widely practiced; the ethos of hospitality is still very strong in Hindu society.

Nudity

Nudity is often seen as both **inauspicious** and forbidden, and is subject to numerous taboos: according to some authorities, one should not bathe (**snana**) naked (a more understandable taboo in times when people would bathe outdoors) and one should not be naked during sexual intercourse. In some cases there are also taboos on a husband seeing his wife naked, since it is widely believed that this will cause **Lakshmi**, the **goddess**, to forsake her, taking away her **auspiciousness** as a married woman. The exception to this taboo on nudity is that some **ascetics** believe nakedness symbolizes the renunciation of all **possessions** and the rejection of all worldly standards, including shame. Few ascetics renounce all clothing; some wear a loincloth in public, rationalizing that one should not mislead or scandalize ordinary people who have limited understanding.

Nyasa

("laying down") A characteristic ritual in **tantra**, a secret religious practice. In the practice of nyasa, the person performing the ritual identifies certain sounds, often in the form of seed syllables (**bijaksharas**), with parts of the human body, **deities**, and material objects. This is done to create a series of identifications between the macrocosm of the universe and the microcosm of the body, such that actions in the microcosmic ritual sphere will cause results in its macrocosmic counterpart.

Nyaya

("method") One of the **six schools** of traditional Hindu **philosophy**, concerned with the examination and validation of the objects of knowledge. It was the Nyayas who first developed and codified the notion of the **pramanas**, the means by which human beings may gain true and accurate knowledge. The Nyayas recognized four such pramanas: perception (**pratyaksha**), inference (**anumana**), analogy (**upamana**), and authoritative testimony (**shabda**). These ideas are accepted by virtually all Indian philosophical schools, and are the Nyayas' major contribution to Indian philosophy.

As did all schools of Indian philosophy, the Nyayas undertook the examination of knowledge not for mere speculation, but to find a way to release the soul from the bondage of reincarnation (**samsara**). The **Nyaya Sutras**, attributed to **Gautama**, are the traditional basis for the school. The **sutras** begin by asserting that the means of knowledge and its elements can bring a person supreme happiness. The text's second sutra describes a five-part **causal chain**: pain, **birth**, activity, defect, and wrong notion. Each of these elements is caused by the one succeeding it, and is eliminated with the destruction of its cause. The primary cause for all of this is "wrong notion," hence the Nyaya were concerned with the investigation of the pramanas.

The Nyayas draw their metaphysics from the **Vaisheshika** school, with whom they become assimilated in the early centuries of the common era. Their philosophical perspective is sometimes described as the "ordinary person's conception." The Nyayas and Vaisheshika are philosophical realists—that is, they believe the world is made up of many different things that exist as perceived, except in cases of perceptual error. All things are composed of nine fundamental substances—the five **elements**, **space**, time, mind, and selves—and that whatever exists is both knowable and nameable. The Nyayas subscribe to the **causal model** known as **asatkaryavada**, which posits that when a thing is created, it is a new entity, completely different from its constituent parts. This causal model tends to multiply the number of things in the universe, since each act of creation brings a new thing into being. It also admits that human efforts and actions are one of the causes influencing these affects, making it theoretically possible to act in a way that brings final liberation of the soul (**moksha**).

One of the unique features of the Nyaya school is their belief in **inherence** (**samavaya**), a weak relational force that functions like a glue connecting various things: wholes and their parts, substances and their attributes, motions and the things that move, and general properties and their particular instances. For the Nyayas, the Self (**atman**) is the locus for all experience. Inherence connects all experiences—

pleasure, pain, happiness, sorrow, and so forth—to the Self. The philosophical difficulties with inherence—particularly the notion that it is one single principle and not a collection of things—caused the Nyaya school great difficulty. These assumptions were ultimately responsible for the rise of **Navyanyaya** school, which attempted to explain these relationships in a more sophisticated way. For further information see Karl H. Potter and Sibajiban Bhattacharyya (eds.), *Indian Philosophical Analysis*, 1992; and Sarvepalli Radhakrishnan and Charles A. Moore (eds.), *A Sourcebook in Indian Philosophy*, 1957.

Nyaya Sutras

Foundational text for the **Nyaya** school, one of the **six schools** of traditional Hindu **philosophy**. The Nyaya Sutras are traditionally attributed to the philosopher **Gautama**; the most significant commentary was written by **Vatsyayana** in the fourth century. The Nyaya Sutras begin with an exposition of the cause of the human bondage, explained as stemming from a five-part **causal chain**: pain, **birth**, activity, defect, and wrong notion. Each of these elements is caused by the one succeeding it, and is eliminated with the destruction of its cause. The root cause for bondage and reincarnation (**samsara**) is thus wrong notions, which must be corrected to attain final liberation of the soul (**moksha**). In their quest for correct understanding, the Nyaya Sutras devote great attention to the **pramanas**, the means by which human beings can gain true and accurate knowledge, and to the rules and procedures for applying them. The Nyaya Sutras describe four such pramanas: perception (**pratyaksha**), inference (**anumana**), analogy (**upamana**), and authoritative testimony (**shabda**). These ideas are accepted by virtually all Indian philosophical schools and are the Nyayas' major contribution to Indian philosophy.

Obscenity

Traditional Hindu culture can be characterized as straightlaced, even prudish, with regard to sexuality; any public mention of sexuality is taboo in polite society. The exception of ritually sanctioned obscenity comes before and during the festival of **Holi**, which usually occurs in March. Holi is a "festival of reversal," in which most social taboos are temporarily suspended. Holi comes very close to the end of the lunar **year**, and symbolizes the end of time, when all norms and standards have been lost. In recent times the license and lawlessness associated with Holi have led many people to stop celebrating it in public, particularly in the cities.

Ocean, Churning of the

Famous mythic event in which the gods and **demons** churned the Ocean of Milk to produce the nectar or immortality. See also **Tortoise avatar**.

Offerings

One of the pervasive realities in Hindu religious life is the importance of transactions or exchanges—both between human beings, and between humans and superhuman beings. The importance of these exchanges makes various offerings a fundamental part of Hindu **worship**. One set of sixteen offerings, known as the **upacharas**, are given to a **deity** as part of worship, on the model of treating the deity as an honored guest—inviting the deity inside, offering the deity a seat, a drink of **water**, and so forth. In the **naivedya**, one offers the deity food, perhaps the most fundamental courtesy of all.

Om

A sacred sound. According to tradition, it should be uttered before and after reading the **Vedas** (the oldest Hindu religious texts), saying any prayer, or performing any sacred rite. When uttered at the beginning of a rite, it is believed to remove obstacles, and when uttered at the end it is seen as a concluding affirmation. Because of its pervasive ritual use, the sound *Om* is regarded as the essence of all holy speech. As early as the **Mandukya Upanishad**, the sound's phonetic elements (A, U, and M) were interpreted as corresponding to different states of consciousness, and ultimately designating the Self (**atman**). See also **four states of consciousness**.

Omens

The notions of **auspiciousness** and **inauspiciousness** are deeply rooted in Hindu life, and are based on the assumption that by their very nature certain things bring good fortune, and certain other things bring ill fortune. The notion of omens is an extension of this idea; omens are important not because they cause good or bad fortune in themselves, but because they indicate conditions that are present. According to this belief, auspicious conditions will automatically give rise to favorable omens, and inauspicious conditions to unfavorable omens. Omens serve as indicators to help judge the current state of affairs and make any necessary adjustments. For example, if on leaving the house to do some business one sees a person deemed inauspicious, one should return to the home and begin again, lest the work be fruitless.

Omkareshvar

Temple and sacred site (**tirtha**) on an island in the **Narmada River** in the state of **Madhya Pradesh**, about fifty miles southeast of the city of Indore. The temple is named after its presiding **deity**, the god **Shiva** in his manifestation as the "Lord of [the sound] **Om**," an utterance claimed to symbolize the entire universe, according to the early speculative texts known as the **Upanishads**. Omkareshvar is one of the twelve **jyotirlingas**, a network of sites at which Shiva is uniquely present. According to the site's mythic charter, Shiva appears there to reward the sage Mandhata, who has performed harsh **asceticism** (**tapas**) to gain a vision of Shiva. The image at the site is a "self-manifested" (**svayambhu**) form of Shiva—an unshaped, roundish black stone emerging from the **earth**, while nearby is a white stone considered to be a manifestation of Shiva's wife, **Parvati**. Viewing this image is believed to grant all of one's desires, just as it did for Mandhata. **Worship** at the site continues all year, but during **Kartik Purnima**, the **full moon** in the **lunar month** of **Kartik** (October–November), there is a major bathing (**snana**) festival at the site.

Onam

The festival of Onam, in the southern Indian state of **Kerala**, is celebrated in the Malayalam month of Chingal, which corresponds to the northern Indian month of **Bhadrapada** (August–September). Onam is a four-day harvest festival highlighted by races in elaborately carved boats known as "snake boats," some of which are large enough to carry 100 paddlers. The most famous of these boat races are held in the Keralan town of Aleppey.

Oraon

Northern Indian tribal (**adivasi**) community. The Oraons are concentrated in the southwestern corner of modern **Bihar**, in the geologic region known as the Ranchi Plateau. The land is quite poor, and for many life is very difficult. For a discussion of the difficulties of Oraon life, see Sudhir Kakar, *Shamans, Mystics, and Doctors*, 1991.

Ordeal, Trial By

Trial by ordeal was one of the traditional means for establishing a person's guilt or innocence. Ordeals were considered a "divine" proof, but could only be used in cases when human proofs such as evidence or eyewitness testimony were inadequate or unobtainable. Crimes committed in secret or in lonely places, questions of sexual consent, or money left for deposit were proven by these trials, following a carefully established ritual procedure. The trial could be done in four different ways: **fire**, **water**, balance, or poison.

The fire ordeal entailed carrying a red-hot iron ball, licking a red-hot plowshare, or removing a ring or coin from a vessel of boiling oil, with guilt or innocence established by whether or not one was burned. The water ordeal entailed remaining underwater for a specified length of time, with guilt determined by the inability to do so. The balance ordeal was done by successive weighings, with the conviction that a guilty person would become progressively heavier. The poison ordeal was performed either by consuming poison, or by safely removing a coin from an earthen pot containing a cobra; innocence was established by surviving.

There were fairly strict prescriptions governing which of these ordeals certain people were allowed to perform. **Women**, the elderly, and the infirm were subjected to the test of balance; **brahmins** were generally forbidden from undertaking ordeal by poison. In every case the actual ordeal was preceded by the person proclaiming his or her innocence, followed by declarations praising the saving **power of truth** and the damning force of untruth. Historians speculate that these required declarations helped make the ordeal more reliable. For instance, in the ordeal of licking a red-hot plowshare, a guilty person might be significantly more nervous and thus have less moisture on the tongue. Similarly, the nervousness during the water ordeal may have impeded

Temple to the sun at Konarak, in Orissa.

a person's ability to hold his breath. Whether or not these speculations have any merit, the most important feature in the original Hindu context was the belief in the power of truth itself.

Organs of Action
See **karmendriya**.

Orissa
A state in modern India on the eastern coast between the states of **Andhra Pradesh** and **West Bengal**. Orissa traces its roots to the kingdom of Kalinga and the bloody conquest by the Mauryan emperor **Ashoka** (r. 269–232 B.C.E.). During the early medieval period the Kesari and **Ganga** dynasties built stunning temples, many of which exist today. Modern Orissa is largely undeveloped, and a large percentage of its people are indigenous tribal peoples (**adivasis**). Historically, Hindu culture has been manifest in the coastal regions, whereas the interior has been tribal land. Orissa's sacred sites include the Ganga-era temples in the state capital of **Bhubaneshvar**, the sacred city of **Puri**, and the temple to the **Sun** at **Konarak**. For general information about Orissa and all the regions of India, see Christine Nivin et al., *India*. 8th ed., Lonely Planet, 1998. See also **Maurya dynasty**.

Orissi
One of the classical **dance** forms of India; some of the others are **Kathak**, **Bharatanatyam**, **Kuchipudi**, **Kathakali**, and **Manipuri**. Dance in **Orissa** dates to the second century B.C.E.; the present Orissi style has its roots in the dance performed at the temple of the god **Jagannath** in **Puri**. The temple itself was built in the eleventh century; the subsidiary part, known as the **natamandira** ("dance-hall"), was built about a century later. The latter period was the era of the poet **Jayadeva**, whose lyric poem, the *Gitagovinda*, is the only non-scriptural poem that can be recited in the temple. According to tradition, Jayadeva's wife, Padmavati, was one of the dancers in the temple, and it was she who first danced parts of the *Gitagovinda* as an **offering** to Jagannath. As dance at the

temple evolved, two categories of temple dancers emerged: those allowed to dance in the inner sanctum, and those allowed to dance in the natamandira. In the seventeenth century, a third type of dance emerged—boys dressed as dancing girls performed for general entertainment both outside and inside the temple. The latter dance tended to be more athletic and acrobatic, whereas the women's dance was more gentle and lyrical.

The modern Orissi style combines both elements. The most characteristic stance is the chauka ("square"), in which the feet are spread wide and pointed in opposite directions, with the knees bent so that the upper leg is parallel to the ground. The arms are held in a mirroring position, bent at the elbow with the upper arms horizontal, and the lower arms and hands pointing straight down. The dance's stylistic impression is one of roundness and fluidity, created by rippling movements in the upper body during the dance. As in all the Indian dances, Orissi has a well-developed vocabulary of **gesture** and expression, making complex story-telling possible. The modern Orissi dance form has been shaped by the shift from temple to stage in the twentieth century; this change of venue has been primarily responsible for its "classical" form becoming more rigidly defined than in the past. For further information see Mohan Khokar, *Traditions of Indian Classical Dance*, 1984.

Osho

The name adopted late in life by **Bhagwan Shri Rajneesh**. See **Bhagwan Shri Rajneesh**.

Owl

In Hindu mythology, the owl is the animal vehicle of **Lakshmi**, the **goddess**. Just as the owl is popularly believed to have trouble seeing in the daytime, a person pursuing "Lakshmi" (money and prosperity) will be single-minded toward it and unable to "see" anything else, such as deeper wisdom. In modern **Hindi**, calling someone an "owl" is a mild insult, referring to the other as a "fool."

P

Pacification of Planets

Indian astrology (**jyotisha**) recognizes nine "**planets**": the **sun**, **moon**, **Mercury**, **Venus**, **Mars**, **Jupiter**, and **Saturn**; the remaining two are **Rahu** and **Ketu**, which do not correspond to any Western astrological features. Each of these planets is considered helpful or harmful by nature. The relative strength of any planet is believed to depend on its position in the horoscope and vis-à-vis the other planets. All are seen as minor divinities rather than as simple material objects, and thus a potentially harmful planet can be "pacified" through rites intended to minimize its disruptive potential. One common means of pacification is to wear the **gemstone** corresponding to the particular planet, so that the stone can neutralize the planet's force. More inauspicious cases demand stronger measures, often involving rites in which the planetary **inauspiciousness** is given away through the medium of gifts (**dana**). For further consideration see Gloria Goodwin Raheja, *The Poison in the Gift*, 1988. See also **Suryia**.

Padma

("lotus") One of the richest symbols in Indian **philosophy** and iconography, both Hindu and Buddhist, and an invariably auspicious object. Its size and colors make it one of the most beautiful Indian flowers, but the lotus is also a potent symbol for spiritual realization. It is rooted in the mud—symbolizing the corrupting world with which all beings must contend—but it blooms above the surface of the water, signifying transcendence. The lotus plant's underwater stems grow as long as necessary to get the flower bud above the water's surface—whether three, five, or ten feet—symbolizing the human ability to overcome obstacles to spiritual progress. Finally, lotus leaves are covered with a waxy coating, upon which water beads up and flows off; one religious text, the **Bhagavad Gita** (5.10), uses this as a simile for the man who renounces all attachment and is untouched by the things of the world.

Aside from its symbolic content, the lotus is also an important element in Hindu iconography. It is one of the four identifying objects carried by the god **Vishnu**, along with the conch shell (**shankha**), club (**gada**), and discus (**chakra**). It is also commonly carried by the **Goddess**, both in her forms as **Durga** and related powerful goddesses, and in her beneficent and benevolent form as **Lakshmi**, who is usually portrayed as standing on a lotus. The lotus even figures in one of the common Hindu creation myths, in which a lotus sprouts from Vishnu's navel and opens to reveal **Brahma**, who proceeds to create the earth. When the universe has run its course and is about to be destroyed, same process happens in reverse.

Padmapada

One of the two attested disciples of **Shankaracharya**—the other being **Sureshvara**—and the founder of the **Vivarana** school of **Advaita Vedanta**. The Advaita school upholds a philosophical position known as monism, which is the belief that a single Ultimate Reality, **Brahman**, lies behind all things, and that all things are merely differing forms of that reality. Advaita proponents claim that reality is nondual (**advaita**)—that is, that, despite the appearance of difference and diversity, all things are nothing but the formless, unqualified Brahman. For the Advaitins, the assumption of diversity is a fundamental misunderstanding of the ultimate nature of things, and a manifestation of **avidya** (lack of genuine understanding).

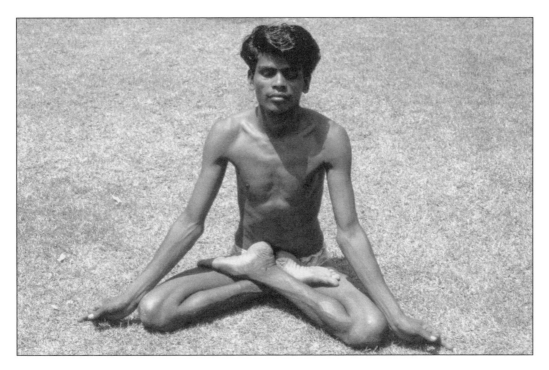

Man sitting in the padmasana, or lotus posture. This sitting position is often used in yoga and meditation.

The defining characteristic of Padmapada's Vivarana school is that he places the locus of ignorance in Brahman, in contrast to the **Bhamati** school, which placed it in the individual. To explain how Brahman can be the locus of ignorance the Vivarana Advaitins invoke the theory of **Reflectionism**: Just as an image appearing in a mirror is based on the original, but different from it, so human selves are identical with Brahman, but appear to be separate. The basis of Padmapada's position is an uncompromising affirmation of Brahman as the sole "reality," to which anything that exists must belong. For further information see Karl H. Potter (ed.), *Advaita Vedanta up to Samkara and His Pupils*, 1981; and Sarvepalli Radhakrishnan and Charles A. Moore (eds.), *A Sourcebook in Indian Philosophy*, 1957.

Padmasana

("lotus posture") Well-known sitting position (**asana**) used in **yoga** and in meditation; the lotus posture is also one of the sitting positions in which **deities** are portrayed in Hindu iconography. In this position the person sits cross-legged, with each foot placed on the thigh of the opposite leg. One of its benefits is that it is extremely stable and well suited for meditation, since the angle of the lower legs keeps the upper part of the legs flat on the ground, making a wide base to support the body. Done properly, it also keeps the spine quite straight, which is thought essential to keep from constricting the channels in the **subtle body**. In Indian iconography, the lotus position is sometimes represented at the base of a statue by the **sculpture** of a lotus, which forms the base on which the image is placed.

Paduka

A wooden sandal used mainly by ascetics. It consists of a wooden sole and a mushroom-shaped front post, which is gripped with first two toes for stability. Padukas are used by **ascetics** not only because of their cheapness and durability, but because they are completely free of animal products such as **leather**, which are considered impure. Aside from their functional use as footwear, after death an ascetic's padukas will often be kept by his (or, more rarely, her) disciples, as a sign of their **guru's** symbolic presence.

Padya

("for the feet") The third of the sixteen traditional **upacharas** ("**offerings**") given to a **deity** as part of **worship**, on the model of treating the deity as an honored guest. In this offering, the deity is offered water for washing the feet, which would be a traditional act of hospitality for a guest coming in from outside. The actual act of offering can be performed in various ways and often depends on the worshiper's inclinations. In some cases the water will simply be presented before the deity's image with the understanding that the deity has taken it, whereas in other cases the devotee (**bhakta**) will physically wash the feet of the image. In either case, the underlying motive is to show love for the deity and to minister to the deity's needs.

Pahari

One of the two influential "schools" of Indian **miniature painting**, the other being the **Rajasthani**. The distinctions between schools are geographical and thus somewhat arbitrary, since, for example, the **Basohli** paintings belong to the Pahari school, but are stylistically closer to those of **Rajasthan** than to the later Pahari style.

The Pahari style flourished in the eighteenth and nineteenth centuries in the small kingdoms in the **Shiwalik Hills** north and west of Delhi. It first appears in the kingdom of **Basohli**, where the influence of the Rajasthani school is the clearest, and later developed in the kingdoms of **Jammu**, **Guler**, **Garhwal**, and **Kangra**. The developed Pahari style differs from the Rajasthani in its emphasis on more linear drawing—perhaps influenced by European art—and a more restrained use of color, both features

tending to give the paintings a more lyrical feel. For further information see W. G. Archer, *Indian Painting*, 1957; and "Pahari Miniatures: A Concise History," in *Marg*, Vol. 28, No. 2, 1975.

Paishacha Marriage

One of the eight ways to perform a marriage recognized in the **dharma literature**, the treatises on religious duty. Paishachas are a class of **demons**, so a marriage named after them is already suspect. The Paishacha marriage takes place when a man has intercourse with a woman who is drunk, unconscious, or asleep. Not surprisingly, this is one of the four reprehensible (**aprashasta**) forms of marriage, and because of the woman's lack of conscious awareness, this form was forbidden, even though it was deemed a valid marriage. Here the writers' concern seems to have been to give the "bride" legal status as a wife, rather to legitimate the actions of the "groom." Although theoretically valid, this form of marriage has always been forbidden, and thus it has never been one of the common forms of marriage. See also **marriage, eight classical forms**.

Paithan

City and sacred site (**tirtha**) on the **Godavari** River in the state of **Maharashtra**, about 175 miles east of Bombay. Although of reduced importance in modern times, it has a long history as a trading city and was an important stopping-point on the central Indian trade route from southern India to **Ujjain**. Since the sixteenth century, Paithan has been famous as the home of **Eknath**, one of the important figures in the **Varkari Panth**, a religious community centered around the **worship** of the Hindu god **Vithoba** at his temple at **Pandharpur** in the modern state of **Maharashtra**. Varkari religious practice primarily consists of two pilgrimages, in which all the participants arrive in Pandharpur on the same **day**. Eknath still symbolically travels to Pandharpur twice each year; a **palanquin** (palkhi) bearing his sandals is at the head of the procession bearing his name.

Paksha

One of the parts in the accepted form of an inference (**anumana**) in Indian **philosophy**. The accepted form for an inference has three terms: an assertion (**pratijna**), a reason (**hetu**), and examples (**drshtanta**); each of these three has its own constituent parts. The paksha is part of the first term, the assertion, and comprises the class of things about which the assertion is to be proved. For instance, in the stock example, "There is fire on that mountain, because there is smoke on that mountain," the paksha in this case is "that mountain," or the class of things about which the assertion must be proved. The class that forms the paksha must also appear in the second term of the inference, the reason, as the common link between the two parts (as in "this mountain is on fire, because this mountain is smoking"). The paksha thus forms the common link between the assertion and the reason, thereby ensuring that the latter is relevant to the former.

In the context of a **lunar month**, the word *paksha* refers to the month's two "parts." The **Shukla Paksha** is the waxing half, while the **Krishna Paksha** is the waning half.

Pakudha Kacchayana

An atomistic early Indian philosopher whose views are mentioned in the Buddhist scriptures. As these scriptures portray him, Pakudha believed that seven things were eternal, unmoving, and unchanging—the four elements, ease, pain, and the soul. According to Pakudha, when a sword cuts a person's head in two, no one is deprived of life, rather the sword merely penetrates the interval between two elementary substances (presumably the soul and the material part of the person's body). This example seems to suggest an antisocial

ethos, but beyond this, very little is known about him.

Pala Dynasty

(8th–12th c.) Eastern Indian dynasty whose ancestral homeland was in **Bihar** but whose core territory also spanned most of modern Bengal. The Pala dynasty's zenith came at the turn of the ninth century, when they controlled the entire northern Indian plain all the way into the **Punjab** region. Their rise to power came as a result of political instability in the Gangetic plain, and the Palas were quickly supplanted by the **Gurjara-Pratihara dynasty** while retaining sway over Bengal and Bihar for several centuries more. Their territory in Bengal was eventually taken by the **Sena dynasty**, and the Palas were finally conquered by the **Gahadavalas** in the middle of the twelfth century. The Palas and Senas are both noted for a particular type of **sculpture**, in which the images were made from black chlorite schist polished to a mirror finish.

Palani

Town and sacred site (**tirtha**) in the eastern part of the state of **Tamil Nadu**, about sixty miles northwest of **Madurai**. Palani is part of a network of six temples in Tamil Nadu dedicated to **Murugan**, a hill **deity** who has been assimilated into the larger pantheon as a form of the god **Skanda**, the **son** of **Shiva**. Five of these temples have been definitively identified, and each is associated with a particular region, a particular ecosystem, and a particular incident in Murugan's mythic career—in the case of Palani, Murugan lived there as a young **ascetic**. Every other shrine to Murugan in Tamil Nadu can be considered the sixth of these temples. The cult of Murugan is thus a symbolic vehicle for Tamil pride and identity, and since the number six has connotations of completeness—as in the six directions, or the six **chakras** in the **subtle body**—it also connotes that nothing external is needed. For

A palanquin is used to carry images of a temple's deity in ritual processions.

further information see Fred Clothey, "Pilgrimage Centers in the Tamil Cultus of Murukan," in *Journal of the American Academy of Religion,* Vol. 40, No. 1 (1972).

Palanquin

Platform or litter supported by poles on the shoulders of two or more men, and used as a respectful way to carry something or someone in procession. A palanquin can be used to carry the image of a **deity** in a ritual procession, or an **ascetic** leader or spiritual teacher (**guru**) by his (or more rarely, her) disciples, or the sandals (**padukas**) or other **possessions** connected with one's spiritual leader, as in the **Varkari Panth's** pilgrimage to **Pandharpur**.

Pallava Dynasty

(6th–9th c.) Southern Indian dynasty whose capital was at the city of **Kanchipuram**, and which ruled over much of the southern Indian peninsula

between the sixth and ninth centuries. The greatest Pallava rulers were king **Mahendravarman** and his successors **Narasimhavarman I** and **II**. The reign of the Pallava dynasty was marked by the explosion of southern Indian culture: the development of Tamil literature, the devotional (**bhakti**) religious fervor of the groups known as the **Alvars** and the **Nayanars**, and the magnificent religious monuments at **Mahabalipuram**. Throughout much of its existence the Pallava empire carried on a running battle with the **Chalukya** and **Pandya** Dynasties, neither of which could prevail against it, but it was eventually absorbed by the next great southern Indian empire, the **Chola dynasty**. See also **Tamil language** and **Tamil epics**.

Palm Leaves

Until commercially produced paper became readily available, palm leaves were the most common writing medium in traditional India. The palm leaves were cut into narrow strips held together by a cord (**sutra**) running through a hole punched in the middle of the leaf. Palm leaf books usually had a top and bottom made from strips of wood, to protect the leaves, and these covers were often ornately decorated. The fragile nature of these palm leaves made regular copying necessary to preserve manuscripts, even though such frequent copying generally introduced errors. If left untended, the life span of a manuscript was at most fifty years, due to the deteriorations caused by the climate and the damage from a species of termite known as "white ants," which fed on palm leaves. See also **pustaka**.

Pan
See **betel**.

Pancha Dravida

Collective name for the five main southern Indian **brahmin** communities, whose names largely correspond to the regions in which they live: the **Gujaratis** in the state of **Gujarat**, **Maharashtris** in the state of **Maharashtra**, **Karnatas** in the state of **Karnataka**, **Andhras** in the state of **Andhra Pradesh**, and **Dravidas** in deep southern India, in the states of **Tamil Nadu** and **Kerala**.

Pancha Gauda

Collective name for the five main northern Indian **brahmin** communities: the **Gaudas** and **Kanaujias**, who stretch over most of northern India; the **Maithilas** in the northern state of **Bihar**; the **Utkalas** in the coastal state of **Orissa**; and the **Saraswats**, traditionally found in several widely separated locations. One group lived in the coastal region of Sindh in modern Pakistan, although after Partition in 1947 most migrated to Bombay. Another group was located in prepartition **Punjab**, although here too they have tended to migrate away from the part of Punjab in modern Pakistan. A third branch, known as the **Gauda Saraswats**, is found on a narrow strip of coastline in the southern Indian state of **Karnataka**.

Panchagavya

("five [products of the] **cow**") A mixture of cow's milk, curds, clarified butter (ghee), urine, and dung. Since each of these products comes from the sacred cow, it is considered a ritually purifying substance. Panchagavya is drunk for purification during rituals of expiation (**prayashchitta**), and it can also be used in other rituals used to purify people, objects, and places.

Panchagni-Tapa

("five-fires **asceticism**") Form of voluntary physical mortification, usually performed in the hot **season**, in which the person sits surrounded by four fires, the fifth fire being the sun overhead. Although this practice is now uncommon, it is very old and routinely named in the **puranas** and other religious texts as one of the standard **ascetic** practices. As with all forms of physical ascetic endurance (**tapas**), this rite is performed under the assumption that voluntarily enduring pain and/or hardship is a way to gain spiritual, religious, and magical power.

Panchak Nakshatra

A group of five (pancha) consecutive **nakshatras** (the twenty-seven signs in the lunar zodiac) in Indian astrology (**jyotisha**). The lunar houses are divided equally throughout the solar zodiac, with 2.25 lunar houses for each solar sign. In a single **lunar month** the **moon** moves through each of these lunar houses in turn, spending about a **day** in each. The Panchak Nakshatra is believed to be a highly inauspicious time, and people who pay attention to astrology will often severely curtail any nonessential activities until this time has passed.

Panchakroshi Yatra

A circular journey (**yatra**) in which pilgrims circumambulate the outer boundary of **Kashi** (the largest of the three concentric ritual areas contained in the city of **Benares**) and visit 108 shrines along the way. The journey's length is reckoned at five kroshas (roughly ten miles), hence the name. The journey measures out the boundaries of the sacred city, and thus pilgrims symbolically circle the entire world. Although the best known Panchakroshi Yatra is in Benares, and the name is most commonly associated with this place, many other sacred sites (**tirthas**) have similar pilgrimage routes, and this process of a circular journey around a sacred spot is a common ritual motif.

Panchala

Name of the region corresponding to the middle part of the state of **Uttar Pradesh**, centered on the **Ganges** River valley around the city of **Kanauj**. Panchala is mentioned as a kingdom as early as the sixth century B.C.E., and although it became a tributary to the great empires such as the Mauryas

(4th–3rd c. B.C.E.), it retained an independent identity until the third century. See also **Maurya dynasty**.

Panchamahayajna

("[the] five great sacrifices") Set of five ritual actions—**brahmayajna**, **pitryajna**, **devayajna**, **bhutayajna**, and **nryajana**—that are prescribed in the **dharma literature**, (texts on religious duty). These five actions are prescribed daily religious observances for a "**twice-born**" householder, that is, a householder who has been born into one of the three "twice-born" groups in Indian society—**brahmin**, **kshatriya**, or **vaishya**—and who has received the adolescent religious **initiation** known as the "second birth." Each **sacrifice** (**yajna**) is directed toward a different class of beings—from the Absolute Reality down to animals—and is satisfied by different actions: to **Brahman** by teaching and studying the **Veda**, to the **ancestral spirits** (pitr) by **offerings** of water (**tarpana**), to the gods (**deva**) by offering clarified butter into the sacred **fire**, to the animals and social outcasts (**bhut**) by putting out food for them, and to human beings (nr) by showing hospitality to guests. In the time since the dharma literature was composed, Hindu life has seen significant changes in emphasis, and although some of these are still important in modern Hindu life—particularly the stress on hospitality to guests—in most cases the others have been either elided or replaced by other religious forms.

Panchamakara

"The Five Forbidden Things," literally, "the five m's": A group of five things used for **worship** in the secret, ritually based religious practice known as **tantra**. This name arises because the names for all five of these begin with the letter "m"—**madya** (wine), **matsya** (fish), **mamsa** (meat), **mudra** (fermented or parched grain), and **maithuna** (copulation). They are used in their actual form in "left hand" (**vamachara**) tantra, and by substitution in "right hand" (**dakshinachara**) tantra.

All five are condemned by "respectable" Hindu society (the last because it is characterized as adulterous), and their use in tantric ritual must be seen in a larger context. One of the most pervasive tantric assumptions is the ultimate unity of everything that exists. From a tantric perspective, to affirm that the entire universe is one principle—often conceived as the activity of a particular **deity**—means that the adept must reject all concepts based on dualistic thinking. The "Five Forbidden Things" provide a ritual means for breaking down duality, since in this ritual the adept violates societal norms forbidding consumption of **intoxicants**, nonvegetarian food, and illicit sexuality, in a conscious effort to sanctify what is normally forbidden. Tantric adepts cite such ritual use of forbidden things as proof that their practice involves a more exclusive qualification (**adhikara**) and is thus superior to common practice. For further information see Arthur Avalon (Sir John Woodroffe), *Shakti and Shakta*, 1978; Swami Agehananda Bharati, *The Tantric Tradition*, 1977; and Douglas Renfrew Brooks, *The Secret of the Three Cities*, 1990.

Panchang

In Indian astrology (**jyotisha**), an almanac documenting the position of the various celestial bodies during the course of a **calendar year**, including the days of the **moon's** monthly cycle, its progression through the **nakshatras**, and the position of the **planets**. Most Hindu religious festivals fall according to a lunar calendar, and thus a panchang is needed to determine when they will arrive. A panchang is also important for helping people to determine auspicious and inauspicious times for the performance of certain activities. The greatest care is taken in fixing marriage times, to avoid any possible **inauspiciousness** that could affect the marriage, but in many cases a panchang will be consulted before initiating any important activity.

Pancharatra

("five nights," of uncertain meaning) The name denotes a particular group of **Vaishnavas** (devotees of the god **Vishnu**). Although there is plenty of evidence that the Pancharatra community is very old, very little is known about its origins. In the earliest Vaishnava sectarian texts, the Pancharatra community is unfavorably compared to another group, the **Bhagavatas**, with the former described as marginal and the latter as "Vedic" and respectable. Despite this seeming disapprobation, in their earliest appearances Pancharatras do not seem theologically different from the Bhagavatas, although their differences may have been rooted in differing practices. In their later history, the Pancharatras become associated with an elaborate theory of **creation**, finalized somewhere around the sixth century and based on the successive appearance of four divine emanations: Vishnu-Narayana, **Sankarshana**, **Pradyumna**, and **Aniruddha**. The successive activity of these divine emanations brings the world into being, but each is also associated with a particular facet of spiritual life through which human beings can reverse the process of creation and gain liberation. The Pancharatra school is also important for its theory of primary and secondary **avatars**, in which the latter can include any properly consecrated image of the **deity**. The doctrine of secondary avatars has become a pivotal idea in the later **Shrivaishnava** community, through which Pancharatra ideas have continued to influence modern Hindu life.

Panchatantra

("Five Treatises") A collection of moralistic fables intended to impart practical and worldly wisdom. The fables themselves are framed by the story of a king who is distressed by his sons' lack of learning and good moral character, which gives him grave misgivings about their ability to rule well after his death. He resolves this problem by hiring a person to teach the boys through fables, each of which usually has several shorter fables embedded in it to give moral lessons along the way. These fables are intended to provide pragmatic advice about how to be successful in the real world, particularly in the art of statecraft. This pragmatic focus can lead one to characterize the text's advice as opportunistic, particularly since it encourages caution and self-interest as the keys to success. The *Panchatantra* exists in several versions, of which the most famous is the *Hitopadesha*. The text has been translated numerous times; a version found its way to Europe, where it became the basis for the fables of La Fontaine.

Panchavati

In the *Ramayana*, the earlier of the two great Indian epics, the place where three of the epic's central characters—the god-king **Rama**, his wife **Sita**, and his brother **Lakshmana**—live during much of their fourteen years of forest exile. It is from here that Sita is kidnapped by **Ravana**, the **demon**-king of **Lanka**. Although the events in the *Ramayana* cannot be definitively set in any specific place, there is a village named Panchavati, outside the city of **Nasik** in the state of **Maharashtra**, which is identified with the mythic site.

Panchayat

In traditional India, a group of five (pancha) elders from a particular community, who were the final authority for the members of that community. Each **jati** (**endogamous** subcommunity, often defined by hereditary occupation) was a self-governing body, for which the panchayat would make all the important decisions. In modern India this institution is being hailed as a paradigm for decentralized government, in which the people themselves take responsibility for their communities, but since there are multiple jatis in any traditional Hindu village, this also means that there were multiple centers of authority.

Panchayatana ("five-abode") Puja

Type of **worship** (**puja**) performed by **Smarta** brahmins, a group of **brahmins** distinguished, not by region or family, but by the religious texts they hold most authoritative—in this case, those known as the **smrtis** rather than sectarian religious texts. The panchayatana puja is marked by the simultaneous worship of five different **deities**—usually **Vishnu**, **Shiva**, **Surya**, **Ganesh**, and the **Goddess**. Individual Smartas may choose one or another from among these as their primary deity, but all these deities are ritually honored since they are all considered manifestations of the divine.

Panchkedar

("The Five Kedars") The collective name for a network of five sites, sacred to the god **Shiva**, spread throughout the **Garhwal** region of the **Himalayas**: **Kedarnath**, **Rudranath**, **Tungnath**, **Madmaheshvar**, and **Kalpeshvar**. Each site is identified with a part of Shiva's body, thus providing a series of connections between the **deity's** body and the land itself—understandably so, since Shiva is believed to dwell in the Himalayas. Kedarnath is identified as Shiva's back, Madmaheshvar his navel, Tungnath his arm, Rudranath his face, and Kalpeshvar his matted locks (**jata**).

Panchvani

("Five Voices") Manuscript collection compiled by the **Dadupanth**, a religious community founded by the northern Indian poet-saint **Dadu** (1554–1603). The collection contains the works of five different devotional (**bhakti**) poet-saints: Dadu, **Kabir**, **Namdev**, **Ravidas**, and Hardas. **Rajasthan's** desert climate has helped to preserve these manuscripts, some of which date from the

early seventeenth century. The Panchvani manuscripts are among the earliest written sources for these poets, which makes them an important resource for the historical study of northern Indian devotional poetry. For further information on the literary resources of the Dadupanth, see Winand Callewaert (trans.), *The Sarvangi of the Dadupanthi Rajab*, 1978; and *The Sarvangi of Gopaldas*, 1993.

Panda

A hereditary priest who assists pilgrims with any rituals they may need or desire to perform, and also with any other needs that the pilgrims may have. Each panda family in any given pilgrimage place (**tirtha**) has the exclusive rights to serve pilgrims coming from a particular geographical area or areas; pilgrims are supposed to seek out the panda serving their native region, whether or not the pilgrims still live in that place. On every visit, pilgrims will make an entry in the panda's pilgrim register (**bahi**), detailing the names of those who visited and the reason that they came. Some of these registers date back hundreds of years, and the documents are the ultimate proof of the hereditary connection between panda and pilgrim families. In earlier times this hereditary relationship was essential for the pilgrims, since their connection with their pandas provided resources while traveling—lodging, food, and other sorts of support. The pandas would minister to their clients, arrange for any needed rites, and even lend them money, if necessary. Pilgrims would usually give the panda a token gift when they departed, along with a pledge for some larger amount, which the pandas would travel to their homes to pick up.

Although pandas are often characterized as greedy and rapacious—based on their tendency to demand what they think a client is able to pay—in its ideal form both parties benefit from the relationship. In recent years, the pandas have become less central figures in

Varkari Panth pilgrims en route to Pandharpur.

many pilgrimage places, and consequently, their status and their income have declined. Many pilgrimage places have been developed as sites for religious tourism, and hotels and facilities that have been built at these places have rendered pilgrims less dependent on their pandas for accommodation. At the same time, recent years have seen a general decline in the performance of ritual acts, except for the most important, particularly those connected with death.

Pandava

("**sons** of **Pandu**") A collective name for the five brothers who are the protagonists of the *Mahabharata*: **Yudhishthira**, **Arjuna**, **Bhima**, **Nakula**, and **Sahadeva**. Although they are named after king Pandu, none are actually his son, since Pandu has been cursed to die the moment he holds his wife in amorous embrace. Rather, they are magically conceived through a **mantra** given by the sage **Durvasas** to **Kunti**, Pandu's senior wife. The mantra gives the woman who recites it the power to call down any god and to have,

by that god, a son equal in power to himself. Kunti uses this mantra to bear Yudhishthira by the god **Dharma**, Arjuna by the storm-god **Indra**, and Bhima by the **wind**-god **Vayu**. With Pandu's blessing Kunti also teaches the mantra to her co-wife **Madri**, who meditates on the **Ashvins** (divine twins who are the physicians to the gods), and delivers the twins Nakula and Sahadeva. The basic theme of the *Mahabharata* is the story of the struggle for royal power between the Pandavas and their cousins, the **Kauravas**, which culminates in a war that destroys the entire family.

Pandharpur

City and sacred site (**tirtha**) on the **Bhima River** in the state of **Maharashtra**, about 185 miles east and south of Bombay. Pandharpur is best known for the temple to the god **Vithoba**, and has been a center of **worship** for the **Varkari Panth** religious community for at least seven hundred years. Varkari rituals center around a twice-yearly pilgrimage to Pandharpur, in which the pilgrims all arrive on the same day. Each pilgrim procession starts from a different place and is identified with one of the poet-saints who helped form the community. At the front of each procession is a **palanquin** (palkhi) bearing the sandals of that group's particular saint, who is thus symbolically leading them into Pandharpur. For more information see G. A. Deleury, *The Cult of Vithoba*, 1960; I. B. Karve, "On the Road," *Journal of Asian Studies*, Vol. 22, No. 1, 1962; and Digambar Balkrishna Mokashi, *Palkhi*, 1987.

Pandrenthan

Historical site south of the city of Shrinagar in **Kashmir**. Pandrenthan is famous for one of the few old Hindu temples still standing in Kashmir, a temple dedicated to the god **Shiva** built in the twelfth century C.E. The shrine itself is fairly small and simple. The floor plan is basically square, with each side 17.5 feet long and an entrance on each side giving the temple an open feel. Each doorway has a gable over it projecting out from a pyramidal roof known to builders as a hip roof. The temple is built entirely of stone but has overlapping courses, in an attempt to mimic wooden construction.

Pandu

In the *Mahabharata*, the later of the two great Hindu epics, the son of the sage **Vyasa** and queen **Ambalika**. Pandu and his brother **Dhrtarashtra** are born as the result of a desperate attempt to preserve the royal line of King **Shantanu** after Shantanu's son **Vichitravirya** dies without heirs. Upon Vichitravirya's death, his mother **Satyavati** calls upon her eldest son, **Vyasa**, to sleep with Vichitravirya's wives, **Ambika** and her sister Ambalika, in the hope that the women will conceive. According to tradition Vyasa is very ugly, and each woman reacts involuntarily when Vyasa appears in her bed: Ambika covers her eyes, causing her son **Dhrtarashtra** to be born blind, and Ambalika turns pale, causing her son

Pandu to be born with an unnaturally pale complexion. Given Dhrtarashtra's blindness, Pandu is the best suited to rule; he marries **Kunti** and **Madri** and lives quite happily as the king.

This idyllic time abruptly ends one day while he is hunting in the forest and shoots a **deer** while it is mating. To his horror, he discovers that the deer is the sage **Kindama**, who has taken this form for sport with his wife; with his dying breath, the sage curses Pandu that he will die the moment he touches his wife in an amorous embrace. Since he has no children, and the **curse** condemns him to die without an heir, Pandu abdicates the throne in favor of his brother Dhrtarashtra and goes with his wives to live as an **ascetic** in the **Himalayas**. At this time Kunti tells him about the **mantra** she has received years before from the sage **Durvasas**, which gives the woman who recites it the power to call down any of the gods and to have by him a son equal in power to himself. With Pandu's blessing Kunti and Madri bear five heroic sons, the five **Pandava** brothers. They all live happily together until one day when Pandu, swayed by the intoxicating influence of spring, ignores Madri's warnings and embraces her. The sage's curse takes effect and Pandu falls dead, although, through the power of the mantra, his family line continues.

Pandurang

("pale") Epithet of the god **Vithoba**, whose primary place of **worship** is in the holy city of **Pandharpur** in the state of **Maharashtra**. See **Vithoba**.

Pandya Dynasty

(6th–14th c.) Southern Indian dynasty whose capital was in the city of **Madurai** in the state of **Tamil Nadu**. The Pandyas existed as a regional power as early as the late sixth century, when they fought the **Pallava dynasty** of **Kanchipuram** for control of the peninsula. The Pandyas at one time became vassals to the **Chola dynasty** when the latter reigned over all of southern India, but with the decline of the Cholas the Pandyas became the dominant regional power, eventually absorbing the Chola kingdom in 1279. At their zenith in the thirteenth century the Pandyas controlled most of the southern part of India, but were in turn conquered and annexed early in the fourteenth century by the Sangama dynasty, also known as the **Vijayanagar dynasty** after their capital city.

Panguni

Twelfth month in the Tamil solar **year**, corresponding to the northern Indian solar month of Mina (the zodiacal sign of Pisces), which usually falls within March and April. This name is a modification of **Phalgun**, the twelfth month of the lunar **calendar**. The existence of several different calendars is one clear sign of the continuing importance of regional cultural patterns. One way that the Tamils retain their culture is by preserving their traditional calendar. Tamil is one of the few regional languages in India with an ancient, well-established literary tradition. See also **Tamil months**, **Tamil Nadu**, and **Tamil language**.

Pani

A group of northern Indian people mentioned in a hymn in the **Rg Veda** (10.108), the oldest Hindu religious text. This reference speaks poorly of this group, since it portrays them as cattle thieves. The hymn is spoken as a dialogue between the Panis and **Sarama**, the divine **dog** who is the servant of the god **Indra** and who has been sent by Indra to recover the cattle the Panis have stolen. This hymn may refer to an actual incident and an actual group of people, but it is impossible to say. Certainly the Vedas were not written as a strict historical record, and it is perilous to read them as such. At the same time, as the earliest textual records they preserve references to the culture and to contemporary times that can be found nowhere else.

Panigrahana

A minor rite, performed in many Hindu marriages, in which the groom grasps the bride's right hand as a symbol of their impending marital union. See also **marriage customs**.

Panini

(4th c. B.C.E.) The greatest **Sanskrit** grammarian, whose descriptive account of that language in his *Ashtadhyayi* ("Eight Sections") became the prescriptive norm for the language in later generations. Panini was not the earliest grammarian, since he names several in his text; his genius lay rather in his skills as an organizer and systematizer. Each of the *Ashtadhyayi*'s eight sections is written as a series of brief aphorisms (**sutras**), each of which provides the foundation and necessary background for those that follow. Panini's use of this form allowed him to provide a complete account of the language in the briefest possible space, and the text's condensed form made it easier to memorize. As with most sutra texts, the *Ashtadhyayi*'s terseness of expression presupposes a commentary, of which the most famous is the *Mahabhashya*, written by the grammarian **Patanjali** in the second century B.C.E.

Panth

General term used for a particular religious community, such as the **Dadupanth**, **Varkari** Panth, or the Nanak Panth—an older name for the Sikh community, which has simply been abridged to "Panth" by contemporary Sikhs. The word is derived from the **Sanskrit** word for "path" and is here used metaphorically to indicate a fixed pattern of belief and behavior, often rooted in a particular individual's teachings. There is a certain amount of semantic overlap between the words *panth* and **sampraday**, both of which denote religious communities, and there is no hard-and-fast rule dividing the two. In general, however, the term *panth* is more closely associated with movements in the **sant** religious tradition, which tended toward rebellion against the prevailing religious establishment, whereas *sampraday* is more commonly applied to groups that evolved within these established religious communities.

Pap

("evil") A word sometimes used as an adjective to describe people and actions, but most often used as a noun, either to denote a particular deed as evil or to refer to the collective evil one has accumulated through the bad deeds in one's karmic career. Since, according to **karma** theory, all one's deeds will eventually come to fruition, the evil that one has done is seen as already existing, even if only in a potential state. The opposite of pap is **punya**, the most general term denoting religious merit.

Papamochani Ekadashi

Religious observance falling on the eleventh day (**ekadashi**) of the dark (waning) half of the **lunar month** of **Chaitra** (March–April). The name Papamochani means "freeing from evil," and the faithful observance of this festival is believed to do exactly that. As with all the eleventh-day observances, it is dedicated to the **worship** of **Vishnu**. Most Hindu festivals have certain prescribed rites, which usually involve fasting (**upavasa**) and worship (**puja**), and often promise specific benefits for faithful performance. On this day one should worship Vishnu with the full complement of the sixteen **upacharas** ("**offerings**").

Papankusha Ekadashi

Religious observance falling on the eleventh **day** (**ekadashi**) of the bright (waxing) half of the **lunar month** of **Ashvin** (September–October). As with all the eleventh-day observances, it is dedicated to the **worship** of **Vishnu**. Most Hindu festivals have certain prescribed rites, which usually involve fasting (**upavasa**) and worship (**puja**), and often promise specific benefits for faithful performance. This ekadashi's name indicates that it is the goad (**ankusha**) to drive away all evil (**pap**), here fancifully conceived as an **elephant**. Thus, faithfully observing this festival is believed to cleanse one of all one's sins.

Parakiya

("belonging to another") Particular type of relationship between lover and beloved, in which the woman is seen as married to another person. Parakiya is said to generate the most intense passion, since the people pursuing it have nothing to gain but love itself—if caught, they risk ridicule and shame, and in any case their liaison has no real future. This is not the conventional, safe love with one's own spouse (**svakiya**) that is sanctioned by marriage, carries social approval, and usually entails procreation, but rather a dangerous love pursued solely for pleasure. This type of relationship is a standard image in **Sanskrit** poetry, and is also the dominant theme for describing the relationship between the god **Krishna** and his human consort **Radha**, which is seen as symbolizing the relationship between god and the human soul.

Paramahamsa

("supreme **Hamsa**") One of four types of Hindu **ascetic**. The four types were based on their supposed means of livelihood, which in practice has been much less important for ascetic identity than sectarian or organizational affiliation. The Paramahamsa is the most prestigious of the four, the others being (in order of increasing status) **Kutichaka**, **Bahudaka**, and Hamsa. Paramahamsas have no fixed abode and always live in an uninhabited place. They are said to have transcended all questions of religious duty (**dharma**), **purity**, and impurity (**ashaucha**), to have broken all attachments to the world, and to be continually immersed in contemplation of the Supreme **Brahman**.

The word Paramahamsa has a more specialized meaning among the **Dashanami Sanyasis**, ascetic devotees (**bhakta**) of the god **Shiva** whose organization is divided into ten sections, each designated by a particular name. Here the name Paramahamsa refers to an ascetic who comes from one of the three **twice-born** (dvija) **varnas**—that is, who is a **brahmin, kshatriya**, or **vaishya**, the three social groups with higher symbolic status—and who has been initiated as a **Sanyasi** in one of the six divisions that will accept non-brahmins. Paramahamsas have higher status in these divisions than the **Naga** or fighting ascetics, who will initiate **shudras**, but lower status than the **Dandis**, who are invariably brahmins.

Paramatman

("the highest self") Term generally used as a synonym for **Brahman**, the unqualified and undifferentiated reality that is seen as the source of all things, and the sole true power in the universe. This name, through its inclusion of the Self (**atman**) as part of the term, also emphasizes the identity in kind between Brahman and atman, between Supreme Reality and the individual Self.

Parampara

("succession") The general term for the spiritual lineage maintained by the transmission of knowledge and power from **guru** to disciple. Such lineages form the basis for tracing spiritual descent within religious communities, particularly in secret traditions such as **tantra**. In a religious context, one's spiritual lineage is an important factor in establishing an identity and connections with others in the school, in the same way a biological lineage places one within a family.

Parashara

In Hindu mythology, a legendary sage who is the grandson of the sage **Vasishtha**. He is credited with authoring the **Parashara Smrti**, an important and early work in the **dharma literature**. Parashara is best known as the father of the sage **Vyasa**, whom he begets through a maiden named **Satyavati**. Satyavati makes her living ferrying people across the **Ganges** River, and although she is a beautiful young woman, she always smells of fish because her mother is a celestial nymph who has been cursed to live as a fish in the Ganges. Struck by Satyavati's beauty while she is ferrying him across the river, Parashara creates an artificial fog to give them the privacy to have sexual intercourse. As a reward, he gives her the boon that, from that day onward, she will smell of musk instead of fish.

Parashara Smrti

One of the **smrtis** or "remembered" texts, a class of literature deemed important but less authoritative than the other textual category, the **shrutis**, or "heard" texts. This smrti is ascribed to the sage **Parashara**, and is an example of one of the **Dharma Shastras**, which were manuals prescribing rules for correct human behavior and ideal social life. Unlike the **Dharma Sutras**, which are ascribed to recognizable individuals, the Dharma Shastras are usually ascribed to mythic sages as a strategy to reinforce the authority of these texts. At 592 verses, the *Parashara Smrti* is relatively short, and it treats only two themes, religious custom (**achara**) and expiation (**prayashchitta**). The text is estimated to have been written between the first and fifth centuries, but in the fourteenth century it received an extensive commentary by **Madhava**, and the resulting work, known as the *Parasharamadhava*, has continued to be influential since then.

The god Vishnu's Parashuram avatar, carrying his battle-axe. He appears in this form to punish the warrior class' abuse of power.

Parashu

("battle-axe") A characteristic object in Hindu iconography, and one that appears in various forms—sometimes with a very light, thin handle and a larger head, at other times with a handle the size of a club (**gada**) and a very small, thin head. This weapon has the strongest mythic associations with **Vishnu's** sixth **avatar** or incarnation, **Parashuram**, who uses it in his war of extermination against the the ruling **kshatriya** class when their pride has grown too strong. The battle-axe is also commonly carried by the god **Ganesh** and signifies his power to cut through obstacles and impediments. It also commonly appears in various images of the deities **Shiva**, **Vishnu**, and the **Goddess**, as one among their galaxy of weapons.

Parashuram Avatar

Sixth **avatar** or incarnation of the god **Vishnu**. As with all the avatars of Vishnu,

the Parashuram avatar comes to restore a cosmic equilibrium that has been thrown out of balance, in this case from the overweening abuse of power by the warrior (**kshatriya**) class. Parashuram is the son of **Jamadagni**, a **brahmin** sage whose most precious **possession** is Surabhi, a **cow** that will grant its owner any desired wish. One day when Parashuram is away, the king comes to Jamadagni's **ashram**. When he sees the cow, he desires it, and when Jamadagni refuses to give it to him, the king takes it by force.

When Parashuram learns of this, he becomes fiercely angry. Taking up his **parashu** (or battle-axe, a weapon particularly associated with him), he enters into battle with the king and eventually kills him. When the king's sons remain rebellious in opposition to him, Parashuram makes twenty-one journeys around India, destroying all of the kshatriyas that he can find, in an effort to wipe them from the face of the earth. The major theme of this story is the conflict between the brahmin and kshatriya classes, and the realities of living in a society in which brahmins had religious authority but kshatriyas had the power of enforcement. This story reveals a strong concern for the sanctity of a brahmin's possessions and highlights the perils of taking them by force. The writers behind the story were almost certainly brahmins, and their remarks on the perils of taking a brahmin's possessions doubtless reflect an insecurity about their ability to supersede governmental power.

In addition to the story of exterminating the kshatriyas, Parashuram appears in the epic *Mahabharata* as the person who teaches the heroic **Karna** the art of weapons and warfare. The epic portrays Parashuram as powerful and irascible, and as possessing such continuing hatred of kshatriyas that he refuses to take them as students. When Parashuram discovers that Karna is a kshatriya and not a brahmin, as he has claimed to be, he lays a curse on Karna that, in his hour of greatest need, he will forget everything he has learned as his student.

Parashurameshvar Temple

Temple constructed about 750 C.E. in the city of **Bhubaneshvar** in the state of **Orissa**, dedicated to the god **Shiva** in his aspect as the "Lord of **Parashuram**." This title refers to Parashuram's long period of **asceticism**, in which he worshiped Shiva as his chosen **deity** and was rewarded with Shiva's **grace**. The temple is an early example of the Orissan variant of the northern Indian **Nagara** temple style. The Nagara style emphasizes verticality, with the whole temple building culminating in a single high point, and the Orissan variant of this style has a single enormous tower (**deul**) over the image of the temple's primary deity, with shorter subsidiary buildings leading up to it. The Parashurameshvar temple is the first example of this basic pattern—a low, flat assembly hall (**jagamohan**), followed by a much taller and narrower tower (deul), in this case about forty feet high. Although later Orissan temples are much larger—some of the deuls tower over 200 feet—and often include additional buildings and structures, they all retain this basic pattern.

Parashuram Jayanti

Festival marking the birthday of **Parashuram avatar**, **Vishnu's** sixth **avatar**. This takes place on the third day of the bright (waxing) half of the **lunar month** of **Baisakh** (April–May), the same day as the festival of **Akshaya Trtiya**.

Parikshit

Mythic king in the **Lunar Line**, who serves as an example that one's fate cannot be escaped. Parikshit is the grandson of **Arjuna**, one of the five **Pandava** brothers who are the protagonists in the *Mahabharata*, the later of the two great Hindu epics.

Parikshit inherits the throne from **Yudhishthira**, Arjuna's elder brother, and according to tradition rules righteously for sixty years, but it is his death that is best remembered. Fond of hunting, Parikshit one day comes across a meditating sage while he is chasing a wounded deer. When the sage refuses to answer to his inquiries about the deer, Parikshit grows angry and, with his bow, drapes a dead cobra around the sage's neck. The sage remains unaware of this, but his **son** finds out about it when his playmates jeer at him. Furious, the son lays a curse that the person responsible will be fatally bitten within seven days by the great serpent **Takshaka**. When he discovers that the king is responsible, the son repents his **curse** to the King.

Parikshit takes all possible precautions to avoid his fate. He builds a house on a huge pillar, has anything brought into the house carefully searched, and surrounds himself with physicians who can cure snakebite. After six days without incident, the king begins to relax his vigilance. As the seventh day is ending, Takshaka conceals himself as a worm in a piece of fruit, changes into his real shape when the fruit is cut open, and bites the king, killing him.

Parinamavada

("transformation-relationship") Philosophical perspective that explains the relationship between the Ultimate Reality or realities and the perceivable world, and describes the world as a genuine transformation of this reality.

This position is espoused by proponents of the **Samkhya**, **Vishishthadvaita Vedanta**, and **Bhedabhada** philosophical schools. All three of these are proponents of a **causal model** called **satkaryavada**. The satkaryavada model assumes that effects preexist in their causes, and that, when these effects appear, they are transformations (parinama) of those causes. The classic example for this model is the transformation of milk to curds, butter, and clarified butter: each of these effects was already present in the cause, emerges from it through a natural transformation of that cause, and is causally related to it.

All three schools believe that the world as perceived is real and has some single ultimate source behind it: for the Samkhyas, the first principles are **purusha** and **prakrti**, for the Vishishthadvaita school, the god **Vishnu**, and for the Bhedabhada school, **Brahman**. All believe that real things come into being because these first principles undergo real transformations. Parinamavada allows for an explanation of the phenomenal world that compromises the transcendence of these first principles by making them part of the world. Philosophically, their difficulties arise in describing how the transcendent can become mundane, and then become transcendent again.

The transformation relationship is vehemently opposed by the **Advaita Vedanta** philosophical school, which upholds a philosophical position known as monism (the belief that a single Ultimate Reality lies behind all things, and that all things are merely differing forms of that reality). Advaita proponents claim that reality is nondual (**advaita**)—that is, that all things are "actually" the formless, unqualified **Brahman**, despite the appearance of difference and diversity in the world. Since Brahman is the only real thing, and Brahman never changes, the parinama model is a fundamental misunderstanding of the ultimate nature of things, since it assumes real change. The Advaita proponents' explanation for the nature of the relationship and the world is known as **vivartavada** ("illusory manifestation"), in which the ultimate appears to become transformed but in reality never changes. For further information see Sarvepalli Radhakrishnan and Charles A. Moore (eds.), *A Sourcebook in Indian Philosophy*, 1957; and Karl H. Potter (ed.), *Presuppositions of India's Philosophies*, 1972.

Parivartini Ekadashi

Religious observance falling on the eleventh day (**ekadashi**) of the bright (waxing) half of the **lunar month** of **Bhadrapada** (August–September). As are all the eleventh-day observances, this is dedicated to the **worship** of **Vishnu**. This day is particularly devoted to the worship of Vishnu's wife **Lakshmi**, the **goddess** presiding over wealth and prosperity. In her form as **Mahalakshmi** (as told in the *Devimahatmya*) she is able to kill **demons** that the gods cannot, and restore to gods the kingdom they have lost. This festival occurs during the time Vishnu is believed to be sleeping on the serpent **Shesha**, on an ocean of milk, with Lakshmi massaging his feet. The name Parivartini means "turning," and on this day Vishnu is believed to be stirring in his sleep. See also **ocean, churning of the**; and **cosmology**.

Parivrajaka

(from **Sanskrit** *parivraj*, "to wander about") A term that can be used to denote any wandering religious mendicant. Continual wandering is a very old Indian **ascetic** practice. It shows the conscious renunciation of the fixed and stable world of the householder, particularly in earlier societies, and it prevents the wanderer from forming any sort of attachments, even to places. This exemplifies the fourth and final stage of life found in the **dharma literature**, the **sanyasi**, in which a person has renounced all attachments of everyday life to search for spiritual attainment.

Parmananddas

(early 16th c.) One of the **ashtachap**, a group of eight northern Indian **bhakti** (devotional) poets. The compositions of these eight poets were used for liturgical purposes by the **Pushti Marg**, a religious community whose members are devotees (**bhakta**) of **Krishna**. In the Pushti Marg's sectarian literature, all eight are also named as members of the community and as associates of either the community's founder, **Vallabhacharya**, or his successor **Vitthalnath**. Little is known about Parmananddas himself, although tradition asserts that he was a **Kanaujia brahmin**, and the corpus of poetry attributed to him is much larger in later sources, suggesting that his name was used by later writers. The evidence from the earliest sources suggests that he was a devoted follower of Vallabhacharya. Much of his poetry is specifically written for the Pushti Marg, such as hymns in praise of Vallabhacharya, or hymns to be sung for the **worship** of Krishna throughout the day, a form of piety that came to characterize the Pushti Marg. To date, his works have not been translated, perhaps because of their sectarian character.

Parvana

A particular type of the memorial rites for the dead known as **shraddhas**. A parvana shraddha can be performed at specific times throughout the **year**, such as the **new moon**, but is most commonly performed during the Fortnight of the Fathers (**Pitrpaksha**), which falls during the waning moon in the **lunar month** of **Bhadrapada**. Whereas an **ekoddishta shraddha** is performed for any particular deceased individual, the parvana shraddha invokes first the paternal father, grandfather, and great-grandfather, then the same ancestors on the mother's side. The rite is performed to give benefits to all of these ancestors, although the father's ancestors are considered the primary recipients.

Parvata Dashanami

One of the ten divisions of the **Dashanami Sanyasis**, renunciant ascetics who are devotees (**bhakta**) of **Shiva**. The Dashanamis were supposedly established by the ninth century philosopher **Shankaracharya**, in an effort create a corps of learned men who could help to revitalize Hindu life. Each of the divisions is designated by a different name—in this case,

parvata ("mountain"). Upon **initiation**, new members are given this name as a surname to their new **ascetic** names, thus allowing for immediate group identification.

Aside from their individual identity, these ten "named" divisions are divided into four larger organizational groups. Each group has its headquarters in one of the four monastic centers (**maths**) supposedly established by Shankaracharya. The Parvata Dashanamis belong to the **Anandawara** group, which is affiliated with the **Jyotir** math in the Himalayan town of **Joshimath**.

Parvati

("**daughter** of the mountain") Wife of the god **Shiva**, and an important Hindu **goddess**, Parvati is the daughter of the minor deity **Himalaya** (the Himalaya Mountains personified), and his wife **Mena**. Parvati appears in human form to draw Shiva out of the **ascetic** isolation in which he has been lost since the death of his first wife, **Sati**, and to induce him to father the son necessary to kill the **demon Taraka**. According to her myths, even in her childhood Parvati vows that she will have only Shiva for her husband. Her parents try to discourage her, since Shiva has taken a vow of **asceticism** and is absorbed in deep meditation on Mount **Kailas**.

Parvati's first effort to arouse Shiva's desire ends in a dismal failure. **Kama**, the god of love, tries to shoot Shiva with an arrow of desire, but Shiva lets loose a stream of fire from the third eye in his forehead, burning Kama to ash. Undeterred, Parvati goes into the mountains and begins a program of harsh physical asceticism (**tapas**) of her own: standing on one foot for immense periods of time, enduring the heat of summer and cold of winter, and practicing severe fasting (**upavasa**) and self-denial. The spiritual power generated by her asceticism eventually awakens Shiva, and he comes to her, disguised as an aged **brahmin**. He tries to discourage

Parvati with her husband Shiva and their sons Ganesh and Skanda.

Parvati by making disparaging remarks about Shiva's lifestyle and personality, but Parvati, unshaken in her resolve, refuses to listen. Eventually Shiva reveals his true form to her, and they are married.

Although in his devotion to his wife Shiva is the Hindu symbol for the ideal husband, their family life is unusual. Since Shiva is the symbol for the perfect ascetic, the couple has no fixed home or means of support, and occasionally Parvati is portrayed as complaining of being an ascetic's wife. Symbolically, their marriage represents the domestication of the ascetic and his entrance into social and family life. Their union highlights the cultural tension between the two most important Hindu religious ideals: the householder and the renunciant ascetic. Perhaps to illustrate the contradiction of being a married ascetic, Shiva and Parvati have children but not in the normal way: **Skanda** develops from Shiva's **semen**, which falls on the ground during their interrupted love-making, while **Ganesh** is formed of the enlivened dirt from Parvati's body.

Parvati, as with all married Hindu goddesses, is generally seen as benign and benevolent. In some mythic stories she can be spiteful, but on the whole she projects a nurturing and motherly presence. Her mythology is almost completely connected with that of Shiva, showing her subordination as the model wife, and her **worship** is generally connected with him as well. She occupies an important position in **tantra**, a secret, ritually based religious practice, since in tantric texts Parvati is usually portrayed as the person questioning Shiva and then as the student receiving his instruction. For more information on Parvati and all the goddesses of Hinduism, see David R. Kinsley, *Hindu Goddesses*, 1986.

Paryanka

("bedstead") One of the postures (**asanas**) described in commentaries to the **Yoga Sutras**, in which the person is lying down with the arms stretched around the knees.

Pasha

("noose") In Indian iconography, one of the weapons carried by some of the divinities, especially **Ganesh** and **Yama**. For Ganesh, as the "Lord of Obstacles," the noose signifies his ability to bind (and release) obstacles, whereas Yama, the god of death, uses the noose to draw the soul from the body at the time of death. In the **Shaiva Siddhanta** religious community, pasha is also the name given to **Shiva's** power of illusion (**maya**), through which he entraps and enthralls unenlightened people (**pashu**). The triad of pasha, pashu, and Shiva as lord (**pati**) are the defining features of the Shaiva Siddhanta school.

Pashu

("beast") In the philosophical school known as **Shaiva Siddhanta**, and in the secret, ritually based religious practice known as **tantra**, the term for an unenlightened person, who is said to have a human form but to be little better than an **animal**. This lack of awareness comes not just through inherent dullness, but through the activity of **maya**, the power of illusion wielded by **Shiva** as lord (**pati**). The triad of pashu, pati and the bonds of illusion (**pasha**) are defining features of the Shaiva Siddhanta school.

Pashupata

An extinct **ascetic** community, of devotees (**bhakta**) of the god **Shiva** in his form as Pashupati, "the Lord of Beasts." Although the Pashupatas have now disappeared, according to the Chinese pilgrim **Hsuan Tsang** they were once the most important ascetic sect in northern India. According to historical reports, its members would engage in strange and antisocial behavior intended to bring disgrace upon themselves, although without lust or malice in their hearts. This practice was in imitation of one of Shiva's mythic tales, in which he exposed himself to the wives of the Sages in the Pine Forest but was without desire for them. For further information see Daniel H. H. Ingalls, "Cynics and Pasupatas: The Seeking of Dishonor," in *Harvard Theological Review*, 55, 1962.

Pashupati

("Lord of Beasts") Epithet of the god **Shiva** in his form as the "Lord of Beasts." See **Shiva**.

The Pashupatinath Temple in Katmandu, Nepal, is dedicated to the god Shiva as "Master of the Lord of the Beasts."

Pashupatinath

Temple and sacred site (**tirtha**) in Katmandu, **Nepal**. The temple is named for its presiding **deity**, who is the god **Shiva** in his form as Pashupatinath, "the Master of the Lord of Beasts." This is a considered an extremely powerful site, and one of its charter myths connects it to **Kedarnath**, a sacred site high in the **Himalayas**. According to the story, the five **Pandava** brothers, who are the protagonists in the epic *Mahabharata*, are making their final journey into the Himalayas in search of a vision of Shiva. They finally see him at a distance, but when they try to get closer, Shiva takes the form of a **bull** and begins running through the snow. The bull burrows into a snow bank, and when the Pandavas follow, they find the body of the bull in the snow. The ridge of rock that forms the Kedarnath **linga** is considered to be the hump of this bull. The bull's head continues traveling over the hills, eventually stopping in Nepal, where it takes form as the deity Pashupatinath.

Patala

A generic name for the realms of the underworld, traditionally numbered at seven to parallel the seven **heavens** that are believed to exist above the visible world. These underworld realms are not considered to be **hells** but rather planes of existence other than the visible world, populated by the **Nagas** and other non-human beings.

Pataliputra

Capital city of the Mauryan empire, identified with modern Patna, the capital of **Bihar** state. See also **Maurya dynasty**.

Patanjali

(2nd c. B.C.E.) **Sanskrit** grammarian and author of the *Mahabhashya* ("Great Commentary") on **Panini's** *Ashtadhyayi*. Panini's text was written as a series of short phrases or aphorisms intended to be a complete description of the language in the briefest possible space. Panini's text was a marvel of economy and was easy to memorize but was so cryptic that it virtually presupposed a commentary, which Patanjali provided. Patanjali's *Mahabhashya* is not only important for his explication of Panini's grammar, but also because his examples often provide useful historical information.

Patanjali is also the person named as the author of the **Yoga Sutras**, but since these are believed to have been composed several centuries after the *Mahabhashya*, the authors are believed to be two different people with the same name.

Pati

("master") In the philosophical school known as **Shaiva Siddhanta**, the name given to the god **Shiva** as the highest being, who wields the noose (**pasha**) of illusion to enthrall and bewilder unenlightened people (**pashu**). The triad of pashu, pati and pasha are the defining features of the Shaiva Siddhanta school.

Patita

("fallen one") In the **dharma literature**, the term for someone who had committed one of the **Four Great Crimes**; murdering a **brahmin** (**brahmahatya**), stealing a brahmin's gold (**steya**), drinking **liquor** (**surapana**), and **adultery** with one's **guru's** wife (**gurutalpaga**). These crimes were considered so heinous that the performer became an outcast from society. Another indication of the gravity of these acts was that their expiations (**prayashchitta**) were so severe they normally ended in death, and in some cases this outcome was specifically prescribed. Aside from prescribing such punishments for the actual offenders, the dharma literature also prescribed similar outcast status for anyone who knowingly associated with such people for more than one year.

Pattadakal

Historical site in the state of **Karnataka**, about twenty miles east of the city of Badami. During the **Chalukya dynasty**, Pattadakal was an important urban center and a sister city to the Chalukya capital at Badami. Although nearly deserted today, the site is important for a collection of temples built in a variety of architectural styles during that era. The Virupaksha temple, dedicated in 740 C.E. during the reign of King **Vikramaditya**, clearly shows the influence of the southern Indian **Dravida** architectural style: a mostly low and extended profile, with a series of terraced roofs over the main sanctuary. It is believed to have been modeled after the temples in the city of **Kanchipuram**, which had been conquered by Vikramaditya, who brought its architects and builders back to Pattadakal with him. At the same time, there are temples showing the early development of the **Nagara** style, in which the major architectural feature is a series of upswept towers (**shikharas**), with the tallest tower directly over the image of the temple's primary **deity**. The best example of this is the Galaganatha temple, dedicated to the god **Shiva**, which has a tall vertical tower perched on a larger, cube-shaped base.

Pattuppattu

("Ten Songs") Collective name for a group of ten Tamil poems written in the style of the eight anthologies of the **Sangam literature** and believed to have been composed later. The dates for the literature are the subject of controversy, but the prevalent scholarly consensus is that it was written in the early centuries of the common era. Like this literature, the Pattuppattu songs fall into two general genres, puram ("the outer part") and akam ("the inner part"). Puram poetry was "public" verse, describing the deeds of kings, war, death, and other heroic actions, whereas akam poetry was about an individual's inner experience, especially love and sexuality. See also **Tamil language** and **Tamil epics**.

Paush

According to the lunar **calendar**, by which most Hindu religious festivals are determined, Paush is the tenth month in the lunar **year**, usually falling within December and January. In northern India, Paush is the coldest month of the year. It is considered inauspicious, and its only holidays are **Saphala Ekadashi** and **Putrada Ekadashi**.

Peacock

Indian bird with several divine associations. It is the **animal** vehicle of the god **Skanda**, the **son** of **Shiva**, who is the leader of the divine armies. The peacock's quickness and resplendent appearance are felt to mirror these qualities in the young god. The peacock also has strong associations with the god **Krishna**, who is usually depicted as wearing a decorative crown containing peacock feathers. This association may come from the peacock's connection with the **monsoon**, which is the peacock mating season, during which they utter piercing calls in the forests and are believed to **dance** with delight on the hillsides. Krishna's dark color often leads to comparisons with rain clouds, and like the peacock he spends his nights dancing in the company of his devotees (**bhakta**), in the celebration known as the **ras lila**.

Penance

The **dharma literature** gave considerable attention to penance and expiation, based on the almost universal Hindu belief in the inexorable workings of **karma**. According to this notion, all good and bad deeds would eventually have their effect, either in this life or the next. Penances were a way to lessen the future consequences of one's past misdeeds, by undergoing voluntary suffering and expiation in one's present life. See **prayashchitta**.

Perception

In Hindu **philosophy**, perception (**pratyaksha**) is universally accepted as one of the **pramanas**, the means by which human beings can gain true and accurate knowledge. Perception is the only pramana accepted by all the schools, but most of the others also accept inference (**anumana**) and authoritative testimony (**shabda**). See **pratyaksha**.

Periyalvar

(9th c.) One of the **Alvars**, a group of twelve poet-saints who lived in southern India between the seventh and tenth centuries. The Alvars were devotees (**bhakta**) of the god **Vishnu**, and their stress on passionate devotion (**bhakti**) to a personal god, conveyed through hymns sung in the **Tamil language**, transformed and revitalized Hindu religious life.

According to tradition, Periyalvar was born into a **brahmin** family. From his youth he showed deep piety, and his primary means of devotion was to grow and pick flowers for the image of his chosen **deity**, **Krishna**. The most famous story about Periyalvar tells of a **dream** in which God commanded him to take part in a scholarly debate to be held by one of the Pandya kings. Periyalvar, despite his reservations about his lack of learning, obeyed this command after he woke. When he spoke, the words flowed out under divine inspiration, and the bag containing the prize money flew off the hook and into his hands as a sign of his victory. For further information see Kamil Zvelebil, *Tamil Literature*, 1975; and John Stirling Morley Hooper, *Hymns of the Alvars*, 1929. See also **Pandya dynasty**.

Periya Puranam

Hagiographical account of the lives of the sixty-three **Nayanars**, written by the twelfth-century figure **Cekkilar**. The Nayanars were a group of **Shaiva** poet-saints, who lived in southern India between the seventh and ninth centuries. Together with their **Vaishnava** counterparts, the **Alvars**, the Nayanars spearheaded the revitalization of Hindu religion within **Tamil Nadu**, which was mostly Buddhist and Jain. Both the Nayanars and the Alvars stressed passionate devotion (**bhakti**) to a personal god—**Shiva** for the Nayanars, **Vishnu** for the Alvars—and conveyed this devotion through hymns sung in the **Tamil language**. According to tradition, Cekkilar was a minister at the court of the **Chola dynasty** king Kullottunga II (r. 1130–50). Cekkilar, distressed by the king's admiration for a Jain epic poem, composed his text in an effort to wean the king away from it. His text portrays these saints as models of devotion to Shiva and as salutary examples to others although at times extreme in their devotion. One example of this intense devotion is Kotpuli Nayanar, who killed his entire family when he discovered that, in order to save their lives in a time of famine, they had eaten rice that belonged to Shiva's temple. Although this is an extreme case, the message is clearly that devotion to God must eclipse all other loyalties.

Peshwa

Originally, title given to the **brahmin** ministers who served as advisers to the kings in the **Maratha** empire. Traditionally, these ministers were **Chitpavan** brahmins, which gave this small group influence far disproportionate to its numbers. During the resurgence of the Maratha confederacy in the early eighteenth century, the Peshwas became *de facto* rulers, although they continued to govern in the name of the Maratha kings. At this time, the position of Peshwa became hereditary. After the Maratha confederation split into different royal states around 1770, the Peshwas retained control over the ancestral Maratha homeland in the western part of the state of **Maharashtra**, where they reigned until it was conquered by the British in 1818.

Pey

(7th c.) With **Bhutam** and **Poygai**, one of the first three **Alvars**, a group of twelve poet-saints who lived in southern India between the seventh and tenth centuries. All Alvars were devotees (**bhakta**) of the god **Vishnu**, and their stress on passionate devotion (**bhakti**) to a personal god, conveyed through hymns sung in the **Tamil language**, transformed and revitalized Hindu religious life.

According to tradition, the three men were caught in a torrential storm and one by one took shelter in a small dry spot, with each making room for the next. As they stood next to one another they felt a fourth presence, that of Vishnu. The Alvars were such great devotees that their combined energy was sufficient to provoke Vishnu's manifestation. Overwhelmed with ecstasy, each burst into song, which formed the first of each of their compositions. For further information see Kamil Zvelebil, *Tamil Literature*, 1975.

Phalgun

According to the lunar **calendar**, by which most Hindu religious festivals are determined, Phalgun is the twelfth month in the lunar **year**, usually falling within February and March. Phalgun concludes with the festival of **Holi**, which is the unofficial end of the cool season. The other holidays in Phalgun are **Janaki Navami**, **Vijaya Ekadashi**, **Shivaratri**, and **Amalaki Ekadashi**.

Phallic Emblem

Designation for the **linga**, the pillar-shaped object that is the symbolic form of the god **Shiva**. The precise sculptural form of the **Gudimallam linga**, which dates from at least the second century B.C.E., leaves little doubt that this phallic element is one aspect of the symbol. What is often overlooked is that an equally important part of the linga's image is the base (**pitha**) in which the shaft is placed, said to represent the female organs of generation. In his symbolic form Shiva is thus both male and female—an appropriate form for a **deity** who is famous for transcending any and all duality.

Philosophy

The Euro-American conception that there is a fundamental distinction between philosophy and religion reflects unique historical and cultural circumstances that have no parallel in many other cultures. The Western philosophical tradition is rooted in Greek thought and culture, whereas Western religious traditions primarily have been shaped by ideas coming out of the Jewish tradition. The ideas from these two different sources developed side by side in Western culture, sometimes in an uneasy alliance and sometimes at odds but they were always seen as separate. In many other cultures, this distinction does not exist, and such imported concepts become less helpful in encountering these cultures. Indian and Hindu culture have a long history of critical and speculative thought, which could be called philosophical. Yet such thought is never exercised simply for its own sake, but always with an underlying religious purpose—to enable one to gain the ultimate religious goal, final liberation of the soul (**moksha**). The different perspectives on how to do this, known as **darshans**, are usually designated as "philosophical schools." See also **six schools**.

Pilgrimage
See **tirthayatra**.

Pilgrimage Places
See **tirtha**.

Pillar Edicts
Set of **inscriptions** commissioned by the Mauryan emperor **Ashoka** (r. 269–32 B.C.E.), containing official pronouncements on royal policy, and advice and instructions to his subjects on a variety of topics, including religious toleration.

Although these edicts were found in widely separated places, the text in each edict was fairly consistent throughout the Mauryan empire. The pillar edicts were inscribed on pillars of polished **Chunar** sandstone and placed on the major roads running through the empire, where they would have been visible to passersby. In this respect they were different from the **rock edicts**, which were carved into large boulders in places near the borders of the Mauryan empire, thus symbolically defining its boundaries. See also **Maurya dynasty**.

Pinaka
In Hindu mythology, the name of the archery bow belonging to the god **Shiva**.

Pinda
("lump") A ball of cooked rice or other grain, one of the important objects used in rites for the dead. A pinda is offered to the departed spirit each day for the first ten days after death, in the belief that the ten pindas progressively help form a new body for the dead person (a secondary meaning of the word *pinda* is "body"). Pindas are also used in the memorial rite known as **shraddha**, which can be performed years after the actual death; in this rite, the performer offers pindas to his or her ancestors as symbolic nourishment.

Pindadan
("giving pindas") In general usage, a synonym for the memorial rite known as **shraddha**. It is given this name because an important element in shraddha is **offering** the balls of cooked grain, known as **pindas**, considered symbolic nourishment for the ancestors.

Pindara River
A Himalayan tributary of the **Ganges**. The Pindara River flows west from the Pindari glacier and joins the **Alakananda River** at the town of **Karnaprayag**. As with all the Himalayan

tributaries of the Ganges, the Pindara is considered sacred along its length, but this region is so mountainous and so thinly settled that Karnaprayag is the river's only noteworthy spot.

Pingala Nadi

One of the vertical channels (**nadi**) in the traditional conception of the **subtle body**. The subtle body is an alternate physiological system believed to exist on a different plane than gross matter, but with certain correspondences to the material body. It is visualized as a set of six psychic centers (**chakras**) running roughly along the course of the spine, connected by three parallel vertical channels. Above and below these centers are the bodily abodes of the two divine principles, **Shiva** (awareness) and **Shakti** (power), the latter as the latent spiritual energy known as **kundalini**. In this model of the subtle body, the pingala nadi is the vertical channel on the right side of the body. As with the rest of the subtle body, the pingala nadi has certain symbolic correspondences; in particular, it is identified with the **sun** and is thus visualized as being a tawny red in color.

Pipa

(15th c.?) Poet-saint in the **Sant** religious community. The name *Sant* is an umbrella term for a group of central and northern Indian poet-saints who share several general tendencies: focus on individualized, interior religion leading to a personal experience of the divine; disdain for external ritual, particularly image **worship**; faith in the power of repeating one's patron deity's name; and the tendency to ignore conventional **caste** distinctions.

According to tradition, Pipa was born into a **Rajput** royal family in the **Malwa** region but eventually renounced his throne and went to **Benares** to become a disciple of the poet-saint **Ramananda**. The hagiographer **Nabhadas** reports that Pipa was a disciple of the powerful

goddess Bhavani (an epithet of **Parvati**), showing the breadth of the Sant tradition. A few of Pipa's verses have been preserved in the **Adigranth**, the sacred text of the Sikh community, and in their language and religious thrust the verses are consistent with these traditions.

Pipal

Common name for *Ficus religiosa*, the fig-tree also known as the **ashvattha**, which has a long history of being considered a sacred tree. See **ashvattha**.

Pippalada

In Hindu traditional lore, one of the ancient sages in the **Atharva Veda**, one of the oldest Hindu religious texts. Pippalada is also mentioned in the **Prashna Upanishad**, one of the speculative religious texts that forms the latest part of the Vedas, as a religious teacher who instructs sages such as Sukesha, **Kashyapa**, and Bhargava. Pippalada supposedly gets his name from his fondness for Pippali fruits, the fruit of the *Ficus religiosa*, the sacred pipal (**ashvattha**).

Pitambara

("clothed in yellow") Epithet of the god **Krishna**, because of his penchant for wearing yellow garments. See **Krishna**.

Pitavasana

("yellow-clad") Epithet of the god **Krishna**, because of his penchant for wearing yellow garments. See **Krishna**.

Pitha

("bench") In its widest meaning, the base or foundation of any object. It can denote the material base or foundation upon which the image of a **deity** is placed. In some cases the foundation becomes an integral part of the image itself, as in the **linga**, the pillar-shaped object that is the symbol of the god **Shiva**. The form of the linga, an upright

During Pitrpaksha, Hindus offer rice balls and water to their ancestors.

shaft set in a horizontal base, represents, not only the union of male and female, but also their transcendence, since Shiva is both male and female at once. At a more symbolic level, a pitha can be the "seat" or residence of a particular deity, that is, the place at which the deity metaphorically sits. The best example of this is the **Shakti Pithas**, a network of sites sacred to the **Goddess**, spread throughout the subcontinent. Each Shakti Pitha marks the site where a body part of the dismembered goddess **Sati** fell to earth, taking up residence in each place as a different goddess.

Pitr

("father") Any and all **ancestral spirits**, to whom funerary **offerings** are due as one of a man's expected duties. See **ancestral spirits**.

Pitrpaksha

The fortnight (**paksha**) dedicated to the **worship** of the **ancestral spirits** (pitr), observed in the dark (waning) half of the **lunar month** of **Ashvin**. This is the period during the **year** in which Hindus remember and give **offerings** for their dead: offerings of **water** and rice-balls (**pinda**) on each day of the fortnight, and as well as special observances on the day of the fortnight corresponding to the day of the ancestor's death. These offerings are believed to sustain the dead by symbolically feeding them, and also to placate the dead by demonstrating that the living still remember and care for them.

Because of its strong connection with the dead, this fortnight is generally considered an inauspicious time, and people often restrict their everyday activities in symbolic recognition of it. Many people will not cut their **hair**, beards, or nails during this time, nor will they wear new clothes. These precautions stem from the conviction that making alterations in one's appearance during an inauspicious time will have adverse future affects, since it will carry the taint forward. Many people also curtail other normal activities during this time, such as buying any article or initiating any new project, unless it is absolutely necessary. The period is also deemed a good time for religious observances, particularly giving gifts (**dana**) to **brahmins**. On the one hand this is a way to propitiate the ancestors, whom the brahmins represent, and thus whatever is given to brahmins is given symbolically to the ancestors. On the other hand, giving such gifts is also a rite of protection against misfortune in an inauspicious time, since the receiver is believed to take away the bad luck along with the gift.

Pitryajna

("**sacrifice** to the ancestors") One of the Five Great Sacrifices (**panchamahayajna**) prescribed in the **dharma literature**, the texts on religious duty. These Five Great Sacrifices are daily observances for a "**twice-born**" householder, that is, one who has been born into one of the three "twice-born" groups in Indian society—**brahmin**, **kshatriya**, or **vaishya**—and who has received the adolescent religious **initiation** known as the "second birth." Each of the five sacrifices (**yajna**) is directed toward a different class of beings—from the Absolute Reality down to **animals**—and is satisfied by different actions. The pitryajna is directed toward one's ancestors, and is satisfied by **offering** them libations of water (**tarpana**). In the time since the dharma literature was composed Hindu life has undergone significant changes, and some of these five rites have been completely elided. Although in certain contexts pitryajna is still an important rite—particularly at pilgrimage sites and in formal rites for the dead—it is no longer performed on a daily basis.

Pitta

("bile") Along with **vata** ("air") and **kapha** ("phlegm"), one of the three humours (**tridosha**) in **ayurveda**, or traditional Indian medicine. Every person has all three of these humours, but usually one is predominant, and this marks a person in certain ways, particularly with regard to health, digestion, and metabolism. Pitta is associated with the elements of **fire** and **water**, since bile is a liquid involved in digestion, which is believed to take place through interior burning. Pitta is hot, intense, and mobile, and those for whom this is the predominant humor are said to have a strong will, be good leaders, and be blessed with good digestion. At the same time, this inner fire gives them bodily difficulties in hot weather, and to do their best they must also learn how to harness their fiery temperaments.

Plakshadvipa

In traditional mythic geography, the second of the seven concentric landmasses (**dvipas**) making up the visible world. See also **cosmology**.

Planets

Indian astrology (**jyotisha**) recognizes nine planets that affect human beings: the five visible ones (**Jupiter**, **Venus**, **Mercury**, **Saturn**, and **Mars**), the **Sun** and **Moon**, and two planets not known to Western astrology, **Rahu** and **Ketu**. Of these, Jupiter, Venus, and Mercury are, by themselves, always benevolent. The moon is changeable, depending on its position in the lunar cycle, and the others are considered to have malefic tendencies, although only Rahu and Ketu are invariably malevolent. Rahu and Ketu move throughout the **zodiac**, but the others are all fixed in place. Each of the planets is part of an elaborate series of associations, including parts of the body, **family relationships**, and personal qualities. The influence of all these planets can be heightened or weakened according to their position in a person's **natal horoscope**, or their position vis-à-vis the other planets. The astrological tradition also recognizes a practice known as **pacification of planets**, through which their good qualities can be heightened, or their malevolent qualities weakened and contained. This can be done either through wearing particular **gemstones** that are believed to correspond to these planets, or by performing certain protective rituals.

Pole Star

In Hindu mythology, the personified form of the boy **Dhruva**, who is a symbol for unrelenting pursuit of a goal. Dhruva is a king's son, but for some unknown reason his father favors Dhruva's half-brother over him. Distressed by this insult, Dhruva takes a vow to attain a place above all others and goes off to the forest to perform austerities (**tapas**). After Dhruva endures many bodily mortifications, the god **Vishnu** appears and grants him a boon. In response to Dhruva's request for a place above all others, Vishnu promises Dhruva that after his death he will be installed as the Pole Star, the pivot around which all the other stars in the sky will turn.

Pollution

In Hindu religious life, a term designating religious contamination and ritual impurity (**ashaucha**). This notion of impurity is strictly concerned with the presence or absence of contamination and carries no necessary sense of moral or ethical lapse. See **ashaucha**.

Polyandry

Having more than one husband. This practice is extremely uncommon in Indian society, either now or in the past. The best-known mythical example comes from the epic *Mahabharata*, in which **Draupadi** is married to all five of the **Pandava** brothers, the epic's protagonists. Textual scholars have argued that this type of marriage was so unusual that it must have been rooted in some ancient practice, but there is no proof for this claim. In contemporary times polyandry can be found only at the outer fringes of Hindu society, such as in the state of **Assam** and in some of the **Himalayan** regions, where traditional practices have allowed for one woman to marry several brothers, following Draupadi's example.

Polygamy

Given the overwhelmingly patriarchal character of Hindu society, polygamy has probably existed since very early times. The practice is attested in both the great epics, the *Ramayana* and the *Mahabharata*, as well as in the historical record. The **dharma literature** permits men to marry wives of lower social status, under the condition that their first wife was of equal status. Despite the existence of polygamy, it was probably unusual and restricted to men of high status and financial resources, who would be able to support several families. For "regular" men, one of the few reasons for taking a second wife was when the first wife was unable to bear children, in an attempt to sire the sons needed to preserve the lineage and ensure performance of the ancestral rites.

Pongal

Southern Indian harvest festival marking the change of **seasons** and the transition of the **sun** into the zodiacal sign of Capricorn, and thus beginning its northward course (**uttarayana**). According to Indian astrology this usually takes place on January 14th; in northern India this day is celebrated as **Makara Sankranti**. Both mark the sun's change in motion from the southerly direction to the northerly, or from the direction considered less auspicious to the one considered more auspicious.

The festivities for Pongal last for three days. The first day is the Pongal of Joy (Bhogi Pongal), on which people visit and exchange sweets and gifts. The second day is dedicated to the Sun (**Surya** Pongal). On this day married women cook rice in milk, and when the pot comes to a boil they shout "Pongal" ("It has boiled"). The milk-rice is made into sweets, which is first offered to the

Sun and to the god **Ganesh**, and then given to friends. On the final day, Pongal of Cows (Mattu Pongal), worshipers walk in a circle around cows while the cows are decorated, garlanded, and worshiped.

Possession

Possession by gods, **ghosts**, and spirits is an accepted element in the traditional Hindu worldview, although whether this is good or bad depends on the nature of the being responsible. Possession is the most common means for **village deities** and certain forms of the **Goddess** to communicate with human beings, although the highest gods in the pantheon virtually never use this medium. Possession by a deity can bring a person high religious status but is generally said to be physically exhausting; through the medium the deities can interact with human beings, both to make their wishes known and to give their help and advice to those who need it. One of the more unusual cases of this occurs at the annual pilgrimage at **Kataragama** in **Sri Lanka**. Devotees (**bhakta**) suspend themselves from trees by hooks stuck into the flesh of their backs and, while suspended, are believed to be speaking for the god **Murugan**.

Possession by departed spirits (**bhut** or **pret**) or by witches and other malefic beings is always seen as an inopportune event and a dangerous imposition on the sufferer that must be remedied as soon as possible through healing or exorcism. As Sudhir Kakar masterfully shows, the language of possession and exorcism can be interpreted as an "idiom," using traditional Indian cultural categories, for what modern psychiatrists might call the diagnosis and treatment of mental illness. For further information see Sudhir Kakar, *Shamans, Mystics, and Doctors*, 1991.

Poygai

(7th c.) With **Pey** and **Bhutam**, one of the first three **Alvars**, a group of twelve poet-saints who lived in southern India between the seventh and tenth centuries. All the Alvars were devotees (**bhakta**) of the god **Vishnu**, and their passionate devotion (**bhakti**) to a personal god, conveyed through hymns sung in the **Tamil language**, transformed and revitalized Hindu religious life. According to tradition, the three men were caught in a torrential storm and, one by one, took shelter in a small dry spot, with each making room for the next. As they stood next to one another, they felt a fourth presence, who was Vishnu. The alvars were such great devotees that their combined energy was sufficient to provoke Vishnu's manifestation. Overwhelmed with ecstasy, each burst into song, which formed the first of each of their compositions. For further information see Kamil Zvelebil, *Tamil Literature*, 1975.

Prabhakara

In Indian **philosophy**, one of the two great seventh-century commentators in the **Purva Mimamsa** school, one of the **six schools** of traditional Hindu philosophy; the other great commentator was **Kumarila**. The Mimamsa school was most concerned with the examination and pursuit of **dharma** ("righteous action"), the Mimamsa school believed all necessary instructions were contained in the **Vedas**, the oldest Hindu religious texts. Much of Mimamsa thought is concerned with principles and methods for textual interpretation seeking to uncover and interpret these instructions. Although both Kumarila and Prabhakara were committed to discovering the boundaries of dharma by interpreting the Vedas, there are significant differences in their philosophical positions, seen most clearly in their **theories of error**.

Prabhakara believes in a concept similar to the **Nyaya** concept of **inherence** (**samavaya**), a weak relational force that is assumed to connect objects and their attributes—for example, connecting the color red with a particular ball, thus making the ball red. This assumption leads him to characterize error as **akhyati** ("nondiscrimination"), the inability to make sharp distinctions. For example, a person mistakes the silvery flash of sea shell for a piece of silver. To Prabhakara, the person errs by uncritically connecting two simple judgments: "that object is silvery" and "silver is silvery." By themselves, both of these statements are true, what is false is their combination into the complex judgment "that object is silver." Kumarila is closer to the **bhedabhada** ("identity-and-difference") philosophical position, which holds that all things both identify with and differ from all other things. Kumarila explains error as **viparitakhyati**, the mistaken pairing of the similarities between two things, rather than the failure to note their differences.

Prabhupada, A.C. Bhaktivedanta

(b. Abhay Charan De, 1896–1977) Devotee (**bhakta**) of the god **Krishna** and founder of ISKCON (International Society for Krishna Consciousness), more popularly known as the Hare Krishnas. ISKCON has its roots in the **Gaudiya Vaishnava** religious community founded by the Bengali saint **Chaitanya**, in which the primary religious action was the repeated recitation of Krishna's name, often in public settings. Prabhupada was initiated into Krishna devotion in his university years, at which time his **guru** commanded him to bring the **worship** of Krishna to the West. At the age of 58, after a successful career as a pharmacist, he boarded a steamer for the United States, arriving with a few books, a typewriter, and eight dollars in his pocket. His timing was exquisite—or, as he put it, reflected Krishna's **grace**—for he came during the countercultural movement in the second half of the 1960s; by the time of his death he had thousands of followers. In his later years he focused on translating and commenting on important **Vaishnava** texts, particularly the **Bhagavad Gita** and the *Bhagavata*

Purana, and this emphasis on publishing has continued after his death. For an insider's perspective on his life, see Satsvarupdas Dasa Goswami, *Prabhupada*, 1983; and Robert D. Baird, "Swami Bhaktivedanta and Ultimacy," in Robert D. Baird (ed.), *Religion in Modern India*, 1998.

Prabodhachandrodaya

("Rising of the **moon** of wisdom") **Sanskrit** drama written by **Krishnamishra**, probably in the latter half of the eleventh century. Clearly allegorical, the play celebrates the triumph of **Vaishnava** piety, that is, of the devotees (**bhakta**) of the god **Vishnu**. The play is particularly notable for its third act, in which representatives for four non-Vaishnava sects appear: a **materialist**, a Jain monk, a Buddhist monk, and a **Kapalika** (a member of an **ascetic** community that worshiped the god **Shiva**). The last is portrayed as thoroughly depraved, indulging in meat, wine, and sexual gratification, and having a penchant for violence. In the play, all four heretical characters plot to capture another character, named Faith, for their king, named Passion. However, they discover that Faith is a devotee of Vishnu and is outside their powers. In the end Faith is reunited with her son Tranquillity and a character named Compassion. Although the reader may safely assume that this play is written from a biased perspective, it is instructive in the attitudes it reveals toward ascetics and all other non-Vaishnava religious groups.

Pracharak

("director") In the **Rashtriya Svayamsevak Sangh** (RSS), a conservative Hindu organization whose express purpose is to provide the leadership cadre for a revitalized Hindu India, the pracharaks are the full-time RSS workers who provide the link between the local units, known as **shakhas** ("branches"), and the RSS higher authorities. The RSS is a highly

A.C. Bhaktivedanta Prabhupada was the founder of ISKCON,
a religious community devoted to the god Krishna that is popularly known as the Hare Krishnas.

authoritarian organization, with all power ultimately vested in a single, unelected leader, the sarsanghchalak, and the pracharaks are the crucial link between this highly centralized leadership and the highly decentralized local units. The pracharaks are responsible for coordinating and managing RSS activities in their area, as well as for reporting on these at RSS meetings at various levels; they may also be sent out on loan to provide leadership to RSS-affiliated organizations. As a rule, pracharaks are completely devoted to the RSS cause, and most have been associated with the RSS since childhood. Their ethos is one of service and sacrifice to the RSS, and by implication to the country as a whole: They are generally unmarried, have no other employment, receive no salary from the RSS (although the local unit generally provides their living expenses), and are famous for living a simple and spartan lifestyle. Most of them are also well educated and are selected for their ability to get along well with others. For further information see Walter K. Andersen and Shridhar D. Damle, *The Brotherhood in*

Saffron, 1987; and Daniel Gold, "Organized Hinduisms: From Vedic Truth to Hindu Nation," in Martin Marty and R. Scott Appleby (eds.), *Fundamentalisms Observed*, 1991.

Pradakshina

("toward the right") Circumambulation of an object or person as a sign of **worship**, reverence, or respect. This is always done in a clockwise direction, so that the walker's right side (considered the purer and more auspicious side) is always turned toward the object or person being circled. Just about anything can be so circled—one's parents or teacher, the image of a **deity**, a temple, a city, or the entire Indian subcontinent. In many larger temples, particularly in the **Nagara** architectural style, the pradakshina is the name for one of the architectural features. In this case, it is a semicircular processional passageway surrounding the temple's main image, so that people can circumambulate the main image either before or after worship. Pradakshina is also the fifteenth of the sixteen traditional **upacharas** ("offerings") given to a deity as part of worship, on the model of treating the deity as an honored guest. The underlying motive here, as for all the upacharas, is to show one's love for the deity and to minister to the deity's needs as one would to a living person's needs.

Pradhana

("principal") In the **Samkhya** philosophical school, pradhana is another name for **prakrti**, the "primal matter" that the Samkhyas consider the first principle from which all material things have evolved. In the secret, ritually based religious practice known as **tantra**, the word *pradhana* is used to denote the goddess **Shakti**, as the active principle behind the formation of the universe. Grammatically, the word is feminine, indicating a connotation of fertility and fecundity.

Pradosh Vrat

("twilight vow") Religious observance celebrated on the thirteenth day of each lunar fortnight, mainly by **women**, often for the birth of children or to sustain the general family welfare. The vow (**vrat**) is dedicated to the god **Shiva**, and its most important part takes place on the evening of the thirteenth day (the word *pradosh* is interpreted as meaning "twilight") when worshipers present Shiva with the sixteen traditional **offerings** (**upacharas**), following which they may take their only meal of the day. In some cases worshipers stay awake through the night so that the observance may finish on the fourteenth day of the month, a lunar day connected with Shiva. When the thirteenth day falls on a **Monday** (associated with Shiva), **Saturday** (associated with **Saturn**), or **Sunday** (associated with the **Sun**), this rite is believed to be especially efficacious.

Pradyumna

In Hindu mythology, the son of the god **Krishna** and his divine queen **Rukmini**.

Pradyumna is the rebirth of the god **Kama**, who has been completely annihilated by the fire from the god **Shiva's** third eye. After Kama's death, Shiva reassures Kama's wife **Rati** that her husband will be reborn as Pradyumna to kill the **demon** Sambhara. Through his **magic** powers Sambhara is well aware of the threat; when he finds the child, he throws it into the ocean and thinks that he has killed it. Pradyumna is swallowed by a great fish, which is caught and presented to king Sambhara; when the fish is split open, the child enchants his wife Mayavati, in whose form Rati has taken birth to aid her husband. Pradyumna kills Sambhara in a ferocious battle and is reunited with Rati.

Prahlada

In Hindu mythology, the **son** of the **demon**-king **Hiranyakashipu**, and a great devotee (**bhakta**) of the god **Vishnu**. Through harsh physical **asceticism** (**tapas**) Hiranyakashipu has gained a series of divine boons that render him virtually invulnerable, yet despite his power, his son Prahlada refuses to abandon his devotion to Vishnu. Prahlada's devotion in the face of his father's ever-growing pride generates an escalating pattern of abuse that culminates in the demand that Prahlada **worship** him rather than Vishnu. At that point Vishnu comes to Prahlada's aid as the **Man-lion avatar**, slays Hiranyakashipu, and establishes Prahlada as king in his place.

Prajapati

("Lord of Creatures") **Deity** appearing late in the **Vedas**, the earliest Hindu sacred texts, who is described as the creator of the universe and is considered superior to the Vedic deities. The means by which Prajapati carries out creation are different in different places. In **Rg Veda** 10.121 he is described as the **Golden Embryo** from which all things developed, whereas in Rg 10.90, also known as the **Purusha Sukta**, he is described as the primal person (purusha) who is sacrificed by the gods and from whose parts the world develops. In later Hindu practice the name *Prajapati* can also be used to refer to the god **Brahma**, as fashioner of the universe, or to the gods **Vishnu** or **Shiva**, as the universe's supreme deities.

Prajapatya Marriage

One of the eight ways to perform a marriage recognized in the **dharma literature**, the treatises on religious duty. In Hindu mythology **Prajapati** was the name of the creator, and this name suggests that the purpose of this marriage was for people to fulfill their duties to the ancestors by procreating. A Prajapatya marriage takes place when a father gives away his **daughter** to a man with the condition that they will perform their civic and religious duties together. This was one of the four approved (**prashasta**) forms of marriage, because it was arranged by the girl's father. However, it was considered less commendable than the other approved forms, because the girl was given in marriage with conditions. In Indian culture, the best way to give a daughter is to impose no conditions. See also **marriage, eight classical forms**.

Prajnanam Brahman

("Wisdom is **Brahman**") In the Hindu philosophical tradition, one of the "great utterances" (**mahavakyas**) expressing the ultimate truth. The truth here is the identity of **prajnanam** (ultimate wisdom) and Brahman (Supreme Reality); this identity is the heart of the speculative texts called the **Upanishads**. Aside from their importance in a philosophical context, as encapsulating fundamental truths, the four mahavakyas were also appropriated as identifying symbols by the four divisions of the **Dashanami Sanyasi** ascetics. Each division had a different **mahavakya**, just as each had a different **Veda**, a different primary monastic center, and a different paradigmatic **ascetic** quality. Prajnanam

Brahman is the mahavakya associated with the **Bhogawara** division of the Dashanami Sanyasis.

Prakamyam

("irresistible will") One of the eight **superhuman powers** (**siddhi**) traditionally believed to be conferred by high spiritual attainment. This particular power removes all obstructions to the movement of one's body, such that one can go wherever one desires, even passing through solid objects as if moving through water.

Prakasha

("illumination") In Hindu **tantra**, a secret, ritually based religious practice, prakasha is one of the bipolar opposites that are used to characterize the nature of all reality, with its counterpart being reflection (**vimarsha**). These two terms are particularly important for the creation of the world, which is said to happen when the pure and radiant consciousness (prakasha) of the ultimate **Brahman** becomes self-conscious through the reflection (vimarsha) of this original consciousness. From one single consciousness, the absolute then evolves into a binary divinity—the god **Shiva** and his consort **Shakti**—whose continued interaction combines to create the world. For further information see Jaideva Singh, *Pratyabhijnanahrdayam*, 1982. See also **cosmology**.

Prakashatman

(13th c.) Proponent of the **Advaita Vedanta** school, one of the **six schools** of traditional Hindu **philosophy**. Prakashatman's **Vivarana**, a commentary on the work of the Advaita philosopher **Padmapada**, provides the name for the Vivarana school of Advaita Vedanta. Prakashatman is traditionally described as Padmapada's disciple, but since the latter is an attested pupil of **Shankaracharya** (9th c. C.E.), the time difference makes this unlikely.

Since **Brahman** is believed to be the locus of all things, Vivarana Advaitins conclude that ignorance must also be a part of Brahman. However, they try to maintain Brahman's integrity by invoking a theory of **reflectionism** to explain the apparent difference between Self and Brahman, even though they are ultimately identical. Just as an image appearing in a mirror is based on the original but different from it, so human Selves are identical with Brahman but appear to be separate. The basic position of the Vivarana school is an uncompromising affirmation of Brahman as the sole "reality," in which anything that exists must belong to it.

Prakrit

("formed") Collective term for the grammatically simpler vernacular languages that developed from **Sanskrit** through the natural process of linguistic change. The existence of Prakrits is evident as early as the fifth century B.C.E., at which time several different dialects are spoken. The Prakrits were contrasted with Sanskrit ("perfected"), the language of temple, court, and other elite contexts, which was subject to strict grammatical canons and did not change. Even those fluent in Sanskrit would have learned it as a second language—as a static, learned language, it is inherently artificial—and would have spoken in Prakrit with lower status people (such as servants, commoners, and most **women**). Despite its "lower" status, Prakrits are vitally important historically: They were the languages for royal **inscriptions** up to the Gupta era (ca. 350–550), and one of the Prakrits, Pali, is famous as the language for the Theravada Buddhist canon. See also **Gupta dynasty**.

Prakrti

("nature") One of the two fundamental principles in the **Samkhya** school, the other being **purusha** ("person"). Samkhya espouses an atheistic philosophical dualism, in which purusha and prakrti—roughly, spirit and nature—are the source of all things. Prakrti is better conceived of as force or power rather than a specific material object. It contains within it three different forces with three different qualities (**guna**): **sattva** tends toward the good, **rajas** towards activity or passion, and **tamas** towards darkness and decay. In the primal prakrti these forces are in perfect equilibrium, each perfectly balancing the others, but when prakrti's equilibrium is disturbed, it sets in motion a pattern of **evolution** that creates both the exterior physical world and the interior psychological world. All of these evolutes—material or psychic—have a differing balance of the three gunas, which ultimately determines their character as wholesome, active, or unwholesome. For further information see Gerald Larson and Ram Shankar Bhattacharya (eds.), *Samkhya*, 1987; and Sarvepalli Radhakrishnan and Charles A. Moore (eds.), *A Sourcebook in Indian Philosophy*, 1957.

Pralaya

In Hindu mythology, the dissolution of the universe that comes at the end of the **kalpa** or **Day of Brahma**. Pralaya is considered the "night" of Brahma, and lasts for the same amount of time as the day (by one estimate, 4.32 billion years). The approach of this "night" is preceded by the destruction of the earth, first by fire, and then by torrential rains that transform the entire planet into one vast ocean. During this time the only living thing is the god **Vishnu**, who reclines on the back of his serpent vehicle **Shesha**, deep in a yogic trance. When the time again comes for creation, a lotus sprouts from his navel, which opens to reveal **Brahma**, and the world begins anew.

Pramana

In Indian **philosophy**, a means by which human beings can gain true and accurate knowledge, generally classified as one of three types: Perception

Pramukh Swami, the present spiritual leader of the Swaminarayan religious community.

(**pratyaksha**), which includes magical or yogic insight as well as direct sensory perception; inference (**anumana**), which ultimately depends upon direct experience; and testimony (**shabda**), which can be either scriptural or the instruction of one's teacher. Some philosophical schools also include a fourth source, analogy (**upamana**), but those who do not recognize this categorize it as another form of inference. The first three are accepted by all philosophical schools except for the **materialists**, who recognize only perception. The **Purva Mimamsa** school affirms two additional pramanas—presumption (**arthapatti**), and knowledge from absence (**abhava**)—which they argue give one knowledge. The root meaning of this term comes from the verb "to measure"; thus these are tools for measuring and interpreting the world we experience.

Pramukh Swami

("President Swami," b. 1921) Title of Shastri Narayanswarupdas Swami, the present spiritual leader of the **Swaminarayan** religious community. Swaminarayan Hinduism is based on the life and teachings of Sahajananda Swami (1781–1830), who because of his piety and charisma was deemed by his followers an **avatar** of the god **Vishnu**. Pramukh Swami is the uncontested head of the **Akshar Purushottam Samstha**, a branch of the Swaminarayan movement that separated from the parent group in 1906. He is a strict **ascetic** who serves as religious teacher (**guru**) to an estimated million followers all over the world. His devotees (**bhakta**) are predominately members of the **Gujarati** community and mostly affluent merchants, making the movement financially robust.

Prana

("breath") As a collective noun, the name for the five "winds" considered to be responsible for basic bodily functions. The first of these, located in the chest, is labeled by the general term *prana*. Because it performs those functions necessary for sustaining life—respiration, the movement of food into the stomach, and the circulation of **blood** through the body—its name is often used to designate all five winds. Of the other four winds, **apana** (in the anal region) is concerned with elimination,

samana (in the navel) aids digestion, **udana** (in the throat) conveys things out of the mouth—like speech, song, burps, etc.—and **vyana** circulates throughout the body, mixing things together. These winds are the focus of the **yoga** exercise known as **pranayama**, the aim of which is to achieve control over the central forces of life.

Pranapratishtha

("establishing the **prana**") Pranapratishtha is the final rite in the **consecration** of a deity's image, usually performed by brahmins, since they have the necessary ritual **purity** and training. The image is infused with the breath of life (prana) through the performance of ritual and the intoning of sacred sounds known as **mantras**. After this rite is performed, the **deity** is believed to be resident in the image, which thereafter must be treated with the care such a spiritual entity requires.

Pranava

Name denoting the sacred sound *Om*. See **Om**.

Pranayama

("restraint of breath") In the **ashtanga** ("eight-part") **yoga** first codified by **Patanjali** (1st c. C.E.?), pranayama is the fourth of the eight constituent elements of yoga practice. Pranayama requires a conscious control of respiration, specifically halting one's breathing before inhaling and exhaling. When both of these actions have become automatic, this is described as "total" restraint. This practice is supposed to weaken and destroy the practitioner's unwholesome **karma**, and render the mind fit for concentration. Removing karma is necessary for liberation of the soul, since all karma (both good and bad) ties one to the cycle of birth and rebirth.

Prapatti

("throwing oneself down") Prapatti refers to a devotee's (**bhakta**) complete surrender to God's power as the only means of salvation. This attitude is particularly stressed among the **Shrivaishnavas**, a southern Indian religious community who are followers of the god **Vishnu** and whose founder was the great philosopher **Ramanuja** (11th c.). Although ultimate power is believed to be vested in God's **grace** by the practitioners of prapatti, believers nevertheless possess a concern for continuing religious practice. Thus, prapatti is not meant to replace conventional religious activities such as **worship**. These activities are still performed, but with the consciousness that God's grace will be sufficient. They are therefore not seen as a means toward salvation, but as reflections of the grace one has already obtained.

Prapti

("acquisition") One of the eight superhuman powers (**siddhi**) traditionally believed to be conferred by high spiritual attainment. This particular power gives one the ability to gain any object simply by desiring it.

Prarthana Samaj

Hindu reformist organization centered in Bombay, whose most important figure was M. G. **Ranade** (1842–1901). The Prarthana Samaj's reformist mission focused more on social issues than on theological or **worship**-related ones. Their primary aim was to rid Hindu society of "evils" such as child marriage and the ban on **widow** remarriage. Although its members were educated and progressive, they were also religiously conservative and devout Hindus with deep roots in the tradition. They saw their work as a slow and gradual process of reforming Hinduism by removing its most objectionable practices rather than by radically remaking it from start. In this they differed from the

Brahmo Samaj, who attempted to remake the tradition wholesale by giving it a strong, quasi-monotheistic emphasis, a quality heavily influenced by European missionaries. The Prarthana Samaj lost its steam by the early 1920s, when social reform associations became absorbed into the Indian National Congress.

Prasad

("favor") Prasad is food or drink that has been offered to a **deity** as part of normal **worship** and, having been sanctified by the deity's power, is later distributed to worshipers as a symbol of the deity's **grace**. In this process, the deity is believed to have "consumed" part of the food **offering**, and thus—in keeping with everyday ideas about the contaminating power of saliva—to have "imprinted" the food with its substance. Since this substance has been "charged" with divine presence, it is given to devotees (**bhakta**) as an emblem of the deity's grace, and worshipers consume it in the belief that this sanctifies them. Its sacred qualities mean that prasad is treated differently than regular food: It cannot be refused and can never be thrown away. If one cannot eat it, the favored method of disposal is to feed it to a **cow**. See also **jutha**.

Prashasta ("Approved") Marriages

In the **dharma literature**, or the texts on religious duty, these are the four approved forms of marriage: the **Brahma** marriage, the **Daiva** marriage, the **Arsha** marriage, and the **Prajapatya** marriage. These forms are deemed commendable because in each case the father of the bride is responsible for arranging the marriage: In the Brahma form the bride is given as a gift without conditions, in the Daiva she is given as a sacrificial fee, in the Arsha she is given in exchange for a pair of cattle for **sacrifice**, and in the Prajapatya she is given with the condition that the husband and wife perform their duties together. The Brahma is the only one of these four practiced in modern India and is the idealized form of marriage. See also **marriage, eight classical forms**.

Prashastapada

(5th c.) Author of the *Padarthadharmasangraha*. This text is the most influential commentary on **Kanada's Vaisheshika Sutras**, the founding text of the Vaisheshika school, one of the **six schools** of traditional Hindu **philosophy**. The Vaisheshika school was atomistic, believing that all things were made up of a few basic constituent substances: the five **elements** (**earth**, **fire**, **water**, **wind**, and **akasha**) along with space, time, mind, and individual selves (**atman**). The five elements combined to form the things in the world, though selves were considered ultimately different from matter.

Prashna ("Question") Upanishad

One of the later and more developed **upanishads**, the speculative religious texts that form the latest stratum of the oldest Hindu sacred texts, the **Vedas**. As with most of the upanishads, the Prashna Upanishad's underlying concern is to investigate ultimate questions, in particular the nature of the Self (**atman**). Considered one of the later upanishads, the Prashna Upanishad is similar to the earliest upanishads, the Brhadaranyaka and the Chandogya, but is far shorter, and the text is much more focused. Like the older upanishads, the Prashna is written as a dialogue. It takes the form of a conversation between the sage **Pippalada** and six questioners. In each section (called a prashna in the text) one of the hearers asks a question, to which Pippalada replies. The six sections all have different themes: the nature of time, **prana** as the most important human power, the nature of life after death, sleep, meditation, the sound *Om*, and the nature of the Self. In this way, it uses the older dialogue form to advance a far more developed and cohesive philosophical perspective.

Pratihara Dynasty

See **Gurjara-Pratihara dynasty**.

Pratijna

("assertion") In Indian logic, a part in the generally accepted form of an inference (**anumana**), or logical statement. The accepted form for an inference has three terms: an assertion (pratijna), a reason (**hetu**), and examples (**drshtanta**). Each of these three also has its own constituent parts. The pratijna's two constituent parts are the **paksha** and the **sadhya**. The paksha is the subject of the assertion and names a class of things, while the sadhya is the claim to be proven about that class. For example, in the assertion "this mountain is on **fire**," the paksha is "this mountain" (the class of things about which a claim is being made), and the sadhya, or thing to be proven, is "is on fire."

Pratiloma

("against the **hair**") Forbidden marriage union, in which the husband has lower social status than the wife. See **hypogamous marriage**.

Pratinidhi

("substitute") In the context of **tantra**, a secret, ritually based religious practice, anything that can correctly be used as a substitute. Certain tantric rites make ritual use of substances or actions that are normally forbidden; the most famous of these rites, the Five Forbidden Things (**panchamakara**), incorporates violating the social taboos on drinking wine, consuming nonvegetarian food, and engaging in illicit sex. The ritual use of such normally forbidden things must be seen in the larger context of tantric practice. One of the most pervasive tantric assumptions is the ultimate unity of everything that exists. From this perspective, adepts affirm that the entire universe is one principle—often, conceived as the activity of a particular **deity**—and therefore reject all concepts based on dualistic thinking. The "Five Forbidden Things," therefore, provides a ritual means for breaking the duality of sacred and forbidden, by sacralizing several things that are ordinarily forbidden.

These five things are used in their actual form in "left hand" (**vamachara**) tantra, and by substitution in "right hand" (**dakshinachara**) tantra. Substitution allows the adept to perform the ritual and at the same time to avoid the disapproval that would result from breaking certain social rules. Although tantric texts allow for substitution in this rite, they are usually quite specific about what sorts of things are acceptable substitutes, a signature quality of strictly defined ritual systems. For further information see Swami Agehananda Bharati, *The Tantric Tradition*, 1975; and Douglas Renfrew Brooks, *The Secret of the Three Cities*, 1990.

Pratyabhijna

("recognition") Doctrine advanced by many different schools of **tantra**, a secret, ritually defined religious practice, and particularly by the Kashmiri philosopher **Abhinavagupta**, the most influential figure in **Trika** Shaivism. It holds that the final realization of the Absolute is simply a "re-cognition" of one's essential unity with the Divine. This unity has always existed and has never been altered, the only factor preventing it from being clearly seen being the obscuring power of false understanding. Final unity with the Divine, therefore, comes not through doing anything, but simply through realizing what has always been the case. This doctrine clearly shows the influence of the **Advaita Vedanta** philosophical school, but with an important shift. The Advaita school upholds a philosophical position known as monism, which is the belief that a single abstract ultimate principle—which they call **Brahman**—lies behind all things, and that all things are only particular manifestations of that one principle. The "Recognition" school

Yoga asanas contribute to the development of pratyahara, or withdrawal from the senses.

adopts this general principle but conceives of Ultimate Reality theistically, as the god **Shiva**. For Trika Shaivism, Shiva is the sole true reality, who is both supreme god, and the source of the material universe. For further information see Jaideva Singh, *Pratyabhijnanahrdayam*, 1982.

Pratyahara

("withdrawal [of the senses]") In the **ashtanga** ("eight-part") **yoga** first codified by **Patanjali** (1st c. C.E.?), pratyahara is the fifth of the eight constituent elements of yoga practice. Pratyahara occurs when one withdraws the senses from the sense objects they ordinarily perceive. It is done after one has mastered the sitting positions (**asanas**)—and thus can sit comfortably for long periods—and after one has gained control of "breath" (**pranayama**), which allows heightened command of one's physiological capacities. Having gained relative mastery over the body, one is then ready to focus attention inward.

Pratyaksha

("concerning the eye") In Indian **philosophy**, pratyaksha is the general term for sense perception. All philosophical schools accept perception as one of the **pramanas**, the means by which human beings can gain true and accurate knowledge, and it is the only pramana accepted by the **materialist** school. Although the word's literal meaning implies only information from the eyes, this pramana includes sense data from the other four human senses, as well as "perceptions" obtained through magical cognition, yogic insight, or any other supernormal abilities or phenomena.

Pravahana Jaivali

A character in the **Chandogya Upanishad**, one of the speculative religious texts that form the latest stratum of the **Vedas**, the oldest Hindu religious texts. In the text, Pravahana Jaivali is a member of the warrior (**kshatriya**) class who serves as teacher to members of the scholarly-priestly (**brahmin**) class. His first students are Silaka Shalavatya and Caikitayana Dalbhya, then **Shvetaketu** Aruneya and his father **Gautama**. This is one of several episodes in the **Upanishads** in which kshatriyas instruct brahmins, thus inverting the accepted pattern that holds brahmins as religious authorities. These episodes reveal the nature of wisdom as conceived in the Upanishads—it is conferred, not by birth or social position, but by individual striving and realization.

Pravara

A lineage system, primarily among **brahmins**, which builds on the assumptions of the **gotra** system (the tracing of brahmin lineage to one of seven mythical sages). In his daily **worship** a brahmin would not only mention the name of his gotra, who is the sage believed to be the family's immediate progenitor, but also the names of other sages believed to be remote ancestors. Both these "lineages" were passed down only through men, since it was customary for a married woman to adopt her husband's gotra as part of her new identity. The only context in which gotra and pravara were really important was in fixing marriages, because of the kinship conferred by these mythic lineages. Marriage within the gotra was strictly forbidden, since the assumption that such people were directly related made this marriage incestuous. Marriage within the pravara was also forbidden, although in medieval times different groups interpreted this prohibition differently. For some groups, any shared pravara ancestry would forbid the marriage, but for other groups one shared "ancestor" was deemed permissible. The more lenient interpretation may well have been spurred by practical difficulties in making matches.

Prayaga

("Place of **Sacrifice**") The traditional Hindu name for **Allahabad**, the city at the junction of the **Ganges** and **Yamuna** rivers. See **Allahabad**.

Prayashchitta

A general term meaning atonement for one's misdeeds. The Hindu religious tradition gives considerable attention to penance and expiation, based on the almost universal Hindu belief in the inexorable workings of **karma**. According to this notion, all good and bad deeds will eventually have their effect, either in this life or the next, and thus one must either atone for the evil one has done or face its consequences in the future. Prescriptions for such expiation can be found as far back as the **Vedas**, and the acts prescribed for atonement fall into several categories: confession, repentance (which was usually seen as preparation for expiation, rather than absolution of the evil itself), restraint of breath (**pranayama**), physical **asceticism** (**tapas**), **fire sacrifice** (**homa**), recitation of prayers (**japa**), gift-giving (**dana**), fasting (**upavasa**), and travel to sacred sites (**tirthayatra**). The prayashchitta literature is quite well developed, both in detailing differing kinds of offenses and their potentially mitigating circumstances, and in laying out the types of atonement to be performed for each offense. For further information see Pandurang Vaman Kane (trans.), *A History of Dharmasastra*, 1968.

Prayoga

("use," "application") In the context of Hindu ritual, any prescribed procedure to be followed during **worship**, meditation, or when performing other ritual actions.

Pregnancy

As in all societies, Hindus regard the impending **birth** of a child as a time of eager expectation tinged with anxiety. Part of this anxiety stems from purely physical worries that the pregnancy and birth proceed normally, and that the mother and child remain in good physical health. Expectant mothers are usually encouraged to rest and are often given food considered especially nourishing (such as milk products and nuts) to build their strength. From the mother's perspective, pregnancy is an extremely significant event, since the birth of children (especially **sons**) will solidify her status in her marital family; but this significance also contributes its own quotient of expectation and anxiety. Since the mother's emotional state during pregnancy is believed to affect the child, all efforts are made to shelter the expectant mother from unpleasant thoughts and situations and to generate happy thoughts.

Aside from protecting the expectant mother's physical and psychological health, Hindus take numerous precautions to guard her from other sorts of misfortune. As at other life transitions, during pregnancy and the child's first days the mother and her child are considered particularly vulnerable to black **magic**, particularly the **witchcraft** of those who might be jealous of the expectant or new mother. Another avenue for harm comes from inauspicious events, such as an **eclipse**, during which a pregnant woman should stay inside (away from its malevolent rays) and remain perfectly still, lest her child be born with missing limbs. These hostile forces can also be countered by various **rites of protection**, such as wearing amulets, charms, or iron (considered to render one impervious to spells), by cutting back on social interaction to avoid possible contact with inauspicious people and things, and by attention to religious rites.

Prenatal Rites

Life-cycle rituals (**samskaras**) performed by a husband before his child's **birth**, as prescribed in the **dharma literature**, the texts on religious duty. According to this literature, there were three such rites: **Garbhadhana**, which ensured conception; **Pumsavana**, which guaranteed that the newly conceived child would be a boy; and **Simantonnayana**, which was performed late in the **pregnancy** to ensure the child's good health and the mother's easy delivery. Although the dharma literature prescribes these rites as obligatory, none of them are widely performed now except by the most orthodox brahmins.

Pret

("departed," "deceased") The spirit of a person who has recently died but is still inappropriately connected to the world of the living, often as a troubling or malevolent presence to the departed's family or the general population. Prets are believed to be the spirits of people who died in childhood and whose untimely death left them with certain unfulfilled desires, particularly longings relating to marriage and family life. Prets make themselves known to the living in two ways, either through **dreams** or **possession**. In some cases they have specific requests and can be placated through **worship** and **offerings**. In such instances, dreams offer a method of communicating with the living, so that necessary actions can be performed for the pret. In other cases, the spirit may resort to bodily possession in an attempt to realize unfulfilled desires directly. These spirits are typically malevolent and require an exorcism to be removed. For further information on the care of unquiet family spirits, see Ann Grodzins Gold, *Fruitful Journeys*, 1988; for a psychological interpretation of spirits, possession, and healing, see Sudhir Kakar, *Shamans, Mystics, and Doctors*, 1991.

Prinsep, James

(1799–1840) British official and amateur Indologist. In 1837, Prinsep became the first modern person to decipher the **Brahmi** script, and was thus able to translate the edicts of the Mauryan emperor **Ashoka** (r. 269–32 B.C.E.). Unfortunately, his career was cut short by an early death, a pattern distressingly familiar for colonial administrators in British India. See also **Maurya dynasty**.

Priyadas

(early 18th c.) Author of the ***Bhaktirasabodhini*** ("Awakening the Delight in Devotion"), a commentary on the ***Bhaktamal*** of **Nabhadas**, completed in 1712. In his text, Nabhadas had given very brief (six line) biographies of over two hundred contemporary **bhakti** (devotional) figures. These original biographies are notably free of marvelous and miraculous events, with their major emphasis being the devotee's (**bhakta**) personal qualities, to serve as a model for others. In his commentary, Priyadas gives greatly expanded accounts for each one of the devotees mentioned by Nabhadas, and usually describes events to which Nabhadas makes no reference. At least in the case of the poet-saint **Ravidas**, Nabhadas clearly drew his material from the texts written by the biographer **Anantadas**, but in many other cases his sources are not clear. The accounts by Priyadas are larded with miracles and wonders, and the prevalence of such events, combined with his chronological distance from his subjects, makes him a less reliable source for the lives of these devotees.

Progress Philosophy

("jativada") Progress philosophy affirms that one can attain complete freedom from bondage—which in the Indian context is identified as the end of reincarnation (**samsara**) and final liberation of the soul (**moksha**)—and that one can also specify the necessary and sufficient conditions that allow human beings to bring about this freedom. As a rule, progress philosophy tends to stress gradual spiritual attainment, in which very small beginnings can gradually lead one to the ultimate goal. Progress philosophers thus tend to stress particular religious paths that will lead one to the final goal, and also tend to place a great significance on actions (especially ritual actions) as essential parts of this path. In the Hindu tradition, most philosophical schools are progress philosophies: the combined **Nyaya-Vaisheshika** school, the combined **Samkhya-Yoga** school, the **Purva Mimamsa** school, and even the **Bhamati** and **Vivarana** schools of **Advaita Vedanta.**

Prohibition

Most traditional Hindus have clearly and strongly disapproved of consuming **liquor**, a substance which, because it may lead to a loss of control, is seen as impure. Among wealthier Indians, drinking alcoholic beverages is seen as a habit that signals the acceptance of Western values and alienation from one's roots, whereas among poorer citizens, particularly laborers, drinking is often seen as a misuse of money needed to support a family. For all these reasons, the imposition of total or partial prohibition has become an effective part of electoral platforms designed to appeal to traditional and conservative Hindus. In 1997, prohibition had been established in three Indian states: **Gujarat**, **Andhra Pradesh**, and **Haryana**. Of these three, Gujarat is the only one with a long-standing history of prohibition, while prohibition in Andhra Pradesh in 1995, and in Haryana in 1996, was imposed to fulfill campaign promises made during the state elections in those years. In both cases, the imposition of prohibition also stimulated widespread bootlegging and illegal distilling.

Prostitution

Prostitutes or courtesans were a regular feature of ancient Indian life. But far from simply offering sexual pleasure, these prostitutes were in many cases women of culture and learning. One of the sections in the ***Kama Sutra*** pertains to such individuals, and the author **Vatsyayana** portrays prostitutes as women who, while clearly outside normal society, have far greater independence than most women. One finds a similar picture in *The Little Clay Cart* (***Mrcchakatika***), a drama in which the courtesan Vasantasena is sought by all the men of the city because of her beauty, wealth, and mastery of the sixty-four aesthetic arts. This picture is doubtless idealized and was probably realistic for only a tiny fraction of the women plying the sex trade, however.

The existence of prostitution also appears in relation to a group of women connected to certain temples. Called servants of the **deity** (**devadasis**), these women were not allowed to marry. Instead, they were considered to be married to the god, for whom they would sing, **dance**, and perform various rites, just as any Hindu wife would for her husband. These women could hold property and resources of their own, but their status was clearly unusual, and it was not uncommon for them to develop long-term liaisons with local men for mutual enjoyment. In some cases this degenerated into prostitution—through which such women became a source of income for the temple—but in other instances they were successful in retaining some autonomy. Since Indian independence in 1947 there has been a prohibition on initiating devadasis, but some older women remain who were initiated before that time. In 1995, a furor developed when the **Jagannath** temple management committee began to explore the possibility of new initiations. For further information see Vatsyayana (tr. Alain Daniélou), *Kama Sutra of Vatsyayana*; and Frederique Apffel Marglin, *Wives of the God-King*, 1985. See also **Yellamma**.

Prthivi

The most common name for the **Earth**, which, in addition to its material form, is conceived of as a **goddess**. This particular name for the Earth goddess comes from a mythic story connecting her to the righteous king **Prthu**.

Prthu

In Hindu mythology, an ancient king who rules over all the **Earth**, and whose reign is considered a golden age. Prthu is magically born from the right hand of king **Vena**, a man so wicked that he has prohibited all sacrifices to the gods. After Prthu's birth the people in his kingdom suffer famine, since the Earth has refused to produce food in protest against Vena's wickedness. Prthu chases the Earth, who has taken the form of a **cow**. She finally agrees that, if Prthu will spare her life, she will produce food again. It is in memory of this deed that the Earth is given the name **Prthivi** ("related to Prthu").

Puja

("homage") The most common word for **worship** in modern Hinduism. The root of the word carries the sense of reverence or respect, but puja is primarily focused on actions, particularly **offerings** to the **deity**, who is treated as an honored guest. Although, according to one list, there are sixteen such offerings (**upacharas**), in practice the worship performed in any particular setting is subject to wide variation—based on regional or local custom, individual inclination, and the person's social status and learning. At the heart of puja, however, is a series of transactions between the deity and devotee (**bhakta**). One such transaction comes in **darshan**, the exchange of glances between an image of the deity and a devotee, which initiates the relationship between the two. The other transactions come from offerings given by the devotee, to which the deity responds by giving **prasad** sanctified by divine contact, most often food or drink for the devotee to consume.

Aside from the transactions, the other most common feature of most puja is the emphasis on **purity**, both of worshiper and of context. The only exception to this arises in certain forms of **tantra**, a secret, ritually based religious practice in which the performer deliberately inverts normal ideas of purity and impurity (**ashaucha**) as a way of symbolically destroying all duality.

Puja offerings, including flowers and red tika powder, are left for a deity as a sign of honor and respect.

Devotees commonly purify themselves before worship, and the purity of the site, and the objects used in worship, must be either established (in the case of a place or things not generally used for worship) or maintained (as in the case of a temple or other regularly established place).

In its most basic conception, the temple is a home for the deity, a ritually pure environment. Most temples have at least two different "purity zones," an outer zone into which the devotees may enter, and an inner zone closest to deity, restricted to the temple priests. In their purity requirements, deities show as much variation as one finds in the human community, and stricter concern for purity indicates higher status, just as for human beings. Whereas **village deities** are often served by non-**brahmin** priests and typically take offerings of meat, **blood**, and **liquor**, the higher deities are always served by brahmin priests, and the food offered to them is invariably vegetarian. As the ritually purest of all human beings, the brahmin priest acts as an intermediary between the high deities and other worshipers, shielding the deity from potentially contaminating contact. His high ritual purity also makes the brahmin a universal donor, from whose hand all people can receive prasad without fear of pollution. For further information see C. J. Fuller, "Hindu Temple Priests," in T. N. Madan (ed.), *Religion in India*, 1991.

Pujari

In its most basic meaning, the word *pujari* denotes "one who does **puja** (**worship**)." In theory this word could refer to any worshiper, but in general usage the meaning is more restricted. It usually designates a man performing worship as his means of livelihood, either as a priest in a temple, or as a religious "technician" hired to perform ceremonies for others. For further information see C. J. Fuller, "Hindu Temple Priests," in T. N. Madan (ed.), *Religion in India*, 1991.

Pulaha

In Hindu mythology, one of the six **sons** of **Brahma**, all of whom become great sages. All are "mind-born," meaning that Brahma's thoughts bring them into being. The others are **Kratu**, **Angiras**, **Pulastya**, **Marichi**, and **Atri**.

Pulakeshin II

(r. 609–42) Greatest king in the **Chalukya dynasty**, which ruled much of the **Deccan** peninsula from the Chalukya capital at modern Badami. Pulakeshin was a contemporary of the Pushyabhuti emperor **Harsha**, whom Pulakeshin defeated in battle to contain Harsha's southward expansion. Pulakeshin also defeated the **Pallava dynasty** king **Mahendravarman**, who was killed in battle with Pulakeshin's army. He, in turn, was finally defeated and killed by Mahendravarman's **son Narasimhavarman**. For several centuries afterward, the Chalukya and Pallava Dynasties warred with one

Farmers harvesting wheat in a field in Punjab.

another, and although each was strong enough to defeat its opponent at various points in this conflict, neither was capable of keeping the other under subjugation. See also **Pushyabhuti dynasty**.

Pulastya

In Hindu mythology, one of the six **sons** of **Brahma**, all of whom become great sages. All are "mind-born," meaning that Brahma's thoughts are enough to bring them into being. The others are **Kratu**, **Angiras**, **Pulaha**, **Marichi**, and **Atri**.

Pumsavana ("engendering a male") Samskara

In traditional calculation, the second of the life-cycle ceremonies (**samskaras**). The Pumsavana samskara was one of the **prenatal samskaras** performed before **birth**, done to ensure that a newly conceived child would be a boy. Various writers give differing prescriptions as to the correct time during the **pregnancy** to perform this rite, but they generally specify that it be performed when the **moon** is in a male

constellation, at which time the woman should have several drops of the juice from the banyan tree inserted into her right nostril (a common practice in traditional medicine). This samskara is seldom performed in modern times.

Pundit

Term still used in modern times to denote a scholar or learned man. In traditional usage, the word *pundit* denoted a person proficient in **Sanskrit** and Sanskrit learning.

Punjab

Modern Indian state that lies south of the state of **Jammu** and **Kashmir** on the border of Pakistan. Modern Punjab is one of the so-called linguistic states, created to unite people with a common language and culture (in this case, Punjabi) under one state government. The present state of Punjab was created in 1966, when the former state (also called Punjab) was divided into three areas: Punjab (the Punjabi-speaking region), the state of **Haryana** (from the

531

Hindi-speaking regions), and **Himachal Pradesh** (from the hill regions). The Punjab region is replete with history, for it has been the traditional route by which invaders have gained access to the northern Indian plains. The first of these were the **Aryans**, who coined its name from the five rivers (pancab) flowing through it. The abundant **water** from these rivers, carried by an extensive irrigation network, has made the Punjab exceptionally fertile, and today it remains the largest wheat-growing area of India.

The Punjab is famous as the birthplace of the Sikh religious community, and is today the only Sikh-majority state. The partition of India into Hindu and Muslim states in 1947 hit the Sikhs the hardest, since the division essentially carved their homeland in half. In the aftermath of the partition millions of people became refugees, and many of them fell victim to the atrocities of the time. For most of the 1980s, Sikh proindependence groups waged an undeclared war against the Indian government. In one of the most dramatic events of this period, the Akal Takht, the traditional symbol for Sikh temporal power, was stormed by the Indian army in June 1984, and the Indian prime minister, Indira Gandhi, was assassinated four months later. By the mid-1990s this movement seemed to have been quelled, although no one can predict whether this is permanent. Punjab is most famous for the Sikh Harmandir (Golden Temple) in Amritsar, a short distance from the **Jallianwala Bagh**, site of a massacre that was one of the pivotal events in the struggle for Indian independence. For general information about Punjab and all the regions of India, an accessible reference is Christine Nivin et al., *India*. 8th ed., Lonely Planet, 1998.

Punya

("holy") Word most often used as a noun to mean "religious merit"—sometimes to denote the religious distinction arising from a particular deed, but more often to refer to the collective body of religious merit one has accumulated through the good deeds in one's karmic career. (According to the theory of **karma**, all of one's deeds will eventually be realized, so the merit one has earned in the past is stored up to bring benefits in the future.) Its opposite is **pap**, the most general word for religious demerit.

Purana

("old") An important genre of **smrti** texts, and the repository of traditional Indian mythology. The smrtis, or "remembered," texts were a class of literature that, although deemed important, was considered less authoritative than the **shrutis**, or "heard" texts. In brief, the shrutis denoted the **Vedas**, the oldest and most authoritative Hindu religious texts, whereas the smrtis included the two great epics, namely the *Mahabharata* and the *Ramayana*, the **dharma literature**, the **Bhagavad Gita**, and the compendia known as the puranas.

According to one traditional definition, a purana should contain accounts of at least five essential things: the creation of the **earth**, its dissolution and recreation, origins of the gods and patriarchs, the reigns of the **Manvantaras**, and the reigns of the **Solar** and **Lunar Lines**. In practice, the puranas are compendia of all types of sacred lore, from mythic tales to ritual instruction to exaltation of various sacred sites (**tirthas**) and actions. Individual puranas are usually highly sectarian and intended to promote the **worship** of one of the Hindu gods, whether **Vishnu**, **Shiva**, or the **Goddess**. By tradition the major puranas number eighteen, but there are hundreds of minor works. Along with the epics, the puranas are the storehouses of the mythic tales that are the common religious currency for traditional Hindus. In this respect the puranas are much more influential than any of the **Vedas**, because the tales in the puranas are common knowledge. The contents of the Vedas, though more authoritative, are less well known. Judgments on the importance of individual puranas vary according to sectarian persuasion, but some of the

Rath Yatra festival in Puri.

most important puranas are the *Agni Purana*, **Shiva Purana**, *Brahma Purana*, **Bhagavata Purana**, **Vishnu Purana**, **Harivamsha**, and **Markandeya Purana**. For a general translation of stories from puranic texts, see Cornelia Dimmitt and J. A. B. van Buitenen, *Classical Hindu Mythology*, 1978.

Purana Kassapa

In early Indian **philosophy**, philosopher opposed to moral rules, whose views are mentioned in Buddhist scriptures. According to these texts, Kassapa believed that there was no religious merit in good acts, and no demerit in evil acts—that neither of these had any affect on the Self at all. Beyond this, very little is known about him.

Purandaradas

(1480–1564) A devotee (**bhakta**) of the god **Vishnu** who was the founder of the **Haridasas**, a sect of saint-composers in the southern Indian state of **Karnataka**. Aside from the literary merits of the poetry Purandaradas wrote, the musical

structure of his songs is believed to have laid the foundations for the Karnatic school of Indian music, the predominant musical form in southern India.

Purattasi

The sixth month in the Tamil solar **year**, corresponding to the northern Indian solar month of Kanya (the zodiacal sign of Virgo), which usually falls within September and October. The existence of several different calendars is one clear sign of the continuing importance of regional cultural patterns. One way that the Tamils retain their culture is by preserving their traditional **calendar**. Tamil is one of the few regional languages in India with an ancient, well-established literary tradition. See also **Tamil months**, **Tamil Nadu**, and **Tamil language**.

Puri

City and sacred site (**tirtha**) on the Bay of Bengal in the state of **Orissa**. Puri is best known for its temple to the god **Jagannath**, a local **deity** assimilated into the pantheon as a form of the god **Krishna** and therefore, by extension, a form of **Vishnu**. The temple was completed in 1198 C.E. and is currently receiving much needed restoration, after several pieces fell off the tower in the early 1990s. The most important annual festival held in Puri is the **Rath Yatra**. During this festival, Jagannath, his brother **Balabhadra**, and his sister **Subhadra** are carried in procession through the city's main street in enormous wooden carts. They travel to another temple about a mile away, where they stay for a week, and then return to Puri. Aside from the spectacle, the ceremony is an important ritual theater used to demonstrate the relationship between Jagannath and the kings of Puri, who were considered to be deputies ruling in his name. Although the kings no longer wield actual power in modern times, by virtue of their status they still play an important ritual role.

Aside from containing the temple of Jagannath, Puri is one of the **four dhams**, which symbolically mark the geographic boundaries of India. It is also the home of the **Govardhan Math**, one of the four **Dashanami Sanyasi** sacred centers supposedly established by the philosopher **Shankaracharya**. Puri's character as a holy city has made it an attractive place for religiously inclined people to make their homes, most notably the Bengali saint **Chaitanya** (1486–1533), who lived there for much of his adult life. The cultural life generated by the **worship** of Jagannath also made Puri a center for the arts, and it is the traditional home of the classical **dance** form known as **Orissi**. For further information see Anncharlott Eschmann, Hermann Kulke, and Gaya Charan Tripathi, *The Cult of Jagannath and the Regional Tradition of Orissa*, 1978; and Frederique Apffel Marglin, "Time Renewed: Ratha Jatra in Puri," in T. N. Madan (ed.), *Religion in India*, 1991.

Puri Dashanami

One of the ten divisions of the **Dashanami Sanyasis**, ascetics who are devotees (**bhakta**) of **Shiva**. The Dashanamis were supposedly established by the ninth century philosopher **Shankaracharya** in an effort to create a corps of learned men who could help to revitalize Hindu life. Each of the divisions is designated by a different name—in this case, **puri** ("city"). Upon **initiation**, new members are given this name as their new surname, thus allowing for immediate group identification.

Aside from their individual identity, these ten "named" divisions are also divided into four larger organizational groups. Each group has its headquarters in one of the four monastic centers (**maths**) supposedly established by Shankaracharya, as well as other particular religious associations. The Puri Dashanamis belong to the **Kitawara** group, which is affiliated with the **Shringeri Math** in the southern Indian town of Shringeri.

Purity

(shaucha) Along with its opposite, impurity (**ashaucha**), purity is one of the fundamental concepts in Hindu culture. Although to outsiders purity can be easily confused with cleanliness, it is fundamentally different—purity is a religious category marked by the presence or absence of pollution or defilement, whereas cleanliness is a hygienic category. In some cases these categories can overlap, but in most their disjunction becomes clear. For example, from a religious perspective, bathing (**snana**) in the **Ganges** River makes one pure, whereas from a hygienic perspective the lower reaches of the Ganges are quite heavily polluted.

On a personal level, purity can be best described as the absence of defilement, gained through removing impurities in some manner, most often by bathing. After becoming purified, one remains pure until coming into contact with a source of impurity. These sources of impurity include essential bodily functions, such as urination and evacuation; sexual activity; contact with impure things both inside and outside one's home; and even contact with certain groups of people deemed impure. Thus, although purity is always easy to regain, it is impossible to retain, since it is breached by many of the actions of everyday life. It is also important to realize that impurity brings no moral stigma to an individual—becoming impure means simply that one has come into contact with some contaminant, and that this must be removed. The only times when purity is particularly important are in **worship** and in **eating**—the former to keep from contaminating the **deities** and their environs, the latter to protect oneself, since the circumstances surrounding what one eats are considered to have long-term effects on an individual.

Aside from its personal dimension, purity has a social dimension as well. Higher status groups, such as **brahmins**, are considered to have inherently higher ritual purity. This social dimension of purity comes with **birth** and is the religious basis determining the hierarchical divisions in the traditional social system. To some extent, a group's purity level corresponds to its hereditary occupation. People who had continual contact with substances considered impure (such as latrine cleaners, **corpse** burners, and scavengers) were seen as tainted by work, and rendered impure. Brahmins, as scholars and priests (the latter a task that brought them in contact with the gods), were the purest. Between these extremes fell the other groups, whose relative status in a specific locale was determined by local factors. For theoretical consideration of the importance that purity plays in modern Hindu life, see Louis Dumont, *Homo Hierarchicus*, 1980; for another analysis of social ordering, see McKim Marriot, "Hindu Transactions: Diversity Without Dualism," in Bruce Kapferer (ed.), *Transaction and*

Pilgrim bathing in the sacred Narmada River. Bathing is believed to be purifying, especially when it is done in sacred waters.

Meaning, 1976; see also Pauline Kolenda, "Purity and Pollution," in T. N. Madan (ed.), *Religion in India*, 1991. See also **caste** and **jati**.

Purochana

In the *Mahabharata*, the later of the two great Hindu epics, Purochana is a minister of **Duryodhana**, the epic's antagonist. He advises Duryodhana to build the **House of Lac** as a means to kill the **Pandavas**, the five brothers who are Duryodhana's cousins, and the epic's protagonists. After the Pandavas move into the House of Lac, Purochana sets **fire** to it. The Pandavas, whose uncle **Vidura** has alerted them to the danger, are able to escape through a secret underground passage, but Purochana himself is killed in the fire.

Purohit

("[one] placed in front") The most important of the priestly functionaries in the cult of **sacrifice** found in the **Brahmanas**. The purohit was

535

responsible for supervising the other sacrificing priests, such as the **rtvij** and the **hotr**, and for making sure that the **animal sacrifices** were completed without error. The purohit would often be attached to a particular ruler and was also called to perform rites for communal well-being. In modern times this latter meaning has persisted, the word is often used to denote one's family priest, who will perform various rituals for the family.

Pururavas

In Hindu mythology, a prominent king of a royal lineage who trace their ancestry to the **moon**. Pururavas is a righteous king who performs one hundred horse **sacrifices** (**ashvamedha**), and the merit from these gives him great power. He is best known for his dalliance with the celestial nymph (**apsara**) **Urvashi**, by whom he has several children. Although the two are forced to spend sixty years apart because of a **curse**, in the end they are happily reunited.

Purusha

("person") One of the two fundamental first principles in the **Samkhya** philosophical school, the other one being **prakrti** ("nature"). Samkhya upholds an atheistic philosophical dualism in which the twin principles of purusha and prakrti—roughly, spirit and nature—are the source of all things. Purusha is conceived as conscious but completely inactive and unchanging. It is the passive witness to the myriad transformations of prakrti going on around it, and as the source of consciousness purusha is ultimately identified with a person's true Self (**atman**). Thus purusha is inferred as plural, given the plurality of conscious beings and the fact that one person can gain final enlightenment while all the rest remain in bondage. According to the Samkhyas, the ultimate source of bondage lies in people's failure to distinguish between purusha and prakrti and in identifying

the Self with the latter rather than the former. For further information see Gerald Larson and Ram Shankar Bhattacharya (eds.), *Samkhya*, 1987; and Sarvepalli Radhakrishnan and Charles A. Moore (eds.), *A Sourcebook in Indian Philosophy*, 1957.

Purushartha

The **Aims of Life**, traditionally numbered at four: material wealth and power (**artha**), pleasure (**kama**), religious duty (**dharma**), and final liberation (**moksha**). All of these were seen as legitimate goals in traditional Hindu society. See **Aims of Life**.

Purusha Sukta

("Hymn to the Primeval Man") The most common name for the hymn in the **Rg Veda** (10.90) that describes the creation of the material and social world as the result of a primordial **sacrifice**. According to the text, in the beginning there was one primeval man, who was dismembered in sacrifice. Different parts of his body became different parts of the physical universe, as well as the four traditional major social groups (**varnas**): the **brahmins** came from the primeval man's mouth, the **kshatriyas** from his shoulders, the **vaishyas** from his thighs (a common euphemism for the genitals), and the **shudras** from his feet. This hymn clearly reflects the sacrificial paradigm that was so central to the later **Brahmana** literature, and is thus believed to be one of the latest hymns in the Rg Veda. It is also notable for giving the first known articulation of the four varnas, as well as the symbolic functions associated with each: for brahmins, speech and the authority of the sacred word; for kshatriyas, protection and military valor; for vaishyas, generation and production, and for shudras, service to others.

Purushottama Mas

Religious observance that occurs when the **intercalary month** falls during the lunar month of Ashadh. The intercalary month is an extra lunar month inserted into the calendar about every thirty months, to maintain general agreement between the solar and lunar calendar. It begins after any "regular" lunar month in which the sun has not moved into the next sign of the zodiac, and takes the name of the preceding month. Since the intercalary month is an unusual phenomenon, it is generally considered to be inauspicious, and the most common colloquial name for this month is the malamasa, the "impure month." When this extra month falls in the lunar month of Ashadh, however, devotees (bhakta) of the god Vishnu take the opposite perspective and treat it as an exceedingly holy time, dedicated to Vishnu in his form as Purushottama ("best of men"). Vaishnavas celebrate this month by reading the sacred texts, chanting Vishnu's divine names, and other sorts of worship. The month of Ashadh, and its intercalary month, are especially important for the Jagannath temple in the city of Puri, whose presiding deity, Jagannath, is considered a form of Krishna and therefore, by extension, a form of Vishnu. During every year Ashadh is the month in which the Rath Yatra festival is performed in Puri, and in years when the intercalary month falls in Ashadh, new images of Jagannath and his siblings are created.

Purva ("Earlier") Mimamsa

One of the six schools of traditional Hindu philosophy, most commonly referred to simply as Mimamsa ("investigation"); it was given the name Purva Mimamsa to distinguish it from the Uttara ("Later") Mimamsa school, better known as Vedanta. The Mimamsa school's name is quite apt, for it emphasizes the investigation of dharma ("righteous action"), particularly as revealed in the Vedas, the earliest and most authoritative Hindu religious texts. Mimamsas affirmed that the Vedas were the source of perfect knowledge, and believed that the Vedas had not been composed either by God or by human beings but were rather simply heard by the ancient sages through their advanced powers of perception, and then transmitted orally from generation to generation.

Since they accepted the Vedas as the primary source of authority and assumed that the Vedas contained codes and prescriptions pertaining to dharma, the Mimamsas then developed complex rules for textual interpretation to discern these, and it is for these rules that they are best known. Mimamsas believed in the existence of the soul and in the necessary connection of actions with their results inherent in the notion of karma—two ideas attested to in the Vedas. In cases where the result of an action comes some time after the act, the Mimamsas believed that the result existed as an unseen force called apurva. This force would invariably bring on the result, thus maintaining the Vedic truth. The Mimamsas were less unified on the existence of God. Jaimini (4th c. B.C.E.?), the author of the *Mimamsa Sutras* and the founder of the school, seems to ignore the issue completely, and 1,000 years later another Mimamsa luminary, Kumarila, argued against the existence of God.

Aside from developing methods for interpreting the Vedas, Mimamsas also contributed to logic and epistemology. One of their notable contributions was postulating two new pramanas, which are the means by which human beings can gain true and accurate knowledge. All the philosophical schools accepted perception (pratyaksha) as a pramana, and most also accepted inference (anumana) and authoritative testimony (shabda). The two new modes developed by the Mimamsas were "presumption" (arthapatti) and "knowledge from absence" (abhava). The Mimamsas justified these additions by claiming that they accounted for knowledge that could not be subsumed under the existing pramanas. Arthapatti is an inference from circumstance, in which a judgment is made about one case based solely on similarities to related cases. An

The city of Pushkar is built around a sacred lake used for ritual bathing.

example would be the presumption that a traveler had reached his or her destination after the train's arrival time had passed. According to Indian philosophy, this is not a true inference, since the latter must always be confirmed by direct perception. In the same way, abhava or the perception of any absence (e.g., the absence of some object before one) could not be accounted for by any of the existing pramanas, and thus required this new one to explain it. Aside from Jaimini, the two most significant figures among the Mimamsas are Kumarila and **Prabhakara**, who both lived in the seventh century. For further information see Karl H. Potter, *Presuppositions of India's Philosophies*, 1972; and Sarvepalli Radhakrishnan and Charles A. Moore (eds.), *A Sourcebook in Indian Philosophy*, 1957.

Pushan

In the **Vedas**, the oldest and most authoritative Hindu religious texts, Pushan is one of the **deities** identified with the **Sun**. Due to this connection, Pushan is described as the witness to all

things; he is also considered to be the keeper and protector of flocks, and bringer of prosperity. By the turn of the common era, and perhaps significantly earlier, his presence had almost completely disappeared, and today he remains only historically important.

Pushan

(2) In Hindu mythology, the name of an **aditya** (minor **deity**) who attends the **sacrifice** sponsored by the demigod **Daksha**. The sacrifice is a disaster, since Daksha insults the god **Shiva** by not inviting him to the ceremony. When Daksha's daughter **Sati**, who is also Shiva's wife, inquires why Shiva has been excluded, Daksha begins to insult her in full view of the company. Mortified and humiliated, Sati commits **suicide**. When Shiva learns of this, he comes with his ghoulish minions and utterly destroys the sacrifice. In the process many of the guests suffer injuries or indignities, and Pushan's teeth are broken and lost.

Pushkar

("blue lotus") City and celebrated sacred site (**tirtha**) a few miles north and west of the city of Ajmer in the state of **Rajasthan**. Pushkar's center is a natural lake, and its major importance is as a bathing (**snana**) place—according to tradition, its lake is so holy that Pushkar is said to be the religious preceptor (**guru**) of all other sacred sites. Pushkar's lake is surrounded by temples. Of these, the best-known is dedicated to the god **Brahma** and is his only temple in all of India. Two nearby temples dedicated to the **Goddess** are said to be **Shakti Pithas**, a network of sites spread throughout the subcontinent and sacred to the Goddess. Each Shakti Pitha marks the site where a body part of the dismembered goddess **Sati** fell to earth. The two temples in Pushkar mark the places where both of Sati's wrists fell. Pushkar's largest festival is known as **Kartik Purnima** (October–November), and falls on a **full moon** (generally associated with enhancing the sanctity of bathing places). Aside from being a time for bathing, this event is also marked by the holding of an enormous livestock market, particularly for camels and horses. The state government is currently promoting this as a tourist attraction, and it has drawn over 200,000 people in recent years. See also **pitha**.

Pushkara ("Blue Lotus") Dvipa

In traditional mythic geography, the name of the seventh and outermost of the concentric land masses (**dvipas**) making up the visible world. See also **cosmology**.

Pushpa

("flower") The tenth of the sixteen traditional **upacharas** ("**offerings**") given to a **deity** as part of **worship**. In this offering (based on the model of treating the deity as an honored guest) the deity is given flowers, valued both for their color and their fragrance. The actual act of offering can be performed in various ways and often depends on the worshiper's inclinations. In some cases the flowers will simply be presented before the deity's image, with the understanding that the deity has taken them, whereas in other cases flowers will be placed on the deity's image, or a garland hung around its neck. In either instance, the underlying motive is to show love and respect for the deity and to minister to its needs as one would to a living person. This particular act of respect and love can also be accorded to other human beings; garlanding a person with flowers is a sign of high esteem or congratulations.

Pushpak Viman

("Flower chariot") In Hindu mythology, the most famous of the **aerial cars**. Pushpak Viman is built by the divine architect **Vishvakarma**. Vishvakarma's daughter **Sanjna** has married the **Sun** but is so overwhelmed by his brilliance that she begs her father to reduce his luster so she can stand to be with him. Vishvakarma does this by trimming some bits off the sun, which are later fashioned into the Pushpak Viman as well as several divine weapons. For some time the Pushpak Viman is held by the minor **deity Kubera**, who obtains it as a reward for performing intense physical **asceticism** (**tapas**). It is later taken from Kubera by the **demon**-king **Ravana**, who uses its powers to wreak all sorts of tyranny, culminating in the abduction of **Rama's** wife **Sita**. After slaying Ravana, Rama uses the Pushpak Viman to return to the city of **Ayodhya** and then returns the car to Kubera.

Pushti Marg

Religious community founded by the philosopher **Vallabhacharya** (1479–1531), whose teachings remain the sect's primary influence. Vallabhacharya characterized his philosophical position as "pure monism" (**Shuddadvaita**); his fundamental position is that the god **Krishna** is the Supreme Being and the ultimate source of everything that exists. The world, and human beings, thus share in his divine nature, although only in a limited fashion, and the human soul is imbued with divinity as its inner light and controller.

Since Krishna is the ultimate source of everything and thus everything depends ultimately on God, the school's primary religious emphasis is on the importance of God's **grace**. This grace is seen as nourishing (pushti) the devotee (**bhakta**) and is best attained by devotion (**bhakti**), which is conceived of as the only effective religious path. This emphasis on grace and devotion has meant that the Pushti Marg have put little stress on **asceticism** or renunciation, and the bulk of Vallabhacharya's followers came from affluent merchant communities. The stress on devotion was soon articulated in elaborately arranged forms of image **worship** in the Pushti Marg's temples. Devotees would visualize themselves as Krishna's companions during his daily activities—waking, eating, taking his cows to graze, coming home, etc.—and thus gain the opportunity to take part in the divine play (**lila**). This emphasis on visualization and participation was fostered through the development of vast liturgical resources, which were composed by eight poets (the **ashtachap**) who were associated with Vallabhacharya and **Vitthalnath**, his **son** and successor. The third leader, Vitthalnath's son **Gokulnath**, further consolidated the developing community, whose major sacred site is now in **Nathdwara** in the state of **Rajasthan**. For further information see R.K. Barz, *The Bhakti Sect of Vallabhacharya*, 1976.

Pushyabhuti Dynasty

(6th–7th c.) Northern Indian dynasty whose capital was at **Kanyakubja**, the modern city of **Kanuaj** in the **Ganges** river basin, and whose territory ran through the northern Indian plain from the **Punjab** to **Bihar**. The Pushyabhutis filled the northern Indian political vacuum after the demise of the Gupta empire and in some measure regained its greatness. The dynasty's greatest ruler was the emperor **Harsha** (r. 606–47), whose reign was chronicled in panegyric fashion by the playwright **Bana**, and perhaps more factually by the Chinese Buddhist pilgrim **Hsuan Tsang**. The latter's journals give a detailed picture both of Harsha himself, in whose court Hsuan Tsang stayed for some time, and of everyday life in Harsha's kingdom. See also **Gupta dynasty**.

Pustaka

A book, traditionally made of **palm leaves** connected by a string running through a hole punched in the middle, with a wooden cover on top and bottom to keep the leaves from being bent or broken. In Indian iconography, the book is most strongly associated with the **goddess Saraswati**, in keeping with her identity as the patron **deity** of the arts, culture, and learning. It also commonly appears as one of the objects held by the god **Brahma**.

Putana

In Hindu mythology, Putana is one of the **demon** assassins sent by **Kamsa**, the king of **Mathura**, in an attempt to kill his nephew, the child-god **Krishna**. Through her **magic** powers, Putana assumes the form of a beautiful young woman and, after cooing over Krishna for awhile, puts him to suckle at her poisoned breast. When Krishna latches on, however, it is Putana who is in dire trouble—Krishna sucks at her breast so hard that he sucks the life right out of her. As she dies, she reverts to her original form, gigantic and hideous, and the crash of her falling body shakes the earth and fells trees.

Putrada Ekadashi

Religious observance that occurs twice per **year**: on the eleventh **day** (**ekadashi**) of the bright (waxing) half of the **lunar month** of **Shravan** (July–August), and on the eleventh day of the bright (waxing) half of the lunar month of **Paush** (December–January). As with all the eleventh-day observances, these are dedicated to the god **Vishnu**. Most Hindu festivals have certain prescribed rites, which usually involve fasting (**upavasa**) and **worship**, and often promise specific benefits for faithful performance. Faithfully observing the ekadashi rites on these days is believed to give one a **son** (putra), which is a major concern in traditional Indian culture. Sons are necessary for this world and the next, not only to care for their parents in their old age, but also to perform certain ancestral rites after one's death. The strength of this desire for sons is demonstrated by the fact that this particular ekadashi occurs twice during the year—the only ekadashi to do so.

Puttaparthi

Town in **Andhra Pradesh** near the border with **Karnataka**, about ninety–five miles north of Bangalore. Puttaparthi is best known in connection with the modern Hindu teacher **Sathya Sai Baba**, not only as the place where he was born and raised, but also the site of his most important religious dwelling (**ashram**) and primary residence.

R

Radha

In later devotional (**bhakti**) literature, Radha is the woman portrayed as the god **Krishna's** lover and companion. Radha's love for Krishna is a symbol of the soul's hunger for union with the divine, expressed through the poetic conventions of **erotic** love.

Although a few references to Radha in poetry date back to the seventh century, her first developed portrayal is in **Jayadeva's** lyric poem the *Gitagovinda,* written around the twelfth century. The *Gitagovinda* tells the story of Radha and Krishna's passion, their conflict and separation, and their eventual reconciliation. Jayadeva's portrayal of Radha is unique. In the poem Radha wishes to have Krishna all to herself, as his sole lover and companion. She sulks jealously when he flirts with other women and angrily dismisses him when he comes to her marked with the signs of another tryst. In the end, however, they reconcile and make passionate love as a symbol of their union.

This picture of love, separation, and reunion between Radha and Krishna gains a sharper focus through the context set by Jayadeva's hymn *Dashavatara Stotra.* In it Jayadeva lists the achievements of Krishna's ten incarnations (**avatars**) immediately after the text's introductory verses. The concluding verses of the hymn explicitly refer to Krishna as the ultimate source of the ten avatars, reminding hearers that the person taking part in this drama of jealousy, repentance, and reconciliation is none other than the Lord of the Universe Himself, who in ages past has acted to preserve the world from destruction. Unlike earlier depictions of Krishna in which his connections with his devotees (**bhakta**) are portrayed as a form of "play" (**lila**), the Krishna found in the *Gitagovinda* seems less lofty and detached, more intimately and intensely involved with Radha as the object of his affection. The poem renders Krishna as one who feels emotions deeply and truly and meaningfully reciprocates the feelings of his devotee.

Jayadeva's poetic focus is on the inner dynamic between the two lovers, and he reveals little about Radha outside this relationship. In the time after the *Gitagovinda*, Radha's character developed in various ways. Some poets describe her as married to another man, thus giving Radha's trysts with Krishna the color of adulterous, forbidden love. This love is considered more intense in Indian poetics, since the lovers have nothing to gain from the liaison but the love itself and stand to lose everything should they be discovered. Here Radha stands as the symbol of one willing to risk and lose all for the sake of love itself.

The other way in which Radha's character is developed runs contrary to this adulterous portrayal. In some traditions Radha is not drawn as a simple woman consumed with love for Krishna, but as his wife, consort, and divine power (**shakti**), through whose agency Krishna is able to act in the world. This deified image of Radha was particularly important for the **Nimbarka** religious community, which conceived of Radha and Krishna as forms of **Lakshmi** and **Narayana**. Another group espousing this equality was the **Radhavallabh** community, whose members particularly stressed the love Krishna felt for Radha. For further information about Radha, see Barbara Stoller Miller (ed. and trans.), *The Love Song of the Dark Lord,* 1977; and David R. Kinsley, *Hindu Goddesses*, 1986.

Radhakrishnan, Sarvepalli

(1888–1975) Modern Indian philosopher and statesman. Like many elite Indians

Radha, the god Krishna's lover and companion.

of his generation, Radhakrishnan was educated at Christian missionary schools, and the contrast between the Hindu piety of his home and the Christian doctrine he encountered at school sparked his interest in comparative **philosophy**. He spent the rest of his life as an interpreter and apologist for classical Hindu thought, particularly the **Vedanta** school, and as a proponent of philosophical idealism, the notion that absolute truth can be found through intuition alone. Aside from his work as a college teacher and administrator, he also served as the vice president of India from 1952 to 1962, and as president from 1962 to 1967. For further information on his thought, see his *An Idealist View of Life*, 1981; Paul A. Schilpp, *The Philosophy of Sarvepalli Radhakrishnan*, 1952; and Robert N. Minor, "Sarvepalli Radhakrishnan and 'Hinduism' Defined and Defended," in Robert D. Baird (ed.), *Religion in Modern India*, 1998.

Radhashtami

("**Radha's** eighth") Festival falling on the eight **day** of the bright (waxing) half of the **lunar month** of **Bhadrapada** (August–September); this day is celebrated as the birthday of **Krishna's** consort Radha. Radha is seen differently by various **Vaishnava** religious communities: For some she is a human woman, the symbol of the perfect devotee (**bhakta**) who forsakes all else to be with her lover, for others she is considered the queen of heaven and an equal to Krishna himself. In either case, her closeness to him is shown by her birth on the same month and lunar day as Krishna, but in the opposite half of the month. Radhashtami festival is celebrated with particular fervor in **Barsana**, the village in the **Braj** region in which Radha is said to have been born.

Radha Soami

Modern Hindu religious community founded in 1861 in the city of Agra by Shiv Dayal Singh, more commonly referred to as Soamiji Maharaj. Soamiji's family had been influenced by **Tulsi** Saheb, a devotional (**bhakti**) saint who lived in that region, and Soamiji's teachings reflect the importance of that contact. The two pillars of Radha Soami doctrine are the importance of the spiritual teacher (**guru**) and the practice of a spiritual discipline called **surat-shabd-yoga.**

According to Radha Soami teachings, contact with a guru is the single most important factor in a person's spiritual development, and this spiritual progress hinges on complete surrender to the guru's **grace**. It is essential for the devotee (**bhakta**) to be associated with a "true guru" (**satguru**), since not only does such an individual have access to the divine, he is considered a manifestation of the divine itself. Surat-shabd-yoga stresses joining (yoga) the devotee's spirit (surat) with the Divine Sound (shabd). The Divine Sound emanates from the Supreme Being and is always present. Most people cannot hear it, due to their preoccupation with worldly things, but with proper training and devotion to a true guru, anyone can eventually become attuned to the Divine Sound and resonate in harmony with it.

In the era since Soamiji Maharaj, the Radha Soami **Satsang** has split numerous times, usually based on disagreements over spiritual authority. Given the Radha Soami emphasis on the satguru as the Supreme Being, disagreements over spiritual succession—in effect, disagreements over the identity of the Supreme Being—made schisms virtually inevitable. It also seems clear that the underlying forces in many of these schisms were disagreements over far more mundane things, such as power, status, and property. Various branches of the Radha Soamis have made successful missionary efforts and established centers in Europe and the United States. For further information see Sudhir Kakar, *Shamans, Mystics, and Doctors*, 1991;

Lawrence Babb, *Redemptive Encounters*, 1987; and Mark Juergensmeyer, *Radhasoami Reality*, 1991.

Radhavallabh Sampraday

Religious community whose members are devotees (**bhakta**) of the god **Vishnu** (that is, **Vaishnavas**), and whose founder was the sixteenth-century poet-saint **Harivamsh**. Harivamsh held distinctive views on the status of **Radha**, which his community has preserved. Whereas earlier poetry had often portrayed Radha as the god **Krishna's** adulterous mistress, the Radhavallabhans conceive of her as his lawful wife and as a **deity** whose status was equal with Krishna's. Their devotion was focused on Krishna and on his status as the "beloved of Radha" (Radhavallabh).

Raga

In Indian music, a concrete melodic mode of at least five notes. Any musician playing a raga is limited by the constraints of its established form. The order of these established notes in the raga does not follow their musical order but differs according to whether the note sequence is ascending or descending. There are over 200 recognized ragas, but only about thirty are in general use. Each raga has very particular symbolic associations—particularly with the time of **day** or with the **seasons**—and is also believed to convey a particular aesthetic mood (**rasa**) to listeners. As in all the Indian arts, the musician who plays a raga endeavors to convey a certain mood to an audience and to awaken corresponding feelings within them.

Raghu

In Hindu mythology, Raghu is a famous king of the **Ikshvaku** dynasty and the grandfather of King **Dasharatha**. One of Dasharatha's **sons** is **Rama**, the protagonist of the *Ramayana*, the earlier of the two great Hindu epics.

Raghuvamsha

("**Raghu's** Lineage") One of the great poetic works by **Kalidasa**, who is generally considered to be the finest classical **Sanskrit** poet. The *Raghuvamsha* is a quasi-historical epic in nineteen cantos, devoted to the kings of the **Solar Line**, and particularly to its most eminent member, the god-king **Rama**. The story of Rama in Kalidasa's poem is fairly close to that of the epic *Ramayana*, although Kalidasa describes Rama as an **avatar** or divine incarnation in a way that **Valmiki** does not. Kalidasa's poem also uses the kings of the Solar Line as examples of devotion to the four **aims of life** (purushartha): wealth (**artha**), pleasure (**kama**), religious duty (**dharma**), and release (**moksha**). In Kalidasa's portrayal, the kings at the end of the line are completely immoral and devoted solely to pleasure. Such abject neglect of their duty to rule righteously brings on the destruction of the line and provides a exemplary lesson for hearers of the poem.

Rahu

A malevolent "**planet**" in Hindu astrology (**jyotisha**) that has no counterpart in Western astrology and was originally the head of a **demon**. According to the story, as the gods drink the nectar of immortality they have churned from the ocean of milk, the demon **Sainhikeya** slips into their midst in disguise. As the demon begins to drink, the **sun** and **moon** alert **Vishnu**, who uses his discus to cut off the demon's head. Sainhikeya's two halves become immortal, however, after coming into contact with the nectar. The severed head becomes Rahu, and the decapitated body another evil planet, **Ketu**. Rahu is regarded not as a physical planet, but as the ascending node of the moon. This is the point where the moon's northward path intersects the path of the sun in the sky, causing an **eclipse**. Rahu has particular enmity for the sun and moon, as the **deities** responsible for his demise, and tries to swallow them whenever he meets them in the **heavens**. He always succeeds, but since he no longer has a body to digest them, they escape unharmed through Rahu's severed neck. This, of course, is the traditional explanation for solar and lunar eclipses; their association with the malevolent Rahu has led eclipses to be seen as highly inauspicious times. See also **Tortoise avatar**.

Raidas

A variant name for the Hindu poet-saint **Ravidas**.

Rajabhiseka

("royal anointing") Royal **consecration** ceremony that replaced the earlier **rajasuya** rite. The Rajabhiseka includes rituals of anointing that were believed to have transformative power, but were less complex than the Rajasuya, and did not involve the ritual slaughter and **sacrifice** of **animals**.

Rajadharma

General name for the "king's **dharma**," or religious duty, which fell to him (or far more rarely, her) by virtue of his role as ruler. This notion proceeded from the assumption in the **dharma literature** that every person had a unique role to play in society, a role that provided for social stability but also brought individual fulfillment. The king's most basic duty was to maintain order in the realm, since such peace enabled all others to fulfill their own individual religious duties (**svadharma**). The dharma literature conceives of maintaining order primarily through inflicting punishment (**danda**), designed to remove some evildoers and frighten the rest into good behavior. If the king succeeded in maintaining social order, then he could otherwise do as he pleased, with the proviso that taxation should not be so high that it was burdensome to the people. Beyond this, the Indian theory of kingship was largely pragmatic.

Rajagrha

Ancient name for the city corresponding to modern Rajgir, in the Nalanda district of the state of **Bihar**. Although contemporary Rajgir is a small and insignificant city, at the time of the Buddha it was the capital of the Magadhan empire and the center of the region's political and intellectual life. According to Buddhist tradition, Rajgir was the site of the first Buddhist council, held shortly after the Buddha's death and organized to document his teachings. This story is almost certainly apocryphal, since the Buddhist scriptures went through a much longer period of development, but its setting illustrates Rajagrha's centrality in the middle of the first millennium before the turn of the common era.

Raja Raja

(r. 985–1014) Monarch under whose rule (and that of his son **Rajendra**) the **Chola dynasty** reached the apex of its power, stretching its influence from the **Tanjore** district of **Tamil Nadu** throughout southern India and into southeast Asia all the way to Malaysia. Raja Raja directed the wealth that such power brought toward the construction of massive temples. Of these, he is most noted for the **Brhadeshvar** temple in the city of Tanjore, dedicated to the "Great Lord" **Shiva**.

Rajas

("passion") One of the three fundamental qualities (**gunas**) believed to be present in all things, the other two gunas being **sattva** ("goodness") and **tamas** ("darkness"). According to this model, differing proportions of these qualities account for differences in the properties of concrete things, and in the range of individual human capacities and tendencies. Unlike sattva and tamas, which, respectively, carry exclusively good and bad associations, rajas and its effects can be either positive or negative, depending on context. Rajas is negative, for example, when it leads to an enslavement to the passions that may blind one to careful and conscious thought. Alternately, the energies derived from passion can also engender useful activity and industriousness. The notion of the gunas originated in the metaphysics of the **Samkhya** school, one of the **six schools** of traditional Hindu philosophy, and although much of Samkhya metaphysics connected with the gunas has long been discredited, the idea of the gunas and their qualities has become a pervasive assumption in Indian culture.

Rajashekhara

(10th c.) Dramatist notable for writing plays both in **Sanskrit** and **Prakrit**. Rajashekhara's Sanskrit plays were highly literary, and it seems that they were probably intended for reading rather than performance.

Rajasimhavarman

(8th c.) Ruler in the **Pallava dynasty** who, like his predecessors, was a great patron of the arts. His reign saw the construction of the last of the magnificent shore temples built on the Bay of Bengal, at **Mahabalipuram** in **Tamil Nadu**. The temple's major **deity** was the god **Shiva**, but a smaller shrine also held an image of the god **Vishnu**. Although these temples have been weathered by time and the elements, they remain some of the most visited sites in southern India.

Rajasthan

("land of kings") Modern Indian state on the border of Pakistan between the states of **Punjab** and **Gujarat**, created by combining a network of princely states with Ajmer, formerly under British control. These principalities were the remnants of small kingdoms, usually maintained by force of arms, giving Rajasthan its well-entrenched martial tradition. Many cities in Rajasthan have large forts originally built as defensive strongholds, which in modern times have been popular tourist attractions.

A miniature painting in the Rajasthani style, circa 1730.

Geographically, the state is split diagonally by the **Aravalli Hills**, creating two distinct climatic zones. The south gets more rainfall and has traditionally been more thickly settled, whereas the north blends gradually into the Thar Desert—rendered cultivable in recent years by a system of irrigation canals. While the state's most important pilgrimage site is the city of **Pushkar**, other locales of interest abound. Among them, the temple of **Hanuman** at **Mehndipur** has gained regional importance as a site for curing mental illness, and the **Karni Mata** temple in the village of **Deshnok** is noted for its sacred rats. For general information about Rajasthan and all the regions of India, an accessible reference is Christine Nivin et al., *India*. 8th ed., Lonely Planet, 1998.

Rajasthani

One of the two influential "schools" of Indian **miniature painting**, the other being the **Pahari**. Distinctions between the two schools are largely geographical and thus somewhat arbitrary, since the

Basohli paintings of the Pahari school are stylistically closer to those of **Rajasthan** than to works in the later Pahari style.

The Rajasthani was the earliest developed school; it flourished in the seventeenth and eighteenth centuries in the small kingdoms of the **Malwa** region such as **Mandu**, and in the kingdoms that now comprise regions in modern Rajasthan—particularly **Bundi**, **Kota**, and **Mewar**, but also Jaipur and Bikaner. The Rajasthani style is generally characterized by a flat perspective and by visual power derived from vivid colors, bands of which often serve as a backdrop to the painting. For further information see W. G. Archer, *Indian Painting*, 1957.

Rajasuya

Royal **consecration** ceremony that is one of the most famous of the sacrificial rites that appear in the **Vedas**, the earliest and most authoritative Hindu religious texts. The ceremony is believed to have developed in the latter part of the Vedic era. Preparations for this rite could last for a **year**, and the rite itself served to raise the king to semidivine status. As with many Vedic sacrifices, an important part of the rajasuya **sacrifice** was the ritual slaughter and **offering** of **animals**. This rite has long fallen into disuse, partly because of the trouble required to prepare for it and partly because of general disapproval over **animal sacrifices**. The coronation rite that has replaced it is the **rajabhiseka**.

Rajatarangini

("River of Kings") Historical chronicle of the kings of **Kashmir**, written in verse by the Kashmiri poet **Kalhana**. The *Rajatarangini* is an unusually descriptive and accurate history of Kashmir and the region's political, social, and religious institutions; the text's only shortcoming is that it pays little attention to the outside world. Kalhana's historical emphasis is unusual for Indian writers, and the *Rajatarangini* is one of the few indigenous Indian histories.

Rajendra I

(r. 1014–42) Monarch under whose rule (and that of his father, **Raja Raja**) the **Chola dynasty** reached the apex of its power, stretching its influence from the **Tanjore** region in **Tamil Nadu**, throughout southern India, and into southeast Asia all the way to Malaysia. In 1023 Rajendra defeated one of the kings of Bengal to extend his empire all the way to the **Ganges** but was unable to maintain authority over this expansive domain for long. He also fought a campaign against the Shrivijaya Empire in modern Malaysia, to retain control of trade from China. Like his father, Rajendra was a great patron of temple-building and other public monuments, including the great temple at **Gangaikondacholapuran**, built to commemorate the victory that opened the way to the Ganges.

Rajneesh, Bhagwan Shri

(b. Mohan Chandra Rajneesh, 1931–1990) Controversial Hindu teacher who mixed traditional Hindu teachings with ideas gleaned from modern psychology. He is most popularly associated with a permissive attitude toward sexuality that attracted many of his followers, both Western and Indian, although the former tended to predominate. This was part of a more generally indulgent attitude in which people were encouraged to act upon their desires, as a way to remove impediments to ultimate realization. For some time his **ashram** was located in Pune in the state of **Maharashtra**, but in 1981 he relocated to southern Oregon, propelled by local opposition and an investigation by Indian tax officials. For several years the new site was highly successful, but local opposition to his teachings and unease about his lifestyle—he reportedly owned ninety-three Rolls-Royces and was protected by Uzi-toting bodyguards—

caused the spectacular collapse of this community in 1985. Rajneesh returned to India, where he eventually took up residence in Pune again. In his last years he changed his name several times—once claiming that the spirit of **Gautama** Buddha had entered him—and at the time of his death had taken the name Osho.

Rajput

("king's son") Traditional Indian society was modeled as a collection of **endogamous**, or intermarried, subgroups known as **jatis** ("birth"). These jatis were organized (and their social status determined) by the group's hereditary occupation, over which each jati had a monopoly. The Rajputs were a martial Hindu jati that at times ruled large parts of western India, and have always claimed to be **kshatriyas**—buttressing this claim by creating genealogies linking their families to the mythical Solar or **Lunar Lines** of kings. Their origin is uncertain, for they first appear around the end of the first millennium, and many scholars speculate that they were descended from the Hunas and later assimilated into the small kingdoms. The four main Rajput clans were known as the **Agnikula** ("fire lineage"), because they claimed descent from a single mythical king who had arisen from a sacrificial fire pit in Mount Abu, **Rajasthan**. These four ruling clans were the Pariharas in southern Rajasthan, the Chauhans in the region around Delhi, the Solankis in **Gujarat**, and the Pawars in western **Madhya Pradesh**.

Whatever their origin, the Rajputs were warrior princes whose martial code stressed death before dishonor and swift reprisals against any insult. During the Moghul Empire era (1525–1707) Rajput kings were often feudal vassals, given kingdoms in exchange for their loyalty and service. After the breakup of the Moghul Empire many of them continued to reign as the rulers of small princely states. They remain an important ruling class even in modern times, through the medium of parliamentary politics.

Rajrajeshvar Temple

Massive temple in the city of **Tanjore** in state of **Tamil Nadu**, dedicated to the god **Shiva** in his form as "Lord of Kings." Tanjore was the capital of the **Chola dynasty**, and this temple, built approximately 1000 C.E. by the Chola king **Raja Raja**, conveys the confidence of a kingdom on the rise. Architecturally speaking, the temple is an enlargement of the simplest sort of Hindu temple, with a **garbhagrha** covered by a spire, but it is breathtaking in its scale. The tower over the central shrine is 190 feet high and looks even higher, since the construction minimizes any distracting elements that would arrest the eye's upward journey. It is capped by a single piece of stone weighing an estimated eighty tons, which required a four-mile-long ramp to put in place. See also **Moghul dynasty**.

Raksha Bandhan

Festival **day** celebrated on the **full moon** in the **lunar month** of **Shravan** (July–August); this festival's theme is the bond of protection (raksha) between brother and sister. On this day sisters tie (bandhan) a string around the brother's right wrist, which is sometimes just a simple thread and sometimes an elaborately constructed ornamental bracelet. Sisters then mark a tilak (**tika**) on the brother's forehead as a sign of respect and feed their brothers sweets. For their part, brothers give their sisters money, clothing, jewelry, or other gifts.

As with the festival of **Bhaiya Duj**, Raksha Bandhan symbolizes the protective bond between brothers and sisters. In the long term, brothers are seen as the family members who will protect their sisters' interests—since in many cases daughters long outlive their fathers and their brothers are the natal relatives on whom they must depend. Sisters perform these rites to protect their brothers from misfortune—the string tied around the wrist is believed to ward off evil. The festival of Raksha Bandhan is also performed by men and **women** who are not related by blood but who are close to one another. Tying on the string "makes" them brother and sister, and thus rules out the potential for any romantic involvement, which would be seen as a form of incest.

Rakshasa

In Hindu mythology, a particular type of asura (**demon**). Rakshasas are generally considered to be extremely powerful—not only in terms of their prodigious physical strength but also in their considerable skill in the magical arts. They are also generally characterized as malevolent toward human beings, whom they not only kill but also eat. According to one myth, rakshasas are born from **Brahma's** anger when he becomes hungry while reciting the **Vedas**. The capital of the rakshasas is in **Lanka**, and their most celebrated leader is **Ravana**, whose death at the hands of **Rama** is the climax of the *Ramayana*, the earlier of the two great Hindu epics.

Rakshasa Marriage

One of the eight ways to perform a marriage recognized in the **dharma literature**, the treatises on religious duty. The **rakshasas** are a class of **demon**, and the rakshasa form of marriage took place when a man had intercourse with a woman after carrying her away by force. Not surprisingly, this was one of the four reprehensible (**aprashasta**) forms of marriage and was forbidden because of the woman's lack of consent, even though it was deemed a valid marriage. (Here the writers' concern seems to have been to give the "bride" legal status as a wife rather than to legitimate the actions of the "groom.") Theoretically valid, this form of marriage has been forbidden since the dharma literature was first codified in the centuries before the common era. Although the rakshasa

marriage has never been one of the accepted forms of marriage, there are groups in which a ritualized battle and capture of the bride is part of the wedding ceremony. One could even interpret the **barat**, the procession of the groom and his family to the wedding location, as a ritualized triumphal entry following conquest. See also **marriage, eight classical forms**, **marriage ceremonies**, and **marriage prohibitions**.

Rakshasi

A female form of the type of **demon** known as a **Rakshasa**.

Raktabija

In the *Devimahatmya*, the earliest and most important textual source for the **worship** of the **Goddess**, Raktabija is the name of one of the **demons** vanquished by the goddess **Kali**. Raktabija has received the boon that any drop of his blood falling to the earth will instantly turn into another version of himself, rendering him practically unconquerable. Kali defeats this demon by drinking his blood as it is shed, until finally it is completely gone, and so is he.

Raktadantika

("bloody teeth") Powerful and protective form of the **Goddess**, particularly noted for killing **demons** and drinking their **blood**. During the fall festival of **Navaratri**, in which the Goddess is worshiped in a different form on nine successive nights, Raktadantika is her manifestation revered on the fifth night.

Rama (Rama Avatar)

The seventh **avatar** or incarnation of the god **Vishnu**, the crown prince of the **Solar Line** and the protagonist of the *Ramayana*, one of the two great Indian epics. As with all of Vishnu's avatars, Rama is born to destroy a being powerful enough to throw the cosmos out of balance, in this case **Ravana**, the **demon**-king of **Lanka**. The focal conflict in the *Ramayana* is **Rama's** quest to regain his wife **Sita**, who has been kidnapped by Ravana. The climactic sequence of the epic features Rama's struggle with Ravana, Ravana's death, and the reestablishment of cosmic equilibrium, signified by Rama's ascension to divine kingship.

Unlike the god **Krishna**, whose divine play (**lila**) often subverts or ignores accepted social values, Rama is a pillar of society. As a whole the *Ramayana* tends to espouse and uphold the traditional social values of religious duty (**dharma**), social hierarchy (**varna**), and the **stages of life** (ashrama). As the epic's protagonist, Rama is the epitome of all these values. He is solid, dependable, stable, righteous, and predictable. In Hindu culture Rama is the model of the perfect **son**, and he shows this by being utterly devoted to his parents, giving far greater weight to his duties as a son than as a husband. Unlike Krishna, who has multiple liaisons with his female devotees (**bhakta**), all in the name of divine play, Rama is married and monogamous. When the time comes for battle, he is the fiercest of combatants, incarnating the warrior (**kshatriya**) ideal of using strength to uphold justice, protect the righteous, and punish the wicked. In all these things he personifies some of the most deeply embedded values of Hindu culture.

Yet there are also some unsettling incidents, particularly in the **Valmiki** *Ramayana*, the epic's earliest version. These incidents either feature Rama inexplicably stepping out of character or else point to problematic tensions in traditional Hindu values. In an attempt to help the monkey-king **Sugriva** against his rival **Bali**, Rama shoots Bali in the back from a concealed place—an action incompatible with the notion of fair and honorable warfare. His actions in enforcing the existing social order also show its oppressive and restrictive nature. In one incident, Rama kills a low-status **shudra** whom he finds

The god Vishnu's Rama avatar. In the Hindu epic the *Ramayana*, Vishnu appears as Rama to defeat Ravana, the demon king.

performing physical **asceticism** (**tapas**), a privilege reserved for his betters, and has molten lead poured in the ears of another shudra who was discovered listening to the sacred **Vedas**—a forbidden act for such a person. Both incidents show the hierarchical nature of idealized Hindu society, and the king's role in preserving and sustaining this hierarchy. When Rama and his brother **Lakshmana** are propositioned by Ravana's sister **Shurpanakha**, they first mislead and ridicule her, then mutilate her by cutting off her ears and nose. These actions seem incompatible with the kshatriya ethic of respect for **women** and the righteous use of force, and prompt Ravana to kidnap Sita in revenge.

Perhaps the most troubling questions arise from Rama's behavior toward his wife Sita. Immediately after being liberated from enslavement, she undergoes an **ordeal** by **fire**, from which her emergence unscathed upholds her claim that she remained chaste while being held captive. Despite this definitive proof, Rama later insists on a second test, in which Sita, in protest, is swallowed up by the **earth**. Thus, the picture of Rama conveyed by the epic is of a figure righteous by the standards of his time but on occasion rigid and inflexible.

In later versions of the *Ramayana*, particularly the ***Ramcharitmanas*** by the poet-saint **Tulsidas** (1532–1623?), this picture subtly shifts, possibly in an attempt to soften or remove these troubling incidents. Certain changes in Tulsidas's text also highlight the centrality of devotion (**bhakti**) over all other religious attitudes. Tulsidas's Rama is more explicitly portrayed as God incarnate, a figure who is aware of his divine status and whose actions are undertaken for the benefit of his devotees. This Rama is still concerned with social values, particularly the kshatriya obligation to uphold and protect religious duty (dharma). Yet this ethic is in tension with—and sometimes in opposition to—the importance of bhakti, which is portrayed as the ultimate religious goal. These subtle shifts in the later text point to an occasional conflict between two differing ideals—dharma and bhakti—both of which are affirmed as essential. For further information on Rama, see the texts of the *Ramayana* (the *Valmiki Ramayana*, *Kamba Ramayana*, and *Ramcharitmanas*) or translations from the Sanskrit puranas, such as Cornelia Dimmitt and J. A. B. van Buitenen (eds. and trans.), *Classical Hindu Mythology*, 1978; secondary sources include V. Raghavan (ed.), *The Ramayana Tradition in Asia*, 1980; Edmour J. Babineau, *Love of God and Social Duty in the Ramcharitmanas*, 1979; and Frank Whaling, *The Rise in the Religious Significance of Rama*, 1980.

Ramakrishna

(1836–86) Bengali mystic and saint who was one of the most remarkable figures in the nineteenth-century revival of Hinduism. Ramakrishna was the son of a village priest and received little formal education during his life. He retained much of his rustic simplicity and spent his adult life as a temple priest at the **Kali** temple at **Dakshineshwar**, outside the city of Calcutta. From his childhood Ramakrishna had been devoted to the **Goddess** Kali, and characterized himself as being "intoxicated with God." He sought and found the divine, first through Kali but later through a variety of other religious paths, including the abstract monism of the speculative **Upanishads**, devotion to the god **Vishnu**, Christianity, and Islam. Out of these experiences came his conviction that the inner experience in all religious traditions was the same and led to the same divine presence. Although Ramakrishna did not publicize himself, he became known in Calcutta's religious circles through his association with **Keshub Chander Sen**, the leader of the reformist **Brahmo Samaj**. This association brought him disciples who would spread his teachings, particularly Narendranath Datta, better known as **Swami Vivekananda**. For a devotee's perspective on Ramakrishna, see Christopher Isherwood, *Ramakrishna and His Disciples*, 1965; for a modern psychological reading, see Jeffrey Kripal, *Kali's Child*, 1995.

Ramakrishna Mission

Hindu religious organization founded in 1897 by **Swami Vivekananda** to propagate the religious message of Vivekananda's teacher, **Ramakrishna**. Since its inception, the Ramakrishna Mission has been equally dedicated to spiritual uplifting and to social service, based on Vivekananda's realization that India needed material development as much as it needed religious instruction. The mission has sought to fulfill part of this charge by publishing inexpensive editions of religious texts, including but not restricted to the teachings of Ramakrishna and Vivekananda, and by sponsoring social service in the fields of education, medical care, and other charitable works. For further information see George M. Williams, "The Ramakrishna Movement: A Study in Religious Change," in Robert D. Baird (ed.), *Religion in Modern India*, 1998.

Ramana Maharishi

(1879–1950) Modern Hindu sage, whose life and message reiterated the fundamental insight of the ancient speculative **Upanishads**, namely, that the inner Self (**atman**) is identical with Supreme Reality (**Brahman**). Ramana was born into a middle-class Indian family and during his youth demonstrated no unusual abilities. In 1895 he obtained a copy of the *Periya Puranam*, a text chronicling the lives of the poet-saints known as the **Nayanars**, and in reading about their lives Ramana began to desire to renounce the world. This inclination was realized the next year, when he imagined the death of his body and reached the conclusion that his real identity was the Self. He left his family and went to the temple of **Tiruvannamalai**, also known as Arunachala, where he remained until his death fifty-four years later. For some time at the start he was deep in meditation and barely attended to his physical needs. Soon he attracted disciples, through whom his family eventually discovered his whereabouts, although Ramana refused to return home with them when they came to see him. His mother moved to Tiruvannamalai in 1916, and after her death five years later Ramana relocated his dwelling to be near her grave. Although he spoke very seldom, he managed to compose two short works—*Self-Enquiry* and *Who am I?*—in which he stated his basic insights. For further information see T. M. P. Mahadevan, *Ramana Maharshi*, 1977.

Ramananda

(14th c.?) **Sant** poet-saint who is traditionally cited as the spiritual teacher (**guru**) of the poet-saints **Kabir**, **Ravidas**, **Pipa**, and others. The Sants were a group of poet-saints from central and northern India who shared several general tendencies: stress on individualized, interior religion leading to a personal experience of the divine; disdain for external ritual, particularly image **worship**; faith in the power of the divine name; and a tendency to ignore conventional **caste** distinctions. Ramananda is said to have been a charismatic spiritual leader, and is claimed to have been a direct disciple of the southern Indian philosopher **Ramanuja**, who sent Ramananda north to help spread the devotional movement. The latter claim is almost certainly false, given that the only verse incontestably attributable to Ramananda is found in the **Adigranth**, the scripture of the Sikh community. This verse does not reflect Ramanuja's **Shrivaishnava** tradition, in which the primary **deity** is **Vishnu**, but instead shows the influence of the **Nathpanthi** ascetics, who stressed **yoga**. There are other verses ascribed to Ramananda in later sources, but their authenticity is doubtful, and little can be definitely known about his life.

Ramanandi

Renunciant ascetics, devotees (**bhakta**) of the god **Vishnu**, who are by far the most numerous and most influential of the **Vaishnava** ascetics. The Ramanandis claim that their order was founded by the religious teacher **Ramananda**, about whom little is definitely known. For some time the Ramanandis maintained that Ramananda had been a disciple of the southern Indian philosopher **Ramanuja**, and thus that their sect had sprung out of Ramanuja's **Shrivaishnava** religious community, but this claim was formally renounced after a dispute at the **Kumbha Mela** festival in the city of **Ujjain** in 1921. Ramananda is also traditionally thought to have been the **guru** of many northern Indian **bhakti** figures, most notably **Kabir**, **Ravidas**, **Pipa**, and **Sen**, although on this matter too there is little hard historical evidence.

All of the stories about Ramananda, however, point to someone who was firm in his commitment to devotion and was willing to initiate people from all walks of society.

The tutelary **deity** for the Ramanandi ascetics is **Rama**, particularly as described in the *Ramcharitmanas*, a vernacular version of the epic *Ramayana* written by the poet-saint **Tulsidas** (1532–1623?). Tulsidas portrays Rama as God incarnate, come to **earth** for the benefit of his devotees, and the text's primary theme is on the power of devotion. Yet within the larger confines of the Ramanandi fold there are several distinct variations on practice, which have little or nothing in common with one another. One strand is that of the **tyagis**, who stress renunciation and **asceticism**. A second strand is that of the **Nagas**, who in earlier times were fighting ascetics but whose military organization is now important only during the bathing (**snana**) processions for the Kumbha Mela. The final strand is that of the **rasiks** ("aesthetes"), whose religious practice is based on highly complex patterns of visualization in which they imagine themselves as present in the court of Rama itself; this sort of visualization was undoubtedly imitated from the patterns of **Krishna** devotion as practiced in the **Braj** region. The rasik tradition is by far the most literate and sophisticated; the tyagis and the Nagas perform similar sorts of rites as other ascetics, although their interpretation and their chosen deity is unique to their order. For further information see Peter van der Veer, *Gods on Earth*, 1988.

Ramanand Sagar

Director of the televised production of the *Ramayana*, which was completed in the late 1980s. The episodes were aired each Sunday morning for about a year, and were wildly successful despite problems with production quality. (Some of these problems undoubtedly derived from the difficulties of preserving the immediacy of the oral experience of traditional storytelling in the modern medium of television.) In the mid-1990s Sagar devoted his attention to other mythological television serials, with an extended series on the life of the god **Krishna**.

Ramanuja

(11th c.) Southern Indian philosopher who was the greatest exponent of the philosophical position known as **Vishishthadvaita** ("qualified nondualism") **Vedanta**, and the most important figure in the **Shrivaishnava** religious community. Ramanuja lived most of his life at the temple-town of **Shrirangam** in the state of **Tamil Nadu**, in service of the temple's resident **deity**, **Ranganatha**, a form of **Vishnu**. Ramanuja was convinced that **Brahman**, or Supreme Reality, was a personal deity rather than an impersonal abstract principle, and he was also convinced that devotion (**bhakti**) was the most important form of religious practice. **Vishishthadvaita Vedanta**, his philosophical position, stressed both of these convictions. According to Ramanuja, in his essential nature God is completely transcendent and free from imperfections. The world develops from God through a process of **evolution**, an idea adapted from the **Samkhya** philosophical school. The world is thus similar to God, since it proceeds from him, but also different, since matter is unconscious and insentient. In the same way, human beings are similar in nature to God, because they have him as their source, though unlike God they are subject to ignorance and suffering. For Ramanuja and his followers, God is not identical to human selves or to the world, all of which are perceived as having real and independent existence. The differences in capacity between God and human beings makes devotion the most effective means to gain final liberation (**moksha**) of the soul, a liberation that is conceived of as eternal communion with God. For further information see Sarvepalli Radha-krishnan and Charles A. Moore (eds.), *A Sourcebook in Indian Philosophy*, 1957; and John B. Carman, *The Theology of Ramanuja*, 1974.

Ramavali

("Series [of poems] to **Rama**") A series of 330 short poems dedicated to the god Rama, written in the **Braj Bhasha** form of **Hindi** by the poet-saint **Tulsidas** (1532–1623?). The *Ramavali* is one of Tulsidas' longest extant works—shorter only than the *Ramcharitmanas*. The seven sections in the *Ramavali* parallel the structure of the *Ramayana*, but differing sections receive unequal emphasis. Tulsidas gives his greatest attention to Rama's childhood and paints lyrical images of the child Rama's divine play (**lila**). Here Tulsidas clearly borrows from devotional poetry to the god **Krishna**, in which such childhood images are well established. Yet the *Ramavali*'s portrayal of Rama de-emphasizes the mischievous qualities associated with Krishna, to stress instead the generally milder nature of Rama, and to highlight the devotee's (**bhakta**) quiet delight in sharing his divine presence.

Ramayana

One of the two great **Sanskrit** epics, traditionally ascribed to the mythical sage **Valmiki**. The *Ramayana* is much shorter than the other great epic, the *Mahabharata*, and in many ways is a less complex work. The *Ramayana*'s text was composed later than the core story of the *Mahabharata*, but the *Mahabharata*'s final recension was compiled after the *Ramayana* had been fixed. The *Mahabharata* is the story of an "evil" royal family for whom greed and power-mongering ultimately lead to destruction. In contrast, the *Ramayana* is the tale of a "good" royal family, and many of the epic's characters are symbols of established Indian family values: **Rama** is the perfect son and the virtuous king, **Lakshmana** and **Bharata** his ideal younger brothers, and **Sita** the model wife. Despite this, the story is not without some troubling moral issues, particularly connected with Rama's treatment of Sita.

The story has been altered somewhat over the years, with the most important change being the elevation of Rama to divine status as an **avatar** or incarnation of the god **Vishnu**. The earliest *Ramayana*, attributed to the sage **Valmiki**, mentions Rama's divinity only in the first and last books, whereas in other portions of the poem he is described merely as a great hero. Given the position of these references to divinity, scholars speculate that they could easily have been added to the original core story of exile, abduction, and revenge.

The text of the *Ramayana* is divided into seven sections (khandas), each of which has a different focus. In the opening section, the Balakhanda ("childhood section"), the text describes the birth of Rama and his brothers (Lakshmana, Bharata, and **Shatrughna**) to King **Dasharatha**, and their lives as young princes. Rama and his brothers take part in an archery contest, sponsored by King **Janaka**, at which Rama's prowess as an archer wins the hand of Janaka's daughter Sita. They are married and live happily at Dasharatha's court.

The Ayodhyakhanda ("**Ayodhya** section") tells how Dasharatha makes preparations to anoint Rama as his successor but how, on the night before the ceremony, these plans are spoiled by Rama's stepmother **Kaikeyi**. Many years before, Kaikeyi receives the offer of two favors from Dasharatha, which she has never used. At the suggestion of her hunchback maid **Manthara**, Kaikeyi demands of Dasharatha that Rama be banished to the forest for fourteen years, and that her son Bharata be crowned in his place. This disaster seems grounded in malice but is presented as the culmination of a **curse** placed on Dasharatha, which predicts he will die bereft of his sons. When informed of his stepmother's

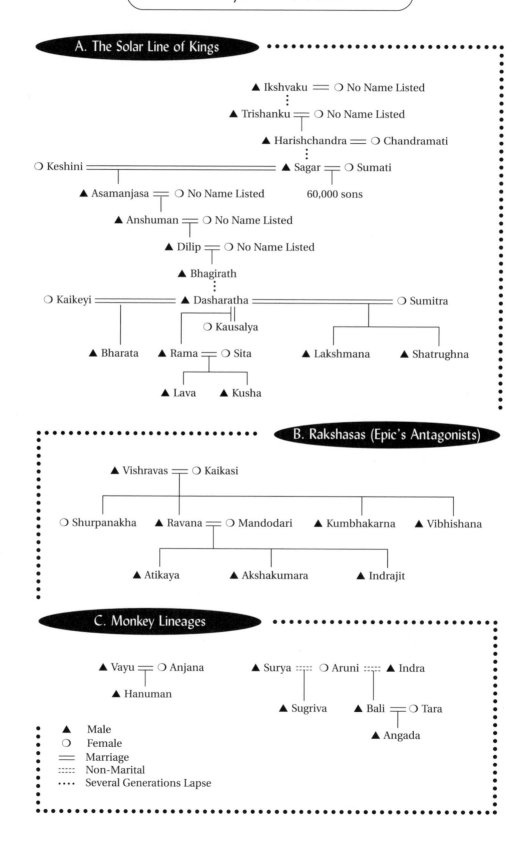

Ramayana Characters

A. The Solar Line of Kings

▲ Ikshvaku ══ ○ No Name Listed

▲ Trishanku ══ ○ No Name Listed

▲ Harishchandra ══ ○ Chandramati

○ Keshini ══════════ ▲ Sagar ══ ○ Sumati

▲ Asamanjasa ══ ○ No Name Listed

60,000 sons

▲ Anshuman ══ ○ No Name Listed

▲ Dilip ══ ○ No Name Listed

▲ Bhagirath

○ Kaikeyi ══════════ ▲ Dasharatha ══════════ ○ Sumitra
○ Kausalya

▲ Bharata   ▲ Rama ══ ○ Sita   ▲ Lakshmana   ▲ Shatrughna

▲ Lava   ▲ Kusha

B. Rakshasas (Epic's Antagonists)

▲ Vishravas ══ ○ Kaikasi

○ Shurpanakha   ▲ Ravana ══ ○ Mandodari   ▲ Kumbhakarna   ▲ Vibhishana

▲ Atikaya   ▲ Akshakumara   ▲ Indrajit

C. Monkey Lineages

▲ Vayu ══ ○ Anjana   ▲ Surya ┅┅ ○ Aruni ┅┅ ▲ Indra

▲ Hanuman

▲ Sugriva   ▲ Bali ══ ○ Tara

▲ Angada

▲   Male
○   Female
══   Marriage
┅┅   Non-Marital
····   Several Generations Lapse

wish, Rama immediately prepares to leave, refusing to seize the throne by force, and Sita and Lakshmana announce their intention to accompany him. Bharata is put on the throne but only as a regent in Rama's place, and the heart-broken Dasaratha dies of grief.

In the Aranyakhanda ("Forest section"), Rama, Lakshmana, and Sita settle into life in forest exile. Rama and Lakshmana kill many of the **demons** (**rakshasas**) who plague the forest-dwellers, thus bringing peace to the area. One day the female demon **Shurpanakha** comes to their dwelling, is smitten by the two young men, and asks them to marry her. The brothers first mock her, then mutilate her by cutting off her ears and nose. Shurpanakha goes to her brother **Ravana**, the demon-king of **Lanka**, and demands revenge for the attack. When frontal assaults fail, Ravana commands his uncle **Maricha** to assume the form of a golden deer in order to lure Rama away from his hut. At Sita's behest, Rama pursues the deer after giving Lakshmana strict orders not to leave Sita's side. Rama slays the deer, which with its dying breath calls out Lakshmana's name in a voice that mimics Rama's. Sita hears the call and flies into a rage when Lakshmana refuses to leave her. She finally drives him off, in an uncharacteristic show of temper, by accusing him of neglecting his brother in a time of peril so that he can have Sita to himself. When Lakshmana departs, Ravana comes to Sita disguised as a mendicant **ascetic**. He lures her out of a protective **magic** circle that Lakshmana has drawn around her, then kidnaps her. Ravana's escape is briefly delayed by a virtuous vulture named **Jatayu**, who attempts to rescue Sita. In the ensuing combat Jatayu is mortally wounded, but he lives long enough for Rama and Lakshmana to find him and learn the identity of Sita's abductor.

The Kishkindhakhanda ("**Kishkindha** section") narrates Rama's and Lakshmana's trip south to the Kishkindha forest. There they become allies with the monkey-king **Sugriva**, whose lost kingdom Rama helps to regain by slaying Sugriva's brother **Bali**. After enjoying the spoils of kingship, Sugriva and his monkey subjects, particularly his lieutenant **Hanuman**, begin searching throughout the country for any trace of Sita. Hanuman decides to leap over the sea, to Lanka, to see if he can find her there.

The Sundarakhanda ("Beautiful section") begins with Hanuman leaping the sea to Lanka and describes how, after much searching, he finally manages to locate Sita. Meanwhile, Ravana unsuccessfully tries to convince Sita to accept him as her husband. The demon's actions are motivated by his desire to avoid a curse, which states that he will drop dead if he ever rapes a woman who resists him. Hanuman reassures Sita that all will be well, and after many adventures makes his way back to Rama, to inform him that Sita has been found.

The Lankakhanda ("Lanka section") describes the beginning of a war between the forces of Rama and Ravana. Aided by armies of monkeys and bears, Rama builds a causeway across the sea to Lanka and begins to besiege the city. In his struggle he is helped by Ravana's youngest brother **Vibhishana**, who opposes Ravana's evil deeds and casts in his lot with Rama. Ravana is assisted by his brother **Kumbhakarna** and his son **Indrajit**, but in the end Ravana and his demon allies are killed in battle. After being rescued, Sita undergoes a trial by **fire** to prove her chastity, and when the fire refuses to burn her, she is shown to have been completely faithful to Rama. They return in triumph to Ayodhya, where Bharata renounces the throne, and the couple rule happily.

In the "Final section" (Uttarakhanda), which was almost certainly added later, Rama has further doubts about Sita's virtue. While roaming the capital one night, he hears a washerman abusing his wife for staying out all night. The washerman says that he is not as big a fool as their king. Rama is troubled by this and, although he is supposedly convinced of Sita's innocence, sends her into exile to please his subjects—here showing a distrust uncharacteristic of a figure who supposedly represents the epitome of virtue. While in exile, Sita gives birth to twin sons, **Lava** and **Kusha**, whose prowess makes them known to Rama, and they are eventually acknowledged as his heirs. Yet after all her suffering, Sita is not amenable to reconciliation. As a final proof she calls on her mother, the **Earth**, to bear witness to her virtue, and as a sign that this is true Sita sinks beneath the earth, never to be seen again. Soon after, Rama himself leaves his body and takes again his true form as Vishnu.

The *Ramayana* has been an extremely influential text, primarily because of the social virtues modeled by its characters. The epic is known throughout the subcontinent, and its popularity can be seen by its numerous retellings in vernacular languages, of which the most famous are the Tamil *Ramayana* of the poet **Kamban** (9th c.), and the ***Ramcharitmanas*** of the poet-saint **Tulsidas** (17th c.). The epic continues to be a prominent text in the modern day, as witnessed by its astounding popularity as a weekly television serial produced in the mid-1980s under the direction of **Ramanand Sagar**. The Valmiki *Ramayana* has been translated numerous times, the most recent partial translation of the work is by Robert Goldman and Sheldon Pollack. See also **Tamil epics**.

Rambha Ekadashi

Religious observance falling on the eleventh day (**ekadashi**) of the dark (waning) half of the **lunar month** of **Kartik** (October–November). As with all the eleventh-day observances, this is dedicated to the **worship** of the god **Vishnu**, on this particular day in his form as **Krishna**. As with most Hindu festivals, Rambha Ekadashi requires that certain rites be performed. These rites involve fasting (**upavasa**) and worship, and promise specific benefits for faithful

performance. This ceremony is named after Rambha, a famous **apsara** or celestial damsel. Its charter myth tells how, by faithfully observing this rite, a certain king was born in **heaven** and served by Rambha and other apsaras.

Ramcharitmanas

("Holy Lake of **Rama's** Deeds") Vernacular retelling of the *Ramayana*, the earlier of the two great **Sanskrit** epics. The *Ramcharitmanas* was written by the poet-saint **Tulsidas** (1532–1623), in the language known as **Avadhi**, an eastern variant of medieval **Hindi**. Evidence indicates that Tulsidas began the text in **Ayodhya** in 1574. At nearly 10,000 lines, this text is by far his longest work and is generally considered to be his greatest. For the most part the poem is structured in groups of six to eight verses written in the **chaupai** form, followed by a verse in the shorter **doha** form. (The doha verse either sums up the essence of the preceding chaupai verses or serves to foreshadow later developments.) There are also verses written in longer meters such as **savaiya**, as well as invocations in fluid Sanskrit poetry at the beginning of each of the seven sections. Tulsidas was a masterful epic poet, as evidenced both by the sheer size of his text and the high poetic quality of the verses contained in it.

As with all the *Ramayana*'s vernacular retellings, Tulsidas did not merely translate the story of Rama but interpreted it according to his own religious convictions. His two most important changes to the poem are the overwhelming emphasis on the importance of devotion (**bhakti**), and the saving power of the name of Rama, to which Tulsidas gives greater importance than Rama himself. Tulsidas also includes mythic material from a variety of other sources, most notably the ***Shiva Purana*** and the *Adhyatmaramayana*. This material is largely added to the first and last chapters, in which Tulsidas makes his greatest changes from the original epic. One theory to explain why Tulsidas brought in this other material argues that he endeavored to transcend narrow sectarian boundaries, for example, by having the god **Shiva** narrate much of the text in the form of a dialogue to his wife **Parvati**. Later, in part of the final book, Shiva is supplanted as narrator by the crow **Bhushundi**, who symbolizes the power of devotion to rescue even a common carrion-eating crow.

The *Ramcharitmanas* has popularly been called the "Bible of northern India," reflecting its enormous influence on ordinary people's piety. Although according to legend Tulsidas faced some opposition from **brahmins** who thought it sacrilegious to translate the *Ramayana* into a vernacular tongue, the text has been immensely popular with ordinary people. Even now there are many people who can recite large sections from memory ("discourses" (**katha**) on the text can draw hundreds or thousands of people) and many of the verses have become proverbial expressions in modern Hindi. Aside from reading or hearing the text, millions of people see it each autumn, in the dramatic presentation known as the **Ram Lila**. The oldest and most traditional Ram Lila, held at **Ramnagar** in **Benares**, uses the text from the *Ramcharitmanas*, and takes great pride in this traditionalism. For further information see Philip Lutgendorf, *The Life of a Text*, 1991.

Ramdev

(1404–58) According to legend, a **Rajput** prince whose piety and ability to perform miracles won him renown during his lifetime, and who was considered an incarnation of the god **Krishna** after his death. His tomb in the village of **Ramdevra**, east of the city of Jaisalmer in the western part of the state of **Rajasthan**, has become a pilgrimage site for devotees (**bhakta**) who come seeking various favors. Little is known about Ramdev's life, and unlike many of the other medieval saints, he has no poetry or body of literature attributed to him,

nor did he serve as the leader of any organized religious community. His original followers came to him because he was able to meet their needs, and for this reason pilgrims come to him still.

Ramdevra

Village and sacred site (**tirtha**) in the northwest corner of the state of **Rajasthan**, about sixty miles east of the city of Jaisalmer. Ramdevra is famous for the grave of the fifteenth-century saint **Ramdev**, as well as the grave of his low-**caste** disciple Dadi Bhai. During his lifetime Ramdev was famous for his piety and generosity, and was credited with performing various miracles to aid those in need. Since his death he has come to be regarded as an incarnation of the god **Krishna**. Although pilgrims can come throughout the **year**, most come during the annual religious fair (**mela**), at which time the near-deserted town takes on the semblance of a bustling city. Many of the visitors come to ask Ramdev for something, often related to concerns over health or prosperity. Others come to show gratitude, especially those whose past wishes have been granted, and to maintain their relationship with him.

Rameshvar

Manifestation of the god **Shiva**, in his form as "**Rama's** Lord" at **Rameshvaram** in the state of **Tamil Nadu**. The image of Rameshvar at this site is a **linga**, a pillar-shaped object said to represent Shiva's symbolic form. The Rameshvar linga is one of the twelve **jyotirlingas**, a network of twelve lingas deemed especially holy and powerful, and at which Shiva is thought to be uniquely present. The site's mythic charter is drawn from the *Ramayana*, the earlier of the two **Sanskrit** epics. According to tradition, Shiva is worshiped here by the god Rama, the epic's protagonist, although there are differing accounts of when this happened. In some stories, it is to gain Shiva's blessing immediately before

Rama's attack on the **demon** kingdom of **Lanka**. In other accounts the **worship** comes after the conquest of Lanka, as a rite of thanksgiving. In either case, both sets of stories portray Rama as a devotee (**bhakta**) of Shiva and thus buttress Shiva's status as the greatest god of all.

Rameshvaram

("**Rama's** Lord") Sacred site (**tirtha**) on an island off the coast of the state of **Tamil Nadu** in the Palk Strait, which separates **Sri Lanka** from the mainland. Rameshvaram is one of the most important sacred sites in India, for several different reasons. It is one of the **four dhams** associated with the philosopher **Shankaracharya**, which mark the geographical boundaries of the subcontinent. It also has specific mythic associations that make it holy both to devotees (**bhakta**) of **Shiva** and **Vishnu**, two of the most important Hindu **deities**. For Shiva's devotees, the pillar-shaped image (**linga**) of Shiva there represents the god in his manifestation as **Rameshvar** ("Rama's Lord"). This image is also one of the **jyotirlingas**, a network of twelve lingas deemed especially holy and powerful, and at which Shiva is said to be uniquely present. For Vishnu's worshipers, Rameshvaram is held to be the place from which the god Rama staged his attack on the **demon** kingdom of **Lanka**. According to tradition, upon Rama's return with his rescued wife **Sita**, the image of Rameshvaram was consecrated in gratitude for his success. Rameshvaram also has very old connections with the sacred city of **Benares**, and even today pilgrims come from there bearing **Ganges** water to offer to Shiva.

Ramgarh

Architectural site in the **Vindhya** Hills, 160 miles south of **Benares**. An **inscription** in one of the caves at Ramgarh, estimated to be from the third century B.C.E., contains the earliest datable reference to **devadasis**, a special class of women who served the **deities** of certain temples.

Ram Janam Bhumi

Site in the city of **Ayodhya**, where some claim the god **Rama** was born; since the early 1980s this spot has witnessed some of India's most intense postindependence religious conflict. The site has long been a source of controversy between the Hindu and Muslim communities, and British sources record hostilities there in 1855 and 1934. Until 1992 Ram Janam Bhumi was occupied by the **Babri Masjid**, a mosque constructed in 1528 by command of Mir Baqi, a general of the Moghul emperor Babar (1483–1530). Local tradition holds that the mosque was built after the razing of an existing Hindu temple there, although there is little evidence for this claim. A few months after India gained independence in 1947, several local Hindus secretly installed images of the child Rama, his wife **Sita**, and his brother **Lakshmana** in the mosque, claiming that the images had miraculously appeared in a ball of light. The government, having only recently quieted the Hindu-Muslim massacres that accompanied the partition of British India into India and Pakistan, was loath to ignite religious passions, and its solution, therefore, was to padlock the compound's gates and send the case to the courts for resolution, where it languished for almost forty years.

The early 1980s saw renewed controversy over the site, when the **Vishva Hindu Parishad** (VHP), a Hindu nationalist organization, first began calling for the site's "liberation," proclaiming that the existing mosque was an insult to all Hindus. The VHP's campaign portrayed the mosque as a symbol of Muslim iconoclasm and depicted government efforts to protect it as an attempt to appease the Muslim community and retain their votes. In 1986, the VHP's drive to liberate the site was aided by Rajiv Gandhi's national government. Together, the VHP and the Gandhi administration

An effigy of Ravana from the Ram Lila, a dramatic presentation of the *Ramcharitmanas*.

succeeded in unlocking the compound's gates so that Hindus could **worship** there, though observers called the action a clear bid to attract the Hindu vote.

Pressure throughout the 1980s, culminated in a series of campaigns to begin construction of a new temple at Ram Janam Bhumi. Many of these campaigns coincided with national elections, and the emotion that they generated boosted the electoral fortunes of the **Bharatiya Janata Party** (BJP), a political group with close links to the VHP. The final campaign came on December 6, 1992, a day that was scheduled to have "symbolic" meaning, and ended a little over five hours later with the mosque's demolition. The whole operation was carefully planned—demolition crews ordered the destruction of all television cameras prior to leveling the building in order to prevent any media coverage by outsiders. The razing was also carried out with the blessing of the BJP-led state government, which made no attempt to protect the temple. Riots ensued, particularly in the city of Bombay, where over three thousand people were killed, most of them Muslims.

Even after the destruction of the Babri Masjid, the site remained an area of contention between Muslims and Hindus. Immediately after the demolition, Prime Minister P.V. Narasimha Rao promised to rebuild the mosque but did nothing to accomplish this during the next five years he was in office. Meanwhile, various Hindu groups have been calling for the construction of a Ram Janam Bhumi temple, including traditional religious leaders such as the **Shankaracharyas**. Seeing nothing but trouble ahead, the government again sent the matter to the courts for resolution, where it remains to this day and may remain for decades to come. For further information see Christophe Jaffrelot, *The Hindu Nationalist Movement in India*, 1996.

Ram Lila

Any public dramatic presentation of the *Ramayana*, the earlier of the two great Hindu epics. The epic's basic plot revolves around the unjust exile of the god-king **Rama**; the abduction of Rama's wife **Sita** by **Ravana**, the **demon**-king of **Lanka**; and Rama's search to regain Sita, a struggle that ultimately ends in Ravana's death. Ram Lilas are prominent during the autumn in northern India, and usually correspond with the festival of **Dussehra** (October–November), which celebrates Rama's victory over Ravana and thus the symbolic triumph of good over evil. Late in the nineteenth century the Ram Lilas were important symbolic vehicles for demonstrating pride in Indian culture. Additionally, they were considered a coded symbol of resistance to British rule. Today, Ram Lilas can be found throughout northern India in many of the larger cities, while neighborhood associations often sponsor their own local productions.

The longest, most elaborate, and arguably the oldest Ram Lila is held at **Ramnagar**, the fortified town where the kings of **Benares** reside. The Ramnagar Ram Lila was begun in the early nineteenth century, during the reign of **Udit Narayan Singh**, and the Maharaja of Benares still plays an important symbolic role in the production even though he no longer wields temporal power over the city. It lasts for thirty-one days, during which the action moves to different places in and around Ramnagar. Thousands of faithful viewers follow the drama for the entire month, but on peak days the audience can reach 100,000. For further information on the Ram Lila, see Norvin Hein, *The Miracle Plays of Mathura*, 1972; and Anaradha Kapur, *Actors, Pilgrims, Kings, and Gods*, 1990.

Ramnagar

Fortified city just south and across the **Ganges** from the sacred city of **Benares** in the state of **Uttar Pradesh**. The Maharajas of Benares built their fort on this site because it was relatively easy to defend, and continue to live there, although they no longer possess ruling power. Ramnagar is famous as the site of the oldest and most traditional **Ram Lila**, a production of the epic *Ramayana* dramatized in a month of nightly shows. Aside from sponsoring this Ram Lila and underwriting its costs, the royal family also continues to play an important symbolic role in the production itself. For further information see Anuradha Kapur, *Actors, Pilgrims, Kings, and Gods*, 1990.

Ram Navami

Festival celebrated on the ninth day of the bright (waxing) half of the **lunar month** of **Chaitra** (March–April). Ram Navami is celebrated as the birthday of the god **Rama**, the seventh **avatar** of the god **Vishnu**, and this festival also ends the spring **Navaratri** festival of the **Goddess**. The Goddess festival of Navaratri, observed twice yearly in the spring and in the fall, ends each time with a celebration for Rama. The reason for this festival sequence is not entirely clear but probably reflects cultural imperatives to contain the explosive but uncontrolled fertile feminine energy personified by the Goddess with the stable and predictable masculine energy of Rama. Ram Navami is widely celebrated across India, but especially in **Ayodhya**, the city traditionally deemed his birthplace. In their celebrations, devotees (**bhakta**) may **worship** in their homes, fast (**upavasa**), attend religious discourses (**katha**), or go to temples for **darshan** and worship. With the recent growth of **Hindutva** (militant, politicized Hinduism) this holiday has become a day for large demonstrations and political action. This has been particularly true in Ayodhya, where the continuing struggle to build the **Ram Janam Bhumi** temple at the site of Rama's birthplace has made this day particularly significant.

Ramprasad

(early 19th c.) Bengali poet-saint and devotee (**bhakta**) of the **goddess Kali**, who is justly renowned for the power and expressive quality of his poems. As with many of the devotional (**bhakti**) figures, little is definitely known about his life. According to tradition, he worked for a short time as a clerk before his indulgent employer, finding him spending his days composing poetry to Kali, became his literary patron to allow him to write full time. Ramprasad's poetry invokes the Goddess in many of her different personae—as the goddesses **Uma**, **Durga**, and **Bhairavi**—but the majority of his poems are addressed to Kali. Despite Kali's fearsome qualities, Ramprasad persistently addresses her as "mother," and, like a child, clings to her despite all her attempts to discourage him. The end result is that his unflinching and unquestioning devotion to Kali removes all fear and brings him liberation. For further reading, see David R. Kinsley, *The Sword and the Flute*, 1975; and Clinton Seely and Leonard Nathan (trans.), *Grace and Mercy in Her Wild Hair*, 1999.

Ram Rajya Parishad

("Organization for Ram's Reign") Northern Indian political party formed immediately after Indian independence in 1947. It was founded by Swami **Karpatri**, an influential modern Hindu **ascetic**. The term Ram Rajya carries mythical significance, referring to the period of righteous rule by the god-king **Rama**, the protagonist of the epic *Ramayana*, after his return from fourteen years of exile in the forest. According to popular belief, Rama's reign was marked by perfect peace, justice, and social harmony.

The Ram Rajya Parishad sought to reshape India according to the vision of this mythical time, and the party's political platform was solidly rooted in conservative Hindu religious ideas. The party strongly supported the **caste** system, with its traditional division of social status and labor, and believed that it was essential for a smoothly functioning society. This position would have condemned most low-caste people to a

life of servitude, although the party did leave them a few meager windows for advancement. One of these was managing shoe factories, since **leather** is considered religiously impure by the higher castes, and thus working with leather is the traditional occupation of certain low status groups. Aside from their views on the validity of the caste system, the Ram Rajya Parishad also supported other conservative Hindu causes, particularly a total ban on **cow slaughter** and a complete ban on the production and consumption of **liquor**. The Ram Rajya Parishad's constituency came mainly from conservative, upper-class Hindus, particularly those in the **Ganges** River basin. Its conservatism gave those outside this group no incentive to support it. Although it had limited electoral success in years immediately after independence, within a dozen years the party had been reduced to a completely marginal presence.

Ram Rasik Sampraday

Religious lineage among the **Ramanandis**, a community of renunciant ascetics. All Ramanandis are devotees (**bhakta**) of the god **Rama**, but members of the Ram Rasik Sampraday stress the **worship** of Rama and his wife **Sita** as the divine couple. They focus their worship on the time of domestic bliss when the newly married couple lived in **Ayodhya**, before Rama's unjust banishment from that city. Rasik ("aesthete") devotion involves complex forms of visualization, in which devotees imagine themselves to be servants and companions of Rama and Sita, and spend their days in service to the divine couple. Rasik devotees also draw up exacting "schedules" of the **deities'** daily routines—in some cases, down to the quarter-hour—so that through this imaginative exaltation they can savor the bliss of being God's companions. (This form of dedication is clearly influenced by devotional patterns to the god **Krishna**, particularly the divine reverence found in the **Gaudiya Vaishnava** religious community.) Because Rasik worship is complex and highly developed, it has remained an elite phenomenon largely confined to a small group of ascetics. For further information see Peter van der Veer, *Gods on Earth*, 1988; and Philip Lutgendorf, *The Life of a Text*, 1991.

Ramsnehi

Renunciant **ascetic** community made up of devotees (**bhakta**) of the god **Vishnu**—in his form as the god **Rama**—whose practice stresses the love (sneha) of Rama. The Ramsnehis have three main centers, all located in the state of **Rajasthan**. These centers are unique in that each pays homage only to its own founder, and no founder or preceptor is honored by all three. Ramsnehi religious practice focuses on the repetition of the name of Rama, but has also been influenced by the Jains. Because of this latter influence the Ramsnehis voluntarily take on many restrictions to avoid destroying life.

Ranade, Mahadev Govind

(1842–1901) Lawyer, judge, and one of the great Hindu social reformers of nineteenth-century India. Along with his younger contemporary, **Gopal Krishna Gokhale**, Ranade was marked by his commitment to reform Hindu life by seeking the cooperation of the British government and by working within established institutions. Ranade was among the first generation of Indians to be educated in British schools and, after earning his degree at Bombay University, chose a career in law. In thirty years as a judge Ranade worked diligently to reform certain religious practices that were deemed social abuses, particularly issues concerning child marriage and **widow** remarriage. He was also a founding member of the **Prarthana Samaj**, a Hindu reformist organization that sought to attain similar goals. In addition to his interests in law, Ranade applied himself to the study

of economics, to provide practical guidance for economic development.

Ranganatha

("the rocking lord") A particular form of the god **Vishnu**, in which the god is depicted as sleeping on the back of his serpent couch, **Shesha**, floating in the sea of cosmic dissolution (**pralaya**). The most famous example of this image is housed in the Ranganathaswamy temple in **Shrirangam**, in the state of **Tamil Nadu**.

Rasa

("tastes") In Indian aesthetics, the nine moods that can be generated in an audience by various types of artistic expression: **erotic**, comic, compassionate, cruel, heroic, terrifying, loathsome, marvelous, and peaceful. These nine rasas correspond to the nine **bhavas** ("states"): sexual excitement, laughter, grief, anger, energy, fear, loathing, wonder, and peace. The nine bhavas are considered to be the most basic unadulterated emotions, and although each of the rasas corresponds to one of the bhavas, there is an important difference. Human emotive states come and go in response to circumstances largely beyond our control. Such emotive states often cannot be sustained, and they are generally not objects of aesthetic satisfaction. The case is very different for an aesthetic mood (rasa), which can be sustained, since it is artificially generated through artistic expression. This emphasis on creating and sustaining such a mood for an audience is the dominant goal of the performing arts in the Hindu tradition.

Rasayana

("method of essences") Alchemical school specializing in the use of certain chemicals, particularly compounds made from elemental **mercury**, in a quest to transmute the body and render it immortal. Some scholars have characterized rasayana as the Buddhist school of **alchemy**, with the Hindu school known as **dhatuvada**. The reported difference is that the latter relied solely on the consumption of mercurials, whereas the former used mercurials only to prolong life until the body could be transmuted through meditation, ritual, and extramaterial means. Despite these differing conceptions of the end of the process, the two schools overlap considerably on many other points. Both also probably draw from a common alchemical tradition. For further information see David Gordon White, *The Alchemical Body*, 1996.

Rashtrakuta Dynasty

(8th–10th c.) Central Indian dynasty whose core area was in the middle of **Maharashtra**, and whose capital was the Maharashtrian city of Achalpur. The **Rashtrakutas** were originally vassals of the **Chalukya dynasty**, but overthrew them in the middle of the eighth century and remained the premier power south of the **Vindhya Mountains** until the middle of the tenth century. The dynasty directly ruled most of the modern states of Maharashtra and **Karnataka**, along with parts of the states of **Andhra Pradesh** and **Tamil Nadu**, but had vassal states through the entire **Deccan** plateau, southern India, and Ceylon. Their hegemony ended in 973, when they were overthrown by the later Chalukya dynasty. The Rashtrakutas' greatest monument is the **Kailasanatha** temple at **Ellora** in the state of Maharashtra, which was completed late in the eighth century.

Rashtriya Svayamsevak Sangh

("National Volunteer Corps," hereafter RSS) Hindu nationalist organization founded in 1925 by **Dr. K. B. Hedgewar**. Since its inception the RSS has ascribed to the ideals of **Hindutva**, the notion that the Hindus are a nation despite their regional, linguistic, and cultural differences. The RSS has historically characterized itself as

In their daily meetings, members of the Rashtriya Svayamsevak Sangh practice martial drills that include sparring with sticks.

a cultural and character-building organization and, for much of its existence, has shunned direct political involvement, although it has exercised considerable influence through its many affiliated organizations.

RSS training stresses loyalty, obedience, discipline, and dedication to the advancement of the Hindu nation, but does not encourage the development of independent thought. The heart of its program are the daily meetings of its neighborhood units known as **shakhas** ("branches"). At these meetings members, known as **svayamsevaks** ("volunteers"), spend part of their time playing games, part of their time practicing martial drill—including sparring with sticks—and part of their time discussing and absorbing RSS ideals. The shakhas in any given area are overseen by a full-time RSS worker known as a **pracharak** ("director"), who serves as a liaison between the local units and the RSS leadership and who oversees RSS activity in his area.

As an organization, the RSS is profoundly elitist, and its self-proclaimed mission is to provide leadership for a renascent Hindu India. Most of its members will never advance beyond the local level, but those who do are generally remarkably efficient, effective leaders. Although the RSS has shunned direct activism that would tarnish its self-proclaimed cultural emphasis, it has exercised considerable influence through the formation of affiliated organizations, for which it has provided the leadership cadre. These organizations are spread throughout every level of Indian society, from labor and student unions to service organizations, religious organizations such as the **Vishva Hindu Parishad** (VHP), and political parties such as the **Bharatiya Janata Party**.

Although the RSS has produced some remarkably effective leaders, it has also generated considerable controversy. One reason is that it is a highly authoritarian organization, run on the model of the Hindu joint family. All authority is vested in a single supreme leader, the sarsanghchalak, and proceeds downward from there. In this way the RSS is profoundly undemocratic, and many of its opponents—particularly in the political arena—have felt uneasy about having it as the controlling hand behind its affiliated organizations. Other opponents have also worried about its anti-Muslim and anti-Christian tone—non-Hindus were not allowed to join the organization until 1979—a tone rooted in the organization's Hindutva ideals. A final reservation about the RSS comes on social grounds. The RSS has long condemned untouchability, and has also long asserted that **caste** distinctions did not exist within its ranks—in keeping with its Hindutva roots, it proclaims that all its members are Hindus and Hindus only. Nevertheless, critics have noted that most RSS members come from **brahmin** and other privileged castes, and that all of its leaders have been brahmins. These critics contend that such public disavowal of caste distinctions is a mask to perpetuate brahmin control and to conceal whose interests the RSS truly serves. For further informa-

tion see Walter K. Andersen and Shridhar D. Damle, *The Brotherhood in Saffron*, 1987; K. Jayaprasad, *The RSS and Hindu Nationalism*, 1991; Daniel Gold, "Organized Hinduisms: From Vedic Truth to Hindu Nation," in Martin Marty and R. Scott Appleby (eds.), *Fundamentalisms Observed*, 1991; Tapan Basu et al., *Khaki Shorts and Saffron Flags*, 1993; Lise McKean, *Divine Enterprise*, 1996; and Christopher Jaffrelot, *The Hindu Nationalist Movement in India*, 1996.

Rasik

Person able to appreciate a developed artistic mood (**rasa**); someone who is cultured and sophisticated. In the context of religious practice, the word refers to a person who has transposed this appreciation of aesthetic mood into a devotional setting. Rasik devotees (**bhakta**) would engage in elaborate visualizations of their chosen divinity and mentally accompany that divinity during the day. These meditative visualizations were said to give the devotee a sense of participation in the divine play (**lila**) of God's presence on earth and thus sharpen his or her enjoyment of it. The two religious communities that laid the greatest stress on this ability were the **Pushti Marg** and the **Ram Rasik Sampraday**, whose objects of devotion were the gods **Krishna** and **Rama**, respectively. This type of **worship** is almost exclusively focused on these **deities**, or on other forms of the god **Vishnu**.

Raskhan

(late 16th c.) Poet-saint and devotee (**bhakta**) of the god **Krishna** who was born a Muslim, specifically a Pathan (Afghan) and whose name may have been Saiyid Ibrahim. According to legend, Raskhan spent the early part of his life in Delhi, where he became enamored of a handsome boy. When the object of his affections proved unattainable, he migrated to **Brindavan**, the town where Krishna is said to have lived as a child, and spent the rest of his life sublimating that attraction through his devotion to Krishna. The main themes in his poetry are the attraction of the cowherd women (**gopis**) to Krishna, sparked by Krishna's physical beauty and, especially, the enthralling music of his flute. With Raskhan one finds a person who was a Muslim by birth but who used images and attitudes belonging to Hindu culture in an absolutely genuine manner.

Ras Lila

In the mythology of the god **Krishna**, the ras lila is the "circle dance" that **Krishna** and his devotees (**bhakta**), the **gopis**, perform on autumn nights on the shore of the **Yamuna River**. In this dance—a symbol of communion with the divine—Krishna offers a form of himself to every woman present, in order to convince each one that God is paying attention to her and to her alone.

Rat

An animal with a prominent place in at least two religious contexts. On one hand, the rat is famous as the animal vehicle of the **elephant**-headed god **Ganesh**, and reinforces Ganesh's identity as the Lord of Obstacles. If Ganesh's elephant head represents his power to remove obstacles by simply knocking them aside, his rat vehicle shows a stealthier approach. Rats are famous for their ability to work their way around obstacles, slipping through the smallest cracks in granaries to get to the grain inside. In their ability to slip around and between obstructing objects, they stand as a worthy complement to Ganesh's power.

Rats are also important to the temple of the **goddess Karni Mata** in the village of **Deshnok**, in the state of **Rajasthan**. The Karni Mata temple is inhabited by thousands of rats, considered to be Karni Mata's **sons** and thus sacred **animals**. According to tradition, when the rats die they are reborn as members of the families that comprise the temple's hereditary servants, and thus the rats and the temple priests are all members of one extended family.

Rath Yatra

Festival falling on the second day of the bright (waxing) half of the **lunar month** of **Ashadh** (June–July). The primary **deity** worshiped in this festival is **Jagannath**, who is considered a form of the god **Krishna**. This festival is celebrated all over India but especially in the sacred city of **Puri**, where the principal temple of Jagannath is located. During the festival in Puri, Jagannath, his brother **Balabhadra**, and his sister **Subhadra** are carried in procession through the city's main street to another temple about a mile away. They stay in this nearby temple for a week, and then return to the Jagannath temple.

The deities are processed by their devotees (**bhakta**) in three enormous wooden chariots (rath), which the devotees pull using long ropes. The largest of the three, belonging to Jagannath, is forty-five feet high, thirty-five feet broad and wide, and travels on sixteen wheels each seven feet high. The English word "**juggernaut**" is a corruption of Jagannath, and the connotation of a juggernaut as an unstoppable force undoubtedly derives from the momentum that these carts attained once they began to move. One of the staple fictions of British colonial lore described Jagannath's frenzied devotees committing **suicide** by throwing themselves under the car's wheels, so that they would die in the sight of God. Despite such tales being widely repeated, suicides of this sort were extremely uncommon. Still, there was some risk in pulling the carts, since people losing their footing in the massed crowd would be unable to get up, and could potentially be crushed by the wheels. For further information see T. N. Madan (ed.), *Religion in India*, 1991.

Relief sculpture of the demon king Ravana from Angkor, Cambodia. As the antagonist of the Hindu epic, the *Ramayana*, Ravana acquires great magical powers, which he abuses until Rama kills him in battle.

Rati

("pleasure," particularly sexual pleasure) The wife of **Kama**, god of love. Rati is both Kama's wife and his ally, reflecting the way that sexual pleasure can both accompany and amplify desire.

Ratri

Name of the **goddess of Night**. See **Night, goddess of**.

Ravana

In the *Ramayana*, the earlier of the two great Indian epics, Ravana is the ten-headed **demon** king of **Lanka**. To destroy Ravana, the god **Vishnu** is born in his incarnation as **Rama**. Ravana is a reincarnation of Vishnu's gatekeeper **Jaya**, who has been cursed by a sage to be reborn three times as a demon and to be killed by Vishnu each time. As a **rakshasa**, a type of demon, Ravana possesses enormous physical strength and various **magic** powers. He augments these natural abilities by performing intense physical **asceticism** (**tapas**), which in Indian culture is widely believed to generate spiritual power and bring boons from the gods. When the god **Brahma** finally appears and directs Ravana to choose his boon, Ravana requests that he be able to be killed by no one but a human being. This seems to make him practically immortal, since his powers are such that no ordinary human will be able to harm him, much less kill him. Ravana then proceeds to terrorize the gods, secure in the knowledge that they will not be able to harm him. He begins with his half-brother, the minor **deity Kubera**, who loses his home and all his possessions to Ravana.

Ravana's virtual invulnerability goes to his head, and the powerful demon begins to disregard all rules of decency and morality. He is particularly guilty of molesting and abducting women, acts which result in various **curses** being laid upon him by his helpless victims, many of them predicting his death. As a result of one of these curses his sister **Shurpanakha** is mutilated by Rama's brother **Lakshmana**. Ravana is determined to avenge this insult, and decides that the best way will be to abduct

Rama's wife **Sita**. Although his wife **Mandodari** and his brothers rebuke him for this act and advise him to return Sita and make peace with Rama, Ravana stubbornly refuses to listen. His inflated pride and desire to avenge the insult to his sister deafen his ears to their good counsel, and he eventually pays for his stubbornness with his life when Rama kills him in battle.

As with all **demons**, Ravana is not completely villainous by nature but rather greatly powerful and greatly flawed at the same time. According to some stories he is a devotee (**bhakta**) of the god **Shiva**, and the hymn to the dancing Shiva known as the Shivatandava **Stotra** is often attributed to Ravana.

Ravidas

(ca. 1500) **Sant** poet-saint who lived his life in the city of **Benares** and is traditionally believed to have been a younger contemporary of the poet-saint **Kabir**. The Sants were a loose group of central and northern Indian poet-saints who shared several general tendencies: stress on individualized, interior religion leading to a personal experience of the divine; disdain for external ritual, particularly image **worship**; faith in the power of the divine Name; and a tendency to ignore conventional **caste** distinctions. Both tradition and references in his poetry describe Ravidas as a **leather** worker (**chamar**), a social group whose contact with dead **animals** and their skins rendered them **untouchable**. He is believed to have supported himself by his hereditary trade, and much of his poetry speaks on issues of worldly **birth** and status. He never denied the importance of heredity but ultimately felt that his devotion to God had helped him to transcend his birth and given him status based on different criteria. His poetry reflects this staunch personal faith, as do his frequent warnings to his listeners that life is short and difficult, and that they should pay great attention to religious practice.

Given his low social status, Ravidas was almost certainly illiterate. His poetic songs were likely first transmitted orally, though their personal appeal made him one of the most popular sant poets. The two oldest attested sources of his work are the **Adigranth**, the scripture for the Sikh community, and the **Panchvani** collections, compiled by the **Dadupanth**. In modern India, Ravidas has also served as a model for the depressed classes; his followers call themselves **Ravidasis**. For further information see John Stratton Hawley and Mark Juergensmeyer, *Songs of the Saints of India*, 1988; and Winand M. Callewaert and Peter Freidlander (trans.), *The Life and Works of Raidas*, 1992.

Ravidasi

Name taken by followers of the **untouchable** poet-saint **Ravidas**. The Ravidasis emphasize many ideas found in the poetry of Ravidas, such as the irrelevancy of ideas of **purity** and impurity (**ashaucha**), the futility of trying to contain the divine in texts and rites, and his vision of a society in which all people can have equal status, whatever their background. It is unlikely that the Ravidasis were established by Ravidas himself, nor is Ravidas an object of **worship** for them, although he is held as a model for religious equality, based on the messages in his poetry. In modern times the Ravidasis have focused on opposing all sorts of **caste**-based discrimination and have also taken up the empowerment of various low-caste groups. This movement is very recent, and to date little has been published about it; for some information see the introduction to Ravidas in John Stratton Hawley and Mark Juergensmeyer (trans.), *Songs of the Saints of India*, 1988.

Ravidas Jayanti

Festival falling on the **full moon** in the **lunar month** of **Magh** (January–

February), celebrated as the birthday of the medieval **bhakti** poet-saint **Ravidas**, born near **Benares**. Ravidas's birth into the **untouchable caste** of **leather** workers (**chamar**) afforded him a very low social status. His poetry is set in a personal voice and contrasts this lowly status with the honor and renown he gained through his devotion to God. In modern times many members of the depressed classes see Ravidas as a model, and his birthday is celebrated with great fervor.

Rawal

Title given to the head priest (**pujari**) at the temple of **Badrinath** in the **Himalayas**. The Rawal is invariably a **Nambudiri brahmin**, who must remain unmarried to retain his position. In Hindu belief, Badrinath is one of the **four dhams** ("divine abodes") connected with the philosopher **Shankaracharya**. Seeking to combat the spread of Buddhism and revitalize Hindu religion, Shankaracharya reportedly chose one Hindu sacred center in each corner of the subcontinent, and at each established a **Dashanami Sanyasi** monastic center (**math**) to train learned monks. Badrinath is associated with the **Jyotir Math** in the Himalayan town of **Joshimath**, forty miles south, which is also the place where the **deity** Badrinath is symbolically transported for the winter.

According to Badrinath temple records, for several hundred years the position of head priest was filled by **Dandi Sanyasis**, who were also Nambudiri brahmins, the same **caste** into which Shankaracharya is supposed to have been born. When the last of these died without a successor in 1776, the local king who served as the protector of the shrine invited a non-**ascetic** Nambudiri brahmin to serve as the temple's priest. This priest was given the title *rawal* (from the word *raja*, "deputy"), and his extended family has run the shrine since then. The rawal was the only person allowed to touch the image of Badrinath, and was responsible for performing **worship** during the six months that the temple is open. Because of these duties, the rawal was required to remain a bachelor, lest the ritual impurity arising from the **birth** of a child (**sutakashaucha**) render him unable to attend to his duties. Until the Badrinath Temple Act of 1939 established a temple board as the ultimate authority, the rawals had sole rights to the **offerings** given at the shrine.

Rawat

A particular subgroup of the warrior princes known as the **Rajputs**; the Rawats' major area of influence was in southwestern **Uttar Pradesh** state.

Reciprocal Dependence

In Indian logic, one of the **fallacies** to be avoided in constructing an argument. Reciprocal dependence occurs when two things each stand as cause and effect to the other—when A depends on B, and B in turn depends on A. This is seen as an extended case of **self-residence**, and equally objectionable.

Reconversion

General name for the rites by which people who have converted to other religious traditions are accepted back as Hindus. See **shuddhi**.

Reflectionism

Theory used in later schools of **Advaita Vedanta** to explain how one single primal ignorance could afflict multiple ignorant selves. Reflectionism is rooted in the idea of an image appearing in a mirror; different from the original, it is nonetheless based on it. In the same way, according to this explanation, the ignorance affecting each individual is simply a reflection of a primal ignorance. For further information see Karl H. Potter, *Presuppositions of India's Philosophies*, 1972.

Reincarnation
One of the fundamental assumptions of Indian religious life. See **samsara**

Religious Duty
See **dharma**.

Religious Law
See **dharma**, **dharmashastra**, and **dharma literature**.

Religious Persecution
In popular belief India is visualized as a land of perfect religious tolerance in which all schools of thought have been allowed to grow unchecked. Although true in its basic form, this picture is greatly simplified. There is a long history of competition between differing religious communities and schools of thought, sometimes fueled by scathing polemics designed to persuade listeners that one was correct and the others false. What has been quite rare, however, are acts of violence accompanying these arguments, or the notion that people should have to fear for their lives because of their ideas. In the literature of the **Nayanar** and **Lingayat** communities—both devotees (**bhakta**) of the god **Shiva**—language toward the Jains has a genuinely hostile edge, and the Nayanar leader **Sambandar** has been persistently implicated in the **impalement** of 8,000 Jains in the southern Indian city of **Madurai**. In the same way, the northern Indian king **Sashanka**, who was also a devotee of Shiva, harbored a pathological hatred of Buddhists. Sashanka reportedly not only persecuted Buddhists themselves, but also tried to destroy the tree in Bodh **Gaya** under which the Buddha purportedly gained enlightenment.

Sectarian competition aside, people whose religious faith has led them to ignore generally accepted social conventions have been quite likely to encounter stiff opposition. Stories of the devotional (**bhakti**) poet-saints are replete with tales of the troubles they faced from guardians of conventional morality, usually said to be **brahmins**. In the eighteenth and nineteenth centuries there was a running and often bloody conflict between two groups of militant ascetics—the **Naga** class of the **Dashanami Sanyasis**, and the **Bairagi Nagas**—although in that case the motives might just as well have been economic, namely, the control of trade in the **Ganges** valley. A final example of religious persecution appears in the rise of **Hindutva** in the 1980s. Propelled by verbal attacks on Muslims and Christians, this persecution has all too often prompted physical violence.

Renuka
In Hindu mythology, the wife of the sage **Jamadagni** and mother of the **Parashuram avatar**, the fifth **avatar** or incarnation of the god **Vishnu**.

Republic Day
Indian national holiday, falling on January 26, that marks the day the Indian constitution was adopted in 1950. As a holiday connected with Indian independence, it is one of the few celebrated according to the common **calendar**. Republic Day is comparable to the Fourth of July in the United States and is celebrated with massive parades in India's major cities. The largest occurs in New Delhi—from which it is televised to the rest of the nation—and includes singers and performers from all over the country, as well as large displays of military hardware, including fly-overs by the newest jet planes.

Reservations
Modern government policy designed to rectify the long-standing economic and social disadvantages faced by certain poor or low-status groups by offering them preferential treatment in employment and education. This is usually done by setting aside, or "reserving," for such groups certain percentages of

government jobs or places in institutions of higher learning, which admit people from disadvantaged communities under much lower standards than those for the general public. Those groups who qualify for such reservations are generally referred to as Scheduled Castes and Scheduled Tribes, after the "schedule" or official government list on which the names of these groups appear. The Scheduled Castes are low-status **caste** Hindus, who in earlier times would have been called **untouchables**, while the Scheduled Tribes are aboriginal peoples (**adivasis**), who mainly live in central India.

Although the reservations policy has been implemented for some time, it remains a continual source of controversy. Proponents claim that it is moving socially disadvantaged people into the mainstream of Indian life and helping to correct centuries of injustice. Opponents decry the fact that less-qualified people are being deliberately chosen, making a mockery of the notion of merit. Critics also argue that the people who benefit the most from such policies are the best-off members of such communities—the so-called creamy layer, designating their position at the top—whereas the truly disadvantaged remain in the same positions as they have always been. Aside from the philosophical debates about this policy, it has had a recognizable impact on people's livelihoods. Such reservations have made competition even more ferocious for the remaining spots, and made reservations a politically volatile issue. Given the benefits derived from reservations, there has also been considerable lobbying to include other, less-disadvantaged groups under its rubric, as a way to spread benefits to other sectors of Indian society.

Rg Veda

The oldest and most important of the four **Vedas**, which are themselves the most ancient and authoritative Hindu religious texts. The Rg Veda is a group of 1,028 hymns collected in ten books. Judging by their content, the hymns were clearly composed over a long period of time, but the actual dates are the subject of sharp disagreement. Traditional Hindus assert that the Vedas were not composed either by God or by human beings but, rather, simply heard by ancient sages through their advanced powers of perception, and then transmitted orally from generation to generation. Because of their origin, the Vedas thus belong to the class of religious texts known as **shruti** ("heard"). Scholarly consensus maintains that the Vedas were begun in the earlier part of the second millennium B.C.E., perhaps 1800–1500 B.C.E., and were finished somewhere around the end of the second millennium B.C.E., perhaps 1200–900. All these dates are highly speculative, since the hymns themselves have no internal evidence to allow precise dating, which has instead been based primarily on a comparative study of changes in the language of certain Vedas. Some of the hymns, for example, are thought to have been created relatively later than others, both because their language is less archaic and closer to classical **Sanskrit** and because the locations mentioned in them reflect a broader geographical area.

Most of the hymns in the Rg Veda are addressed to a particular **deity**. The primary deities are **Indra**, **Agni**, and **Soma**, although **Varuna** is prominent in the earliest hymns. It is generally accepted that the hymns were chanted at sacrifices as a way to invoke these deities. Evidence from the hymns themselves describes these sacrifices as large public rites, usually involving the slaughter of **animals**, which were burned on a sacrificial **fire**, and the preparation and consumption of the mysterious beverage soma. In this context, the Vedic hymns reflect a body of sacred learning known to only a small group of religious specialists. Accordingly, these hymns were never meant for universal public dissemination, since all except **twice-born** men were forbidden to hear them.

The Rg Veda's tenth and final book differs sharply from the preceding ones. Its language is closer to classical Sanskrit, and its content is far more speculative than that of the earlier books, hinting at a major conceptual shift. This book features the famous **Creation Hymn** (10.129), in which the poet speculates on how the world came to be, only to conclude that the answer may be unknown even to the creator. Another notable hymn in this book is the **Purusha Sukta** (10.90), which describes both the earth and human society as the product of a primeval **sacrifice**. The former hymn foreshadows the religious and cosmological speculation found in the texts known as the **Upanishads**. The latter, which contains the first known articulation of the four major social groups (**varnas**), along with their symbolic functions, is distinguished as foreshadowing the later **dharma literature**.

Rhythm, in Music
See **tala**.

Right Hand Tantra
Name for a type of **tantra**, a secret, ritually based religious practice. Certain tantric rituals make use of substances that are normally forbidden, such as **liquor** and nonvegetarian food, in an effort to unify the world by destroying all conceptual dualities, including that between sacred and forbidden. These substances are used in their actual forms in "left hand" (**vamachara**) tantric ritual, and by substitution in "right hand" (**dakshinachara**) tantric ritual. See **dakshinachara**.

Rishabha
According to Jain tradition, Rishabha was the founder of the Jains. He is considered the first of the Jain tirthankaras, the founding figures in the Jain religious tradition. He is one of three Jain tirthankaras who are mentioned in the **Yajur Veda**, one of the earliest

The city of Rishikesh lies on the Ganges River. It contains many ashrams and is a popular place for ritual bathing.

Hindu religious texts. The figure most often credited with developing the teachings used by the Jains today is Mahavira, who is considered the twenty-fourth tirthankara.

Rishi
Common word to designate a sage, seer, or inspired religious leader. It is most often used to indicate religious figures of the distant past, and is not usually applied to contemporary figures.

Rishikesh
City and sacred site (**tirtha**) in the Himalayan foothills of the state of **Uttar Pradesh**. Rishikesh lies about fifteen miles up the **Ganges** River from the sacred city of **Haridwar**. As with many sites on the Ganges, Rishikesh is famous primarily as a bathing (**snana**) place, although it is also noted as a dwelling-place for **ascetics**, particularly at the **ashrams** in the area around **Lakshman Jhula**. As a sacred site, Rishikesh is also notable for having no single charter myth. According to one story, this is the place where the god **Rama** kills several **demons**, enabling the sages to carry out

their sacrifices undisturbed. Another story names this as the place where Rama does penance (**prayashchitta**) for killing the demon-king **Ravana**. A third story names Rishikesh as the site where a sage named Raibhya receives a vision of the god **Vishnu**. The most famous temple in Rishikesh is named after Rama's brother **Bharata**.

Rishi Panchami

Festival falling on the fifth **day** (panchami) of the light (waxing) half of the **lunar month** of **Bhadrapada** (August–September). This festival is dedicated to the Seven Sages (**rishi**) born of **Brahma: Bhrgu, Pulastya, Kratu, Pulaha, Marichi, Atri**, and **Vasishtha**. Worshiping these seven sages on this day is said to bring prosperity and happiness.

Rishyashringa

A sage in the *Ramayana*, the earlier of the two great Indian epics. King **Dasharatha** commissions Rishyashringa to perform a great **sacrifice**, to enable the king's wives to conceive. At the conclusion of Rishyashringa's sacrifice, a shining figure emerges from the sacrificial fire, places a pot of milk-rice before Dasharatha, and directs him to feed it to his wives. Dasharatha divides the contents among his wives **Kausalya, Kaikeyi**, and **Sumitra**, and in due time they all bear **sons**. Kausalya is the mother of **Rama**, the *Ramayana*'s protagonist. Kaikeyi is the mother of **Bharata**, and Sumitra is the mother of **Lakshmana** and **Shatrughna**.

Rites of Passage

General term for rites that recognize and mark transitions in an individual life-cycle, and that often signify a change of state or status. See **samskara**.

Rites of Protection

For many Hindus, the world is a ritually dangerous place. Certain hours, days, and periods of the **year** are considered inauspicious. At these times the very tone of the cosmos is disagreeable and all sorts of bad fortune can befall the ignorant or the unwary. Rites of protection are used to counter these dangers, as well as the problems of one's past **karma**, which can be diagnosed through an inauspicious conjunction in one's birth horoscope (**natal horoscope**).

Some inauspicious times are unlucky only for certain types of activities. Potential misfortune can be avoided simply by refraining from these activities. However, certain events that cannot be avoided, such as **eclipses**, are also believed inauspicious. In such cases, one can prevent the negative effects of **inauspiciousness** by transferring it to another person, usually through the medium of gifts (**dana**); giving gifts is also the preferred means for getting rid of inauspiciousness stemming from a bad conjunction in one's birth horoscope. People also safeguard themselves by performing prayer and **worship** as positive protective forces.

Inauspicious forces are also generated by human jealousy, greed, and hatred, which can find their agency in black **magic**, the evil eye (**nazar**), or other sorts of **witchcraft**. Finally, some Hindus believe there are a host of non-human beings, such as spirits, **ghosts**, and witches, who sometimes seek to harm human beings through the exercise of supernormal powers. Despite the power and prevalence of all of these malevolent forces, if one is aware and careful of them there are ways to counter them.

For problems stemming from human malice, there are well-established solutions. One is to avoid those people who are considered inauspicious, such as **widows**. Another strategy is to avoid inciting people's jealousy by never proclaiming one's good fortune too openly, praising a child too lavishly, or flaunting one's wealth too freely. In many cases, people will counter potentially vulnerable moments in the life cycle by various protective rites. It is still common for people to wear talismans or amulets, which are believed to protect the wearer. Another common protective measure is to carry iron, which is believed to render the person carrying it impervious to witchcraft. Young children will often have a black smudge of lamp-black put on their faces, to symbolically disfigure them and take away the motive for jealousy. Another protective strategy is to hang up an object (such as a clay pot with a painted face) intended to absorb all the bad feelings, which is then discarded. For further information see Lawrence Babb, *The Divine Hierarchy*, 1975; Gloria Goodwin Raheja, *The Poison in the Gift*, 1988; and David F. Pocock, "The Evil Eye," in T. N. Madan (ed.), *Religion in India*, 1991.

Rock Edicts

Name for a set of **inscriptions** commissioned by the Mauryan emperor **Ashoka** (r. 269–32 B.C.E.). The inscriptions were official pronouncements on royal policy, and advice and instructions to his subjects on a variety of topics, including religious tolerance. In general, the rock edicts were carved into large boulders or rock faces in places that would have been at the borders of the Mauryan Empire, thus symbolically defining its boundaries. The text was fairly consistent throughout the empire, even though different examples of these edicts were found in widely separated places. The other major class of Ashokan inscriptions, the **pillar edicts**, were inscribed on pillars of polished **Chunar** sandstone and set up on the major roads running through the empire, where they would have been visible to passersby. See also **Maurya dynasty**.

Rohini

In Hindu mythology, a daughter of the demigod **Daksha** who, along with her twenty-six sisters, is married to the **Moon**. The Moon favors Rohini over all her sisters, despite Daksha's entreaties to give them all equal time. In the end Daksha lays a curse on the Moon to lose his luster. The **curse** is later modified so that the moon will alternately wane and wax, but that its disappearance will never be final.

Rohini

(2) In Hindu mythology, birth mother of **Balarama**, the god **Krishna's** brother. Balarama's birth is unusual. After his conception the fetus is magically transported from the womb of **Devaki** to that of Rohini. This is done to protect him from harm, as Devaki's wicked uncle **Kamsa** has already killed her first seven children and will certainly do the same to Balarama if she carries him to term.

Roy, Ram Mohan

(1774–1833) First major Indian proponent of Hindu social and religious reform, who founded the organization **Brahmo Samaj** for this purpose. He came from a wealthy Bengali family and was a successful businessman and civil servant. He moved to Calcutta in 1815, at the time when the British were first beginning to take serious notice of traditional Indian society, especially the aspects they considered "evil." Roy's reformist interests largely meshed with that of the British. From an early age Roy had rejected the practice of using images in **worship**, perhaps through exposure to Sufi ideas, and his first public crusade was against such worship of gods and goddesses. Like most Indian reformers, Roy used **Sanskrit** texts selectively, and for him the most important ones were the speculative **Upanishads**, which (under the influence of the English Unitarians) he translated to reflect a monotheism (belief in the existence of only one God). In his later years he promoted many different educational and social works, but is especially known for his opposition to **sati**, the custom of burning a **widow** on her husband's funeral pyre. Although later seen as too heavily influenced by the British, his reinterpretation of the past provided a model for others to use. For further consideration see Robert D. Baird (ed.), *Religion in Modern India*, 1998.

Rta

In the **Vedas** (the oldest and most authoritative Hindu texts) rta is the cosmic order and regularity that allows the rhythms of time and the **seasons** to occur in orderly succession. According to the texts, rta also had a moral dimension, which human beings had an obligation to support. One such moral dimension was truth, which was seen as upholding the cosmos, whereas its opposite, **anrta**, came to signify falsehood. The connection between natural and moral world came through the Vedic god **Varuna**, who was both the guardian of rta and the **deity** who punished untruth, usually by affliction with **dropsy**.

Rtvij

In the Hindu sacred texts (**Vedas**), one of the priests who officiated at **sacrifices**. The four chief priests at sacrifices were the **hotr**, **udgatr**, **adhvaryum**, and **brahman**.

Rudra

("howler") Fearsome **deity** who first appears late in the **Vedas**, the oldest Hindu religious texts, later identified with the god **Shiva**. Several hymns in the **Rg Veda** are dedicated to Rudra, where he is identified with the storm-god **Indra**, and the fire-god **Agni**. A more developed picture of Rudra appears in the **Shvetashvatara Upanishad**, one of the later speculative texts known as the **Upanishads**. In the third chapter (adhyaya) of this text, Rudra is identified as the ruling power in the universe and the source and origin of the gods themselves. Rudra's depiction in this upanishad shows considerable ambivalence, both mentioning the destructive arrows that he bears and imploring him to appear in a form that is auspicious (shivam) and peaceful. This ambivalence

perhaps reflects the religious tension associated with the figure of Shiva, who was a deity outside the Vedic sacrificial cult but was gradually absorbed into established religion and is now one of the primary Hindu deities.

Rudraksha

("eye of **Rudra**") The dried seed of the tree *Elaeocarpus ganitrus*, which is considered sacred to the god **Shiva**. Rudrakshas are often strung into garlands and worn by Shiva's devotees (**bhakta**). The seed itself is round with a knobby, pitted surface, with a natural channel in the middle through which a thread can easily be drawn. Each seed also has natural longitudinal lines running from top to bottom, which divide the seed into units known as "faces" (mukhi). The most common rudrakshas have five faces, but they can have up to fourteen. Each differing number of faces has been given a symbolic association with a particular **deity**. The rarest form is the **ekmukhi** rudraksha, which has no faces at all and is considered to be a manifestation of Shiva himself. This rudraksha is so valuable that street sellers routinely make counterfeit versions by carving them out of wood. Another rare form is the **Gauri-Shankar**, in which two rudraksha seeds are longitudinally joined; this is considered a manifestation of Shiva and **Shakti**. Aside from the number of "faces," the quality of rudrakshas is judged by their color and size. The color runs from reddish brown to a light brown, with the former considered more desirable, while the smaller sizes are preferable to the larger ones.

Rudranath

Temple and sacred site (**tirtha**) in the **Garhwal** region of the **Himalayas** in the valley between the **Mandakini** and the **Alakananda** rivers, about thirty miles from the district headquarters at Chamoli. The temple's presiding **deity** is the god **Shiva** in his manifestation as "Lord **Rudra**."

Rudranath is one of the **Panchkedar**, a network of five sacred sites spread throughout the Garhwal region; the other four sites are **Kedarnath**, **Kalpeshvar**, **Tungnath**, and **Madmaheshvar**. This network of five sites is seen as a symbolic representation of Shiva's body, since Shiva is believed to dwell in the Himalayas. Rudranath is believed to be Shiva's face.

Rudraprayag

Himalayan town and sacred site (**tirtha**) at the junction of the **Mandakini** and **Alakananda** rivers, two Himalayan tributaries of the **Ganges** River. As with all the other river junctions in the **Garhwal** region, Rudraprayag is considered an especially holy place for bathing (**snana**), although the raging currents make it dangerous. Above the junction of the rivers is a temple to **Shiva** in his form as **Rudra**. According to local tradition, this marked the place where the sage **Narada** performed physical **asceticism** (**tapas**) to gain his skill as a bard. Shiva, pleased with Narada's efforts, instructed Narada in music and remained at the spot.

Rudra Sampraday

One of the four branches (**sampraday**) of the **Bairagi Naga** ascetics. The name *Bairagi* denotes ascetics who are devotees (**bhakta**) of the god **Vishnu**. The name *Naga* describes a class of fighting ascetics recruited to protect the other Bairagi ascetics who, because they were saintly, scholarly men, could not protect themselves. Bairagi Nagas were organized in military fashion into different **anis** or "armies." Until the beginning of the nineteenth century the Nagas' primary occupation was as mercenary soldiers, although they also had substantial trading interests. The Nagas lent money at interest, engaged in trade, and often owned large amounts of property. They were particularly powerful in parts of the country where the centralized government had broken down. Their roles as mercenaries and in trade have both largely disappeared in contemporary times.

Rudraksha seed. Devotees of the god Shiva often identify themselves by wearing necklaces made of these seeds.

The Rudra Sampraday traces its spiritual lineage through the philosopher **Vallabhacharya** and the earlier religious teacher, **Vishnuswami**. The followers of Vallabhacharya tend to be householders rather than ascetics; Vallabhacharya himself was married and had many children. It is the smallest and least important of the Bairagi Naga sampradays, and the only event at which it figures is the bathing (**snana**) processions at the **Kumbha Mela**.

Rukmini

In Hindu mythology, the chief queen of the god **Krishna** in his later life as the king of the city of **Dwaraka**. Rukmini is the daughter of the king of Vidarbha, and although both she and her parents favor her marriage to Krishna, her brother, who is Krishna's bitter enemy, makes arrangements to marry her to his friend **Shishupala**. On her wedding day, with all the guests assembled, Krishna carries Rukmini off in his chariot. They are married, and, according to tradition, have ten **sons**.

S

Sabarmati

Northern Indian river that rises in the **Aravalli Hills** in the state of **Rajasthan**, and flows south to the Gulf of Cambay in the state of **Gujarat**. It is best known as the site of the Sabarmati **Ashram**, across the river from the city of Ahmedabad in Gujarat. The Sabarmati Ashram was home to **Mohandas K. Gandhi** for sixteen years after he returned from **South Africa** in 1915. He organized much of the struggle for Indian independence from this ashram.

Sacchidananda

Sanskrit compound word denoting the three generally accepted attributes of the supreme **Brahman** (the Ultimate Reality of the universe according to some Hindu traditions): being (**sat**), consciousness (chit), and bliss (**ananda**). The differences between the form of the individual words and their form in the compound are the result of **sandhi** or euphonic combination.

In certain Hindu philosophical traditions, but particularly in the **Advaita Vedanta** school, the supreme Brahman is considered the Ultimate Reality behind all things. Although Brahman is considered to be without particular qualities, these three attributes are believed to be inseparable from its very nature. It has the attribute of being, because it is the reality from which all other "being" comes. In the same way, it is consciousness, as the source of all conscious thought. Finally, bliss proceeds from its perfection, which is ultimate and complete.

Sacred Ash

Substance used in rituals and by devotees (**bhakta**) of the god **Shiva** to mark their bodies, in imitation of their patron **deity**. The name given to this ash is **vibhuti**. See **vibhuti**.

Sacred Sites

Hindu religious life is intimately connected to the land of India itself, which is studded with sacred sites, known as **tirthas**. These can be lakes, rivers, mountains, or any other natural feature; they can also be cities, temples, or any other created environment; they can even be the presence of holy men and **women**. Pilgrimage (**tirthayatra**) to any sacred site is a means of spiritual and religious advancement. See **tirtha**.

Sacred Thread

A circular cord made of three strands (in which each strand itself has three strands), which is worn over the left shoulder, crossing the body to fall on the right hip. The sacred thread is given to a boy as part of the **upanayana samskara**, which is the adolescent religious **initiation** also known as the "second birth." Second birth entitles a boy to study the **Vedas**, the oldest Hindu religious texts. In the **dharma literature** this initiatory rite is prescribed for all young men belonging to the three "**twice-born**" social groups (**varnas**)—that is, the **brahmins**, **kshatriyas**, and **vaishyas**. The sacred thread would have been the most visible sign of a twice-born man, for whom wearing the thread was mandatory, since any religious acts performed without wearing it were said to be ineffective.

In modern times its presence generally means that the wearer is a brahmin, since it is mainly the brahmins who carry out this rite today. The sacred thread is worn for extended periods of time, although it must be changed at certain times: after the wearer has suffered violent impurity (**ashaucha**), such as that of death; after performing any rite of expiation (**prayashchitta**); and after **eclipses** or other highly inauspicious times. For further information see Pandurang Vaman Kane, *A History of Dharmasastra*, 1968; and Raj Bali Pandey, *Hindu Samskaras*, 1969. The former is encyclopedic and the latter more accessible; despite their age, they remain the best sources on traditional Hindu rites.

Sacrifice

Generally a rite involving a sacred **fire** and, often, an **offering** in that fire. This sort of ritual is rooted in the oldest part of the Hindu tradition, although it has undergone some profound changes, particularly in the decline of **animal** sacrifice. This sort of sacrificial rite is known as a **yajna**.

Sadachara

("practice of good [people]") One of the traditional sources for determining religious duty (**dharma**) for matters not treated in the **dharma literature**, or for cases in which the literature itself gave conflicting opinions. This was the least authoritative source of dharma, after the **Vedas** (the oldest Hindu scriptures) and the dharma literature. Sadachara recognizes that life has many ambiguities and uncertainties, and at the same time provides a resource for determining the appropriate action, by taking as a model the practice of established and upright people. Another term to designate this sort of authority was **shishtachara**, the "practice of learned [people]."

Sadasatkhyati

("discrimination of the unreal as the real") **Theory of error** propounded by the **Samkhya** philosophical school. All theories of error attempt to explain why people make errors in judgment, the stock example being of mistaking the silvery flash of a sea shell for a piece of silver. The Samkhya theory of error is based on dualistic metaphysics, in which the fundamental error comes in confusing **purusha** and **prakrti**—roughly, spirit and nature—which are the sources of all things. These are the two Samkhya first principles—purusha as conscious witness, and prakrti as insentient matter—which are always separate from each other, and whose attributes can never coincide. For the Samkhyas, the fundamental error is to confuse these two completely different principles—that is, to attribute powers of motion and development to purusha, and consciousness to prakrti. Purusha is conceived as conscious, but completely inactive and unchanging. It is the passive witness to the myriad transformations of prakrti going on around it.

This initial misidentification causes the **evolution** of the entire world, both the interior, subjective world and the exterior world the subject perceives. Against this background, confusing the shell for silver is just an extension of this original mistake and is rooted in it. According to the Samkhyas, perfect knowledge would protect one from all sorts of errors, both cosmic and mundane. For further information see Karl H. Potter (ed.), *Presuppositions of India's Philosophies*, 1972.

Sadashiva

In certain schools of **tantra** practice, particularly in the **Trika** school of Kashmiri Shaivism, the name for the first step in the **evolution** of the cosmos. According to the Trika school, the Ultimate Reality, conceived as **Shiva**, is utterly nondual, and thus neither masculine nor feminine. The first step in cosmological evolution comes when the divine consciousness becomes conscious of itself through the reflection (**vimarsha**) of its original illumination (**prakasha**). Moved by this self-consciousness, the unqualified divine being transforms itself into a divine being containing a masculine and feminine nature, the first of many such bipolar dyads from which the universe is born. The masculine part of this first dyad is Sadashiva, which is considered the

A man smokes from a chillum wrapped with a safai, a cloth used to cool the smoke before it is inhaled.

material cause of the universe. The energy for creation comes from the creative and dynamic power of the dyad's female principle, **Shakti**. For further information see Jaideva Singh, *Pratyabhijnanahrdayam*, 1982.

Sadhana

("accomplishing") The most common colloquial Hindu term designating established and regular religious practice. It is given this name because it is through such practice that one gains spiritual attainments. In modern **Hindi**, the word can also be used to refer to anything to which one has devoted a great deal of time, attention, and hard work.

Sadharana ("common") Dharma

In the **dharma literature**, the religious duties required of all human beings, including truth, generosity, and compassion. One's essential obligation, however,

is to fulfill one's own **dharma** (**svadharma**), which may supersede or even contradict the requirements of the common dharma. For instance, it is generally accepted that a king must occasionally disregard truth to be an effective ruler. Since a king's primary duty is to maintain peace and order in the country, so that other people have the opportunity to do their duties, he is required to do whatever it takes to accomplish this.

Sadhu

("virtuous man") A general term that can be used for any **ascetic**, although it more often refers to an ascetic who has not undergone formal **initiation** into an established ascetic order.

Sadhubela

In the time before the partition of India in 1947, Sadhubela was the name of the most important **ascetic** center for the **Udasi** ascetics; it was in Sukkur in the province of Sindh province, now in Pakistan.

Sadhya

("to be proved") Element in the accepted form of an inference (**anumana**) in Indian **philosophy**. An acceptable inference has three terms: an assertion (**pratijna**), a reason (**hetu**), and examples (**drshtanta**); each of these three has its own constituent parts. The sadhya is, along with the **paksha**, one of the two parts of the assertion. The paksha is the subject of the hypothesis and names a class of things, while the sadhya contains the claim to be proven about that class. In the standard example, in which the hypothesis is "this mountain is on fire," the paksha is "this mountain" (the class of things about which a claim is being made); and the sadhya, or thing to be proven, is "is on fire."

Safai

Small cloth wrapped around the base of a **chillum**, a clay cylinder used for smoking a mixture of tobacco and hashish (**charas**). The safai serves two purposes, one ritual and one physical. On one hand, it forms a barrier intended to prevent passing the ritual impurity (**ashaucha**) carried by saliva when the chillum is being passed from person to person. Ascetics who are very conscious of **purity** or status will often wrap their own safai around the base of the chillum before smoking. Aside from helping to protect personal purity, the safai also serves a practical purpose–it is usually dipped in **water** before being wrapped around the chillum, which serves to cool and mellow the smoke being drawn through it.

Sagar

In Hindu mythology, a celebrated king of the **Solar Line**. Sagar, the son of King Subahu and his wife Yadavi, gets his name because one of Yadavi's co-wives has given her poison (gara) while she is pregnant with him. Sagar has a very hard early life. His father is driven from his kingdom even before he is born, and Sagar is raised at the **ashram** of the sage Aurva, where his mother has taken asylum. When he comes to maturity Sagar embarks on a series of military campaigns in which he wins back all the lands his father lost, and becomes a righteous and religious king whose only concern is his lack of progeny.

To beget **sons**, Sagar calls on the sage **Bhrgu**, who gives Sagar's two wives a choice: one wife will bear 60,000 sons who will all die childless, and one wife will bear one son who will carry on the line. Each of his wives chooses, and in due course both have their children—**Keshini** delivers her one son in the normal way, whereas **Sumati** delivers a lump of flesh that is divided and put into 60,000 pots, each of which develops into a handsome son.

In his prosperity King Sagar continues to sponsor religious rites, and is on the verge of completing his hundredth horse **sacrifice** (**asvamedha**), which will entitle him to the throne of **Indra**, the god who is the king of **heaven**. To forestall this, Indra steals the sacred horse and hides it in the ashram of the sage **Kapila**. Sagar sends his 60,000 sons to search for the horse, but they make the mistake of insulting the sage, who burns them all to ash through his yogic powers. To rescue their souls it is necessary to bring down the **Ganges** from heaven, a job that Sagar's descendants diligently attempt to complete. After several generations of frustration, his great-great-grandson **Bhagirath** is finally successful.

Sagara Dashanami

One of the ten divisions of the **Dashanami Sanyasis**, renunciant ascetics who are devotees (**bhakta**) of **Shiva**. The Dashanamis were supposedly established by the ninth-century philosopher **Shankaracharya** in an effort create a corps of learned men who could help to revitalize Hindu life. Each of the divisions is designated by a different name—in this case, sagara ("ocean"). Upon **initiation**, new members are given this name as a surname to their new **ascetic** names, thus allowing for immediate group identification.

Aside from their individual identity, these ten "named" divisions are divided into four larger organizational groups. Each group has its headquarters in one of the four monastic centers (**maths**) supposedly established by Shankaracharya, as well as other particular religious associations. The Sagara Dashanamis belong to the **Anandawara** group, which is affiliated with the **Jyotir math** in the Himalayan town of **Joshimath**.

Saguna

("with qualities") Anything having distinguishing qualities. In the context of ideas about divinity it refers to particular **deities** with particular attributes. In the religious traditions based on the ideas of the **Upanishads**, the speculative texts that are the final texts in the **Vedas**, any manifestation of a deity with qualities is seen as ultimately inferior to the unqualified (**nirguna**) **Brahman**. This assumption is adamantly opposed by certain theistic traditions, such as the **Gaudiya Vaishnava** religious community, which insists that the highest deity, in this case **Krishna**, has a particular form (and thus certain qualities).

Sahadeva

Fifth of the five **Pandava** brothers who are the protagonists in the great Hindu epic, the *Mahabharata*. Sahadeva's mother is **Madri**, who is the junior wife of King **Pandu**. None of the Pandava brothers are actually Pandu's sons, since he has been cursed to die the moment he holds his wife in an amorous embrace. Madri conceives her sons magically, using a **mantra** given to her co-wife, **Kunti**, by the sage **Durvasas**. The mantra gives the woman who recites it the power to call down any of the gods and to have by him a son

equal in power to the god. With Pandu's blessing Kunti teaches the mantra to Madri, who meditates on the **Ashvins**, the divine twins who are the physicians of the gods, and thus bears the twins **Nakula** and Sahadeva. As the sons of the physicians of the gods, both are skilled healers of animals and human beings. Although they are among the five Pandava brothers, they are less important to the *Mahabharata* than their three elder siblings.

Sahajiya

Religious community originating in medieval Bengal. The Sahajiyas synthesize devotional practices to the god **Vishnu** and the ritual practices of the secret tradition known as **tantra**, particularly the extreme practices associated with the "left-hand" (**vamachara**) tradition of tantra. The name *sahajiya* comes from the word *sahaja* ("natural" or "spontaneous"), indicating the group's belief that one's natural passions, qualities, and tendencies should not be suppressed but should be channeled to help one gain final liberation of the soul (**moksha**). Over this foundation of tantric ritual practice was added the devotion to the god **Krishna** and his consort **Radha**, a devotional thrust strongly influenced by the **Gaudiya Vaishnava** religious community, founded by the Bengali saint **Chaitanya**. For further information see Shashibhushan B. Dasgupta, *Obscure Religious Cults*, 1962; and Edward C. Dimock Jr., *The Place of the Hidden Moon*, 1989.

Sahasradalapadma

In many schools of **yoga**, and in the religious tradition known as **tantra**, one of the sites in the **subtle body** (an alternate physiological system believed to exist on a different plane than gross matter but with certain correspondences to the material body). The subtle body consists of a set of six psychic centers (**chakras**), which are visualized as six multipetaled lotus flowers running roughly along the course of the spine and connected by three vertical channels. Each of these chakras has important symbolic associations—with different human capacities, with different subtle elements (**tanmatras**), and with different seed syllables (**bijaksharas**) formed from the letters of the **Sanskrit** alphabet, thus encompassing all sacred sound. Above and below these centers are the bodily abodes of **Shiva** (awareness) and **Shakti** (power), the two divine principles through which the entire universe has come into being. The underlying assumption behind this concept of the subtle body is thus the homology of macrocosm and microcosm, an essential Hindu idea since the time of the mystical texts known as the **Upanishads**.

The sahasradalapadma is the site at the apex of the **subtle body**, visualized as a "thousand-petaled lotus" located in the crown of the head. This is identified as the bodily abode of Shiva, where he is ever-present. In tantra, final liberation (**moksha**) comes through the divine union of Shiva and Shakti in one's own body. This is done through awakening the **kundalini**, the bodily correlate of Shakti that lies dormant at the base of the spine, and drawing the kundalini up to the sahasradalapadma to effect the divine union. The sahasradalapadma is identified with the seed syllable *Om*, the symbol of completeness and perfection. For further information see Arthur Avalon (Sir John Woodroffe), *Shakti and Shakta*, 1978; Philip S. Rawson, *The Art of Tantra*, 1973; and Douglas Renfrew Brooks, *The Secret of the Three Cities*, 1990.

Sai Baba

Name used by two different charismatic Hindu teachers, now distinguished by the addition of other names. The earlier of the two is **Shirdi Sai Baba** (d. 1918), so named for the town in the state of **Maharashtra** where he lived much of his life. The latter figure, **Sathya** ("true") **Sai Baba** (b. 1926), is a modern Hindu religious figure of the type known as a **godman**, who claims to be the reincarnation of Shirdi Sai Baba.

Sainhikeya

In Hindu mythology, **demon** who appears in the story of churning the Ocean of Milk. After the gods and demons join forces to churn the Ocean of Milk and obtain the nectar of immortality (**amrta**), the gods succeed in tricking the demons out of their share. As the gods divide this nectar among themselves, the demon Sainhikeya slips into the distribution line and is mistakenly served some as well. As the demon drinks it, the **Sun** and **Moon** alert the god **Vishnu** to his presence and Vishnu cuts off the demon's head with his discus. Although the head and body are separated, both parts become immortal through their contact with the nectar. The head becomes **Rahu**, while the body becomes **Ketu**, both of which are considered malevolent **planets** in Indian astrology (**jyotisha**). According to tradition, Rahu is also the cause of **eclipses**: He roams the sky, chasing the Sun and Moon, and tries to get revenge by swallowing them, but the two planets always pass unharmed out of his severed neck. See also **Tortoise avatar**.

Sakata Chauth

Festival falling on the fourth **day** (chauth) of the dark (waning) half of the **lunar month** of **Magh** (January–February), which is celebrated as the birthday of the god **Ganesh**. Those who observe this festival are believed to gain Ganesh's blessings—wisdom, freedom from troubles, and prosperity. The fourth day of every lunar fortnight is sacred to Ganesh, and vows marking this day may be performed by his devotees (**bhakta**). The biggest Ganesh festival of the **year** is not his birthday, but **Ganesh Chaturthi**, which falls on the fourth day of the bright (waxing) half of the lunar month of **Bhadrapada** (August–September).

Sakha ("companion") Bhava

The third of the five **modes of devotion** to the Supreme Being that were most prominently expressed by **Rupa Goswami**. Rupa used different types of human relationships as models for the possible relationships between **deity** and devotee (**bhakta**). These five models increased in emotional intensity from the peaceful (**shanta**) sense that comes from realizing one's complete identity with **Brahman**, or Supreme Reality, to conceiving of God as one's master, friend, child, or lover. In the sakha bhava, devotees consider themselves as God's friends and companions and thus as taking part in his regular, everyday activities.

Sakhi

("friend," "companion") The motif of friendship as a religious ideal was well developed by the devotees (**bhakta**) of the god **Krishna**, and to a lesser extent by devotees of the god **Rama**. Both of these **deities** are **avatars** (incarnations) of the god **Vishnu**, and **Vaishnava** devotion tends to stress not only **worship** of the chosen deity, but also the notions of relationship and communion—both between the deity and devotee, and among devotees themselves. Vaishnava religious practice often involved elaborate visualization exercises, in which devotees would envision the deity's daily activities—for Krishna, the simple life of a village cowherd, and for Rama, the life of a prince. Some devotional manuals give detailed daily schedules of the deity's activities to facilitate this process of visualization. Such elaborate visualization allowed the devotees to symbolically enter the deity's world and take part in the deity's divine play (**lila**) on **earth**, building a relationship with God through sharing the mundane elements of everyday life. In this sort of visualization, devotees commonly considered themselves to be the deity's sakhis or companions—in some cases male companions, and in other cases female companions of the deity's consorts, **Radha** and **Sita**. Taking on the persona of a sakhi provided a devotee with a concrete place in the divine world, in which he or she could both observe and participate in the god's earthly activity.

Sakshin

("witness") The perceiving consciousness believed to be the inner Self (**atman**), which observes changes going on around it but is utterly unaffected by them. It is described in a primitive way as early as the **Upanishads**, the speculative texts that form the final layer of the **Vedas**, the most authoritative Hindu religious texts. The **Katha** Upanishad describes the Self as a thumb-sized person inside the head. The **Samkhya** philosophical school develops this notion in a more subtle and sophisticated way: of its two fundamental first principles, one is the **purusha**, which is the conscious but inert witness to the transformations of **prakrti**, or nature. Later philosophical schools such as **Vedanta** reject the Samkhya school's dualism by collapsing all reality into a single ultimate principle known as **Brahman**. Vedanta's conception of Brahman as "being-consciousness-bliss" (**sacchidananda**) also conceives of the Self as the conscious and unchanging witness to the material flux surrounding it.

Sala

In **Hindi**, "wife's brother." The term can be used as a serious insult if applied to someone who is not related in this way. Calling someone "sala" implies that the other is in a position of relative subservience, since he is a member of the family that "gives" the bride. It also implies that one is having sexual relations with that person's sister, an allegation that is an insult to a family's honor, whether or not it is true.

Salmala ("Silk-Cotton Tree") Dvipa

In traditional mythic geography, the third of the seven concentric landmasses (**dvipas**) making up the visible world. See also **cosmology**.

Samadhi

("trance") In the **ashtanga yoga** first codified by the philosopher **Patanjali**, the last of the eight elements of yoga practice. Along with **dharana** ("concentration") and **dhyana** ("meditation"), samadhi is one of the three practices that make up the "inner discipline" (**samyama**), the culmination of yogic training. Samadhi is described as a state in which the mind is conscious of only the object of concentration, and is devoid of any notion of the self as perceiver. Once one has attained samhadi on the conscious plane, one supposedly pursues it on more subtle inner planes.

The loss of subjectivity in samadhi is believed to make people unaware of the outside world, such that they will not respond to stimuli and may sometimes appear almost dead. For this reason, the **burial** places of deceased ascetics are usually referred to as **samadhi shrines**, since it is popularly believed that they are not dead, but only rapt in deep meditation.

Samadhi Shrine

Burial place of a deceased ascetic. Part of the process of **ascetic initiation** is the initiate's ritualized death, in which he (or far more rarely, she) performs his (or her) own funeral rites, followed by rebirth with a new name and a new identity. Consequently, upon the physical death of an ascetic the funeral rites (**antyeshthi**) are not performed, since the ascetic is (ritually speaking) already dead. The body is often disposed of by being weighted down with rocks and thrown into a river, but well-known and powerful ascetics are often buried, usually in a sitting position as if in meditation. Such people are often buried in

places associated with their presence during their lives—whether a room, building, or particular outdoor site. In popular wisdom such ascetics are believed not to be dead but only rapt in deep meditation (**samadhi**). The samadhi shrines of very renowned ascetics often have shrines built over them, which can become places of pilgrimage for those seeking the ascetic's continuing blessings (**ashirvad**).

Samana

In traditional Indian physiology, one of the five bodily **winds** considered responsible for basic bodily functions, the others being **prana**, **apana**, **vyana**, and **udana**. The samana wind is considered to reside in the navel, and to aid in the process of digestion.

Samasthana

In **yoga** practice, sitting position in which the legs are bent, with the soles of the feet pressed flat against one another and the outer edges of the feet on the ground. See **utkutikasana**.

Samavartana ("return") Samskara

The fourteenth of the life-cycle ceremonies (**samskaras**), which marks the end of a young man's life as a celibate student (**brahmacharin**) and the return to his parental home. The most important element in this rite is a bath, after which the young man changes into new clothes, marking his change in status. The young man is supposed to ask his **guru's** permission before performing the ceremony, and gives him his teacher's fee (**dakshina**), both as payment for services rendered and as a sign of respect. Shortly after his return to his natal home, the young man usually gets married. In modern times this rite is not often observed, due to the decline of the traditional paradigm of the brahmacharin **stage of life**, although sometimes it is performed in preparation for a marriage.

The four Vedas in Sanskrit. The Sama Veda is the second of the four Vedas.

Samavaya

("**inherence**") Fundamental category in the worldview of the **Nyaya-Vaisheshika** philosophical school. This school conceives of the world as made up of atomistic parts, which are connected to form larger things. The fundamental function of samavaya is as a subtle glue to connect various things: wholes and their parts, substances and their attributes, motions and the things that move, and general properties and their particular instances. It also connects both pleasure and pain to the Self. Thus samavaya is the fundamental thing holding the universe together. The philosophical problems raised by the idea of inherence—particularly the claim that inherence was one single principle, and not a collection of things—were ultimately responsible for the rise of **Navyanyaya** school, which attempted to explain these relationships in a more sophisticated way.

Sama Veda

Traditionally considered the second of the four **Vedas**, the oldest and most authoritative Hindu religious texts. The Sama Veda is a collection of hymns, arranged for singing as one of the components of the Vedic sacrifices (**yajna**). While drawn mostly from the **Rg Veda**, the singing patterns are far more elaborate than the simple chanting generally associated with the Rg Veda. Thus it is believed that the Sama Veda developed later than the Rg Veda.

Sambandar

(7th c.) One of the earliest of the **Nayanars**, a group of sixty-three southern Indian poet-saints who were devotees (**bhakta**) of the god **Shiva**. Along with their contemporaries the **Alvars**, who were devotees of **Vishnu**, the Nayanars spearheaded the revitalization of Hindu religion through their passionate devotion (**bhakti**) to a personal god, conveyed in hymns sung in the **Tamil language**. Along with his contemporary

Appar, Sambandar actively opposed the unorthodox sects of the times, particularly the Jains, whom he reviles in his poems. The depth of his hatred can be seen in a well-established tradition that, after converting the king of **Madurai**, of the **Pandya dynasty**, from Jainism to Shaivism, Sambandar was instrumental in having eight thousand Jain ascetics executed by **impalement**. The collected hymns of the three most important Nayanars—Appar, Sambandar, and **Sundaramurtti**—comprise the *Devaram*, the most sacred of the Tamil Shaivite texts. See also **Shaiva**.

Samharakrama

("destruction method") Ritual in the **Shrividya** school of the secretive religious practice known as **tantra**. This ritual uses the **shrichakra**, a symbolic diagram used in **worship**. The adept's ritual journey starts at the outer edges of the shrichakra, which represents the apparently "real" everyday world, and gradually moves toward the center, where a single point (**bindu**) represents absolute unity. This process is called "destruction" because the ritual process systematically deconstructs the notion of the dualistic world and destroys the notion of a Self that is separate from the Absolute Reality. For further information see Douglas Renfrew Brooks, *The Secret of the Three Cities*, 1990.

Samhita

("collection") The most archaic textual layer in the **Vedas**, comprising hymns to the Vedic **deities**, benedictions, prayers, spells, and litanies. The term indicates that this group of texts is a collection of various things important, not only for their cognitive meaning, but for their power as **mantra** (sacred sound). The samhitas were chanted during rites of **sacrifice** and remain the oldest living part of the Hindu tradition. Following the samhitas are the three later textual levels: the **Brahmanas**, which are essentially manuals detailing correct performance of the sacrifice, and the **Aranyakas** and the **Upanishads**, which ask speculative questions about the power behind the sacrifice.

Samkalpa

("intention") Important ritual sequence at the beginning of many religious rites in which the person performing the rite states his or her identity, the time and place at which the action is being performed, the performer's intention to carry out this particular ritual act, and the benefits desired from the action. The samkalpa is important as the formal commitment to perform the stated action. For ritual actions that promise several different possible benefits—for example, **birth** in **heaven** or final liberation—performing the samkalpa is believed to give one the result one desires.

Samkhya

("enumeration") One of the **six schools** of traditional Hindu **philosophy**, whose founding text is the *Samkhyakarikas*, written by **Ishvarakrishna** in the third century B.C.E. Samkhya espouses an atheistic philosophical dualism positing two fundamental principles as the source of all things. The first of these is called **purusha** ("person"), which is conscious, but completely inactive and unchanging. It is seen as a passive witness to the transformations going on around it. As the source of consciousness, purusha is ultimately identified with an individual's true and eternal Self. Purusha is inferred as plural, given the plurality of conscious beings, combined with the fact that one person can gain enlightenment while all the rest remain in bondage.

The other fundamental principle is **prakrti**, ("nature"), which provides the object to the purusha's subject. Prakrti is better conceived of as force or power rather than a specific material object. Prakrti contains within it forces with three different primordial qualities (**gunas**):

sattva tends toward the good, **rajas** towards activity or passion, and **tamas** towards darkness and decay. In the primal prakrti these three forces are in perfect equilibrium, each perfectly balancing the others. The two principles of purusha and prakrti are distinct, separate, and alone.

When prakrti's initial equilibrium is disturbed, it sets in motion a pattern of **evolution** that creates both the exterior physical world and the interior psychological world. From prakrti emerges **mahat** ("the great one"), which has as its psychological counterpart the subtlest form of mental activity (**buddhi**). From buddhi evolves **ahamkar**, which contains the first real ideas of individual identity. From ahamkar evolves the mind (**manas**), the sense organs (**jnanendriyas**), the organs of action (**karmendriyas**), and the subtle elements (**tanmatras**); from the last evolve the gross elements that actually make up the material world. All of these evolutes—material or psychic—have a differing balance of the three gunas, which ultimately determines their character as wholesome, active, or unwholesome. Throughout this process of evolution, purusha remains unchanged, a mere witness to prakrti's unceasing transformations. Their mutual functioning is described using the metaphor of the lame man (purusha) being carried by the blind man (prakrti).

The ultimate source of bondage, according to the Samkhya school, comes because people do not recognize the difference between these two principles. Through this lack of discrimination between the two, the Self (purusha) appears as if it is an agent, and the evolutes (from prakrti) as if they are conscious. The Samkhyas illustrate this misunderstanding using the example of the rose behind the crystal, in which the latter appears to be colored but is in fact unchanged. Although for the Samkhyas prakrti undergoes real transformations, the primary problem is epistemological—that is, how one comes to know things—rather than ontological, or rooted in the nature of things themselves. Since the purusha never changes, there is no question of making it into anything else or regaining the way that it used to be; the real problem is making the distinction between the differing realities of these two principles. Once this has been done, the evolution of prakrti is said to reverse, leaving the purusha again in its state of magnificent isolation (**kaivalya**). Of course, once one has a developed (if erroneous) idea of (conventional) personality, this discrimination becomes all the more difficult. This mistaken idea becomes the basis for one's volitional actions (**karma**) and one's emotional dispositions. One's actions and dispositions reinforce each other, and both of these are undergirded by the notion of a Self.

The Samkhya metaphysics were adopted wholesale by the **yoga** philosophical school, and the two schools are usually mentioned together—Samkhya as the theoretical foundation, and Yoga as the practical component. One of Samkhya's lasting contributions to Indian thought is the idea of the gunas, a basic concept running through Hindu culture. Another influential but less pervasive idea is their model of evolution, which has been adapted by other schools but often subsumed under theistic assumptions in which God is the source of both consciousness and the material world. The one philosophical problem that the Samkhya could never surmount was to explain the source of bondage, given their starting assumptions. If purusha and prakrti are completely separate, how could the two of them interact—much less mistake one for the other—and how did the process of evolution begin? Although their contributions remain significant, they were largely eclipsed by **Vedanta**, which claimed that the problem is ignorance of the Self and not-Self, and that the world around us is not an actual evolution, but only an illusory transformation (vivarta). This philosophical model is called **Vivartavada**. For further information see Sarvepalli Radhakrishnan and

Charles A. Moore (eds.), *A Sourcebook in Indian Philosophy*, 1957; and Gerald Larson and Ram Shankar Bhattacharya (eds.), *Samkhya*, 1987.

Sampraday

("tradition") Literally, "that which is handed down," or the transmitted body of teachings that distinguishes one religious group from another. Belonging to a particular sampraday is based on having received teachings from one's spiritual preceptor (**guru**), thus becoming part of a spiritual lineage, and continuing the life of that sampraday by transmitting the teachings to disciples. Although the sampraday is often translated as "sect," this loses its sense of uniqueness within particular theistic traditions. For example, one can speak of different sampradays among Tamil **Shaiva** brahmins, by virtue of their differing spiritual lineages, even though they **worship** the same **deity** and share a common cultural heritage.

Samsara

("wandering") The cycle of reincarnation, one of the most fundamental assumptions throughout all Indian religion. In the Indian worldview, reincarnation involves a series of births and rebirths in different realms and forms, all based on the quality and quantity of **karma**, formed through previous actions and patterns of thought. Beings with good karma may be born into the **heavens**, which are essentially realms of pleasure and carefree enjoyment; those with bad karma may be reborn as **animals** or as **ghosts**, or into realms of punishment, such as **hells**. Neither pleasure nor punishment is eternal, although they may last an extremely long time. Beings in heaven enjoy the results of their past actions, but when their good karma is exhausted they must take another, lower birth; beings in realms of punishment are paying for their evil deeds, but when this has been done they will take another birth, presumably in some higher status.

Between these two lies the human realm, which comprises infinite possibilities, based on various factors—such as high status or low, wealth or poverty, health or disability, and the religious piety of one's natal family. Varying mixtures of good and bad karma combine for many different human circumstances, and according to popular belief one's present life and body are a record of one's past. The notion that people are, in life, where they deserve to be because of karma can be seen as the basis for the **caste** system. Fulfilling one's particular social role (**svadharma**), no matter how humble, not only upholds the social order but is a means for individual spiritual advancement.

The human realm is widely believed to be the best of all for spiritual life, partly because human beings can make rational choices, including the decision to take part in religious life. In this humans are different from animals, which are driven mainly by their instincts, and from ghosts or hell-dwellers, who are simply expiating their past acts. At the same time human life, unlike life in the heavens, is full of reverses and sorrow continually reminding human beings about the transience of life and possessions and the need to engage in spiritual development. Embodied existence is a constant cycling from one realm to the next, leaving one body and assuming another, and the inherent uncertainty of this condition has led to the search, dating from the time of the speculative texts known as the **Upanishads**, for an unchanging state, completely out of this cycle of rebirth. This unchanging state is widely accepted as life's supreme goal, although in any generation very few actively seek it, with most people content to relegate it to some indefinite future lifetime. For further information see Wendy Doniger O'Flaherty (ed.), *Karma and Rebirth in Classical Indian Traditions*, 1980.

The chudakarana samskara, in which a child's head is shaved as a rite of purification.

Samskara

("making perfect") Collective name for the various life-cycle ceremonies in Hindu society. Although status in Indian society depends most on one's **birth**, this alone is not sufficient to become a complete and finished person. In an individual's development, the raw material given by nature must be refined through the process of culture, or the action of samskaras. This process of transformation begins before birth, with the three **prenatal** samskaras, and continues to death with the **antyeshthi** samskaras. In general, samskaras transform people in two ways: by removing latent or residual impurities, such as the childhood **chudakarana samskara**, or by generating new capacities and entitlements, such as the **upanayana (initiation)** and **vivaha** (marriage) **samskaras**.

Although different writers in the **dharma literature** disagree on the number of samskaras, traditionally, sixteen are accepted. Three were prenatal samskaras: one to ensure conception (**Garbhadhana**), one to ensure the birth of a boy (**Pumsavana**), and one to ensure an easy delivery and a healthy child (**Simantonnayana**). Six samskaras were associated with childhood: ritual actions immediately after birth (**Jatakarma**), name-giving (**Namakarana**), the first outing (**Nishkramana**), the first solid food (**Annaprashana**), head-**shaving (Chudakarana)**, and piercing of the ears (**Karnavedha**). Five samskaras were connected with life as a celibate student (**brahmacharin**): beginning of learning (**Vidyarambha**), adolescent religious initiation (**Upanayana**), the beginning of **Veda** study (**Vedarambha**), the first shave (**Keshanta**), and the return home at the conclusion of studies (**Samavartana**). The final two samskaras were marriage, and the last rites for the dead (**antyeshthi samskara**).

These sixteen samskaras were the rites for a **twice-born** man, whom this literature considered the default person. A twice-born man was one born into one of the three "twice-born" **varnas**—**brahmin**, **kshatriya**, or **vaishya**—who were ritually eligible for the adolescent religious initiation known as the "second birth." **Women** in the twice-born groups would undergo all the rites through the **childhood rites**, but would have no further rites until marriage, which was considered equal to all samskaras for them. People born outside the twice-born groups—namely, **shudras** and **untouchables**—would perform few if any of these rites.

These life cycle rites drive and govern the formation of the individual. In modern times many of these samskaras are still performed, but mainly by brahmins who, because of their traditional role as priests and scholars, conserve this practice to help maintain their traditional prestige. For further information see Pandurang Vaman Kane, *A History of Dharmasastra*, 1968; and Raj Bali Pandey, *Hindu Samskaras*, 1969. The former is encyclopedic and the latter more accessible; despite their age, they remain the best sources about traditional Hindu rites.

Samudra Gupta

(r. 335–376) The second monarch in the **Gupta dynasty, son** of **Chandra Gupta I**. During his reign Samudra Gupta made significant territorial gains from the Gupta dynasty's home base in eastern **Uttar Pradesh** and **Bihar** westward to the **Ganges** basin and eastward into Bengal and **Assam**. **Orissa** and much of the **Coromandel** Coast gave tribute as independent but vassal states. Samudra Gupta left a personal account of his prowess inscribed on a stone column at **Allahabad**. This column had originally been carved to display one of the **Pillar Edicts** of the Maurya emperor **Ashoka** (r. 269–232 B.C.E.), and in claiming it as his own Samudra Gupta was attempting to appropriate some of the **Maurya dynasty's** luster.

Samvad

("dialogue") Technical term for the speaking parts in the **Ramnagar Ram Lila**, a dramatic presentation of the *Ramayana* staged annually at the fortified town of Ramnagar, near **Benares**. The dialogues are interspersed with recitations from the *Ramcharitmanas*, a vernacular retelling of the *Ramayana* written by the poet-saint **Tulsidas** (1532–1623?), and render the archaic language of the *Ramcharitmanas* into modern vernacular **Hindi**. The action in the Ram Lila alternates between contemporary and archaic text.

Samyama

("inner discipline") In the **ashtanga yoga** first codified by the philosopher **Patanjali**, a collective name for the last three stages in yoga practice, namely **dharana**, **dhyana**, and **samadhi**. These stages are concerned with focusing and disciplining the mind, and are the most subtle and internalized elements in yogic practice.

Sanaka

In Hindu mythology, one of four sages born of the god **Brahma**, who are paradigms of **asceticism**; the other three are **Sanandana**, **Sanatana**, and **Sanatkumara**. When Brahma emanates these four sages, he commands them to begin the work of creation, but they are so detached from worldly concerns that they refuse to do so. They are celibate their entire lives, study the **Vedas** from childhood, and always travel together.

Sanakadi

("**Sanaka** and the others") In Hindu mythology, a collective name for four sages born of **Brahma** who are paradigms of **asceticism**; the four sages are Sanaka, **Sanandana**, **Sanatana**, and **Sanatkumara**. When Brahma emanates them, he commands them to begin the work of creation, but they are so detached from worldly concerns that they refuse to do so. They are celibate their entire lives, study the **Vedas** from childhood, and always travel together.

Sanaka Sampraday

One of the four branches (**sampraday**) of the **Naga** class of the **Bairagi** ascetics. Bairagi ascetics are devotees (**bhakta**) of the god **Vishnu**. The Nagas are fighting ascetics hired by the other Bairagis to protect them. The Naga class is organized in military fashion into different **anis** or "armies." Until the beginning of the nineteenth century their primary occupation was as mercenary soldiers, although they also had substantial trading interests; both of these have largely disappeared in contemporary times. The Sanaka Sampraday traces its spiritual lineage from the **Nimbarki** sect, founded by **Nimbarka**. Members of this sect **worship Radha** and **Krishna** as a divine couple, with both **deities** holding equal status.

Sanandana

In Hindu mythology, one of four sages born of the god **Brahma** who are paradigms of **asceticism**; the other three are **Sanaka**, **Sanatana**, and **Sanatkumara**. When Brahma emanates these four sages, he commands them to begin the work of creation, but they are so detached from worldly concerns that they refuse to do so. They are celibate their entire lives, study the **Vedas** from childhood, and always travel together.

Sanatana

In Hindu mythology, one of four sages born of the god **Brahma** who are paradigms of **asceticism**; the other three ascetics are **Sanaka**, **Sanandana**, and **Sanatkumara**. When Brahma emanates these four sages, he commands them to begin the work of creation, but they are so detached from worldly concerns that they refuse to do so. They are celibate their entire lives, study the **Vedas** from childhood, and always travel together.

Sanatana ("eternal") Dharma

In the **dharma literature**, the ultimate and eternal moral order of the universe. It is the eternal ideal pattern revealed in the **Vedas** (the oldest and most authoritative Hindu religious texts). This pattern must be upheld to maintain the stability of society. All aspects of religious duty (**dharma**) aim ultimately toward the maintenance and fulfillment of this order, including common religious duties (**sadharana dharma**), religious duties stemming from social status (**varna dharma**) and **stage of life** (ashrama dharma), and individualized religious duty (**svadharma**). In more recent times, the term has been used by Hindus to identify the religious tradition known to the outside world as "Hinduism."

Sanatana Sampraday

Another name for the **Nimbarki** religious community. The philosopher **Nimbarka** was the community's historical founder, but, according to the Nimbarkis, the actual founder was the god **Vishnu** himself. One of Vishnu's disciples was named **Sanatana** ("eternal"), hence the name of the **sampraday**.

Sanatkumara

In Hindu mythology, one of four sages born of the god **Brahma** who are paradigms of **asceticism**; the other three are **Sanaka**, **Sanandana**, and **Sanatana**. When Brahma emanates these four sages, he commands them to begin the work of creation, but they are so detached from worldly concerns that they refuse to do so. They are celibate their entire lives, study the **Vedas** from childhood, and always travel together

Sandarshana ("expositing") Mudra

In Indian **dance**, **sculpture**, and ritual, a particular symbolic hand **gesture** (**mudra**), in which the tips of the thumb and index finger are touching, with the rest of the fingers extended and the palm facing the viewer. This is the hand gesture used to signify explanation or exposition, and for this reason it is also known as the **vyakhyana** ("teaching") **mudra**. Since the teaching gesture indicates a person of higher spiritual attainment, it is also known as the chit ("consciousness") mudra.

Sandhabhasha

Symbolic language used in **tantra**, a secret, ritually based religious practice. The literal translation of the term is disputed; it is often translated as "twilight language" because of its shadowy and mysterious character, but Agehananda Bharati is emphatic that the term means "**intentional language**." The elements of tantric **worship** and practice are described in a coded language drawn from the parts and functions of the human body considered private by most standards. Such coded discourse is used to hide the tradition's essentials from noninitiates and also to project the speakers into an altered understanding. For noninitiates, such language reinforces the general conception of tantric practitioners as completely debased. Douglas R. Brooks reports in *The Secret of the Three Cities*, 1990, that although widely used in Buddhist tantra, Sandhabhasha is less common among Hindus, who for their coded language favor using common words with contextually technical meanings. For further information see Swami Agehananda. Bharati, *The Tantric Tradition*, 1977; Appendix A in Linda Hess and Shukdev Singh (trans.), *The Bijak of Kabir*, 1983; and Douglas Renfrew Brooks, *The Secret of the Three Cities*, 1990.

Sandhi

("junction") In classical **Sanskrit** grammar, a term for the euphonic (harmonic) combination of words. In general this is done by modifying the final phoneme of one word, based on the initial phoneme of the following word, to facilitate a smooth verbal transition between the two. An example is the compound word **sacchidananda**, which designates the three essential aspects of the ultimate unqualified **Brahman**, and is formed from the words *sat* ("being"), *chit* ("consciousness") and *ananda* ("bliss").

Sandhya

("union") Morning and evening twilight, the two transitional times between day and night and thus, metaphorically, the times when day and night are united. The word also often denotes certain rites performed daily at morning, noon, and evening, the three times when different parts of the day are in union. These rites are prescribed in the **dharma literature** as mandatory for all **twice-born** men, that is, all men from the **brahmin**, **kshatriya**, or **vaishya** groups who have undergone the adolescent religious **initiation** known as the "second birth." At present time these rites are performed only by the most orthodox brahmins.

Sangam

("coming together") Meeting-place for two rivers and the point at which their capacity for purification is believed to be heightened. The most famous such site is the confluence of the **Ganges** and the **Yamuna** rivers at the city of **Allahabad**, but numerous other such sites exist throughout the Indian subcontinent.

Sangama Dynasty
See **Vijayanagar dynasty**.

Sangam Literature

Collection of classical literature from the Tamil culture, composed during the early centuries of the common era; Sangam (also spelled Cankam) means "academy." The most famous texts in Sangam literature are eight collections of short poems. Three of these collections fall into the genre called puram ("the outer part"); the other five are in the genre called akam ("the inner part"). Puram poetry was "public" verse, describing the deeds of kings, war, death, and other heroic actions. Akam poetry was about an individual's inner experience, especially cultured love, of which the Sangam poets distinguished five developed moods: union, patient waiting, unfaithfulness, separation, and hardship. Each of these moods had well-developed symbolic associations, including associations with a specific type of landscape, time of **day** and **year**, flora, fauna, and types of people; such richly developed symbolism gives these poems incredible symbolic depth. The akam poems are arguably the literary antecedents to devotional (**bhakti**) poetry, which first developed in **Tamil Nadu**. For further information see A.K. Ramanujan (trans.), *The Interior Landscape*, 1994; and Glenn Yocum, "Shrines, Shamanism, and Love Poetry: Elements in the Emergence of Popular Tamil Bhakti," in the *Journal of the American Academy of Religion*, Vol. 41, No. 1, 1973. See also **Tamil epics** and **Tamil language**.

Sanjaya

Minister of the blind king **Dhrtarashtra**, an important older figure in the Hindu epic the *Mahabharata*. Sanjaya tries valiantly to avert the war that is the epic's climax by counseling the king to better control his son **Duryodhana**, and to deal more equitably with his nephews the **Pandavas**, the five brothers who are the epic's protagonists. In the end, the king ignores Sanjaya's advice. Sanjaya is most famous for his ability to see anything he thinks about ("tele-vision"). This power is given to him as a gift from the sage **Vyasa** so he can describe the progress of the war to Dhrtarashtra without actually having to be there. After the war, Sanjaya goes to live in the forest with Dhrtarashtra, and it is he who informs the Pandavas about the blind king's death in a forest fire.

Sanjaya Belatthiputa

Agnostic thinker in early Indian **philosophy** whose views are alluded to in the Buddhist scriptures. The scriptures portray Sanjaya as an advocate of profound agnosticism with regard to another world, the effects of good and evil deeds, and just about every facet of religious life.

Sanjna

In Hindu mythology, the daughter of **Vishvakarma**, workman and architect for the gods. Sanjna has been married to **Surya**, the **Sun**, but finds his dazzling radiance too much to bear. To help his daughter adjust to her husband, Vishvakarma trims off some bits of the sun with his divine tools, removing enough of his radiance that Samjna can bear to be with him. The trimmed-off parts of the sun are used to build the **Pushpak Viman**, an **aerial car**, as well as the god **Vishnu's** discus (**chakra**), the god **Shiva's** trident, and various other divine weapons.

Sankalpa

Spoken ritual performed before a religious act. The person about to perform the act identifies himself by name, tells the location of the act, and gives the lunar **calendar** date and time. He goes on to describe the religious act and what benefits he wants to receive as a result. Sankalpa is done before rituals such as **suicide** and doing morning **puja** to the **Ganges**. See **samkalpa**.

Sankarshana

("dragging away") Epithet of the god **Krishna's** brother **Balarama**, referring to Balarama's unusual prenatal development—he is conceived by Krishna's mother **Devaki** but is magically transferred into the womb of her co-wife **Rohini**. This is done to protect him from harm, since Devaki's wicked uncle **Kamsa** has already killed her first seven children, and will certainly do the same if she carries Balarama to term. See **Balarama**.

Sankat Mochan

("freeing from distress") Epithet of a particular form of the monkey-god **Hanuman**, whose main temple is on the southern part of **Benares**. Sankat Mochan has been an increasingly popular form of Hanuman since the 1970s. As with all manifestations of Hanuman, Sankat Mochan is considered a strong protective **deity**, with the power to rescue his devotees (**bhakta**) from all kinds of trouble and misfortune.

Sankat Mochan

(2) A temple in the southern part of **Benares** dedicated to the monkey-god **Hanuman** in his form as Sankat Mochan. The temple does not have a long history but first became famous in the nineteenth century through some **Ramanandi** ascetics living there, whose piety drew visitors to the spot. In modern times, the temple has become popular because the image of Hanuman is believed to be very powerful, but also accessible—qualities that lead petitioners to come with requests and leave with the assurance that help is forthcoming.

Sankranti

("transition") The transition of a celestial body (**sun**, **moon**, or **planet**) from one sign of the **zodiac** to another. Such transitions can give the celestial bodies or the time in question positive or negative qualities. The most important of these celestial bodies is the sun, whose two directional transitions—northward at **Makara** Sankranti, and southward at **Karka** Sankranti—define more and less auspicious times for the entire **year**.

Sanskrit

("perfected") For much of Indian history, Sanskrit was the language of the cultural and religious elite. Even in the twentieth century, it is still the language with the highest religious status. Its name reflects the religious conviction that it was the perfect language—the language of the gods. Sanskrit was essentially fixed in the fourth century B.C.E. by the **grammarian Panini** in his *Ashtadhyayi*. Since it has not changed from Panini's time, Sanskrit is no longer considered a "natural" language. Even in Panini's time, Sanskrit would have been a person's second language, learned by conscious study after acquiring a grammatically simpler mother tongue (one of the **Prakrits**)

An illustrated page of Sanskrit from the first chapter of the *Devimahatmya*.
The illustration depicts the opening episode, in which a king and a merchant visit a hermit.

through the normal process of language learning. In a religious context Sanskrit has primarily been the province of **brahmins**, serving both as a sacred language and a common language through which the brahmins from various areas could communicate with each other. Its place of pride as the religious language *par excellence* has been somewhat undercut by the influence of the devotional (**bhakti**) religious movement. One of this movement's pervasive features was poetry composed in vernacular languages, which reflected the conscious choice to speak in a language that everyone could understand.

Sant

Literally, someone who has found the truth, or who is searching for it. The word is derived from the **Sanskrit** word **sat** ("truth"). More generally it refers to two major groups of devotional (**bhakti**) poet-saints. One group was centered around the temple of **Vithoba** at **Pandharpur** in the state of **Maharashtra**, and includes saints from the **Varkari Panth** community such as **Namdev**, **Tukaram**, **Chokamela**, and **Eknath**. The other group included later poet-saints from various places in northern India, among them **Kabir**, **Ravidas**, **Dadu**, and Guru Nanak, the founder of the Sikh community.

As a group the sants shared certain general tendencies rather than an explicit body of doctrine. Sant religion was inclined to stress an individualized, interior religion leading to a personal experience of the divine, rather than participation in established cults. One of the most common sant themes was their disdain for external ritual, and the general rejection of any **worship** using images. The northern Indian sants are the most uncompromising advocates of **nirguna** devotion, in which the divine is seen as beyond conception; but even among the Pandharpur devotees (**bhakta**) the stress was on devotion to the god Vithoba, rather than actual worship. The sants stressed the power of the divine Name and its ability to remove all obstacles. They disregarded **caste** distinctions, viewing them as an arbitrary barrier dividing the human community. They stressed instead the value of **satsang**, and the transforming effects that such "good company" could bring. Satsang thus formed an egalitarian community through the common bonds of faith and devotion, as an alternative to the hierarchical society established by birth.

It is sometimes suggested that all of these themes can be traced to the sants' social background, since many of them came from very low caste communities. It is certainly true that devotees of low social status would have been forbidden even to enter temples, much less worship the images in those temples, and thus a religious path emphasizing the Name and interior religious experience, which are accessible to everyone, might have seemed a more viable option. In the same way, the socially oppressed might find the notion of an alternative, egalitarian community immensely attractive. Yet to reduce the sant tradition to a simple reaction by marginal social groups cannot explain why one of its major figures is Eknath, a **brahmin**. Such reductionist analyses ignore the sant movement's real thrust, namely the passionate search for the divine that permitted no compromises and no excuses. For further information see Karine Schomer and W. H. McLeod, *The Sants*, 1985.

Santal

Tribal (**adivasi**) community in northern India, particularly in the border districts of **Bihar** and **West Bengal**. As with most tribals in India, many are very poor and make a precarious living as cultivators.

Santoshi Ma

("the mother who satisfies") **Goddess** who is one of the most fascinating Hindu **deities**, and whose recent explosive popularity illustrates both the flexibility of the Hindu pantheon, and the way that Hindu religion reflects and responds to changes in Indian society. Santoshi Ma's popularity was largely inspired by a film released in 1975, *Jai Santoshi Ma* ("Victory to Santoshi Ma"). The film first details the birth of Santoshi Ma as the daughter of the god **Ganesh**, but then cuts to the earthly problems suffered by one of her devotees (**bhakta**), **Satyavati**. Satyavati is a new bride having problems adjusting to her marital home, particularly because of tensions with her wicked sisters-in-law. By the end of the film, through Satyavati's steadfast devotion to Santoshi Ma, all of her problems are resolved.

This film did not invent Santoshi Ma, although it was largely responsible for spreading her **worship**. The prescriptions for Santoshi Ma's religious vow (**vrat**) had existed before the film was made, and both the rite's charter myth and the film focus on the problems of a new bride and their eventual resolution through her steadfast devotion to Santoshi Ma. Santoshi Ma's ultimate source is a mystery, but her iconography suggests that she is an amalgam of other female deities. She is seated on the lotus, a feature associated with the goddess **Lakshmi**; she wields the sword associated with the goddesses **Kali** and **Durga**, as well as the trident associated with the god **Shiva**. She shows the attributes associated with both married and unmarried goddesses: Like the married goddesses, she is nurturing and caring to her devotees, playing the role of the benevolent Indian mother, and like the independent unmarried goddesses, she is powerful and and potentially dangerous—one of the film's climactic scenes shows her utterly destroying a temple after Satyavati's sister-in-law intentionally ruined the sanctified food (**prasad**) meant for her devotees. Yet she is also believed to have the power to grant her devotees' requests, no matter how large. Through her nurturing, benevolent character coupled with power, she crosses the usual boundaries associated with Hindu goddesses.

Part of the popularity of Santoshi Ma's vrat comes from its simplicity, cheapness, and promise of benefits. The observance is usually kept by **women** with the aim of attaining concrete goals for themselves and their families: getting a job, passing an exam, conceiving a child, or arranging a marriage. The rite involves weekly fasting (**upavasa**) and worship. One of the social factors cited in Santoshi Ma's explosive popularity is the steadily growing uncertainty in Indian (and South Asian) life, which makes very ordinary things difficult to attain and necessitates the use of all possible resources. In this context, an inexpensive rite that promises concrete benefits for assiduous devotion is an attractive option. See also **Santoshi Ma Vrat**.

Santoshi Ma Vrat

Religious observance celebrated on **Fridays** in homage to the **goddess Santoshi Ma** ("the mother who satisfies"). This religious vow (**vrat**) is usually kept by **women** with the aim of attaining concrete goals for themselves or (more commonly) their families: getting a job, passing an exam, conceiving a child, or arranging a marriage. When one's wish has been granted, a final ceremony calls for the observant to feed eight **brahmin** boys a meal of rice, yogurt, and bananas. After this concluding rite, one is no longer required to observe the vow, although many women choose to continue performing it as a means to maintain the household's general good fortune.

The Santoshi Ma Vrat has become extremely popular throughout northern India since the late 1970s, one reason being that it is simple and inexpensive. On the day of the fast (**upavasa**) the worshiper should not eat until the evening meal, although tea and other beverages are generally allowed. In the late afternoon the worshiper should light a lamp in front of a picture of Santoshi Ma, offer her small amounts of chickpeas and raw sugar—things that can be found in even the poorest households—and read aloud the rite's charter myth, which tells how a poor, unfortunate woman solved all her family's troubles through her devotion to Santoshi Ma. After this, the worshiper may eat the evening meal, although it is also subject to restrictions: Since Santoshi Ma is a goddess associated with sweetness, the food must not contain any sour, spicy, or bitter seasonings. This observance thus carries the two common features of most religious vows: some form of **worship** and modification of one's diet, with the promise of benefits in return.

Sanyasi

("renunciant") According to the **dharma literature**, the last of the idealized **stages of life** (ashrama) for a **twice-born** man, that is a man born into the **brahmin**, **kshatriya**, or **vaishya** communities. Boys born into these communities are eligible for the adolescent religious **initiation** known as the "second birth." After engaging in religious learning as a celibate student (**brahmacharin**), marrying and raising a family as a householder (**grhastha**), and gradually detaching himself from the world as a forest-dwelling recluse (**vanaprastha**), a twice-born man should finally renounce all possessions and all attachments to devote himself exclusively to the search for ultimate truth. Although in a general sense the word *Sanyasi* can (and sometimes does) refer to any such renunciant, it is most used as the name of a particular **ascetic** community, the **Dashanami Sanyasis**, who are believed to have been founded by the great philosopher **Shankaracharya**, and who are devotees (**bhakta**) of the god **Shiva**.

Sanyasi Rebellion

Name given by the British to a long-term struggle in the Bengal region in the latter half of the eighteenth century. This was the period in which the British East India Company was consolidating its economic, political, and military control over the region, causing wide-ranging dislocations in traditional Bengali society. Among the entrenched powers with which the British clashed were organized bands of soldier-ascetics, both Hindus and Muslims. These soldier-ascetics were significant local forces, with both military and economic power gained through mercenary services, trading, and money-lending, and they competed with the British East India Company for political authority and land revenue.

Conflict between the British and the ascetics peaked shortly after the Bengal famine of 1770–1771. The rebellion was caused partly by competition for greatly reduced agricultural revenue and by British-sponsored changes in land ownership patterns, in which officials in the East India Company replaced many of the "unprofitable" traditional landowners with their own Company employees. Many of the traditional landowners owed money to **ascetic** moneylenders (Sanyasis), and had pledged their land revenue as security. The Sanyasis were upset when the landowners were replaced and the debts not honored. For their part, the Company's officials were reluctant to allow the ascetics, who traveled in heavily armed bands, to pass through the company's territories while on religious pilgrimage, as the ascetics had traditionally done. Ultimately the ascetic attacks were disorganized and local, and the disparate **Sanyasi** bands were unable to withstand British resources and organization. A fictionalized account of the Sanyasi Rebellion appeared in the novel ***Anandamath***, by **Bankim Chandra Chatterjee** (1838–1894), who used the Sanyasi Rebellion as a coded call for resistance to contemporary British rule.

Sapaksha

One of the parts of an acceptable form of inference (**anumana**) in Indian **philosophy**. An acceptable inference has three terms: an assertion (**pratijna**), a reason (**hetu**), and examples (**drshtanta**); each of these three has its own constituent parts. The sapaksha is part of the third term, the examples. It is a positive example given to support the claim made in the initial assertion, by showing that similar things happen in comparable cases. For example, in the inference, "there is **fire** on the mountain, because there is smoke on the mountain," the sapaksha could be "as in a kitchen," since this place has both fire and smoke, and thus supports the initial assertion. Conventionally, an inference also has to have a negative example, to show that the claim made in the assertion does not happen in some other cases.

Saphala Ekadashi

Religious observance falling on the eleventh day (**ekadashi**) of the dark (waxing) half of the **lunar month** of **Paush** (December–January). All the eleventh-day observances are dedicated to the **worship** of **Vishnu**. Most Hindu religious festivals have certain prescribed rites, which usually involve fasting (**upavasa**) and worship and often promise specific benefits for faithful performance. Those performing this rite must stay up all night singing and telling of Vishnu's exploits. The name *Saphala* means "successful," and those who faithfully observe this will be successful in all their endeavors.

Sapinda

("having a common body") Term for people having common ancestry, who could thus be said to share the same body through the ancestor. This relationship was held to cease after seven generations on the father's side, and after five on the mother's. Men and women who were sapinda were theoretically forbidden to marry, although this prohibition has been routinely ignored in southern India since very early times. See also **marriage prohibitions**.

Sapindikarana

Funerary rite (**antyeshthi samskara**) performed on the twelfth day after death, which symbolically represents the one-year anniversary of the death. In this rite, the departed person is transformed from a potentially dangerous wandering spirit (**pret**) to a benevolent **ancestral spirit** (pitr). Each day for ten days following a person's death, mourners leave a ball of cooked grain (**pinda**) for the departed spirit. Gradually the ten pindas "construct" a new body for the departed person. Then sapindikarana is performed on the twelfth day. A large pinda, representing the departed, and three smaller ones are collected, representing the departed's father, grandfather, and great-grandfather. The rite's

A groom and bride circle the sacred fire during the marriage ceremony,
a rite often combined with the saptapadi, or the seven steps.

central moment comes when the departed's pinda is divided into three parts, one part is mixed with each of the other three pindas, and finally all three pindas are combined into one. At the moment the three pindas are combined, the departed is believed to have become one (sapindi) with his ancestors, and to

have been transformed from a wandering spirit into an ancestor as well. This twelfth day rite is the last of the funerary rites performed on a strict timetable. Mourners may wait for years before performing the final rite of **asthi-visarjana**, in which bone and ashes from the dead person's **cremation** pyre are immersed in a sacred river, although with the advent of better transportation this is sometimes now performed before the twelfth day rites. In addition, people still perform annual memorial rites for the deceased. For an excellent account of this rite, see David M. Knipe, "Sapindikarana: The Hindu Rite of Entry into Heaven," in Frank E. Reynolds and Earle H. Waugh (eds.), *Religious Encounters With Death*, 1977.

Saptapadi

("seven steps") The most important rite in the Hindu **marriage ceremony**, in which the bride and groom take seven steps together to symbolize their marital union. The seventh step completes the transfer of the bride from her natal family to the groom's family and is also the point when the marriage becomes permanent. As described in the **dharma literature**, the bride and groom would perform this rite by taking seven steps in a straight line. In contemporary times this rite is often combined with the **agnipradakshinam** ("circumambulating the **fire**"), in which the bride and groom make seven revolutions around a small fire—considered to be a form of the god **Agni** and thus the divine witness to the marriage. While circling the fire, the bride and groom are often physically joined by tying part of his turban to the edge of her sari as a visible sign of their marital union.

Saptasindhu

("seven seas") In traditional mythic geography, the seven oceans surrounding the seven concentric landmasses (**dvipas**) that make up the visible world. Each of these seven seas is composed of a different substance. The ocean accessible to human beings is composed of salt water, but the oceans beyond that are composed of sugarcane juice, wine, ghee (clarified butter), yogurt, milk, and sweet water. Few specific details exist about most of these oceans, but the Ocean of Milk has a prominent place in Hindu mythology, since it was by churning this that the gods obtained the nectar of immortality (**amrta**). See also **Tortoise avatar**.

Sarama

In the **Rg Veda**, the earliest Hindu sacred text, a servant of the storm-god **Indra**. In Rg Veda 10.108, Sarama is sent as an emissary to Indra's enemies, the **Panis**, to inquire where they have hidden the **cows** they have stolen, and to threaten them with Indra's wrath if they do not reveal their location.

Saraswat

Traditional Indian society was modeled as a collection of **endogamous**, or intermarried, subgroups known as **jatis** ("birth"). Jatis were organized (and their social status determined) by the group's hereditary occupation, over which each group has a monopoly. This sort of differentiation applied even to **brahmins**, whose role has been to serve as priests, scholars, and teachers. The Saraswats are a brahmin jati counted as one of the five northern Indian brahmin communities (**Pancha Gauda**); the other four are the **Gaudas**, the **Kanaujias**, the **Maithilas**, and the **Utkalas**. Unlike most other brahmin communities, which had a well-defined core region, the Saraswats are found in several widely separated locations. One group lived in the coastal region of Sindh in modern Pakistan, although after Partition in 1947 most of the group migrated to Bombay. Another group was located in prepartition **Punjab**, although here too they have tended to migrate away from the part of Punjab in modern Pakistan. A third branch, known as the Gauda Saraswats, is found on a narrow strip of coastline in the southern Indian state of **Karnataka**. The Saraswat community takes its name from **Saraswati**, patron **goddess** of speech and learning, and, as a group, is famous for its erudition and piety.

A depiction of Saraswati, the goddess associated with art, aesthetics, learning, sacred speech, and wisdom.

Saraswati

Goddess associated with art, aesthetics, learning, sacred speech, and wisdom. Saraswati is the patron **deity** of culture in all its manifestations. The spoken word is considered very powerful in Hindu culture and Saraswati can either promote or frustrate one's efforts by conferring or withdrawing the ability to speak clearly. Her association with sacred speech goes back to the time of the sacrificial manuals known as the **Brahmanas**, in which the cult of **sacrifice** was based on the precise performance of sacred speech and ritual.

Her iconography emphasizes her connection with the life of the mind: She holds a book, a crystal (symbolic of a purified mind), a **vina** (musical instrument), and a rosary (associated with religious rites, and particularly with the repetition of the sacred sounds known as **mantras**). Her animal vehicle is the swan, whose white color is a symbol of **purity** and whose high flight is a symbol of transcendence. Through Saraswati's blessings (**ashirvad**) human beings can transcend their biological condition to create works of art and culture.

Saraswati is usually believed to be married, although different mythic sources give her different husbands. In some cases she is described as the wife of the god **Brahma**, the creator; here their joint activity encompasses the formation of the material world and its transformation through human cultural activity. In other stories she is described as the wife of the god **Vishnu**, and thus a co-wife of **Lakshmi**. Here the realms of Lakshmi and Saraswati can be seen as giving differing messages about the "good things" in life—while Lakshmi grants wealth and material prosperity, Saraswati brings wisdom and culture. A popular Indian saying reports that Saraswati's devotee (**bhakta**) will never make money, while a follower of Lakshmi (whose vehicle is the **owl**) will be "blind" to spiritual wisdom. For more information on Saraswati and all the goddesses of Hinduism, see David R. Kinsley, *Hindu Goddesses*, 1986.

Saraswati Dashanami

One of the ten divisions of the **Dashanami Sanyasis**, renunciant ascetics who are devotees (**bhakta**) of **Shiva**. The Dashanamis were supposedly established by the ninth-century philosopher **Shankaracharya** in an effort to create a corps of learned men who could help to revitalize Hindu life. Each of the divisions is designated by a different name—in this case, **Saraswati** (the patron **goddess** of learning and culture). Upon **initiation**, new members are given this name as a surname to their new **ascetic** names, thus allowing for immediate group identification.

These ten "named" divisions of Dashanami Sanyasis are divided into four larger organizational groups. Each group has its headquarters in one of the four monastic centers (**maths**) supposedly established by Shankaracharya, as well as other particular religious associations. The Saraswati Dashanamis belong to the **Bhuriwara** group, which is affiliated with the **Shringeri math** in the southern Indian town of **Shringeri**. The Saraswati division is elite in that it is one of the few that will initiate only **brahmins** (the other such divisions are **Ashrama**, **Tirtha**, and part of the **Bharati** order).

Saraswati River
One of the seven sacred rivers of India, along with the **Ganges**, **Yamuna**, **Godavari**, **Narmada**, **Indus**, and **Cauvery**. The Saraswati is particularly interesting because no one is sure exactly where this river is located. A river by this name is mentioned in the hymns of the **Vedas**, the earliest and most authoritative Hindu religious texts, and thus the Saraswati River would seem to have been in the northeastern part of India, in which these hymns are set. In modern times a Saraswati River flows through the northern Indian state of **Haryana** and dries up in the desert of the state of **Rajasthan**. Archaeologists have found extensive settlements from the **Indus Valley civilization** on its banks, indicating that in earlier times the river was an active tributary of the Indus. Popular belief holds that the Saraswati continues to flow underground, and joins the Ganges and Yamuna Rivers at their confluence in **Allahabad**. This reputed confluence of three sacred rivers is the source for one of the site's names, **Triveni** ("triple stream").

Sarmanochegas
According to the Greek writer Strabo, the name of an **ascetic** who was part of a delegation sent to Athens by a king of the **Pandya dynasty**, met by Augustus in

Athens in 20 B.C.E. In Athens, Sarmano-chegas, tired of a life of bondage on earth, committed religious **suicide** by burning himself on a pyre.

Sarvadarshanasangraha

("Collection of all [philosophical] views") A philosophical encyclopedia composed by **Madhava** in the late four-teenth century. In this text, Madhava compiled the views of all the existing philosophical schools, which he placed in hierarchical order, based on his judg-ment of their truth value. The **material-ist** schools were ranked the lowest and least reliable since their proponents completely denied the virtue of any reli-gious life. After this came various Buddhist schools, whose low standing can be attributed to the widespread per-ception that they were nihilists (**nas-tikas**). Madhava then moves through the various Hindu philosophical schools, finishing with the **Advaita Vedanta** school—his own—which was judged the highest and most perfect expression of the truth. Although the Sarvadarshanasangraha is a polemical text with a clear bias, it is one of the few extant sources that considers the per-spectives of all the existing schools.

Sarvam Idam Khalu Brahman

("Truly, this universe is **Brahman**") In the Hindu philosophical tradition, one of the "great utterances" (**mahavakyas**) expressing the ultimate truth, here the sameness of the individual Self (**atman**) with the Supreme Reality (Brahman).

Sarvasvara

Sacrificial rite found in the **Vedas**, the oldest and most authoritative Hindu religious texts. The most notable feature of the sarvasvara is that it involved the **suicide** of the sacrificer, who concluded the rite by entering the sacrificial fire. The sarvasvara is an extreme example of the class of ritual actions known as **kamya karma**, which consists of action performed solely because of the

performer's desire (**kama**) to obtain cer-tain benefits. This element of desire makes kamya karma different from the other two classes of ritual action, **nitya karma** and **naimittika karma**, which were each in some way obligatory. The sarvasvara could be undertaken to obtain any outcome, such as **birth** in **heaven** as a god, or rebirth in a royal family. The sac-rificer declares the benefit in the part of the rite called the **samkalpa**. Although the sarvasvara had extreme elements, it was completely voluntary.

Sashanka

(7th c.) King of Bengal who was an ardent devotee (**bhakta**) of the god **Shiva** and a fierce opponent of Buddhism, which was deeply entrenched in his domain. According to reliable historical reports, Sashanka not only persecuted the Buddhists themselves but also tried to destroy the tree in Bodh **Gaya** under which the Buddha gained enlightenment. This is one of the few well-documented cases of **reli-gious persecution**.

Sat

In Indian philosophical thought, the most basic denotation for "that which (really and truly) exists." The term is a present participle of the verb "to be," so a fairly common translation is "Being," but the word also carries connotations relating to the idea of Truth—that things that exist are both "real" and "true." Sat is the first of the three attributes tradi-tionally ascribed to the unqualified, ulti-mate **Brahman** as **sacchidananda**, along with consciousness (chit) and bliss (**ananda**).

Satavahana Dynasty

Central Indian dynasty whose core area was in the **Deccan** plateau in the west-ern state of **Maharashtra**, and whose capital was in the city of **Paithan**. The Satavahana dynasty was at its peak from the first to the third centuries, when it ruled an area spanning the modern states of **Gujarat**, **Madhya Pradesh**, Maharashtra, **Karnataka**, and **Andhra Pradesh**. It was in the Satavahana domains that the first cave temples were constructed in the **chaitya** and **vihara** architectural styles, which paved the way for later architectural forms.

Satguru

("true **guru**") In the **sant** religious tradition, an epithet (label) that can refer either to the Supreme Being or to a genuinely realized religious teacher, through whose instruction a disciple attains the Supreme Being. The sants were a loose group of central and northern Indian poet-saints who lived between the fifteenth and seventeenth centuries and who shared several general tendencies: stress on individualized and interior religion, leading to a personal experience of the divine; disdain for external ritual, particularly image **worship**; faith in the power of the divine Name; and a tendency to ignore conventional **caste** distinctions. Many of the sants, particularly in northern India, thought of the divine as without qualities (**nirguna**) and beyond human powers of conception. Given these aniconic and occasionally iconoclastic tendencies, it is not surprising that the sant tradition highlights the importance of the spiritual teacher (guru), since the guru's human form is the only image that a disciple has to work with. In human form, the satguru guides the disciple's spiritual practice and thus becomes the vehicle for spiritual attainment. Yet a true guru, according to the tradition, always remains a servant rather than a master, maintaining and transmitting the teaching of his or her particular lineage. The sant notion of the satguru has been adopted into many modern Hindu movements, most notably the **Radha Soami Satsang**.

Sathya Sai Baba

(b. Satya **Narayana** Peddi Venkappa Raju, 1926) Modern Hindu teacher and religious figure who presides as religious teacher (**guru**) over millions of devotees (**bhakta**), both Indian and foreign. He was born in the small village of **Puttaparthi** in the state of **Andhra Pradesh**, where his main **ashram** is still located. He first claimed to be an incarnation of **Shirdi Sai Baba**, a Maharashtrian saint, at thirteen—a move that gave him religious authority and obviated the need to accept a human guru and a spiritual lineage. Sathya Sai Baba has since stated that he will be reincarnated a third time, thus eliminating awkward questions about a successor. His fame rests upon his supposed **magic** powers, particularly the ability to heal and to materialize objects from thin air. Sai Baba has many middle- and upper-class Indian devotees, whom he obliges to perform service (**seva**) to others. Some observers are highly skeptical about his reputed powers and about Sai Baba in general. For further information see Lawrence Babb, "Sathya Sai Baba's Saintly Play," in John Stratton Hawley (ed.), *Saints and Virtues*, 1987; "Sathya Sai Baba and the Lesson of Trust," in *Redemptive Encounters*, 1987; and "Sathya Sai Baba's Miracles," in T. N. Madan (ed.), *Religion in India*, 1991.

Sati

Hindu **goddess**, **daughter** of the demigod **Daksha** and wife of the god **Shiva**, whose death and dismemberment are pivotal incidents in the mythology of both Shiva and the **Goddess**. According to legend, after Sati marries Shiva, her father Daksha feels that Shiva has not shown him proper respect and develops bad feelings toward him. Inflated with pride, Daksha plans a great **sacrifice** to which he invites all the gods but deliberately excludes Shiva. When Sati learns about the sacrifice, she insists that she wants to go, since it is in her natal home. Shiva, after trying to discourage her by pointing out that one should not go without an invitation, finally gives her his permission. When Sati arrives at the sacrificial grounds and asks

Daksha why he has excluded her husband, Daksha responds with a stream of abuse, excoriating Shiva as worthless and despicable. Humiliated by these public insults, Sati commits **suicide**—in some versions, by leaping into the sacrificial **fire**, in others by withdrawing into yogic trance and giving up her life.

Shiva, furious at what has happened, creates the fierce **deity Virabhadra** (or in some versions, Virabhadra and the fierce goddess **Bhadrakali**), and dispatches them to destroy Daksha's sacrifice. They gleefully carry out his command, scattering the guests and killing Daksha. The resulting carnage ends only when the assembled gods praise Shiva as the supreme deity. Daksha is eventually restored to life with the head of a goat, and he too repents his arrogance and worships Shiva. At Daksha's request, Shiva agrees to remain at the sacrificial site forever and sanctify it. Shiva takes the form of a **linga**, the pillar-shaped object that is his symbolic form, and can still be seen at the **Daksha Mahadev** temple in the town of **Kankhal**.

Although Shiva's anger has been pacified by this **worship**, he is disconsolate at Sati's death and wanders the **earth** carrying her body on his shoulders. In his grief, Shiva neglects his divine functions, and the world begins to fall into ruin. The gods, concerned over the world's imminent destruction, go to the god **Vishnu** for help. Vishnu then follows behind Shiva and uses his razor-sharp discus to gradually cut away pieces of Sati's body, until finally there is nothing left. When the body is completely gone, Shiva leaves for the mountains, where he remains absorbed in meditation until it is broken by **Kama**. Sati is reborn as the goddess **Parvati** and later remarries Shiva.

The myth connected with the figure of Sati is important for several reasons. First, it provides the charter myth for the **Shakti Pithas** ("bench of the Goddess"), a network of sites sacred to the Goddess that spreads throughout the subcontinent. Each of these Shakti Pithas—in some lists there are fifty-one, and in others 108—marks the site where a part of Sati's body fell to earth, taking form there as a different goddess. These differing goddesses, spread all over the subcontinent, are thus seen as manifestations of this one primordial goddess, united by the symbolism of the human body. Aside from establishing this network, the myth has several other important messages: It graphically illustrates the supremacy of devotion (in this case, to Shiva) over the older sacrificial cult; it illustrates some of the tensions in the joint family, in which **women** feel the conflict of loyalty between their natal and their marital homes; and it is the charter myth for the **Daksha Mahadev** temple in the town of Kankhal, just south of the sacred city of **Haridwar**, where Daksha's sacrifice is claimed to have taken place. See also **pitha**.

Satkaryavada

One of the three **causal models** in Indian **philosophy**, along with **asatkaryavada** and **anekantavada**. All three models seek to explain the relationship between causes and their effects in the everyday world, which has profound implications for religious life. All the philosophical schools assume that if one understands the causal process correctly, and can manipulate it through one's conscious actions, it is possible to gain final liberation of the soul (**moksha**). Thus, disagreements over different causal models are not merely academic disputes but are grounded in basically different assumptions about the nature of things. The satkaryavada model assumes that effects preexist in their causes, which can thus be seen as transformations (real or apparent) of those causes. The classic example is the transformation of milk to curds, butter, and clarified butter. According to satkaryavada proponents, each of these effects was already present in the cause, and emerges from it through a natural transformation of that cause.

This causal model tends to reduce the number of causes in the universe, since anything can be seen as a transformation of other things. Given these strong

Women singing hymns at a neighborhood temple during a satsang in Ahmedabad, Gujarat.

relationships, if one can understand how these relationships work, they can be manipulated to one's advantage. The disadvantage of this model is that it can lead to **fatalism**. In a world in which everything occurs through natural transformation, it can seem as if the universe is running under its own power, and that human actions may not be able to influence such strong relationships. The philosophical schools espousing this model are the **Samkhyas**, proponents of **Bhedabhada**, **Ramanuja's Vishishthadvaita Vedanta**, and the various branches of **Advaita Vedanta**. The first three believe that the difference between cause and effect is a genuine transformation of the cause, whereas the Advaita school stresses that this transformation is only apparent, and that the real source of bondage (and liberation) lies in **avidya**, the fundamental lack of understanding that causes one to misperceive the nature of things. For further information see Karl H. Potter (ed.), *Presuppositions of India's Philosophies*, 1972.

Satkhyati

("discrimination of the real") **Theory of error** propounded by **Ramanuja**, the eleventh century philosopher who was the founder of **Vishishthadvaita Vedanta**. This theory is also known as yathakhyati ("discrimination [of things]

as they are"). All the theories of error aim to explain why people make errors in judgment, the stock example being mistaking the silvery flash of sea shell for a piece of silver. Ramanuja's analysis is based on the understanding that all things are composed of the five **elements**, and that the different proportions of the elements account for their differences. The viewer is correct in perceiving the silvery flash, since this is a property shared by both shell and silver. The error comes in supposing that the object is silver—that is, taking the part of the judgment that is true, and making an incorrect assumption based on that. As for some of the other theories, the ultimate reason one "sees" silver and not other silvery things comes from karmic dispositions stemming from **avidya**, specifically the greed for silver that prompts us to look for such items of value. For further information see Bijayananda Kar, *Theories of Error in Indian Philosophy*, 1978; Karl H. Potter (ed.), *Presuppositions of India's Philosophies*, 1972.

Satsang

("company of the good") Quasi-congregational meeting and **worship** that was particularly emphasized in devotional (**bhakti**) religious life as a way to

607

associate with fellow devotees (**bhakta**). The word covers an enormous range of activities and contexts, from an informal gathering for singing and conversation in someone's home, to highly orchestrated meetings in which a **guru** may preach to thousands of devotees, and anything in between. In all these cases the importance of satsang lies in the wholesome religious atmosphere generated by the presence of good people, which is believed to create beneficial effects in terms of reinforcing one's own good qualities and reforming one's faults.

Sattan

(7th c.) Tamil poet who was the author of the *Manimegalai*, a text that was clearly written as a sequel to the earlier poem "The Jeweled Anklet" (*Shilappadigaram*). Sattan's story focuses on a young woman named Manimegalai, who was wooed by the local prince but eventually became a Buddhist nun. Although the story's bias clearly favors the Buddhists, the Manimegalai has numerous debates with people from competing religious traditions, thus giving a rounded if somewhat subjective picture of contemporary religious life. See also **Tamil epics** and **Tamil language**.

Sattva

("goodness") One of the three fundamental qualities (**gunas**) believed to be present in all things. The other two gunas are **rajas** ("passion") and **tamas** ("darkness"). According to this model, the differing proportions of these qualities account for the differences between the properties of concrete things, and in individual human capacities and tendencies. Of the three, sattva is invariably positive and carries associations with goodness, truth, wholesomeness, health, cognitive thought, and deep-rooted religious life. The notion of these three gunas originated in the metaphysics of the **Samkhya** school, one of the **six schools** of traditional Hindu **philosophy**. Although much of Samkhya metaphysics connected with the gunas have been long discredited, the idea of the gunas and their qualities has become a pervasive assumption in Indian culture.

Saturday

(Shanivar) The sixth **day** of the Hindu **week**, whose presiding planet is **Saturn** (Shani). Saturn is by far the most feared of all the **planets**, and Saturday is considered by far the most inauspicious day of the week. In Hindu iconography, Saturn is depicted as a terrifying black figure holding a sword and riding a buffalo; he is also considered easily affronted and extremely thorough in avenging any offenses. Any misfortune Saturn brings will last for fourteen years—a figure doubtless drawn from the fourteen years of Saturn's orbit.

Hindus counter this danger by avoidance and **rites of protection**, just as they do on **Tuesday**, the other day considered to be generally inauspicious. Movements and activities are often widely restricted on Saturday, and certain activities, in particular buying things made from iron (whose black color is associated with Saturn), are avoided except when absolutely necessary. As on Tuesday, people **worship** protective **deities** and give as charity (**dana**) items associated with Saturn: iron, mustard oil, black sesame seed, black cloth, and black lentils. Giving away such items associated with Saturn is believed to transfer any potential **inauspiciousness** from Saturn to the recipient, providing a way to get rid of one's bad luck.

Saturn

In Hindu astrology (**jyotisha**), a strongly malevolent **planet** associated with obstruction and death. Saturn's power and malevolent nature make him extremely dangerous, particularly since any misfortune he brings will last for fourteen years—a figure doubtless drawn from the fourteen years of Saturn's orbit. During the **week** Saturn presides over **Saturday**, considered by far the most inauspicious **day** of the week. On this day people refrain from numerous activities and also commonly perform **rites of protection**, such as giving alms (**dana**) as a way to give away any potential misfortune.

Satyabhama

In Hindu mythology, one of the wives of the god **Krishna**, when he has assumed his kingly station as the ruler of **Dwaraka**.

Satyagraha

("Holding Fast to the Truth") Organized campaign of nonviolent resistance or non-cooperation as a political tool, a technique best refined by **Mohandas K. Gandhi**. For Gandhi himself, the basis of this technique was rooted in his commitment to the truth and his conviction that his opponents could be swayed by the **power of truth**, if it was put before them. Gandhi's satyagraha campaigns would begin by publicly pointing out the injustice in question, in the hope that this alone could lead to the matter being rectified. If nothing was done, a campaign would then begin, but the adversary would always be informed of what was to happen next. The real goal was not to humble the adversary but to persuade the other party to see the rightness of one's position and to accept it. The most important thing of all was to retain one's own commitment to the truth and never to compromise it, even if doing so could gain one some immediate advantage. For Gandhi, in the end the truth was the only thing that mattered, and winning or losing could only be measured insofar as one kept this in perspective.

Satyakama

("He whose desire is truth") Legendary figure in the early speculative text **Chandogya Upanishad**, renowned for his adherence to the truth. Desiring to take **initiation** as a celibate student (**brahmacharin**), Satyakama asks his mother about his extended family, so that he can have this information to give his teacher. His mother Jabala replies that she does not know who his father is and tells him to take her name, and call himself Satyakama Jabala. Satyakama, when asked by his teacher **Gautama** to tell about his family roots, tells the whole story. Impressed by his honesty, Gautama initiates him at once. This story is often cited in modern times, to emphasize the importance of one's actions over one's **birth**.

Satyanarayan Vrat

Religious observance that may be observed any day of the month but is most commonly performed on the day of the **full moon**. The presiding **deity** is **Vishnu**, worshiped in his form as Satyanarayan ("Lord of Truth"). The rite is believed to destroy evil and to promote the prosperity of its sponsors (those who hire a **brahmin** to perform the rite), its performers, and even its hearers. The rite's major features involve modification of diet and **worship**, the two general characteristics of most Hindu religious observances. On the day this rite is performed, the observant must keep a strict fast (**upavasa**) until the ceremony is over. A pavilion is prepared in which an image of Satyanarayan is installed and worshiped (part of the worship includes reading the rite's charter myth), and after which **prasad** is given to all those present.

Satyavan

In Hindu mythology, the husband of **Savitri**, a woman famous both for her devotion to her husband and for her cleverness in outwitting Death to regain her husband after he dies.

Satyavati

In Hindu mythology, the mother of the sage **Vyasa**. Satyavati is born in an unusual way. Her mother, a celestial nymph who lives as a fish in the **Ganges** as the result of a **curse**, one day swallows some **semen** that has fallen into the Ganges, becomes pregnant, and delivers a **son** and a **daughter**. Satyavati grows into a beautiful young woman, but because of her origins she always smells of fish, and because of this is also called Matsyagandhi ("fish-scent"). She works ferrying passengers across the Ganges and one day ferries the sage **Parashara**, who is struck by her charms. Parashara creates an artificial fog to give the two of them privacy, has sexual relations with her, and grants that from that day onward Satyavati will smell of musk instead of fish. The son born of this union is Vyasa.

Satyavati continues to ply her trade, and one day ferries King **Shantanu**, who is also struck by her beauty. Before she will marry him she demands that her sons will rule Shantanu's kingdom. Shantanu agrees; and to give her absolute certainty, his son **Bhishma** takes a vow that he will never marry, so that his line will never compete with hers. Satyavati has two sons: Chitrangada dies in childhood, and **Vichitravirya** dies after he marries the princesses **Ambika** and **Ambalika** but before having any children. In desperation, Satyavati thinks of her first son Vyasa, who conceives a son with each of the wives: **Pandu** from Ambalika, and **Dhrtarashtra** from Ambika. The descendants of these two sons are the warring families in the **Sanskrit** epic *Mahabharata*, of which Vyasa is famed as the narrator.

Saumya

("mild") Term used to refer to the **deities** in their benevolent, beneficent, and gentle manifestations, as opposed to their terrifying (**ghora**) manifestations. This distinction is particularly applicable to **Shiva** and the **Goddess**, both of whom can appear in either form and whose **worship** can focus on either aspect.

Saundaryalahari

("waves of beauty") Poetic text dedicated to the praise of the **Goddess** as the supreme power in the universe. The text is traditionally ascribed to the philosopher **Shankaracharya**, who is also believed to have written other hymns in praise of Hindu gods and goddesses, despite being the greatest exponent of the philosophical school known as **Advaita Vedanta**, in which the Supreme Reality, called **Brahman**, is believed to be completely devoid of specific attributes. If Shankaracharya did in fact author these poetic texts, one possible explanation is that Shankaracharya was an intensely religious man and expressed this devotion in various ways. The text has been an enormously influential, particularly in those schools of **tantra** (a secret, ritually based religious practice) in which the Goddess is considered the single Ultimate Reality.

Savaiya

Syllabic **meter** in **Hindi** poetry, composed of four lines of between twenty-two and twenty-six syllables each. Its loose form gives the poet some flexibility, but the challenges of working with such an extended meter place considerable demands on the poet's skill, making this one of the more "literary" meters.

Savarkar, Vinayak Damodar

(1883–1966) Hindu nationalist leader and thinker whose ideas have had lasting influence. Savarkar spent his entire life opposing British rule, often by violent means. He was also virulently opposed to Muslims, whom he saw as invaders and intruders in the Indian homeland. After being expelled from college for organizing a political rally, he spent four years in London, where he and his compatriots learned bomb-making and planned political assassinations. In 1911 he was

Image of the sun god Savitr, more commonly known as Surya, sculpted in Bengal during the Pala dynasty.

sentenced to life imprisonment in the Andaman Islands but was released because of political pressure in 1924, although he was barred from politics until 1937. In the time after that he served for seven years as president of the **Hindu Mahasabha**, until failing health finally forced him to resign. Throughout his life he had sharp differences with **Mohandas Gandhi**, first over the latter's commitment to nonviolence and later over the partition of India, which Savarkar characterized as the "vivisection" of the Indian motherland. Savarkar was brought to trial when Gandhi was assassinated by one of his former associates, **Nathuram Godse**. Savarkar was acquitted, but the accusation had a negative affect on the rest of his life.

Savarkar's keynote work, *Hindutva*, was composed and committed to memory while he was imprisoned in the Andamans. His central thesis was that the Hindus were a nation, despite all of their differences—social, regional, cultural, linguistic, and religious—because for them India was their motherland, fatherland, and holy land. He called on Hindus to transcend the particular identities that divided them and to gain strength through unity to resist the oppression of outsiders. Savarkar's formulation equates Hinduism and Indian nationalism and thus marginalizes both Muslims and Christians as "outsiders." His ideas profoundly influenced **Dr. K. B. Hedgewar**, founder of the **Rashtriya Svayamsevak Sangh** (RSS). The RSS and its affiliates have continued to stress some of Savarkar's ideas, which, during the 1990s, have gained a national audience with the rise of the RSS-affiliated **Bharatiya Janata Party** (BJP). For further information see Lise McKean, *Divine Enterprise*, 1996; and Christophe Jaffrelot, *The Hindu Nationalist Movement in India*, 1996.

Savikalpika

("with conceptions") In certain schools of Indian **philosophy**—among some Buddhists, the **Nyayas**, and the **Prabhakara** school of **Mimamsa**—a term referring to complex conceptual knowledge in which the mind puts together and interprets data from the senses or from memory. Since such knowledge involves the activity of the mind, it is susceptible to error. The opposite sort of knowledge, called **nirvikalpaka**, nonconceptual awareness, is produced directly by the operation of the senses without any interpretation. According to these schools, if the senses producing this awareness have no defect, such an awareness is true.

Savitr

("generator") Epithet of **Surya**, the **sun**, in his aspect as the progenitor and nourisher of all things. This particular name appears in the **Gayatri Mantra**, a sacred formula whose daily recitation is required of all **twice-born** men.

According to the **dharma literature**, a twice-born man was one born into the **brahmin**, **kshatriya**, or **vaishya** communities, who was thus eligible for the adolescent religious **initiation** known as the "second birth." See **Surya**.

Savitri

In Indian culture, a mythic figure and the model for a virtuous and faithful wife, who by her cleverness is able to rescue her husband **Satyavan** from the clutches of Death himself. Before Savitri is betrothed to Satyavan, she has been told that he will die within a **year**. Savitri replies that she has chosen him for her husband and will not be deterred. On the day that he is fated to die, Satyavan goes to the forest to cut wood, accompanied by Savitri. After Satyavan falls unconscious while working, Savitri sees **Yama**, the god of Death, draw out Satyavan's soul and start his journey back to the underworld. Savitri follows them. When Yama tells her that she cannot follow where they are going, she meekly replies that it is her wifely duty to follow her husband. Yama grants her some wishes, although she is forbidden to ask for her husband's life. Savitri first requests that her blind father-in-law shall regain his sight, then that he shall regain the kingdom from which he has been exiled, and finally that she shall have many **sons**. All of these requests are granted, and when she points out that the return of her husband will be necessary for her to have many sons, Yama acknowledges that he has been outwitted, and leaves the two of them to many happy years together.

Savitri Puja

Religious observance on the **new moon** in the **lunar month** of Jyeshth (May–June), celebrating the virtue of **Savitri**, who rescued her husband **Satyavan** from the clutches of **Yama**, the god of Death. This observance is usually kept only by **women**, to promote the health and longevity of their husbands, and thus ensure them a long married life. As a woman whose entire energies were directed toward the well-being of her family, Savitri is a cultural model for Indian women; her ability to save her husband from death demonstrates her virtue and cleverness as well. Women observing this rite **worship** Savitri, Satyavan, and Yama; keep a strict fast (**upavasa**) before the worship; and after worship eat only fruit for the rest of the day.

Sayana

(14th c.) A southern Indian **brahmin** scholar most famous for his commentaries on the **Vedas**, the oldest and most authoritative Hindu religious texts. Sayana's commentary is notable, in part because it is an outstanding scholarly work, but also because this is generally believed to be the first time that the Veda was ever written down, an estimated three thousand years after some of the hymns were composed. Part of Sayana's commentary was simply explanatory because, in the time since the Vedas had been composed, the meanings of many of the words had been forgotten. Sayana's text is noted as a careful and credible clarification of the text.

Sculpture

Branch of the visual arts most important in Hindu religion for its use as decoration in **architecture** and in the construction of images of Hindu **deities** for **worship**. Both these sculptural forms were regulated by precisely defined canons. See also **shilpa shastra**.

Seasons

According to the most traditional enumeration, there are six seasons, each spanning two **lunar months**: Vasanta (spring) in the lunar months of **Chaitra** and **Baisakh**; Grishma (hot season) in **Jyeshth** and **Ashadh**; Varsha (rains) in **Shravan** and **Bhadrapada**; Sharad (fall) in **Ashvin** and **Kartik**; Hemanta (winter) in **Margashirsha** and **Paush**; and

Shishira (late winter) in **Magh** and **Phalgun**. In actual practice, there are three major seasons, at least in northern India: the hot season (April–June), the **monsoon** (July–September), and the cool season (October–March). All these seasons are approximate, because they are ultimately determined by larger climatic phenomena. In the hot season the sun bakes the northern Indian plains, eventually setting in motion air currents that suck moist air north from the Indian ocean; the resulting monsoons break the heat and provide rain for the crops. The weather then gets gradually cooler until January, when it becomes gradually hotter until the hot season returns. The monsoon arrives at different times in different parts of the country—earlier to regions further south, later to regions further north—and at times the monsoons are sporadic or do not come at all. Each of these three seasons has general correlations with certain festivals.

The hot season is a time of gradually increasing heat, and many of the festivals during this time have associations with heat: **Holi**, **Navaratri**, **Ram Navami**, **Shitalashtami**, and **Ganga Dashahara**. Although the rising heat can make life difficult, it is considered a generally auspicious time.

The rainy season is a time of both physical and ritual danger. The sudden influx of rain drives venomous animals such as snakes and scorpions from their holes, and their search for other habitations often brings them into contact with human beings. On a bacteriological level, the runoff from the rains often leads to the contamination of water supplies by sewage and to a sharp rise in sickness and death from gastrointestinal ailments, as well as other infections. On the ritual level, the gods are considered to be sleeping during part of the rainy season and thus less available to protect their devotees (**bhakta**). At the same time, the coming of the rains is greatly anticipated, and the moisture is essential for crops to grow. Consequently, although this is a time of great fertility and abundance, it is also associated with danger, and some of the festivals are **rites of protection**: **Nag Panchami**, **Raksha Bandhan**, **Ganesh Chaturthi**, **Anant Chaturdashi**, and the **Pitrpaksha**. Other ceremonies are associated with water or with the rains, such as the **Shravan** festival and **Janmashtami**.

In the cool season the gods awaken from their sleep, and crops that have been fed by the rains are ready for harvest. This is the most ritually active time of the **year**, and is generally auspicious. Major festivals include the fall Navaratri, ending with the festival of **Dussehra** (Vijaya Dashami), **Diwali**, **Karva Chauth**, **Kartik Purnima**, **Makara Sankranti**, and **Shivaratri**. The last major festival of the year is Holi, which marks the unofficial beginning of the hot season. In ending with Holi, a festival celebrating license, excess, and the dissolution of all social boundaries, followed by an abrupt reestablishment of propriety and social order, the lunar year thus mirrors the cycle of the cosmos, which is subject to degeneration and periodic renewal.

Seed Syllable

A syllable, or set of syllables, that are believed to have an intimate connection with a **deity**—either as a way of gaining access to the deity's power or as the subtlest form of the deity itself. They are seed syllables in that they contain the deity in its briefest form, just as a seed contains the potential for a plant. These seed syllables are called **bijaksharas**. See **bijakshara**.

Self-Residence

In Indian logic, one of the **fallacies** in constructing an argument. Self-residence occurs when the cause and effect are believed to be the same thing. Although the simplest forms of this fallacy are almost never found, since it is so patently unconvincing, one does find extended forms of it, such as **reciprocal dependence**, **vicious circle**, and **infinite regress**.

Self-Revealing Knowledge

In Indian **philosophy**, the notion that certain things, such as knowledge, are self-revealing and do not need proof or substantiation to be known. Whether such knowledge (or things) exists, and what they would be if they did, was a source of lively disagreement among Indian thinkers. See **svaprakasha**.

Self-Validating Knowledge

In Indian **philosophy**, a name denoting a sort of knowledge believed to carry its own stamp of truth, which does not need to be verified by anything outside itself. See **svatahpramanya**.

Semen

As with all bodily fluids, semen is considered to make a person ritually impure through emission or contact, although it is obviously necessary for procreation, which is an auspicious event. Semen is also considered the concentrated essence of a man's vital energy, distilled drop by drop from his **blood**; in Hindu mythology the semen from the gods is portrayed as having wondrous generative powers, as in the story of the god **Skanda**, who spontaneously developed when the god **Shiva's** semen fell on the ground. Although a married man is obliged to have intercourse with his wife at certain times during her menstrual cycle, this is also seen as a potentially dangerous depletion of his vital energy. Since in Indian culture women are seen as having stronger sex drives than men, men are faced with the constant demand on their resources, which must be carefully husbanded to maintain their vitality. This problem of depletion is particularly pronounced in the unusual case when a man is younger than his wife, for in that case her needs are believed to be far greater than his capacity. Because all seminal emission depletes one's vital forces, there are strict taboos on masturbation, which is seen not only as an abject surrender to one's baser instincts, but as posing actual physical danger.

Sen

(15th c.) Poet and saint of the **Varkari Panth**, a religious community centered around the **worship** of the Hindu god **Vithoba**. According to tradition, Sen was a barber—a very low-**caste** occupation—at the court of the king of Bidar. Sen renounced this occupation to wander and sing Vithoba's praises. Little is known about him, but he is mentioned as a model of devotion in one of the hymns by the northern Indian poet-saint **Ravidas**, which indicates that he was well known outside **Maharashtra**. For traditional hagiography, see Justin Abbott and Narhar R. Godbole, *Stories of Indian Saints*, 1988.

Sen, Keshub Chander

(d. 1884) Reformist Hindu and leader of the **Brahmo Samaj**, to which he gave most of his life. His emphases on the ideal of ethical monotheism and rejection of many rituals were heavily influenced by English Unitarianism. In 1865, the Samaj split over Keshub's insistence that members should no longer wear the **sacred thread**. Then in 1878 Keshub had an inexplicable lapse in principles when he arranged for the marriage of his thirteen year-old **daughter**. Most of his followers left him in protest, and he spent his remaining years creating what he called the New Dispensation, a new religion using elements drawn from various religious traditions. At his death he had few followers but had been influential through his earlier efforts to reform Hindu society, and to look critically at Christian culture and religion. In his curiosity for religious ideas, he happened to meet the Bengali mystic **Ramakrishna**, and it was through association with Keshub that Ramakrishna began to attract disciples from Calcutta's middle class, most notably Narendranath Datta, who became famous as **Swami Vivekananda**.

Sena Dynasty

(11th–13th c.) Eastern Indian dynasty whose ancestral homeland was in the Bengal region but whose territory also

The ashram established by Mohandas K. Gandhi in Sevagram, Maharashtra.

included the western part of the state of **Bihar**. The Senas were originally vassals of the **Pala dynasty** but became independent in 1097 and later seized much of the Pala domain in Bihar. The Sena dynasty survived until 1245, when it was finally conquered by the Mamluks, who had been seizing Sena territory since the beginning of that century. The Senas (and their predecessors, the Palas) are particularly noted for a certain type of **sculpture** in which the images were carved from black chlorite schist that was polished to a mirror finish.

Setubandha

("Building the Bridge") Early medieval poem whose theme is taken from the epic *Ramayana* and describes **Rama's** invasion of **Lanka** by building a bridge across the ocean straits. The poem is written in **Prakrit**, an umbrella term for the grammatically simpler vernacular languages that developed from **Sanskrit** through natural linguistic change. The poem has been falsely ascribed to **Kalidasa**, the greatest Sanskrit poet. The true author is unknown.

Seva

("service") Actions springing from an attitude of loving devotion, manifested as attendance on and service to a **deity**, religious teacher (**guru**), or any superior person. The notion of seva is particularly important in the relationship between religious teacher and disciple. The teacher's task is to further the disciple's spiritual development, which may sometimes entail harsh criticism to reform some of the disciple's faults. The ideal disciple will accept such direction in a spirit of self-effacement and carry out the teacher's instructions faithfully and without protest, as a sign of submission and service. Such arrangements are often necessary for spiritual growth, and a teacher can often give a much more objective assessment of the disciple's true spiritual state and what must be done for advancement. Still, when one of the parties is not sincere, this model has great potential for abuse. In such circumstances the teacher's call for obedience and service—in which any "resistance" to the teacher's demands can be cited as a sign of spiritual immaturity—can be a way to take advantage of a devotee (**bhakta**).

Sevagram

("service village") City in the eastern part of the state of **Maharashtra** about fifty miles south and west of **Nagpur**. It is most famous for the **ashram** established there by **Mohandas K. Gandhi** in 1933, which was founded to promote his ideal of a decentralized village economy. This economic model had political and cultural symbolism, since it was independent of the industrialized economy run by the British and intended to counterbalance it by providing a model of an economy based on indigenous "Hindu" values.

Seven Sacred Cities

Seven sacred cities (**tirthas**) spread throughout the Indian subcontinent in which death is traditionally believed to bring final liberation of the soul (**moksha**). The seven cities are **Ayodhya**, **Mathura**, **Haridwar**, **Benares**, **Kanchipuram**, **Ujjain**, and **Dwaraka**.

Shabara

In the **Purva Mimamsa** school of Hindu **philosophy** Shabara was the author of the earliest and most famous commentary on **Jaimini's *Mimamsa Sutras***, the school's founding text. The commentary is called Shabara-**bhashya**. The date of the text is highly uncertain, and estimates range from the first century B.C.E. to the fourth or sixth century C.E. As often happens, later commentators have accepted Shabara's commentary as part of the text itself and commented on it as well as on the original sutras.

Shabarabhashya

("**Shabara's** commentary") Extensive commentary on the ***Mimamsa Sutras*** of **Jaimini**, the founding text of the **Purva Mimamsa** school of **philosophy**. The date of the text is uncertain. It is believed to have been written by Shabara in either the first century B.C.E., or the fourth or sixth century C.E. As often happens, later commentators have accepted Shabara's commentary as part of the text itself and commented on it as well as on the original sutras.

Shabari

In the ***Ramayana***, the earlier of the two great Indian epics, a tribal woman who is a sincere devotee (**bhakta**) of the god **Rama**. Shabari belongs to a group known as the Shabaras, and so her name conveys a sense of anonymity, since it is simply the feminine form of the group's name. Rama and **Lakshmana** stop for some time at Shabari's dwelling during their search for Rama's kidnapped wife **Sita**. Although as a tribal she has very low social status, Rama graciously receives her hospitality as a reward for the devotion with which it is given. In the ***Ramcharitmanas***, the vernacular retelling of the ***Ramayana*** written by the poet-saint **Tulsidas** (1532–1623?), Shabari tastes each fruit before she gives it to Rama, to be sure that he will get only the very sweetest—an act that violates one of the most pervasive ritual taboos barring the exchange of any food that has come into contact with saliva, and particularly from lower to higher status people. Yet in the story Rama eats the fruits very happily because of the love with which they are given. The message in this episode is consistent with a primary theme in the ***Ramcharitmanas***, namely, the power of devotion to override or overturn conventional social norms. Soon after Rama and Lakshmana's visit, Shabari dies a happy death.

Shabari Malai

Temple and sacred site (**tirtha**) in the hills of the southern state of **Kerala**, about seventy miles north of Trivandrum. Shabari Malai is renowned for the temple to **Aiyappa**, a regional divinity who has been assimilated into the larger pantheon as the son of the gods **Vishnu** and **Shiva**; he is born when Vishnu takes the form of the enchantress **Mohini**. Shabari Malai's annual month-long pilgrimage occurs from the middle of December to the middle of January, with the exact dates determined by astrological calculations.

This pilgrimage is most often taken by men, since, according to the charter myth, the site is forbidden to **women** of childbearing age. The pilgrimage itself is a highly structured ritual process. Pilgrims carry out their spiritual training for the journey in well-defined village groups, each headed by a local leader, who supervises their strict religious discipline. Their preparatory vows commence forty-five to sixty days before the actual journey begins, and entail strict **celibacy** and avoiding the company of women, distinctive dress, a ban on **shaving** and wearing shoes, a strict vegetarian diet, daily **worship**, and the erasing of all social and status distinctions among members. In essence, the men training for this pilgrimage live as renunciant ascetics for this period and later revert to their normal identities. The pilgrimage itself is an arduous and exhausting journey over the twisted ridges of the Periyar Hills, during which pilgrims symbolically divest themselves of their egos, to be filled with the **grace** of God. For a first person account of the Shabari Malai pilgrimage, see E. Valentine Daniel, *Fluid Signs*, 1984.

Shabda

("word") In Indian **philosophy**, the general term for authoritative testimony. This is generally accepted as one of the **pramanas**, the means by which human beings can gain true and accurate knowledge, except by the **materialists**, who reject all pramanas except perception (**pratyaksha**). Such authoritative testimony is of two sorts. It most often refers to authoritative scriptural texts, such as the **Vedas**, but it can also refer to verbal instruction given by one's **guru**, which is considered to have equal authority, at least by members of that spiritual lineage. Shabda is an important **pramana** because it tells people about those things that the other pramanas cannot uncover, such as the nature of the

heavens, the course of the soul after death, proper religious life, and so forth. With regard to the liberation of the soul, it is often the most important pramana, since this cannot be discovered in any other way.

Shabdabrahman

("**Brahman**-as-sound") This term refers to the notion that the Supreme Reality (Brahman) exists in its most subtle form, not as matter, but as sound. This idea is particularly prevalent in **tantra**, a secret, ritually based system of religious practice, and helps to explain the tantric stress on **mantra**, or sacred sound, as the essential means through which one gains access to this reality. In this understanding, the primary mantra (**mula-mantra**) of one's particular **deity** would be the clearest articulation of shabdabrahman, with other mantras conceived as derivative forms of that primary mantra; these latter mantras were the source for everyday speech and the mundane sounds of ordinary experience.

Shachi

In Hindu mythology, the wife of the god **Indra**, also known as **Indrani**. See **Indrani**.

Shaddarshana

("six perspectives") Collective name for the **six schools** of classical Hindu **philosophy**. These six were usually grouped in three pairs: **Nyaya** and **Vaisheshika**, **Samkhya** and **Yoga**, and **Purva Mimamsa** and **Vedanta**. See **six schools**.

Shaiva

Devotee (**bhakta**) of the Hindu god **Shiva**, who along with **Vishnu** is one of the major figures in the Hindu pantheon. From the evidence at hand, it seems that the earliest sectarian Shaivites were the **Kapalikas**, **Kalamukhas**, and

Pashupatas. All three of these were communities of renunciant **ascetics**, perhaps to accord with the example set by their patron deity. The information for all three must be reconstructed, since the sects have all disappeared. Shaivas can still be found in ascetic life in the **Dashanami Sanyasis** and the **Nathpanthis**, two living ascetic communities. The major current through which Shaiva devotionalism (**bhakti**) came into mainstream society was through the devotional hymns of the **Nayanars**, a group of sixty-three poet-saints who lived in southern India in the seventh and eighth centuries. Their passionate devotion, conveyed in hymns in the **Tamil language**, was later systematized into the southern Indian philosophical school known as **Shaiva Siddhanta**. As the bhakti movement moved northward, it found Shaiva expression in the **Lingayat** community in modern **Karnataka**, as well as the Krama and **Trika** schools of Kashmiri Shaivism. Shaivism has had a long association with **tantra**, a secret, ritually based religious practice, and the influence of tantra is evident in the Kashmiri schools as well as in the doctrines of the Nathpanthi ascetics.

Shaivism does not show the bewildering sectarian variety characterizing **Vaishnavas**, devotees of the god **Vishnu**, and Shaivites tend to be less strict about membership in a particular sect. Nevertheless, Shiva has millions of devotees in modern India, and a well-established network of pilgrimage places (**tirtha**), particularly in the **Himalayas**.

Shaiva Nagas

Naga ("naked," i.e., fighting) ascetics who are devotees (**bhakta**) of the god **Shiva**, organized into different **akharas** or regiments on the model of an army. The other major Naga division was the **Bairagi** Nagas, who were devotees of the god **Vishnu**. Until the beginning of the nineteenth century the Nagas' primary occupation was as mercenary soldiers, although they also had substantial trading interests. Such resources allowed many Naga leaders to become rich and powerful men despite often coming from lower social strata, and in earlier times such opportunities would have made a career as a Naga an attractive proposition for an ambitious young man. Both these sources of income have largely disappeared in contemporary times, although some Naga communities are still landowners with extensive properties and thus both rich and influential. See also **shaiva**.

Shaiva Siddhanta

Southern Indian religious community that was particularly developed in the Tamil country, and whose members are devotees (**bhakta**) of the god **Shiva**. Shaiva Siddhanta is based on a series of fourteen texts, all completed by the fourteenth century C.E., in which the ideas about Shiva found in **Sanskrit** texts were reinterpreted in light of the devotional faith of the **Nayanars**. The Nayanars were a group of sixty-three poet-saints who lived in southern India in the seventh and eighth centuries. The most famous and influential of these interpreters was the ninth-century poet **Manikkavachakar**. Central to Shaiva Siddhanta is the triad of Shiva as the "Lord" (**pati**), human souls held in bondage (**pashu**), and the "bonds" (**pasha**) holding these souls. Shiva is conceived as the supreme divinity, who wields the bonds of **maya**, or illusion, to keep souls in bondage. Yet he is also pictured as gracious and loving to his devotees, a far cry from the capricious and somewhat dangerous figure in his earliest mythology. As the supreme lord, Shiva is the source of all spiritual illumination and energy, and also the power through which the world is created, sustained, and reabsorbed again. Souls are conceived as different from Shiva, since they are subject to imperfections, although here too his power is their ultimate source. The only path to liberation is devotion to Shiva, through whose **grace** the bonds of maya can be broken or transcended. Even after liberation souls remain distinct from Shiva, although they remain in his presence. For further information see M. Dhavamony, *Love of God According to Saiva Siddhanta*, 1971. See also **shaiva** and **Tamil Nadu**.

Shaka ("Teak") Dvipa

In traditional mythic geography, the sixth of the seven concentric landmasses (**dvipas**) making up the visible world. See also **cosmology**.

Shaka Era

One of the dating systems in India, which is claimed to mark the defeat of the Shakas by King Salivahana. For any given **year** in the common era, the Shaka era date is either seventy-eight or seventy-nine years earlier, a discrepancy that stems from the differing days on which the years begin in these two systems. In the common era the year begins on January 1, but in the Shaka era it begins with the **sun's** transition into Aries, determined in India as falling on April 14. Hence, to convert a Shaka era date to a common era date, one adds seventy-nine years for dates from January 1 to April 14, and seventy-eight years for dates from April 15 to December 31.

Shakata

("cart") One of the **demon** assassins sent by **Kamsa**, the demon-king of **Mathura**, to kill his nephew, the child-god **Krishna**. Shakata takes the form of a cart, intending to take the infant Krishna unaware. Yet Krishna is not fooled by this deception: With a kick of his infant toes Krishna launches the cart into flight, killing the demon with the force of the blow.

Shakha

("branch") The name given to a local "branch" of the **Rashtriya Svayamsevak Sangh** (RSS), whose membership is often drawn from a particular neighborhood or section of a city. The RSS is a conservative Hindu organization whose express purpose is to provide the leadership cadre for a revitalized Hindu India. The RSS has historically characterized itself as a cultural and character-building organization, and for much of its existence has shunned direct political involvement, although it has exercised considerable influence through its many affiliated organizations. Each shakha, or local RSS unit, holds a daily meeting for its members, who are known as **svayamsevaks** ("volunteers"). The meeting's typical activities include an opening ceremony in which the organization's saffron banner is raised; traditional games or exercises, including martial drill, and a discussion period in which RSS ideals can be disseminated and propagated. The shakhas in any given area are overseen by a full-time RSS worker known as a **pracharak** ("director"), who serves as a liaison between the local units and the RSS leadership, and who oversees RSS activity in his area. Most of the shakha's members will never advance beyond this local level, and those who do are usually gifted leaders. Thus, the primary stress at the shakha level is on forming personal relationships with other members, as a way to develop loyalty to the organization. Although the shakhas often have very high attrition, the bonds developed there are often very strong as well and are particularly beneficial in helping displaced and newly urbanized people develop a sense of community. For further information see Walter K. Andersen and Shridhar D. Damle, *The Brotherhood in Saffron*, 1987.

Shakra

An epithet of the god **Indra**. See **Indra**.

Shakta

Worshiper of the **Goddess** in any of her myriad forms. The name itself is derived from **shakti**, the divine feminine "power" that gives the Goddess her vitality. Among the most famous forms of the Goddess are **Durga** and **Kali**, who are both powerful and dangerous goddesses. Aside from these, there are a host of other goddesses, who are often the presiding **deities** of a particular place. See also **Lakshmi**, **Nirriti**, **Parvati**, **Prithvi**, **Sati**, **Shiwalik goddesses**, and **Ushas**.

Shakti

("power") In Hindu iconography, the name of the spear carried by the god **Skanda**. The spear's head is shaped either like a leaf or a diamond, and it is fitted with a wooden shaft.

Shakti

(2) Epithet of the **Goddess**. Shakti is believed to be a divine feminine power that is present in each person as the **kundalini**. See also **Goddess** and **kundalini**.

Shakti Pithas

("benches" or "seats" of Shakti) General term for a network of sites connected with the **worship** of the Mother **Goddess**. Although their number differs from source to source— some list fifty-one, and others 108—in both cases the sites are spread throughout the subcontinent, from Baluchistan (in modern Pakistan) to **Assam** to the deep south. According to the charter myth, each of these places marks the site where a body part of the dismembered goddess **Sati** fell to **earth**, taking form as a different goddess in each place. This myth provides a way to connect the myriad local Hindu goddesses by conceiving them as differing manifestations of a single primordial Goddess. It also connects the subcontinent into a single conceptual unit, knit together by this network of sites as the body is connected by its members. One should also note that different places may claim the same body part in the drive to enhance the religious prestige of any particular site. As but one example, according to most "official" lists Sati's vulva, the most powerfully charged part of the female body, fell at the temple of **Kamakhya** in **Assam**, but the same claim is made at **Kalimath** in the **Himalayas**. Suffice it to say that there is no single authoritative list of sites, and competing claims are not unusual. See also **pitha**.

Shakumbhari Devi

Presiding **deity** of the Shakumbhari Devi temple in the district of Saharanpur in **Uttar Pradesh**, and one of the nine **Shiwalik goddesses**. This site is one of the **Shakti Pithas**, a network of sites sacred to the **Goddess** that spreads throughout the subcontinent. Each Shakti Pitha marks the site where a body part of the dismembered goddess **Sati** fell to **earth**, taking form there as a different goddess; in the case of Shakumbhari Devi, the body part is said to have been Sati's head. The temple is in a thinly settled region, and the major time of **year** that pilgrims come to visit is during the **Navaratri** festivals.

Although **Hindi** literature identifies Shakumbhari Devi as a form of **Durga**, the site's charter myth shows the nurturing capacities of the Goddess as well as the warrior aspect more commonly associated with Durga. According to the story, a **demon** named Durgam gains the boon that he cannot be conquered by any of the gods. After subduing all the gods, Durgam prevents the storm-god **Indra** from sending rain to the earth for one hundred years. Seeing the earth's distress, the gods approach the Goddess and beg for her help. The Goddess, filled with pity, takes a form with one hundred eyes, because of which one of her epithets is Shatakshi ("hundred eyes"). From each eye comes a stream of tears, and when these fall to the earth, plants begin to grow again. Further, when her tears do not reach some places, she puts forth vegetables (Shak) from her own body to nourish the creatures of the earth. Her final action is to kill the demon Durgam, reasserting the Goddess as a strong and protective figure. Although there is little information on Shakumbhari Devi in English, there are further references to her in David R. Kinsley, *Hindu Goddesses*, 1986. See also **pitha**.

Shakuni

In the *Mahabharata*, the later of the two great Hindu epics, the maternal uncle of **Duryodhana**, the epic's antagonist. Shakuni's most famous episode in the *Mahabharata* is as a player in the game of dice against **Yudhishthira**, the eldest of the five **Pandava** brothers who are the epic's protagonists. The epic describes Shakuni as the world's best dice player, whereas Yudhishthira is enthusiastic but completely unskilled. As Yudhishthira begins to lose, he keeps betting bigger and bigger stakes in an effort to win back what he has lost. After losing his family's kingdom and all their possessions, Yudhishthira wagers himself and his brothers, and after losing this bet, he wagers and loses their common wife, **Draupadi**. As a result, Draupadi is paraded through the assembly hall by Shakuni's nephews, Duryodhana and **Duhshasana**, her clothes stained with her menstrual blood, sharpening the already strong enmities between these two groups. Shocked at such treatment, Duryodhana's father, King **Dhrtarashtra**, gives the Pandavas back their freedom. Then, because of a loss in a subsequent game of dice, the Pandavas agree to go into exile for twelve years and live incognito for the thirteenth, with the condition that, if they are discovered in the thirteenth year, the cycle will begin anew. In the ensuing Mahabharata war Shakuni fights on the side of his nephew and is eventually killed by the fourth Pandava brother, **Sahadeva**.

Shakuntala

A figure in Hindu mythology and the protagonist in the drama *Abhijnana-shakuntala* written by the poet **Kalidasa**. Shakuntala is the daughter of the **apsara Menaka** and the sage **Vishvamitra**, conceived when Menaka is sent to seduce Vishvamitra in an attempt to reduce his spiritual powers. Shakuntala is raised at the **ashram** of the sage Kanva, where she grows into a beautiful young woman. One day she attracts the eye of King **Dushyanta**, who has been hunting in the forest, and they are married by the **gandharva** form of marriage (consensual sexual intercourse), conceiving their son **Bharata**. Shakuntala's happiness, however, is short-lived. As she is thinking one day about Dushyanta, who has traveled back to his capital without her, she fails to notice the arrival of the sage **Durvasas**. In his anger at being ignored, Durvasas lays a curse that her beloved will completely forget her. Shakuntala, horrified, manages to convince Durvasas to modify the **curse**: Dushyanta will remember everything, as soon as Shakuntala shows him proof of their union. Shakuntala has Dushyanta's signet ring as proof, but she loses it on her way to see Dushyanta. Dushyanta (as expected) denies that he has ever met Shakuntala, and she eventually ends up working as one of the palace cooks. Her salvation comes unexpectedly, when she finds the missing ring in the belly of a fish she is preparing for the king's dinner. When she shows him the ring, Dushyanta immediately recognizes Shakuntala and acknowledges her as his wife, and the couple live happily ever after.

Believed to be a manifestation of the god Vishnu, a shalagram is a black stone that contains the fossilized spiral shell of a prehistoric sea creature.

Shalagram

Black stone containing an **ammonite**, the spiral-shaped fossil shell of a prehistoric sea creature. The shalagram is primarily found in the upper reaches of the **Gandaki** River in **Nepal**. The circular ammonite fossil is understood to be **Vishnu's chakra**, and the shalagram is thus understood as a "self-manifest" (**svayambhu**) form of Vishnu. As with all such "self-manifest" forms, the shalagram is believed to be especially holy, since in it Vishnu has chosen to reveal himself to his devotees (**bhakta**) rather than coming to an image fashioned by human hands. Because of its holiness, the shalagram is often an object of **worship**. Its portability (and durability) made it the preferred form of Vishnu for wandering **Vaishnava** ascetics. One also finds cases in which small images are claimed to have been revealed when a shalagram was broken open; these images carry the glamour of a finished image as well as the **divine power** that accompanies spontaneous manifestation.

Shambhu

("causing happiness," "granting prosperity") Epithet of the god **Shiva**. See **Shiva**.

Shamvuka

Shudra ascetic who appears both in the *Ramayana*, the earlier of the two great Indian epics, and in the poet **Kalidasa's** *Raghuvamsha*, whose story line is based on the *Ramayana*. According to the story a **brahmin** comes to **Rama**, the epic's protagonist, and complains that his son has died because of the unrighteousness running through the land. Since the king is considered responsible for the general moral climate in his kingdom, Rama immediately asks the brahmin for more information. He is told that a man named Shamvuka has been doing physical **asceticism** (**tapas**) in a bid to generate spiritual powers through his suffering, even though Shamvuka is a member of the servant (**shudra**) class, and these sorts of religious exercises are forbidden to people of such low social status. Rama finds Shamvuka hanging his head downward over a smoking **fire**, and when he refuses to desist from his ascetic practices, Rama kills him. This episode conveys several important messages. One of these is the Indian cultural belief that physical suffering generates spiritual and/or **magic** powers. When this belief is combined with a profoundly hierarchical model of society, it becomes important for the higher-class people to control the people who are allowed to do this, lest the lower classes gain power over their "betters." Finally, this story shows the *Ramayana*'s general tendency to uphold established social values and boundaries.

Shankara

("auspicious") Epithet of the god **Shiva**. With the honorific suffix *acharya* ("teacher"), this is also the name of the most significant figure in the **Advaita Vedanta** philosophical school, **Shankaracharya**, who is popularly considered to be Shiva incarnate. As noted above, the generally accepted meaning of the name

Shankara has intensely positive connotations, yet the verb *shank*, from which this name is almost certainly derived, has associations with doubt, uncertainty, and anxiety. This sort of ambivalence has a long association with Shiva; the earliest accepted reference, in the **Shvetashvatara Upanishad**, mentions both his death-dealing arrows, and his kindness to his devotees (**bhakta**). The traditional meaning of this name may thus be a form of propitiation—knowing that Shiva wields awesome and unpredictable power but describing him as "auspicious" in the hope that he will show his kinder side.

Shankaracharya

(788–820?) Writer and religious thinker who is unquestionably the most significant figure in the **Advaita Vedanta** philosophical school, and arguably the single greatest Hindu religious figure. Very little is known about his life—even his dates are a matter of speculation—but popular tales abound. According to one story, he was the god **Shiva** incarnate, who descended to earth to reveal the knowledge of the absolute. This connection is shown by his name—**Shankara** is one of the epithets of Shiva, and **acharya** ("teacher") is an honorific suffix. He is traditionally believed to have been born in a **Nambudiri brahmin** family at Kaladi in the state of **Kerala**, to have become an **ascetic** at a very young age, and to have traveled widely engaging in religious disputes, particularly with the Buddhists, whose religious influence he put in permanent decline. He is believed to have established the ten **Dashanami Sanyasi** orders and the four **maths** that are their centers, to have written commentaries on the three texts central to the Vedanta school—namely the **Upanishads**, the *Vedanta Sutras*, and the **Bhagavad Gita**—and to have gone finally to the high **Himalayas**, where he died at the age of 32.

Many of these claims cannot be substantiated, but the significance of his work cannot be denied. His commentary on the *Vedanta Sutra*s, the **Brahmasutra Bhashya**, gives the classic formulation of Advaita Vedanta, with its emphasis that the Ultimate Reality is the unqualified (**nirguna**) **Brahman**, which is eternal and unchanging, and to which the human soul is identical. The changing phenomenal world (the world we see and sense) is an illusion, created through the superimposition (**adhyasa**) of mistaken ideas upon the unqualified Brahman. Since Shankaracharya believes that one is released from bondage by replacing this mistaken understanding with the correct one, insight and not action is the means to liberation. This moment of understanding can be described as a flash of realization, but it seems mistaken to characterize Shankaracharya as a mystic. This is because he strongly emphasizes the authority of the sacred texts as a source of accurate knowledge about the ultimate truth. Although this stress on insight devalues the ultimate worth of ritual action, except in a preparatory role by removing defilements, Shankaracharya also believed that required ritual actions should be performed from a sense of duty.

Shankaracharya is as philosophically significant for his silence as for his speech. He gives no definitive answer on many philosophical issues: about whether selves are one or many, about whether the locus of ignorance (**avidya**) was Brahman or the individual, about the nature of ignorance itself, and about the real nature of the material world. His refusal to take a position on these issues left many different routes open to those who came after him. Shankaracharya himself tended to emphasize epistemological issues—how human beings come to know things, and particularly how to correct the mistaken ideas through which human beings are held in bondage. The image that comes through his writing is of a deeply religious man whose primary concern was

A shankha, or conch shell. Used as a musical instrument, it is an identifying object carried by the god Vishnu.

to help his hearers destroy their illusions and gain final liberation of the soul (**moksha**). Given this underlying goal and his acute philosophical mind, one can argue that he was aware of such metaphysical questions but chose to ignore them, since they were unrelated to his primary goal. For further information on Shankaracharya's thought, see Sarvepalli Radhakrishnan and Charles A. Moore (eds.), *A Sourcebook in Indian Philosophy*, 1957; and Karl H. Potter (ed.), *Advaita Vedanta up to Samkara and His Pupils*, 1981.

Shankaracharyas

The philosopher **Shankaracharya** (788–820) is traditionally said to have established centers for the **Dashanami Sanyasi** ascetics, devotees (**bhakta**) of the god **Shiva**, at four places in India: **Badrinath**, **Puri**, **Shringeri**, and **Dwaraka**. The head monk at each of these centers has been given the title *Shankaracharya*, as a sign of the status of his office. The head of the **Kamakotipith**, an **ascetic** center in the southern Indian city of **Kanchipuram**, has also come to be described as a Shankaracharya, even though this site is not one of the original four; this reflects the Kamakotipith's importance as an ascetic center and Kanchipuram's general status as a religious center. Although by this reckoning there are five places, at present there are only four Shankaracharyas, since Swami Swaroopanand Saraswati holds the seat for both Badrinath and Dwaraka. The other Shankaracharyas are Swami Nishchalanand (Puri), Swami Bharati Tirtha (Shringeri), and Swami Jayendra Saraswati (Kanchipuram). Their traditional office gives the Shankaracharyas a great deal of religious status and prestige, and because of this they have become highly influential figures, even in an intensely decentralized religious tradition.

Shankaradigvijaya

("**Shankara's** victory tour") A written account of the life of the philosopher **Shankaracharya** traditionally attributed to the fourteenth-century writer Madhavacharya, although evidence within the work points to composition several centuries later. The story is clearly hagiographical, for it is filled with fantastic legends intended to highlight Shankaracharya's achievements and his ultimate identity with the god **Shiva** himself. According to this story, after gaining full wisdom, Shankaracharya embarks on a "victory tour" (digvijaya) of India. During this tour he travels throughout the country, debates all opponents, and defeats them all convincingly, thus establishing the supremacy of his **Advaita Vedanta** philosophical school. The motif of the digvijaya (literally, "conquest of [all] directions") was a common theme in works about political and military leaders, and here it has been adapted to tell a religious story.

Shankha

("conch shell") In Hindu religious imagery, one of the identifying objects always carried by the god **Vishnu**, along with the club (**gada**), lotus (**padma**), and discus (**chakra**). Vishnu's conch is considered both a musical instrument and an instrument of war, since through its powerful sound he is said to have struck terror in the hearts of his enemies. The conch is also commonly carried by certain powerful forms of the **Goddess**. The reason for this can be found in her charter myth, in which she is formed from the collected radiance of all the gods and receives duplicates of all their weapons.

Shanta ("peaceful") Bhava

The first of the five **modes of devotion** to God that were most prominently articulated by **Rupa Goswami**, a devotee (**bhakta**) of the god **Krishna** and a follower of the Bengali saint **Chaitanya**. Rupa used five different models of human relationships to explain the variety of links followers might have with the **deities**. These five models showed growing emotional intensity, from the peaceful (shanta) sense that comes from realizing one's complete identity with **Brahman**, or Supreme Reality, to conceiving of god as one's master, friend, child, or lover. The shanta bhava, in which one finds mental peace through the realization of complete identity with Brahman, is the only one of these modes in which the devotee does not have a personalized relationship with God. Given Rupa's assumption that Krishna was the highest manifestation of godhead, and that true religious life involved having a relationship with him, the shanta bhava was thus judged inferior to the other four modes.

Shantanu

In the *Mahabharata*, the later of the two great **Sanskrit** epics, Shantanu is the father of **Bhishma** by his first wife, and the husband of **Satyavati** in his second marriage. Satyavati has agreed to marry Shantanu on the condition that her sons reign, despite the fact that Bhishma is the eldest and thus is rightly entitled to the throne. Shantanu agrees to this condition, and to please his father Bhishma

vows never to marry, so that he will have no heirs to compete with Satyavati's. Bhishma upholds his promise until his death, but Shantanu's willingness to put aside the rightful heir has terrible consequences. When Satyavati's son **Vichitravirya** dies childless, she calls on her elder son **Vyasa** to sire children by his wives. From this union comes **Pandu** and **Dhrtarashtra**. The struggle for royal power by their respective sons culminates in the Mahabharata war, in which the family is destroyed.

Shantiniketan

("abode of peace") Town in the Birbhum district of **West Bengal**, about ninety miles northeast of Calcutta. It is most famous for Vishva-Bharati University, founded in 1921 by the Indian poet and Nobel laureate **Rabindranath Tagore** (1861–1941). As an educational institution, the university was dedicated to providing an education that would satisfy people's material and spiritual needs and thus develop an integrated human being. It did this in part by promoting the arts and by stressing the interconnection between nature and human beings, both themes that were close to Tagore's heart.

Sharada Math

One of the four **maths** or sacred centers for Hindu **ascetics** (often translated as "monasteries") traditionally believed to have been established by the great philosopher **Shankaracharya**; the others are the **Jyotir Math**, **Shringeri Math**, and **Govardhan Math**. These four sacred centers are each associated with one of the four geographical corners of the Indian subcontinent; the Sharada Math is in the western quarter, in the city of **Dwaraka** in the state of **Gujarat**, on the shore of the Arabian Sea. Shankaracharya is traditionally cited as the founder of the **Dashanami Sanyasis**, the most prestigious Hindu ascetic order. The Dashanami ("ten names") ascetics are devotees (**bhakta**) of the god

Shiva who are divided into ten divisions, each with a different name. These ten divisions are organized into four larger organizational groups—**Anandawara**, **Bhogawara**, **Bhuriwara**, and **Kitawara**—each of which has two or three of the ten divisions and is associated with one of the four maths. Of these, the Sharada Math is associated with the Kitawara group.

Sharva

(from *shara*, "arrow") Epithet of the god **Shiva**. In his earliest description in the **Shvetashvatara Upanishad**, the god **Rudra** (later identified with Shiva) is identified as a god whose primary weapons are infallible arrows. This characterization of Shiva as an archer has continued ever since; his bow **Pinaka** is one of few divine weapons famous enough to have a name. See **Shiva**.

Shastra

("order") A shastra is the name given to a technical treatise explaining the standards of a particular cultural or artistic discipline in Hinduism, as in **Bharata's** *Natyashastra*, a technical manual that discusses **dance** and the theater. When it is placed at the end of a compound (as in "**Shilpa Shastra**"), the word *shastra* can also serve to denote the whole body of teaching on that particular subject. All of the classical arts were placed under well-defined canons, each with its own specific rules and standards to guide artists: **Sculpture** and **architecture** were under Shilpa Shastra, music under Sangita shastra, and dance and theater under **Natya** shastra. Given the prevailing emphasis on upholding such strict rules, artistic genius meant doing something unusual within the larger confines of the tradition rather than creating something entirely new or original.

Shastri Narayanswarupdas Swami

The **ascetic** name of the spiritual leader of the **Akshar Purushottam Samstha**, a branch of the **Swaminarayan** religious community. He is more commonly known by his title **Pramukh Swami** ("President Swami"). See **Pramukh Swami**.

Shatakatrayam

("The Three Hundred") Collection of **Sanskrit** poems ascribed to the poet-philosopher **Bhartrhari**, who is believed to have lived in the fifth century. The text is a three-part collection of poems about political life, love, and renunciation, which explore all of the conventional ends of life: The first two sections are about power (**artha**), sensual or physical desire (**kama**), and righteous action (**dharma**), whereas the final section is concerned with liberation of the soul (**moksha**). Much of the poetry carries a cynical, slightly bitter tone, suggesting the world-weariness of a man who has seen too much of the harsh realities of life. For further information see Barbara Stoller Miller (trans.), *The Hermit and the Love-Thief*, 1978.

Shatakshi

("[having] one hundred eyes") Epithet of the **goddess Shakumbhari Devi**, based on a story that tells of a time when the **earth** is parched with drought, and she takes a form with a hundred eyes, watering the earth with her tears. See **Shakumbhari Devi**.

Shatapatha ("Hundred-Path") Brahmana

One of the two most important texts in the **Brahmana** branch of sacred Vedic literature, along with the **Aiteraya Brahmana**. The Brahmanas were primarily manuals describing the correct performance of Vedic ritual sacrifices. Each Brahmana was in theory connected with one of the **Vedas**, which gave them Vedic authority, but in fact they were quite different from the Vedas in scope and content. According to tradition, the Shatapatha Brahmana was connected with the "white" recension of the **Yajur Veda**, a variant form of the text in which the explanatory notes connected with the Vedic mantras have been collected into a separate appendix. This is in

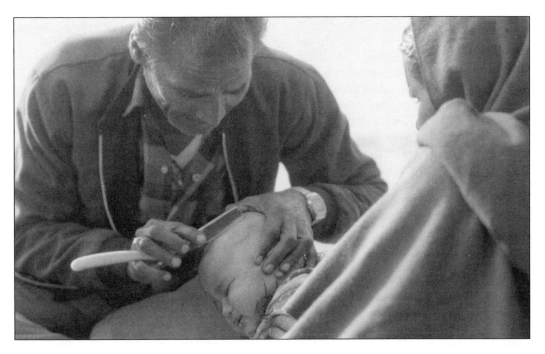

A man shaves an infant boy's head. Hair is believed to trap impurities.

contrast with the "Black" Yajur Veda, in which these notes have been incorporated into the body of the text itself. Aside from giving instruction on the practice of rituals, the Shatapatha Brahmana includes a wide variety of texts, one of which is the **Isha Upanishad**. The upanishad's presence in a Brahmana text clearly shows that there was considerable overlap in the times of composition of various Vedic literary styles, rather than clear-cut "periods."

Shatrughna

("Foe-slayer") In the *Ramayana*, the earlier of the two great Indian epics, Shatrughna is the second son of King **Dasharatha** and his wife **Sumitra**, and the youngest brother of **Rama**, the epic's protagonist. Whereas Rama's brothers **Lakshmana** and **Bharata** play important roles in the epic—the former as Rama's minion and shadow, the latter serving as Rama's regent during his exile—Shatrughna is virtually invisible and does not play an important part in the larger epic narrative.

Shattila Ekadashi

Religious observance falling on the eleventh day (**ekadashi**) of the dark (waning) half of the **lunar month** of **Magh** (January–February). As with all the eleventh-day observances, this is dedicated to the **worship** of the god **Vishnu**. Most Hindu festivals have certain prescribed rites, which usually involve fasting (**upavasa**) and worship and often promise specific benefits for faithful performance. On this day one should bathe an image of Vishnu with the five auspicious things (milk, curds, honey, ghee, and sugar water), placing some sesame seed (tila) into each. One should also eat food containing sesame seed. During the night one should sleep before the image of the **deity**. This ekadashi's name comes from the six (sat) ways in which the sesame seed has been used. Faithfully observing this festival is said to cause one to be reborn in Vishnu's realm, **Vaikuntha**.

Shaving

An act of ritual purification as well as an act of hygiene. The **hair** of the head and face is believed to trap impurity (**ashaucha**), and shaving one or both is a significant part of many rites of purification. Body hair, however, is rarely shaved, since the **Sanskrit** language has different words for these two types of hair, and they are considered to be different things entirely. During the period of impurity associated with death (**maranashaucha**) the mourners will not shave for the entire ten days, signifying their continuing impurity, but at the end of that period they will shave completely to signify their final purification. Hindu men will sometimes also refrain from shaving as a sign of austerity while they are keeping religious vows, and shave when the vow has been completed. One example occurs during the **lunar month** of **Shravan**, in which men who are devotees (**bhakta**) of the god **Shiva** will often refrain from shaving. Another example can be found in the ritual preparation for the annual pilgrimage to **Shabari Malai**; men must keep a strict **ascetic** discipline for forty-one days before the pilgrimage, in which one element is a ban on shaving.

Shesha

("remnant") Mythical thousand-headed serpent upon which the god **Vishnu** reclines, as on a couch; Shesha is also considered to support the various regions of the **earth**, particularly the underworlds. His name comes from the fact that he is considered a partial incarnation of Vishnu and is thus related to Vishnu, both as incarnation and through his status as Vishnu's couch. As with most of the gods' animal associates, Shesha does not play a prominent role in his own right. The one mythic episode in which he does play an important part is that of churning the Ocean of Milk in which Shesha serves as the churning-rope to turn Mount **Mandara**, with all the gods pulling from one side, and the **demons** pulling from the other. Yet here too he is only instrumental, necessary for the episode to unfold but with the main focus lying

elsewhere. Shesha is seen as having a protective role. In Hindu astrology (**jyotisha**) he is identified as the protective **deity** for the fifth **day** of each half of the **lunar month**. See also **Tortoise avatar**.

Shibi

In Hindu mythology, sage-king who is famous for his virtue and commitment to his word. Shibi's reputation reaches the ears of the gods, who decide to test it. The god **Dharma**, who is righteousness personified (or in some other versions, the god **Agni**) takes the form of a dove, and is pursued by the god **Indra**, in the form of a hawk. The dove flies into Shibi's lap and entreats him for asylum, which Shibi grants. The hawk observes that it is inappropriate for Shibi to deprive him of the food he needs to eat, and demands in exchange an equal weight of flesh cut from Shibi's body. Shibi agrees, but no matter how much of his flesh he throws into the balance, the dove is still heavier. Finally Shibi sits his whole body into the balance, as a sign that he will sacrifice his life for the dove. At this point the gods resume their divine forms and bless Shibi for his steadfastness.

Shikhandi

In the *Mahabharata*, the later of the two great Hindu epics, the rebirth of the maiden **Amba**, daughter of the king of **Kashi**. Amba and her sisters have been kidnapped by **Bhishma** to be married to his nephew **Vichitravirya**, but when she informs Bhishma that her heart already belongs to King Salva, Bhishma gallantly releases her. Yet Salva refuses to marry her, for since she has been kidnapped he is not certain of her virginity. Amba then returns to Bhishma, who refuses to marry her because of his vow to remain a lifelong bachelor. In her anger Amba swears to get revenge on Bhishma and performs harsh physical **asceticism** (**tapas**) to generate the spiritual powers necessary to do this. Her austerities eventually please the god **Shiva**, who promises her that she will be rewarded in her next **birth**. Amba then raises a pyre and burns herself to death.

Amba is reborn as Shikhandi to King **Drupada**, whose wife has received a boon that she will give birth to a girl, but that the girl will later be transformed into a boy. When Shikhandi is born, it is announced that the child is a boy and the child is given the training appropriate for a prince. It is only upon fixing a marriage for Shikhandi that the issue of the child's gender comes up and it is finally resolved when Shikhandi exchanges sexes with a nature spirit (**yaksha**) named **Sthunakarna**, who becomes a woman, and Shikhandi a man. The switch is originally intended to be for only a short period, but is later extended until Shikhandi's death, at which time Sthunakarna again becomes male.

During the Mahabharata war Shikhandi challenges **Bhishma** in battle but the latter refuses to fight him, since Shikhandi has been born a woman. Shikhandi takes advantage of this gallantry to shoot a barrage of arrows at Bhishma, as does the warrior **Arjuna**, who hides behind Shikhandi for protection. With this assault, Bhishma finally decides that the time has come for him to give up the fight and die. In the battle that follows after Bhishma falls, Shikhandi is killed by **Ashvatthama**, the **son** of **Drona**, who fights on the side of the **Kauravas** in the war. Based on Shikhandi's role in shielding Arjuna from harm, in modern **Hindi** the name Shikhandi is used to designate a scapegoat, someone behind whom another person hides and escapes blame.

Shikhara

Temple tower that was the central feature of the **Nagara** architectural style, prevalent in northern and eastern India. The temple's tallest tower was always directly over the image of the temple's primary **deity**, although there were often also smaller, subsidiary towers to lead the eye up to that primary one. Within this general pattern there are two important variations, exemplified by the temples at **Khajuraho** and **Orissa**. In the Khajuraho style a group of shikharas is unified into one continuous upward swell, which draws the eye upward like a series of hills leading to a distant peak. In contrast, the Orissan style tends to emphasize the differences between the temple's parts, with a low entrance hall (**jagamohan**) next to a beehive-shaped temple tower (**deul**), which is often three or four times taller than the entrance hall.

Shiksha

("learning") One of the six **Vedangas**. These were the supplemental branches of knowledge connected with the **Vedas**, the oldest Hindu religious texts, and all the Vedangas were associated with the use of the Vedas. Shiksha was concerned with articulation, proper pronunciation, and the laws of euphonic combination (**sandhi**), that is, sounds combined in a certain way to have a pleasant effect. Although this may sound trivial, it was a central concern in the cult of **sacrifice** laid out in the **Brahmana** literature. This was because the power of these sacrifices was believed to depend on the proper delivery of the Vedic **mantras**, with any mistake being potentially ruinous. Aside from shiksha, the other Vedangas are **vyakarana** (**Sanskrit** grammar), **chandas** (Sanskrit prosody), **kalpa** (ritual instructions), **nirukta** (etymology), and **jyotisha** (favorable times for sacrifices).

Image of the god Vishnu. Crafted according to the rules of shilpa shastra, the image's proportions are strictly defined and he holds identifying objects.

Shilappadigaram

("the Jeweled Anklet") The greatest epic poem in classical Tamil literature. It is traditionally ascribed to the poet **Ilangovadigal** (2nd c.) but almost certainly was written several centuries later. The poem is a symbolic theater for several important themes that have pervaded Hindu culture, particularly the need for a king to rule righteously and the power gained by a wife through her devotion to her husband. The story tells the tale of a married couple, Kannaki and her husband Kovalan. In his infatuation with a dancer, Kovalan squanders the family's wealth, selling nearly all their possessions. When he finally returns to his wife, their only remaining valuables are one pair of her jeweled anklets. The couple decides to travel to the town of **Madurai** to sell the anklets, and use the proceeds to reestablish their family as traders.

When they reach Madurai, however, tragedy strikes. The night before the couple's arrival, a dishonest jeweler has stolen an identical pair of anklets from the queen of Madurai, and when Kovalan goes to sell the anklets, the same jeweler accuses him of being the thief. Kovalan is executed, and when Kannaki hears of this she comes into the city, bearing the other anklet as a sign of his innocence. She gains an audience with the king, who falls dead with remorse when he realizes the disaster he has caused. Still furious, Kannaki rips off her left breast, pronounces a **curse** on the city, and hurls the breast onto the street; the breast bursts into flames that consume the city. In the end, Madurai's patron **goddess** persuades Kannaki to withdraw her curse, and Kannaki dies a few days later.

One of the forces assumed to be operating here is the power of a woman's devotion to her husband. Even though Kovalan squanders all their money through unfaithfulness, Kannaki readily takes him back when he returns, and is willing to give up her last resource to help him. The power of her devotion gives her the ability to cause widespread destruction through a single curse, and the strength of this power is still an article of faith among many Hindus even today. For further discussion of the themes in this play, and more general consideration of images of Hindu **women**, see Sarah Mitter, *Dharma's Daughters*, 1991. See also **Tamil language** and **Tamil epics**.

Shilpa Shastra

General name for rules and standards governing the mechanical arts and handicrafts—traditionally numbered at sixty-four—through which anything was formed, made, or fashioned. In the context of art and **architecture**, the term *shilpa shastra* is most often associated with two specific areas, which by the medieval era had had their conventions strictly fixed. One of these governed the creation of sculptural images, according to which the images of the **deities** had to be carved to exactly defined proportions, along with their identifying attributes. The other area was in regard to buildings, whether individual structures such as temples, or collections of buildings in city planning. The layout of temples was modeled after the human body (and thus mirrored the sculptor's precision regarding the images of the divine); entire towns were similarly modeled to create a harmonious urban environment.

Shipra River

A distant tributary of the **Yamuna River**, which has its headwaters in the **Vindhya Mountains** in **Madhya Pradesh**. The Shipra is considered a holy river because it flows through **Ujjain**, a central Indian city with great religious and historical significance.

Shirdi

Small town in the state of **Maharashtra**, about 120 miles northeast of Bombay. It is famous as the home of the modern saint **Shirdi Sai Baba**, who appeared there as an adolescent boy in 1872 and lived there until his death in 1918. He was greatly esteemed by people from all religious communities, and the shrine built in the place in which he lived receives considerable traffic even today.

Shirdi Sai Baba

(d. 1918) Hindu **ascetic** and religious teacher whose disciples came from many different religious communities—Hindu, Muslim, Parsi, and Christian. His origins are mysterious, for in 1872 he simply appeared in the town of **Shirdi** in **Maharashtra**, as a boy of about sixteen. He was dressed in the manner of a Muslim **faqir** (religious mendicant, or beggar), but claimed to have forgotten his birthplace and his family. Because of his dress a local priest forbade him from staying at a Hindu temple, so he moved into a small, unused mosque, where he lived for the rest of his life. He kept a perpetual fire burning in a fire pit, and for religious rituals performed both Muslim prayers and Hindu **worship**. He was most famous for his supernatural powers: healing (for which he often gave people ash from his fire pit to eat), foretelling the future, multilocation (the ability to be in two places at the same time), and appearing in **dreams** to guide his followers. His response to people's immediate needs made him famous through much of India, but he always maintained that his purpose in performing miracles was to attract people to spiritual life. He gradually attracted disciples, and in the time since his death the town of Shirdi has become an important regional pilgrimage place (**tirtha**). Although he referred to himself as **Sai Baba**, he is now usually called Shirdi Sai Baba, to distinguish him from **Sathya Sai Baba**, another religious leader who claims to be Shirdi Sai Baba's reincarnated form.

Shishtachara

The "practice of learned [people]," which was one of the traditional sources for determining religious duty (**dharma**) for matters not discussed in the **dharma literature**, or for cases in which the literature itself gave conflicting opinions. Although Shishtachara was the least authoritative source of dharma, after the Vedic scriptures and the dharma literature, making it an authority recognizes that life has many ambiguities and uncertainties and at the same time provides a resource for determining the appropriate action by taking as a model the practice of established and knowledgeable people. Another term to designate this sort of authority was *sadachara*, the "practice of good [people]."

Shishupala

In the *Mahabharata*, the later of the two great Hindu epics, Shishupala is the son of the king of Cedi. He is also described as a reincarnation of **Jaya**—one of the gatekeepers of the god **Vishnu's** heavenly dwelling, **Vaikuntha**—who has been cursed by the sages to be born three times as a **demon** and killed by the god Vishnu each time. Shishupala is born with three eyes and four hands, but as his horrified parents are about to abandon him, a celestial voice informs them that the child will grow up into a powerful king. The heavenly voice also says that Shishupala can be killed by only one person on **earth**, that Shishupala's third eye will disappear when he sees that person, and that two of his hands will disappear when the person takes him in his lap. After some time the god **Krishna** pays a visit to Cedi, and when the signs take place as foretold, Shishupala's parents know that Krishna is the only person who can kill their son. Shishupala's mother is Krishna's aunt, and when she begs him not to kill her son, Krishna promises to forgive Shishupala's misdeeds one hundred times. Krishna sticks to his word, but such forbearance only makes Shishupala more reckless, and after the one hundred and first insult, Krishna throws his discus and cuts off Shishupala's head.

Shishupala-Vadha

("Slaughter of **Shishupala**") Sanskrit drama written by the seventh-century poet **Magha**, which is traditionally reckoned as one of the six **mahakavyas**. The play's theme is the death of the mythic figure Shishupala, whose mother has been promised by **Krishna** that he will forgive her son one hundred times. This promise only makes Shishupala more reckless, and after the one hundred and first insult, Krishna throws his discus and cuts off Shishupala's head. Aside from its mythic theme, the play is notable for a number of unusual verses, such as verses that are perfect palindromes (verses that are the same when read backward or forward), or that use only one or two consonants, as a sign of the poet's skill.

Shishya

("to be taught") A word that in its literal meaning can refer to any student but in its most common sense refers to the disciple of a religious instructor (**guru**).

Shitala

Hindu **goddess** who is both worshiped and feared. Shitala was traditionally believed to be the physical representation of smallpox, a deadly virus, and a person infected with the disease was thought to be possessed by the goddess, a notion reinforced by the fever and delirium that often accompany this disease. Shitala is also associated with heat—both because of the fever caused by smallpox and because her major religious observance, **Shitalashtami**, comes near the advent of the hot **season**. Shitala is considered a jealous, spiteful goddess whose wrath is visited upon those who ignore and displease her. The literal meaning of her name, "Cool One," can be seen as an attempt to appease her wrath through flattery. Shitala has retained prominence even though the World Health Organization has declared that smallpox has been completely eradicated. In a fascinating example of religious change, one writer details how Shitala has shifted the disease through which she shows herself, and now appears in the guise of tuberculosis. See Margaret Thrice Egnor, "The Changed Mother, or What the Smallpox Goddess Did when There Was No More Smallpox," *Contributions to Asian Studies XVIII*, 1984.

Shitalashtami

Religious observance celebrated on the eighth day of the bright (waxing) half of the lunar month of **Baisakh** (April–May), in honor of the **goddess Shitala**. In northern India this festival falls at the advent of the hottest time of **year**; the climate thus mirrors the heat and fevers brought on by contact with Shitala herself, in her form as smallpox. Although Shitala is conceived as spiteful and jealous, she cannot be ignored, since this will be sure to provoke her wrath.

Shiv Sena

("Army of **Shivaji**") Militant Hindu organization formed in Bombay in the late 1960s by Bal Thackeray. It was originally a movement made up of people native to **Maharashtra**, a modern Indian "linguistic state" formed to unite people with a common language, to resist the perceived dominance of outsiders, in this case migrants from **Tamil Nadu** who were taking away jobs from the Maharashtrian "sons of the soil." This nativist bent is reflected in its name, taking as its symbol the Maharashtrian hero Shivaji, who successfully resisted the power of the Moghul Empire. In more recent times the movement has associated itself with **Hindutva** or Hindu nationalism, projecting itself as defending the interests of the larger Hindu community against the "outsiders," in particular Muslims. The Shiv Sena's potential for violent action is well known, and they have always been ready to defend their interests with physical force, as well as working through official channels. The Sena's ability to provide "muscle power" has given them political strength in Maharashtra, both in the municipal government of Bombay, and most recently as a partner (with the **Bharatiya Janata Party**) in running the state government. This political strength is being translated into a strong presence in other areas, particularly in labor unions, in which the Sena-affiliated union is gaining greater influence and membership. See also **Moghul dynasty**.

Shiva

(auspicious) Along with the god **Vishnu** and the **Goddess**, one of the three most important **deities** in the Hindu pantheon. All three are notable for being virtually absent from the Vedas, and their collective rise to dominance (and the gradual eclipse of the original Vedic gods) points clearly to a definitive change in the Hindu tradition. Of the three, Shiva is not mentioned at all in the **Veda**. He is identified with the god **Rudra**, who first appears in a few of the late Vedic hymns and who is later identified in the **Shvetashvatara Upanishad** as the single supreme deity behind all things. The word *Shiva* ("auspicious") first appears in this upanishad, but as an adjective modifying the feminine noun *body*.

Despite Rudra/Shiva's appearance in the upanishad as a supreme divinity, his position is not clear-cut. He is described as a master of archery who dwells in the mountains (and thus away from human beings) and is implored not to use his arrows to harm either man or beast. It is certain that Rudra/Shiva is not a Vedic deity, and some have claimed that his roots lie in the ancient urban-cultural center known as the **Indus Valley civilization**, citing as evidence one of the seals found in **Harappa**, an ancient city of Pakistan, which shows a horned figure sitting cross-legged as if in meditation. This identification is possible but hardly compelling. A more likely possibility is that he entered the pantheon as a god worshiped by **ascetics**, who have always been associated with mountain dwellings. His connection with ascetics is reinforced by several ascetic characteristics attributed to Shiva, such as the matted locks and ash-smeared body. Ascetic origins would also account for his marginal status among the gods, since this would have rendered him an "outsider" to Vedic sacrificial cult, which was the "established" religion of the time. Shiva's dramatic entry into the pantheon comes in the story of the death of his wife **Sati**. In this story, his

Statue of the god Shiva from the Kumbha Mela festival in Allahabad. Living outside of society with his hair in matted locks and his body smeared with ash, Shiva is often regarded as the model for the Hindu ascetic.

father-in-law **Daksha's** insulting remarks—that Shiva was an ascetic with no money, job, or family, and was unfit to join respectable society—finally resulted in the destruction of Daksha's **sacrifice** as a sign of Shiva's supremacy.

Shiva has retained this ambivalent, sometimes marginal quality in his iconography, his mythology, and his character. Perhaps his most basic and important characteristic is that he is a divinity whose nature allows him to move beyond the opposing forces (or dualities) within himself and the world by being at all times the possibility of both forces at once. Shiva can represent both the wild and dangerous side of life and the respectable and refined side. On the one hand, he is the typical ascetic, with matted hair, ash-smeared body, and a home on Mount **Kailas** in the remote **Himalayas**. On the other hand, he is Hindu society's ideal for the good husband, who dotes upon his wife **Parvati**. His body is adorned with snakes and clothed with a bloody **elephant** skin, but he also wears the **Ganges** River and the crescent **moon**, which are associated with beauty, **purity**, and **auspiciousness**. His mythic deeds stress his overwhelming power, against which no enemy can stand, and his sudden and sometimes impetuous temper, seen best in the destruction of **Kama**, the god of love; yet this sudden violence contrasts with his **grace** and favor toward his devotees (**bhakta**), by whom he is given the name "quickly satisfied" (Ashutosh) and to whom he will give almost everything. Although he is portrayed as simple and without deceit (as **Bholanath**, the "simple lord"), he is also traditionally described as the expositor of the **tantras**, the most secret and hidden religious practice of all. This transcendence of all opposites can be seen in the images that commonly represent him: in his form as **Nataraja**, in which many of these contrary attributes are shown, or as **Ardhanarishvara**, in which the image is half male and half female. This transcendence of duality is also visible in the **linga**, the pillar-shaped object that is his symbolic form, whose base and shaft are interpreted as symbolizing male and female reproductive organs. Finally, one can see this transcendence in the tantric conception of the **subtle body** (the system of psychic centers, or **chakras**, that run throughout the human body), in which religious practice aims for the union of Shiva and **Shakti**. As Wendy Doniger O'Flaherty points out, through his actions Shiva embodies all the contradictory possibilities for human experience, and in mythic form provides a resolution that one ordinary human life can never provide.

In medieval times Shiva's devotees developed a doctrine of **avatars** (incarnations of Shiva who take the form of a variety of saints, sages, and minor deities who appear on earth to restore balance and perform other necessary acts), probably in response to the older and better developed notion of avatars of Vishnu. Unlike Vishnu's avatars, Shiva's do not seem to have been a way to create a place for smaller existing deities in the larger pantheon. Of Shiva's twenty-one avatars, the most important one is **Hanuman**, who is the only one with a well-established independent cult. The others were sages (such as **Durvasas**) and important beings, but the worship of Shiva's avatars has never upstaged the worship of Shiva himself, as has often happened with Vishnu. For further information on the mythology of Shiva, see Wendy Doniger O'Flaherty *Shiva*, 1981; and Stella Kramrisch, *The Presence of Shiva*, 1981. See also **Shaiva**.

Shivaga-Sindamani

By far the latest of the three **Tamil epics**, written perhaps in the late sixth century. The story describes the adventures of Shivaga, a man who excels at every possible manly art, who with each new challenge wins a new wife for his harem but in the end renounces everything to become a Jain monk. Although the story clearly has a Jain bias, the *Shivaga-Sindamani* paints a

Ascetics observing Shivaratri.

useful picture of contemporary southern Indian life.

Shivaji

(1627–1680) **Maratha** chieftain who carved out an independent kingdom in western **Maharashtra** and **Goa**, and was able to hold onto it despite the efforts of the Moghul emperor **Aurangzeb** to take it back. Shivaji's father Shahji was a Moghul governor in the city of Bijapur, and Shivaji began his operations as a robber chief there. He gained the support of the local Maratha people, and his first important conquest was a hill fort near the city of Pune. From there he expanded his territory and consolidated his power, building forts to hold the territory. Shivaji was a devout Hindu, which undoubtedly helped gain him support from the common people. In modern times his Hindu roots, and his opposition to Moghul rule, have transformed him into a Hindu nationalist hero, particularly in Maharashtra. See also **Moghul dynasty**.

Shivananda, Swami

(1887–1963) Hindu **ascetic**, teacher, and founder of the **Divine Life Society**. Shivananda's first calling was to be a doctor; after getting his degree, he spent some time practicing medicine in Malaysia, spurred by a passion to serve others. Later in life he felt the call of renunciation and, in 1924, settled in **Rishikesh**, where he was based for the rest of his life. Shivananda's message stressed the teachings of the **Advaita Vedanta** school, which is devoted to a belief in monism (the belief in a single Ultimate Reality where all things are united), and the practice of **yoga** for a disciplined life. He saw his own mission as teaching others, a mission fostered by the Divine Life Society's publications, which continue to be important today. Shivananda's learning and religious charisma made him greatly respected, and in keeping with his original vocation, one of the charitable works sponsored by the Divine Life Society is a free medical clinic. For further information see David Miller, "The Divine Life Society Movement," in Robert D. Baird (ed.), *Religion in Modern India*, 1998.

Shiva Purana

One of the eighteen traditional **puranas**, which were an important genre of **smrti** texts and the repository of much of traditional Indian mythology. The smrtis, or "remembered" texts, were a class of literature, which, although deemed important, were considered less authoritative than the **shrutis** or "heard" texts. In brief, the shrutis included the **Vedas**, the oldest and most authoritative Hindu religious texts, whereas the smrtis included the *Mahabharata* and the *Ramayana*, the **dharma literature**, the **Bhagavad Gita**, and the puranas. The puranas are the collection of all types of sacred lore, from mythic tales to ritual instruction to exaltation of various sacred sites (**tirthas**) and actions. Most of the puranas stress the **worship** of one deity as supreme over all others and as this one's name clearly shows it is focused on the worship of **Shiva**. The *Shiva Purana* is one of the longer and larger puranas. It gives an exhaustive account of Shiva's mythic deeds—many of which have become the common mythology for many traditional Hindus—as well as instructions for how, where, and when Shiva is to be worshiped.

Shivaratri

("Night of **Shiva**") The most important annual festival for devotees (**bhakta**) of the god Shiva, celebrated on the fourteenth day of the dark (waning) half of the **lunar month** of **Phalgun** (February–March). Worshipers of Shiva on this night are said to receive unlimited religious benefits. The observances for this festival fall into three general categories: fasting (**upavasa**), wakefulness, and **worship**. Those fasting on Shivaratri must abstain from all grains—which define the difference between a "snack" and a "meal"—but are free to eat all other things. During the night observers stay awake, preferably at a temple, relating and listening to Shiva's mythic exploits, and worship Shiva early the next morning. Shivaratri is a major Indian festival, and in many places the readings and discourses are broadcast through loudspeakers, so that those nearby may also share the religious merit.

The charter myth for this festival describes the power of any religious observances performed on this day, even if unknowingly. According to the story, a hunter lost in the woods on the evening of Shivaratri climbs a tree for safety, and spends the night. Unknown to him, at the base of the tree is a **linga**, the pillar-shaped object which is Shiva's symbolic form. The hunter passes a cold and miserable night, and through his shivering shakes the tree, sending dew and leaves from the tree as **offerings** onto the linga; upon descending the tree he kneels to pick up an arrow he has dropped during the night and thus kneels before the linga. Despite a lifetime of bad **karma** generated by his livelihood as a hunter, the religious merit from this unknowing observance brought this hunter to the abode of Shiva on his death, and to a later rebirth as a king.

Shiwalik Goddesses

Local goddesses from the **Shiwalik hills** separating the **Himalayas** from the northern Indian plain. Some have little importance beyond the borders of their particular villages, whereas others have become important regional **deities**. As with all the goddesses of India, the Shiwalik goddesses are considered to be manifestations of the same feminine divine energy—the **Goddess**. As one sign of this identity, many of these sites are claimed to be **Shakti Pithas**—places where a part of the dismembered goddess **Sati** fell to **earth** and took form as a different goddess. Shiwalik goddesses are also thought of as relatives. Kathleen Erndl mentions seven goddesses, known as the Seven Sisters: **Vaishno Devi**, **Jwalamukhi**, **Vajreshvari Devi**, **Chintapurni**, **Naina Devi**, **Chamunda**, and **Mansa Devi**. Modern **Hindi** language sources list nine—the seven just mentioned plus **Shakumbhari Devi** and **Kalika Devi**. This group of nine is scattered in three different Indian states along the Shiwalik Range: Seven are in **Himachal Pradesh**, Vaishno Devi is in **Jammu** and **Kashmir**, and Shakumbhari Devi is in **Uttar Pradesh**. The pantheon here is fairly flexible, and the goddesses mentioned in these lists will probably vary over time, partly reflecting the success or failure to establish the holiness of these sites. For further information on the Shiwalik goddesses and **worship** of the Mother Goddess in northwestern India, see Kathleen Erndl, *Victory To The Mother*, 1993. See also **pitha**.

Shiwalik Hills

Himalayan foothills running through the Indian states of **Uttar Pradesh**, **Himachal Pradesh**, and **Jammu** and **Kashmir**. The hills are an ecological transition zone between the plains and the mountains but have their own religious ecology as well. Whereas the sites high in the **Himalayas** are often associated with **Shiva**, the primary sacred sites (**tirthas**) in the Shiwaliks are associated with the **Goddess**. See also **Shiwalik goddesses**.

Shraddha

("faithful") Ancestral memorial rite, performed either for one specific person (**ekoddishta**), or for a group in which the primary beneficiaries were one's three paternal ancestors (**parvana**).

An ekoddishta shraddha is usually first performed on the eleventh day after a person's death, although it may be repeated on the anniversary of the death. It is also usually performed every year during the **Pitrpaksha**, a two-week period specifically devoted to such rites, on the lunar day during this period that corresponds to the lunar day of death.

A parvana shraddha can be performed on a number of different occasions, for a number of different reasons. In the **dharma literature** and its commentaries, shraddhas are classified as falling in all three categories of ritual action: **nitya**, **naimittika**, and **kamya**. Certain shraddhas are obligatory (nitya) because they are prescribed for certain particular times, such as during the Pitrpaksha. Other shraddhas are occasional (naimittika) because they are necessary only under certain conditions, such as the obligation to give a **tirtha** shraddha when one visits a pilgrimage place (tirtha). Finally, certain shraddhas are freely performed because of the desire (**kama**) for certain benefits from them—usually conceived as the well-being of one's ancestors—and these are desiderative (kamya) shraddhas.

Whatever the motive for giving the shraddha, the general procedure always has two particular features: symbolically feeding one's ancestor(s) by **offering** balls of cooked grain (**pindas**), and feeding real food to a group of brahmins (the group with the highest social status in Hinduism) representing one's ancestors. Each of these parts is given a great deal of ritual elaboration, and there is considerable disagreement about which should come first, but in modern times offering the pindas generally precedes the meal. Many texts exalt the spiritual merits generated from feeding brahmins, but this is hardly surprising, since most of these texts were written by brahmins, and for many brahmins living at pilgrimage places these shraddhas were (and remain) an important part of their livelihood. However, many people deem this livelihood parasitic, and it is also potentially inauspicious, since it is gained through rites performed for the dead. For further information see Pandurang Vaman Kane, *A History of Dharmasastra*, 1968; and Raj Bali Pandey, *Hindu Samskaras*, 1969.

Shraddhanand, Swami

(b. Lala Munshi Ram, d. 1926) Key figure in the development of the **Arya Samaj**, a modern Hindu reformist movement. Shraddanand was born in **Punjab** and got a law degree from the Government College in Lahore, but was most influential through his support for the Arya Samaj's educational institutions. His greatest work was establishing the Gurukul Kangri near the sacred city of **Haridwar** in 1901. The Gurukul ("teacher's household") was a boarding school where Arya Samaj children could be raised with "progressive" Arya values, far from the corrupting influences of traditional mainstream Hindu society. This model was based on the **Vedas**, the earliest Hindu religious texts, which the Arya Samaj took as the sole religious authority, and in which a student would live as a member of his teacher's family. Educationally, the curriculum stressed the arts and sciences necessary for a "modern" education, but also traditional **Sanskrit** learning, particularly of the Vedas. Shraddhanand became a **Sanyasi** in 1917 but continued to support political causes, particularly Indian social and political leader **Mohandas Gandhi's** 1919 call for non-cooperation with the British government. His fervor and strength of character made him an unpopular figure, and he was assassinated by a Muslim in 1926.

Shramana

(from the **Sanskrit** verb *shram*, "to strive") General term denoting religious adepts from the middle of the first millennium before the common era whose beliefs stressed renunciation, **ascetic** practices, and the search for intuitive insights. Shramana religious practice was individualist, experiential, free-form, and independent of society. All of these qualities put them in religious competition with the **brahmin** priests, whose practice stressed mastery of sacred texts and performing enormously complex rituals; the need for sponsors for these rituals made brahmin religion "establishment" religion, serving its patron classes. Indian grammarians use the pair shramana and brahmin to illustrate typically bitter opponents, along with examples such as mongoose and cobra, and their difference seems to be between a religious model stressing individual charisma (shramana), and one stressing highly trained technical expertise (brahmin). Part of the shramana tradition remained outside the Hindu fold by virtue of resolutely rejecting the authority of the **Vedas**; the Jains, Buddhists, Ajivikas, and other religious groups developed as a result of this rejection of the Vedas. Part of the shramana tradition was absorbed into traditional Hinduism in the **dharma literature**, which found a place for renunciant **asceticism** in the form of the **Sanyasi**, the last of the four traditional **stages of life** (ashramas). For further information on the shramanas and the development of this tradition, see Padmanabh S. Jaini, "Sramanas: Their Conflict with Brahmanical Society," in Joseph Elder (ed.), *Chapters in Indian Civilization*, 1970.

Shrauta Sutras

("aphorisms on Vedic rituals") A set of brief sayings (4th c. B.C.E.) explaining the ritual instructions for performing the public sacrifices prescribed in the **Vedas**, the earliest and most authoritative Hindu religious texts. Such sacrificial instructions had been prescribed in the **Brahmana** literature—itself considered part of the Veda—but with the passage of time the Brahmanas had become too complex and difficult to understand. The Shrauta Sutras were essentially manuals for the priests presiding over the Vedic sacrifices, composed to ensure that the sacrifices would be performed correctly. Aside from instructions for performing the **sacrifice**, the Shrauta Sutras also contained an appendix with the exact measurements for the sacred altar, known as the **Sulva Sutras**. In theory, the Shrauta Sutras were the first part of a **Kalpa Sutra**, which would also contain prescriptions for domestic rites (**Grhya Sutras**) and appropriate human behavior (**Dharma Sutras**), with each Kalpa Sutra being connected to one of the four Vedas. But in practice the story of the Shrauta Sutras is far more complex, since aside from the three complete Kalpa Sutras that have survived, by **Apastamba**, **Baudhayana**, and **Hiranyakeshin**, there are other Shrauta Sutras, indicating a more independent composition.

Shravan

According to the lunar **calendar**, by which most Hindu religious festivals are determined, Shravan is the fifth month in the lunar **year**, usually falling within July and August. In northern India Shravan is associated with the rains, the breaking of the heat and revival of the land, and a general feeling of release. The major holidays in Shravan are **Nag Panchami**, **Kamika Ekadashi**, **Tulsidas Jayanti**, **Putrada Ekadashi**, and **Raksha Bandhan**. In addition, the entire month is deemed sacred to the god **Shiva**, with all **Mondays** and the **Shravan Vrat** marked out as times for particular observances.

Shravan Vrat

Religious vow (**vrat**) performed during the entire **lunar month** of **Shravan** (July–August), which is dedicated to the god **Shiva**. During this month devotees (**bhakta**) will perform various acts of homage, abstinence, and **worship**, although the strictness of this observance depends largely on individual inclination. Some worshipers observe a vow on each **Monday** of Shravan to worship Shiva (Monday is the day of the **week** over which he presides). The observant will fast (**upavasa**) during the

day, worship Shiva and members of his "family" (**Ganesh**, **Parvati**, and **Nandi**), and sometimes stay up late into the night reciting Shiva's mythic deeds. Some devotees will also refrain from cutting their **hair** and **shaving** their beards during this month, in imitation of Shiva's primary identity as the great **ascetic**.

Another observance falling in Shravan is the festival of **kanvars**, in which devotees draw pots of **water** from the **Ganges**, suspend them from a bamboo pole (kanvar), and carry this water to a Shiva temple, where it is offered to Shiva. This practice occurs in many places throughout northern India, but the most famous place is at **Deoghar** in the state of **Bihar**. There Shiva is present in his form as **Vaidyanath** ("Lord of Physicians"), and the image of Vaidyanath at Deoghar is one of the twelve **jyotirlingas** (images considered especially sacred). Pilgrims going to Deoghar draw their water from the Ganges at Sultanganj, and then walk to Deoghar to offer the water, a distance of over sixty miles. This particular observance combines devotion to God with the willingness to suffer hardship; it is often performed to fulfill a vow made when asking for some divine favor. See also **Solah Somvar Vrat**.

Shri

("auspicious," "bringing good fortune") Epithet of the **goddess Lakshmi**, reflecting her identification with luck, fortune, and prosperity. See **Lakshmi**.

Shri Aurobindo

Name taken by the Indian philosopher and social activist **Aurobindo Ghose** after retiring from political life to become an **ascetic**. See **Aurobindo Ghose**.

Shrichakra

Symbolic diagram (**yantra**) used in **worship** by the **Shrividya** school, a branch of the secret, ritually based religious practice known as **tantra**. The

Shrichakra is a set of nine interlocking triangles with four pointing up and five pointing down. The figure is surrounded by a double series of lotus petals, then an enclosing circle, and finally angular exterior walls. In the center of the diagram is a single point known as the **bindu**, representing the ultimate divinity that is the source of all things. The shrichakra is considered a subtle form of the **goddess** Lalita Tripurasundari, a goddess who is identified with different local goddesses throughout southern India. Lalita Tripurasundari is considered a "textual" goddess since she appears as an object of worship in the Shrichakra diagram but has no temple or image. The Shrichakra is used as a ritual aid during the rite known as **samharakrama**, in which the adept symbolically destroys the external world and ideas of a separate Self to become completely identified with this goddess, who is considered the source of all reality. For extensive information on the Shrichakra, see Douglas Renfrew Brooks, *The Secret of the Three Cities*, 1990.

Shrichandra

(b. 1494–1612?) Historical founder of the **Udasi** ("indifferent") **ascetic** community. Shrichandra was the elder son of Guru Nanak, the first of the Sikh community's ten gurus. By all accounts, Shrichandra was a devout and pious man, but Nanak passed over Shrichandra to designate one of his followers, Angad, as the second Sikh guru. According to tradition this was because Guru Nanak, believing that his followers should live married lives in regular society, disapproved of Shrichandra's status as ascetic. Due to his pedigree and his piety, Shrichandra gained a considerable following of his own, but the Udasis have always been considered as belonging in the Hindu fold. During the **Kumbha Mela**, an important bathing (**snana**) festival held in different places in northern India, the Udasis march third in the bathing procession, behind the **Sanyasis** and the **Bairagis**.

Shrikrishnavali

("Series [of poems] to **Krishna**") Series of sixty-one short poems dedicated to the god Krishna, written in the **Braj Bhasha** form of **Hindi** by the poet-saint **Tulsidas** (1532–1623?). This collection is unusual, since Tulsidas is renowned as a devotee (**bhakta**) of the god **Rama**, and most of his literary work describes Rama's exploits. The *Shrikrishnavali* is a poetic cycle about Krishna's life, so it begins with poems devoted to Krishna's childhood and youth in the **Braj** region. Most of the text, however, describes the sorrow of the cow herd girls (**gopis**) after Krishna's departure for his kingdom in **Mathura**, and their scornful rejection of Krishna's messenger **Uddhava**, who tries to convince them that since Krishna is the supreme **deity**, he is everywhere. This work is an example of the ecumenical, or universal, tendencies found throughout Tulsidas's work. Not only did he compose poems in praise of another deity, thus transcending sectarian barriers, but he also transcended linguistic barriers by writing these poems in Braj Bhasha, the most widely read language of his time, rather than his own native **Avadhi**.

Shrinathji

The name of a particular image of the god **Krishna**, the presiding **deity** of the Shrinathji temple in **Nathdwara**, **Rajasthan**. According to tradition, the image was originally hidden on top of Mount **Govardhan**, a famous mountain in the **Braj** region that is mythically associated with Krishna's humiliation of the storm-god **Indra**. The image's location was revealed in a **dream** to **Vallabhacharya**, the founder of the religious community known as the **Pushti Marg**. Vallabhacharya built a temple to house the image on Mount Govardhan, and his descendants have remained Shrinathji's hereditary servants since that time. The image was taken to Rajasthan in 1669, a move prompted by fears that it would be destroyed by the Moghul emperor **Aurangzeb**. According

Shrirangam, an island in the Cauvery River, contains the Ranganathaswamy Temple, dedicated to the god Vishnu.

to tradition Shrinathji revealed his wish to stay in Nathdwara by sinking his wagon's wheels deep into the earth, so that it could not go further. A new temple was erected and dedicated in 1672, and the image has remained there ever since.

Whether or not one accepts the claim of the divine mandate, much of the story seems reasonable. Given the proximity of Braj to Agra, the Moghul capital, keepers of well-known images might have been concerned about their safety, and since the neighboring state of Rajasthan was controlled by the Moghuls' Hindu vassals, this would have been an obvious place to go. Even today Nathdwara is in a remote and thinly settled region of Rajasthan, which indicates that in earlier times it would have been a place of refuge. The Nathdwara temple is particularly important to the Pushti Marg, a religious community devoted to the god Krishna, who play the major role in administering it. For more information see Rajendra Jindel, *Culture Of a Sacred Town*, 1976. See also **Moghul dynasty**.

Shringeri

Town and sacred site (**tirtha**) in eastern **Karnataka**, about 160 miles west of Bangalore. Although Shringeri is a very small town, it is religiously significant as the home of the Shringeri **Math**, one of the four **Dashanami** maths, the monastic centers believed to have been established by the philosopher **Shankaracharya**. The **ascetics** of the Shringeri math have a reputation for very strict adherence to traditional practice, and the town has a long standing as a center for religious learning.

Shringeri Math

One of the four **maths** or monastic centers traditionally believed to have been established by the great philosopher **Shankaracharya**; the others are the **Jyotir Math**, **Sharada Math**, and **Govardhan Math**. These four sacred centers are each associated with one of the four geographical corners of the Indian subcontinent; the Shringeri Math is in the southern quarter, in the city of **Shringeri** in the southern Indian state of **Karnataka**. Shankaracharya is traditionally cited as the founder of the **Dashanami Sanyasis**, the most prestigious Hindu **ascetic** order. The Dashanami ("ten names") ascetics are devotees (**bhakta**) of the god **Shiva**, who are divided into ten divisions, each with a different name. These ten divisions are organized into four larger organizational groups—**Anandawara**, **Bhogawara**, **Bhuriwara**, and **Kitawara**—each of which has two or three of the ten divisions, and each of which is associated with one of the four sacred centers. Of these, the Shringeri Math is associated with the Bhuriwara group.

Shrirangam

Island in the **Cauvery** River, just north of the town of **Tiruchirappalli** in the state of **Tamil Nadu**. The site is most famous for the Ranganathaswamy Temple, dedicated to the god **Vishnu** in his form as **Ranganatha**, who is sleeping on the back of his serpent couch **Shesha** in the sea of cosmic dissolution (**pralaya**). The temple is built in the **Dravida** style of **architecture**, in which the temple buildings are of modest height but cover an immensely large area and are surrounded by a boundary wall with massive towers (**gopurams**) over each wall's central gateway. In the temple's outer zones one often finds shops and houses, making such temples veritable cities in their own right. The Ranganathaswamy temple has a series of seven concentric processional streets, making it one of the largest temples in India. It was built in stages by the various dynasties that controlled this part of southern India—**Chera**, **Pandya**, **Chola**, **Hoysala**, and **Vijayanagar**—although the bulk of the construction was done by the last two. Since Vishnu's image is that of the divine king, it is hardly surprising that each of these regional dynasties patronized this site, as a way of using this divine imagery to support and validate their own right to rule.

Shrirangapatnam

Demolished fortress city just outside the city of Mysore in the state of **Karnataka**. Shrirangapatnam formerly served as the capital of Tipu Sultan (r. 1782–1799), the last ruler of Mysore. Throughout his reign he fought against the encroachment of outside powers. However, in 1799 he unsuccessfully took up arms against the British and was killed in battle, leaving the city largely destroyed. The city got its name from a temple there to the god **Ranganatha**, a form of **Vishnu** in which he is sleeping on his serpent couch **Shesha** in the sea of cosmic dissolution (**pralaya**). The temple survived the demolition and is still functioning today. Ranganatha is considered a divine king, and his most famous image, on the island of **Shrirangam** in **Tamil Nadu**, has strong associations with southern Indian kings and kingship. Even though Tipu was a Muslim, invoking Ranganatha's powerful symbolism would have been an astute political move, to legitimate his rule in the eyes of his Hindu subjects.

Shri Sampraday

One of the four branches (**sampraday**) of the **Bairagi Naga** ascetics. The Bairagi Nagas are devotees (**bhakta**) of the god **Vishnu**, organized in military fashion into different **anis** or "armies." Until the beginning of the nineteenth century their primary occupation was as mercenary soldiers, although they also had substantial trading interests; both of these have largely disappeared in contemporary times. The Shri Sampraday traces its spiritual lineage through the poet-saint **Ramananda** to the southern Indian philosopher **Ramanuja**, who is claimed to have been Ramananda's **guru**. This claim can also be seen in the name of the sampraday, since Ramanuja's followers, the **Shrivaishnavas**, focus their **worship** on Vishnu and Shri (**Lakshmi**). Yet the **Ramanandi** ascetics worship an entirely different pair of **deities**—**Rama** and **Sita**—and the claim of any connections between the Ramanandis and the Shrivaishnavas was formally renounced at the **Ujjain Kumbha Mela** in 1921, at the insistence of the Shrivaishnavas. As with another Bairagi order, the **Brahma Sampraday**, the claim to be connected to a famous religious figure seems to be a way to gain the authority and prestige of an ancient and established tradition. Even without this claim, the Shri Sampraday is the largest and the most important of the Bairagi Naga orders. For further information see Peter van der Veer, *Gods on Earth*, 1988.

Shrishaila

("holy mountain") Sacred mountain in the center of the state of **Andhra Pradesh**, about 185 miles south and slightly east of Hyderabad. The site is remote and difficult to reach but is famous for a temple sacred to the god **Shiva**, in his manifestation as **Mallikarjuna**, "[Lord] White as Jasmine." Shiva's image as Mallikarjuna is in the form of a **linga**, the pillar-shaped image that is his symbolic form, and the Mallikarjuna linga is one of the twelve **jyotirlingas**, a network of sites deemed especially sacred to Shiva, and at which **Shiva** is uniquely present.

Shrivaishnava

Southern Indian religious community who are devotees (**bhakta**) of the god **Vishnu** and Shri (**Lakshmi**), and whose religious life is rooted in the devotional hymns of the **Alvars**, a group of twelve poet-saints who lived in southern India between the seventh and tenth centuries. All the Alvars were devotees of Vishnu, and their stress on passionate devotion (**bhakti**) to a personal god, conveyed through hymns sung in the **Tamil language**, transformed and revitalized Hindu religious life. Two centuries later, the Alvars' devotional outpouring was organized and systematized by the philosopher **Ramanuja**, considered the Shrivaishnava founder. Ramanuja was convinced that **Brahman**, or Supreme Reality, was a personal **deity**, rather than an impersonal abstract principle, and was also convinced that devotion was the most important form of religious practice. **Vishishthadvaita Vedanta**, his philosophical position, stressed both of these convictions, and thus opposed the **Advaita Vedanta** school founded by the philosopher **Shankaracharya**, which stressed that the Supreme Being was impersonal and that realization (**jnana**) was the best spiritual path. In the time after Ramanuja the Shrivaishnava community split into two smaller groups, the **Tengalai** and the **Vadagalai**. The schism stemmed from a disagreement over whether human action was necessary to attain final liberation, or whether the hope came in complete surrender (**prapatti**) to God's **grace**; the Vadagalais held the former position, and the Tengalais the latter.

In practice, the Shrivaishnava community has been strongly influenced by the doctrine of divine "emanations" originated by the **Pancharatra** religious community, particularly the notion that a properly consecrated image becomes a form of the deity itself. Shrivaishnava piety has tended to center around temples, and particularly the service of the temple's image, which is considered a genuine form of the deity. Given this stress on learning and temple-based **worship**, it is not surprising that the community has been dominated by **brahmins**, and the few non-brahmins in the community have distinctly inferior status. For further information see K. Rangachari, *The Sri Vaisnava Brahmans*, 1931; and

John Braisted Carman, *The Theology of Ramanuja*, 1974.

Shrivatsa

An auspicious mark on the god **Vishnu's** chest, also found on Vishnu's form as **Krishna**, which is sometimes described as a mole and sometimes as a curl of **hair**. In statues and pictures, the Shrivatsa is usually portrayed as a four-petaled flower, and it is believed to be the **kaustubha** jewel, which was one of the precious things churned from the Ocean of Milk along with the **goddess Lakshmi**, the wishing-**cow** Surabhi, and **amrta**, the nectar of immortality. See also **Tortoise avatar**.

Shrividya

Southern Indian school of **tantra**, a secret, ritually based religious practice, in which the principal **deity** is the **goddess** Lalita Tripurasundari. The Shrividya tradition is noted for its ritual use of the **shrichakra**, a particular symbolic diagram (**yantra**) composed of a series of interlocking triangles. The Shrichakra ritual is known as **samhara-krama**, and is a systematic ritual deconstruction of the perceivable world and all illusions of duality, to attain union with the single true reality. The interior counterpart to this exterior ritual is the practice of **kundalini yoga**, which is based on the tantric idea of the **subtle body**—the six psychic centers (**chakras**) running along the spine—and seeks to gain ultimate union within the aspirant's own body by bringing together the microcosmic forms of the deities **Shiva** and **Shakti** that exist within the body. For a careful and considered picture of the Shrividya tradition, see Douglas Renfrew Brooks, *The Secret of the Three Cities*, 1990.

Shriyantra

Another name for the **Shrichakra**, a symbolic diagram (**yantra**) used in **worship** by the **Shrividya** school, a particular branch of the secret, ritually based religious practice known as **tantra**. See **Shrichakra**.

Shrutashravas

In the *Mahabharata*, the later of the two great Hindu epics, **Krishna's** paternal aunt and the mother of **Shishupala**.

Shruti

("[that which is] heard") The most authoritative type of Hindu sacred literature, made up of all the **Vedas**, the oldest Hindu religious texts. The Vedas are generally considered to have four types of texts: the hymns to the gods known as **samhitas**, the ritual manuals called the **Brahmanas**, and the speculative texts known as the **Aranyakas** and the **Upanishads**. The term comes from the traditional Hindu belief that these texts were not composed by human beings but are based in the primordial vibrations of the cosmos itself. The ancient sages, whose faculties of perception had been sharpened through persistent religious practice, were able to "hear" and understand these vibrations, and transmitted them to others in a lineage of learning. Thus, the belief that their origin is nonhuman makes the shruti the highest religious authority.

Shuddadvaita

("pure monism") Philosophical school first propounded by **Vallabhacharya** (1479–1531). Vallabha called his school shuddadvaita, or "pure monism," to distinguish it from the **Advaita Vedanta** school founded by the philosopher **Shankaracharya**. The latter school propounds "nondual" (advaita) monism, in its claim that a single Ultimate Reality lies behind all things, and that all things are merely differing forms of that reality. The Advaitins call this single reality **Brahman**, which they conceive as formless, impersonal, and having no defining attributes except for being, consciousness, and bliss (**sacchidananda**). In the Advaita understanding, since all conceptions of particular **deities** have specific attributes, they are thus conditioned forms of the ultimate Brahman. In fact, any assumption that the world as it appears is real is a fundamental misunderstanding that ultimately causes human beings to be trapped in karmic bondage, reincarnation (**samsara**), and suffering.

Shankaracharya's philosophical position was based primarily on the **Vedas**, the oldest and most authoritative Hindu texts, and particularly on the **Upanishads**, the speculative texts that are the latest part of the Vedas. Vallabhacharya used both of these sources in framing his Shuddadvaita school, but also used the *Bhagavata Purana*, which he considered to be of equal authority. The *Bhagavata Purana* is one of the later sectarian collections known as **puranas**. It is the most important source for the **worship** of the god **Krishna**, whom Vallabha considered to be the ultimate manifestation of the Supreme Being, rather than the unqualified Brahman promoted by Shankaracharya. Aside from promoting a personal conception of the deity over an impersonal conception, another difference in the two schools concerned the status of the world. For Vallabhacharya, the world as perceived is not an illusion but is real, because it and human beings have both evolved from God through the exercise of his supreme power. Krishna is conceived in the traditional threefold divine aspect as being–consciousness–bliss. Living beings possess being and consciousness, but not the divine bliss, whereas the material, nonliving, world has only being. Since this conception gives real value to the everyday world, Vallabhacharya described it as "pure monism."

In Vallabhacharya's system God is the inner controller of all souls, which makes human beings dependent on God for thinking and perception (**pratyaksha**). This dependence on God highlights the importance of **grace**, which he refers to as pushti, meaning "that which nourishes the soul."

Because of this emphasis on grace, Vallabhacharya's religious community is also known as the **Pushti Marg**. The Pushti Marg believes that God's favor is gained through devotion (**bhakti**), which is open to all and for which there are no prerequisites. The emphasis on devotion has marginalized all other forms of religious practice, and the Pushti Marg is particularly known for rejecting all **ascetic** endeavors, such as **celibacy**, fasting (**upavasa**), or renunciation. Its members tend to be householders coming from merchant families, particularly from the state of **Gujarat**. The community's primary temple is at **Nathdwara** in the state of **Rajasthan**. For further information see Richard Barz, *The Bhakti Sect of Vallabhacarya*, 1976.

Shuddhi

("purification") Any ritual purification that removes impurities and thus returns one to a state of ritual **purity**. In a more specialized context the term denotes the "reconversion" back to Hinduism of people who had either converted to another religion or who had adopted practices characteristic of other religious traditions. This practice was first instituted in the 1890s by the reformist **Arya Samaj**, led by **Swami Dayanand Saraswati**. There was a tremendous stir in the Sikh community when several Sikhs were a part of a group thus "purified," and in Sikh accounts this threat of reabsorption into the Hindu community was one of the major forces behind the Singh Sabha movement, which defined the Sikhs as a separate religious community. In modern times this practice has been employed by the Hindu nationalist organization **Vishva Hindu Parishad**, which has used it to "purify" certain groups who had adopted some Islamic practices.

Shudra

Among the four major social groups (**varnas**) in the traditional Hindu society, the shudras are the lowest and least influential. In this model, the shudras' social function was to serve all the others. This low social status is reflected in the creation story known as the **Purusha Sukta**, in which the shudras are described as being created from the Primeval Man's feet. The feet are the lowest and basest part of the body, and the shudra was correspondingly seen as the lowest level of **caste** Hindu society. Unlike members of the "twice-born" varnas—**brahmin, kshatriya,** and **vaishya**—whose adolescent males were entitled to have a ritual second birth that entitled them to study the **Veda**, shudras were always once-born, and thus forbidden to study or even to hear the Veda. In practice the status of shudras differed widely from region to region—in southern India, many of the land-owning **jatis** (**endogamous** social subgroups) were shudras, and they were very influential communities. At the very least, they were accorded a definitive place in caste Hinduism, unlike the **untouchables**, who were considered completely impure, usually because of their hereditary occupations.

Shudraka

(early 5th c.) Playwright and author of the *Mrcchakatika* ("The Little Clay Cart"). This drama describes the love between a poor but noble **brahmin**, Charudatta, and a wealthy but virtuous courtesan, Vasantasena, set in the context of a complicated political intrigue. It is notable for its detailed portrayal of everyday urban life, exemplified by the little clay cart, which is a child's toy. It has been translated into several languages, and is periodically performed for modern American audiences.

Shuka

("parrot") In Hindu mythology, a sage whose life story upholds the traditional doctrine of the four **stages of life** (ashramas). Shuka was the **son** of the sage **Vyasa**, born when Vyasa had a seminal emission upon seeing a celestial nymph (**apsara**) in the form of a parrot. From boyhood Shuka was interested only in spiritual life and had the firm desire never to marry, but despite intensive spiritual study he could not find contentment. He eventually decided to visit the sage-king **Janaka**, who advised Shuka that he could rightly consider renunciation only after having married and raised a family. Shuka returned home to his father and lived the householder's life; later in life he took up renunciation again and became perfectly realized.

Shuka Sampraday

Another name for the **Charanadasi** religious community, since their founder **Charanadas** was believed to have received **initiation** from the sage **Shuka**. See **Charanadasi**.

Shukla Paksha

("light half") Name denoting the waxing half of a **lunar month**, so called because the **moon's** light increases every night.

Shukra

In Hindu mythology, the religious teacher (**guru**) of the type of **demons** known as **asuras**. Shukra is a well-known figure who appears most prominently in the tale of the **Vamana avatar**. In this tale, the Asura king **Bali** is performing a great **sacrifice**. He is approached by the god **Vishnu**, who has taken the form of a dwarf (**vamana**), and asks Bali for three paces of land to build a sacrificial altar. Shukra suspects a trick, and warns Bali not to grant it, but Bali ignores Shukra's cautionary advice. As soon as Bali grants the gift, the dwarf grows immensely large. With his first two steps Vishnu measures out the cosmos, and with his third pushes Bali down into the underworld, where he is allowed to reign as king.

The god Shiva carrying a shula, or lance, beside his wife Parvati.
The type of shula with which Shiva is associated is the trishul, or trident.

Shula

A lance or pike; one of the characteristic weapons in Hindu iconography. The most famous example of this is the trident (**trishul**), which has three points, although the center one may be larger than the side ones. This weapon is most intimately associated with **Shiva**, but it is also commonly carried by certain powerful forms of the **Goddess**. This may reflect her charter myth, in which she was formed from the collected radiance of all the gods and received duplicates of their weapons from all of them. The lance with a single blade is associated with the god **Skanda**, particularly in his southern Indian manifestation as **Murugan**. When carried by Skanda-Murugan, the lance is usually called **shakti** ("power"), rather than shula.

Shumbha

In Hindu mythology, demon killed by the **goddess Kali** in the *Devimahatmya*, the earliest and most important text for the mythology of the **Goddess**. Together with his brother **Nishumbha**, Shumbha is a general in the army of a **demon** named **Mahishasura**, the figure whom the Goddess takes form to destroy. Due to a divine boon given to Mahishasura,

Shumbha and Nishumbha are able to conquer the gods and assume control of **heaven**, but they are unable to resist the power of the Goddess.

Shurpanakha

([having] "nails [like] winnowing-fans") In the *Ramayana*, the earlier of the two great Indian epics, Shurpanakha is the sister of **Ravana**, the demon-king of **Lanka**. Although she is a minor character in the epic, she plays a pivotal role in advancing the action of the story. As Ravana's sister, Shurpanakha is a **demon** woman of high status, and is free to choose her own husband according to her inclinations. As she roams through the forest one day, she happens to see **Rama**, the epic's protagonist, and is immediately smitten by his handsome form. Assuming the shape of a beautiful woman, she approaches him and expresses her desire for him. Rama tells her that since he is already married, his brother **Lakshmana** will be a more appropriate match for her. When Lakshmana gives her reasons why he too cannot marry her, Shurpanakha becomes angry. Realizing that Rama's wife **Sita** is the real impediment to her desires, Shurpanakha tries to harm her, and in the struggle that follows, Lakshmana mutilates her by cutting off her ears and her nose. Shrieking with pain and humiliation, Shurpanakha returns to her brother Ravana's court, who swears that her insult will be avenged. After their brothers **Khara** and **Dushana** are killed in a direct attack on Rama, Ravana decides to get revenge by kidnapping Sita, an action that eventually causes his own death.

Shvetaketu

A character in the **Chandogya Upanishad**, one of the speculative texts that form the latest stratum of the **Vedas**. In the upanishad, Shvetaketu is the **son** of **Uddalaka Aruni**, and a paradigm for a seeker of knowledge. Shvetaketu's education also symbolizes the conception of true knowledge found in the Upanishads and the way that this differs from earlier conceptions. According to a story in the upanishad's sixth chapter, Shvetaketu is sent away by his father to study the Vedas, and when he returns twelve years later having mastered all the Vedas, he incorrectly considers himself learned. Shvetaketu's father punctures his arrogance, showing him the difference between memorization and true knowledge, by asking Shvetaketu questions about the nature of the cosmos. When Shvetaketu cannot answer these, he admits his ignorance and accepts instruction from his father on the nature of the Self (**atman**). This instruction contains the teaching "That thou art" (**tat tvam asi**). This is one of the "great statements" (**mahavakya**) in Indian **philosophy**, and asserts the ultimate nondifference between **Brahman** and **atman**, the cosmos and the individual Self.

Shvetashvatara Upanishad

A text generally regarded as one of the latest **upanishads**, the speculative religious texts that themselves form the most recent stratum of the **Vedas**. This judgment is based on both the Shvetashvatara Upanishad's form and on its content. Stylistically, the earliest upanishads tend to be written in prose, or prose mixed with verse, whereas the later upanishads, including the Shvetashvatara, are completely in verse. In terms of content, the earlier upanishads tend to be long and rambling, whereas in the later ones the ideas are far more concise and clearly developed. The Shvetashvatara Upanishad's most original idea is its description of the Supreme Being in completely theistic terms, in contrast to the abstract, impersonal representations in the earlier upanishads. It identifies Ultimate Reality as the god **Rudra**, who was later identified with the god **Shiva**, one of the most important modern Hindu **deities**. The text is also notable for an explicit description of the process and results of yoga, which is the first known written explanation of this tradition.

Although it is best noted for these new ideas, the upanishad also reveals continuity with the older tradition. The second chapter begins with an extended invocation to the god Savitr (**Surya**), the **sun**, using verses drawn directly from Vedic texts composed a thousand years earlier. Such anachronisms indicate that there was no clear dividing line between the four differing types of Vedic text—**samhita**, **Brahmana**, **Aranyaka**, and **upanishad**—but rather that these textual styles were composed in overlapping periods.

Shyam

("black") Epithet of the god **Krishna**, based on the dark color of his skin. See **Krishna**.

Siddha

("perfected one") Name for a religious adept who is believed to have attained the perfect knowledge, enlightenment, and ultimate spiritual realization.

Siddhapith

("seat of the perfected") Name denoting a site believed to have particular power in conferring spiritual attainments upon those who carry out religious practices there. This power is usually tied to a mythic charter in which a **deity** became resident at the site—and is thus still present to assist people—but such sites have often been further sanctified by the presence of charismatic ascetics whose lives and spiritual discipline serve as examples to others.

Siddhasana

("perfected posture") One of the common sitting postures (**asana**) used for meditation. In this position one foot (often the left) is placed with the heel in the area between the anus and genitals, with the other foot resting on the opposite calf, turned so that the heel is straight up. This is called the "perfected" posture partly because of its difficulty—only those perfected in **yoga** can do it—but also because it is believed to bring substantial spiritual benefits.

Siddhi

("attainment") The most common word used to denote a superhuman power or faculty. The siddhis are first referred to in **yoga's** founding text, the **Yoga Sutras** of **Patanjali** (3.45), and are traditionally said to number eight: minuteness (**anima**), lightness (**laghima**), greatness (**madhima**), acquisition (**prapti**), irresistible will (**prakamyam**), control (**vashitvam**), superiority (**ishitvam**), and suppression of desire (**kamavasayitvam**).

The **possession** of such siddhis is generally seen as the evidence of high spiritual attainment, but the attitude toward the powers is mixed. They give one great abilities, but they are also seen as being highly seductive, since they can be used for both good and evil. The ability to keep from being beguiled by them is the true sign of spiritual maturity, and a spiritually immature person could easily fall into using them for selfish purposes. For this reason, religious aspirants are discouraged from aiming to gain such powers, since the very act of seeking is considered a selfish desire. In contrast, when one has gained such powers as a by-product of spiritual attainment, one is believed to be able to keep them in proper perspective.

Simantonnayana Samskara

Traditionally, the third of the life-cycle ceremonies (**samskaras**), and the last of the **prenatal samskaras**. This was performed when the **pregnancy** was further advanced, although various writers gave differing times for this. The major element in this rite is the husband parting the **hair** of his wife, supposedly to protect her from the misfortune and black **magic** that are supposed to plague pregnant **women**. One can also interpret parting the hair as symbolizing an easy delivery, and since this was a rite of protection, it would also give the expectant mother psychological assurance that everything would be all right. One bit of evidence supporting this interpretation is that many of the **dharma literature** writers classify this samskara as being for the woman rather than the unborn child, and as only needing to be performed during the first pregnancy. This samskara is seldom performed in modern times.

Simhakarna

("**lion's** ear") Another name for the hand **gesture** (**hasta**) known as **kataka hasta**, in which the fingers are loosely pressed onto the thumb, creating a ring. This particular name comes from the fanciful notion that the shape of the hand resembles a lion's ear. See **kataka hasta**.

Simuka

(1st c. B.C.E.) Founder of the **Satavahana dynasty**, which for over three centuries ruled over much of central India and the **Malwa** region from their capital in the city of **Paithan**.

Singh, Ishvari Prasad Narayan

(r. 1835–1889) A Maharaja of **Benares** who, with the help of local scholars, wrote the dialogues (**samvads**) for the characters in the **Ramnagar Ram Lila**. The Ram Lilas are dramatized versions of the epic *Ramayana*, which transcend simple theater to become a form of **worship**. The Ram Lila at Ramnagar, the fort that is home to the kings of Benares, is the most famous and traditional of all these Ram Lilas. The Ramnagar Ram Lila began because of the royal family's patronage, and the annual performance is still sponsored by them. Although they are no longer the actual political rulers, the royal family continues to play an important ceremonial role. For further information see Anaradha Kapur, *Actors, Pilgrims, Kings, and Gods*, 1990.

Singh, Udit Narayan

(r. 1796–1835) Maharaja of **Benares** whose reign saw the first performances of the **Ram Lila** at his palace in **Ramnagar**. The Ram Lilas are dramatized versions of the epic *Ramayana*, which transcend simple theater to become a form of **worship**. The Ram Lila at Ramnagar, the fort that is home to the kings of Benares, is the most famous and traditional of all these Ram Lilas. According to tradition, the Maharaja was a great devotee (**bhakta**) of the god **Rama** and a patron of the Ram Lilas in Benares itself, but on several occasions found it difficult to get across the **Ganges** because of the seasonal flooding. As a solution to the problem, he sponsored his own Ram Lila—no doubt also symbolically intended to reinforce his kingship—which has become the oldest, most traditional, and most important Ram Lila in Benares. Udit Narayan Singh finalized the locations of the Ram Lila, which is performed throughout the city, whereas his son **Ishvari Prasad Narayan Singh** was responsible for writing the dialogues (**samvads**) spoken by the characters. For further information see Anaradha Kapur, *Actors, Pilgrims, Kings, and Gods*, 1990.

Sinhastha Mela

Name for the **Kumbha Mela** festival held in the holy city of **Ujjain**. The festival is called Sinhastha because it is celebrated when **Jupiter** is in Leo (Sinha). The Sinhastha Mela's climactic bathing (**snana**) day comes on the **full moon** in the **lunar month** of **Baisakh** (April–May). The Kumbha Mela is a massive religious festival celebrated at three-year intervals in four different cities: **Haridwar**, **Allahabad**, **Ujjain**, and **Nasik**; the festival thus comes to each city every twelve years. The Kumbha Mela is chiefly a festival at which participants bathe in sacred rivers. The festival's primary participants are ascetics, who come from all over South Asia to bathe in the sacred waters. According to

Depiction of Sita and her husband Rama. In the epic the *Ramayana*,
Sita is abducted by the demon king Ravana and Rama must search the earth for her.

tradition, the Kumbha Mela was organized by the great philosopher **Shankaracharya** to promote regular gatherings of learned and holy men, as a means to strengthen, sustain, and spread Hindu religion.

The charter myth for the Kumbha Mela is taken from the story of Churning the Ocean of Milk. After the ocean has been churned and the nectar of immortality (**amrta**) has been extracted, the gods and their **demon** opponents begin to quarrel over the pot of nectar. The gods snatch the pot and run off with it, but the one carrying the pot grows tired, and in twelve days of carrying it sets it on the ground in twelve different places. Eight of the places are in heaven, but the other four are on earth and these are the four sites where the Mela is held. In each place a bit of the nectar splashes on the ground, sanctifying the site, and since a divine day is considered to be a human year, the twelve-year cycle is established. According to popular belief, at each Kumbha Mela's most providential moment, the waters in which people are bathing become the nectar of immortality, and all those who bathe in these waters gain immeasurable religious merit.

Historically speaking, the two most important sites have been Haridwar and Allahabad; one measure of their dominance is that they have held "half" (**ardha**) Kumbha Melas after six years, and that these have consistently drawn bigger crowds than the "full" Kumbha Melas at Ujjain and Nasik, which fall during those times. In recent times, however, political considerations have increased the attendance at the Sinhastha Mela. Ujjain is located in central India, in the heartland of the Hindu nationalist groups such as the **Rashtriya Svayamsevak Sangh**, **Vishva Hindu Parishad**, and **Bharatiya Janata Party**. The city of Ujjain is also close to the ancestral kingdom of Vijaya Raje Scindia, the matriarch of a former royal family and a prominent figure in the Bharatiya Janata Party. In such a political climate and local environment, the Sinhastha Mela has been seen as a good opportunity for religious-political theater, in order to generate publicity, deliver patronage, and give the people in these organizations greater status and visibility. See also **Tortoise avatar**.

Sita

("furrow") Daughter of King **Janaka**, wife of the god-prince **Rama** (himself the seventh **avatar** or incarnation of the god **Vishnu**), and the major female character in the ***Ramayana***, the earlier of the two great **Sanskrit** epics. Unlike many other Hindu goddesses, Sita's identity stems almost completely from her husband, and she has little independent **worship** or personality of her own. Her abduction by the **demon**-king **Ravana** is the single major event driving the plot of the *Ramayana*, prompting

her husband and his allies first to search the **earth** for her and then to fight a climactic battle to regain her, concluding with Ravana's death. Throughout all the tumult Sita simply waits to be rescued, sure that this will provide her husband with greater glory.

According to her charter myth, Sita is not born in the normal way but is found in a furrow by King Janaka as he plows his field. Sita thus carries a strong association with the earth, fertility, and prosperity; as David Kinsley points out, her marriage to Rama symbolizes the union between the fecund earth and a righteous king that will make it prosper. Her connection with the earth is also seen in her disappearance, when in response to Rama's accusations of unfaithfulness, she calls on the earth to swallow her up as a witness to her chastity, and disappears forever.

Sita's primary virtue is her devotion to her husband, and in her unflagging love for him she is a model Hindu wife, just as many of the *Ramayana's* other characters incarnate cultural ideals. An early sign of her devotion is shown when Rama has been wrongly exiled in the forest for fourteen years. Even though Sita has never known anything but luxury and ease, she is determined to accompany him into exile, based on the conviction that a faithful wife should always accompany her husband. Rama objects, reasons, and even forbids her, but Sita does not give in—perhaps the only time that she does not observe her husband's wishes. She goes to the forest with Rama and her brother-in-law **Lakshmana**, cheerfully taking on the difficult life of an **ascetic**, since this means she can remain with her husband.

The more difficult test of her devotion to her husband comes when she is abducted and held captive by Ravana. She holds steadfast despite Ravana's unceasing persuasion, threats, and attempts to convince her that Rama has been killed. According to one story, the only part of Ravana that she ever sees is his feet, since as a devoted wife she kept her eyes modestly downcast rather than look directly at another man. When Rama's ally **Hanuman** discovers where Sita is hidden, she refuses to let him carry her away, since this will have meant touching another man, as well as depriving her husband of the opportunity to rescue her.

Her devotion is severely tested after her rescue, when Rama insists that she must have been unfaithful to him during her long captivity. This accusation reflects the Indian cultural assumption that **women** have much higher sex drives than men, and much less ability to control these drives. Stung by this accusation, she asks Rama to have a funeral pyre built for her and enters it with the wish that, if she is innocent, the **fire** will not harm her. When the blaze dies down she emerges unscathed, with the god **Agni** (fire personified) as a witness to her chastity. Despite this proof, Rama banishes her from **Ayodhya** after their return. When Rama later demands a second **ordeal**, Sita calls on the earth to swallow her up as a witness to her **purity**, and disappears forever.

Sita's ability to withstand both ordeals reflects the widespread Indian belief that women gain power through their devotion to their husbands, power that can be so great that they can even **curse** the gods themselves. Encoded in this notion are cultural messages about the role of women and the importance of their relationships with others. Sita represents the model Indian woman, whose primary loyalty is to her husband and his family. This reflects the northern Indian marriage pattern in which brides are brought into the groom's home and become part of their marital families, severing their connection with their **birth** family. Wives are expected to place other people's welfare before their own, so that they may live a happily married life. In return for such self-**sacrifice**, a wife becomes a model for all to respect and honor.

For more information on Sita and all the goddesses of Hinduism, see John Stratton Hawley and Donna Wulff (eds.), *The Divine Consort*, 1986; David R. Kinsley, *Hindu Goddesses*, 1986; and Sara Mitter, *Dharma's Daughters*, 1991.

Sitamarhi

City in the northern part of the state of **Bihar**, about ten miles from the border with **Nepal**. It is in the **Panchala** region traditionally reckoned as the kingdom of King **Janaka**, and Sitamarhi is believed to be the place where the **goddess Sita** was found in a furrow of the **earth** while King Janaka was plowing.

Six Schools

Collective name for the six developed schools of traditional Hindu **philosophy**. All six schools consider the religious texts known as the **Vedas** to be the most authoritative **pramana**, the means by which human beings can gain true and accurate knowledge. All six schools also assume that philosophical reflection must ultimately serve religious goals, to release the embodied soul (**atman**) from an otherwise unending cycle of transmigration. Aside from these basic similarities, each of these schools developed distinctive and characteristic perspectives. Despite their differences, by the early centuries of the common era the schools had become associated in pairs: **Nyaya-Vaisheshika**, **Samkhya-Yoga**, and **Purva Mimamsa**-Uttara Mimamsa, with the final school more commonly known as **Vedanta**.

Of these, the Nyaya school focused on examining and cataloguing the pramanas, the means by which human beings can gain true and accurate knowledge, and their conclusions became accepted by all six schools. The Vaisheshika school was a descriptive ontology that categorized the world in atomistic fashion, in which all things were considered to be constructed from smaller parts. This school had inherent philosophical problems that contributed to its eclipse. **Samkhya** is an atheistic dualism based on the distinction between a conscious but inert

Skanda, the god Shiva's son. Skanda is a warrior prince, born to defeat the demon Taraka.

purusha ("person," or spirit), and an unconscious but active **prakrti** ("nature"). According to the Samkhya proponents, failure to discriminate between the two leads to the **evolution** of the world and the individual person, whereas correct understanding reverses this process. Samkhya provides the theoretical basis for the Yoga school, which essentially details techniques to help one gain the correct understanding between these two entities. Purva Mimamsa stresses the study of the Vedas as the source of instruction for human beings, an emphasis that led it to develop sophisticated theories of language and methods for textual interpretation. These tools were used by the Vedanta school in its efforts to reveal the ultimate meaning of the Vedas. Most of the first millennium during the common era was a time of lively debate among these schools, each of which held varying positions on basic things such as the reality of the world. By the end of the millennium Vedanta had become the most significant philosophical perspective, largely eclipsing the others, although it had absorbed certain influences from them. For further information see Sarvepalli Radhakrishnan and Charles A. Moore (eds.), *A Sourcebook in Indian Philosophy*, 1957.

Skanda

Hindu **deity** who is the son of the god **Shiva**. Skanda is born to destroy the **demon Taraka**, who has received the divine boon that he can only be killed by a son of Shiva. When Taraka makes this request, Shiva is deep in meditation in his grief after the death of his wife **Sati**, and it seems unlikely that such a son can ever be born. After Taraka grows too strong, the other gods begin the process of trying to encourage Shiva to marry, which results in his wedding with the **goddess Parvati**.

Despite the marriage of Shiva and Parvati, Skanda is born in an unusual way. According to the legend, Shiva and Parvati are disturbed while making love, and Shiva inadvertently spills his **semen** on the ground (the verb *skand* means "to leap" or "to ooze"). In Indian culture semen is seen as a man's concentrated essence, and for a deity like Shiva this means that the semen is inordinately powerful, capable of destroying the **earth**. The semen is first held by the god **Agni**, who is fire personified, but it proves too powerful for him. Agni then puts it in the River **Ganges**, and after 10,000 years the river deposits a shining child in the reeds by its bank. The child is discovered by the **Krittikas** (the Pleiades personified), each of whom want to nurse him. To oblige them Skanda grows five extra heads. As a mark of the Krittikas' care, one of his epithets is Kartikkeya. Skanda grows rapidly, assumes command of Shiva's heavenly host (**gana**), and kills the troublesome Taraka. His persona remains that of a warrior prince, unlike that of his brother **Ganesh**, who is a scholar and sage.

In northern India Skanda is considered a member of Shiva's household, and although his power is acknowledged, he is generally not a primary object of **worship**. In southern India Skanda has been identified with **Murugan**, a regional deity associated primarily with the hunt, but also with war. In this atmosphere he has taken on a much greater role, particularly in **Tamil Nadu**, and has assumed the mantle of a philosopher and exponent of the **Shaiva Siddhanta** school.

Smallpox

In traditional Hindu belief, smallpox was personified as the **goddess Shitala** ("Cool One," a euphemism), and the fever and skin eruptions accompanying the disease were interpreted as signs of **possession** by this goddess. In the time since the World Health Organization has declared smallpox officially eradicated, in some regions Shitala has been identified with tuberculosis. See **Shitala**.

Smara

("memory") Epithet of the god **Kama**, the deification of desire, reflecting the importance of memory in generating and maintaining desire. See **Kama**.

Smarana

("remembering") One of the standard religious practices mentioned in lists of religiously meritorious actions. Smarana is most often associated with **deities** but is also mentioned in conjunction with sacred sites (**tirthas**), one's spiritual teacher (**guru**), or even particular acts of **worship**. This practice involves thinking constantly upon the deity, person, place, or object, and in the case of a deity this often involves mental recitation of the deity's name. The primary emphasis in this practice is to create habitual behavioral patterns that, over the long term, will have beneficial effects on one's character.

Smarta

Name for a particular group of brahmins distinguished not by region or family, but by the religious texts that they hold most authoritative. For the Smartas, the most authoritative texts are the texts known as the **smrtis**—either the texts themselves or commentaries and compilations based on them. The smrtis or "remembered" texts were a class of literature that, although deemed important, were considered less authoritative than the **shrutis** or "heard" texts. In brief, the shrutis denoted the **Vedas**, the oldest and most authoritative Hindu religious texts, whereas the smrtis included the **dharma literature**, the **Bhagavad Gita**, the *Mahabharata*, and *Ramayana*, and the collection known as the **puranas**. The Smartas thus stand in contrast with sectarian brahmins, whether **Shaiva** (devotees of **Shiva**) or **Vaishnava** (devotees of **Vishnu**), for whom their particular sectarian scriptures have the highest religious authority. Smarta brahmins can therefore claim to be following the oldest and best established religious texts and thus in some way to be the most orthodox. Since Smartas are distinguished by their authoritative texts and practice rather than by the **deity** they **worship**, individual Smartas may worship different Hindu deities, and many do. Yet particularly in southern India, many Smartas perform the **panchayatana puja** to the five divine forms—Vishnu, Shiva, **Surya**, **Ganesh**, and the **Goddess**—which is intended to show the ultimate unity behind the differing manifestations of divinity.

Smrti

("[that which is] remembered") An important class of Hindu religious literature that, despite its sacrality, is deemed less authoritative than the other major category, **shruti**. According to tradition, the shruti ("heard") texts were not composed by human beings but are based in the primordial vibrations of the cosmos itself. The ancient sages, whose faculties of perception had

Snana, or bathing, at a festival in Rajasthan. Before performing any ritual, one must obtain purity by bathing.

been sharpened through rigorous religious practice, were able to "hear" and understand these vibrations, and transmitted them to others in a lineage of learning. The smrti texts, in contrast, are attributed to human authors, who are putting forth matters that are "remembered" and thus carry with them the possibility of error. The smrti literature is wider and much more varied than the shruti, which is restricted to the texts in the **Vedas**; smrti literature includes the **dharma literature**, the sectarian compilations known as **puranas**, the two great epics (*Mahabharata* and *Ramayana*), the **Bhagavad Gita**, and the **tantras**, which are manuals detailing the secret, ritually based religious practice of tantra followers. Although theoretically the smrtis have less religious authority than the shrutis, in practical terms they are often far more important, in part because their contents are much better known. This is particularly true for sectarian Hinduism, in which a group's sectarian literature will often be given the highest religious authority.

Snana

("bath") Bathing is arguably the single most commonly performed Hindu religious act, and it is a necessary one before performing any rite or **worship**. An early morning bath is the norm for just about all Hindus, and this has been true for centuries. The earliest European visitors invariably remarked on this practice, since some of these visitors bathed only a few times in their lives. For Hindus, bathing not only keeps one clean but is a way to regain ritual **purity** by using water (most commonly) to remove any source of defilement.

Bathing is normally the last part of one's morning rites, preceded by cleaning one's teeth and tongue, rinsing the mouth (**achamana**), and (immediately before bathing) voiding one's bladder and bowels. These latter acts are a necessary part of life, but they also render one ritually impure, a state that the bath removes. People generally perform any daily worship immediately after bathing, while this ritual purity is still unbroken.

Most people bathe only in the morning, although those scrupulously concerned with purity (generally brahmins or ascetics) will bathe more often. The bath itself is usually quite brief and some in cases consists of simply immersing oneself in a natural body of water, or pouring a bucket of water over one's head. In modern times people often use soap, but the traditionally prescribed cleansing medium is **earth**. It is preferable to bathe in running water, since the bath purifies by removing the impurity (**ashaucha**) and carrying it away and although bathing in a large pond is seen as acceptable, bathing in a bathtub is seen as simply spreading the impurity around rather than getting rid of it. Although the most common medium for bathing is water, when this is impossible one can ritually cleanse oneself with oil, or one can perform ritual cleansing with **mantras** by using sacred sounds to remove defilement and bring one to a state of ritual purity.

In the context of worship, snana is the sixth of the sixteen traditional **upacharas** ("offerings") given to a **deity** as part of worship, on the model of treating the deity as an honored guest. In this offering, the deity is bathed, either literally or symbolically. The underlying motive here, as for all the upacharas, is to show one's love for the deity and minister to the deity's needs.

Snataka

("[one who has] bathed") In the **dharma literature**, this is the name for a young man who had performed the **samavartana samskara**, the life-cycle ceremony that marks the end of his **stage of life** as a celibate student (**brahmacharin**) and return to his parental home. The most important element in the rite was a bath, after which he changed into new clothes, marking his change in status. Before doing this he was supposed to ask his **guru's** permission, and also to give him his teacher's fee (**dakshina**), both as payment for services rendered and as a sign of respect. A young man who had performed this rite would be eligible to get married, and the literature prescribes that this should follow in short order.

Solah Somvar Vrat

A religious vow (**vrat**) that is a variant of the **worship** of the god **Shiva** prescribed for every **Monday** (**Somvar**), the day of the **week** over which he is believed to preside. In the Solah Somvar Vrat, the observer vows to do perform this rite for sixteen (solah) consecutive Mondays. Each week's observance is marked by fasting (**upavasa**), worship, and reading aloud the charter myth for this particular observance. As with most literature pertaining to such rites, the text ends with a catalog of the benefits brought by the rite—in essence, it gives whatever one desires.

According to the vow's charter myth, as Shiva and his wife **Parvati** are playing dice in a temple, Parvati asks a nearby **brahmin** which of them will win, and when he replies that it will be Shiva, she angrily curses him to be afflicted with leprosy. The curse comes true (as with all **curses** in Indian mythology) and the brahmin is in a terrible state. Shiva takes pity on the brahmin, tells him to perform the Solah Somvar Vrat, and on the sixteenth Monday, the brahmin is completely cured. Some time later Parvati sees him and is amazed at his recovery. When she asks how he has been cured, the brahmin tells her about the vow, which she later uses to cure her son of disobedience (thus emphasizing the power of the vow, since it is even used by the gods themselves).

Solar Line

In Hindu mythology, one of the two great lineages, the other being the **Lunar Line**. The Solar Line traces its descent from **Ikshvaku**, the grandson of the **Sun** himself. Its descendants include many of the principal characters in the *Ramayana*, the earlier of the two great Indian epics. One of these descendants is **Rama** himself. In many of the small former princely states in **Rajasthan**, the rulers claimed descent from the Solar Line as a way to establish and support their royal authority. Although they no longer wield ruling power, many of these royal houses still exist, and thus this lineage is believed to be still extant.

Soma

Soma is one of the most enigmatic **deities** in the Hindu tradition. The 120 hymns to soma in the **Rg Veda**, the oldest Hindu sacred text, variously describe soma as a plant, as the juice pressed from that plant, and as the deified form of both juice and plant. The Vedic hymns give detailed descriptions of how the sacrificial priests pressed it, strained and filtered it, and finally consumed it, which then brought visions upon them. These hymns portray soma as some sort of mind-altering substance, although there is no general agreement on what the soma plant might be. Its identity has been lost since late Vedic times, and since then various substitutes have been used in rituals.

Although the hymns describe soma as hallucinogenic, one need not take this literally. One can explain such visions in purely psychological terms, as induced or fostered by the priests' heightened expectations in the sacrificial arena. If one assumes that soma was actually mind-altering, it could not have been an alcoholic beverage—since it was prepared and consumed on the same day, this would have given no time for fermentation. One theory is that soma was hashish (**charas**), which is still consumed in certain ritual contexts. The most intriguing theory was proposed by R. G. Wasson, who contended that soma was *Amonita muscaria*, a mind-altering mushroom that has a long history of use in Asian shamanic traditions. Although Wasson's theory would explain soma's ability to take immediate effect, many Indologists have taken issue with this claim. See Robert Gordon Wasson, *Soma*, 1971; for contrary remarks, see J. Brough, "Soma and Amonita Muscaria," in *The Bulletin of the School of Oriental and African Studies,* Vol. 34, 1971.

Somavati Amavasya

Religious observance celebrated when a **new moon** (**amavasya**) falls on a **Monday**, which can thus occur in any month in the **year**. On the new moon day the **sun** and moon travel together during the daylight sky, and when this happens on the Monday, whose presiding **planet** is the moon, this confluence is deemed particularly favorable. Another auspicious connection arises because Monday's presiding **deity**, the god **Shiva**, also has mythic connections with the moon. A Somavati Amavasya is thus judged a particularly beneficial time to **worship** Shiva, as well as to bathe (**snana**) in a sacred river such as the **Ganges**, or to perform any other religious act.

Someshvara I

(r. 1042–1068) Monarch in the **Chalukya dynasty**. Aside from his long reign, he is most noted for performing religious **suicide** by intentionally drowning himself in the **Tungabhadra River** when his mental faculties began to wane. Although in general suicide was strongly condemned, suicide by a person suffering from a terminal disease or enduring chronic pain was a well-attested exception to this rule. This sort of suicide was performed according to a well-defined ritual, which was intended to put the performer in the proper frame of mind. In about the twelfth century this was declared one of the rites "forbidden in

Somnath Shore Temple, Gujarat.

the **Kali** [Age]" (**Kalivarjya**), although it had been permitted in earlier times.

Somnath

Temple and sacred site (**tirtha**) in the state of **Gujarat**. The temple is named for its presiding **deity**—the god **Shiva** in his manifestation as the "Lord of the **Moon**." Shiva is present at Somnath in the form of a **linga**, the pillar-shaped image that is his symbolic form, and the Somnath linga is one of the twelve **jyotirlingas**, a network of sites deemed especially sacred to Shiva, and at which he is uniquely present. According to the site's charter myth, the moon is married to all of the twenty-seven **nakshatras**, or signs in the lunar **zodiac**, but he loves **Rohini** nakshatra so much that he stays with her all the time, and neglects his other twenty-six wives. His father-in-law **Daksha** protests to the moon, but when he refuses to give them equal time, Daksha lays a curse on him that he will lose all his light. The moon overcomes this **curse** by worshiping Shiva at Somnath for six continuous months and is given the boon that he will only shrink during half the **lunar month**, and that

during the other half he will grow. As a sign of this gift, Shiva takes residence there as Somnath, and remains to this day.

Aside from its importance as a sacred site, the Somnath temple is a potent political symbol. The original temple was razed and pillaged by **Mahmud of Ghazni** in 1024, who reportedly carried off astounding booty. The present temple at Somnath was built after Indian independence in 1947 and consecrated in 1951. As a symbol, Somnath is thus associated with past oppression and depredation, and with the revitalization of Hindu culture in India. For this reason, the Somnath temple is a popular image for proponents of **Hindutva**, an idea that identifies Hindu identity and Indian citizenship.

Sonar

In traditional northern Indian society, a Hindu **jati** whose hereditary occupation was gold smithing and jewelry making. Traditional Indian society was modeled as a collection of **endogamous**, or inter-married, subgroups known as jatis ("birth"). These jatis were organized (and their social status determined) by the group's hereditary occupation, over which each group held a monopoly.

Song of Manik Chandra

Traditional **Bengali** song describing the adventures of the mythical king Manik Chandra, his wife Mayana, and their **son Gopi** Chand; the latter figures are the primary characters, since Manik Chandra dies early in the story. The text is a romance but also contains many of the doctrines associated with the **Nathpanthi** ascetics. In particular, Queen Mayana has power over **Yama** (death personified), which was one of the primary aims of the Nathpanthi ascetics. Furthermore, she acquired this power through the spiritual instruction given by her **guru Gorakhnath**, the Nathpanthi founder.

Her power over death is shown in various ways. When her husband dies, Mayana descends to Yama's realm and physically abuses both Yama and his minions. In his flight Yama changes into various forms to escape Mayana's wrath, but she is never deceived and continues to harass him. On other occasions, she shows her power over death by her inability to be killed. She mounts her husband's funeral pyre, and although the **fire** burns for seven days and nine nights, not even her clothing is scorched. Many years later, Mayana survives seven fearsome ordeals, such as boiling in oil. When asked how she acquired these magical arts, she replies that Gorakhnath himself taught her. The appearance of such ideas in an essentially popular tale shows how deeply these ideas had sunk into the popular mind.

Sons

It is difficult to overstate the importance traditional Hindu culture has placed on the need for sons, and the cultural bias for sons over **daughters**. Religious motives underlie one important reason for this bias, since only sons are entitled to perform the memorial **offerings** for the dead known as **shraddhas**. The men in each generation are responsible for making these offerings to their ancestors. They are in turn obliged to have sons of their own, so that the family lineage and the chain of ancestral offerings remains unbroken through the generations. Sonless couples are not completely out of luck, since sons can be obtained through **adoption**.

The other major reason behind the preference for sons lies in far more pragmatic motives. According to the traditional Indian marriage pattern, daughters move into their marital homes and become members of their marital families, whereas sons bring their brides into the home and through their own families continue the family line. Thus, parents sometimes see their daughters as "temporary" family members, while their sons are "permanent." The sons will dwell in their natal house their entire lives, support their parents in old age, and produce the family's future generations. These traditional practices and beliefs still hold very strong, although the forces of modernity have affected the joint family. It has become more common for husbands and wives to live separately from the husband's parents.

The religious, economic, and social factors behind this preference for sons have sometimes had terrible consequences. Consciously or unconsciously, sons may be favored over daughters in many significant ways. Sons are often given better access to education and economic opportunities, because men are traditionally required to support their families. A similar presumption lies behind the inequities in traditional Hindu **inheritance** laws, which give the sons a much larger share of the inheritance. In poorer families, sons may even get preference for basic needs such as food and access to medical care. Despite these patterns, in contemporary times many families treat all their children with equal love and care. Given the trend toward smaller families, the birth of a daughter can be cause for as much rejoicing as that of a son.

Sopashraya

("using a support") One of the sitting postures (**asana**) described in commentaries to the **Yoga Sutras** of **Patanjali**, the foundational text for the practice of **yoga**. The name of this posture derives from a wooden support used by the sitter to keep erect, often portrayed as a crutch-shaped prop under the chin.

Soratha

Metrical form in northern Indian devotional (**bhakti**) poetry, made up of two lines of twenty-four metric beats, divided unevenly after the eleventh beat. The metric pattern for the first line is 6+4+1, with the pattern for the second line being 6+4+3. The soratha is thus an inversion of the metrical form **doha**. Although the soratha was a common poetic form, the doha was far more popular and widely used.

South Africa

One of the countries with significant Hindu **diaspora populations**. This is particularly true in Natal province, where Hindus were first brought as indentured agricultural laborers, but there is a significant Hindu presence in other parts of the country as well. South Africa is best known as the place where **Mohandas K. Gandhi** first developed and refined his program of nonviolent resistance, or **satyagraha**, which he employed in the service of the Indian community there. In contemporary times the South African Hindu community, as with many Hindu diaspora communities, has loosened religious ties to India, and is in the process of forming a Hindu religious life in another geographical setting.

Space

One of the five **elements** in traditional Indian **cosmology**, the others being **earth**, **fire**, **water**, and **wind**. **Akasha** or "space" is not conceived in the sense of "outer space," but rather the space between or within visible objects on earth. For example, an "empty" pitcher was not actually empty, but was filled with space, until it was displaced by some fluid. This elemental sense of space was thus something closer to what might be considered the "atmosphere," and was actually seen as having fluidlike properties. In some philosophical schools, each of the elements is paired with one of the five senses; here akasha is associated with hearing, since it is believed to convey the sound from place to place.

Sphota

("disclosure") Crucial element in the theory of language propounded by **Bhartrhari** (7th c.). Bhartrhari was the founder of the **Grammarians**, a philosophical school that conceived of **Brahman**, the Supreme Reality, as being manifested in sound, particularly the sound of the spoken word. According to this theory, a verbal utterance had three elements: the sound or sounds produced by the speaker and heard by the listener; a phonological pattern, of which that utterance is an instance; and finally the sphota, which was expressed by the sounds and signified the object of that utterance. According to Bhartrhari, sphota had to be postulated to explain how words could carry meaning. They do so because they are connected to the sphota, which designated a particular object, and in producing the sounds the speaker expressed that sphota.

Sri Lanka

Island nation off the southeastern coast of India, formerly known as Ceylon. Local tradition claims that Sri Lanka was the place at which the biblical Adam alighted from paradise. Yet despite the island's idyllic natural beauty, its human geography has been far more troubled. Since 1981 the nation has been in the throes of civil war between the Sinhalese and the Tamils, the island's two major ethnic groups. The Sinhalese comprise about 70 percent of the population, are largely Buddhist, live mainly in southern, western, and central Sri Lanka, and consider themselves the island's traditional inhabitants. The Tamils comprise little more than 20 percent of the population, are both Hindu and Christian, and are concentrated in the north and east. The Tamils came to Sri Lanka in two different ways—about half are descended from medieval invaders, who established Tamil kingdoms in northern Sri Lanka after crossing the straits from southern India, others were brought to Sri Lanka in the nineteenth and early twentieth centuries, to serve as laborers on tea plantations.

Since independence in 1948, the Tamils have been at a distinct disadvantage *vis-à-vis* the Sinhalese, whose majority has allowed them to control virtually all aspects of national life. This precarious position was often further undermined by anti-Tamil riots, particularly in Colombo, the nation's capital. In 1981 Tamil groups began a struggle for an independent nation in the Tamil-majority areas. The Sinhalese majority was deathly opposed to this notion, and since then Sri Lanka has been marked by periods of vicious civil war. Given their slimmer resources, the Tamils have tended to wage guerrilla warfare. Their soldiers are famous for wearing a cyanide capsule around their necks with which to commit **suicide** if captured. These soldiers are also notorious for their willingness to serve as human bombs, striking against civilian populations in urban areas. In 1991 one such human bomb was responsible for the assassination of former Indian Prime Minister Rajiv Gandhi in revenge for Gandhi's perceived treachery in cooperating with the Sri Lankan government. Although the Tamil regions have been offered limited autonomy by Chandrika Kumaratunga, Sri Lanka's present prime minister, the conflict has been so bitter that it is not likely to be easily resolved.

Sri Lanka has traditionally been part of the Indian cultural orbit and has a long history of cultural exchanges with India. According to local tradition, Buddhism was brought to Sri Lanka from India in the third century B.C.E. by Mahinda, who was the son of the Mauryan emperor **Ashoka**. Another sign of this connection is that Sri Lanka contains an important Hindu pilgrimage place (**tirtha**), **Kataragama**, located near the island's southern coast. Kataragama's perceived power draws Hindus from abroad as well as Sri Lankans from all religious communities. Although Kataragama is Sri Lanka's only major Hindu site, the northern regions strongly reflect the Tamil culture of the region's population, which stems from their geographic roots. See also **Tamil Nadu**.

Stages of Life

As described in the **dharma literature**, there were four stages (ashramas) in the life of a **twice-born** man, that is, a man born into one of the three "twice-born" groups in Indian society—**brahmin**, **kshatriya**, or **vaishya**—who are eligible for the adolescent religious **initiation** known as the "second birth." In the first stage, immediately after this initiation, the young man would live as a celibate student (**brahmacharin**) studying the Vedas in his **guru's** household. The second stage was that of the householder (**grhastha**), in which he would marry, raise a family, and engage in worldly life. In the third stage, as a forest-dwelling hermit (**vanaprastha**), he would gradually detach himself from worldly entanglements. The final stage was as a total renunciant (**Sanyasi**), who had given up all things in a search for the ultimate religious truth. These four stages are an idealized progression and should not be understood as describing actual practice, since most men never pass beyond the householder stage of life and have no desire to do so.

Beneath this idealized progression lies the tension between two differing modes of religious life—that of the householder, which is based in the world, and that of the **ascetic**, which renounces the world. The latter ideal originated with the religious adepts known as the **shramanas** and evolved into the monastic **asceticism** of the Buddhists and Jains, which was portrayed as a superior religious path than the householder's life. Both these groups were highly influential—the Jains had a significant presence in southern Indian society up to the eighth century C.E.—and it is generally accepted that the pattern of the four ashramas was evolved as a way to appropriate and transform this stress on ascetic life. The doctrine of the four stages provided a place and time for asceticism, but as the last stage, at the end of one's life. The clear message was that one should engage in the search for religious truth only after fulfilling one's social and ancestral duties.

Steya

("theft") In the **dharma literature**, one of the **Four Great Crimes** whose commission made one an outcast from society; steya was theft of a **brahmin's** gold, above a certain specified amount. One guilty of this crime was to go to the king bearing an iron club and receive a blow to the head intended to be fatal. This blow would absolve the sin, whether or not one actually died, although one was also expected to restore the stolen property. For lesser amounts of gold the punishment was less severe and satisfied by fasting (**upavasa**) and other penance (**prayashchitta**). The stress on the seriousness of this sin clearly reflects the interests of the brahmins, who undoubtedly wrote most of the dharma literature.

Sthala Murti

("fixed image") Image of a **deity** that is fixed in a certain place and does not move from it (in the case of stone images, this is often because such images are so large and heavy that moving them is virtually impossible). The other sort of image is the **utsava murti**, a movable image used during festival processions.

Sthunakarna

In the *Mahabharata*, the later of the two great Hindu epics, Sthunakarna is a nature spirit (**yaksha**) who exchanges sexes with **Shikhandi**, the rebirth of the maiden **Amba**, daughter of the king of **Kashi**.

Stridhan

("woman's wealth") Term denoting any property owned or inherited by a woman, which usually included any gifts given to her by her family or money that she earned herself. In the patrilineal **inheritance** systems prescribed by texts such as the *Mitakshara* and the *Dayabhaga*, stridhan was not considered part of the family property, but a woman's personal property that she could dispose of as she pleased. Stridhan could be inherited, but the inheritance patterns were different than those for family property. The primary inheritors were a woman's **daughters**; for **women** with no daughters, the ownership would devolve to her husband and his heirs, or to her birth family.

Stridharma

Term denoting "**women's** religious duty" (**dharma**), the set of social roles, rules, and duties broadly conceived as applying to all women. In the **dharma literature**, it was generally assumed that appropriate women's roles were as daughters, wives, and mothers, and that their lives would be primarily defined by their relationships with men—whether fathers, brothers, husbands, or sons. As described in the dharma literature, their position seems to have had status, but little authority. One well-known passage from the *Manu Smrti* warns that a woman must never be independent, but always under the guardianship of a man; this is followed by an equally famous passage warning that the treatment of women was a marker of the family's honor, and that a household in which the women were badly treated would disappear. In real life women exercised considerably more power than in this theoretical model, but such power usually came later in life, when a woman's sons had formed families of their own, and she had thus become the matriarch of an extended family.

Subhadra

The divine sister of the god **Jagannath**, who is invariably pictured with him and their brother **Balabhadra**. The most important site for these three **deities** is the Jagannath temple in the city of **Puri**, at which Jagannath is the presiding deity. Although Jagannath is identified with the god **Krishna**, he is generally considered an autochthonous ("of the land") deity who was originally the local deity of Puri. He has been assimilated into the Hindu pantheon by his identification with Krishna.

One piece of evidence for this theory is the deities' invariable appearance, with Jagannath (Krishna) on the right, his brother Balabhadra (**Balarama**) on the left, and Subhadra as a smaller figure in the center. Such a triadic grouping is virtually unknown in Krishna devotion, which tends to stress either Krishna alone or the divine couple of Krishna and **Radha**. The female figure of Subhadra is also very unusual, since as Jagannath's sister she is ineligible for the amorous adventures usually associated with Krishna. Although Jagannath is the most important of the three deities, the identifications with the other two also reveal larger syncretizing tendencies. Balabhadra is sometimes identified as a form of the god **Shiva**, and Subhadra as the powerful **goddess Durga**. In this way, Puri's divine trio embody the three most important Hindu deities. For further information on Subhadra and her brothers, the best source is Anncharlott Eschmann, Hermann Kulke, and Gaya Charan Tripathi, *The Cult of Jagannath and the Regional Traditions of Orissa*, 1978.

Subodhini

("Greatly enlightening") A name given to commentaries on various texts—presumably because of the commentary's ability to illuminate the text. The most famous of these commentaries, to which the name *Subodhini* is often understood to refer, is the one by **Vallabhacharya** (1479–1531) on the ***Bhagavata Purana***. The *Bhagavata Purana* is one of the later sectarian compendia known as **puranas**, and it is the most important source for the mythology of the god **Krishna**, whom Vallabhacharya considered the Supreme Being. Vallabhacharya's *Subodhini* lays out the basic doctrines of his religious community, known as the **Pushti Marg** because of their stress on god's **grace**, which they called *pushti*, meaning "that which nourishes the soul."

Subrahmanya

("dear to brahmins") Epithet of the god **Skanda**, particularly in his southern Indian manifestation as **Murugan**. See **Skanda** and **Murugan**.

Subtle Body

Alternate human physiological system that exists on a different plane than gross matter, but has certain correspondences with the anatomy of the material body. Different parts of the subtle body contain the microcosmic forms of the **deities Shiva** and **Shakti**, the bipolar forces believed to be the powers behind the cosmos. The subtle body is thus based on the principle of the homology, or essential similarities, of macrocosm and microcosm, a fundamental Hindu idea since the time of the **Upanishads**. The **Sanskrit** texts describing the subtle body assume that there are different planes of reality, and thus that the subtle body actually exists, but given the network of symbols associated with it, one

Vishnu, surrounded by worshipers, wielding Sudarshana, his discus weapon.

need not accept its literal reality for it to be religiously meaningful.

The subtle body is visualized as a set of six psychic centers (**chakras**), running roughly along the course of the spine: the **muladhara chakra** at the base of the spine, the **svadhishthana chakra** in the genital region, the **manipura chakra** in the navel region, the **anahata chakra** in the heart region, the **vishuddha chakra** in the throat region, and the **ajna chakra** is in the forehead between the eyebrows. Associated with each of these chakras is an elaborate symbolic system: All six can be seen as symbols for a human physiological capacity; the first five are associated with one of the subtle elements (**tanmatras**), and the sixth with thought.

The lotus petals on each chakra contain a letter of the Sanskrit alphabet, thus encompassing all sacred sounds. Some models of the subtle body are even more developed, with each chakra associated with a certain color and a certain presiding deity.

These centers are capped at the top of the head by the "thousand-petaled lotus" (**sahasradalapadma**), which is the abode of Shiva in the human body. Connecting all of the centers are three vertical channels (**nadi**)—the **ida nadi** on the left, the **pingala nadi** on the right, and the **sushumna** in the center. Coiled three times around the muladhara chakra is the **kundalini**, the latent spiritual force in all human beings. This is considered an aspect of the universal Shakti, or feminine **divine power**, but in most people is regarded as dormant, symbolized by its coiled state. The separation of Shakti and Shiva at the opposite ends of the subtle body also symbolizes the ordinary person's unenlightened state, since enlightenment transcends this duality, and the two deities are united and identical.

The subtle body is a fundamental aspect of **tantra** practices and some forms of **yoga**. In the types of yoga that focus on the subtle body, including **kundalini yoga**, the ultimate aim is to awaken and straighten the kundalini, moving it up the sushumna through the chakras to the abode of Shiva. Since the kundalini is nothing but raw energy, the process must be carefully controlled to prevent the aspirant from unleashing uncontrollable forces, and manuals warn against doing this without being under the supervision of a spiritual teacher (**guru**). The union of Shiva and Shakti in the aspirant's body mirrors the action of these divine forces in the macrocosm, and with this union the aspirant gains bliss and final liberation of the soul (**moksha**). For further information see Arthur Avalon (Sir John Woodroffe), *Shakti and Shakta*, 1959; Philip S. Rawson, *The Art of Tantra*, 1973; Swami Agehananda Bharati, *The Tantric Tradition*, 1977; and Douglas Renfrew Brooks, *The Secret of the Three Cities*, 1990.

Suchi Hasta

In Indian **dance**, **sculpture**, and ritual, a particular hand **gesture** (**hasta**), in which the hand is closed except for the index finger, which is pointing downward to indicate something to the viewer. The word *suchi* means "needle" but is derived from a verb that can mean either "to pierce" or "to indicate"—both meanings that imply focusing on a particular place.

Sudama

In Hindu mythology, one of the god **Krishna's** childhood friends who is a symbol for god's **grace** and providence. In later life Sudama is desperately poor and, at his wife's urging, goes to beg for help from his childhood friend, who is now the king of **Dwaraka**. Sudama is so poor that the only gift he can bring for Krishna is a small packet of parched rice, but Krishna greets him and graciously accepts it. The two have an enjoyable visit in which they reminisce about old times, and Sudama goes home without asking for anything. Some of the stories explain this lapse as stemming from shame, but in others Sudama is portrayed as having had such a nice time that he simply forgets. During his homeward journey Sudama worries over the reception he will get from his wife, but when he arrives he discovers that his hut has been transformed into a palace by Krishna's **divine power**, and from that day he is never poor again.

Sudarshana

In Hindu mythology, the name for the god **Vishnu's** discus weapon (**chakra**), which is fashioned by **Vishvakarma**, the workman and architect of the gods. According to the story, Vishvakarma has married his daughter **Sanjna** to the **sun**, but she finds her husband's brightness too much to bear. To help his daughter adjust, Vishvakarma trims off some bits

667

of the sun with his divine tools, removing enough of his radiance that Sanjna can bear to be with him. He then fashions the trimmed-off portions into Vishnu's Sudarshana chakra, **Shiva's** trident, and various other divine weapons, as well as the **Pushpak Viman**, an **aerial car**. Sudarshana's divine source makes it a fearful weapon, and it is thus able to decimate any enemy.

Sudarshana Sampraday

Another name for the **Nimbarki** religious community, since their founder **Nimbarka** was believed to be an incarnation of **Sudarshana**, **Vishnu's** weapon.

Sugriva

In the *Ramayana*, the earlier of the two great Indian epics, a monkey king and an ally of the god **Rama** in his struggle to regain his kidnapped wife **Sita**. Sugriva and his brother **Bali** jointly rule the kingdom of **Kishkindha** but become enemies because of a misunderstanding. On one occasion the two are fighting a magician who has taken refuge in a cave. Bali goes in, after instructing Sugriva on certain signs that will indicate which of them has been killed. Sugriva waits outside the cave for a year, and then sees the sign indicating his brother's death, which the cunning magician has engineered during his own death. Thinking that his brother is dead, Sugriva rolls a stone over the mouth of the cave to trap the magician, and returns home. Bali eventually manages to get out of the cave and, thinking that his brother has used this opportunity to get rid of him, forces Sugriva into exile and keeps Sugriva's wife as his own. Sugriva lives in exile until he makes an alliance with Rama, who kills Bali by shooting him while Bali fights with Sugriva. After regaining his kingdom, Sugriva is a faithful ally to Rama, and with his monkey armies aids in the conquest of **Lanka**.

Suicide

An act whose permissibility and consequences have elicited varying opinions over time. In medieval times commentators distinguished between several types of suicide, depending on the circumstances surrounding the act. Any suicide prompted by an overpowering emotional impulse such as rage or grief was always strictly forbidden, and those who did this were said to reap dire karmic consequences. Another case entirely was suicide performed as an expiation (**prayashchitta**) for one's sins, which was often prescribed to expiate one of the **Four Great Crimes**. A third type was suicide by people suffering from a terminal disease, or who were in chronic pain. This sort of suicide was performed according to a well-defined ritual, intended to put the performer in the proper frame of mind. This third category was one of the rites designated as "forbidden in the **Kali** [Age]" (**Kalivarjya**), although it had been permitted in earlier times. The most fascinating sort of suicide was at pilgrimage places (**tirtha**), particularly at **Allahabad**. This was also done according to a very specific ritual, and part of the ritual required the performer to name the benefit for which the rite was being performed—in some cases liberation of the soul (**moksha**), in other cases life in **heaven** for many eons. This practice is well documented up to the seventeenth century, although it is no longer done in contemporary times.

Sulfur

A pivotal substance in Indian **alchemy**, the conceptual foundation for which is its analysis of the world as a series of bipolar opposites in tension with one another, and the conviction that unifying these opposing forces brings spiritual progress and the end of reincarnation (**samsara**). Hindu alchemy shares this model of uniting or transcending opposing forces with Hindu **tantra**, a secret, ritually based system of religious practice, and with **hatha yoga**, which is based on a series of physical exercises that are also believed to affect the **subtle body**.

In the alchemical tradition, the governing metaphor for this combination of opposites is the union of **sun** and **moon**. Both are connected to other opposing principles through an elaborate series of associations, in keeping with this bipolar symbolism. In Hindu alchemical conceptions, sulfur is conceived of as the uterine **blood** of **Shakti**, and thus a powerful element. It is also identified with the sun, with heat, dryness, and withering force. When sulfur is mixed and consumed with elemental **mercury**, which is identified with the god **Shiva's semen**, the aspirant's gross body is purified and refined, eventually rendering it immortal. Modern descriptions of this practice invariably warn that it should only be carried out under the direction of one's **guru** (spiritual teacher), since otherwise the combination will be harmful. This warning is not surprising, since by itself mercury is a deadly poison. For further information see Shashibhushan B. Dasgupta, *Obscure Religious Cults*, 1962; and David Gordon White, *The Alchemical Body*, 1996.

Sulva Sutras

("aphorisms on measurement") A collection of brief sayings giving the exact rules for constructing the sacrificial altars for the public Vedic sacrifices. The Sulva Sutras were connected to the **Shrauta Sutras**, which laid down the ritual prescriptions for these rites, of which the preparation of the site was an obvious necessity. Given the premise that the **sacrifice** would be unsuccessful unless it was performed exactly right, such precise attention to the altar's construction seems a necessary consequence.

Sumantra

In the *Ramayana*, the earlier of the two great Indian epics, Sumantra is one of the ministers of King **Dasharatha**, the father of **Rama**. As Rama, his wife **Sita**, and his brother **Lakshmana** are going into exile, Sumantra accompanies them to the River **Ganges** to make sure that the trio will comply with their orders. When the three board the boat on which the boatman **Guha** will take them over the river, Sumantra bids Rama a tearful farewell.

Sumati

In Hindu mythology, one of the wives of King **Sagar**. Through a sage's boon, Sumati and her co-wife **Keshini** are given a choice in the number of children they would bear—one will bear a single son through whom the lineage will continue, whereas the other will bear sixty thousand sons who will die before they have any offspring. Sumati chooses the latter, and when her sixty thousand handsome sons go out to search for their father's sacrificial horse, they are burned to ash by the fury of the sage **Kapila**. Although these sons die without issue they still have a profound affect on the world, since Keshini's descendants bring the River **Ganges** down to earth to bring peace to their souls.

Sumitra

In the *Ramayana*, the earlier of the two great Indian epics, Sumitra is one of the three wives of King **Dasharatha** and the mother of **Rama's** half-brothers, the twins **Lakshmana** and **Shatrughna**. In their fidelity and service to Rama, her **sons** are important characters in the epic, but aside from bearing them, Sumitra has little importance.

Sun

In Hindu astrology (**jyotisha**), a **planet** generally associated with strength and vitality, although it can be malevolent, possibly reflecting the relentless destructive power of the Indian sun. The sun's vitality makes it a strong planet, and as in Western astrology the sun's position in the **zodiac** plays a major role in fixing a person's **natal horoscope**

The Sun Temple at Konarak, Orissa. It was built in the thirteenth century to resemble the chariot that was believed to carry the sun.

(janampatrika). The sun presides over **Sunday**, a **day** of the **week** that is not strongly marked as either auspicious or inauspicious. See also **Surya**.

Sundaramurtti

(8th c.) The last of the **Nayanars**, a group of sixty-three southern Indian poet-saints who were devotees (**bhakta**) of the god **Shiva**. Along with their contemporaries the **Alvars**, who were devotees of **Vishnu**, the Nayanars spearheaded the revitalization of Hindu religion through their passionate devotion (**bhakti**) to a personal god, conveyed through hymns sung in the **Tamil language**. Along with his predecessors, **Appar** and **Sambandar**, Sundaramurtti actively opposed the heterodox sects of the times, particularly the Jains, whom he reviles in his poems. The collected hymns of the three most important Nayanars—Appar, Sambandar, and Sundaramurtti—comprise the *Devaram*, the most sacred of the Tamil Shaivite texts. Sundaramurtti is also important for his catalog of the sixty-three Nayanars, which forms the first literary source for Tamil Shaivite hagiography.

Sundareshvara

(The "Handsome Lord") Epithet of the god **Shiva** in his manifestation as the husband of the **goddess Minakshi**. Minakshi is the presiding **deity** of the Minakshi temple in the city of **Madurai** in the state of **Tamil Nadu**. See **Shiva**.

Sunday

(Ravivar) First **day** of the Hindu **week**, whose presiding **planet** (and **deity**) is the **sun** (ravi). As a day, Sunday is considered generally auspicious but not particularly powerful, probably because the sun is acknowledged as a deity but is not widely worshiped as a primary one.

Sun Temple

The most famous temple to the **sun** is at **Konarak** in **Orissa** state, right on the shore of the Bay of Bengal. The temple was built by King Narasimhadeva (r. 1238–1264), a monarch in the **Ganga dynasty**, and the entire temple was intended to be a likeness of the sun's chariot. It has twelve great wheels carved on the sides at the temple's lowest level, and in front, statues of several colossal horses. As at the temples of **Khajuraho**, the lower levels here are covered with **erotic** and sexually explicit carvings, to which people have given differing interpretations: Some claim that these sanction carnal pleasure as a religious path, some interpret them allegorically as representing human union with the divine, and still others view them as teaching that the desire for pleasure must ultimately be transcended to attain the divine.

The temple was built on a massive scale; according to one estimate, the central spire would have been over 200 feet high. It is uncertain whether this spire was ever actually completed, since the sandy soil on which the temple platform was built would have been unable to support the weight of such an enormous structure. This same unstable soil has been the greatest contributor to the temple's increasing deterioration. The primary structure left at the site is the **jagamohan** (assembly hall), which was filled with sand in the nineteenth century, in an effort to prevent further collapse. For further information see Roy Craven, *Indian Art*, 1997.

Suparna

("having beautiful wings") Epithet of the god **Vishnu's** vehicle, the divine eagle **Garuda**. See **Garuda**.

Superhuman Powers

Widely believed to be attainable, either through voluntarily suffering harsh physical **asceticism** (**tapas**) or as products of high spiritual attainment. See **Siddhi**.

Surapana

("**liquor**-drinking") In the **dharma literature**, one of the **Four Great Crimes** whose commission made one an outcast from society. Although in modern times the word *sura* is the term for "wine," here it was believed to refer to a particular type of spirituous liquor made from rice flour. For members of the three highest social groups—**brahmins**, **kshatriyas**, and **vaishyas**, the most commonly prescribed penance (**prayashchitta**) for habitually drinking sura was to drink this same beverage boiling hot, until one died. Interestingly, this penalty does not apply to members of the lowest social class, the **shudras**. This difference reflected their lower status, in which they were not held to the same sorts of scrupulous standards as the "**twice-born**." Despite the harsh penalty for drinking sura, there were other sorts of **intoxicants** that kshatriyas and vaishyas could drink without penalty, although brahmins who drank these had to perform mild penances.

Surasa

In Hindu mythology, Surasa is the mother of all the **Nagas**, a class of minor divinities conceived in the form of serpents. In the *Ramayana*, the earlier of the two great Indian epics, Surasa takes the form of a gigantic serpent to test the fortitude of the monkey-god **Hanuman**, who jumps over the sea to **Lanka** to search for **Sita**, the god **Rama's** kidnapped wife. Surasa tells Hanuman that no one can go by without passing through her mouth, and in response Hanuman makes himself larger and larger. Surasa in turn opens her jaws wider and wider, and finally Hanuman becomes very small and darts in and out of her mouth. Surasa, pleased with Hanuman's ingenuity and courage, gives him her blessing.

Surat-Shabd-Yoga

Mystical discipline in the **Radha Soami** religious community, which stresses the joining (**yoga**) of the spirit (surat) with the Divine Sound (shabd). The Divine Sound emanates from the Supreme Being and is always present. Most people cannot hear it due to their preoccupation with worldly things. With proper training and devotion to a true **guru** (**satguru**), anyone can eventually become attuned to the Divine Sound, and resonate in harmony with it. The most important part of this path is contact with a true guru, since only a true guru has access to the divine and is considered a manifestation of the divine itself. Devotion to a true guru is the single most important factor in a person's spiritual development, and this spiritual progress hinges on complete surrender to the guru's **grace**.

This metaphor of the Divine Sound, and human resonance with it, has much in common with the images used by Guru Nanak, the first of the Sikh gurus, and with the **Nathpanthis** before him. The overwhelming stress on a guru makes it possible for this religious discipline to be practiced by just about anyone, and most of the Radha Soami followers are householders living in the world rather than ascetics. For further information see Sudhir Kakar, *Shamans, Mystics, and Doctors*, 1990; Lawrence Babb, *Redemptive Encounters*, 1987; and Mark Juergensmeyer, *Radhasoami Reality*, 1991.

Surdas

(early 16th c.) One of the **ashtachap**, a group of eight northern Indian **bhakti** (devotional) poets. The compositions of these eight poets were used for liturgical purposes by the **Pushti Marg**, a religious community whose members are devotees (**bhakta**) of **Krishna**. In the Pushti Marg's sectarian literature, all eight poets are also named as members of the community and as associates of either the community's founder, **Vallabhacharya**, or his successor **Vitthalnath**. In this literature, as recounted in the *Chaurasi Vaishnavan ki Varta* ("Lives of eighty-four

Vaishnavas"), it was at Vallabhacharya's order that **Surdas** began to compose poems about **Krishna's lila**, his playful interactions with the world and his devotees. He then proceeded to compose the 5,000-odd poems of the *Sursagar*.

The oldest manuscripts paint a much different picture of Surdas, for most of them contain only a few hundred poems, which are usually quite short. The most important themes in the early poetry are supplication (**vinaya**) and separation (**viraha**), and although one also finds the depictions of Krishna's childhood for which Surdas has become most famous, these themes are more important later in the poetic tradition. Surdas's poetry thus shows a wide range of themes, from his own spiritual life to devotional "glimpses" of Krishna; the latter most commonly explore the religious tension between the image of Krishna as a charming child and his alter ego as lord of the universe. As in much of **Vaishnava** devotional poetry, Surdas composed these poems to invite his hearers to enter Krishna's world.

The difference between these pictures raises doubts about the connection between Surdas and Vallabhacharya. Although songs by Surdas have been worked into the rites of the **Pushti Marg**, Surdas composed no poetry in praise of Vallabhacharya, unlike the other ashtachap poets. It seems just as likely that, as the popularity of Surdas's poems grew, he was "claimed" by the Pushti Marg as a fellow Krishna devotee. In fact, there is very little definitely known about him, including whether or not he was actually blind, as is generally accepted. Only two of the oldest poems mention blindness; one of these is clearly metaphorical, and the other is part of a litany of the woes of old age. As with so many of the bhakti poets, one knows a great deal more about the poems than the poet. For further information see John Stratton Hawley, *Krishna: The Butter Thief*, 1983; and *Surdas: Poet, Singer, Saint*, 1984; see also John Stratton Hawley and

Mark Juergensmeyer (trans.), *Songs of the Saints of India*, 1988.

Sureshvara

Philosopher in the **Advaita Vedanta** school, and one of two attested disciples of the school's founder, **Shankaracharya** (788–820?), the other being **Padmapada**. The Advaita school upholds a philosophical position known as monism, which is the belief that a single Ultimate Reality lies behind all things, and that all things are merely differing forms of that reality. Advaita proponents exemplify this belief in their claim that reality is nondual (**advaita**)—that is, that all things are nothing but the formless, unqualified **Brahman**, despite the appearance of difference and diversity. For Advaita proponents, the assumption that the world is real as perceived is a fundamental misunderstanding of the ultimate nature of things and a manifestation of **avidya**. Although often translated as "ignorance," avidya is better understood as the lack of genuine understanding, which ultimately causes human beings to be trapped in karmic bondage, reincarnation (**samsara**), and suffering.

In Hindu thought, Sureshvara is the only explicit proponent of **leap philosophy**, although one can see traces of this in the other figures in **Advaita Vedanta**, particularly in his teacher. Leap philosophy affirms that one can attain complete freedom from bondage, which in the Indian context is identified as the end of reincarnation and final liberation of the soul (**moksha**), but that such freedom cannot be gained by a precisely specified sequence of causes and effects. According to Sureshvara, since the ultimate problem stems from one's mistaken understanding, the only solution can come from purified, correct understanding. Sureshvara's path, such as it is, is to use a negative dialectic to distinguish clearly what the Self is not, and when one's mind has been prepared, to gain a flash of mystic insight through hearing one of the **mahavakyas** ("great utterances") that identify the Self with **Brahman**. Sureshvara affirms that actions can have no part in this process, since action is bound up with the world and is pervaded by ignorance. For further information see A. J. Alston (trans.), *The Naiskarmya Siddhi of Sri Suresvara*, 1959; and Karl H. Potter (ed.), *Advaita Vedanta up to Samkara and His Pupils*, 1981.

Sursagar

("Ocean of Sur") Corpus of poetry in the **Braj Bhasha** language ascribed to the northern Indian poet-saint **Surdas**. Traditional versions of the *Sursagar* are divided into twelve parts, to mirror the structure of the **Bhagavata Purana**, which is the most important **Sanskrit** source for the mythology of the god **Krishna**. Surdas was a Krishna devotee (**bhakta**), and this arrangement is a way to confer the luster of an authoritative Sanskrit text on vernacular religious poetry. Just as the *Bhagavata Purana* lavishly describes Krishna's youthful exploits, the *Sursagar* is most commonly associated with poems painting intimate and affectionate pictures of Krishna's childhood.

Although the poetry published in editions of the *Sursagar* is ascribed to Surdas, most of it is certainly pseudonymous. The oldest manuscripts of Surdas's poetry have at most a few hundred poems, and the size of this corpus roughly doubles every century, reaching the five thousand poems in the present Sursagar. The general tone of the earliest poems also shows a marked thematic difference. Although they include Krishna's childhood, a far greater percentage express the poet's pangs of separation (**viraha**) from Krishna or complaint (**vinaya**) about his spiritual troubles. Even the earliest manuscripts show no common body of poems, and it seems likely that from the very beginning the "Surdas" poetic tradition was drawn from the songs of wandering singers, a characterization that fits well with the image of the poet himself. For

673

A painted relief of Surya, the sun god.

further information see John Stratton Hawley, *Krishna: The Butter Thief*, 1983, and *Surdas: Poet, Singer, Saint* 1984; see also John Stratton Hawley and Mark Juergensmeyer (trans.), *Songs of the Saints of India*, 1988.

Surya

The **sun**, both in its physical form as a celestial phenomenon and personified as a **deity**. The sun has been an important deity as far back as the **Vedas**, the earliest and most authoritative Hindu religious texts, and has retained a position of some importance since that time. One example of this is the **Gayatri Mantra**, a sacred formula that is supposed to be recited every day by **twice-born** males, that is, men from the three "twice-born" groups—**brahmin, kshatriya**, and **vaishya**—who have undergone the adolescent religious **initiation** known as the "second birth." The Gayatri Mantra invokes the sun as the generator and nourisher of all things, and requests him to stimulate the minds

of those who perceive him. Surya is still worshiped by many **Smarta** brahmins as one of the "five-fold" (panchayatana) deities (the others being **Shiva**, **Vishnu**, the **Goddess**, and **Ganesh**), a practice attributed to the Advaita philosopher **Shankaracharya**. For some time Surya was also the primary deity for certain communities, particularly in eastern India, although his cult has been largely eclipsed in recent times. The most spectacular example of this **worship** is the temple of the sun at **Konarak** (now ruined), whose claims to fame stem from its enormous size and the profuse **erotic** sculptures on its exterior walls. For further information see Vibhuti Bhushan Mishra, *Religious Beliefs and Practices of North India During the Early Medieval Period*, 1973; and Sarat Chandra Mitra, *The Cult of the Sun God in Medieval Eastern Bengal*, 1986. See also **panchayatana puja**.

Suryapraksha

("effulgence of the **sun**") Name given to the banner that is the symbolic emblem of the **Mahanirvani Akhara**, a particular group of the **Naga** class of the **Dashanami Sanyasis**. The Nagas are devotees (**bhakta**) of the god **Shiva**, organized into different **akharas** or regiments on the model of an army. Until the beginning of the nineteenth century the *Nagas*' primary occupation was as mercenary soldiers, although they also had substantial trading interests; both of these have largely disappeared in contemporary times. All of the akharas have particular features that signify their organizational identity, and this particular banner—one with strong connections to a martial identity—is one such feature.

Suryavarman II

(r. 1112–1153) Ruler of the Khmer people in Cambodia, whose reign saw the construction of the massive temple complex at **Angkor** Wat. Although Suryavarman and his people were native Cambodians, the temples at Angkor Wat were dedicated to Hindu **deities**, showing the vast influence of contemporary Indian culture.

Sushruta

(4th c.) Physician and writer who is traditionally regarded as the author of the *Sushruta Samhita*. Along with the slightly earlier *Charaka Samhita*, the *Sushruta Samhita* is one of the two major sources for **ayurveda**, an Indian medical tradition.

Sushruta Samhita

Along with the slightly earlier *Charaka Samhita*, one of the two major sources for the Indian medical tradition known as **ayurveda**. Underlying ayurveda is the theory of the three bodily humors—**vata** (**wind**), **pitta** (bile), and **kapha** (phlegm). Each is composed of different elements, and although everyone has all three humors, their varying proportions are used to explain differing body types, metabolic dispositions, and personalities. The cause of disease is an imbalance of these humors—whether caused by environmental sources or personal habits—whereas the state of this equilibrium is the state of health. The *Sushruta Samhita* has been edited and translated into various languages, and served as a source for secondary studies, such as Debiprasad Chattopadhyaya, *Science and Society in Ancient India*, 1977.

Sushumna

One of the vertical channels (**nadi**) in the traditional conceptions of the **subtle body**. The subtle body is an alternate physiological system believed to exist on a different plane than gross matter but with certain correspondences to the material body. It is visualized as a set of six psychic centers (**chakras**) running roughly along the course of the spine, connected by three parallel vertical channels. Above and below these centers are the bodily abodes of the two divine principles, **Shiva** (awareness) and **Shakti** (power)—the latter as the latent spiritual energy known as **kundalini**—conceived in the form of a coiled serpent. In the types of **yoga** that focus on the subtle body, the ultimate aim is to awaken the kundalini, and move it up through the chakras to the abode of Shiva. The union of Shiva and Shakti in the aspirant's body mirrors the action of these divine forces in the macrocosm, and with this union the aspirant gains bliss and final liberation of the soul (**moksha**).

The sushumna is the middle of the three vertical channels in the subtle body—the side channels are the **ida nadi** and the **pingala nadi**—and it is by far the most important of the three. The sushumna provides the pathway for the rising kundalini as it awakens and straightens during the aspirant's spiritual exercises, piercing through the chakras on its way. In most people the sushumna is closed where it intersects the chakras, which blocks the flow of energy from moving smoothly through it. When the chakras have been pierced and opened by the rising kundalini, the passageway has been opened for the kundalini to rise to the abode of Shiva, and effect the union of Shakti and Shiva that will bring ultimate realization. For further information see Arthur Avalon (Sir John Woodroffe), *Shakti and Shakta*, 1978; Philip S. Rawson, *The Art of Tantra*, 1973; Swami Agehananda Bharati, *The Tantric Tradition*, 1975; and Douglas Renfrew Brooks, *The Secret of the Three Cities*, 1990.

Suta

In Hindu mythology, a disciple of the sage **Vyasa**, who is said to have recounted the **puranas** to other renunciants in the **Naimisha** forest. The puranas are an important genre of religious texts that collect all types of sacred lore, from mythic tales to ritual instruction to exaltation of various sacred sites (**tirthas**) and actions. Individual puranas are usually highly sectarian and intended to promote the **worship** of one of the Hindu gods, whether **Vishnu**, **Shiva**, or the **Goddess**. The traditional puranas are numbered at eighteen, and in many of them Suta is named as the narrator, in accordance with the legend mentioned above.

Sutakashaucha

The impurity (**ashaucha**) caused by childbirth (sutaka). All bodily effluvia (**hair**, spittle, pus, **blood**, etc.) are considered to be sources of impurity, and because **birth** is attended with these it is considered impure, even though it is always regarded as an auspicious and happy event. There is also impurity caused by death, known as **maranashaucha**, but the presence of the **corpse** renders this impurity more violent; needless to say, it is also considered inauspicious.

Sutra

("thread") In a metaphorical sense, a sutra is a short phrase or aphorism that can easily be committed to memory. Many early philosophical and grammatical texts were collections of such sutras, which are so brief that they virtually presuppose a commentary to explain their meaning. In many cases the commentary would have been an oral exchange between teacher and student, thus effecting the living transmission that is still the norm in **tantra**, a secret, ritually based religious practice. Memorizing such sutras was a way to gain mastery over an entire text, and the sutras could also serve as an aid to memory for the commentary, thus enabling a person to preserve the "thread" of the argument. In a more literal sense, the word sutra can also refer to the cord or cords strung through the centers of **palm leaf** manuscripts, which kept the pages of the text in their proper order.

Svadharma

("one's own **dharma**") In the **dharma literature**, svadharma is an individual's unique religious duty (dharma), based on that person's social position, **stage of life**, and gender. The governing assumption behind this notion is that every person has a social role to fulfill, and each of these roles is necessary for the maintenance of society, no matter how humble it might be. For each person, his or her svadharma carries the highest authority, and supersedes all other religious laws. As one example, violence is generally prohibited, but it is a necessary part of a ruler's svadharma—both to protect the land from external invaders, and to punish criminals within the country. In both cases the use of violence helps to maintain social order, which is the king's primary duty. In the same way, society depends on a host of other people fulfilling their particular social roles. This notion of social responsibility and interconnectedness is tied to religious fulfillment through the notion of the Path of Action (**karmamarga**). According to this idea, selflessly performing one's social duty, for the good of the world rather than through selfish desire, was also a path to ultimate spiritual fulfillment and final liberation of the soul (**moksha**). According to this conception, since every svadharma is potentially a path to final liberation, each person has a path that only he or she can tread.

Svadhishthana Chakra

In many schools of **yoga**, and in the esoteric ritual tradition known as **tantra**, the svadhishthana chakra is one of the six psychic centers (**chakras**) believed to exist in the **subtle body**. The subtle body is an alternate physiological system, believed to exist on a different plane than gross matter but with certain correspondences to the material body. It is visualized as a set of six psychic centers, which are conceived as multipetaled lotus flowers running roughly along the course of the spine, connected by three vertical channels. Each of these chakras has important symbolic associations—with differing human capacities, with different subtle elements (**tanmatras**), and with different seed syllables (**bijaksharas**) formed from the letters of the **Sanskrit** alphabet, thus encompassing all sacred sound. Above and below these centers are the bodily abodes of **Shiva** (awareness) and **Shakti** (power), the two divine principles through which the entire universe has come into being. The underlying assumption behind this concept of the subtle body is thus the fundamental similarity and interconnectedness of macrocosm and microcosm, an essential Hindu idea since the time of the mystical texts known as the **Upanishads**.

The six chakras are traditionally listed from the bottom up, and the svadhishthana chakra is the second. It is visualized as a six-petaled lotus located in the region of the genitals. The petals each contain a seed syllable formed from a letter of the Sanskrit alphabet, in this case the consonants from "ba" to "la." On a symbolic level, the svadhishthana chakra is associated with the human capacity for reproduction. It is also identified as the bodily seat for the subtle element of **water**, the fluid medium through which reproduction is possible. For further information see Arthur Avalon (Sir John Woodroffe), *Shakti and Shakta*, 1978; and Philip S. Rawson, *The Art of Tantra*, 1973.

Svadhyaya

("study") Study of the sacred texts, which connotes oral recitation, since these texts were traditionally studied by reciting them. This is one of the methods named in the **Yoga Sutras** as one of the preparatory elements to yoga, since the text claims that such study attenuates one's karmic hindrances and fosters the ability to enter trance. Even in modern times the act of reciting a religious text is seen to have multiple spiritual benefits and, if performed over a long period of time, to be able to transform the person reciting.

Svakiya

("belonging to oneself") Mode of conceiving the relationship between lover and beloved, in which the man and woman are married to each other. The **svakiya** relationship is socially respectable—sanctioned by society, upholding social propriety, fruitful, and procreative in its course. Although this mode of relationship is rich and celebrated, this very social approval is said to make it less intense than the adulterous **parakiya** relationship, in which the lovers gain nothing but their love itself. Although in most cases the union between the god **Krishna** and his consort **Radha** is described as parakiya, some **Vaishnava** communities—such as the **Radhavallabh** community—claim that this relationship is svakiya, perhaps reflecting reservations about endorsing **adultery**, even by the **deities**.

In Indian traditions the image of a svastika, arms pointed in a clockwise direction, symbolizes life, prosperity, and good fortune.

Svaprakasha

("self-revealing") In Indian **philosophy**, the notion that certain things such as knowledge are self-revealing and do not need anything else in order to be known. The issue about whether these things existed, and what they were if they did, was a source of lively disagreement among Indian thinkers.

Svarup

("own-form") In popular devotional dramas such as the **Ram Lila**, which is based on the story of the *Ramayana*, svarup is the name for the child-actors (most often **brahmin** boys) playing the parts of the gods and goddesses. Viewing these performances is not simply entertainment but also an act of religious devotion, since such dramas are considered to be ways in which the gods reveal themselves to their devotees (**bhakta**). When the actors are in make-up and in character—or wearing crowns, as in the case of the **Krishna**

lilas in the town of **Brindavan**—they are actually considered to be forms of the **deity**, revealed within the context of the lila. As one sign of this status, a regular feature of such performances is time set aside for **darshan**, in which the actors sit perfectly still for the viewers to view them as an act of **worship**, in the same way that people would interact with an image in a temple.

Svastika

Although in the modern mind the svastika is indelibly associated with Adolph Hitler's Germany, it has a long and venerable history as an Indian symbol, predating the Nazis by several thousand years. The name is compounded from *su* ("good") + *asti* ("to be") + *ka* ("making"), and a general translation would be something like "bringing good fortune." In Hindu India the svastika is a symbol of life, prosperity, and good fortune, at least when the arms are pointing in a clockwise direction. Circling an object in this direction presents one's right side to the central object, and since this side is considered purer, the svastika with arms pointing clockwise is considered more auspicious than its counterclockwise counterpart.

Svastikasana

("**svastika**-posture") One of the sitting postures (**asana**) described in commentaries to the **Yoga Sutras**. In this position, the right foot is inserted into the space between the left thigh and calf, and the left foot into the space between the right thigh and calf (one of the feet is pointing upwards, and the other downward). The opposing directions of the feet and the crossed legs evokes images of the svastika, hence the name.

Svatahpramanya

("self-validating") In Indian **philosophy**, the notion that certain things, such as knowledge, are self-validating. This means that they can be definitively known to be true in themselves, without reference to any of the other **pramanas**, the means by which human beings can gain true and accurate knowledge. The issue about whether these things existed, and what they were if they did, was a source of lively disagreement among Indian thinkers.

Svayambhu

("self-born") Epithet of the god **Brahma**. This name underscores his role as the fashioner of the worlds—as the agent responsible for arranging the cosmos, he cannot himself be a created being. According to Hindu mythology, at the beginning of each cycle of creation Brahma emerges from the calyx of a lotus that sprouts from the god **Vishnu's** navel; at the time of cosmic dissolution he again enters the lotus, and is reabsorbed into Vishnu's body. See **Brahma**.

Svayambhu ("self-manifested") Images

Name denoting any image of a Hindu divinity believed to exist by virtue of divine self-revelation, rather than by being made or established by human hands. These images are believed to be intensely holy and powerful, and to have a more pronounced sense of the **deity's** presence. They mark instances where these deities have revealed themselves out of **grace**, in order to become accessible to their devotees (**bhakta**), and they are places where the deities are believed to be particularly present and "awake," and thus more receptive to requests for favors.

Svayambhu images can be found for each of the three major Hindu deities. Images of the **Goddess** are often natural rock formations, such as the image of the goddess **Kamakhya**, which is a natural cleft in the rock, or the stone images of many of the **Shiwalik goddesses**; they can take other forms as well, such as the image of the goddess **Jwalamukhi**, which is a burning vent of natural gas. For the god **Vishnu**, the best-known self-manifested form is the **shalagram**, a black stone containing the spiral-shaped fossil shell of a prehistoric sea creature, which is believed to be a symbol of his discus (**chakra**). The god **Shiva's** pillar-shaped symbol known as the **linga** appears in the widest variety of self-manifested forms. Many of these self-manifested lingas are found in natural rock formations, such as at **Kedarnath**; **Amarnath**, where the linga appears as a pillar of ice; and the **bana linga**, which is a naturally rounded stone, usually small enough to be easily portable. Further, in the Hindu religious groups that stress the **subtle body**, both Shiva and the Goddess are believed to be present within one's own body. In some cases for all these deities, carved images are claimed to be self-manifest forms; in their usual motif the statue's location is revealed to a favored devotee in a **dream**. A self-manifested image is a powerful claim for any site and will bolster its importance as a place of divine access.

Svayamsevak

("volunteer") Rank-and-file member of the **Rashtriya Svayamsevak Sangh** (RSS). The RSS is a conservative Hindu organization the express purpose of which is to provide the leadership cadre for a revitalized Hindu India; for most of its history it has characterized its mission as cultural and character-building rather than religious or political. The svayamsevaks are the rank-and-file members of the local RSS branches (**shakhas**), and are thus "foot soldiers" who make up the organization's core membership. The shakhas in any given area are overseen by a full-time RSS worker known as a **pracharak** ("director"), who serves as a liaison between the local units and the RSS leadership, and oversees RSS activity in his area.

The svayamsevak is the lowest level of RSS membership. Most members do not advance beyond this rank, since to do so requires complete commitment to the RSS and its ideals; those who do, however, are usually gifted leaders. The primary stress at the shakha level is on forming personal relationships with other members, as a way to develop loyalty to the organization. Each shakha, or local unit, holds a daily meeting. Activities include an opening ceremony in which the organization's saffron banner is raised; traditional games or exercises, including a martial drill; and a discussion period in which RSS ideals can be disseminated and propagated.

Svayamvara

("self-choice") In Hindu mythology, a form of marriage in which the bride would choose the groom she wanted, indicating her choice by placing her garland around his neck. In the stories in which a svayamvara occurs, the bride-to-be is usually of royal lineage, as are her suitors, so the bride's choice was an exercise fraught with potential political consequences. One famous mythic svayamvara was that of **Nala** and **Damayanti**, in which Damayanti prefers Nala even to the gods who have come as suitors. This story also illustrates the dangers of such a choice, when an unhappy suitor cursed the couple to endure separation and privation.

Swami Malai

Temple and sacred site (**tirtha**) on a hill in the **Tanjore** district of **Tamil Nadu**, just outside the temple-town of **Kumbhakonam**. Swami Malai is part of the network of six temples in Tamil Nadu built to honor **Murugan**, a hill **deity** who has been assimilated into the larger pantheon as a form of the god **Skanda**, the son of **Shiva**. Five of these temples have been definitively identified, and each is associated with a particular region, a particular ecosystem, and a particular incident in Murugan's mythic career. In the case of Swami Malai, it is said to be where he taught the meaning of the sacred syllable (**Om**) to his father **Shiva**, and thus presents him in the aspect of a teacher, which is one of his identifying features in **Shaiva**

Siddhanta (a series of fourteen texts, all completed by the fourteenth century C.E., which reinterpret the ideas about Shiva found in **Nayanar** devotional poetry). The sixth of these temples is said to be every other shrine to Murugan in Tamil Nadu. This belief seems to stress Murugan's presence throughout Tamil Nadu and sacrilize the entire landscape, giving mythic significance to every Murugan temple, no matter how small. The cult of Murugan is thus a symbolic vehicle for Tamil pride and identity, and since the number six has connotations of completeness—as in the six directions, or the six **chakras** in the **subtle body**—it also suggests that nothing outside is needed. For further information see Fred Clothey, "Pilgrimage Centers in the Tamil Cultus of Murukan," in the *Journal of the American Academy of Religion*, Vol. 40, No. 1, 1972.

Swaminarayan Sect

Modern religious community devoted to the god **Vishnu**; its practice is based on the life and teachings of Sahajananda Swami (1781–1830), who was born near the sacred city of **Ayodhya** in eastern India but spent much of his life in the western Indian state of **Gujarat**. Sahajananda took **initiation** as an **ascetic** and soon became a **mahant**, or ascetic leader. His followers revered him first as a religious preceptor (**guru**), and later as a partial incarnation of the god **Krishna** himself. They believed that manifestations of the god Vishnu, such as Krishna, are born on earth in times of extreme trouble. It was in this latter aspect that he was given the name Swaminarayan ("Lord Narayan"), and his followers believed that he was the highest manifestation of God in human form. The Swaminarayan sect has several million lay devotees (**bhakta**), most of whom are affluent **Gujarati** merchants. In keeping with the community's ascetic roots, however, its most important figures are the ascetics who run the organization and who serve as teachers and advisers to them. For further information see Raymond Brady Williams, *A New Face of Hinduism*, 1984.

SYDA

(**Siddha Yoga** Dham America) Religious organization founded by Swami **Muktananda** (1908–1982), which has ashrams and centers around the world. Siddha Yoga's metaphysics are a modified form of Kashmiri Shaivism, but its signature teaching is the notion that the **guru's grace** can immediately awaken the disciple's latent **kundalini** (spiritual power, the most vital substance of the **subtle body**) and speed the process of spiritual development. This teaching puts an even greater emphasis on the importance of the guru as spiritual teacher, and the overwhelming emphasis pervades the whole movement. Although it has Indian members, most of its followers are non-Indian converts, who may be engaged in a spiritual search but who have little interest in becoming culturally Indian. The organization was headed by Muktananda until his death in 1982; for most of the time since then it has been presided over by his successor, **Chidvilasananda**.

T

Tad Ekam

("That One") Epithet used in **Rg Veda** hymn 10.129, the so-called **Creation Hymn**, to designate the first living being on the **earth**. The four **Vedas** are the oldest Hindu religious texts, and based on its style and content, the Rg Veda is the oldest of the Vedas. Most of the hymns in the Rg Veda are invocations addressed to various divinities, sung to propitiate these divinities so that human beings may enjoy the good things of this life. The Creation Hymn takes a far more speculative tone, standing in marked contrast to the confidence and optimism found in the earlier hymns. In the Creation Hymn, the poet begins by imagining a time before the existence of Being and Nonbeing and speculates on how the world came to be.

In the end, the poet ascribes all creation to a single impersonal agent, That One (Tad Ekam). This hymn is noteworthy for ascribing the creation of the world to a single power, an idea that foreshadows the notion of **Brahman** in the **Upanishads**, the speculative texts that form the final stratum of the Vedic literature. The name Tad Ekam, which is grammatically a neuter noun, also foreshadows the notion found in the Upanishads that Brahman is an impersonal force. After describing how That One formed the cosmos and knew all its secrets, the poem ends with the conjecture that perhaps That One may not be omniscient and omnipotent after all. This hymn thus further foreshadows the Upanishads in its speculative tone and its admission that the ultimate answer may be unknown.

Tagore, Rabindranath

(1861–1941) Poet and Nobel laureate in Literature, an honor bestowed in 1912 for his *Gitanjali* ("Garland of Songs"). Tagore came from an influential and extremely wealthy landed family and was thus able to focus all his energy on his literary work. Aside from his prodigious literary output, he lectured extensively both in India and in other countries; in the latter he emphasized the need to retain spiritual values, whereas in India he more often gave his attention to the need to fulfill people's material needs. In 1921 he established the Vishva-Bharati University at **Shantiniketan** in the state of **West Bengal**. The university was dedicated to providing an education that would satisfy both of these needs and thus develop an integrated human being. For further information see Krishna Kripalani, *Rabindranath Tagore: A Biography*, 1980; and Donald R. Tuck, "Rabindranath Tagore: Religion as a Constant Struggle for Balance," in Robert D. Baird (ed.), *Religion in Modern India*, 1998.

Tagore Jayanti

Holiday marking the birth date of the Bengali poet, writer, and thinker **Rabindranath Tagore**, celebrated on May 8, the day he was born in 1861. As with most twentieth-century figures, Tagore's birthday is celebrated according to the solar **calendar** of the common era, rather than the lunar calendar that governs most religious observances. Although Tagore is best known for his literary work, he was also considered a religious preceptor (**guru**), and thus his birthday carries extra meaning.

Tai

Tenth month in the Tamil solar **year**, corresponding to the northern Indian solar month of Makara (the zodiacal sign of Capricorn), which usually falls within January and February. The existence of several different **calendars** is one clear sign of the continuing

Teens drum and dance in Ghoom, Darjeeling. Tala, or rhythm, is a typical part of festival celebrations.

importance of regional cultural patterns. One way that the Tamils retain their culture is by preserving their traditional calendar. Tamil is one of the few regional languages in India with an ancient, well-established literary tradition. See also **Tamil months**, **Tamil Nadu**, and **Tamil language**.

Takshaka

In Hindu mythology, a venomous serpent-king from whose bite King **Parikshit** is killed. After insulting a powerful sage, Parikshit is cursed to die of a snakebite within seven days. Parikshit takes all possible precautions to avoid his fate: He builds a house on a huge pillar, has all things entering the house carefully searched, and surrounds himself with physicians who can cure snakebite. Six days pass without incident, but as the seventh day ends, people begin to relax and bring in some fruit to eat. Takshaka has concealed himself as a tiny worm in one of the pieces of fruit and, when the fruit is cut open, changes into his real shape, bites the king, and kills him.

Despite his fearsome role in this story, an earlier story illustrates that Takshaka is not entirely evil. Takshaka's mother, **Kadru**, bets her sister **Vinata** that the tail of a certain celestial horse is black, whereas Vinata claims it is white; the sister agrees that the loser will become a servant to the winner. Kadru asks her children, the serpents, to hang from the back of the horse to make it appear as if it is black and thus takes unfair advantage. Some of her children, including Takshaka, refuse to take part in such deceit, and Kadru curses them to be killed by **Janamjeya**, King Parikshit's **son**. Takshaka manages to escape this **curse**—one of the few times that this happens in Hindu mythic stories—but most of his siblings are not so lucky.

Tala

In Indian music and **dance**, the most general term for "rhythm," either as an accompaniment to music or dance or played on a drum as a solo instrument. The rhythmic systems in all varieties of Indian music are extremely rich and complex and require years of study to master.

Talikota

City in the Bijapur district of the state of **Karnataka**, which in 1565 was the site of a battle between the **Vijayanagar dynasty** king Rama Raja and a coalition of Muslim sultans from farther north in the **Deccan** peninsula. Rama Raja's disastrous defeat brought the Vijayanagar dynasty to an abrupt end. The sultans sacked the empire's capital at **Hampi**, and it has never been inhabited since that time.

Tamas

("darkness") One of the three fundamental qualities (**gunas**) believed to be present in all things, the other two being **sattva** ("goodness") and **rajas** ("passion"). According to this model, the differing proportions of these qualities account for the differences both in the inherent nature of things and in individual human capacities and tendencies. Of the three, tamas is always negative and is associated with darkness, disease, ignorance, sloth, spoilage, and death. The notion of these three gunas originated in the metaphysics of the **Samkhya** school, one of the **six schools** of traditional Hindu **philosophy**, and although much of Samkhya metaphysics connected with the gunas has long been discredited, the idea of the gunas and their qualities has become a pervasive assumption in Indian culture.

Tamil Epics

Collective name for three early Tamil epic poems: the *Shilappadigaram*, the *Manimegalai*, and the *Shivaga-Sindamani*. These poems were composed in about the sixth and seventh centuries of the common era, when religious forms and cultural influence (among them, the composition of epic poems) were seeping in from the north and influencing indigenous forms. Aside from **Sanskrit**, Tamil is the only major ancient literary language. All three of these poems provide important information about life in their contemporary times, including religious life. In brief, the *Shilappadigaram* ("The Jeweled Anklet") is a tragedy that highlights several important themes that have pervaded Hindu culture, particularly the need for a king to rule righteously and the power gained by a wife through her devotion to her husband. The *Manimegalai* focuses on a young woman of the same name, who is wooed by the local prince but eventually becomes a Buddhist nun. Although the story clearly has a Buddhist bias, Manimegalai has numerous debates with people from competing religious traditions. Finally, the *Shivaga-Sindamani* describes the adventures of Shivaga, a man who excels at every possible manly art, who with each new challenge wins a new wife for his harem but in the end renounces everything to become a Jain monk. Although the later two epics are respectively biased toward Buddhist and Jain religious values, they all give valuable information about contemporary religious life. See also **Tamil language**.

Tamil Language

One of the four **Dravidian** languages, along with **Kannada**, Telegu, and Malayalam; all four languages are spoken primarily in southern India. Tamil is the predominant language in modern **Tamil Nadu**, which is one of the "linguistic states" formed after the Indians gained independence. This state was formed to unite people with a common language and culture under one state government. Although all four languages have literary and cultural significance, Tamil has by far the richest history as a literary language. Tamil literature begins in the early centuries of the common era with the **Sangam literature**, eight collections of poetry that focused equally on the external description of battle or internal descriptions of love. The Sangam literature was followed by the three **Tamil epics**: the *Shilappadigaram*, the *Manimegalai*, and the *Shivaga-Sindamani*. Between the seventh and tenth centuries came the devotional (**bhakti**) literature composed by the **Alvars** and the **Nayanars**, with the former expressing their devotion to the god **Vishnu** and the latter to the god **Shiva**. Their devotional poetry was unprecedented in Hindu religious history because it utilized everyday vernacular language as a spectacular vehicle for profound religious expression. The Alvars' poems became a foundational text for the **Shrivaishnava** community, and the Nayanars' for **Shaiva Siddhanta**, and thus both of these collections continue to be important in Hindu religious life. Even today Tamil is a vibrant literary language and a source of intense regional pride to the people living there; some of the most violent recent demonstrations in southern India were the so-called language riots, protesting the imposition of **Hindi** as the government language, a move that was seen as a conscious attempt to marginalize Tamil language and culture.

Tamil Months

Although the lunar **calendar** is by far the most important means for determining the Hindu religious calendar, these **lunar months** are also set in the framework of a solar calendar. The latter is used for the calculation of the **intercalary month**, which helps keep the lunar and solar calendars in rough correspondence. In northern India the months of the solar calendar correlate with the **zodiac**, with each month named after the sign into which the sun is reckoned as entering at the beginning of that month. In southern India the divisions of the solar calendar are exactly the same as in the north, but the twelve months are given different names. The Tamil months take their names from some of the **nakshatras**, or features in the lunar zodiac, or from modifications of the lunar months. The Tamil **year** begins with the month of **Chittirai**, which corresponds to the northern Indian solar month of Mesha (the zodiacal sign of Aries), which by the Indian calculations, falls within April and May.

The eleven months following Chittirai are **Vaikasi**, **Ani**, **Adi**, **Avani**, **Purattasi**, **Aippasi**, **Kartigai**, **Margali**, **Tai**, **Masi**, and **Panguni**. Such different calendars are one clear sign of the continuing importance of regional cultural patterns. This regional culture is particularly important in the Tamil cultural area because Tamil is one of the few regional languages with an ancient, well-established literary tradition.

Tamil Nadu

("land of the Tamils") Modern Indian state at the southern tip of the subcontinent, on the Bay of Bengal. Tamil Nadu is one of the so-called linguistic states, formed after Indian independence in 1947 to unite people with a common language and culture under one state government. Tamil Nadu was thus formed from the Tamil-speaking areas of the former state of Madras. Tamil Nadu has a long and rich history, and the Tamil literary tradition stretches back to the early centuries of the common era. Successive regional dynasties—the **Pallavas**, **Cholas**, and **Pandyas**—built a host of temples in the characteristic **Dravida** architectural style, and even today Tamil Nadu has hundreds of temple towns, that is, towns in which the urban hub is an enormous temple complex that includes shops, markets, offices, and residential space. Modern Tamil culture is the product of this long and ancient tradition, and Tamils pride themselves in having been influenced little by outsiders—neither by the Hindu influences from northern India, nor by the Muslim culture whose influence was so profound in regions farther north. Tamil Nadu has so many cultural sites and holy places that it is impossible to name them, but the most important are **Rameshvaram**, **Chidambaram**, **Madurai**, **Tiruchirappalli**, **Kanchipuram**, **Mahabalipuram**, **Kumbhakonam**, **Thiruvaiyaru**, **Tanjore**, and **Kanyakumari**; there is also a network of six temples to the god **Murugan** scattered in different areas of the state,

Tamil Nadu is home to the tallest temple tower in India, which is part of the Ranganathaswamy Temple in Shrirangam.

which between them lay out the parameters of the Tamil country. For general information about Tamil Nadu and all the regions of India, an accessible reference is Christine Nivin et al., *India*, 8th ed., Lonely Planet, 1998. See also **Tamil language**.

Tamoyoga

One of the three classes of beings in the **Dvaita Vedanta** philosophical school, founded by the philosopher **Madhva** (1197–1276). Madhva's fundamental assumption was that God was utterly transcendent, above and beyond the world and human beings. The strength of this conviction led him to stress the importance of **grace** as the sole means of salvation because human beings were unable to save themselves. Given this dire view of human capacities, Madhva divided the beings of the world into three classes: The **muktiyogas** were destined for final liberation, the **nityasamsarins** were destined for eternal rebirth, and the **tamoyogas** were predestined for eternal damnation.

Tandava

Name denoting one of the two broad categories in Indian **dance**. The tandava style is athletic and dramatic and conveys violence and power, whereas the other dance form, **lasya,** is soft and lyrical and conveys a mood of love. The tandava style received its name from the tandava dance of the god **Shiva**. According to tradition, this is the dance through which Shiva destroys the world when its time has come. Not all of the dance's mythic connotations are violent, since this athletic dance is also said to be the one through which Shiva vanquished the **goddess Kali** in a dance contest, when her feminine modesty prevented her from imitating his style.

Tanjore

City and district in the southern Indian state of **Tamil Nadu**, the eastern boundary of which is the Bay of Bengal. The Tanjore district lies in the **Cauvery River** delta, south of the river's main channel; even today this extremely fertile area grows a large percentage of India's rice. This district was the core homeland of the **Chola dynasty**, and the land's agricultural fecundity was the underlying source of the dynasty's power, which at one point stretched through most of southern India and even extended to Malaysia. The Chola dynasty used their wealth and power to build enormous temples throughout Tamil Nadu, but especially in the Tanjore district and Tanjore city, their capital. The Chola zenith came with King **Raja Raja** (r. 985–1014 C.E.), who built Tanjore

city's **Brhadeshvar** temple, and his **son Rajendra** (r. 1014–1042 C.E.), whose greatest monument is the temple at **Gangaikondacholapuran**. The Brhadeshvar temple is dedicated to **Shiva** as the "Great Lord"; some of the most notable of the other temples built or improved by the Cholas were at **Kumbhakonam**, **Thiruvaiyaru**, **Chidambaram**, and **Shrirangam**.

Tanka

Name for a small chisel used by stone workers, one of the characteristic objects in Hindu iconography. The tanka is mainly associated with **Shiva** and is a minor artifact because it generally appears only when the **deity** has multiple arms and is holding a number of objects.

Tanmatras

The tanmatras are the subtle elements, the subtle forms of the five gross elements (**earth, air, fire, water, and akasha**) from which the gross elements are derived. The senses corresponding to the subtle elements are gandha (smell) for earth, sparsha (touch) for air, rupa (shape) for fire, rasa (taste) for water, and **shabda** (sound) for akasha. The tanmatras first appeared in the account of the **evolution** of the universe propounded by the **Samkhya** school, one of the **six schools** of traditional Hindu **philosophy**. In the Samkhya account, the subtle elements are the stage of evolution preceding the evolution of the gross elements. The Samkhya school espoused an atheistic dualism in which the two fundamental principles were **purusha** (spirit) and **prakrti** (matter); all of this evolution was associated with prakrti because, according to the Samkhyas, the purusha never changed. The Samkhya account of evolution was appropriated by other groups—although these groups often adapted it to reflect theistic assumptions in which the world came from God—and thus the notion of the subtle elements became an accepted philosophical convention.

Tantra

General term for a genre of secret ritually based religious practices. These are most often laid out in texts also known as tantras ("loom"), so named because these texts weave a distinctive picture of reality. In popular Hindu culture, tantric practitioners (**tantrikas**) are associated with illicit sexuality, with consuming forbidden things such as meat and **liquor**, and with having the ability to kill or harm others through black **magic**. Such power and perceived amorality make tantrikas objects of fear, a quality that some people have used to their advantage. A more neutral assessment of tantra would stress three qualities: secrecy, power, and nondualism, the ultimate unity of all things.

Secrecy in tantra serves two functions. On the one hand, it conceals the rites and practices from the uninitiated, who are seen as unqualified to receive it, and on the other, it creates a religious subcommunity with a particularly defined identity and sense of privilege. This sense of exclusivity, of being privy to something to which few have access, is one of the reasons that tantra is seen as a higher religious practice. Even when the text of a tantra has been written down, it is always assumed that the texts are lifeless without the instruction of a qualified person. This stress on personal transmission means that **diksha** (a type of **initiation**) is the only way to gain access to this tradition, and thus tantra stresses the importance of the **guru**-disciple relationship even more strongly than does the Hindu tradition as a whole. Gurus are free to initiate anyone they deem qualified. Although many tantrikas are **twiceborn** men, that is, members of the three highest classes (**varnas**)—**brahmins**, **kshatriyas**, and **vaishyas**—who have received the adolescent religious initiation known as the second birth, in theory tantric practice is open to all people, regardless of gender or social status.

Power in tantra is manifested in various ways. One of these comes in the transmission of the teaching itself, in which the guru's empowerment is believed necessary to "activate" the transmitted material, particularly **mantras**. Tantric practice is also claimed to be far more powerful than regular religious practice and thus more efficacious in bringing final liberation of the soul (**moksha**). The usual claim is that tantra's potency can bring such liberation in a single lifetime, whereas other forms of religious practice take untold aeons. Such powerful forces must be kept secret from the uninitiated, thus the stress on secrecy. It is widely accepted that the spiritual attainments gained through tantric practice also bring superhuman powers (**siddhi**), as a natural byproduct of such attainment. Although aspirants are discouraged from seeking such powers because the act of seeking is seen as rooted in selfish desire, those who gain such powers without seeking are believed to be able to exercise them without being corrupted.

For tantrikas, nondualism—the assertion that all reality is ultimately one thing—is both a philosophical affirmation and the operative principle behind their religious practice. Tantrikas usually conceive of this unity theistically, seeing their chosen **deity** (**ishtadevata**) as the material, efficient, and final cause of all reality. For tantrikas, definitively realizing the essential oneness of all things removes the mistaken understanding that causes bondage and rebirth and brings final liberation. Tantric practice affirms this nondualism, often through rituals stressing the unification of opposites. For this reason, some tantrikas make ritual use of things that are normally forbidden, most notably the "Five Forbidden Things" (**panchamakara**): fish, wine, meat, parched grain, and sexual intercourse. In theory, this rite is a means to break down duality because it violates societal norms forbidding consumption of **intoxicants**, nonvegetarian food, and illicit sexuality, in a conscious effort to sacralize what is normally forbidden. Although this rite collapses conventional boundaries of good and bad, pure and impure, the goal is to replace external rites (**bahiryaga**) with interior ones (**antaryaga**), thus exploding the duality of subject and object. The paradigm for this interior practice is tantric **yoga**. This is usually some variant of **kundalini yoga**, in which the two divine principles of **Shiva** and **Shakti** are ultimately united in the expert's **subtle body**. The final vehicle for tantric practice comes in rituals using symbolic diagrams (**yantra**), of which one example is the **shrichakra**. These are often particular to specific tantric lineages (**parampara**) and thus ground the aspirant in a particular tradition. For further information see Arthur Avalon (Sir John Woodroffe), *Shakti and Shakta*, 1978; Swami Agehananda Bharati, *The Tantric Tradition*, 1977; and Douglas Renfrew Brooks, *The Secret of the Three Cities*, 1990.

Tantrika

Name denoting a practitioner of **tantra**, a secret ritually based religious practice.

Tapas

("heat") Term denoting any physical **asceticism**, or what in earlier times was referred to as mortification of the flesh. The term *tapas* encompasses rites of denial, such as fasting (**upavasa**) or **celibacy**, as well as rites of enduring physical pain, such as the "five fires" (**panchagni**) rite. In this rite a person sits during the hot **season** surrounded by four fires, with the fifth fire being the sun overhead. Other rites include enduring cold from bathing (**snana**) in snow-fed rivers, and enduring any other sort of physical discomfort. The word *tapas* can also describe bizarre and even masochistic behaviors, such as remaining standing for years on end; keeping an arm upraised until the muscles atrophy, and it cannot be lowered; lying on beds of thorns and nails, and so forth. The governing assumption behind all of these practices is that they generate spiritual power (seen figuratively as "heat") and that a person who generates and amasses enough of this power will gain supernormal powers or the ability to demand boons from the gods themselves. Even though many contemporary Hindus are skeptical of the more extreme practices and may dismiss them, there is still great cultural respect for **ascetic** self-control, and combined with the right personality, such practices can still confer considerable religious authority.

In Hindu mythology **Indra**, king of the gods, pays close attention to those amassing such powers to protect himself from being replaced by someone more powerful. When an ascetic starts to amass enough power to displace him, Indra's heavenly throne becomes hot through the "heat" generated by the tapas. Indra must search for the aspirant and defuse this power in one of two ways—either by giving the aspirant a boon, which in many cases is the reason for performing the tapas in the first place, or by sending a celestial nymph (**apsara**) to seduce the ascetic, whose power will be discharged along with his **semen**. This mythology reflects the basic Hindu belief that the starting point for ascetic power is celibacy, which conserves a man's vital energies by conserving his semen.

Taraka

In Hindu mythology, an extremely powerful **demon**, who endures such severe physical **asceticism** (**tapas**) that he receives a boon that he can be killed only by a **son** of the god **Shiva**. This boon seems to make Taraka invulnerable because at the time, Shiva is lost in meditation and is still grieving for his dead wife **Sati**. For a long time Taraka grows more powerful and more arrogant until he is eventually able to defeat the gods in battle and exile them from **heaven**. In their despair the gods turn to the god of love, **Kama**, and beg him to shoot Shiva with an arrow of desire so that he will marry the **goddess Parvati**, and thus make it possible to bring about Taraka's death. Shiva, however, destroys Kama before he can shoot, burning him to ash with a stream of fire from his third eye. Shiva later marries Parvati, and their son, **Skanda**, kills Taraka in battle.

Tarakeshvar

City and sacred site (**tirtha**) thirty miles northwest of Calcutta in the state of **West Bengal**, which because of its proximity to Calcutta, is the most widely visited pilgrimage place in the state. Tarakeshvar is famous for the temple of **Baba** Tarakanath, who is the god **Shiva** in his form as the "Lord of Liberation." Shiva is present at Tarakeshvar in the form of a **linga**, the pillar-shaped object that is Shiva's symbolic form. The Tarakeshvar linga is claimed to be a "self-manifested" (**svayambhu**) image, which was not made by human hands but established through an act of divine self-revelation. The site's charter myth describes how the linga of Shiva is buried in the **earth** but is discovered when a **cow** habitually lets down her milk on the spot above it as an act of **worship**. The charter myth also describes how a man afflicted with agonizing hemorrhoids finds relief by drinking the **water** that has been poured on the linga as an **offering** and thus is blessed by Shiva's touch. With these two stories, the charter conveys the image of a **deity** who is present and responsive to his devotees (**bhakta**) as well as the sense of a place where human beings can go to find relief from their afflictions. One of the most unusual manifestations of this is the practice of **dharna**, in which pilgrims lie on the temple's outer porch, fasting (**upavasa**) for as long as it takes the deity to communicate with them, usually in a **dream**. For further information see E. Alan Morinis, *Pilgrimage in the Hindu Tradition*, 1984.

Tarapith

("Tara's seat") Town and sacred site (**tirtha**) in the state of **West Bengal**, about 130 miles northwest of Calcutta. Tarapith is famous as one of the **Shakti Pithas**, a network of sites sacred to the **Goddess** that spreads throughout the subcontinent. Each Shakti Pitha marks the site where a body part of the dismembered goddess **Sati** fell to **earth**, taking form there as a different goddess; in the case of Tarapith, the body part was Sati's cornea (tara). Tarapith's presiding goddess, Tara, is a fierce form of the Goddess, who has strong associations with **tantra**, a secret ritually based religious practice. In modern times much of the shrine's fame comes from an unusual **ascetic** named **Vamakhepa** (1843–1911), whose apparent irrationality and lack of respect for generally accepted norms—he once urinated on the temple's image of Tara to show his contempt for a **deity** made of iron—was a perfect match for Tara herself. Tarapith is said to bestow supernormal powers (**siddhis**) on those who **worship** there; this makes Tarapith not only a very powerful place but also a potentially dangerous one. For further information see E. Alan Morinis, *Pilgrimage in the Hindu Tradition*, 1984. See also **pitha**.

Tarjini Hasta

In Indian **dance**, **sculpture**, and ritual, tarjini hasta is the name for a particular hand **gesture** (**hasta**) in which the hand is closed except for the index finger, which is pointing upward as if to admonish or scold the viewer. The word *tarjini* is derived from a verb that can mean either "to threaten" or "to censure"—both of which can be understood from this gesture.

Tarka

("reasoning") In Indian logic, tarka denotes the mode of argument that focuses on the identification and classification of **fallacies**. When it is used in argumentation, tarka does not advance one's own point of view but is used to discredit an opponent's assertion, either by reducing it to absurdity, by showing that the argument does not fulfill necessary conditions, or by showing that it suffers from a fallacy that renders it untenable.

Tarpana

("satisfying") Tarpana is a memorial rite performed for the satisfaction of one's ancestors, in which one offers them libations of **water** to quench their thirst. Tarpana satisfies the "**sacrifice** to the ancestors," which is one of the Five Great Sacrifices. These five sacrifices are mandatory daily religious observances (**nitya karma**) for a "**twice-born**" householder, that is, a householder who has been born into one of the three "twice-born" groups in Indian society—**brahmin**, **kshatriya**, or **vaishya**—and who has received the adolescent religious **initiation** known as the second birth. Tarpana is also sometimes an occasional religious act (**naimittika karma**), which should be performed on occasions when one is bathing (**snana**) at pilgrimage places (**tirthas**). The rite itself is quite simple. The performer first bathes to become ritually pure, scoops up water in his joined hands, then tips his fingers forward to let the water drain out. Some sources also specify that the water should be mixed with sesame seeds, a substance associated with **offerings** to the dead. Tarpana was considered a companion rite to the memorial ceremony known as **shraddha**, although as an obligatory daily act, tarpana was performed much more frequently. In the shraddha ritual, one symbolically feeds one's ancestors to satisfy their hunger, whereas in the tarpana ritual, one gives them water to quench their thirst.

Tat Tvam Asi

("You are that") In the Hindu philosophical tradition, one of the "great utterances" (**mahavakyas**) expressing the ultimate truth. The truth referred to here is the identity of **atman** (the individual Self) and **Brahman** (Supreme Reality); this identity is the heart of the speculative

Bather performs the tarpana memorial rite in the sacred Ganges River, Varanasi.

texts called the **Upanishads**. This particular passage is found repeatedly in the sixth book of the **Chandogya Upanishad**, in which the boy **Shvetaketu** is being instructed by his father. The boy's father uses a series of analogies to convey his instruction regarding the identical natures of the **atman** and Brahman, ending every such analogy with this concluding phrase, which contains the wisdom of the whole.

In addition to its textual importance, this and three other mahavakyas—as utterances that capsulize fundamental truth—were appropriated as identifying symbols by the four divisions of the **Dashanami Sanyasi** ascetics. Each division had a different mahavakya, just as each had a different **Veda**, a different primary sacred center, and a different paradigmatic **ascetic** quality. Tat tvam asi is the mahavakya associated with the **Kitawara** division of the Dashanami Sanyasis.

Teej

Teej is a name denoting two different Hindu religious observances, both falling in the **lunar month** of **Bhadrapada** (August–September). Kajari Teej falls on the third day of the dark (waxing) half of the month and Hartalika Teej two weeks later, on the third day of the bright (waxing) half. Both of these observances have a mythic charter connected with the god **Shiva** and his wife **Parvati**, but the latter is far more important. Kajari Teej is a festival marking the coming of the **monsoons**, a season that once rendered travel impossible. For lovers who were together, the monsoon months were very sweet, but for those who were apart, the coming of the rains foretold a time of separation. One of the standard poetic images is the woman watching the darkening sky, wondering whether her beloved will make it home in time. On this day people sing songs in the Kajari **raga**, a melodic mode associated both with the rains and with songs of separation and longing. On this day people also welcome the rainy season by setting up swings and swinging on them. The festival is celebrated through much of India, but especially in the **Benares** and Mirzapur districts of the eastern part of **Uttar Pradesh**.

Hartalika Teej (also known as Hariyali Teej) is a religious observance practiced by young unmarried **women** in order to gain a good husband and have a happy marriage. In Hindu culture the model for the ideal husband is the god Shiva, who despite his wild appearance and his unusual habits, is completely devoted to his wife. One sign of this devotion is that Shiva and his wife Parvati are married only to each other, no matter which forms they take—as, for instance, when one or the other is cursed to be born as a human being. As the ideal divine couple, Shiva and Parvati are the patron **deities** of this religious observance. Women observing this festival should **worship** Shiva and Parvati (as the model couple whose happiness they hope to share), decorate their houses, put on new clothes, and pass the night singing songs of **auspiciousness**. This festival reveals the cultural importance of marriage for Indian women. Because the identity for many Indian women is still formed primarily through their traditional roles as wives and mothers, for many women their marriage is the most important event in their lives.

The charter myth for Hartalika Teej not only underlines the importance of a happy marriage but also points to the woman's role in gaining her husband. After the death of the **goddess Sati**, she is reborn as Parvati in the house of **Himalaya**, the mountains personified. Very early in life, Parvati vows that she will have no husband except for Shiva. Her parents try to discourage her from this wish because Shiva has taken a vow of **asceticism** and passes his time deep in meditation on Mount **Kailas**. Undeterred, Parvati goes up into the mountains and begins to do harsh physical asceticism (**tapas**) of her own. The power generated by her asceticism eventually awakens Shiva, and on Hartalika Teej he comes to where she is staying, disguised as an aged **brahmin**. He first tries to discourage Parvati by making disparaging remarks about Shiva's lifestyle and personality, but Parvati refuses to listen and remains unshaken in her resolve. Eventually Shiva reveals his true form to her, and on that day they are betrothed to be married.

Teli

Traditional Indian society was modeled as a collection of **endogamous**, or intermarried, subgroups known as **jatis** ("birth"). These jatis were organized (and their social status determined) by the group's hereditary occupation, over which each group had a monopoly. In traditional northern Indian society, the Telis were a Hindu jati whose hereditary occupation was making vegetable oil by pressing oil seeds.

Temple car from the city of Shrirangapatnam, in the state of Karnataka. It is used to transport an image of the temple's primary deity during festival processions.

Temple Cars

Name for the ceremonial carts in which the movable image of a **deity** (**utsava murti**) can be transported throughout the town or, in the case of the temples of southern India, around the processional streets that often ring the temple in concentric layers. In some cases the carts are made new every **year**, as at the temple of the god **Jagannath** in the city of **Puri**; in other cases (as one finds in many of the southern Indian temples) the temple car is one of the deity's standard accouterments, and it is made from precious metals and is richly decorated. In either case the deity is being treated in a manner parallel to that of a king, and the car is a means to move the deity in procession to view his or her earthly domain.

Tengalai

One of the two main subsects in the **Shrivaishnava** religious community, the other being the **Vadagalai**. The

Shrivaishnavas are devotees (**bhakta**) of the god **Vishnu**, and their roots lie in the devotional hymns of the **Alvars**, a group of twelve poet-saints who lived in southern India between the seventh and tenth centuries. Two centuries later, the Alvars' devotional outpouring was organized and systematized by the philosopher **Ramanuja** (11th c.), who is considered the Shrivaishnava founder. Ramanuja was convinced that **Brahman**, or Supreme Reality, was a personal **deity** rather than an impersonal abstract principle, and he was also convinced that devotion (**bhakti**) was the most important form of religious practice. **Vishishthadvaita Vedanta**, his philosophical position, stressed both of these convictions and thus opposed the **Advaita Vedanta** school, founded by the philosopher **Shankaracharya**, which believed that the Supreme Being was impersonal and that realization (**jnana**) was the best spiritual path.

The split between the Tengalais and the Vadagalais came several centuries after Ramanuja and stemmed from differing perspectives on what the individual must do to gain final liberation of the soul (**moksha**). The Tengalais emphasize the need for absolute surrender (**prapatti**) to the **grace** of God, through which devotees will be saved with no action of their own; the Vadagalais stress that devotees must also exert themselves on their own behalf. The Tengalai founder was Pillai **Lokacharya** (14th c.), who is also the community's most important figure.

Thakur

("master") The model for traditional Indian society was as a collection of **endogamous** subgroups (i.e., groups in which marriages occurred only between members of the same group) known as **jatis** ("birth"). These jatis were organized (and their social status determined) by the group's hereditary occupation, over which each group had a monopoly. In northern India, the Thakurs were a jati considered to be **kshatriyas**, who have traditionally functioned as landlords and village leaders. Its most famous member was the Nobel laureate **Rabindranath Tagore**.

Thandai

("cooling") A refreshing sweetened drink made of milk or yogurt, ground nuts, and spices often used as the medium for the consumption of ground marijuana (**bhang**). As with all milk products, the thandai is considered to have cooling properties; this effect may be intended to balance the bhang, which is considered to be "hot" because of its intoxicating properties.

Thanesar

City and sacred site (**tirtha**) adjoining the sacred site of **Kurukshetra** in the northern part of the state of **Haryana**. Thanesar is a famous site in the *Mahabharata*, the later of the two Sanskrit epics. The epic's climax comes at Kurukshetra in an eighteen-day battle between two factions of an extended family, along with their allies and supporters. On one side, there are the five **Pandava** brothers, who are the epic's protagonists, and on the other, their cousins the **Kauravas**, who are the antagonists. According to the epic, on the eve of the battle, the Pandavas worshiped the god **Shiva** in a temple at Thanesar, and after their **worship** Shiva assured them that they would be victorious. Aside from the temple, Thanesar also has a renowned bathing tank said to contain all the sacred rivers of India, at which the primary bathing (**snana**) day is **Sunday**. Nearby is the Gita **Mandir**, at which **Arjuna**, one of the Pandava brothers, is said to have received the teaching of the **Bhagavad Gita** from **Krishna** in the moments before the battle began.

Thanjavur

A variant name for the southern Indian city of **Tanjore**. See **Tanjore**.

Thief Castes

The model for traditional Indian society was as a collection of **endogamous** subgroups (i.e., groups in which marriages occurred only between members of the same group) known as **jatis** ("birth"). These jatis were organized (and their social status determined) by the group's hereditary occupation, over which each group had a monopoly. Although it sounds bizarre, this specialization extended to all occupations, and there were hereditary occupational groups whose profession was thievery and banditry. The most famous individual from these was **Tirumangai** (9th c.), by far the most picturesque of the **Alvars**, a group of twelve poet-saints who lived in southern India between the seventh and tenth centuries. In the nineteenth century the British composed a list of several hundred such groups, who were subject to relentless scrutiny, opposition, and in many cases resettlement.

Thiruvaiyaru

Temple town and sacred site (**tirtha**) in the **Tanjore** district of **Tamil Nadu**, about 170 miles south and west of Madras. Thiruvaiyaru's major temple is dedicated to the god **Shiva**, but the site is most famous for being the home of the late-eighteenth-century saint and musician Tyagaraja.

Thoreau, Henry David

(1817–1862) American writer and philosopher, who by his own account was powerfully influenced by the Hindu religious text known as the **Bhagavad Gita**, particularly the text's instruction to perform one's duties selflessly for the good of society, without any thought of personal reward. Thoreau refers to this text in both *Walden* and *A Week on the Concord and Merrimack Rivers*, and in letters to his friends, Thoreau talks about his desire to practice **yoga**.

Three Debts

According to tradition, repayment of three "debts" was incumbent on all "**twice-born**" men, that is, men born into one of the three "twice-born" groups in Indian society—**brahmin**, **kshatriya**, or **vaishya**—who had undergone the adolescent religious **initiation** known as the second birth. The first of these debts was to the gods and was repaid by **offering** sacrifices. The second debt was to the sages and was satisfied by studying the **Vedas**, the oldest and most authoritative religious texts. The final debt was to the ancestors (**pitrs**) and was satisfied by procreating a **son**, to ensure that the ancestral rites would be carried out without interruption.

3HO/Sikh Dharma Brotherhood

Modern religious organization founded by **Yogi Bhajan**; the movement's two names reflect differing emphases in the phases in Yogi Bhajan's teaching. His initial teachings were the traditional disciplines of **hatha yoga** and **kundalini yoga**, with his followers organized into a group known as the Happy, Healthy, Holy Organization (3HO). Hatha yoga is a system of religious discipline (**yoga**) based on a series of bodily postures known as **asanas**; this practice is widely believed to provide various physical benefits, including increased bodily flexibility and the ability to heal chronic ailments. Kundalini yoga is the religious discipline whose primary focus is awakening the **kundalini**, the latent spiritual force that exists in every person in the **subtle body**. The kundalini is awakened through a combination of yoga practice and ritual action and is believed to bring further spiritual capacities and final liberation (**moksha**) of the soul.

These two disciplines remain an important part of Yogi Bhajan's teachings, for he claims to be a master of **tantra**, a secret, ritually based religious practice. In the 1970s his teaching widened to include traditional Sikh teachings and symbols. The most prominent of these symbols are the "five

K's" that all Sikhs are supposed to wear, so called because each of them begins with the letter *k*: uncut **hair** (kesh), a comb (kangha), a bangle on the right wrist (kara), shorts (kacch), and a ceremonial sword (kirpan). Many of Yogi Bhajan's followers keep the Sikh symbols far more strictly than most people born as Sikhs, but the movement has two important divergences with the traditional Sikh community. One of these is its emphasis on tantra, which has little importance in the Sikh community. The most significant difference, however, is the religious authority that Yogi Bhajan holds over his followers, which is very different from the decentralized, essentially democratic form of the traditional Sikh community.

Thug

In the colonialist mythology describing the savagery of the East and the demonic qualities of Hinduism, one of the most compelling stories is that of the Thugs, a group of robbers who were devotees (**bhakta**) of the **goddess Kali**. According to popular belief, the Thugs were widespread throughout India and frequented the highways, seeking travelers as their prey. They would travel with their victims, sometimes for days on end, and then kill them—sometimes after giving them sweets laced with **drugs**, and sometimes simply by taking them by surprise. The victims would be strangled with a silken scarf, and whenever possible, no **blood** would be shed, for the victims' blood was considered an **offering** to the goddess Kali and thus should not be spilled and wasted. The victims' worldly possessions were claimed by the Thugs themselves, in a division of the spoils between **deity** and devotee. This demonic practice persisted until the 1830s, when it was finally uprooted and destroyed by the British.

Although the tale of the Thugs makes a gripping story, much of it has been dispelled by more careful recent scholarship. One of the major factors in the rise of the Thugs was the radical economic dislocation caused by the arrival of the British themselves. Many of the people marginalized by these forces took to wandering and, in their desperation, resorted to banditry. These small-scale and essentially local depredations were transformed into a widespread religious conspiracy. The myth of the Thugs certainly showed concern about the prevailing law-and-order situation in central India, but it may also have reflected British colonial fears about their ability to control their territory. Even though there are references to the Thugs in texts predating British contact, on the whole, this was one of the more enduring colonial stereotypes. For further information see C. A. Bayly, *Indian Society and the Making of the British Empire*, 1988; and *The Raj*, 1990.

Thursday

(Brhaspativar) The fifth day of the **week**, whose presiding **planet** is **Jupiter** (**Brhaspati**). Since in Hindu mythology the sage **Brhaspati** is the religious preceptor (**guru**) of the gods, another common name for Thursday is Guruvar. In Hindu astrology (**jyotisha**) Jupiter is an extremely powerful planet, and because in religious life one's spiritual preceptor is often likened to a god, this makes Thursday a ritually important and powerful day. One of the "**deities**" to be honored and served on this day is one's religious preceptor.

Another deity worshiped on this day is the **goddess Lakshmi**, who is worshiped mainly by **women**. Lakshmi is the wife of the god **Vishnu** and the embodiment of wealth, prosperity, and good fortune, which she brings with her wherever she goes and removes when she leaves. As the human counterpart to Lakshmi, married women **worship** her to obtain these things or to retain them if they already have them. Because it is well known that good fortune is not permanent and can often change, Lakshmi is also seen as a capricious and somewhat fickle divine presence. One of the taboos for women, at least in parts of northern India, is changing their jewelry on that day because this is said to annoy Lakshmi and raise the danger that she might depart because of her vexation.

Tiger

In Hindu mythology, a tiger or **lion** is the animal vehicle of the powerful forms of the **Goddess**, such as **Durga**. Modern iconography shows both lions and tigers with no apparent difference between them, perhaps reflecting the fact that the **Hindi** word *sher* can refer to either animal. In either case, the fact that the Goddess rides such a dangerous animal is clearly a symbol of her power and capacity, because in her mythology these **animals** are often described as her allies, doing battle on her part in response to her command.

Tika

In modern **Hindi**, a word denoting either a commentary on a text or a colored mark (often red vermilion) on one's forehead. These forehead marks are applied for various reasons: for sheer ornamentation, to indicate sectarian affiliation, or as an outward symbol of having worshiped in a temple that day (since a common element in this **worship** is to receive some of the vermilion daubed on the feet of the **deity's** image, as a sign of **grace** and one's subordinate status). The former of these two meanings is the original sense of the word, but the latter meaning is far more common in contemporary times. The connection between these two meanings could be the notion that just as a primary text is ornamented and highlighted by a commentary, in the same way a forehead mark could ornament the body.

Tilak

A mark on the forehead, also colloquially known as a **tika**, made from colored powders mixed with oil, sandalwood paste, or cosmetics. These forehead marks are applied for various reasons: for sheer ornamentation, to indicate

This ascetic's tika markings indicate that he belongs to the Ramanandi group.

sectarian affiliation, or as an outward symbol of having worshiped in a temple that day. See **tika**.

Tilak, Bal Gangadhar

(1856–1920) Maharashtrian political activist who was once characterized as "the father of Indian unrest." Unlike his Maharashtrian contemporaries **Ranade** and **Gokhale**, who stressed working within existing institutions, Tilak never compromised his conviction that the British had no right to rule India. He resigned from Gokhale's reformist group in 1890 and devoted himself to educating and organizing ordinary people in **Maharashtra**. One vehicle for such organizing comprised two newspapers, one written in English and one in Marathi. The other involved organizing and promoting two new festivals. One of these festivals was devoted to the **Maratha** king **Shivaji**, a regional hero who had spent his life fighting

697

domination by the Moghul empire. The other festival was **Ganesh Chaturthi**, which Tilak promoted as a visible way to assert and celebrate a Hindu nationalist identity during the time of British imperial rule. Given British power, outright rebellion was simply impossible, and the British government heavily restricted all forms of political dissent. The Ganesh festival provided a way to circumvent these restrictions because the British had a long-standing policy of not interfering with religious observances. Tilak was imprisoned several times on the charge of inciting political assassinations, but he always returned directly to the political fray. Aside from his political agitation, his greatest intellectual work is a commentary on the **Bhagavad Gita**, a religious text, in which he stresses the need for this-worldly activism to defeat evil, including violence if necessary. See also **Moghul dynasty**.

Time

For various articulations of time in traditional Hindu culture, see **cosmic time**, **calendar**, and **lunar month**.

Tirruppavai

One of the two collections of poetry composed by the poet-saint **Andal** (9th c.), the other being the *Nacciyar Tirumoli*. Andal was the only woman among the **Alvars**, a group of twelve poet-saints who lived in southern India between the seventh and tenth centuries. All of the Alvars were devotees (**bhakta**) of the god **Vishnu**, and their stress on passionate devotion (**bhakti**) to a personal god, conveyed through hymns sung in the **Tamil language**, transformed and revitalized Hindu religious life. Andal's chosen **deity** was **Ranganatha**, the particular form of Vishnu presiding at the temple of **Shrirangam**, yet both collections of her poetry are dedicated to **Krishna**, a different form of Vishnu.

This seeming divergence may reflect her conviction that all manifestations of Vishnu were the same or else may indicate a difference between personal devotion and literary expression. Ranganatha was a specific form of Vishnu presiding over a specific place—which at the time was true for most southern Indian temples—whereas Krishna was a form of Vishnu for whom there was already a large body of literature, but who was not geographically limited. The contents of the *Tirruppavai* are poems of separation in which Andal mourns the absence of Krishna, using the language and images of the forlorn lover, feverishly hoping for Krishna's return.

Tirtha

("crossing place") The most general name for any holy place. Just as a ford on a riverbank provides a safe place to cross from one side to the other, in the same way a tirtha provides a way for one to "cross over" from mundane life to a sanctified one or, on an even greater scale, to "cross over" from this ephemeral and ever changing world to the unchanging, blissful, final liberation of the soul (**moksha**). Many tirthas are actual places—and many of them are on the shores of India's sacred rivers, particularly the **Ganges**—and in its most colloquial meaning, the word *tirtha* connotes a pilgrimage place. Yet the traditional pilgrimage literature is emphatic that tirthas are not just restricted to mere physical places: The word can also refer to holy people (such as **ascetics**, saints, **gurus**, and sages) as well as to virtues such as charity, wisdom, compassion, and **purity** of heart.

A tirtha is first and foremost a place or thing that gives one access to sanctity and religious power, and in the case of the physical places (rivers, mountains, cities, temples, or images), this power is accessible to all. Such holy places are seen not only as giving easier access to the divine but also as being areas where religious merit is more readily and bountifully obtained. When one surveys the literature connected with certain areas, one of the most common themes is the claim that the merit from religious acts performed at place X (the physical tirtha) equals that of a thousand (or a million, or a billion) such religious acts done in ordinary places. The rarefied atmosphere at tirthas has a similar effect on evil acts, multiplying their consequences manifold. In this way the action of a tirtha can be compared to that of a microphone; just as a microphone magnifies any sound, whether harsh or pleasant, in the same way a tirtha magnifies, for good or ill, the consequences of any action. The pilgrimage literature thus commonly reminds people of the religious merit that their acts can bring, and it warns them that careless or evil actions can have equally severe consequences. For this reason, people performing religious pilgrimage (**tirthayatra**) were encouraged to live an austere, self-conscious life, both to save themselves from any lapses and to make the journey a self-conscious process of transformation. For further information see Diana Eck, *Banaras*, 1999; E. Alan Morinis, *Pilgrimage in the Hindu Tradition*, 1984; A. W. Entwistle, *Braj*, 1987; Ann Grodzins Gold, *Fruitful Journeys*, 1988; and Peter van der Veer, *Gods on Earth*, 1988.

Tirtha Dashanami

One of the ten divisions of the **Dashanami Sanyasis**, renunciant **ascetics** who are devotees (**bhakta**) of the god **Shiva**. The Dashanamis were supposedly established by the ninth-century philosopher **Shankaracharya**, in an effort to create a corps of learned men who could help revitalize Hindu life. Each of the divisions is designated by a different name—in this case, *tirtha* ("sacred site"). On **initiation**, new members are given this name as a surname to their new ascetic names, thus allowing for immediate group identification.

Aside from their individual identity, these ten "named" divisions are divided into four larger organizational groups. Each group has its headquarters in one of the four monastic centers (**maths**) supposedly established by Shankaracharya, as well as other particular religious associations. The Tirtha Dashanamis belong to the **Kitawara** group, which is affiliated with the **Sharada math** in the city of **Dwaraka**, on the shore of the Arabian Sea. The Tirtha division is unique in that it is one of the few that will initiate only **brahmins**. (The other such divisions are **Saraswati**, **Ashrama**, and part of the **Bharati** order.)

Tirtha Shraddha

Name for a particular type of **shraddha** (ancestral memorial rite) performed when visiting a pilgrimage place (**tirtha**). A shraddha has two major features: symbolically feeding one's ancestor(s) by **offering** balls of cooked grain (**pindas**), and feeding real food to a group of **brahmins** representing one's ancestors. Tirtha shraddhas belong to a class of action known as occasional actions (**naimittika karma**) because they are incumbent only under certain conditions. Under ordinary circumstances one would not have to perform this action, but it becomes required when one visits a pilgrimage place. The traditional pilgrimage literature, much of it clearly written by the brahmins who received such meals and other gifts, is emphatic that this obligation should not be neglected.

Tirthayatra

("Journey to a **tirtha**") The general term denoting religious pilgrimage, which is seen as an act generating considerable religious merit (**punya**). The major focus of such travel was a visit to a "crossing place" (tirtha), a sacred site or person through which one could more easily communicate with the worlds beyond. One of the major themes in the traditional pilgrimage literature was the inherent holiness of whatever place was being described at that time, which was invariably described as bringing

A group of pilgrims on a tirthayatra
(pilgrimage), Tibet.

incalculable benefits, even for actions performed unknowingly or in jest. A second and seemingly contradictory theme was the stress on the inner state of the pilgrims themselves and the warning that they would gain no benefits unless they were serious about their visit. In its ideal, pilgrimage to the holy places was not a pleasure tour but a vehicle for spiritual development, through bathing (**snana**) in holy rivers, visiting and worshiping powerful **deities**, enduring hardships, making **offerings** to the ancestors, gift-giving, and living a sober, disciplined life.

In fact, the traditional literature affirms both sides of this tension—the need for individual commitment and the inherent sanctity of the places themselves—although the emphasis may shift depending on the needs of the moment. One explanation, combining both of these themes, is that these holy places amplified the effects of all of one's actions there, whether good or bad. Pilgrims were thus encouraged to benefit from performing meritorious actions but warned of the heightened consequences from evil deeds, which were much more severe than normal.

In earlier times pilgrimage required a large investment of time and money. People would often spend months or years on pilgrimage, usually visiting a series of pilgrimage places. This was seen as a religiously meritorious use of one's money, a notion still current in contemporary times. For most people, such an opportunity would come only once in their lifetime, generally in their later years, and this long-awaited fulfillment must have heightened their experience. The advent of railroad travel in the late 1800s largely reshaped this pattern, although it persisted in the **Himalayas** until well into the twentieth century. With the advent of railroad travel, people were able to visit places with relative ease and speed. This convenience encouraged multiple visits, but also ones in which the person stopped at fewer places on the way.

The most recent change in pilgrimage patterns has come with the development of tourism, which is being marketed by state governments as a way to generate income for the local people. It cannot be denied that "seeing the sights" has always been a part of pilgrimage, which provided a religiously sanctioned motive for travel. Yet the ideal, then as now, was that this journey should not be undertaken merely for enjoyment, but for serious purposes. Some contemporary Hindus worry that the growth of tourism has commercialized the sanctity of their holy places; other more sanguine souls consider the stress on tourism simply a stronger manifestation of trends that have always existed, which will have no effect on the truly pious.

Tiruchendur

Temple and sacred site (**tirtha**) on the Bay of Bengal in **Tamil Nadu**, sixty miles up the coast from **Kanyakumari**. Tiruchendur is part of the network of six temples in Tamil Nadu built to honor **Murugan**, a hill **deity** who has been assimilated into the larger pantheon as a form of the god **Skanda**, the **son** of **Shiva**. Five of these temples have been definitively identified, and each is associated with a particular region, a specific ecosystem, and a particular incident in Murugan's mythic career. In the case of Tiruchendur, it is said to be where he killed a **demon** enemy and thus presents him in his warrior aspect. The sixth of these temples is said to be every other shrine to Murugan in Tamil Nadu. The cult of Murugan is thus a symbolic vehicle for Tamil pride and identity, and because the number six has connotations of completeness—as in the six directions or the six **chakras** in the **subtle body**—it also connotes that nothing outside is needed. For further information see Fred Clothey, "Pilgrimage Centers in the Tamil Cultus of Murukan," in *Journal of the American Academy of Religion,* Vol. 40, No. 1, 1972.

Tiruchirappalli

City on the **Cauvery** River in the central part of the state of **Tamil Nadu**, and the capital of the district with the same name. The city's strategic position meant that it was contested by various southern Indian dynasties, of which the most recent were the **Nayaks** of **Madurai**, who built an imposing fort on a stone outcrop in the center of the city. It is most famous, however, for the great temples of **Shrirangam** and **Jambukeshvar**, both of which are on an island in the Cauvery, north of the city. The former is a temple to the god **Vishnu**, which has important symbolic associations with southern Indian kings and kingship; the latter is dedicated to the god **Shiva** in his aspect as "Lord of the Rose-Apple (**jambu**) Tree."

Tirukkural

One of the most important pieces of early Tamil literature, along with the slightly later *Naladiyar*. The Tirukkural

Depiction of Tirumalai Nayak.

is a collection of brief verses on religious, social, and moral life, organized according to various themes; it is attributed to the poet **Tiruvalluvar** and is believed to have been written late in the fifth century. The *Tirukkural*'s underlying assumptions are theistic, and in this it differs from the *Naladiyar*, the tone of which is primarily ethical, with no mention of divinity. Many of these epigrams have become proverbial expressions in Tamil and have become the cultural property of Tamils from all religious communities. See also **Tamil language** and **Tamil epics**.

Tirumalai Nayak

(r. 1623–1659) Greatest ruler in the southern Indian **Nayak dynasty**, who took advantage of the collapse of the **Vijayanagar dynasty** to rule much of modern **Tamil Nadu** from the capital city of **Madurai**. The peace and prosperity during Tirumalai's reign was expressed with two large pieces of monumental **architecture**—his royal palace, and the enormous **Minakshi** temple, named after the **goddess** considered to be Madurai's patron **deity**. Interestingly, the temple was the real ritual center of the city, as is clearly shown by its placement and the processional streets surrounding it.

Tirumalisai

(9th c.) One of the **Alvars**, a group of twelve poet-saints who lived in southern India between the seventh and tenth centuries. All of the Alvars were devotees (**bhakta**) of the god **Vishnu**, and their stress on passionate devotion (**bhakti**) to a personal god, conveyed through hymns sung in the **Tamil language**, transformed and revitalized Hindu religious life. According to tradition, Tirumalisai was the son of a sage and a celestial nymph (**apsara**), who was abandoned by his parents at birth. He was found and raised by a man of very humble status who called his foster son by the name of their village. For further information see Kamil Zvelebil, *Tamil Literature*, 1975.

Tirumangai

(9th c.) By far the most picturesque of the **Alvars**, a group of twelve poet-saints who lived in southern India between the seventh and tenth centuries. All the Alvars were devotees (**bhakta**) of the god **Vishnu**, and their stress on passionate devotion (**bhakti**) to a personal god, conveyed through hymns sung in the **Tamil language**, transformed and revitalized Hindu religious life. According to tradition, Tirumangai was born into a **caste** of thieves, and theft, robbery, and deceit play an important role in the stories associated with him. One story reports that after taking a vow to feed 1,008 **Vaishnavas** for a year, he resorted to highway robbery to raise the necessary funds; on another occasion he took to robbery to raise funds to enlarge the temple at **Shrirangam**. In these and other works, he had the continual help of Vishnu, his chosen **deity**; regardless of

their truth or falsity, these stories reveal a great deal about the passionate devotional commitment of his time. For further information see Kamil Zvelebil, *Tamil Literature*, 1975; and John Stirling Morley Hooper, *Hymns of the Alvars*, 1929.

Tirunavukkarashu

(7th c.) This was the given name of the **Nayanar** poet-saint most commonly referred to as **Appar** ("father"). Appar was one of the earliest of the Nayanars, a group of sixty-three southern Indian poet-saints who were devotees (**bhakta**) of the god **Shiva** and who lived in southern India in the seventh and eighth centuries. Along with their contemporaries the **Alvars**, who were devotees of **Vishnu**, the Nayanars spearheaded the revitalization of Hindu religion through their passionate devotion (**bhakti**) to a personal god, conveyed through hymns sung in the **Tamil language**.

Tirupati

Town in the far southern part of the state of **Andhra Pradesh**, about 160 miles northwest of Madras. It is most famous for the Holy Hill (Tirumalai) eight miles to the north, which is the location of the temple to **Venkateshvara** and for which Tirupati is the major gateway.

Tirupati/Tirumalai Devasthanam

Official name for the managing committee of the **Venkateshvara** temple, near the town of **Tirupati** in the state of **Andhra Pradesh**. This temple is the richest one in India, based largely on the popular belief that any wish made in the **deity's** presence will invariably come true. In earlier times all of the temple receipts were taken by the priests running the temple, but since Indian independence in 1947, the temple committee has been responsible for them. The committee has channeled these funds into hundreds of charities, but particularly into education and temple building: the former in schools from the primary to the university level, and the latter in providing the funds to help build many of the larger Hindu temples in the United States and Europe.

Tiruppan

(9th c.) One of the **Alvars**, a group of twelve poet-saints who lived in southern India between the seventh and tenth centuries. All of the Alvars were devotees (**bhakta**) of the god **Vishnu**, and their stress on passionate devotion (**bhakti**) to a personal god, conveyed through hymns sung in the **Tamil language**, transformed and revitalized Hindu religious life. According to tradition, Tiruppan was a foundling who was adopted by a musician. As he grew up, he developed deep devotion for **Vishnu** in his form as **Ranganatha** at the temple of **Shrirangam**, but because his family status was unknown, he never went into the temple itself out of fear that his presence might render it impure. Tiruppan finally gained entrance when one of the temple's **brahmin** priests, who had earlier insulted him, received a divine command to carry Tiruppan on his shoulders to Ranganatha's image. As with many stories in the lives of the bhakti saints, the lesson here clearly emphasizes the superiority of devotion over birth. For further information see Kamil Zvelebil, *Tamil Literature*, 1975; and John Stirling Morley Hooper, *Hymns of the Alvars*, 1929.

Tirupparankunram

Tirtha (sacred site) ten miles southwest of **Madurai** in central **Tamil Nadu**. Tirupparankunram is famous for one of the six temples in Tamil Nadu built to honor **Murugan**, a hill **deity** assimilated into the pantheon as a form of **Skanda**. It is said to be where he marries **Devasena**, the bride given by **Indra** and the gods after he has proven his mettle in battle, and thus reflects his acceptance into the larger pantheon. Five of these temples are definitively identified and scattered throughout the state, but

the sixth is said to be every other shrine to Murugan in Tamil Nadu. The cult of Murugan is thus a symbolic vehicle for Tamil pride and identity, and because the number six has connotations of completeness—as in the six directions, or the six **chakras** in the **subtle body**—it also connotes that nothing outside is needed. For further information see Fred Clothey, "Pilgrimage Centers in the Tamil Cultus of Murukan," in *Journal of the American Academy of Religion*, Vol. 40, No. 1, 1972.

Tiruttani

Tirtha (sacred site) in the hills of **Tamil Nadu**, seventy-five miles of Madras. It is famous for one of the six temples in Tamil Nadu built to honor **Murugan**, a hill **deity** assimilated into the pantheon as a form of **Skanda**. Tiruttani is celebrated as the place where he marries his tribal bride **Valli**, which gives him a family connection with southern India. Five of these temples are definitively identified and scattered throughout the state, but the sixth is said to be every other shrine to Murugan in Tamil Nadu. The cult of Murugan is thus a symbolic vehicle for Tamil pride and identity, and because the number six has connotations of completeness—as in the six directions or the six **chakras** in the **subtle body**—it also connotes that nothing outside is needed. For further information see Fred Clothey, "Pilgrimage Centers in the Tamil Cultus of Murukan," in *Journal of the American Academy of Religion*, Vol. 40, No. 1, 1972.

Tiruttontar Puranam

("history of the holy servants [of **Shiva**]") Another name for the *Periya Purana*, a hagiographical account (an idealizing biography of saints or venerated figures) of the lives of the sixty-three **Nayanars**, written by the twelfth-century figure **Cekkilar**. The Nayanars were a group of **Shaiva** poet-saints who lived in southern India in the seventh and eighth centuries. See *Periya Purana*.

Tiruvachakam

("holy utterances") Collection of poetry composed in the ninth century by the Tamil poet-saint **Manikkavachakar**, who was a passionate devotee (**bhakta**) of the god **Shiva**. Manikkavachakar's work comes in the tradition of the **Nayanars** (a group of sixty-three **Shaiva** poet-saints who lived in southern India in the seventh and eighth centuries), although he is not counted as one of them because he was about a century later than the last Nayanar, **Sundaramurtti**. The hymns in the *Tiruvachakam* bear witness to Manikkavachakar's intense devotion to Shiva, and in their devotional fervor, they can be seen as the culmination of the earlier devotional (**bhakti**) tradition. Manikkavachakar's hymns are also the basis for the development of the philosophical tradition known as **Shaiva Siddhanta**, which makes Manikkavachakar a pivotal figure in southern Indian Shaivism. For further information see Glenn Yocum, *Hymns to the Dancing Siva*, 1982. See also **Tamil language** and **Tamil epics**.

Tiruvalluvar

(5th–6th c.) According to tradition, the author of the *Tirukkural*, one of the most important pieces of early Tamil literature. The *Tirukkural* is a collection of brief verses on religious, social, and moral life, organized according to various themes. Many of these epigrams have become proverbial expressions in Tamil and have become the cultural property of Tamils from all religious communities. See also **Tamil language** and **Tamil epics**.

Tiruvannamalai

Temple town and sacred site (**tirtha**) in the northern part of the state of **Tamil Nadu**, about 100 miles southwest of Madras, the capital. Tiruvannamalai is most famous as a temple to the god **Shiva** in his form as Arunachaleshvar, "the Lord of Arunachal [Hill]," the hill on which the temple is built.

Tiruvannamalai is also one of the **bhutalingas** ("elemental **lingas**"), a network of five southern Indian sites sacred to Shiva. In each of these sites, Shiva is worshiped as a linga, the pillar-shaped object that is his symbolic form, and at each site the linga is believed to be formed from one of the five primordial **elements** (bhuta)—**earth**, **wind**, **fire**, **water**, and **space** (**akasha**). Tiruvannamalai's linga is associated with the primordial element of fire, making this an extremely powerful image. Aside from the image and the temple, Tiruvannamalai is also famous as the place in which the modern Indian saint **Ramana Maharshi** spent most of his life, from 1896 until his death in 1950.

Tiruvaymoli

("Holy words") Collection of 1,102 stanzas written in the tenth century by the poet-saint **Nammalvar**. Nammalvar was one of the **Alvars**, a group of twelve poet-saints who lived in southern India between the seventh and tenth centuries. All of the Alvars were devotees (**bhakta**) of the god **Vishnu**, and their stress on passionate devotion (**bhakti**) to a personal god, conveyed through hymns sung in the **Tamil language**, transformed and revitalized Hindu religious life. Nammalvar's *Tiruvaymoli* is an outpouring of ecstatic **Vaishnava** devotionalism and forms the concluding section of the *Nalayira Divyaprabandham*, the collected compositions of the Alvars. For further information see Kamil Zvelebil, *Tamil Literature*, 1975; John Stirling Morley Hooper, *Hymns of the Alvars*, 1929; A. Shrinivasa Raghavan, *Nammalvar*, 1975; and A. K. Ramanujan (trans.), *Hymns for the Drowning*, 1981.

Tiruvayur

Southern Indian temple town about thirty-five miles east of the city of **Tanjore** in the state of **Tamil Nadu**. The town is most famous for an enormous temple to the god **Shiva**, and as with many southern Indian temples, the temple is located in the heart of the city and forms a substantial part of the city itself.

Tithi

A lunar **day**, that is to say, one of the thirty days occurring during a single **lunar month**, from **full moon** to full moon. Because these thirty lunar days take place in about twenty-eight solar days, each lunar day is thus slightly shorter than a solar day. Even in contemporary times, most Hindu religious observances are determined by the lunar **calendar**, which makes the determination of these lunar days an important matter. Most people keep track of these holidays with a **panchang**, an almanac that gives all the lunar days.

Toddy Palm

Palm tree that is both the source of the slightly fermented beverage tapped from its sap known as toddy, and the long, flat leaves that were traditionally used for writing down all sorts of texts, including religious ones. The former use led this tree to be considered unclean, since alcoholic beverages are proscribed in "respectable" Hindu society; the manuscripts written on the leaves, however, could be the holiest of texts. The poet-saint **Ravidas** uses this palm to illustrate how the power of the divine name can transform something normally believed to be base and vile. In doing so he is also referring to himself, who as a tanner and **leather** worker was believed to be defiled because his work involves handling the skins of dead **animals**.

Tondaradippodi

(9th c.) One of the **Alvars**, a group of twelve poet-saints who lived in southern India between the seventh and tenth centuries. All of the Alvars were devotees (**bhakta**) of the god **Vishnu**, and their stress on passionate devotion (**bhakti**) to a personal god, conveyed through hymns sung in the **Tamil language**, transformed and revitalized Hindu religious life. According to tradition, **Tondaradippodi** was born as a **brahmin** named Vipra **Narayana**, and his family's hereditary labor was to arrange the flowers for the **worship** of **Ranganatha**, a form of Vishnu who is the presiding **deity** at the temple of **Shrirangam**. He became enamored of a courtesan who cast her spell on him, and for a time paid attention to nothing else. In the end he was saved by Ranganatha, to whom Vipra Narayana devoted himself for the rest of his life, taking as a symbol of this his new name ("Dust of the Feet of the Slaves [of God]"). For further information see Kamil Zvelebil, *Tamil Literature*, 1975; and John Stirling Morley Hooper, *Hymns of the Alvars*, 1929.

Tortoise Avatar

Second **avatar** or incarnation of the god **Vishnu**. As with all of Vishnu's avatars, the Tortoise avatar came into being in a time of crisis and served to restore the cosmic balance that had been thrown out of equilibrium. In this case the source of trouble was the sage **Durvasas**, who had cursed the gods to become mortal and their heavenly luster to fade. To counter this, the gods made a pact with the **demons** that they would jointly churn the Ocean of Milk to obtain the nectar of immortality, which would be equally divided.

The image of churning here is based on traditional dairy practices, in which the person churning uses a string to rotate a churning paddle. In this instance, however, the churning takes place on a cosmic scale: The churning stick is Mount **Mandara**, the mountain that is at the center of the earth; the churning string is the divine serpent **Vasuki**, who encircles the world; and Vishnu himself, in the form of a tortoise, dives to the bottom of the ocean to provide a stable base for the churning stick. The gods and demons pull Vasuki back and forth, spinning the mountain and churning the Ocean of Milk. The churning separates the Ocean of Milk into

The god Vishnu's Tortoise avatar. He takes this form to help the gods regain their immortality.

various components, both good and bad. One product is the deadly **halahala** poison, which is neutralized by having **Shiva** hold it in his throat. Some of the other products are the **Kaustubha** jewel, the wishing **cow** Surabhi, the **goddess Lakshmi**, and finally the physician of the gods, **Dhanvantari**, who emerges from the sea bearing the pot containing the nectar of immortality.

The demons grab the pot of nectar and begin to escape, but Vishnu takes the form of the enchantress **Mohini** and beguiles the demons into giving the pot back to her. She gives the pot to the gods, who take off with the demons in hot pursuit. According to more recent traditions, in their flight the gods stop at four different holy places on earth—**Allahabad**, **Haridwar**, **Ujjain**, and **Nasik**—over a twelve-(divine) day span; this latter incident is cited as the charter myth for the celebration of the **Kumbha Mela** at these sites on a twelve-**year** basis (because a divine day is believed to equal a human year).

The gods finally manage to escape their pursuers and divide the nectar among themselves, but they fail to notice that the demon **Sainhikeya** slips into their midst in disguise. As the demon begins to drink, the **sun** and **moon** alert Vishnu, who uses his discus to cut off the demon's head. Sainhikeya's two halves become immortal because they have come into contact with the nectar, and both halves are considered malevolent celestial beings: the head as **Rahu**, the body as **Ketu**. Rahu has particular enmity for the sun and moon, since these **deities** are responsible for his demise, and tries to swallow them whenever he meets them in the **heavens**. He always succeeds, but because he no longer has a body to digest them, they escape unharmed through Rahu's severed neck. This, of course, is the traditional explanation for solar and lunar **eclipses**; the association with the malevolent Rahu has thus led eclipses to be seen as highly inauspicious times. See also **ocean, churning of the**.

Tota Puri

An **ascetic** initiated into the **Puri** order of the **Dashanami Sanyasis**, as can be seen from his surname. Tota Puri was one of the teachers of the Bengali saint **Ramakrishna**, who appeared to instruct Ramakrishna in **Advaita Vedanta** as part of the latter's continuing exposure to many different types of religious practice. In his earlier religious practice, Ramakrishna had been a fervent devotee (**bhakta**) of the **goddess Kali**, whereas the Advaita Vedanta **philosophy** claims that behind all things lies a single impersonal reality that has no defining attributes except for being, consciousness, and bliss (**sacchidananda**). In the Advaita understanding, because all conceptions of particular **deities** have specific attributes, they are thus conditioned forms of the ultimate **Brahman** (Supreme Reality).

Although this conception ran counter to his own previous experience, Ramakrishna practiced diligently under Tota Puri's direction. When Ramakrishna attained enlightenment through the practices of Advaita, he discovered that the essence of this experience was the same as that gained from his earlier devotional practices. This inner experience of identity was a pivotal experience for Ramakrishna and reinforced his conviction that all forms of religious practice led the seeker to the same place. After Ramakrishna's experience of enlightenment, Tota Puri disappeared.

Transcendental Meditation

Religious organization founded by **Maharishi Mahesh Yogi**, whose teachings on meditation comprise its major thrust. As its name would indicate, Transcendental Meditation (TM) stresses the multiple benefits of meditation: For the individual, it promotes physical, mental, and spiritual health, whereas for the larger environment, it is claimed to have pacific effects, resulting in reduced crime and hatred. All of these results can be obtained only by diligent practice, but the **initiation** itself is easy to obtain—all one has to do is to attend a seminar sponsored by a TM instructor and pay the required fee to obtain one's **mantra**, or sacred utterance. In more recent years, TM has offered programs leading to the acquisition of superhuman powers (**siddhis**) at its headquarters at Maharishi International University in Fairfield, Iowa. The claims of these programs have been toned down since a disgruntled buyer—who had been unable to learn to levitate—won a lawsuit for damages.

Although meditation and the use of mantras are well-established Hindu practices, many traditional Hindus are uncomfortable with other elements of TM's marketing. One controversial point is the practice of buying (or selling) a mantra, which was traditionally transmitted from teacher (**guru**) to disciple only after significant association. A similar problem comes from the notion that one can buy and sell superhuman powers. These powers are seen as highly seductive because they can be used for both good and evil and as having the potential to destroy a spiritually immature person. Traditional wisdom is unanimous that a person should not consciously seek such powers, because the very act of seeking is seen as being rooted in selfish desires. In contrast, when one has gained such powers as a byproduct of spiritual attainment, one is believed to be able to keep them in proper perspective.

Treta Yuga

A particular age of the world in **cosmic time**. According to traditional belief, time has neither a beginning nor an end, but alternates between cycles of creation and activity, followed by cessation and quietude. Each of these cycles lasts for 4.32 billion years, with the active phase known as the **Day of Brahma**, and the quiet phase as the Night of Brahma. In cosmic time, the Day of Brahma is divided into one thousand **mahayugas** ("great cosmic ages"), each of which lasts for 4.32 million years. Each mahayuga is composed of four constituent **yugas** (cosmic ages), named the **Krta Yuga**, Treta Yuga, **Dvapara Yuga**, and **Kali Yuga**. Each of these four yugas is shorter than its predecessor and ushers in an era more degenerate and depraved. By the end of the Kali Yuga, things have gotten so bad that the only solution is the destruction and recreation of the **earth**, at which time the next Krta era begins.

The Treta Yuga is the second of the four yugas, lasting for 1,296,000 years. Although the Treta Age is still relatively **auspicious**, it is less so than the Krta Age, symbolized by its identification with the metal silver—not as valuable as the gold associated with the preceding Krta Yuga, but more valuable than the bronze and iron associated with the two following yugas. In popular belief the Treta Yuga is believed to be the time when the god **Rama** reigned on earth.

Tribhanga

("three breaks") Name denoting one of the best-known poses in Indian **dance** and **sculpture**, in which the line of the body has three distinct breaks, or changes in direction. In this pose, the body's weight is mainly supported on one foot, with the corresponding knee and shoulder inclined toward one side and the hips inclined in the opposite direction.

Tridosha

In **ayurveda**, the term for the set of three bodily humours, **vata** ("air"), **pitta** ("bile"), and **kapha** ("phlegm"). Each of these humours is associated with certain physiological tendencies, particularly with regard to digestion and metabolism. Every person has all three of these humours, although one of them is generally dominant. In a healthy person the three humours are in general equilibrium, but an imbalance can lead to illness or chronic health problems. The solution to these lies in regaining the proper balance between the doshas, or humours, for which one of the major solutions is **eating** a proper diet.

Trika

Kashmiri religious community whose members were devotees (**bhakta**) of the god **Shiva**; the greatest figure in the Trika school was the tenth-century philosopher and aesthetic theorist **Abhinavagupta**. Trika Shaivism is a tantric tradition—that is, a secret, ritually based religious practice—whose philosophical underpinnings merge two philosophical positions, theism and monism. Theism is the notion that a divinity is the Supreme Reality in the universe, whereas monism conceives a more abstract principle as the basis of all reality. For Trika Shaivism, the sole true reality is the god Shiva, who is both Supreme God and the source for emanations from which the material universe is formed. Final liberation of the soul (**moksha**) comes through a process of "recognition" (**pratyabhijna**), in which one realizes that the entire universe is nothing but a manifestation of Shiva

alone. Here one "recognizes" something that has always been true but until that time had been obscured by a mistaken understanding. For further information see Paul Eduardo Muller-Ortega, *The Triadic Heart of Siva*, 1989. See also **tantra** and **Shaiva**.

Trilochan

(15th c.?) A **sant** poet who is generally associated with the poet-saint **Namdev**. The name *sant* is an umbrella term for a loose group of central and northern Indian poet-saints who shared several general tendencies: a stress on individualized, interior religion leading to a personal experience of the divine; a disdain for external ritual, particularly image **worship**; a faith in the power of the divine name; and a tendency to ignore conventional **caste** distinctions. Trilochan's only existing poems are a few verses in the **Adigranth**, the sacred scripture of the Sikh community. These verses describe his devotion to **Vithoba**, the presiding **deity** of the temple at **Pandharpur** in **Maharashtra**, who was also Namdev's chosen deity. Thus, the poems seem consistent with Maharashtrian origins. Trilochan is also mentioned as a devotee (**bhakta**) by other **bhakti** poets, most notably by the poet-saint **Ravidas**.

Trimbak

Sacred site (**tirtha**) at the headwaters of the **Godavari River**, in the **Nasik** district of the state of **Maharashtra**. Trimbak is famous as the site for **Tryambakeshvar**, one of the twelve **jyotirlingas**, the most sacred spot for devotees (**bhakta**) of the god **Shiva**.

Trimurti

("three forms") The three **deities** of **Brahma**, **Vishnu**, and **Shiva**, often represented as three faces on a single image, to symbolize the ultimate identity of all three forms of divinity and divine activity: Brahma as creator, Vishnu as preserver and sustainer, and Shiva as destroyer.

Triphala

Another name for the **Urdhvapundra**, the characteristic forehead mark of renunciant **ascetics** who are devotees (**bhakta**) of the god **Vishnu**. Although there is considerable variation, the basic form is three vertical lines, in contrast to the three horizontal lines worn by **Shaivite** ascetics. See **Urdhvapundra**.

Tripundra

Sectarian mark of three horizontal lines, most commonly applied to the forehead but which can also be applied to the back, heart, shoulders, arms, and legs. The tripundra marks the person wearing it as a devotee (**bhakta**) of the god **Shiva**, and although this mark is most commonly worn by renunciant **ascetics**, householders also wear it. According to one interpretation, the three lines represent the three prongs of Shiva's trident; according to another, they symbolize Shiva's third eye. The three lines are drawn by dipping the first three fingers of the right hand into a sacred ash known as **vibhuti** ("power") and then drawing them across the forehead. In earlier times vibhuti was made from wood ash that had been sifted through cloth until it was as fine as talcum powder. This is still done today, primarily by ascetics who usually use the ash from a **dhuni**, or smoldering ascetic **fire**, which has sacred characteristics; vibhuti can also be bought in stores selling religious supplies.

Tripura

("three cities") In Hindu mythology, the triple city built by the three sons of the **demon Taraka**: Kamalaksha, Tarakaksha, and Vidyunmali. **Shiva** eventually destroyed the demons' three cities, and as a result one of Shiva's epithets is **Tripurari**, the "Enemy of the Three City."

Tripurari

Epithet of **Shiva** as the enemy (ari) of the Triple City (**Tripura**). According to the mythic charter, three **demons** are

An ascetic wearing tripundra markings, three horizontal lines that indicate he is a devotee of the god Shiva.

dismayed by their continuing defeats at the hands of the gods, and they begin to perform harsh **asceticism** (**tapas**) to find the means to counter this. The god **Brahma** finally comes to them, willing to reward them with boons. However, when the demons learn that absolute invulnerability is impossible, they lay down the condition that each of them should build a city that can move over the earth, which will come together only once in a long time, and that these cities can be destroyed only by a single arrow that pierces through them all at the same time.

This boon renders the demons practically invulnerable, and they proceed to build three magnificent cities—one of iron, one of silver, and one of gold. They grow rich and prosperous, but over time they are corrupted by power and began to oppress the earth. Finally the gods petition Brahma for help, and Brahma informs them that the only one with the strength to fulfill this condition is the god Shiva. The gods build him a bow and arrow, and when the conjunction of the three cities takes place, Shiva sends a single arrow through all three, kindling a fire that burns the cities and destroys their inhabitants.

This story illustrates one important facet of Shiva's character—unlike the god **Vishnu**, who often manages to trick those he subdues, Shiva is much less complex and attains his end by using power against which no one can stand. In some of the stories, one of the three demons is himself a devotee (**bhakta**) of Shiva, and when the arrow is loosed and hurtles to destroy the Triple City, Shiva himself rescues his devotee and his family. This is in character, for Shiva is portrayed as gracious to his devotees and will do just about anything for them. It also shows that the demons are conceived not as completely debased but as another race of beings with different powers and capacities, and who have as much potential as **deities** and human beings.

Trishanku

("three sins") In Hindu mythology, a celebrated king of the **Solar Line**. He is named Satyavrata at **birth** but is cursed by the sage **Vasishtha** to bear the name Trishanku because of three major sins: He abducts another man's wife, he incurs the anger of his father, and he eats beef (which he has earlier obtained by slaughtering Vasishtha's **cow**). Along with this uncomplimentary name, Vasishtha also curses Trishanku to be a chandala (**untouchable**), which Trishanku suffers for some time before being restored to his kingship.

After regaining his throne, Trishanku is a good king, but he desires to be taken bodily into **heaven**. Vasishtha and his sons ridicule this desire, but Trishanku finds an ally in the sage **Vishvamitra**, who has a long history of conflict with Vasishtha. Vishvamitra performs the **sacrifice** to take Trishanku to heaven, but when he arrives there, he is pushed back down by **Indra**, the ruler of heaven, and Trishanku falls head downward. Vishvamitra orders Trishanku to remain where he is, and since Indra will not let

him up and Vishvamitra will not let him down, he is suspended in midair. Indra begins to construct a separate heaven for Trishanku, but when Vishvamitra threatens to create a new Indra for the new heaven, Indra relents and takes Trishanku to heaven in his material body. The name *Trishanku* has since become proverbial to refer to a person trapped between two options.

Trishiras

In the *Ramayana*, the earlier of the two great Hindu epics, Trishiras is a **demon** ally of **Ravana**, the demon-king of **Lanka**. Along with Ravana's brothers, **Khara** and **Dushana**, Trishiras leads a frontal attack against the god **Rama**, the epic's protagonist. The attack is an effort to avenge the insult to Ravana's sister **Shurpanakha**, who has been mutilated by Rama's brother **Lakshmana**. Although he is a valiant warrior, Trishiras is eventually killed by Rama, as are Khara and Dushana. The failure of such frontal attacks convince Ravana that Rama is too powerful to kill in combat, so he decides to take revenge by kidnapping Rama's wife **Sita**.

Trishul

("three points") The trident, which is an important weapon associated with both the god **Shiva** and the **Goddess**. The trident is a modified form of the spear (**shula**).

Tristhalisetu

("The bridge to the Three Holy Cities") Pilgrimage text written by the great scholar **Narayana Bhatta** (approx. 1513–1570) that was intended to give the readers precise instructions for correctly performing the pilgrimage rites at three important sites: **Allahabad**, a bathing (**snana**) place at the junction of the **Ganges** and **Yamuna Rivers**; **Benares**, which is renowned as a city of culture and religious learning; and **Gaya** in **Bihar**, a major site for the **shraddha** rites for the dead. The text begins with a section devoted to pilgrimage in general, giving the rules for its performance, and continues with three sections giving the prescriptions for pilgrimages to Allahabad, Benares, and Gaya. The Tristhalisetu is an important example of the class of commentarial literature known as **nibandhas** ("collections"). The nibandhas were compendia of Hindu lore, in which the compilers culled references on a particular theme from the **Vedas**, **dharma literature**, **puranas**, and other authoritative religious texts, and then compiled these excerpts into a single volume, often with their own commentary. Narayana Bhatta was one of the most learned men of his time, and he was attempting to define everything precisely, based on his sources, so that people would know how to do the right thing. The initial section of this text has been edited and translated by Richard Salomon as *The Bridge to the Three Holy Cities*, 1985.

Triveni

("Triple stream") Traditional epithet for the confluence of the **Ganges** and **Yamuna Rivers** in the city of **Allahabad**, in the state of **Uttar Pradesh**. Although only two rivers can be seen at the confluence, the name Triveni comes from the traditional belief that they are joined by a third river, the **Saraswati**, which flows underground and is unseen to the naked eye.

Trivikrama

("[taking] Three Steps") Epithet of the god **Vishnu** in his **avatar**, or incarnation, as a dwarf (**Vamana**). The name exists because diminutive Vamana begs three paces of land from the **demon**-king **Bali** and then grows to such a large size that these three paces measure out the universe. See **Vamana avatar**.

Triyuginarayan

Village and sacred site (**tirtha**) in the **Mandakini River** valley in the **Garhwal** region of the **Himalayas**, fifteen miles down from **Kedarnath**. The site for Triyuginarayan is on the top of a mountain, surrounded by forest. Triyuginarayan's major temple is dedicated to the god **Vishnu** in his form as **Narayana**, and in front of the temple is a pit in which a **fire** is said to have been smoldering for the past three cosmic ages (triyugi). According to its charter myth, Triyuginarayan is the site at which the **deities Shiva** and **Parvati** were married, a ceremony to which this continuously smoldering fire (in its guise as **Agni**, the fire-god) stands as the witness.

Trnavarta

In Hindu mythology, Trnavarta is one of the **demon** assassins sent by **Kamsa**, the **demon**-king of **Mathura**, in an attempt to kill his nephew, the child-god **Krishna**. Trnavarta is a whirlwind that sweeps Krishna up into the air, but Krishna holds tight to Trnavarta until he simply blows himself out.

Truth, Power of

In popular Hindu belief, truth is seen as having magical power of its own, a power to which people can appeal in their time of distress. One way of appealing to this power is through the famous **act of truth**, a conditional statement in which the first part is a true statement about one's past behavior and the second part a request for some specific result (for example, "If I have always given to those who begged from me, may this fire not burn me"). The power of truth was also invoked in trial by **ordeal** and was seen as the power that made the ordeal a valid means of testing people.

Tryambakeshvar

Temple and sacred site (**tirtha**) in the village of **Trimbak** in the **Nasik** district of the state of **Maharashtra**, at the headwaters of the **Godavari River**. The temple is named for its presiding **deity**, the god **Shiva** in his manifestation as the "Three-Eyed Lord." Shiva is present at

Tryambakeshvar in the form of a **linga**, the pillar-shaped image that is his symbolic form. The Tryambakeshvar linga is one of the twelve **jyotirlingas**, a network of sites deemed especially sacred to Shiva and at which Shiva is uniquely present. The charter myth for Tryambakeshvar begins with the sage **Gautama**, who unwisely hits an old **cow** with a stick, killing it, and thus incurs the sin of cow slaughter. Gautama is told that to expiate his sin, he first has to amass enough merit to bring the **Ganges** down to **earth**, and after he has purified himself by bathing (**snana**) in the Ganges, he has to make and **worship** 10 million Shiva lingas formed from the sand on its banks. Gautama undertakes his penance (**prayashchitta**) diligently. Upon worshiping the 10 millionth linga he is rewarded by a vision of Shiva, who grants his wish that both the Ganges and Shiva will remain there forever—the former in her form as the Godavari, the latter as Tryambakeshvar.

Tuesday

(Mangalvar) The third day of the **week**, presided over by the **planet Mars** (Mangal). The planet Mars is deemed inauspicious, both because of its red color (reminiscent of **blood**) and because of its associations with war and disorder. Tuesday is widely considered an unlucky day, and many people abstain from certain kinds of activity on it. Travel is particularly discouraged unless absolutely necessary. Cutting the **hair** and beard is also discouraged, and in much of northern India, barbers take Tuesday off. To counter the day's potential **inauspiciousness**, many people also perform **rites of protection**, such as worshiping strong protective **deities** such as **Hanuman**—who is close enough to human beings to understand the problems they face, but divine enough to be able to protect them. Paradoxically, the literal meaning of the name for Tuesday is the "auspicious" (mangal) day. Giving it this euphemistic name may simply be a bit of reverse

magic; that if one calls it the lucky day, it may, in fact, turn out to be.

Tukaram

(1598–1650) Poet and saint in the **Varkari Panth**, a religious community centered on the **worship** of the god **Vithoba**, at his temple at **Pandharpur** in the modern state of **Maharashtra**. According to tradition, Tukaram was a **shudra** (in traditional Hinduism, there are four main social groups, the **shudras** being the lowest and least influential) born in the small village of **Dehu**, where his father was a petty merchant. Tukaram continued in the family business, which eventually failed because he had little interest in worldly life. He longed instead for the life of a renunciant, in which he could completely devote himself to God. As with many of the other **bhakti** saints, he is reported to have suffered considerable persecution by traditionally minded **brahmins**, who were uneasy about a person of his low status gaining spiritual greatness. An unlettered man, he is most famous for the songs known as **abhangs**, which are still widely sung in Maharashtra. He had many disciples, including the poet-saint **Bahina Bai**, and according to tradition, he ended his life by being taken up to **heaven** in a chariot of fire. For further information see G. A. Deleury, *The Cult of Vithoba,* 1960; and Justin E. Abbott (trans.), *The Life of Tukaram,* 1980.

Tulsi

A small shrublike plant commonly denoted the "holy basil." For devotees (**bhakta**) of the god **Vishnu**, the tulsi plant is a form of Vishnu's wife **Lakshmi**, who is cursed to take birth as a plant. According to the story, Lakshmi sits with **Vishnu's** wives, the goddesses **Ganga** and **Saraswati**. Ganga makes amorous eyes at Vishnu, and when Saraswati protests this indecency, a quarrel breaks out. By the time it is over, Ganga and Saraswati have cursed each other to be born on earth as rivers. Vishnu has been cursed to be born as a stone (the **shalagram**); and Lakshmi, who tries only to mediate the quarrel, is cursed to be born as a plant. This plant is thus a form of Lakshmi, and pious **Vaishnavas** cultivate a tulsi plant as an act of devotion. The plant is especially dear to Vishnu, and it is believed that all parts of the plant are purifying. Any parts of it used in **worship** are especially meritorious—whether grinding the leaves to a paste to mark one's body, taking the leaves as **prasad** (food offered to a **deity** as an act of worship), or using tulsi wood for implements or sacrificial fuel.

Tulsidas

(1532–1623) Poet-saint and devotee (**bhakta**) of the god **Rama**, whose greatest work, the *Ramcharitmanas*, retells the epic *Ramayana* in the vernacular language of his day. According to evidence in his poetry, Tulsidas was born into a desperately poor **brahmin** family, but his life was transformed by the power of Rama's name. This can be taken as a reference to his teacher, who is believed to have been a **Ramanandi**, but it can also be taken literally. Tulsidas continually stresses that the name of Rama embodies the divinity's power and thus makes that power accessible to devotees. According to tradition, he lived a fairly hard life despite his fame, and because of his emphasis on devotion, he reportedly faced problems from other brahmins, who were concerned about maintaining their social status.

As with all of the *Ramayana*'s vernacular retellings, Tulsidas did not merely translate the story of Rama but interpreted it according to his own religious convictions. The two most important shifts are his overwhelming emphasis on the importance of devotion (**bhakti**) and the saving power of the name of Rama, to which Tulsidas gives greater importance than Rama himself. Tulsidas also brings in mythic material from a variety of other sources, most notably the *Shiva Purana* and the *Adhyatmaramayana*. This material is largely added to the first and last chapters, where Tulsidas makes his greatest changes from the original epic. One theory to explain why Tulsidas brought in this other material is that he was trying to transcend narrow sectarian boundaries, and a sign of this is that much of the text is narrated by the god **Shiva**, in the form of a dialogue to his wife **Parvati**. For part of the final book, Shiva is supplanted as narrator by the crow **Bhushundi**, who symbolizes the power of devotion to rescue even a common carrion-eating crow. Aside from the *Ramcharitmanas*, Tulsidas composed many other works in varying regional languages and dedicated to various **deities**; the most important are the *Kavitavali*, the *Vinaya Patrika*, the *Ramavali*, and the *Shrikrishnavali*. Tulsidas himself refers to writing down his poems, and although the manuscript tradition is uncertain for some of his texts, the transition from song to written text took place much faster than for most of his contemporary poet-saints, many of whom were illiterate. For further information see F. Raymond Allchin (trans.), *Kavitavali*, 1964; W. Douglas P. Hill (trans.), *The Holy Lake of the Acts of Rama*, 1971; and John Stratton Hawley and Mark Juergensmeyer (trans.), *Songs of the Saints of India*, 1988.

Tulsidas Jayanti

Festival falling on the seventh day of the bright (waxing) half of the **lunar month** of **Shravan** (July–August), celebrating the birthday of the medieval devotional (**bhakti**) poet-saint **Tulsidas** (1532–1623). Tulsidas composed many different texts, and he is one of the few medieval poet-saints believed to have been literate and to have actually written down his work. His most celebrated text is the *Ramcharitmanas*, a vernacular retelling of the epic *Ramayana*.

Tulsi Vivah

Festival marking the marriage of the **goddess Lakshmi** and the god **Vishnu**,

Tulsi plant used in Tulsi Vivah festival.

celebrated on the eleventh day of the bright (waxing) half of the **lunar month** of **Kartik**. It is also celebrated as **Devotthayan Ekadashi**. On this day devotees (**bhakta**) place a **shalagram** (a black stone containing the spiral-shaped fossil shell of a prehistoric sea creature, understood as a "self-manifest" form of Vishnu) in a pot containing a **tulsi** plant (considered a form of Lakshmi). Thus they symbolically unite Vishnu and Lakshmi and perform the **marriage ceremony** for them, complete with festive songs.

Tumari

Vessel used by renunciant **ascetics**. In earlier times it would have been made of a gourd, although today the shape is often replicated in brass or some other metal. The tumari is taller than it is wide, with an open top over which the carrying handle arches. Unlike another piece of ascetic equipment, the **kamandalu**, which has both a spout and a covered top, the tumari is an open vessel. When made of a gourd, it would simply have entailed cutting parts off of the top for the opening, with the remaining top parts forming the vessel's handle. Because of its simplicity and use of readily available materials, the tumari was a symbol of ascetic life.

Tungabhadra River

Important tributary of the **Krishna River**, which has its source in the Western Ghats in southern **Karnataka** and then flows north and east toward the Krishna. The most important place on its banks is **Hampi**, the ruined city that was the capital of the Vijayanagar empire. See also **Vijayanagar dynasty**.

Tungnath

Temple and sacred site (**tirtha**) in the **Garhwal** region of the **Himalayas** in the valley between the **Mandakini** and the **Alakananda Rivers**, fourteen miles by footpath north of the village of **Ukhimath**. The temple's presiding **deity** is the god **Shiva** in his manifestation as the "Lofty Lord." Tungnath is one of the **Panchkedar**, a network of five sacred sites spread throughout the Garhwal region; the other four are **Kedarnath**, **Kalpeshvar**, **Rudranath**, and **Madmaheshvar**. This network of five sites is seen as a symbolic representation of Shiva's body, understandably so, since Shiva is believed to dwell in the Himalayas. Of these five, Tungnath is believed to be Shiva's arm.

Turiya

("fourth") The name for the innermost quarter of the Self (**atman**), as described in the **Mandukya Upanishad**, one of the speculative religious texts that form the latest stratum of the **Vedas**, the oldest Hindu sacred texts. As with most of the Upanishads, the Mandukya Upanishad's underlying concern is to investigate ultimate questions, in particular the nature of the Self. The upanishad describes the Self as having four quarters, each of which removes another layer of egoism. The first quarter is waking consciousness, which is characterized by perceptions of subject and object; the second is **dream** sleep, which is sheer subjectivity; the third is deep sleep, which has neither subject nor object; and the last is a mysterious state simply called "the fourth" (turiya), which is the Self. This state is identified as the ultimate truth, and knowledge of this brings final liberation of the soul (**moksha**).

Tvashtr

("maker of carriages") In the **Vedas**, the oldest and most authoritative Hindu religious texts, Tvashtr is a minor **deity** known as the workman of the Vedic gods. The Vedic hymns frequently mention wheeled chariots as military devices, and his name's literal meaning shows the esteem in which this craft was held, as the apex of creative work. In the Vedas, Tvashtr is famous for crafting the weapons of the gods, especially the mace with which the storm-god **Indra** slays the serpent **Vrtra** (**Rg Veda** 1.32). In later times Tvashtr is identified with the minor deity **Vishvakarma**, who in later Hindu life becomes the architect and craftsman of the gods. Since Tvashtr has a much older textual presence than Vishvakarma, this seems to be an attempt to identify one divine workman as another, based on their similar functions.

Twice-Born

(dvija) In its most specific sense, this word denotes a man from the highest traditional social groups (**varnas**)—**brahmin**, **kshatriya**, and **vaishya**—who has undergone the adolescent ritual **initiation** known as the **upanayana samskara**. This initiation gives the entitlement and the obligation to study the **Vedas**, the oldest Hindu religious texts, and definitively divides society between those who have this entitlement and those who do not—namely, all children, **women**, and men not belonging to these three groups. Because of this initiation's ritual significance,

Sadhu carrying a tumari.

it was known as the second birth, and thus the initiates were "twice-born." The first birth was biological and based on nature, whereas the second was cultural and marked higher religious status. Although in its strictest sense this word refers only to such initiates, in a more general sense it can denote any person belonging to a varna whose members are eligible for this initiation—that is, any brahmin, kshatriya, or vaishya.

Twilight Language

One of the translations for the term *Sandhabhasha*. Sandhabhasha is a symbolic language used in **tantra**, a secret, ritually based religious practice, in which the elements of tantric **worship** are described in a coded language often drawn from the private parts and functions of the human body. This is done to hide the tradition's particulars from the uninitiated. See **Sandhabhasha**.

Tyag

("renunciation") Practice of renunciation stressed most by **ascetics**, but even among this group, some stress it more than others. Some ascetics carry this to extreme lengths. One famous ascetic, Swami **Karpatri**, was famous for receiving the food he was given as alms into his cupped hands, signifying the renunciation of an eating-vessel. The most extreme examples are ascetics who have given up all clothing as a symbol of renunciation of conventional standards, including shame. The ultimate purpose in such renunciation varies with the individual, but one of the common themes is to serve as a model of how little one really needs to live a happy and fulfilling life and thus to illustrate the fundamental values that people often forget in the bustle of everyday life. Many ordinary people also share this value in seeking to simplify their lives through giving up attachments and entanglements.

U

Udana

In traditional Indian physiology, one of the five bodily "**winds**" considered to be responsible for basic bodily functions, the others being **prana**, **apana**, **vyana**, and **samana**. The udana wind is considered to reside in the throat and to be the force that conveys things out of the mouth—primarily speech and song, but also burps and (presumably) vomit.

Udasi

Ascetic community founded by **Shrichandra** (traditional dates 1492–1612), the elder son of Guru Nanak, the first of the ten Sikh gurus. According to one tradition, Nanak passed over Shrichandra as his successor because Shrichandra had become an ascetic. Guru Nanak disapproved of this, believing that his followers should live married lives in society. The Udasis have always been an ascetic sect, and since their formation they have been seen as distinct from the two other major ascetic communities, the **Sanyasis** and the **Bairagis**. The latter are separated on sectarian grounds: The Sanyasis **worship** the god **Shiva**, and the Bairagis the god **Vishnu**, whereas the Udasis worship the Panchayatana grouping of five Hindu **deities** (Shiva, Vishnu, **Ganesh**, **Surya**, and **Durga**) rather than one or another alone. During the bathing (**snana**) processions at the **Kumbha Mela**, the Udasis march third, behind the Sanyasis and the Bairagis. Through the legacy of their founder, they have retained some informal connections with the Sikh community, but by and large they have always been considered to belong in the Hindu fold. There was considerable friction between the Udasis and the Sikh community in the early twentieth century because the Sikhs were more self-consciously asserting their separate identity. See also **Panchayatana Puja**.

Udayagiri

Village just north of the city of Bhopal in the state of **Madhya Pradesh**. Udayagiri is famous for its rock-cut cave sculptures from the Gupta era (350–550 C.E), particularly a twenty-foot **sculpture** of the god **Vishnu** in his form as the **Boar avatar**, with the **earth** balanced on his tusk. See also **Gupta dynasty**.

Uddalaka Aruni

A character in the **Chandogya Upanishad**, one of the speculative texts that form the latest stratum of the **Vedas**. In the upanishad, Uddalaka is the father and teacher of the boy **Shvetaketu** Aruneya, and the two are a model for the transmission of secret teachings passed between **guru** and disciple. According to a story in the upanishad's sixth chapter, Shvetaketu is sent away by his father to study the Vedas, and when he returns twelve years later, having mastered all the Vedas, he incorrectly considers himself learned. His father punctures his arrogance by asking Shvetaketu questions about the nature of the cosmos and thus shows him the difference between memorization and true knowledge. When Shvetaketu cannot answer these, he admits his ignorance and accepts instruction from his father on the nature of the Self (**atman**). This instruction contains the teaching "That thou art" (**Tat tvam asi**). This is one of the "great statements" (**mahavakya**) in Indian **philosophy** and asserts the ultimate identity between **Brahman** and atman, the cosmos and the individual Self.

Uddhava

In Hindu mythology, one of the god **Krishna's** friends and companions. In

The Mahakaleshvar Temple in Ujjain.
It is dedicated to the god Shiva
in the form of the "Lord of Death."

the devotional (**bhakti**) literature, Uddhava is most famous for the message he carries from Krishna back to the **gopis**, the cowherd **women** of **Braj** (a northern Indian region on the **Yamuna River** south of the modern city of Delhi) who are Krishna's devotees (**bhakta**) and who love him more than life. Uddhava tells the gopis not to be concerned with Krishna's physical absence, since as the supreme divinity, Krishna is always with them, even though he may not be visible. The gopis reply that such talk is fine for intellectual folk such as Uddhava, but that for simple women like themselves, who have had the delight of associating with Krishna in the flesh, such abstractions are absolutely useless. Uddhava and the gopis are symbols for two different types of religious life: one cool and abstract, focused on an impersonal divinity, and the other based on passionate love for a particular **deity**. Differing accounts of this story give different endings, according to the writers' inclinations. In some of the stories, including the earliest version in the ***Bhagavata Purana***, the story ends in a

standoff, with each side unable to convince the other. Yet in at least one of the accounts, Uddhava is converted to the gopis' point of view. For further information see R. S. McGregor (ed. and trans.), *Nanddas*, 1973.

Udgatr

Type of sacrificial priest in the **Brahmana** literature, one of the later strands in the sacred literature known as the **Vedas**. The Brahmanas largely functioned as manuals describing how to perform sacrificial rites—which primarily involved burning **offerings** in a sacred **fire**—and the care and attention devoted to detailing these **sacrifices** leads to the inference that these were the primary religious act. These rites were so complex that they required specialized ritual technicians: the **adhvaryum**, the **hotr**, the udgatr, and the **brahman**. Of these, the udgatr was the sacrificial priest who chanted the hymns from the **Sama Veda** that were used in the sacrifice.

Udupi

Town and sacred site (**tirtha**) on the Arabian Sea in the state of **Karnataka**, about thirty miles north of Mangalore. Udupi's most famous temple is to the god **Krishna**, but it is best known as the home of the philosopher **Madhva**, founder of the **Dvaita Vedanta**.

Ugrasena

In Hindu mythology, the king of **Mathura** who is the grandfather of the god **Krishna**. Ugrasena is supplanted by the evil **Kamsa**, who is believed to be Ugrasena's son but is actually not. According to legend, Kamsa is the son of a **demon** who has taken Ugrasena's form, and who under this guise has intercourse with Ugrasena's wife.

Ujjain

City and sacred site (**tirtha**) on the **Shipra River** in the state of **Madhya**

Pradesh, about 100 miles west of Bhopal, the state capital. Ujjain is the traditional center of the **Malwa** plateau and has a long history as a commercial, political, cultural, and sacred center. In earlier times Ujjain was a major stop on the central trade route, through which goods from southern India were funneled to other places farther north. Just before the common era, Ujjain is said to have been the capital of King **Vikramaditya**, after whom the **Vikram era** was named. Vikramaditya's stepbrother, **Bhartrhari**, reportedly renounced the throne to become an **ascetic** but is best known for his poetry. In later days Ujjain was the *de facto* capital of the Gupta ruler **Chandra Gupta II** (r. 380–414 C.E.), under whose patronage the greatest **Sanskrit** poet, **Kalidasa**, is said to have worked.

As a sacred center, Ujjain has multiple attractions, and this is its major source of contemporary importance. It is one of the **Seven Sacred Cities** of India. Dying in one of these cities is said to bring liberation. Every twelve years Ujjain plays host to the bathing (**snana**) festival known as the **Kumbha Mela**, although the **mela** there is smaller than the ones at **Haridwar** and **Allahabad**. Given its history, Ujjain is studded with important religious sites. The most important site is the temple to **Shiva** in his form as **Mahakaleshvar**, the "Lord of Death." Shiva is present at Mahakaleshvar in the form of a **linga**, the pillar-shaped image that is his symbolic form. The Mahakaleshvar linga is one of the twelve **jyotirlingas**, a network of sites deemed especially sacred to Shiva and at which Shiva is uniquely present. Ujjain is also famous for a temple associated with **Matsyendranath**, the religious preceptor (**guru**) of **Gorakhnath**, the founder of the **Nathpanthi** ascetics. In addition, Ujjain has a temple to the nine **planets**, as well as one of the **baithaks**, a group of 108 sacred sites associated with the life and activity of the philosopher **Vallabhacharya**. Ujjain's most unusual site is the temple to the **deity** Kal

Bhairav. Kal Bhairav is another name for **Bhairava**, a horrific form of Shiva, and the traditional **offering** at the temple is **liquor**—a substance proscribed and condemned by "respectable" Hindus and thus the ideal offering for a marginal deity such as Bhairava. See also **Gupta dynasty**.

Ukhimath

Himalayan town on the **Mandakini River** in the hills of **Uttar Pradesh**, across the river from **Guptakashi**. Ukhimath is the winter seat of **Kedarnath**, a form of **Shiva** whose summer home is a temple in the village of Kedarnath, high in the mountains at the Mandakini's headwaters. The village is at such high altitude that it is only accessible between late April and October, after the snows have melted; in October the temple is ritually closed until the next spring. When the temple at Kedarnath has been closed for the winter, the **deity** (symbolically represented by a movable image) takes residence in Ukhimath for the winter and then moves back to Kedarnath the following spring.

Ulatbamsi

("upside-down language") Word denoting paradoxical language in which the speaker's utterances are reversals of "normal" events, such as "The cow is sucking the calf's teat," "Mouse stalks cat," "Rain falls from **earth** to sky." The most famous composer of such utterances was the devotional (**bhakti**) poet-saint **Kabir**, who inherited a tradition of coded language (**sandhabhasha**) from the **Nathpanthi** and **Sahajiya** religious communities. Ulatbamsi utterances are not intended to be simply nonsensical, nor is it simply a coded language in which one term stands for another; they are rather intended to stimulate the hearer to active listening, interpretation, and searching for a truth that lies beyond right side up and upside down. For a long discussion of ulatbamsi, see Appendix A in Linda Hess and Shukdev Singh (trans.), *The Bijak of Kabir*, 1983.

Uma

Epithet of the **goddess Parvati**, wife of the god **Shiva**. The name supposedly comes from the exclamation uttered by Parvati's mother, **Mena**, when Parvati announces that she intends to perform **asceticism** to win Shiva as a husband. According to the story, Mena covers her ears with her hands and replies "U Ma!" (Oh, don't!) As with all forms of Parvati (and all married goddesses), Uma is a beneficent and benevolent presence, maternal and life affirming, although at times she can be capricious and spiteful if insulted. For more information on Uma and all the goddesses of Hinduism, see David R. Kinsley, *Hindu Goddesses*, 1986.

Untouchable

Name denoting certain **jatis** who were considered so impure that their very presence was polluting to **caste** Hindus, that is, Hindus belonging to the four **varnas** (major social divisions). Jatis are **endogamous** social subgroups—groups in which members are forbidden to marry outside of their particular group—that were often defined by the group's hereditary occupation. Untouchability usually stemmed from occupations considered impure or debased, such as working with **leather**, in the case of the **Chamars**, or the groups whose hereditary occupation was to remove night soil, often by carrying it in baskets balanced on their heads. In traditional society, untouchables were subject to numerous restrictions and prohibitions on where they could live, work, draw water, and even move about. In many cases they had to announce their presence to allow caste Hindus to remove themselves from the area. Although untouchability has been illegal since independence, social attitudes supporting it persist, and in a country in which one's name often conveys one's jati, such discrimination is difficult to escape. In many places these people are still underprivileged and desperately poor, as a legacy of the past. In recent years they have become more militant—among other things, adopting the name **dalit** ("oppressed") to describe themselves—and have begun to exercise their power at the ballot box, trying to take advantage of their considerable numbers.

Upachara

("honoring," "entertaining") In its literal meaning, this word denotes the act of showing politeness, courtesy, or honor to any superior. In the context of **worship**, the meaning has been extended to refer to the things that are normally offered to the **deity** as part of the standard hospitality that would be offered to any honored guest. Although there are differing enumerations of these **offerings**, one of the most common lists has sixteen of them: summoning (**avahana**), offering a seat (**asana**), water for washing the feet (**padya**), thirst-quenching beverages (**arghya**), water for rinsing the mouth (**achamaniya**), bathing (**snana**), clothing (**vastra**), affixing the **sacred thread** (yajnopavit), fragrant unguents (**anulepana**), flowers (**pushpa**), incense (**dhupa**), lamp (**dipa**), food (**naivedya**), reverential salutation (**namaskara**), circumambulation (**pradakshina**), and dismissal (**visarjana**). To give all sixteen offerings is a long and detailed ritual, and the most common of the offerings is the eleventh, the offering of light, which is also known as **arati**.

Upadana

In Indian **philosophy**, the word *upadana* denotes the "material cause" for something, that is, the stuff from which it is formed. Although this notion seems obvious to modern materialist ears, it carries several important assumptions that not all Indian philosophical schools were willing to concede—namely, that there were real objects in the world, that they were made from other things, and that these things underwent real transformations. The notion of a material cause was held by the "realist" schools, most notably the **Samkhya, Nyaya-Vaisheshika**, and **Vishishthadvaita Vedanta**. It was opposed by the Buddhist schools, whose assumption that reality was constantly changing made the notion of real things problematic. It was also opposed by the **Advaita Vedanta** school, whose starting assumption was that ultimately there was only one "real" thing—the formless **Brahman** (Supreme Reality)—and thus that the notion of anything becoming anything else was in error.

Upadhi

("obstruction") In Indian logic, a counterexample that renders an inference (**anumana**) invalid by showing that the reason (**hetu**) given as evidence for the initial assertion (**sadhya**) is not invariably true. For example, the inference that "there is smoke because there is fire" was judged invalid because of the counterexample of the red-hot iron ball, which was considered fiery but not smoky. Since the red-hot iron ball was a class of fiery things that did not smoke, it showed that the reason given for the inference did not account for every case of the thing to be proved (sadhya)—and thus raised the possibility that there were other such cases as well. This invalid inference fails the requirement known as pervasion (**vyapti**), in which the reason must account for every possible case; this is critical for validity in an inference. Needless to say, the search for such counterexamples was an essential part of Indian logic, since one such example could discredit an opponent's argument. For further information and elaboration, see Karl H. Potter (ed.), *Presuppositions of India's Philosophies*, 1972.

Upamana

("analogy") According to some philosophical schools, upamana was one of the **pramanas**, or the means by which human beings can gain true and accurate knowledge. The classic example of this pramana describes a traveler going to a certain region who is told that he will encounter a certain animal that looks somewhat like a cow; upon going there this analogy helps him identify the animal. Some philosophical schools deny that this is a separate pramana and classify it as a variety of inference (**anumana**). Those who accept it as a fourth pramana—primarily the **Nyaya-Vaisheshika** school—stress that according to the rules of inference, a valid inference must be grounded in previous perceptions. In the case of the traveler, his ability to identify is not based on any differences drawn from previous perceptions of that type of animal, since he has never before seen the type of animal he actually encounters. He knows what it is because it looks "somewhat like a cow." Thus an additional pramana was needed to account for this. See also **philosophy**.

Upanayana
("bringing-near") Samskara

Traditionally, the eleventh of the life cycle ceremonies (**samskaras**), in which a young man received a religious **initiation** that functioned as a symbolic "second birth," conferring on him new capacities and responsibilities. This ceremony marks the symbolic end of childhood and, as with many such rites of passage, the creation of a new social identity. After this rite the initiate becomes a **brahmacharin**, the first of the **stages of life** (ashramas) for a "**twice-born**" man. This initiation gives the entitlement and the obligation to study the **Vedas**, the oldest and most authoritative Hindu religious texts, and according to the traditional model, the young man would have done this while living in the household of his **guru**. With

721

this entitlement came responsibilities, particularly to observe **purity** laws, to which younger children were not subject. If nothing else, this rite is an essential prerequisite to marriage, since without it the young man is still considered a child, and in some contemporary cases it is performed immediately before the wedding.

According to the **dharma literature**, this rite was restricted to young men from the three highest traditional social classes (**varnas**), namely, **brahmins**, **kshatriyas**, and **vaishyas**. Indeed, it is the entitlement for this rite that makes these three the "twice-born" groups. For each group, a different age was prescribed for initiation and a different duration fixed for study, with brahmins being both earliest to start and the longest to study. The heart of the upanayana samskara is investing the young man with the **sacred thread** (janeu), which he must wear from that day forth, and teaching him the sacred formula known as the **Gayatri mantra**. This rite is still important and still widely performed, although it tends to be stressed most by brahmins. This is not surprising, given their traditional position as teachers and scholars and their concern for conserving that status, even in modern times. For further information see Pandurang Vaman Kane (trans.), *A History of Dharmasastra*, 1968; and Raj Bali Pandey, *Hindu Samskaras*, 1969. The former is encyclopedic and the latter more accessible; despite their age, they remain the best sources for traditional Hindu rites.

Upanishad

The latest textual stratum in the **Vedas**, the oldest and most authoritative Hindu religious texts. The literal meaning of the word *upanishad* is "to sit near [a teacher]," but a better sense of its true meaning would be "secret teaching." The Upanishads mark a clean break from the immediately preceding Vedic literature, the **Brahmanas**, in which the essential concern was to lay out the

concrete procedures for performing highly complex **sacrificial** rites. In contrast, the Upanishads were concerned with more speculative and abstract questions: the essential nature of the cosmos, the essence of the human being, and the relationship between these two. The conclusion in the Upanishads is that the essence of the universe is an impersonal reality known as **Brahman**, and that the essence of the human being is called the "Self" (**atman**). The fundamental insight and essential teaching in the Upanishads is the identity of Brahman and atman, and thus of the macrocosm and the microcosm. This identity is one of the most fundamental Hindu religious ideas and underlies religious thought up to the present time.

The twelve or thirteen oldest upanishads are not a cohesive set but a series of independent documents, although the later ones were clearly influenced by the earlier ones. The two oldest are the **Brhadaranyaka Upanishad** and the **Chandogya Upanishad**. Each is much longer than all the others combined, they are written in prose as a series of dialogues between famous sages, the **Sanskrit** language in them is clearly more archaic, and their ideas are embryonic and undeveloped. Later upanishads—such as the **Isha**, **Kena**, **Katha**, **Prashna**, and **Mandukya**—are much shorter, are written in verse, and have well-developed ideas. Some of these introduce the notion of theism, but not until the **Shvetashvatara Upanishad** is the Supreme Being identified as a god, in this case **Rudra**. For much of their history, the Upanishads would have been transmitted orally from master to student; this makes it unlikely that these texts were widely known because they would have been secret and carefully guarded teachings.

The Upanishads are important because of the speculative questions they ask and because many of their teachings are fundamental assumptions in Hindu religious life, even today: the notion of an eternal Self that gives a being continuous identity; the idea of reincarnation (**samsara**) commensurate with one's deeds; the concept that some single unifying power lies behind the world's apparent diversity; and the conviction that this can be attained only through individual realization, usually described as a flash of mystic insight. As texts carrying the religious authority of the Vedas, the Upanishads were also extremely important in the development of Hindu philosophical schools, particularly **Advaita Vedanta**, which shares this overriding emphasis on inner realization. For information on the Upanishads themselves, see Robert Ernest Hume (trans.), *Thirteen Principal Upanisads*, 1965. See also **philosophy**.

Upasaka

("servant") A person engaged in **upasana**—that is, having an intent focus on serving and worshiping a **deity**.

Upasana

("service") General term denoting religious practice or spiritual discipline as a whole. Aside from the explicit notion of serving the **deity** (or **guru**), the word also connotes an intent focus on the part of the performer—not so much the particular things one is doing, but the overall attitude of care and attention with which one does them.

Upavasa

General term denoting fasting, which is sometimes performed as a prescribed action for particular religious observances such as festivals and vows (**vrats**), and which is also done as a means of expiating one's sins. Although upavasa can refer to total abstinence from food and drink, it usually entails modification of one's diet. In some cases, as on the festival of **Shivaratri**, such "fasting" entails abstaining from cooked grains, which are considered such an essential element in a meal that in parts of India the word rice is also used to mean

"food." In other cases one will abstain from certain types of food, such as for the **Santoshi Ma Vrat**, in which the person must not eat anything containing sour or bitter flavors.

When fasting is performed as expiation (**prayashchitta**), the prescriptions are usually concerned with the amount of food eaten rather than the particular type. The best-known rite of this kind is the **chandrayana**, a penitential rite lasting for one **lunar month** in which the penitent's food consumption mirrors the monthly course of the **moon**. The performer begins by eating fourteen mouthfuls of food on the first day of the waning moon, then one less mouthful on each successive day, with a complete fast on the **new moon** day. On each successive day during the waxing moon, the penitent eats one more mouthful, finishing at fifteen on the day of the **full moon**.

Upendra

("junior **Indra**") Epithet of the god **Vishnu**. It is first used in some late hymns in the **Vedas**, the earliest Hindu religious texts, in which Vishnu is portrayed as a subordinate and companion of the storm-god Indra, who is the primary Vedic **deity**. The epithet continues to be used later despite Indra's eclipse as a significant deity, and thus its literal meaning is no longer true. See **Vishnu**.

Upside-Down Language

Term designating the type of utterances known as **ulatbamsi**, so called because these utterances intentionally describe things contrary to the way they are in the "normal" world. See **ulatbamsi**.

Urdhvabahu

("[one whose] arm is upraised") Name for a person practicing a particularly severe form of physical mortification, in which one or both arms are kept continually raised. After some time the muscles atrophy, and the arms cannot be lowered again. Although urdhvabahu is

723

An ascetic with the urdhvapundra mark on his forehead.
It consists of three vertical lines and indicates that he is a devotee of the god Vishnu.

not very common, it has a long-attested history as an **ascetic** practice. As with all such harsh physical **asceticism**, this is believed to give one the great benefits of spiritual awareness and magical power. This belief is based partly on the culturally accepted notion that the willingness to endure physical suffering generates such spiritual power, but this belief could also stem from the strength of will needed to carry this out—a strength of will that would presumably have correlates in other dimensions of one's personality.

Urdhvapundra

Name denoting the characteristic forehead mark (**tika**) worn by the **ascetic** devotees (**bhakta**) of the god **Vishnu**. The urdhvapundra's basic pattern is made of three vertical lines, in contrast to the three horizontal lines worn by the **Sanyasis**, who are devotees of **Shiva**. There are many variations in the design, and many different materials can be used: sandalwood paste, white clay, yellow clay, and red vermilion. The only thing that is never used is the sacred ash (**vibhuti**) characteristic of the Sanyasis. The design and materials used for the urdhvapundra are quite distinctive among various **Vaishnava** ascetic communities, and from this, one can easily identify a particular ascetic's affiliation. For further information see A. W. Entwistle, "Vaishnava Tilakas—Sectarian Marks Worn by Worshipers of Visnu," *IAVRI-Bulletin* 11 and 12, 1982.

Urdhvaretas

("[one whose] **semen** is drawn upward") Epithet for someone keeping a vow of **celibacy**, particularly a lifelong vow. In the Hindu tradition, celibacy is important not only for removing one from enjoying the pleasures of the flesh but because on a more basic level, semen is considered the concentrated essence of a man's vital energies. Expending semen is necessary for procreation, but otherwise it should be retained, as a way to conserve one's vital forces. In popular belief, when a man has been celibate for a certain time, the semen is drawn upward to the brain, where it nourishes one's intellectual and spiritual faculties.

Urushringa

Architectural detail in the temple **architecture** of **Khajuraho**, one of the major forms of the northern Indian **Nagara** style. The Nagara style's primary feature is a **shikhara**, or tower. This primary shikhara is often surrounded by smaller, subsidiary towers, to lead the eye up to the highest point, which is directly over the image of the temple's primary **deity**. The urushringas are turrets built on the sides of these towers, whose shape replicates that of the tallest central tower and that serve to draw the eye upward to the highest tower.

Urvashi

In Hindu mythology, a particular celestial nymph (**apsara**) who is most famous for her association with King **Pururavas**. Urvashi comes to stay with Pururavas under several conditions, including that she should never see him naked. When she has been gone from **heaven** for a while, the god **Indra** notices her absence and schemes to get her back. One night he sends several minor **deities** to steal two lambs of which Urvashi is very fond, and when Pururavas leaps up to regain them, a flash of lightning reveals him naked, and Urvashi leaves him. They are separate for some time but are eventually reunited—in some accounts for good, and in others for only one night a year.

Ushas

In the **Vedas**, the oldest and most authoritative Hindu religious texts, Ushas is a **goddess** associated and sometimes identified with the dawn. She is described as lighting the path for the **sun** and driving away the darkness and evil; her presence is thus associated with the regularity of the cosmic order. Ushas is most notable not for what she does—she is a minor **deity**, mentioned in only a handful of the Vedic hymns—but because she is one of the few goddesses in the Vedas. The virtual absence of female divinities in the Vedas is one of the factors behind the notion that the great Goddess, one of the three major deities in later religious life, has her roots in indigenous goddess **worship**. For more information on Ushas and all the goddesses of Hinduism, see David R. Kinsley, *Hindu Goddesses*, 1986.

Utkala

Northern Indian **brahmin** group that makes up one of the five northern brahmin communities (**Pancha Gauda**); the other four are the **Kanaujias**, the **Maithilas**, the **Gaudas**, and the **Saraswats**. Utkala brahmins are found only in the coastal regions of **Orissa**, on the Bay of Bengal, but their ritual control over the pilgrimage sites there, particularly the city of **Puri**, have helped them remain a significant group.

Utkutikasana

Sitting posture (**asana**) in **yoga** practice in which the legs are contracted, with the soles of the feet pressed against each other and the outer part of the feet and legs flat on the ground. This posture is the one in which images of the **deities** are portrayed in Hindu iconography, and it seems to be the position called samasthana in the commentaries to the **Yoga Sutras**. This position is also notable because it appears to be portrayed on one of the seals from the **Indus Valley civilization**; the figure in this position is the mysterious horned deity that some viewers have sought to identify as a "proto-**Shiva**."

Utpanna Ekadashi

Religious observance falling on the eleventh day (**ekadashi**) of the dark (waning) half of the **lunar month** of **Margashirsha** (November–December). As for all of the eleventh-day observances, this is dedicated to the **worship** of **Vishnu**, and on this day especially, in his form as **Krishna**. Most Hindu festivals have certain prescribed rites, which usually involve fasting (**upavasa**) and worship and often promise specific benefits for faithful performance. Those observing this vow should fast completely on the tenth and perform full worship during the **brahma muhurta** of the eleventh. On this ekadashi, only fruits should be offered as food for the **deity**. Faithfully keeping this festival is believed to bring liberation of the soul (**moksha**). The name *Utpanna* means "born," and the charter myth for this celebration is that of **Anasuya**, wife of the sage **Atri**. Anasuya is famous for her devotion to her husband, and the wives of the gods become jealous of her. **Lakshmi**, **Parvati**, and **Saraswati** send their husbands (Vishnu, **Shiva**, and **Brahma**) to try to compromise her fidelity; the gods come **begging** for food, but they refuse to accept it unless Anasuya gives it to them naked. Through the power she has gained from her devotion to her husband, Anasuya turns the three gods into infants and then nurses them until they are satisfied; these three gods are later "born" into her household: Vishnu as **Dattatreya**, Shiva as **Durvasas**, and Brahma as **Chandra**.

Utsava Murti

("festival image") Image of a **deity** that is able (and intended) to be moved. These are used mainly during festivals, when the image of the deity is paraded around the town or city on the model of a kingly procession, symbolically surveying his or her realm. The other general class of Hindu images is the **sthala murti**, which is fixed in one place and never moves from it.

Uttara ("Later") Mimamsa

Another name for the philosophical school also known as **Vedanta**, which was called Uttara Mimamsa to distinguish it from **Purva Mimamsa**, another philosophical school. See **Vedanta**.

Uttararamacharita

("Later Acts of **Rama**") Drama written by the **Sanskrit** playwright **Bhavabhuti** (8th c.), which retells the story of the *Ramayana*, the earlier of the two Sanskrit epics. Bhavabhuti's play largely follows the plot of the original **Valmiki** *Ramayana*, with one important difference. Valmiki's text ends with Rama's banishing **Sita** because of suspicions about her virtue and Sita's being swallowed up by the **earth**, which is her mother and witness to her chastity. The *Uttararamacharita*, on the other hand, ends with a complete reconciliation between Rama and Sita. This change may have been prompted solely by the desire for a happy ending, which is one of the characteristic features of Sanskrit drama. It may also indicate that some people were not comfortable with the moral ambiguities of the original text, in which Rama, although claimed to be divine, sometimes acts in unscrupulous and disturbing ways.

Uttarayana

Term denoting the six months of the solar **year** in which the **sun** is believed to be moving northward. In the common era, this would be the period between the winter solstice and the summer solstice (roughly December 20 to June 20) and would be based on the actual motion of the sun with respect to the **earth**. The Indian solar year is based on the motion of the sun through the **zodiac**, which is calculated differently than in Western astrology. The uttarayana begins on **Makara Sankranti** (the **day** the sun is calculated as entering Capricorn, usually January 14) and ends the day before **Karka Sankranti** (the day the sun enters Cancer, usually calculated as July 14). The uttarayana is considered a more **auspicious** time than the **Dakshinayana** (in which the sun is traveling toward the south) because the guardian **deity** for the southern direction is **Yama**, who is death personified.

Uttarkashi

("northern **Benares**") Himalayan town and sacred site (**tirtha**) on the **Bhagirathi River** in northern **Uttar Pradesh**. As its name indicates, Uttarkashi is claimed as the northern form of the city of Benares, the city of the god **Shiva** that is one of the most sacred sites in India. Uttarkashi's charter myths also claim that in the present age, Shiva no longer dwells in Benares, but instead lives in Uttarkashi. To buttress the claim to being the northern Benares Uttarkashi shows many parallels and homologies with Benares itself: In both, the **Ganges River** flows in a northern direction through the city; both have their core region defined as the area between the **Varuna** and Asi Rivers; both are enclosed by a **panchakroshi** pilgrimage route; and in both, the primary **deity** is Shiva in his form as **Vishvanath**. Uttarkashi is a site of great antiquity—**inscriptions** have been discovered from the seventh century C.E.—and although these parallels to Benares might seem slavish, the basis of this claim is not just that Uttarkashi is a holy place, just as Benares is a holy place, but that the holiness of Uttarkashi is equal to that of Benares. Aside from its importance as a pilgrimage town, Uttarkashi is also the district headquarters and a major supply point to the other sites in the region. The town was severely damaged in an earthquake in early 1993 and has been rebuilding slowly since that time.

Uttar Pradesh

("northern state") Modern Indian state running along the border with **Nepal**. Uttar Pradesh is India's most populous state and is thus one of its most politically important. The state has a range of different ecosystems, from the high **Himalayas** to the rice-growing plains in its eastern basin, which gives it immense natural and social variety. Uttar Pradesh also contains the sources and much of the length for both the **Ganges** and **Yamuna Rivers**, and the state thus contains many of the holiest sites in India. Although a full catalog would be difficult to give, some of the state's major sacred sites (**tirthas**) are the four Himalayan Dhams ("[divine] abodes"), **Yamunotri**, **Gangotri**, **Kedarnath**, and **Badrinath**; the sacred cities of **Haridwar**, **Allahabad**, and **Benares**; the city of **Ayodhya**, the mythic home of the god **Rama**; and the **Braj** region south of Delhi, which is mythically associated with the god **Krishna**. For general information about Uttar Pradesh and all the regions of India, an accessible reference is Christine Nivin et al., *India*, 8th ed., Lonely Planet, 1998. See also **four dhams**.

Vachaspati Mishra

(ca. late 15th c.) Commentator and compiler of the **dharma literature**. He composed dozens of texts in his working life, including a number of digests (**nibandha**) organized around various subjects, including daily religious rites, purification, **pilgrimage**, death rites (**antyeshthi samskara**), political life, judicial procedures, and funeral rites. In these digests Mishra would draw material relating to the theme from a number of different religious texts, weigh them, and sometimes interpret their position on a religious issue. Mishra was much respected for his learning and piety, and his texts were an important resource to those who followed him.

Vadagalai

One of the two main subsects in the **Shrivaishnava** religious community, the other being the **Tengalai**. The Shrivaishnavas are devotees (**bhakta**) of the god **Vishnu**, and the community's roots lie in the devotional hymns of the **Alvars**, a group of twelve poet-saints who lived in southern India between the seventh and tenth centuries. Two centuries later, the Alvars' devotional outpouring was organized and systematized by the philosopher **Ramanuja** (11th c.), who is considered the Shrivaishnava founder. Ramanuja was convinced that **Brahman**, or Supreme Reality, was a personal **deity** rather than an impersonal abstract principle, and he was also convinced that devotion (**bhakti**) was the most important form of religious practice. **Vishishthadvaita Vedanta**, his philosophical position, stressed both of these convictions and

thus opposed the **Advaita Vedanta** school, founded by the philosopher **Shankaracharya**, which believed that the Supreme Being was impersonal and that realization (**jnana**) was the best spiritual path.

The split between the Tengalais and the Vadagalais came several centuries later and stemmed from differing perspectives on what the individual must do to gain final liberation of the soul (**moksha**). The Vadagalais not only stress the saving power of God's **grace**, but also assert that the individual must respond to that grace and take an active role in his or her salvation. This belief is in complete contrast to the Tengalais, who emphasize the need for absolute surrender (**prapatti**) to the grace of God, through which devotees are saved with no action of their own.

Vagish

("Lord of Speech") Epithet of the poet-saint **Appar**, reflecting the power of his devotional poetry. Appar was one of the earliest of the **Nayanars**, a group of sixty-three southern Indian poet-saints of the seventh and eighth centuries who were devotees (**bhakta**) of the god **Shiva**. See **Appar**.

Vaidyanath

Form of the god **Shiva**, in his manifestation as the "Lord of Physicians" (vaidya). A temple is named for him at **Deoghar** in the state of **Bihar**. Shiva is present at Vaidyanath in the form of a **linga**, the pillar-shaped image that is his symbolic form, and the Vaidyanath linga is one of the twelve **jyotirlingas**, a network of sites deemed especially sacred to Shiva, and at which Shiva is uniquely present. Vaidyanath's charter myth is associated with the **demon**-king **Ravana**, who is said to be a great devotee (**bhakta**) of Shiva. Ravana travels to Shiva's home on Mount **Kailas** and practices harsh **asceticism** for years, hoping to gain a vision of Shiva. When his asceticism proves unsuccessful, the ten-headed

Ravana proceeds to cut off his heads, one by one, and to offer them to Shiva. As he is about to cut off the last of his heads, Shiva appears before him and grants Ravana a boon. Ravana asks for Shiva to come and live in his palace in **Lanka**, a request that would have made Ravana invincible. Shiva agrees to come in the form of a linga, but warns Ravana that wherever the linga touches the **earth**, it will stay there forever. As Ravana begins traveling back to Lanka, he feels the urge to urinate (which in some versions is described as being caused by Shiva himself, because the other gods have begged Shiva not to go to Lanka). Given the condition of his boon, he cannot put the linga down; moreover, since urination renders one ritually impure, the linga would be defiled if he holds it while answering nature's call (or touches it before he has taken a purifying bath). Ravana ends up handing the linga to a cowherd, giving him strict orders to keep it off the ground. The linga is so heavy, however, that the cowherd eventually has to let it rest on the ground, where it sticks fast, and remains there to this day.

Vaijayanti Shakti

In the *Mahabharata*, the later of the two great Hindu epics, this is the name of an all-conquering weapon that the storm-god **Indra** gives to the warrior **Karna**. Karna has been born wearing earrings and a suit of armor, and Karna's father, the **sun**-god **Surya**, has ordained that as long as Karna wears these, he cannot be harmed. Indra gains them from Karna by taking the guise of a **brahmin**, and **begging** for them as alms from Karna, who is famous for his generosity. Despite being warned in a **dream**, Karna cannot bring himself to refuse and gives them to Indra. When Indra gives him a boon in return, Karna asks for the Vaijayanti Shakti. Karna keeps this weapon in reserve to kill his nemesis, **Arjuna**, but is forced to use it against another mighty warrior, **Ghatotkacha**, when the latter proves

unconquerable during the Mahabharata war. The loss of this weapon leaves Karna at a disadvantage against Arjuna, and Karna is eventually killed.

Vaikasi

Second month in the **Tamil year**, corresponding to the northern Indian solar month of Vrshabha (the zodiacal sign of Taurus), which usually falls within May and June. This name is a modification of **Baisakh**, the second month in the lunar **calendar**. The existence of several different calendars is one clear sign of the continuing importance of regional cultural patterns. One way that the Tamils retain their culture is by preserving their traditional calendar. Tamil is one of the few regional languages in India with an ancient, well-established literary tradition. See also **Tamil language**, **Tamil months**, and **Tamil Nadu**.

Vaikuntha

In Hindu mythology, the name of the **heaven** in which the god **Vishnu** lives.

Vaishali

City and region in northern **Bihar**; the region's western border is the **Gandaki** River, and its southern border the **Ganges** river. Although now the region is extremely backward, at the time of the Buddha, Vaishali was one of the largest cities in India and a center of intellectual culture of the time. Vaishali is famous as the birthplace of Mahavira. He was the last of the Jain tirthankars, the founding figures in the Jain religious tradition. Tradition also holds Vaishali as the site of the second Buddhist council, convened one hundred years after the death of the Buddha (ca. 386 B.C.E.), at which the Buddhist community split between the Sthaviravadins and the Mahasanghikas.

Vaisheshika

("noting characteristics") One of the **six schools** of traditional Hindu

One of the many forms of Vishnu. Vishnu's followers are known as Vaishnavas.

philosophy, and a school whose special concern was the elucidation of physics and metaphysics. The Vaisheshika analysis of the categories for the universe was later combined with the stress on reasoning in another of the six schools, the **Nyayas**, to form the Nyaya-Vaisheshika school, sometimes called the **Naiyayikas**. The Vaisheshika school was atomistic—that is, it espoused the belief that all things were made up of a few basic constituent things—and this atomism was the root of the school's metaphysics. Philosophically speaking, the Vaisheshikas were realists—that is, they thought that the world was made up of many different things and that these things actually existed as perceived, except in cases of perceptual error. They believed that all things were composed of nine fundamental substances—the five **elements**, **space**, time, mind, and Selves—and that whatever exists was both knowable and nameable. The Vaisheshikas subscribed to the **causal model** known as **asatkaryavada**, which posited that when a thing was created, it was a whole new aggregate, completely different from its constituent parts. This causal model tends to multiply the number of things in the universe because each act of creation brings a new thing into being. It also admits that human efforts and actions are one of the causes influencing these effects, making it theoretically possible to act in a way that brings final liberation of the soul (**moksha**).

According to the Vaisheshika analysis, the objects of experience can be divided into six categories: substances, qualities, activity, universals, particulars, and **inherence** (**samavaya**); some later Vaisheshikas add a seventh category, absences. The first three categories can be perceived, whereas the others must be inferred, but the concept of inherence is central to their system of thought. Inherence is the subtle glue connecting all the elements of the universe: wholes and their parts, substances and their qualities, motions and the things that move, general properties with their particular instances, and most important, pleasure and pain to the Self. The philosophical problems with inherence—particularly the notion that it was one single principle and not a collection of things—caused them great difficulty and were responsible for the rise of **Navyanyaya** school, which attempted to explain these relationships in a more sophisticated way. For further information see Karl H. Potter and Sibajiban Bhattacharyya (ed.), *Indian Philosophical Analysis*, 1992; and Sarvepalli Radhakrishnan and Charles A. Moore (eds.), *A Sourcebook in Indian Philosophy*, 1957.

Vaishnava

Name denoting a devotee (**bhakta**) of the god **Vishnu**, in any of his myriad forms. Vaishnava theology is most prominently characterized by the doctrine of the ten **avatars**, or divine incarnations: **Fish**, **Tortoise**, **Boar**, **Man-Lion**, **Vamana** (dwarf), **Parashuram**, **Rama**, **Krishna**, **Buddha**, and **Kalki**. It is generally accepted that the avatar doctrine provided a way to assimilate smaller regional **deities** into the larger pantheon by designating them as forms of Vishnu, and it is in the form of these avatars that Vishnu is most commonly worshiped. Of the ten avatars, the two most important ones have been Rama and Krishna, although in the early centuries of the common era, the Boar avatar and the Man-Lion avatar were influential regional deities.

Early Vaishnava religion is cloudy and mysterious. Although Vishnu appears in several hymns in the **Vedas**, the oldest Hindu religious texts, he was clearly a minor deity, and it is difficult to get from there to being the supreme power in the universe. Some scholars have speculated that the cult of Krishna—a deified local cowherd hero—originally came from outside the Vedic religious matrix, and that Krishna was identified with Vishnu as a way to assimilate Krishna's cult into respectable Vedic religion. Such ideas are intriguing but have little hard evidence to support them. Inscriptional evidence clearly shows that the **worship** of Krishna was well-established by the first century B.C.E. These devotees are generally described as **Bhagavatas** ("devotees of the Blessed One"), a name that for the next thousand years is used to refer to Vaishnavas in general. One particular subset of this early Bhagavata community was known as the Pancharatrikas ("followers of the **Pancharatra**"), who later evolved distinctive cosmological doctrines. These mainstream Bhagavatas expressed their devotion to Krishna by composing texts, including parts of the **Bhagavad Gita**, the *Harivamsha*, and various **puranas**, culminating with the *Bhagavata Purana* in about the tenth century.

The tone of Vaishnava devotion took a dramatic turn with the advent of the

Alvars, a group of twelve devotional (**bhakti**) poet-saints who lived in southern India between the seventh and tenth centuries. Singing their hymns in the **Tamil language**, the vernacular tongue of their times, the Alvars propounded a bhakti that was marked by passionate devotion to God and characterized by a profound emotional attachment between deity and devotee. Along with their **Shaiva** counterparts, the **Nayanars**, the Alvars spearheaded the revitalization of Hindu religion *vis-à-vis* the Buddhists and the Jains, and in the process, transformed the tradition as the devotional wave they had begun moved northward. The period between the twelfth and sixteenth centuries saw the development of various Vaishnava communities, often stemming from a particular charismatic religious figure.

This process began in southern India, where the philosopher **Ramanuja** (11th c.) founded the **Shrivaishnava** community, while the philosopher **Madhva** (1197–1276) founded the community that bears his name. The next great center was in **Maharashtra**, particularly in the **Varkari Panth**, which was centered on the temple of **Vithoba** in **Pandharpur**; some of this community's greatest figures were **Jnaneshvar** (1275–1296?), **Namdev** (1270–1350), **Chokamela** (d. 1338), **Eknath** (1533–1599), and **Tukaram** (1598–1650). The Maharashtra region also saw the rise of the **Mahanubhav** sect, from the thirteenth century. At **Puri** on India's eastern coast one finds the worship of **Jagannath**, a tribal deity assimilated into the pantheon as a form of Krishna. This was well established by the twelfth century, as the poet **Jayadeva's** *Gitagovinda* clearly shows. Finally, in northern India one finds several vibrant religious groups. A very early figure is the twelfth-century philosopher **Nimbarka**, whose **Nimbarki** community bears his name; several centuries later came **Vishnuswami**, about whom little is known. The greatest explosion of northern Indian devotionalism came in the sixteenth century, with the

philosopher **Vallabhacharya** founding the **Pushti Marg**, the Bengali saint **Chaitanya** founding the **Gaudiya Vaishnava** community, and the poet-saint **Harivamsh** (d. 1552) founding the **Radhavallabh** community. All these were based in the **Braj** region that is Krishna's mythic home, and all of them worshiped Krishna: The Pushti Marg and the Gaudiya Vaishnavas considered him to be the supreme divinity, whereas the Nimbarkis and the Radhavallabh community worshiped him in conjunction with his consort **Radha**, whom they considered Krishna's wife and equal. It is also in northern India that the worship of Rama has its deepest roots, as exemplified in the songs of the poet-saint **Tulsidas** (1532–1623?). Many of these schools with long histories are still vital in modern times.

The final Vaishnava community that must be addressed is comprised of **ascetics**. Vaishnava **asceticism** is a more recent development than that of the Shaivas (though dates are uncertain), and it is largely located in the northern part of India (the Shaivas are spread throughout the country). Vaishnava ascetics are known as **Bairagis** ("dispassionate") and are primarily organized into four **sampradays** (religious sects distinguished by unique bodies of teachings), each connected with a major Vaishnava figure. By far the most powerful is the **Shri Sampraday** of the **Ramanandi** ascetics, which traces its spiritual lineage through the poet-saint **Ramananda** to the southern Indian philosopher Ramanuja, whom they claim was Ramananda's **guru**. The **Sanaka Sampraday** of the Nimbarki ascetics traces its spiritual lineage to the philosopher Nimbarka. The **Rudra Sampraday** of the Vishnuswami ascetics traces its lineage through the philosopher Vallabhacharya to an earlier figure, Vishnuswami. Finally, the **Brahma Sampraday**, an ascetic subset of the Gaudiya Vaishnava ascetics, traces its spiritual line through the Bengali saint Chaitanya to the southern Indian philosopher Madhva.

Each of these sampradays is differentiated not only by its founder, but also by its tutelary deity or deities. The Ramanandis **worship** the god Rama, whereas the others worship the god Krishna and his consort Radha, but differ in the position that they give to Radha. Scholars have noted that these historical claims are either highly suspect or completely spurious and that the distinctions among the sampradays are largely academic. Given that the overwhelming majority of these ascetics are Ramanandis, the others seem important only for symbolic reasons, to include a representative from each of the great Vaishnava religious figures.

Vaishno Devi

Presiding **goddess** of the Vaishno Devi shrine, located in a cave on Trikut mountain in the hills near **Jammu**, and one of the nine **Shiwalik goddesses**. Pilgrims to Vaishno Devi travel by road via Jammu to the village of Katra, whence they walk the ten miles to the shrine itself. As with many of the images of the Shiwalik goddesses, the images at Vaishno Devi are "self-manifested" (**svayambhu**), in the form of three stone outcrops. These outcrops are considered to be **Mahakali**, **Mahalakshmi**, and **Mahasaraswati**, the three forms of the Goddess mentioned in the *Devimahatmya*, the earliest and most authoritative source for the mythology of the Goddess. The presence of all three goddesses is believed to make this site extremely powerful, and according to popular belief, Vaishno Devi grants whatever request her devotees (**bhakta**) make. According to some accounts, those whose wishes are granted are highly advised to make a second trip, both to thank the Goddess and to bear witness to her **grace**. The number of visitors to the site has increased dramatically in the recent past, perhaps reflecting anxieties about modern Indian life.

There are several stories connected with Vaishno Devi's charter myth. The name *Vaishno* is a derivation of **Vishnu**, reflecting the claim that Vaishno Devi was born as a partial **avatar** of Vishnu. One sign of this connection is that Vaishno Devi is a vegetarian goddess, for whom no **animal sacrifices** can be performed. According to another story, Vaishno Devi was the spot at which the arms of the dismembered goddess **Sati** fell to **earth**. Since this story is never further connected to Vaishno Devi, this seems a transparent attempt to tie into the network of the **Shakti Pithas**, a group of shrines sacred to the Goddess, which stretch throughout the subcontinent. The longest version of the charter myth reports that the cave is discovered by a **brahmin** named Shridhara. Shridhara, a great devotee of the Goddess (who tested him in various ways), is disturbed by the fact that he has no children. The Goddess reveals the location of the Vaishno Devi cave to him in a **dream**. After an extensive search he finally finds the cave and is soon blessed with four **sons**, emphasizing the claim that Vaishno Devi will grant the desires of her devotees, whatever they may be. For further information see Kathleen Erndl, *Victory to the Mother*, 1993. See also **pitha**.

Vaishya

In the traditional Hindu social theory of the four major social groups (**varnas**), the vaishyas were the third group—less influential than the **brahmins** and **kshatriyas**, but with greater status than the **shudras**. In this model of society, the vaishyas' social function was economic activity, to provide the material basis for social life. This image is reflected in the creation story known as the **Purusha Sukta**, in which the vaishyas are described as being created from the Primeval Man's (**purusha's**) thighs—a standard euphemism for the genitals, and thus the most direct connection with fruition and procreation. In fact, the **jatis** (**endogamous** social subgroups, often determined by hereditary occupation) considered to be vaishyas did all sorts of economic activity, from farming to **animal** husbandry to all sorts of trades and services.

Vaitarani

In Hindu mythology, a river flowing through the underworld over which souls must cross on the way to their audience with the god **Yama**, the god of the dead. For righteous people the crossing is fairly easy, and they are widely believed to get over by holding the tail of a **cow**. For wicked people, on the other hand, the Vaitarani is a river of pus, **blood**, spit, and other polluting substances, in which various ferocious beasts lie in wait.

Vajapeya

Along with the **Rajasuya**, one of the two most famous of the Vedic sacrifices. The Vajapeya **sacrifice** was essentially intended to provide an established king with continuing strength and vitality, magically rejuvenating him after a long reign and in the face of advancing age. In ancient times the rite was elaborate and entailed the sacrifice of **animals**; when it is performed in modern times it is performed in one day, and the **animal sacrifice** is symbolic.

Vajra

Name for the thunderbolt, conceived as one of the divine weapons. It has two symmetrical sides, sometimes pointed, with a handle in the middle. The vajra is an enormously important symbol in Buddhism, particularly the tantric forms (i.e., secret, ritually based religious practices) found in Tibet, but it appears very seldom in Hindu iconography. It is attested to be an attribute of certain forms of the gods **Ganesh** and **Vishnu**, but on the whole it is not as important as some of the other symbols. See also **tantra**.

Vajreshvari Devi

("**Goddess** of the Thunderbolt") Presiding **deity** of the Vajreshvari temple in **Kangra**, **Himachal Pradesh**, and the only one of the nine **Shiwalik goddesses** whose temple is in an urban center. Kangra has a long tradition as a center of Goddess **worship** and may have been a site for practitioners of **tantra**, a secret, ritually based religious practice. The charter myth identifies Vajreshvari Devi as one of the **Shakti Pithas**, a network of sites sacred to the Goddess, which spreads throughout the subcontinent. Each Shakti Pitha marks the site where a body part of the dismembered goddess **Sati** fell to **earth**, taking form there as a different goddess; in the case of Vajreshvari Devi the body part was Sati's breast—certainly a highly charged part of the female body, thus making it a more attractive place for tantric practitioners. Another indication of her possible connection comes from her name, in which the image of the thunderbolt carries associations with Buddhist tantric practice. For further information see Kathleen Erndl, *Victory to the Mother*, 1993. See also **pitha**.

Vajroli Mudra

Yogic practice attributed to **Nathpanthi** ascetics, as part of their effort to attain physical immortality through the practice of **hatha yoga**. The dominant metaphor used in describing the process of gaining immortality in this manner is the union of **sun** and **moon**, in which the sun stands for the processes of change and destruction, and the moon for stability and immortality. In some cases this union was described in very abstract terms, as a process in the **subtle body**, at other times in the most concrete possible fashion, for which the best example is vajroli mudra. This is urethral suction or the "fountain-pen technique," in which a man, having ejaculated into his female partner, draws his **semen**, now refined through contact with the woman's uterine **blood**, back into his body, along with a certain amount of his partner's blood. Despite some commentators' discomfort and denials (characteristic of most references to sexual activity as part of Hindu spiritual practice), vajroli mudra is consistently named as one of the Nathpanthi practices. For further information see George W. Briggs, *Gorakhnath and the Kanphata Yogis*, 1982.

Vakataka Dynasty

(4th–6th c.) Central Indian dynasty whose ancestral homeland was in the center of modern India. The Vakataka zenith came between the fourth and sixth centuries, during which their sway extended through most of the **Deccan** plateau. At the turn of the fifth century, the Vakataka king Rudrasena II married Prabhavati Gupta, creating a marriage alliance with the northern Indian **Gupta dynasty** that gave the two dynasties sway over much of India. Prabhavati Gupta ruled as regent following Rudrasena's untimely death, during which the Vakataka kingdom was a virtual part of the Gupta empire, but in the time after that the Vakatakas regained greater autonomy.

Vallabhacharya

(1479–1531) Philosopher, teacher, and founder of the religious community known as the **Pushti Marg**. Vallabhacharya propounded a philosophical position called **Shuddadvaita** ("pure non-dualism"), in which the Ultimate Reality was conceived as personalized, in the form of **Krishna**, rather than the impersonal **Brahman** propounded by the **Advaita Vedanta** school. Since Vallabhacharya had personalized his conception of the Supreme Reality, the supreme religious goal was conceived in terms of relationship with that divine person. This stress on devotion was soon articulated in elaborately arranged forms of image **worship** in the Pushti Marg's temples. The devotees (**bhakta**) would visualize themselves as Krishna's

companions during his daily activities—waking, **eating**, taking the **cows** to graze, coming home, etc.—and thus gain the opportunity to take part in the divine play (**lila**). This emphasis on visualization and participation was fostered through the development of vast liturgical resources, which were composed by eight poets (the **ashtachap**) who were associated with Vallabhacharya and **Vitthalnath**, his **son** and successor. For further information see R.K. Barz, *The Bhakti Sect of Vallabhacharya*, 1976.

Vallabhite

Popular name for the followers of **Vallabhacharya**. As the suffix clearly shows, this term is one term formed by non-Hindus that was used to describe a particular Hindu group. In earlier times it was used by British government officials, but today it is used mainly by scholars, usually foreigners. Vallabha's own followers would be far more likely to describe themselves as belonging to the **Pushti Marg**.

Valli

In the mythology of southern India, the god **Skanda** (in his southern Indian form as **Murugan**) becomes enamored of and marries Valli, a young girl from a group of tribal hunters. The marriage takes place despite his earlier marriage to the **goddess Devasena**, who has been given to him by **Indra** and the established Hindu gods. Murugan's marriage with Valli is a sign of his connection with the land and probably reflects his earlier past as a tribal **deity**. The marriage is described as taking place at **Tiruttani** in **Tamil Nadu**, but he is also described as settling at **Kataragama** in **Sri Lanka**.

Valmiki

In Hindu mythology, a sage who is regarded as the first poet, and who is traditionally cited as the author of the ***Ramayana***, the earlier of the two great **Sanskrit** epics. According to legend,

The god Vishnu's Vamana avatar, a dwarf. Vishnu takes this form to release the universe from the control of the demon Bali.

Valmiki is a bandit in his early life. One day, one of his victims asks him whether his family will also share the sins he is committing, and when Valmiki finds out that they will not, he has a change of heart. He sits down in a secluded place and begins to do **japa** (recitation), but his heart is so blackened by his sins that the only words he can say are "mara mara" ("death, death"). After a long time the syllables become reversed, and by reciting "Rama Rama" he expiates his former sins. This recitation is so long that a colony of white ants (in Sanskrit, named "valmika") builds a hill over him, and when he emerges from this he is given the name Valmiki.

After his emergence, Valmiki builds an **ashram** on the banks of the Tamasa River and lives a quiet life. He gives shelter to **Sita** after she has been exiled from **Ayodhya** by her husband, **Rama**, and also cares for her **sons**, **Lava** and **Kusha**. One day when Valmiki is walking by the Tamasa River, he sees a hunter shoot a pair of courting Krauncha birds, and in his intense anger, his rebuke to the hunter comes out in verse; according to legend, this is the first poem ever composed. After this first verse composition, the god **Brahma** appears, and at Brahma's encouragement Valmiki composes the *Ramayana*.

Valmiki Jayanti

Festival celebrated on the **full moon** in the **lunar month** of **Ashvin** (September–October). This day is considered to be the birthday of the poet **Valmiki**, who according to tradition is the author of the ***Ramayana***, the earlier of the two **Sanskrit** epics.

Vamachara

("left-hand practice") In the secret, ritually based religious practice known as **tantra**, this term denotes a type of tantric practice that makes ritual use of forbidden substances, such as the Five Forbidden Things (**panchamakara**), or promotes behavior that the orthodox would consider scandalous or objectionable. When seen in a tantric context, the use of such normally forbidden substances is not mere license, but a powerful ritual tool. One of the most pervasive tantric assumptions is the ultimate unity of everything that exists. From a tantric perspective, to affirm that the entire universe is one principle—often, conceived as the activity of a particular **deity**—means that the adept must reject all concepts based on dualistic thinking. The "Five Forbidden Things" provide a ritual means for breaking down duality because in this ritual the adept breaks societal norms forbidding consumption of **intoxicants**, nonvegetarian food, and illicit sexuality, in a conscious effort to sacralize what is normally forbidden. Within the tantric tradition itself there is a long-standing debate about the propriety of such acts, and whereas the vamachara practice uses these elements in their actual forms, in the **dakshinachara** ("right-hand") practice, other items are substituted for the forbidden ones. This distinction between "right" and "left" hand also reveals the pervasive polarity between right and left in

Indian culture, with the former being deemed better.

Vamakhepa

(1843–1911) **Ascetic** devotee (**bhakta**) of the **Goddess** in her fierce and powerful form as Tara; his presence and supposed miraculous powers are largely responsible for the importance of **Tarapith** as an important regional sacred site (**tirtha**) in **West Bengal**. From his earliest childhood, Vamakhepa was occupied with thoughts of the Goddess, and from an early age he took up residence in the **cremation ground** at Tarapith, where he undertook the **worship** of Tara. Various stories describe his power to heal people of all sorts of ailments, as well as his complete disregard for all accepted standards—according to tradition, he once urinated on the temple's image of Tara, to show his contempt for a **deity** made of iron, and was struck in punishment by the Goddess.

Vamana Avatar

Fifth **avatar** of **Vishnu**, this one in the form of a dwarf ("vamana"). As with all of Vishnu's avatars, the Vamana avatar comes into being in a time of crisis and serves to restore the cosmic balance that has been thrown out of equilibrium. In this case the source of trouble stems from a **demon** (asura) named **Bali**, who has grown so powerful that he is able to rule the entire universe, doing as he wishes. As in many other cases, Vishnu is able to counter and conquer this disruptive force through cunning and trickery, rather than simple overt power.

The mythic tale describes how Bali is sponsoring a great **sacrifice**, to which all the gods and sages have come. Vishnu comes in the form of a dwarf, disguised as a mendicant **brahmin**. Bali gives many rich gifts to those attending, as part of the gift-giving (**dana**) associated with sacrifice, and he offers to give Vamana anything that he asks for. Vamana refuses the offer of riches, land, and material wealth, and asks only for three paces worth of land to set up his own sacrificial altar. Bali is amused by the request and grants it flippantly despite the warnings of **Shukra**, his religious preceptor (**guru**), that he should not do this.

As soon as Bali pours **water** on Vamana's hand, marking that the gift has been given irrevocably, Vamana suddenly begins to grow. He grows so large that he takes up all the space in the cosmos and then begins to take his three steps. With his first step he traverses the **earth**, with his second the **heavens**, and with his third step there is nowhere else to go. Bali realizes that he has been defeated, and as a **gesture** of submission indicates that Vishnu's third step should fall on his head. Vishnu's third step pushes Bali down into the netherworld, where he still remains as the ruler. As for many of the other avatars, Bali's fate gives an important lesson: Vishnu's purpose is not to destroy him, but to restore the cosmic balance that has been lost through one being gaining disproportionate or inappropriate power. Through his submission to Vishnu, Bali remains a powerful being, but on a diminished scale.

The motif of measuring out the universe in three steps is part of the oldest stratum of Vishnu's mythology. In one of the few hymns to Vishnu in the **Rg Veda** (1.154), the oldest Hindu religious text, he is described as a protective and benevolent **deity**, who with three steps defines the boundaries of the universe. This manifestation of Vishnu is named Trivikrama ("[taking] three steps"); it seems likely that the motif from this hymn was grafted onto the Vamana story as part of the process of assimilation into the pantheon.

Vana Dashanami

One of the ten divisions of the **Dashanami Sanyasis**, renunciant ascetics who are devotees (**bhakta**) of **Shiva**. The Dashanamis were supposedly established by the ninth-century

Varanasi ghats with pilgrims bathing in the Ganges.

philosopher, **Shankaracharya**, in an effort to create a corps of learned men who could help revitalize Hindu life. Each of the divisions is designated by a different name—in this case, vana ("forest"). Upon **initiation**, new members are given this name as a surname to their new **ascetic** names, thus allowing for immediate group identification.

Aside from their individual identities, these ten "named" divisions are divided into four larger organizational groups. Each group has its headquarters in one of the four monastic centers (**maths**) supposedly established by Shankaracharya, as well as other particular religious associations. The Vana Dashanamis belong to the **Bhogawara** group, which is affiliated with the **Govardhan Math** in the city of **Puri**, on the bay of Bengal.

Vanamalin

("wearing a garland of forest flowers") Epithet of the god **Krishna**. See **Krishna**.

Vanaprastha

("forest-dweller") According to the **dharma literature**, the vanaprastha was the third of the idealized **stages of life** (ashrama) for a **twice-born** man, that is, a man born into the **brahmin**, **kshatriya**, or **vaishya** communities, who had undergone the adolescent religious **initiation** known as the "second birth." According to this idealized pattern, after engaging in religious learning as a celibate student (**brahmacharin**), the first stage; marrying and raising a family as a householder (**grhastha**), the second stage; a man should, in the third, gradually disengage himself from the world by giving up his attachments and withdrawing to a more secluded place. The renunciation in this third stage of life is less severe than the last stage, the **Sanyasi**—the texts are very clear that he should remain with his wife and that he should continue to perform the prescribed daily domestic sacrifices. Although in contemporary times it is fairly common for older people to live a more retired life, bequeathing the bulk of the family affairs to their children, few people live by the strict prescriptions for the vanaprastha. The prescription for this third stage of life is generally considered to be a reaction to the growth of **asceticism** in the centuries before the turn of the common era, particularly the monastic asceticism of the Buddhists and Jains, which they claimed was religiously superior to the life of a householder. The vanaprastha is a transitional stage that paves the way for an **ascetic** life, but it is set in one's old age and thus allows for the fulfilling of one's duties to family and society.

Varada Hasta

In Indian **dance**, **sculpture**, and ritual, a particular hand **gesture** (**hasta**), in which the left hand is held with the fingers pointing downward and the palm exposed to the viewer, with the fingers either fully extended or slightly curled. The word *varada* means "boon-granting," and the gesture is meant to indicate beneficence and generosity.

Varaha Avatar

The third **avatar** or incarnation of the god **Vishnu**, in the form of a boar. See **Boar avatar**.

Varanasi

Traditional name for the sacred city of **Benares**. The name *Varanasi* may be generally used to denote the whole city, but in a more specific context this refers to one of the concentric sacred zones surrounding the **Vishvanath** temple, the city's ritual center. The smallest of these zones is called **Avimukta**, the second is Varanasi, and the largest is named **Kashi**. The sacred zone of Varanasi is conceived as the area between the Varana and the Asi rivers—the traditional boundaries of the city of Benares—but Varanasi's boundaries do not stretch inland as far as those of Kashi.

Varkari

Religious community of devotees (**bhakta**) of the god **Vishnu**, in his manifestation as **Vithoba**. Varkari **worship** has centered on Vithoba's temple at **Pandharpur** in the southern part of the state of **Maharashtra**. The community's history begins with a series of extraordinary devotional (**bhakti**) poet-saints, dating from the twelfth to the seventeenth century: **Jnaneshvar**, **Namdev**, **Eknath**, **Tukaram**, **Chokamela**, **Gora**, **Janabai**, **Bahina Bai**, and many others. One of the ways that these saints expressed their devotion was in pilgrimage to Pandharpur, and this pilgrimage is still the major ritual act in the Varkari community. Twice a **year** Varkaris come on pilgrimage to Pandharpur and time their travel so that all the pilgrims arrive on the same **day**—the eleventh day (**ekadashi**) in the bright half of **Ashadh** (June–July) in the summer, and the eleventh day in the bright half of **Kartik** (October–November) in the fall. Individual pilgrims travel in small groups called **dindis**, often made up of people from the same neighborhood or locality. The dindis are organized into larger groups known as **palkhis**, each of which is associated with one of the Varkari poet-saints and is led by a **palanquin** (palkhi, an enclosed single-person litter borne on the shoulders of bearers by means of poles) bearing the sandals of that saint. Each palkhi departs from a place associated with its particular saint—for example, the palkhi of Jnaneshvar leaves from the town of **Alandi** in which he lived—and thus he and all the other saints are still symbolically journeying to Pandharpur twice a year. During their journey pilgrims sing the devotional songs composed by these poet-saints. In this way, the pilgrims are emulating the saints

Child celebrating Vasant Panchami.

before them, both by treading in their physical footsteps and by singing their songs of devotion. Although the pilgrimage concludes with the entry to Pandharpur and the worship of Vithoba, the most important part is the journey itself. For more information see G. A. Deleury, *The Cult of Vithoba*, 1960; I. B. Karve, "On the Road," in the *Journal of Asian Studies*, Vol. 22, No. 1, 1962; and Digambar Balkrishna Mokashi, *Palkhi*, 1987.

Varna

("color") Theoretical system dividing Indian society into four major groups, each with a differing occupation and status: **brahmin**, **kshatriya**, **vaishya**, and **shudra**. The highest status was held by the brahmins, who were priests and scholars, next came the kshatriyas, who were kings and soldiers, then the vaishyas, whose purview was economic life, and finally the shudras, who were supposed to serve the others. This picture is articulated as early as the **Vedas**, the oldest Hindu religious texts, in particular by a hymn in the **Rg Veda** (10.90)

known the **Purusha Sukta**. The Purusha Sukta describes the creation of the world and of society as stemming from the **sacrifice** of the Primeval Man (**purusha**), with the brahmins coming from his mouth, the kshatriyas from his shoulders, the vaishyas from his thighs (a common euphemism for the genitals), and the shudras from his feet.

This four-fold scheme is conceptually neat, but the real picture was far more complex. For one thing, none of these four varnas was as uniform as this scheme might lead one to suppose: Each of the varnas had multiple occupationally defined subcommunities known as **jatis**, which often competed for status with one another, even though they may have been members of the same varna. The other discrepancy was that local circumstances had a great effect on any particular community's social status. As one example, the **Vellala** community in **Tamil Nadu** had a great deal of status and power, even though they were technically **shudras**, because they were a landholding community. On the opposite end, it is not uncommon for brahmins in northern

India to earn their living by trading or other businesses. This four-fold varna plan does give the general status picture, but the specifics are much more detailed.

Varnashrama Dharma

In the **dharma literature**, varnashrama dharma is the ordering of **dharma** or religious duty based on the hierarchical social ordering of the four major social groups (**varnas**) and the four successive **stages of life** (ashramas). According to this theory, all people would be able to discern their social status and appropriate function based on their social class and stage of life. The interrelationship between these two sets of categories is often used to denote traditional Hindu society, in theory if not always in fact. The term survives in modern times, but because the doctrine of the ashramas is now largely ignored, those who uphold varnashrama dharma are primarily defending the hierarchical social divisions commonly known as the **caste** system.

Varuna

In the **Vedas**, the oldest and most authoritative religious texts, Varuna is a **deity** associated with the sky, with waters, with justice, and with truth. Varuna belongs to the earliest layer of the Indo-**Aryan** deities; this is clearly shown by comparisons with the Avesta, an ancient Iranian sacred text that shows many parallels with the Vedas, and with even older epigraphic sources. As portrayed in the Vedas, however, Varuna's influence has clearly declined—there are far fewer hymns addressed to him than to deities such as **Indra**, **Agni**, and **Soma**, and he seems to have played a far less important role than these other deities in Vedic religion.

In the Vedas, Varuna is portrayed as the guardian of **rta**, the cosmic order through which the world proceeds. As the deity associated with the high **heaven**, he also watches over the deeds of human beings and punishes them for any transgressions. The best known hymn to Varuna, **Rg Veda** 7.86, shows Varuna's connection with justice, moral order, and the waters. The hymn is the lament of a person who has committed some offense against Varuna and whose sin has become visible through being afflicted with **dropsy**, in which the body retains its fluids and swells. The speaker begs Varuna to reveal the forbidden act, "committed under the influence of **liquor**, anger, or heedlessness," so that Varuna may be propitiated and the sufferer healed.

Despite his virtual eclipse early in the tradition, in the later tradition, Varuna retains his association as the god presiding over the waters. He is also considered to be one of the eight **Guardians of the Directions**, each of which is associated with one of eight points on the compass. Varuna presides over the western direction.

Vasant Panchami

Festival falling on the fifth **day** (panchami) of the bright (waxing) half of the **lunar month** of **Magh** (January–February), celebrated as the first day of spring (vasant). This day is considered sacred to the **goddess Saraswati**, patron **deity** of the arts, music, and learning. In her honor, celebrants sing songs in melodic modes (**ragas**) associated with spring. Given Saraswati's connection with learning, this is also traditionally reckoned as the day on which young children should begin their studies.

Vasant Panchami is also associated with **Kama**, the god of love, since the coming of spring brings the reappearance of flowering plants, with their scents and colors. This is supposedly the day that Kama attempts to instill **erotic** desire in the god **Shiva's** heart, first by bringing spring to Mount **Kailas**, where Shiva is meditating, and then shooting Shiva with one of his flower arrows. Shiva awakens from his meditation, becomes angry at Kama, and reduces him to ashes with a burst of flame from his third eye. Despite being destroyed, in the end Kama is successful—after being awakened, Shiva becomes aware of **Parvati's ascetic** practice and eventually becomes her husband.

Vashitvam

("control") One of the eight superhuman powers (**siddhi**) traditionally believed to be conferred by high spiritual attainment. This particular power gives one the ability to control others, while remaining free from outside control.

Vasishtha

In Hindu mythology, one of the Seven Sages whose names mark exogamous clan "lineages" (**gotra**; in exogamous groups members must marry outside the group); the others are **Gautama, Bharadvaja, Kashyapa, Bhrgu, Atri,** and **Vishvamitra**. All **brahmins** are believed to be descended from these seven sages, with each family taking the name of its progenitor as its gotra name. In modern times, these gotra divisions are still important, since marriage within the gotra is forbidden. After her marriage, the new bride adopts her husband's gotra as part of her new identity.

In the *Ramayana*, the earlier of the two great Hindu epics, Vasishtha is a very powerful sage who is the **guru** to the kings of the Solar dynasty, including King **Dasharatha** and his **son, Rama**. Vasishtha is also famous for his long-standing feud with the sage Vishvamitra, which causes numerous confrontations. The feud's genesis is ultimately rooted in the difference in status between **kshatriyas** and brahmins. Vishvamitra is a king who stops with a host of retainers at the forest **ashram** of the brahmin Vasishtha. Upon asking for food, Vishvamitra is amazed at the ability of Vasishtha's **cow**, the **Kamadhenu**, to provide food for everyone. Vishvamitra first tries to buy the Kamadhenu, then tries to take it by

force, but his minions are defeated by the **magic** powers generated by Vasishtha's **tapas** (**ascetic** practices). Vishvamitra finally admits defeat and begins to do ascetic practices to generate power of his own. Two of their most celebrated clashes are over King **Trishanku** and his son, **Harishchandra**; in each case the real issue is the mutual antipathy of these two sages. See also **marriage prohibitions**.

Vastra

("clothing") The seventh of the sixteen traditional **upacharas** ("**offerings**") given to a **deity** as part of **worship**, on the model of treating the deity as an honored guest. In this offering, the deity is offered clothing, either through symbolic presentation or through physically dressing the image. The underlying motive here, as for all the upacharas, is to show one's love for the deity and minister to the deity's needs.

Vastradhari

("wearing the clothes") Name for a newly initiated **Sanyasi ascetic**, one who has put on the ascetic robes, but still has to undergo a period of training as a disciple to his **guru**.

Vasudeva

The god **Krishna's** father. His most important role in Krishna's mythology comes on the night of Krishna's **birth**, when Vasudeva is able to spirit the infant Krishna out of prison, his birthplace, to the home of his foster parents, **Nanda** and **Yashoda**. Vasudeva returns that night, bearing Yashoda's newborn girl, who is really the **goddess Bhadrakali** in disguise. The next morning **Kamsa** kills the child by dashing it against a stone, but from the body arises the goddess, who taunts Kamsa that the person who will slay him has escaped.

Vasudeva

(2) ("**son** of Vasudeva") Epithet of the god **Krishna**, a patronymic formed from the name of his father, Vasudeva, by lengthening the initial vowel. See **Krishna**.

Vasuki

In Hindu mythology, a famous **Naga** (mythical serpent). Vasuki's most famous mythic role comes in the story in which the gods and **demons** churn the Ocean of Milk to obtain the nectar of immortality (**amrta**). In the form of his **Tortoise avatar**, the god **Vishnu** serves as the churning-base, Mount **Mandara** serves as the churning-stick, and Vasuki, with his enormous length, as the churning-rope. With the gods on one side and the demons on the other, they pull Vasuki back and forth until the sea of milk gives up its treasures.

Vata

("air") Along with **pitta** ("bile") and **kapha** ("phlegm"), one of the three humors (**tridosha**) in **ayurveda**, the traditional system of Indian medicine. Every person has all three of these humors, but usually one is predominant, and this marks a person in certain ways, particularly with regard to health, digestion, and metabolism. Vata is associated with the element of air, which is quick, light, and dry. People whose predominant humor is vata are said to have quick minds, light bodies, and tend to always be doing something. At the same time, they lack substantiality and can run down easily if not careful.

Vatsalya ("calf-like") Bhava

The fourth of the five **modes of devotion** to God that were most prominently articulated by **Rupa Goswami**, a devotee (**bhakta**) of the god **Krishna** and a follower of the Bengali saint **Chaitanya**. Rupa used differing types of human relationships as models for differing conceptions of the link between **deity** and devotee. These five models showed growing emotional intensity, from the peaceful (**shanta**) sense that comes from realizing one's complete identity with **Brahman** or Supreme Reality, to conceiving of God as one's master, friend, child, or lover. In the Vatsalya mode of devotion, devotees consider themselves as God's parents, lavishing love and care on the deity as a **cow** cares for her calf. This is an emotionally intense mode of relationship, but without the **erotic** element present in the fifth mode, **madhurya bhava**.

Vatsyayana

According to tradition, the author of the *Kama Sutra*. This text is usually associated with an exhaustive catalog of sexual positions and pleasures, which it certainly contains, but in fact, the text goes far beyond this. Vatsyayana was interested in exploring desire in all its manifestations, and the text begins with a consideration of the four **aims of life** (purushartha): worldly goods (**artha**), desire (**kama**), religious duty (**dharma**), and liberation of the soul (**moksha**). Vatsyayana argued that because desire was one of the established ends of human life, its pursuit was thus a good thing, as long as this pursuit did not interfere with the other ends.

Having established the legitimacy of desire, Vatsyayana then talks about how to foster it. The *Kama Sutra*'s second book contains the text's best-known material, the discussion and categorization of various types of sexual union. It begins by characterizing various types of sexual endowment, both male and female, then proceeds to describe different sorts of embracing, kissing, scratching, and biting as symbols of passion, sexual positions, and oral sex. This is followed by chapters on gaining a wife, attracting other men's wives (which the text discourages, except in cases where one's passion is "too strong"), courtesans, and general remarks on attraction. The text is thus a manual for all phases of **erotic** life, in which sex can be refined into a vehicle for aesthetic experience, as well as pure carnal pleasure.

Vatsyayana

(2) (4th c.) Writer and commentator in the **Nyaya** school, one of the **six schools** of traditional Hindu **philosophy**, which since early in the common era has been combined with another of the six schools, the **Vaisheshikas**. Vatsyayana is best known for his commentary on **Gautama's Nyaya Sutras**, themselves the foundational text for the Nyaya school.

Vayu

In Hindu mythology, the **deity** who is **wind** personified. Vayu is a minor deity who is one of the eight **Guardians of the Directions**; his direction is the northwest. Aside from being the external winds, Vayu is also believed to be present inside the body, in the five "**vital winds**" (**prana**) through which all physiological processes are believed to occur. Although Vayu is a minor deity, two of his **sons** are extremely significant. His son, **Bhima**, is one of the five **Pandava** brothers who are the protagonists in the *Mahabharata*, the later of the two great **Sanskrit** epics. Bhima is famous for his size and strength, and also for his earthy appetites, both of which reflect the wind's raw, uncontrollable nature. Vayu's other famous son is the monkey-god, **Hanuman**. Even though mythically Hanuman is most famous for his devotion and service to the god **Rama**, in practical terms he is one of the most popular and widely worshiped deities in northern India. This popularity may stem from his intermediate status; because Hanuman is also a servant, he is less remote and majestic than Rama and, therefore, accessible to human petitions. Another important factor is that this accessibility is coupled with power and the ability to protect those who call on him.

Veda

("knowledge") The oldest and most authoritative group of Hindu sacred texts, also designated by the term **shruti** ("heard"). According to tradition, these texts were not composed by human beings, but are based in the primordial vibrations of the cosmos itself. The ancient sages, whose faculties of perception had been honed through arduous religious practice, were able to "hear" and understand these vibrations, and transmitted them to others in a lineage of learning. On one level, the term *veda* is part of the names of four individual texts—the **Rg Veda**, **Sama Veda**, **Yajur Veda**, and **Atharva Veda**, each of which has a differing focus and content. The term *veda* is also a collective term for the material in these texts or their associated appendices: the Vedic hymns (**samhitas**), the **Brahmanas**, the **Aranyakas**, and the **Upanishads**. Although these four groups of texts are all considered part of the Vedas, they have very different forms and characteristics. The samhitas are hymns of praise addressed to particular **deities**, and are found mainly in the Rg Veda and the Sama Veda. In contrast, the Brahmanas are detailed ritual manuals, giving the instructions for performing complex sacrificial rites; the Aranyakas and the Upanishads are speculative ponderings on the nature of the cosmos. The Vedas were considered so sacred that for 3,000 years they were not written down, but transmitted orally, a mode of transmission that still persists today. The Vedas' power comes not from their literal meaning, but from their very sound, which is the identical sound heard by the sages long ago. To safeguard this tradition, Hindus developed an elaborate system of **mnemonics** to ensure that the texts would not be altered or corrupted, thus preserving their efficacy.

Vedanga

("[subsidiary] member of the **Veda**") General name for six classes of works considered auxiliary to the Vedas because they were intended to facilitate its use. These six were guides to proper articulation and pronunciation (**shiksha**), metrical forms (**chandas**), **Sanskrit** grammar (**vyakarana**), etymological explanations of archaic words (**nirukta**), determining astrologically appropriate times for **sacrifice** (**jyotisha**), and ritual and ceremonial guides (**kalpa**).

Vedanta

The latest of the **six schools** in traditional Hindu **philosophy**. The name Vedanta literally means "the end of the Vedas," and reflects their contention that they were revealing the ultimate meaning of these sacred texts. Vedanta proponents gave particular attention to the **Upanishads**, which were also the latest stratum of Vedic texts, and thus their "end" in a different sense. These texts have served as authoritative sources for several major schools, with widely differing philosophical positions. The best known and most important of these is the **Advaita Vedanta** school, propounded by the philosopher **Shankaracharya** and his followers. The Advaita school upholds a philosophical position known as monism, which is the belief in a single impersonal Ultimate Reality that they call **Brahman**. For Advaita proponents, reality is thus "nondual" (advaita)—that is, all things are nothing but the formless, unqualified Brahman, despite the appearance of difference and diversity. For the Advaitins, this assumption of diversity is a fundamental misunderstanding of the ultimate nature of things and a manifestation of **avidya**. Although often translated as "ignorance," avidya is better understood as the lack of genuine understanding, which causes human beings to be trapped in karmic bondage, reincarnation (**samsara**), and suffering.

Whereas the Advaita school conceives of this Ultimate Reality in abstract impersonal terms, the other Vedanta schools are theistic—that is, they conceive the Ultimate Reality as a personal God, namely the god **Vishnu**. The two other major schools are the **Vishishthadvaita** vedanta ("qualified nondualism") propounded by **Ramanuja** and the **Dvaita** Vedanta ("dualist") propounded by **Madhva**. The major differences between these two schools stem from assumptions about connections between God, human souls, and the world. Ramanuja tends to see these in a continuum, with the world and human souls sharing in the divine nature, whereas Madhva stresses the great gulf between God and all other things. Another minor school is the **dvaitadvaita** vedanta ("dualism and nondualism") of **Nimbarka**, which strives to find some middle ground between Advaita Vedanta's monism, and Dvaita Vedanta's dualism. Nimbarka stressed that the world and souls were dependent on God, in whom they exist, and with whom they had a subtle connection. Even from their names, it is obvious that there are significant differences between these positions.

Vedanta Deshika

(13th c.) Writer and commentator in the **Vishishthadvaita Vedanta** philosophical school. Vedanta Deshika was a follower of **Ramanuja** and interpreted Ramanuja as teaching that there were two sorts of liberation: a lower one in which one was subject to no outside forces, and a higher one in which one's entire being was focused on the Lord, whom Ramanuja identified as the god **Vishnu**. The human being is considered both identical to and different from the Lord, which means the perfect identity is never possible; God's transcendence leads to the exaltation of devotion (**bhakti**) and the stress on submission to God's **grace**.

Vedanta Society

The oldest Hindu missionary organization in America, established in 1897 by **Swami Vivekananda**. The society stresses the philosophical teachings of **Vedanta**, which it understands as referring solely to the **Advaita Vedanta** school, Vivekananda's major emphasis. The society's tone has been nontheistic, nonritual, and rationalist; its constituency has been drawn from liberals and intellectuals, such as the writer Aldous Huxley.

Vedanta Sutras

Text ascribed to the sage **Badarayana** in the third to fifth century B.C.E. Along with the **Upanishads** and the **Bhagavad Gita**, the *Vedanta Sutras* is one of the three traditional sources for the **Vedanta** school, one of the **six schools** of traditional Hindu **philosophy**. The text itself is a collection of 555 brief aphorisms (**sutras**), which are so terse that they presuppose a commentary. The sutras focus particularly on the ideas about **Brahman**, hence their other common name, the **Brahma Sutra**. In content, the first section describes the nature of Absolute Reality, the second responds to objections and criticizes other positions, the third details the means to acquire knowledge, and the fourth describes the benefits of such knowledge.

Vedarambha ("beginning of Veda [study]") Samskara

Traditionally, the twelfth of the life-cycle ceremonies (**samskaras**). In this ceremony, a newly initiated **brahmacharin**—a young man who had entered the celibate student phase of life—would commence to study the Vedas, the oldest Hindu religious texts. This rite is not mentioned in the earliest texts in the **dharma literature**, perhaps under the assumption that **Veda** study would commence at an appropriate time, after learning had commenced with the earlier **vidyarambha samskara**.

Vegetarianism

A dietary practice that carries extremely high status among Hindu people, probably because of its associations with strict **brahmin** practice; even people who are nonvegetarian themselves will commonly think of a vegetarian diet as "purer." Strict vegetarians eat no flesh or eggs, but milk and milk products are always eaten and are considered pure and health-giving, probably because they come from the **cow**. Those people who keep the strictest diets will also often refrain from onions and garlic, which are considered to excite the passions. This religious commitment to vegetarianism by a certain part of the population, and the general status given to "pure" vegetarian food, are both responsible for the great variety of vegetarian cooking found in Indian culture. Despite the higher status given to a vegetarian diet, most modern Hindus are not vegetarian—a recent poll of urban Hindus found that only about 25 percent were pure vegetarian, although the number may be higher in villages, which tend to be more traditional.

Vellala

The landlord community throughout much of traditional **Tamil Nadu**. Although technically the Vellalas were of **shudra** status, their control over the land gave them considerable influence and prestige in the region. The Vellala community was the source for many of the **Alvars**, a group of twelve poet-saints whose stress on passionate devotion (**bhakti**) to the god **Vishnu** transformed and revitalized Hindu religious life. Most of the Alvars' influence undoubtedly stemmed from the strength of their religious devotion, but this was undoubtedly reinforced by Vellala status as a land-holding community.

Velur

Village in the Aurangabad district of the state of **Maharashtra**, a few miles from the cave temples at **Ellora**. Velur is famous as the site for the temple to the god **Shiva** in his form as **Ghrneshvar**, the "Lord of Compassion." Shiva is present at this temple in the form of a **linga**, the pillar-shaped image that is his symbolic form, and the Ghrneshvar linga is one of the twelve **jyotirlingas**, a network of sites deemed especially sacred to Shiva, and at which Shiva is uniquely present.

Vena

In Hindu mythology, a wicked king who prohibits all religious rites and gift-giving except those dedicated to him. He is finally killed by a group of outraged sages, who through their **magic** powers transform blades of sacred **kusha** grass into spears. After Vena has been killed, the problem of the royal succession arises. The sages first churn from his thigh a small, malformed, dark-skinned man named Nishada, who is believed to be the ancestor of the tribal people known as the Nishadas. Nishada takes upon himself all Vena's manifold sins, thus purging them from Vena. After Vena has been cleansed, the sages churn his right hand, from which emerges a radiant and shining boy, who is King **Prthu**.

Venkateshvara

("the Lord of Venkata [Hill]") Presiding **deity** of the Venkateshvara temple near the town of Tirupati in the state of **Andhra Pradesh**; the temple is north and east of Madras. Venkateshvara is a local deity who has been assimilated into the larger pantheon as a form of the god **Vishnu**. The temple is in the Tirumalai hills, a cluster of seven hills believed to represent the seven cobra hoods of **Shesha**, the mythic serpent who serves as Vishnu's couch. Venkateshvara's image is unusual, in that his forehead is covered with a plate. The two branches of the **Shrivaishnava** community, the **Tengalais** and the **Vadagalais**, each wear distinctive sectarian markings, and this plate conceals these markings on the image and thus allows both communities to claim him as their own.

Venkateshvara is also famous for having the single richest temple in India. People come to Tirupati from all over the country, largely because of the popular belief that any wish made in the deity's presence will invariably be granted. Aside from significant monetary **offerings**, it is also very common for pilgrims to have their heads shaved, as a sign of their visit and to make an offering of the **hair**, as well. In the time since independence the temple's wealth has been administered by a trust, which has been particularly attentive in fostering publishing, educational institutions, and in helping to build Hindu temples outside India.

Venu

("bamboo") A bamboo flute, which is an important instrument in Indian classical music. In Hindu iconography, it is the characteristic instrument of the god **Krishna**, who used its sweet sounds to summon his devotees (**bhakta**) to him, to spend their nights dancing on the shores of the **Yamuna River**.

Venus

In Hindu astrology (**jyotisha**), a planet associated with love and pleasure. It is considered a strong planet, with pronounced benevolent qualities, although like all the other **planets**, its powers will vary according to context. Venus presides over **Friday**, and its positive qualities make this an auspicious **day**.

Veshara

One of the three developed styles in medieval Hindu temple **architecture**, the others being the **Nagara** and the **Dravida**. The Veshara style is primarily found in western India and the **Deccan** and was the least significant and widespread of the three styles. Whereas the Nagara style was characterized by vertical uplift achieved by a temple's towers (**shikharas**), and the Dravida style by lower temples covering enormous tracts of ground, the Veshara style's most identifiable feature is a barrel roof above the

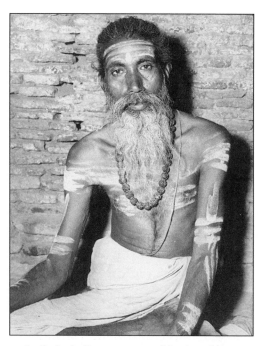

A pilgrim in Benares wears vibhuti markings, which consist of three horizontal lines and identify him as a devotee of the god Shiva.

sanctuary, which has its roots in the rock-cut caves (**chaityas**) first sculpted by the Buddhists. This sort of roof is midway between the Nagara towers and the Dravida horizontal tiers, just as the Deccan was the intermediate region between the two.

Vetala

In Hindu mythology, one of the classes of malevolent spirits that can be subsumed under the general rubric of **demons**. Vetalas are usually described as **eating** human flesh and are sometimes said to haunt battlefields to get their fill.

Vibhishana

In the **Ramayana**, the earlier of the two great Indian epics, Vibhishana is the youngest brother of **Ravana**, the **demon** king of **Lanka**. In their youth Vibhishana, Ravana, and their third brother, **Kumbhakarna**, have performed harsh physical **asceticism** (**tapas**) to gain boons from the gods. Whereas his brothers have chosen boons designed to advance their military ability and glory, Vibhishana asks that he remain righteous in times of danger, and this quality marks his life. When Ravana holds a council of war preceding the battle with **Rama's** army, Vibhishana is the only one to vote against battle and instead advises Ravana to return Rama's kidnapped wife, **Sita**, and to beg Rama's pardon. For these words, Ravana expels his brother from the city, and Vibhishana goes over to Rama's army, where he fights valiantly throughout the war. After the death of Ravana, Rama crowns Vibhishana the king of Lanka, as a reward for his fidelity and his virtue. Vibhishana is a perfect example of the fact that **demons** (in this case the type of demons known as **rakshasas**) are not inherently evil in Indian mythology. They are powerful beings who may clash with gods and men, but they have many virtues as well. In the **Ramcharitmanas**, the vernacular retelling of the *Ramayana* written by the poet-saint **Tulsidas** (1532–1623?), Vibhishana is portrayed as a great devotee (**bhakta**) of Rama, in keeping with the emphasis of Tulsidas on the primacy of devotion over all other forms of religious life.

Vibhuti

("power") Name for the sacred ash with which devotees (**bhakta**) of the god **Shiva** mark their bodies, usually with three horizontal lines (**tripundra**). According to one interpretation, the three lines represent the three prongs of Shiva's trident, according to another, they symbolize Shiva's third eye. Ash is associated with Shiva in several different contexts. On one hand, he is said to smear his body with ashes from the **cremation ground**, which indicates his lack of concern for all conventional distinctions between **purity** and impurity (**ashaucha**); the ash could also symbolize Shiva's destruction of **Kama**, the god of love, who is burned to ash by Shiva's third eye. In earlier times vibhuti was made from wood ash that had been sifted through cloth until it was as fine as talcum powder. This is still done today, particularly by ascetics who usually use the ash from a **dhuni** or smoldering **ascetic fire**, which is believed to give the ash a sacred quality; in modern times vibhuti has become available in stores that sell religious supplies.

Vichitravirya

In Hindu mythology, the **son** of **Satyavati** and king **Shantanu**. Vichitravirya dies after his marriage to **Ambika** and **Ambalika**, but before he has fathered any children. In her desperation to perpetuate King Shantanu's lineage, Satyavati calls on her eldest son, **Vyasa**, to sleep with the two wives. From this union Vyasa sires **Pandu** and **Dhrtarashtra**, whose descendants form the major warring factions in the *Mahabharata*, the later of the two great **Sanskrit** epics.

Vicious Circle

In Indian logic, one of the **fallacies** to be avoided in constructing an argument. A vicious circle occurs when a series of things stand in a cause-and-effect relationship to one another, with any one of them standing as both cause and effect. For example, when "a" causes "b," and "b" causes "c," (somewhere down the line) "x" causes "a." This is seen as an extended case of **self-residence**—saying that "a" is both cause and effect—and is equally objectionable.

Vidhi

Philosophical concept that is found in the *Mahabharata* and *Ramayana*, the two great **Sanskrit** epics. As portrayed there, vidhi is an impersonal force controlling and constraining both the gods and human beings; this notion corresponds best to the idea of fate.

Vidura

In Hindu mythology, the son of the sage **Vyasa** and the serving maid of Queen **Ambika**. Ambika and her sister **Ambalika** are the wives of King **Vichitravirya**, who has died without heirs. In a desperate attempt to save the lineage, Vichitravirya's mother, **Satyavati**, summons her son, **Vyasa**, to sleep with his brother's two wives. Ambika and Ambalika both spontaneously recoil from Vyasa, and each of their **sons** is born with a defect: Ambalika turns pale, causing her son **Pandu** to be born with an unnaturally pale complexion; Ambika covers her eyes, causing her son **Dhrtarashtra** to be born blind. Ambika is so repulsed by Vyasa's appearance that when she is told to sleep with him again, she sends her serving maid instead. In contrast to the two sisters, Ambika's maid gives herself willingly to Vyasa, and as a reward delivers a handsome son named Vidura.

According to one legend, Vidura is a partial **avatar** of **Dharma**, the god who is righteousness personified. Vidura always shows his righteousness in his dealings with the **Pandavas** and the **Kauravas**, the epic's two warring factions. As the Kauravas become more and more wicked, this inclines him more toward the Pandavas, for whom he serves as a trusted and faithful adviser. It is Vidura who realizes the danger in the **House of Lac**—a house built entirely of highly flammable materials—and makes arrangements for the Pandavas to escape from it. During the **Mahabharata** war, he remains neutral, but after the war is over he again serves as an adviser to King **Yudhishthira**, the eldest of the Pandavas, and to Yudhishthira's brothers.

Vidyadhara

("wisdom-bearer") Class of semidivine beings. The Vidyadharas are generally believed to live in the **Himalayas** and are thus often associated with the god **Shiva**, whose home is also said to be there. Vidyadharas are generally benevolent toward human beings and are often (as their name suggests) associated with bringing wisdom to those they favor.

Ruins of Vijayanagar, capital of the Vijayanagar dynasty.

Vidyapati

(ca. 1400) **Brahmin** court poet in the Hindu kingdom of **Mithila** in northern **Bihar**. Although Vidyapati wrote works in **Sanskrit**, he is best known for his love poetry, which was written in the vernacular Maithali language. In this poetry he drew on the literary traditions of Sanskrit love poetry, but his favorite subjects for this poetry were the divine lovers **Radha** and **Krishna**. Although later **Vaishnavas** considered Vidyapati's love poetry as devotional works, Vidyapati's own religious writings definitively describe **Shiva** as the Supreme Being, clearly showing that he was a **Shaiva**. For further information see Edward C. Dimock Jr. and Denise Levertov (trans.), *In Praise of Krishna*, 1981; and R. S. McGregor, *The Love Songs of Vidyapati*, 1987.

Vidyarambha ("beginning of study") Samskara

Traditionally, the tenth of the life-cycle ceremonies (**samskaras**), in which the child begins formal education, usually by starting to learn the alphabet. Although people in modern India may not perform this rite according to its prescribed form (which includes making **offerings** to a sacrificial **fire** and giving gifts to **brahmins**), families in which education is taken seriously usually have a ritualized commencement of study, often when the child is as young as three.

Vighneshvar

("Lord of Obstacles") Epithet of the god **Ganesh**, reflecting the belief that he wields control over all obstacles, and thus can make things easy or hard on a person. See **Ganesh**.

Vihara

An early architectural form, in which a central courtyard was surrounded by a series of small rooms. This was originally a Buddhist architectural form, intended to create a living space for the monks—individual cells in the small rooms and a common area in the large center space. The design was adapted into the earliest forms of the Hindu temples, such as those at **Aihole**.

Vijaya

In Hindu mythology, one of the gate-keepers of **Vaikuntha**, who with his brother **Jaya**, is cursed by the sage **Sanaka** to be born three times as an asura (**demon**), and to be killed each time by **Vishnu**. In their first birth Jaya and Vijaya incarnate as **Hiranyaksha** and **Hiranyakashipu**, who are killed by the **Boar avatar** and the **Man-Lion avatar**, respectively. In their second they are born as **Ravana** and **Kumbhakarna**, who are killed by **Rama**. In their final birth they take form as **Shishupala** and **Dantavaktra**, who are killed by **Krishna**. After this they return to their duties as Vishnu's gatekeepers.

Vijaya Dashami

("victory tenth") Another name for the festival of **Dussehra**, which falls on the tenth **day** of the **lunar month**. The festival has two mythic charters, one with the god **Rama** and one with the **Goddess**, and both these myths point to this as the day on which the **deity** wins a definitive victory. See **Dussehra**.

Vijaya Ekadashi

Religious observance falling on the eleventh **day** (**ekadashi**) of the dark (waning) half of the **lunar month** of **Phalgun** (February–March). As for all the eleventh-day observances, this is dedicated to the **worship** of **Vishnu**. Most Hindu festivals have certain prescribed rites, which usually involve fasting (**upavasa**) and worship and often promise specific benefits for faithful performance. Those performing this vow should fill an earthen pot with the seven kinds of grain, set an image of Vishnu on the pot, and for twenty-four hours, remain engaged in chanting the names of Vishnu. On the twelfth the pot

of grain should be given to a **brahmin**. As for results, faithfully observing this festival is said to bring victory (**vijaya**) over poverty and unhappiness.

Vijayanagar Dynasty

("City of Victory") The last of the great southern Indian Hindu kingdoms, which took its name from its capital city, near modern **Hampi** in **Karnataka**. The kingdom was founded in 1336 by **Harihara**, a regional governor in the Tughluq dynasty who broke away to carve out a kingdom in the central **Deccan** plateau. The kingdom went through several periods of expansion and decay. In the early fifteenth century it controlled most of southern India, but then passed through a period of decline and loss of territory; this was followed by renewal in the early sixteenth century, during the reign of **Krishna Deva Raya**, and finally ended after the battle of **Talikota** in 1565, in which the ruling prince Rama Raja was decisively defeated by a coalition of the sultans from the northern part of the Deccan. The city of Vijayanagar was abandoned almost immediately, and although it has suffered the ravages of time, it still contains stunning examples of late medieval Hindu art and **architecture**.

Vijnaneshvara

(12th c.) Author of the *Mitakshara*, a voluminous commentary on the *Yajnavalkya Smrti*, itself an example of the **dharma literature**, or texts on religious duty. This particular commentary played a pivotal role in the British administration of India. The British were largely content to have their Indian subjects governed by traditional religious laws, but to do so, they needed an accepted standard. For large sections of British India, the *Mitakshara* was given the status of traditional law and was used as a legal code. The only major part of India in which Hindus were not subject to this was in Bengal, where the legal authority was the *Dayabhaga*. One of the major differences between the two was in matters of **inheritance**. The *Mitakshara* stresses inheritance by survivorship, in which only living males can inherit property, whereas the *Dayabhaga* stresses inheritance by succession, in which a dead man's heirs can inherit in his name.

Vikramaditya

("**Sun** of Prowess") Title taken by King **Chandra Gupta II** (r. 376–415) as a symbol of his royal mastery. This monarch is traditionally identified as the Vikramaditya who established the **Vikram era**, but because the Vikram era was established a little less than sixty years before the common era, this claim is clearly untenable.

Vikram Era

One of the most common dating systems, particularly in northern India. It is generally believed that the Vikram era takes its name from King **Vikramaditya** of **Ujjain**, who is supposed to have ruled over much of India. The Vikram era date is fifty-six or fifty-seven years later than that of the common era; the discrepancy stems from the differing first days of the **year** in the two systems. In the common era the year begins on January 1, but in the Vikram era the year begins with the **sun's** transition into Aries, considered in India as occurring on April 14. Hence, to convert a Vikram era date to a common era date, one subtracts fifty-six years for dates between January 1 and April 14, and fifty-seven years for dates between April 15 and December 31.

Vikramorvashiya

("**Urvashi** won by valor") Drama written by the poet **Kalidasa**, generally considered the greatest classical **Sanskrit** poet. The *Vikramorvashiya* is a musical play in five acts, whose mythic theme is the liaison of King **Pururavas** and the celestial nymph Urvashi, a story mentioned both in **Rg Veda** 1.95 and in the **Shatapatha Brahmana**. In both these earlier sources the story ends unhappily, with the separation of Urvashi and Pururavas, but in

Kalidasa's version the estranged lovers are finally happily reunited. This change may have been prompted solely from the desire for a happy ending, which is one of the most characteristic features of Sanskrit drama.

Village Deities

According to popular Hindu tradition, the universe has 330 million gods. The richness of this mythic imagination can be seen in the composition of the Hindu pantheon, in which hundreds of major and minor **deities** have been given form, identity, and mythic history. Yet aside from these deities, who have been given an identifiable form, there are also a host of village deities found throughout India. In most cases, the village deity is exactly that—the deity who protects, watches over, and acts as a divine overseer for a particular village or locale. One of their most common functions is to protect the village from disease, either of people or livestock, and to provide remedies when disease strikes. They are also the guardians of the village, defending it from **ghosts** and unseen powers, as well as protecting the villagers from danger and misfortune.

The authority of these deities is generally quite limited—in most cases, it does not extend beyond the village itself. In most cases, village deities have no well-defined mythic history, form, or personality. At times they will have a temple dedicated to them, but in other cases the village deity is believed to be associated with a particular tree or is represented by a post in the village square. Village deities are usually nonvegetarian, demanding **animal sacrifices** and **offerings** of **blood** in exchange for their services. Relationships with these deities are highly pragmatic—the villagers make offerings, and the deities protect, but beyond these offerings there is usually little organized **worship**. If these deities have any organized priesthood, it is almost always non-**brahmin** because the impurity (**ashaucha**) generated by animal sacrifices would be unacceptable to brahmins. These priesthoods are intermediaries between the deity and the villagers, usually communicating with the deities through **dreams** or **possession**. In this way the deities' wishes become known, and problems or concerns can find their solution.

In some cases, local deities have gained greater stature and have been assimilated into the pantheon. For female deities, this process is fairly simple, since they can be brought into the pantheon by claiming that their temples are one of the **Shakti Pithas**, a network of sites sacred to the **Goddess** that spreads throughout the subcontinent. Each Shakti Pitha marks the site where a body part of the dismembered goddess **Sati** fell to **earth**, taking form there as a different goddess; all these individual goddesses are thus seen as manifestations of a single great Goddess. Male deities are more commonly assimilated into the pantheon as manifestations of the god **Vishnu**, and three prominent examples of the former are **Jagannath**, **Vithoba**, and **Venkateshvara**. Village deities are less commonly said to be forms of the god **Shiva**, but this has happened with **Khandoba**, an important regional deity in the state of **Maharashtra**. See also **pitha**.

Vimana

("vehicle") A word with different specific meanings in different contexts, a common feature in the **Sanskrit** language. It can refer to the vehicles used by a **deity**—either in a mythic sense, because each of the **deities** has an **animal** considered to be his or her vehicle, or in a literal sense as the cart used to carry them in procession, or to the human being who "carries" them through becoming possessed. In the context of **architecture**, the word *vimana* is used to refer to that part of the temple that "carries" the deity, that is, the sanctuary as a whole.

Vimarsha

("reflection") In Hindu **tantra**, a secret, ritually based religious practice, **vimarsha** is one of the bipolar opposites that are used to characterize the nature of all

The vina is a classical Indian musical instrument.

reality, with its counterpart being illumination (**prakasha**). These two terms are particularly important for the creation of the world, which is said to happen when the pure and radiant consciousness (prakasha) of the ultimate **Brahman** becomes self-conscious through the reflection (vimarsha) of this original consciousness. From one single consciousness, the absolute then evolves into a binary divinity—the god **Shiva** and his consort **Shakti**—whose continued interaction combines to create the world. This dyad of prakasha-vimarsha is particularly important in the **Trika** school of Kashmiri Shaivism. For further information see Jaideva Singh, *Pratyabhijnanahrdayam*, 1982.

Vina

Multistringed musical instrument with a long hollow body and a sounding box at the bottom; the top has a large hollow gourd projecting from the back, which further amplifies the sound. The vina is one of the classical musical instruments, particularly in southern India, where its mastery is still held in high regard. In Indian iconography, the vina is most strongly associated with the **goddess Saraswati**, in keeping with her identity as the patron **deity** of the arts, culture, and learning.

Vinata

In Hindu mythology, the **daughter** of the divine sage **Daksha**, and the sister of **Kadru**. Vinata gives **birth** to a line of eagles—of whom the most famous is **Garuda**—whereas Kadru gives birth to a line of serpents. The proverbial antipathy between these two kinds of **animals** is described as stemming from conflict between these two sisters. One day the sisters get into an argument about the tail color of a certain celestial horse, with Vinata arguing that it is white, and Kadru asserting that it is black. The disagreement becomes more intense, until they finally agree that the person who is wrong will become a slave to the other. To ensure her victory, Kadru persuades a number of her children to hang from the back of the horse, which from a distance makes the tail appear to be black. When Vinata sees the black snakes, she accepts her defeat, and for many years has to serve Kadru under extremely harsh conditions. She is finally rescued by her **son**, Garuda, who when he discovers what has happened, embarks on a program of killing snakes that has never abated.

Vinaya Patrika

("letter of petition") One of the later poetic works by the poet-saint **Tulsidas** (1532–1623?), in the form of a series of 280 short poems written in the **Braj Bhasha** dialect. The entire work is presented as a letter of petition to Tulsidas's chosen **deity**, **Rama**,

using as his intermediary the monkey-god **Hanuman**. The letter's general theme is a plea for deliverance from the evils of the current degenerate age (**kali yuga**). The first sixty-odd verses are a series of invocations paying homage to various deities, showing the ecumenical quality that more generally marks Tulsidas's devotion. The remainder of the poem is directed to Rama and stresses other themes that run throughout Tulsidas's poetry. One theme is the corrupted nature of the present cosmic age, the kali yuga, which makes devotion the only effective means to salvation. Another pervasive theme is the power of God's name and its incomparable ability to rescue the devotee (**bhakta**). Finally, there are warnings to the hearers not to waste the opportunity of a human **birth**. Much of the poetry has an intimate personal quality, and it seems to reflect both the poet's despair at his own frailty and his eventual hope for salvation. From this general tone, the *Vinaya Patrika* is generally assumed to have been written in the later part of the poet's life, although it cannot be precisely dated.

Vindhya Mountains

Mountain range running from east to west in central India. Despite their modest height, they have traditionally served as the cultural dividing line between northern and southern India. The Vindhyas themselves were seen as an uncivilized and potentially dangerous place, inhabited by **ghosts**, **demons**, and tribal peoples; these dangers were exemplified by the untamed nature of its presiding **goddess**, **Vindhyavasini**.

Vindhyavasini

("dweller in the Vindhyas") Powerful form of the great **Goddess**. The **Vindhyas** are a mountain range in central India that are difficult to reach, inhabited by tribal peoples, and seen as a place at the margins of civilized society. As the goddess who dwells in that place, Vindhyavasini is equally marginal, often seen as a fierce and dangerous **deity** who demands **blood sacrifices** from her devotees (**bhakta**). The mythology of Vindhyavasini is associated with various places in the Vindhyas, but for centuries, her primary temple has been in the village of Vindhyachal near the city of Mirzapur in the state of **Uttar Pradesh**, although she is worshiped in other places in northern India. One of her charter myths identifies her as the goddess (in infant form) exchanged for the infant god **Krishna** and killed by Krishna's wicked uncle, **Kamsa**. After taunting Kamsa that the child he seeks has already escaped, she flies off and takes up residence in the Vindhyas. Since other accounts identify this goddess as **Bhadrakali**, this points to the fluidity of the Hindu pantheon, in which the renditions differ in the various accounts, according to the purpose of the writers. For further information see David R. Kinsley, *Hindu Goddesses*, 1986; and Cynthia Humes, "The Goddess of the Vindhyas in Banaras," in Cynthia Humes and Bradley R. Hertel, *Living Banaras*, 1993.

Vipaksha

In Indian **philosophy**, one of the parts in the accepted form of an inference (**anumana**). The accepted form of an inference has three parts: an assertion (**pratijna**), a reason (**hetu**), and examples (**drshtanta**); each of these three have their own constituent parts. The vipaksha is part of the third term, the examples, and is a negative example given to show that the claim made in the initial assertion is one that reflects the action of particular causes. For example, in the inference, "there is fire on the mountain because there is smoke on the mountain," the vipaksha could be "unlike a lake" since lakes are places with neither fire nor smoke, and thus shows that these conditions are not universally present (fire is found in mountains, but not in lakes). By convention, an inference also had to have a positive example, the **sapaksha**, to show that similar things happened in similar cases (i.e., that there were other cases in which there was both fire and smoke).

Viparitakhyati

("contrary discrimination") **Theory of error** propounded by the **Mimamsa** philosopher **Kumarila**, who lived in the seventh century C.E. All the theories of error aim to explain why people make errors in judgment, such as the stock example of mistaking the silvery flash of seashell for a piece of silver.

Like **Prabhakara** and the **Naiyayikas**, Kumarila believes that the simple judgments "that object is silvery" and "silver is silvery" are both true and indisputable. Kumarila also agrees with the Naiyayika that the error comes from a discrimination that is contrary to reality. His difference with the Naiyayikas comes with the latter's postulation of the **inherence**-relationship as connecting subjects and predicates ("silver color" and "silver"). Kumarila's theory is identity-and-difference (**bhedabhada**) in which all things are what they are and are not what they are not. Thus the perception (**pratyaksha**) of the shell on the beach would involve its similarities and differences from silveriness, combined with silver's similarities and differences from silveriness. One can combine the similarities and get a false judgment, or the differences and come up with a true one. As in the Naiyayika theory of error, the root cause for combining the similarities rather than the differences comes from karmic dispositions stemming from **avidya**, specifically the greed for silver that prompts us to look for such items of value. For further information see Bijayananda Kar,

The Theories of Error in Indian Philosophy, 1978; and Karl H. Potter (ed.), *Presuppositions of India's Philosophies*, 1972.

Vira

("hero") In the context of **tantra**, a secret, ritually based religious practice, the vira is one of the modes of ritual expression. The tantric "hero" is said to be one who not only partakes of the Five Forbidden Things (**panchamakara**)—wine, fish, meat, parched grain, and sexual intercourse—in their elemental forms, but also uses this inversion of normal moral rules as a way to affirm the ultimate unity of all things in the universe. Aspirants adopting a heroic mode will often **worship** a powerful but dangerous **deity**, in which the ultimate affirmation of this unity is to affirm one's identity with that deity. If one can do this successfully, it is believed to confer various powers, but if one fails it is said to lead to illness, insanity, or death. This is not a path without hazards, but through it the heroes quickly attain their desired goals.

Virabhadra

In Hindu mythology, a powerful being who is created by the god **Shiva** to humble the demigod **Daksha** and to destroy Daksha's **sacrifice**. Daksha gives his **daughter**, **Sati**, to marry Shiva, but later he feels that Shiva has not shown him proper respect. To humble Shiva, Daksha plans a great sacrifice and invites all the gods except Shiva. When Sati asks her father why he has done so, Daksha responds with a stream of abuse, excoriating Shiva as worthless and despicable. Humiliated by these public insults, Sati commits **suicide**—in some versions, by leaping into the sacrificial **fire**, and in others by withdrawing into a yogic trance and giving up her life.

In the most common version of Virabhadra's creation, Shiva is so enraged when he learns of Sati's death that he tears out two matted locks (**jata**) from his head and dashes them to the ground. One matted lock takes form as Virabhadra, and the second takes form as **Bhadrakali**, a powerful and terrifying form of the **Goddess**. Just as Virabhadra represents Shiva's destructive aspect, Bhadrakali represents the ferocious and dangerous side of the Goddess, in contrast with the gentle and loyal Sati. At Shiva's orders, the two demolish Daksha's sacrifice, scattering the guests and destroying the sacred fires, until Daksha finally repents and worships Shiva as the supreme **deity**. Although Virabhadra's actions in this story are destructive, he is and remains Shiva's servant, carrying out his divine master's commands, a mandate that ultimately upholds the created order.

Viragal

("Hero-stone") Stone erected in memory of a warrior, often the village headman, who perished in battle while defending the village cattle from pillage. Such stones can be found all over the **Deccan** region, and Deleury speculates that the origins of the Maharashtrian god **Vithoba** lay in such a deified hero, who was later assimilated into the pantheon as a form of **Vishnu**.

Viraha

("separation") Well-established poetic genre in classical **Sanskrit** poetry and in much of vernacular devotional (**bhakti**) poetry. The genre focuses on describing the pain resulting from the separation of lover and beloved, whether the separated lovers are two human beings or devotee (**bhakta**) and **deity**. Such separation is believed to bring on specific physical symptoms, which the poets describe in detail—lack of appetite, insomnia, inability to attend to daily life, or to think about anyone but the beloved. The sort of love felt in such separation is believed to engender an even more intense love for the beloved than love in union because the latter is sweetened by the presence of the beloved, whereas the former has to stand by itself.

Viramamunivar

Pseudonym of Father Constanzio Beschi (1680–1747), an Italian Jesuit who lived in **Tamil Nadu** for thirty-six years. Like many of the other early Jesuits, Beschi learned the local language and adopted the local way of life. As part of his missionary work, he translated parts of the Old and New Testament into literary Tamil, and his facility with the language and its poetic conventions make this work a significant milestone in later Tamil literature.

Viramitrodaya

One of the latest and the largest of the **nibandhas** ("collections"), compiled in the early seventeenth century by the scholar **Mitra Mishra**. The nibandhas were compendia of Hindu lore, in which the compilers culled references on a particular theme from the **Vedas**, **dharma literature**, **puranas**, and other authoritative religious texts, and then compiled these excerpts into a single volume. The *Viramitrodaya* is a massive compendium of Hindu lore, each of whose twenty-two sections is devoted to a particular aspect of Hindu life, such as daily practice, **worship**, gift-giving (**dana**), vows, pilgrimage, penances (**prayashchitta**), purification, death rites (**antyeshthi samskara**), law, and so forth, finally ending with liberation (**moksha**). Aside from citing the relevant scriptural passages, Mitra Mishra also provides extensive learned commentary, and his work became an important source for later legal interpretation, particularly in eastern India.

Virasana

One of the sitting postures (**asana**) described in commentaries to the **Yoga Sutras**; this is also one of the sitting postures in which **deities** are portrayed in Hindu iconography. As described in the commentaries to the Yoga Sutras, in this position one foot rests on the ground, under the opposite thigh, while the other foot rests on top of the opposite knee. In modern yoga manuals this posture is described quite differently, as a sitting posture with the legs folded back outside the body, with the feet pressed against the thighs and buttocks.

Virashaiva

("Heroic Shaivas") Another name for the **Lingayat** religious community, stemming from the Lingayat insistence that the god **Shiva** was the only real god. See **Lingayat**.

Virata

In the *Mahabharata*, the later of the two great Hindu epics, Virata is the king who shelters the five **Pandava** brothers, the epic's protagonists, during the year they spend incognito, following their twelve years of exile in the forest. This year is critical because according to the agreement that the Pandavas have made with their adversary, **Duryodhana**, if they are discovered during this year the cycle of exile and living incognito will begin again. Due to Virata's care and foresight the Pandavas are not discovered, even though Duryodhana has sent legions of spies to find them. During the Mahabharata war he continues to support the Pandavas and is eventually killed by the archery master **Drona**.

Visarjana

("dismissing") The sixteenth and last of the traditional **upacharas** ("offerings") given to a **deity** as part of **worship**, on the model of treating the deity as an honored guest. In this offering, the devotee (**bhakta**) gives the deity leave to go, as the concluding rite in worship. Although the word dismissal sounds presumptuous in any interaction with a deity, this term really refers to the words of parting that one would say to any departing guest. The underlying motive here, as for all the upacharas, is to show one's love for the deity and minister to the deity's needs.

Vishakhadatta

(6th c.) **Sanskrit** dramatist whose only surviving work is the play *Mudrarakshasa* ("**Rakshasa's** Ring"). The play is of some historical interest, for its major theme is the rise of **Chandragupta Maurya** (r. 321–297 B.C.E.), founder of the **Maurya dynasty**, although the play ascribes his success to the machinations of his cunning **brahmin** minister, **Chanakya**. The play paints the king as a weak figure, with the minister as the real power behind the throne, although in fairness to the historical king this portrayal seems inaccurate. The drama's plot is highly complex, as with many **Sanskrit** plays, but its climax comes when the principal characters are dramatically rescued from execution at the last moment. The play has been translated into English by Michael Coulson, and published in an anthology titled *Three Sanskrit Plays*, 1981.

Vishishthadvaita ("Qualified Non-Dualism") Vedanta

One of the branches of **Vedanta**, the philosophical school purporting to reveal the ultimate meaning and purpose (anta) of the **Vedas**, the oldest and most authoritative Hindu religious texts. Vishishthadvaita's greatest figure is the eleventh-century philosopher, **Ramanuja**, who was central to its formation, although he was building on earlier work. Ramanuja was convinced that **Brahman** or Supreme Reality was a personal **deity**, rather than an impersonal abstract principle, and he was also convinced that devotion (**bhakti**) was the most important form of religious practice. Vishishthadvaita Vedanta, his philosophical position, stressed both of these convictions and thus opposed the position of the **Advaita Vedanta** school, founded by the philosopher **Shankaracharya**.

The Advaita school upholds a philosophical position known as monism, which is the belief in a single impersonal Ultimate Reality, which they call Brahman. For Advaita proponents, reality is "nondual" (**advaita**)—that is, all things are nothing but the formless Brahman, despite the appearance of difference and diversity in the perceivable world. For the Advaitins, this assumption of diversity is a fundamental misunderstanding of the ultimate nature of things and a manifestation of **avidya**. Although often translated as "ignorance," avidya is better understood as the lack of genuine understanding, which ultimately causes human beings to be trapped in karmic bondage, reincarnation (**samsara**), and suffering. Since for the Advaitins the real problem is this mistaken understanding, this means that realization (**jnana**) was the best spiritual path to gain final liberation (**moksha**).

According to Ramanuja's formulation, the material world and selves have real and independent existence, although their existence is ultimately rooted in God, whom he identifies as **Vishnu**. The world comes from God in a process of **evolution** adapted from the **Samkhya** model, but since matter is unconscious, it is both similar to and different from God. In the same way, human beings share similarity to God in having God as their source, and difference from him in being subject to ignorance and suffering. For Ramanuja and his followers, God is not identical to Selves or the world, all of which are perceived as having real and independent existence. This doctrine of identity and difference makes the perceivable world real, in a sense that the Advaita proponents would never admit. This same contention of simultaneous identity and difference distinguishes Ramanuja's position from that of a later thinker, **Madhva**, whose **Dvaita Vedanta** stressed the great gulf between God and all other things. Given this difference in capacities between deity and devotee (**bhakta**), Ramanuja and his followers have stressed bhakti as the most efficacious means to salvation. Even after liberation the souls retain enough of a distinction

Vishnu as depicted in a granite carving, Hampi.

from God to make devotion possible; liberation is seen not as loss of identity, but as eternal communion with God. For further information see John Braisted Carman, *The Theology of Ramanuja*, 1974; and Sarvepalli Radhakrishnan and Charles A. Moore (eds.), *A Sourcebook in Indian Philosophy*, 1957.

Vishnu

("all-pervasive") Along with **Shiva** and the **Goddess**, one of the three most important **deities** in the Hindu pantheon. All three of these are notable for being almost unmentioned in the **Vedas**, the earliest Hindu religious texts, and the ascendancy of these three and the gradual eclipse of the Vedic gods points clearly to a definitive shift in Hindu religious life. Of the three, Vishnu has the most significant presence in the Vedas. Many of the hymns in which he is mentioned describe him as a helper to the storm-god **Indra**, the primary Vedic god, and one of Vishnu's epithets here is Upendra ("junior Indra"). Yet he also appears in some of the late hymns as an independent agent, who is associated with marvelous deeds for the good of the cosmos, such as taking three steps to measure out the universe. Vishnu is also associated with the **sun**, both in his ability to move through the **heavens**, and to fall on (and thus "observe") all things.

In the divine triad of **Brahma**-Vishnu-Shiva, Vishnu is identified as the sustainer or maintainer of the cosmos. One manifestation of this can be seen in a common creation myth, which begins with Vishnu lying on the back of his serpent couch, **Shesha**, in the primordial ocean at the time of cosmic dissolution (**pralaya**). A lotus sprouts from Vishnu's navel, which opens to reveal Brahma, the creator, who begins the work of creation. Vishnu presides over the creation, and when the time for dissolution comes again, the entire process reverses, and the universe is drawn back into Vishnu, who is thus seen as the source of all.

The other way that Vishnu sustains the cosmos is through the action of his **avatars** or incarnations, who come into the world to restore balance to a universe dangerously out of equilibrium, usually because of a **demon** grown disproportionately strong. There are ten generally reckoned avatars. The first four are in nonhuman forms: the **Fish avatar**, **Tortoise avatar**, **Boar avatar**, and **Man-Lion avatar**. The other six are in human form, often as sages or heroes: **Vamana avatar**, **Parashuram avatar**, **Rama avatar**, **Krishna avatar**, **Buddha avatar**, and **Kalki avatar**; the last has yet to come. In each of these cases, Vishnu takes form to avert some sort of disaster and to maintain the integrity of the cosmos. The doctrine of the avatars provided a mechanism to assimilate existing deities into the larger pantheon and to give them recognizable status of their own. Although most of the avatars are no longer objects of **worship** (the Boar and Man-Lion avatars each had a substantial following early in the common era), in much of northern India the worship of Rama and Krishna has largely eclipsed that of Vishnu himself, who has largely faded into the background. In southern India, Vishnu is still an important object of worship, particularly in the **Shrivaishnava** community. Aside from the doctrine of the avatars, important local deities have also been assimilated into the pantheon as forms of Vishnu; the most significant examples are **Jagannath**, **Venkateshvara**, and **Vithoba**.

In medieval Hinduism sectarian rivalry developed between **Vaishnavas** and **Shaivas**, with each claiming that their chosen deity (Vishnu and Shiva, respectively) was supreme. Although Vaishnavas see Vishnu as the supreme power in the universe, his mythic character and activity differ sharply from Shiva's. Whereas Shiva is associated with **ascetic** life and practices (**tapas**), and thus with the religious power generated by such practices, Vishnu's headdress is a crown, and his persona is that of an all-ruling king. Whereas Shiva destroys his mythic adversaries using raw power, from which all subtlety is absent, Vishnu more often triumphs through cunning, cleverness, and trickery. Each deity's adherents affirm their divinity as the preeminent power in the universe, from which all the other gods gain their power, and both are seen as gracious and loving to their devotees (**bhakta**).

Vishnuchittar

An epithet of the **Alvar** poet-saint **Periyalvar**. The Alvars were a group of twelve poet-saints who lived in southern India between the seventh and tenth centuries. All the Alvars were devotees (**bhakta**) of the god **Vishnu**, and their stress on passionate devotion (**bhakti**) to a personal god, conveyed through hymns sung in the **Tamil language**, transformed Hindu religious life. See **Periyalvar**.

Vishnu Purana

One of the eighteen traditional **puranas**, which were an important genre of **smrti** texts, and the repository of much of traditional Indian mythology. The smrtis or "remembered" texts were a class of literature that although deemed important, were considered less authoritative than the **shrutis** or "heard" texts. In brief, the shrutis denoted the **Vedas**, the oldest and most authoritative Hindu religious texts, whereas the smrtis included the *Mahabharata* and the *Ramayana*, the **dharma literature**, the **Bhagavad Gita**, and the puranas. The puranas are compendia of all types of sacred lore, from mythic tales to ritual instruction to exaltation of various sacred sites (**tirthas**) and actions. Most of the puranas are highly sectarian, and as this one's name clearly shows, it is focused on the **worship** of **Vishnu**. It gives an exhaustive account of Vishnu's mythic deeds—many of which have become the common mythic currency for many traditional Hindus—as well as instructions for how, where, and when Vishnu is to be worshiped.

Vishnuswami

("[He whose] Lord is **Vishnu**") According to tradition, the founder of the **Rudra Sampraday** of the **Vaishnava** ascetics. (The Rudra Sampraday is one of the four branches, "sampraday," of the **Bairagi Naga** ascetics, who are devotees (**bhakta**) of the god Vishnu; vaishnava refers to devotees of Vishnu.) Vishnuswami was an **ascetic**, whom some sources name as the **guru** of both **Jnaneshvar** and **Namdev**. As his name clearly shows, Vishnuswami was a Vaishnava, although other than this little is known about him. His ascetic line and its position as one of the four Vaishnava ascetic sampradays have been appropriated by the followers of **Vallabhacharya**, whose **Shuddadvaita**, or "Pure Monism," stresses the **worship** of **Krishna**, with **Radha** as his consort.

Vishuddha Chakra

In many schools of **yoga**, and in the secret, ritually based religious practice known as **tantra**, the vishuddha chakra is one of the six psychic centers (**chakras**) believed to exist in the **subtle body**. The subtle body is an alternate physiological system, believed to exist on a different plane than gross matter, but with certain correspondences to the material body. It is visualized as a set of six psychic centers, which are visualized as multipetaled lotus flowers running roughly along the course of the spine, connected by three vertical channels. Each of these chakras has important symbolic associations—with differing human capacities, with different subtle elements (**tanmatras**), and with different seed syllables (**bijaksharas**) formed from the letters of the **Sanskrit** alphabet, thus encompassing all sacred sound. Above and below these centers are the bodily abodes of **Shiva** (awareness) and **Shakti** (power), the two divine principles through which the entire universe has come into being. The underlying assumption behind this concept of the subtle body is thus the homology of macrocosm and microcosm, an essential Hindu idea since the time of the mystical texts known as the **Upanishads**.

The six chakras are traditionally enumerated from the bottom up, and the vishuddha chakra is the fifth. It is visualized as a sixteen-petaled lotus, located in the region of the throat. The petals each contain a seed syllable formed from a letter of the Sanskrit alphabet, in this case all sixteen of the Sanskrit vowels, the essential connecting elements for any meaningful speech. On a symbolic level, the vishuddha chakra is associated with the human capacity for speech and respiration. It is also identified as the bodily seat for the subtle element of **space** (**akasha**), through which hearing is believed to take place. For further information see Arthur Avalon (Sir John Woodroffe), *Shakti and Shakta*, 1978; and Philip S. Rawson, *The Art of Tantra*, 1973.

Vishva Hindu Parishad

("World Hindu Organization," hereafter VHP) Modern Hindu religious organization affiliated with the **Rashtriya Svayamsevak Sangh** (RSS), a conservative Hindu organization whose express purpose is to provide the leadership cadre for a revitalized Hindu India. The VHP was formed in 1964, when RSS leader **Madhav Sadashiv Golwalkar** met in Bombay with a group of Hindu religious leaders. Their immediate concern was the upcoming visit of Pope Paul VI to India, which they interpreted as a concealed attempt to convert Hindus to Christianity, and resolved to oppose by forming an organization dedicated to the propagation of Hinduism. For the next fifteen years, the VHP focused its attention on countering Christian missionary efforts in northeastern India, with little fanfare and little impact on the public consciousness.

A watershed in the VHP's public image came in 1982, following the conversion of some untouchables to Islam in the **Tamil Nadu** village of Minakshipuram. The VHP used this much-publicized event as evidence that Hindu identity was endangered and countered it by launching a series of innovative public actions, first in Tamil Nadu, but later extending throughout the entire nation. The VHP's renewed activity corresponded with a more activist bent in its parent organization, the RSS, as well as the decision by the **Bharatiya Janata Party** (BJP), a political organization that is also an RSS affiliate, to assume a more militantly Hindu identity. Many of the VHP's national campaigns coincided with national or state elections, and many of these centered on the campaign to build a temple to the god **Rama** in the city of **Ayodhya**, at the site claimed to be Rama's birthplace. The site on which they proposed to build the temple was occupied by a Muslim mosque, the **Babri Masjid**, which the VHP claimed had been built only after tearing down the original Rama temple. This temple campaign thus carried powerful images of past oppression, as well as the assertiveness of a renascent Hindu identity. The VHP's activism has enormously boosted the BJP's political fortunes, and helped make it the dominant political party through much of northern India.

The VHP's activism has generated sharply contrasting emotions throughout India. Proponents point to its long record of social service and its role in helping strengthen and define a modern Hindu identity. Detractors point to its disregard for the niceties of law, which was epitomized by the destruction of the Babri Masjid in December 1992, its often vitriolic anti-Muslim rhetoric, and its ultimate control by the RSS, despite its separate institutional identity. Other critics have censured the VHP for attempting to declare certain "required" Hindu rites as antithetical to the Hindu tradition and for attempting to define and control the nature of "Hinduism." Other critics question the organization's claim to speak for all Hindus, noting that its real power lies in the hands of **brahmins** and other privileged classes; these critics see the VHP as an organization designed to conceal its true purpose, the maintenance of upper-class influence and privilege. For further information see Walter

K. Andersen and Shridhar D. Damle, *The Brotherhood in Saffron*, 1987; James Warner Björkman, *Fundamentalism, Revivalists, and Violence in South Asia*, 1988; Tapan Basu et al., *Khaki Shorts and Saffron Flags*, 1993; Lise McKean, *Divine Enterprise*, 1996; and Christophe Jaffrelot, *The Hindu Nationalist Movement in India*, 1996.

Vishvakarma

("doing all things") A minor **deity** whose mythic roles include being the architect of the gods; creator of innumerable handicrafts, ornaments, and weapons; the finest sculptor; and the inventor of the aerial chariots used by the gods. He is the patron and paradigm for all the skilled crafts in which materials are shaped and formed, and in particular he is said to have fixed the canons for carving images of the gods. According to one story, Vishvakarma's **daughter**, **Sanjna**, is married to **Surya**, the **sun**, but because of the sun's radiance cannot bear to be with him. Vishvakarma takes the sun to his workshop and trims off enough of his effulgence so that Sanjna can bear his brightness. He then shapes the cut-off pieces of the sun into the god **Vishnu's** discus (**Sudarshana**), the god **Shiva's** trident (**trishul**), various other divine weapons, and the **Pushpak Viman**, the most famous of the aerial chariots.

Vishvakarma is sometimes identified with **Tvashtr**, the workman of the gods in the **Vedas**, the oldest Hindu religious texts. Yet it seems that these are two different deities, homologized to each other through their common function. Tvashtr's name means "builder of carriages," and this seems to have been his primary function, although he is also noted for crafting the weapons of the gods, especially the mace with which the storm-god **Indra** slays the serpent **Vrtra**. Still, his name seems to indicate that his major function is in building carriages, which is believed to be highly significant in a Vedic context, since many Vedic hymns mention the use of military chariots. Vishvakarma, on the other hand, has much more wide-ranging skills, and this would seem to indicate that the two are not the same deity.

Vishvamitra

In Hindu mythology, one of the Seven Sages whose names mark exogamous clan "lineages" (**gotra**; in exogamous clans, members marry outside their own clan); the others are **Gautama**, **Bharadvaja**, **Kashyapa**, **Bhrgu**, **Atri**, and **Vasishtha**. All **brahmins** are believed to be descended from these seven sages, with each family taking the name of its progenitor as its gotra name. In modern times, these gotra divisions are still important because marriage within the gotra is forbidden. After her marriage, the new bride adopts her husband's gotra as part of her new identity.

Vishvamitra is most famous for his long-standing feud with the sage Vasishtha, which causes numerous confrontations. The feud begins as a result of the difference in status between **kshatriyas** and brahmins. Vishvamitra is a king, who once stops with a host of retainers at the forest **ashram** of the brahmin Vasishtha. Upon asking for food, Vishvamitra is amazed at the ability of Vasishtha's **cow**, the **Kamadhenu**, to provide food for everyone. Vishvamitra first tries to buy the Kamadhenu, then tries to take it by force, but his minions are defeated by the **magic** powers generated by Vasishtha's **tapas** (**ascetic** practices). Vishvamitra finally admits defeat and begins to do ascetic practices to generate power of his own. Two of their most celebrated clashes are over King **Trishanku** and his **son, Harishchandra**; in each case the real issue is the mutual antipathy of these two sages. See also **marriage prohibitions.**

Vishvanath

Form of the god **Shiva**, in his manifestation as the "Lord of the Universe" at the

Vishvanath Temple

Vishvanath temple in **Benares**. Shiva is present at Vishvanath in the form of a **linga**, the pillar-shaped image that is his symbolic form; the Vishvanath linga is one of the twelve **jyotirlingas**, a network of sites deemed especially sacred to Shiva, and at which **Shiva** is uniquely present. Benares, or **Varanasi**, is one of the most sacred cities in India; it is considered particularly sacred to Shiva, and of all the Shiva temples there, Vishvanath is the most important. The original temple was destroyed by the Moghul emperor **Aurangzeb**, who built a mosque on the site, and the only remaining part of the original temple is the **Gyan Vapi** ("well of knowledge"), into which the original Shiva linga was reportedly cast (to save it from desecration by Aurangzeb's soldiers). The present temple was built in 1776 by the **Maratha** queen **Ahalya Bai Holkar**, on a site adjoining the original temple. It was later roofed with gold by Maharaja Ranjit Singh of Lahore, and thus one of its nicknames is the "Golden Temple."

Even in preceding centuries the history and proximity of the Vishvanath

Dancer displaying the vismaya hasta.

temple and Aurangzeb's mosque made for delicate relations between the Hindu and Muslim communities, and like many northern Indian cities Benares has seen its share of bloodshed between these two communities. In recent times the destruction of the original Vishvanath temple has been taken up as a political issue by the **Vishva Hindu Parishad** (VHP), a Hindu activist organization calling for the "return" of this and other northern Indian sites by force if necessary. The VHP's presence and activity have significantly escalated tensions between Hindus and Muslims as a whole. Given the political gains that these confrontational strategies have brought, it seems likely that they will continue in the future and that the Vishvanath temple will be a site connected with conflict.

Vishva Nirmala Dharam

Religious organization founded by the modern Hindu teacher **Nirmala Devi** (b. 1923), to propagate her teachings throughout the world.

Vishvedevas

This name can either be construed as referring to all the gods, based on the term's literal meaning ("all the gods"), or it can refer to a group of **deities** reckoned as the **sons** of **Vishva**, the **daughter** of the divine sage **Daksha**. The number of sons differs according to different texts and is reckoned at either ten or thirteen. The Vishvedevas are especially worshiped at the memorial rites for the dead known as **shraddhas**, although the *Manu Smrti*, one of the authoritative texts in the **dharma literature**, prescribes **offerings** to them every day. These prescribed daily offerings are said to have been their reward for having performed particularly harsh **asceticism** (**tapas**).

Vismaya ("surprise") Hasta

In Indian **dance**, **sculpture**, and ritual, a particular hand **gesture** (**hasta**), in which the forearm and the fingers are pointing upward, with the back of the hand turned toward the viewer. This particular hasta is meant to convey any sort of surprise, including wonder and astonishment.

Vital Winds

General term to designate the five internal winds collectively known as **prana**, through which all human physiological processes are believed to occur.

Vithoba

Presiding **deity** of the temple with the same name in the city of **Pandharpur** in the state of **Maharashtra**; other epithets for Vithoba include Vitthala and Pandurang. Vithoba was originally a local deity—according to some theories, a deified hero—who has been assimilated into the larger Hindu pantheon as a form of the god **Vishnu**. According to the temple's charter myth, Vishnu comes to Pandharpur drawn by the filial devotion of a young boy named Pundalika. When Vishnu arrives Pundalika is massaging his father's feet, and when Vishnu asks for the hospitality due to any guest, Pundalika stops only long enough to throw a brick over his shoulder, to give the god a place to stand out of the mud. Impressed that Pundalika's devotion to his parents supersedes even his devotion to God, Vishnu becomes rooted to that spot and has remained there ever since; Vithoba's image shows him with his hands on his hips (still waiting, perhaps, for Pundalika). Aside from this story, Vithoba has surprisingly little mythic history, although he has become an important regional deity.

Vithoba is most famous for the activities of his devotees (**bhakta**), the **Varkari Panth** religious community, who make pilgrimages to Pandharpur twice a year. Pandharpur sits in the **Bhima River** valley on the edge of the Maharashtra-**Karnataka** border, and pilgrims come from all directions. Individual pilgrims travel in small groups called **dindis**, often made up of people from the same neighborhood or locality. The dindis are organized into larger groups known as **palkhis**, each of which is associated with one of the Varkari poet-saints, and which is led by a **palanquin** (palkhi) bearing the sandals of that saint. Each palkhi departs from a place associated with its particular saint—for example, the palkhi of **Jnaneshvar** leaves from the town of **Alandi** in which he lived, and thus he and all the other saints are still symbolically journeying to Pandharpur twice a year. Each of these palkhis travels a prescribed route, and pilgrims time their departure and their travel to arrive in Pandharpur on the same day—the eleventh day (**ekadashi**) in the bright half of **Ashadh** (June–July) in the summer, and the eleventh day in the bright half of **Kartik** (October–November) in the fall. Pilgrims compare their journey to that of a small stream merging with other streams, gradually forming a mighty river converging on Pandharpur. During their journey pilgrims sing the devotional songs composed by these poet-saints, among them **Jnaneshvar**, **Namdev**, **Eknath**, **Tukaram**, **Chokamela**, **Gora**, **Janabai**, and **Bahina Bai**. In this way, the pilgrims are emulating the saints before them, both by treading in their physical footsteps and by singing their songs of devotion. Although the pilgrimage ends with the entry to Pandharpur and the **worship** of Vithoba, the most important part is the journey itself. For more information on Vithoba and the Varkari sect, see G. A. Deleury, *The Cult Of Vithoba*, 1960; I. B. Karve, "On the Road," *Journal of Asian Studies*, Vol. 22 No. 1, 1962; and Digambar Balkrishna. Mokashi, *Palkhi: An Indian Pilgrimage*, 1987.

Vitthala

Common epithet of **Vithoba**, the presiding **deity** of a famous temple at **Pandharpur** in the state of **Maharashtra**. The name *Vitthala* is a more literary form, and according to **Deleury**, the oldest attested name for the Pandharpur deity. See **Vithoba**.

Vitthalnath

(r. 1566–1585) Second **guru** of the **Pushti Marg** (a religious community), which was founded by his father, **Vallabhacharya**. Vitthalnath continued the consolidation of the Pushti Marg, in particular the organization of its rites, and in fostering the composition of songs and poetry to accompany them. According to tradition, the eight poets known as the **ashtachap** were all active during his tenure, although four of them are more closely associated with his father. The four poets associated with Vitthalnath were clearly members of the Pushti Marg, for among their poetry can be found hymns praising him and his leadership. He was succeeded by his **son Gokulnath**, under whose direction the lives of these and other saints were finally written down, with each being given a **Vallabhite** emphasis.

Vivaha ("uplift") Samskara

Traditionally, the fifteenth of the life-cycle ceremonies (**samskaras**), in which a man and woman became husband and wife. Except for those rare individuals who remained lifelong celibates (**naisthika brahmacharin**), marriage was an essential element in the life of every man (and woman), since the children procreated through marriage allowed him to retire one of the **three debts**, this one to the **ancestral spirits** (pitr). One mark of the importance given to marriage can be seen in the literal translation of the word *vivaha*—it signifies that by which a man is "uplifted" and made complete. Given the stress on family in Indian society, marriage has also been a gravely important matter, and for many Indians, it remains the most important day of their life. The **dharma literature** underlines the importance of marriage by cataloging eight different forms. See also **marriage**, **eight classical forms**.

Vivarana Advaita

One of the later schools of **Advaita Vedanta**, a philosophical school, the greatest figure in which was **Shankaracharya**. The Advaita school upholds a philosophical position known as monism, which is the belief in a single impersonal Ultimate Reality, which they call **Brahman**. For Advaita proponents, reality is "nondual" (**advaita**)—that is, all things are nothing but the formless Brahman, despite the appearance of difference and diversity in the perceivable world. For the Advaitins, this assumption of diversity is a fundamental misunderstanding of the ultimate nature of things and a manifestation of **avidya**. Although often translated as "ignorance," avidya is better understood as the lack of genuine understanding, which ultimately causes human beings to be trapped in karmic bondage, reincarnation (**samsara**), and suffering. Because the real problem for the Advaitins is this mistaken understanding, this means that realization (**jnana**) was the best spiritual path to gain final liberation (**moksha**).

The Vivarana Advaita school is based on the thought of **Padmapada** (9th c.), one of Shankaracharya's disciples, but takes its name from a commentary written by the thirteenth-century **Prakashatman**. The latter is traditionally a disciple of Padmapada's, but this seems problematic. As with the **Bhamati** school, the Vivarana school took definitive stands on several points on which Shankaracharya had remained silent. One of these was on the locus of ignorance, which the Vivarana school describes as being located in Brahman. In explaining how this can be, since it seems to compromise the integrity of Brahman, the Vivarana Advaitins invoke the theory of **reflectionism** to explain the apparent difference between Brahman and the Self, although, in fact, the Selves are identical with Brahman. Their position seems based more than anything on an uncompromising affirmation of Brahman as the sole "reality," in which anything that exists must belong to it.

Vivartavada

A philosophical model used to explain the relationship between the Ultimate Reality or Realities and the perceivable world; this model describes the world as an illusory transformation of this reality. The vivartavada model is unique to the **Advaita Vedanta** philosophical school. The Advaitins are proponents of a **causal model** called **satkaryavada**, which assumes that effects already exist in their causes, and that when these effects appear, they represent transformations (**parinama**) of those causes. The classic example is the transformation of milk to curds, butter, and clarified butter. According to asatkarya's proponents, each of these effects was already present in the cause and emerges from it through a natural transformation of that cause.

The Advaita school upholds a philosophical position known as monism, which is the belief that a single Ultimate Reality lies behind all things and that all things are merely differing forms of that reality. Advaita proponents exemplify this belief in their claim that reality is nondual (**advaita**)—that is, that all things are "actually" nothing but the formless, unqualified **Brahman**, despite the appearance of difference and diversity in the world. The Advaitins' belief that an effect already exists in its cause comes from the principle that all things in the universe ultimately depend on Brahman as a first cause. At the same time the Advaitins are unwilling to admit that Brahman ever undergoes actual change because this would nullify its eternal and unchanging nature. For this reason, they speak of an illusory transformation (vivartavada). For the Advaitins, Brahman never really changes, because it is eternal and thus unchanging; the apparent changes are only illusory, based on human ignorance through changing patterns of superimposition (**adhyasa**). In this way the Advaitins can maintain the transcendence of Brahman and at the same time account for the (apparent) changes in the phenomenal world.

This position is contested by proponents of another model, which describes the perceivable world as an actual transformation of this single reality. This position is espoused by proponents of the **Samkhya**, **Vishishthadvaita Vedanta**, and **Bhedabhada** philosophical schools, who like the Advaitins are also proponents of satkaryavada. Each of these three schools believes that the world as perceived is real, that it has some single ultimate source behind it, and that this first principle undergoes a real transformation by which the world comes into being. This parinama relationship allows these schools to explain the phenomenal world but in a way that compromises the transcendence of these first principles by making them part of the world. Philosophically, their difficulties come in describing how the transcendent can become mundane, and then become transcendent again.

Vivasvan

("shining forth") Epithet of the god **Surya**, the **Sun**. See **Surya**.

Vivekananda, Swami

(b. Narendranath Datta 1863–1902) Best-known disciple of the Bengali mystic **Ramakrishna** and also the first Hindu missionary to the West. Narendranath had received a good education and had originally intended to be a lawyer; on meeting Ramakrishna he was initially skeptical and questioning but in the course of a year became transformed. After Ramakrishna's death he spent several years roaming through India, gradually coming to the conclusion that religious life had to address India's material needs as well as its spiritual ones. Vivekananda is most famous for his address to the First **World Parliament of Religions** in Chicago in 1893, in which Hinduism—in its rational, Vedantic form—was first seriously received by his Western hearers. For the next four years, he lectured in America and in England and returned to India to widespread acclaim. He devoted the rest of his short life to fostering the **Ramakrishna Mission**, a religious organization intended to promote social uplift as well as religious education. For further information see Christopher Isherwood, *Ramakrishna and His Disciples*, 1965; Swami Vivekananda, *The Complete Works of Swami Vivekananda*, 1970; and George M. Williams, "Swami Vivekananda," and "The Ramakrishna Movement: A Study in Religious Change," both in Robert D. Baird (ed.), *Religion in Modern India*, 1998.

Vraj

Variant form of the region known as **Braj**. This is the land in which the god **Krishna** is believed to have lived, located in the southwestern part of the state of **Uttar Pradesh** just south of Delhi, the national capital. See **Braj**.

Vrat

Term denoting a religious vow, usually thought to be derived from the verb meaning "to choose." As religious observances, vrats are an important part of modern Hindu life. They may refer to religious practices performed once a **year** with particular festivals, such as the vrat performed on **Shivaratri**, or to more regular religious observances, such as those connected to the monthly lunar **calendar** (e.g., the **ekadashi** rites) or those performed on the day of the **week** associated with a particular patron **deity**. The specific prescriptions for these vrats vary widely, but there are several common features. They usually involve modification of diet—sometimes through fasting (**upavasa**), and other times by **eating** or avoiding certain types of food. Another constant feature is **worship** of the presiding deity. Part of this worship usually involves reading or hearing the vrat's charter myth, which tells how the vrat was established, how one should perform it, and what sort of benefits it brings. Vrats connected with festivals are performed by all sorts of people, but weekly vrats (such as the **Santoshi Ma Vrat**) are most often performed by married **women** to promote the health, safety, and prosperity of their families. Although such

weekly vrats are theoretically voluntary, they have become an expected element in women's religious life, through which women by their sacrifices can safeguard their family's welfare. For further consideration of women's rites, see Mary McGee, "Desired Fruits: Motive And Intention in the Votive Rites of Hindu Women," in Julia Leslie, ed., *Roles and Rituals for Hindu Women*, 1991; and Doranne Jacobson and Susan S. Wadley, *Women in India*, 1992.

Vratya

In the **Atharva Veda**, one of the earliest Hindu religious texts, the vratyas were a particular class of vagrant ascetics who were priests of a non-Vedic fertility cult. Not much is known about them because there are no other sources, but they were clearly outside the Vedic cult and thus looked down upon. In later times, the word is used to designate a person who has lost **caste** through nonobservance of one of the necessary **samskaras** (life-cycle ceremonies).

Vrindavan

Variant form of **Brindavan**, the village in southeastern part of the state of **Uttar Pradesh** in which the god **Krishna** is believed to have lived from infancy to adolescence. See **Brindavan**.

Vrtra

("obstruction") The name of the **demon** killed by the storm-god **Indra** in one of the hymns from the **Rg Veda** (1.32), the oldest Hindu religious text. In this hymn Vrtra is described as a serpent obstructing the free flow of waters, hence his name. The action in this hymn is one of Indra's defining deeds, in which he destroys the serpent, cuts it into pieces, and releases the waters to run free. Some interpreters inclined to read the **Vedas** as historical record have seen in this hymn the breaching of the dams constructed by the **Indus Valley civilization** by the incoming **Aryans**, but there is little proof that such an incident ever happened.

Vyakarana

("analysis") One of the six **Vedangas**. These were the auxiliary branches of knowledge connected with the **Vedas**, the oldest Hindu religious texts, and all the Vedangas were associated with the use of the Vedas. In its essence, vyakarana is the study of **Sanskrit** grammar, which was obviously essential to understanding the Vedic texts (which were written in Sanskrit). Vyakarana's role as the gatekeeper to the Sanskrit language made grammar the queen of the traditional learned sciences, and in many contexts it is what is meant by the term *vidya* ("knowledge"). Aside from vyakarana, the other Vedangas are **shiksha** (correct pronunciation), **chandas** (Sanskrit prosody), **kalpa** (ritual instructions), **nirukta** (etymology), and **jyotisha** (auspicious times for sacrifices).

Vyakhyana ("teaching") Mudra

In Indian **dance**, **sculpture**, and ritual, a particular symbolic hand **gesture** (**mudra**), in which the tips of the thumb and index finger are touching, with the rest of the fingers extended, and the palm facing the viewer. This is the hand gesture used to signify explanation or exposition; for this reason, it is also known as the **sandarshana** ("expositing") **mudra**. Since the teaching gesture indicates a person of higher spiritual attainment, it is also known as the **chin** ("consciousness") **mudra**.

Vyana

In traditional Indian physiology, one of the five bodily "**winds**" considered to be responsible for basic bodily functions, the others being **prana**, **apana**, **udana**, and **samana**. Unlike all the others, which are given specific locations in the body, the vyana **wind** is believed to pervade throughout the body, to keep things moving and mixed together.

A vyas, or stage director, at a performance of the Ram Lila, Bombay.

Vyapti

("pervasion") In classical Indian **philosophy**, vyapti is the key condition determining the validity of an inference (**anumana**). The accepted form of an inference has three terms: An assertion (**pratijna**) containing the thing to be proved, a reason (**hetu**) containing evidence to support the assertion, and supporting examples (**drshtanta**). In the stock example "there is fire on the mountain, because there is smoke on the mountain," the assertion is that there is fire, and the reason is that there is smoke—with the underlying assumption that smoke invariably accompanies fire. In a valid inference, the reason accounts for every case of the thing to be proven; vyapti, or pervasion, is the term for this invariable association between cause and effect. For further information see Karl H. Potter (ed.), *Presuppositions of India's Philosophies*, 1972.

Vyas

In the traditional **Ram Lila** (name given to any public dramatic presentation of the *Ramayana*, the earlier of the two great Hindu epics), vyas is the name given to the stage directors. The Ramnagar Ram Lila is the longest, most elaborate, and arguably the oldest of these dramas. In the Ramnagar Ram Lila, one vyas is responsible for the **svarups**, the **brahmin** boys who are playing the parts of the divinities, and who are considered manifestations of the **deities** when they are "in character." The other vyas is responsible for the rest of the cast. Between them they shift the action between chorus and cast, give the actors minute directions for their acting, and prompt them when they forget their lines. As such, they are visible agents themselves and an important part of the Ram Lila.

Vyasa

In Hindu mythology, a sage who is traditionally considered to be the author of the *Mahabharata*, the later of the two great **Sanskrit** epics. Vyasa is the **son** of the sage **Parashara** as a result of his dalliance with the ferrywoman **Satyavati**. Later in life Satyavati marries King **Shantanu** but only after extracting the promise that their children will rule, instead of Shantanu's eldest son, **Bhishma**. Satyavati's first son dies in childhood, and the second dies after his marriage but before having any children. In her desperation to preserve Shantanu's line, Satyavati calls on Vyasa to sleep with her younger son's wives, **Ambika** and **Ambalika**. According to tradition Vyasa is very ugly, and both of the **women** involuntarily react when Vyasa appears in her bed. Ambalika turns pale, causing her son, **Pandu**, to be born with an unnaturally pale complexion, and Ambika covers her eyes, causing her son, **Dhrtarashtra**, to be born blind. Vyasa also has sexual relations with Ambika's maidservant, who gives herself to him willingly, and from her is born **Vidura**. The descendants of Pandu and Dhrtarashtra are the **Pandavas** and **Kauravas**, respectively, who are the two warring factions whose enmity drives the *Mahabharata*. Thus Vyasa is not only the author of the *Mahabharata*, but also the source of the two families whose struggle is described in it.

Water

One of the five elements in traditional Indian **cosmology**, the others being **earth**, **fire**, **wind**, and **akasha**. In some philosophical schools, each of the elements is paired with one of the senses; here water is associated with taste. Within the body, water is also associated with certain bodily functions, especially reproduction (involving the mixing of fluids) and the elimination of fluid wastes.

Wednesday

(Budhvar) The fourth **day** of the **week**, the presiding **planet** of which is **Mercury** (Budh). Although not inauspicious, the day has few strong associations and is not linked to the **worship** of any major **deity**. The planet Mercury is seen as an auspicious but weak planet, based on its small size and its quick rotation around the **sun**.

Week, Structure of

The Hindu week has seven days, just like the European **calendar**. Each of the days has a presiding planet, is associated with one or more presiding **deities**, and (in keeping with the general Indian attitude toward time) is deemed more or less auspicious. The most unlucky days are **Tuesday** and **Saturday**, associated respectively with the **planets Mars** and **Saturn**. **Monday** (the **moon**), **Thursday** (**Jupiter**), and **Friday** (**Venus**) are usually regarded as auspicious days since these are judged to be benevolent and powerful planets. **Sunday** (the **sun**) and **Wednesday** (**Mercury**) have no strong associations, because although

these bodies are seen as benevolent, they are also seen as relatively weak in their influence.

West Bengal

Modern Indian state. It was formed after Indian independence in 1947, after the partition of the state of Bengal into West Bengal and West Pakistan, the latter now known as Bangladesh. Most of the state lies in the lowland of the **Ganges** River delta, although in the north, Darjeeling extends into the **Himalayas**. West Bengal's capital, Calcutta, was the administrative center of British India until the beginning of the twentieth century. It was also a hotbed of anti-British resistance and has remained one of India's great artistic and intellectual centers. West Bengal has a number of important religious sites: **Kalighat**, in the heart of Calcutta, and **Dakshineshwar**, **Tarakeshvar**, **Tarapith**, and **Navadvip**. For general information about West Bengal and all the regions of India, an accessible reference is Christine Nivin et al., *India*, 8th ed., Lonely Planet, 1998.

West Indies

A cluster of Caribbean islands with a significant Hindu **diaspora population**. As in many other cases, they were originally brought to the West Indies as indentured agricultural laborers, particularly on the sugar plantations, but have now lived there so long that they have become a part of the local community. On some of the islands, particularly Trinidad, Hindus have constructed temples and established sacred sites (**tirthas**) there, as a way of connecting their religious lives to their local environment.

White Yajur Veda

Along with the **Black Yajur Veda**, this is one of the two major forms of the Yajur Veda, one of the oldest Hindu religious texts. The major difference between these two forms comes from the

Women carry water from the lake in a wedding procession in the town of Udaipur.

differing placement of explanatory notes on the Vedic mantras and their significance. The "White" Yajur Veda gathers these notes into an appendix known as a **Brahmana**—namely, the **Shatapatha Brahmana**, which gives its name to the second major stratum of Vedic texts. In contrast, the four recensions of the Black Yajur Veda include these notes in the text itself.

Widows

Given the traditional assumption that a Hindu woman's central role is as a wife and mother, becoming a widow is deemed the worst fate that can befall a woman and is seen as the karmic fruition of some ghastly former deed. Because the underlying assumption of the **marriage ceremony** is that the bride's identity becomes assimilated to the groom's, a woman without a husband was seen as having lost her identity. Furthermore, because she had already taken on her dead husband's identity, remarriage was not an option for her. Immediately after her husband's death a woman was supposed to remove all the symbols of a married woman—rubbing the red vermilion from the part in her **hair**, breaking her glass bangles, and in southern India, cutting the thread on her **mangal sutra**. For the rest of her life, she was forbidden to wear jewelry, colored clothing, or other bodily adornments, was supposed to keep her hair cropped short, and was supposed to devote herself to religious acts for the benefit of her dead husband. Because she had been widowed, she was also considered an unlucky and inauspicious person, banned from any and all auspicious events, living out her life doing the drudge work in the household. In certain parts of India, it was common practice to burn a widow on her husband's funeral pyre, a rite known as **sati**, although there were many other regions in which this practice was unheard of.

In real life, there was considerable variation on this grim picture. The most significant factors were a woman's age at the time she was widowed, whether she had children, and the social status of her husband's family. A woman widowed in old age would likely continue as matriarch of the family, a young widow with

sons would retain family status through her children, while even a **child widow** in a wealthy family could have a fairly comfortable life, although subject to numerous restrictions. Where one or another of these factors was lacking, then a widow's position would be much more precarious, and there is no doubt that in earlier times many widows led very difficult lives. Even in modern times a woman whose husband dies at a young age is often considered to be inauspicious, and thus a source of bad fortune. Ameliorating the condition of widows was one of the major goals of nineteenth-century Hindu reformers, and it has become more common for widows to remarry, although some of the most traditionally minded people do not accept this.

Wind

One of the five elements in traditional Indian **cosmology**, the others being **earth**, **fire**, **water**, and **akasha**. In some philosophical schools, each of the elements is paired with one of the five senses; here wind is associated with touch. The various "**vital winds**" (**prana**) inside the body are also associated with a number of bodily functions, including respiration and circulation.

Witchcraft

The existence of witchcraft is generally accepted in many segments of contemporary Hindu culture, even by many "modern" urban Hindus. The root forces behind witchcraft are malevolence, envy, and greed, through which some people try to harm others or to ruin what they have gained. Witches may work through spells, through the evil eye (**nazar**), or through pronouncing **curses** on others. Pregnant **women** and young children are thought to be particularly susceptible to their powers, and these parties are also deemed particularly likely to be cursed, because the envy over their good fortune is said to excite a witch's passion. The appropriate counteraction is to perform various **rites of protection**, which will safeguard the person from being affected. Those afflicted by witchcraft may exhibit this as an unusually persistent illness or as strange behavior; for these people, stronger remedies are needed. As Sudhir Kakar masterfully shows, the language of **possession** and exorcism can be interpreted as an "idiom" (using traditional Indian cultural categories) for what modern psychiatrists might call the diagnosis and treatment of mental illness. For further information see Sudhir Kakar, *Shamans, Mystics, and Doctors*, 1991; and David F. Pocock, "The Evil Eye," in T. N. Madan (ed.), *Religion in India*, 1991.

Women

In the **dharma literature**, women from all social groups were considered at the same ritual level as **shudras**—they could not undergo a second birth, were forbidden to hear the **Vedas**, were forbidden to perform certain religious rites, and in many places could not own property or resources, except by extension through their husbands. At the same time, women played (and play) an immensely important part in Hindu religious life, as **daughters**, mothers, wives, and patrons. According to the traditional dharma literature women had their own special role to play, based on their status as women. See also **stridharma**.

Woodroffe, Sir John

(1865–1936) Calcutta High Court Justice who also, under the pseudonym of Arthur Avalon, translated and published works on **tantra**, a secret, ritually based religious practice. Woodroffe was one of the earliest European exponents of tantra as a coherent religious path and served as an apologist for the seemingly "impure" or "immoral" ritual acts described in the texts. In his expositions of the tantras, Woodroffe was trying to convince a dual audience, both of whom were horrified at the licentiousness described in the tantric texts, which involve violating deeply embedded taboos on nonvegetarian food, consumption of alcohol, and illicit sexuality. On the one hand, Woodroffe was addressing the British, who were the political masters of the time, and on the other, educated Indians, many of whom would have preferred to dismiss the tantras as an aberration. His publications and lectures were instrumental in helping make tantrism respectable, although more careful scholarly work has been done since that time.

World Parliament of Religions

Meeting in Chicago in 1893 to which representatives from major world religions were invited, including Asian religions. It marks a watershed in the Euro-American conception of non-Christian religions, in which they were no longer seen as simple idolatry but taken seriously as genuine religious paths. It is also notable that many mainline Christian churches were not represented there, and that the main Christian presence came from historically black churches. One of the Parliament's highlights was the address by **Swami Vivekananda**, in which Hinduism—in its rational, Vedantic form—was first seriously received by his Western hearers. Vivekananda's presence was charismatic enough that he spent the next four years living in America and in 1897 founded the **Vedanta Society**.

Worship

Two separate words can be used to describe Hindu worship, with two groups of assumptions that come with it. The first and most common act of worship is called **darshan** ("seeing"), in which devotees (**bhakta**) view the image of the **deity**, and believe that the deity is also looking at them. Darshan is thus an interaction between deity and devotee, an exchange of glances that carries understanding. Worship involving **offerings** and objects usually falls under the rubric of the word **Puja** ("homage").

Worship of Tools

A rite traditionally performed on the festival of **Dussehra** by members of certain artisan groups. This festival has two different charter myths, both of which mark the triumph of good over evil. It is celebrated as the day that the god **Rama** slew the demon **Ravana**, and is also associated with the triumph of the **Goddess** over a **demon** named **Mahishasura**. For the artisans, such **worship** ritually marks the importance of their tools as a means to earn their livelihood, and such propitiation is also believed to guarantee success for the following **year**.

Worship of Weapons

In earlier times, a common rite among the warrior classes on the festival of **Dussehra** (usually occurring within October and November). This festival has two different charter myths, both of which mark the triumph of good over evil. It is celebrated as the day that the god **Rama** slew the demon **Ravana**, and is also associated with the triumph of the **Goddess** over a **demon** named **Mahishasura**. Given the martial tone of both charter myths, it is easy to see how it would be associated with soldiers and fighting, and thus this was considered a day to **worship** one's weapons, as a symbol of the **deity**. According to popular belief, any endeavor begun on this festival day will invariably succeed, and for this reason, Dussehra has been a favored day to begin military campaigns. Since Dussehra comes after the end of the monsoon rains, in which any travel is nearly impossible, this is a favorable time from a strategic perspective as well.

Y

Yadava

In Hindu mythology, the tribe from which the god **Krishna** is said to have come and over which he ruled after he gained his kingdom in the city of **Dwaraka**. In Indian history, the Yadava dynasty controlled the **Deccan** region in modern **Maharashtra** between the thirteenth and fourteenth centuries. In northern Indian society, this is the name of a particular **jati**, an **endogamous** social subgroup that was organized (and whose social status was determined) by the group's hereditary occupation. In past generations the Yadavas had fairly low status, but they have recently gained much greater political power—Mulayam Singh Yadav has twice been elected chief minister of **Uttar Pradesh** and has also served as India's minister of Defense; Laloo Prasad Yadav has been the chief minister of **Bihar** (either directly or by proxy through his wife) throughout the 1990s.

Yadunandana

("joy of the **Yadus**") Epithet of the god **Krishna**. The Yadus were reckoned as Krishna's clan, and thus he was their joy. See **Krishna**.

Yajamana

("patron of the **sacrifice**") In the cult of sacrifice found in the **Vedas**, the oldest Hindu religious texts, the yajamana was the person who commissioned the sacrifice and paid for its performance, and who thus stood to gain its anticipated benefits. This term draws a crucial distinction between priest and patron and points to the relationship between them—the former were learned men and ritual technicians, who knew how to perform complex sacrificial rites, but they were dependent for their livelihood on the patronage of their sponsors.

Yajna

("**sacrifice**") A **fire** sacrifice, which was the primary religious act in the earliest stratum of Indian religion. This cult of sacrifice is elaborated in the greatest detail in the **Brahmana** literature, in which sacrifice is portrayed as the means by which the universe came into being. The performance of sacrifice needed highly trained priestly technicians (**rtvij**), who were differently responsible for chanting parts of the **Rg**, **Sama**, and **Yajur Vedas**, as well as building and maintaining the sacred fire that was the heart of the sacrificial action. This cult of sacrifice was essentially based on burning things in this sacred fire, conceived as the god **Agni**, so that Agni could convey the **offerings** to the other **deities**. These rites were so elaborate and expensive that they eventually fell into disuse; by the turn of the common era, there was also considerable ambivalence about the **animal sacrifices** that were originally an important part of many of these sacrifices. These ancient rites are rarely performed today, but in the present context the word *yajna* can be used for any rite involving the sacred fire, particularly one carried out by a **brahmin** for a patron.

Yajnavalkya

In the **Upanishads**, the speculative texts that form the latest textual stratum in the **Veda**, Yajnavalkya is named as a sage associated with the court of King **Janaka**, who was able to show that he had greater wisdom than the others. He is also ascribed as the author of the ***Yajnavalkya Smrti***, one of the texts that comprise the **dharma literature**, based on the pattern of mythic ascription found in these texts.

Yajnavalkya Smrti

One of the **smrtis** or "remembered" texts, a class of literature deemed important but less authoritative than the other textual category, the **shrutis** or "heard" texts. This smrti is ascribed to the sage **Yajnavalkya** and is an example of one of the **Dharma Shastras**, which were manuals prescribing rules for correct human behavior and ideal social life. Unlike the **Dharma Sutras**, which are ascribed to recognizable individuals, the Dharma Shastras are usually ascribed to mythic sages, as a strategy to reinforce the authority of these texts. The extant text is about a thousand verses, divided into sections on religious custom (**achara**), the administration of justice (vyavahara), and expiation (**prayashchitta**). Estimates on its date of composition range from the first to the sixth century, but it is clearly later than the *Manu Smrti* because some parts of the middle section are far more developed. The *Yajnavalkya Smrti* was the subject of numerous commentaries, one of which, the **Mitakshara**, was given the status of a legal code for the greater part of India during the British empire.

Yajnopavit

Another name for the **sacred thread**. See **sacred thread**.

Yajur Veda

Traditionally, the third of the four **Vedas**. As with the **Rg Veda** and the **Sama Veda**, the Yajur Veda was associated with sacrificial rituals, and the text itself consists mainly of the **mantras** to be uttered while the **sacrifice** was being carried out. The Yajur Veda exists in five major recensions, of which four are "black" and one is "white." Their differences stem from the placement of explanatory notes on the mantras and their significance: The recensions of the **Black Yajur Veda** contain these notes in the text itself, whereas the **White Yajur Veda** gathers these notes into an appendix known as a **Brahmana**—namely, the **Shatapatha Brahmana**—and this Brahmana literature becomes the next major stratum of Vedic texts.

Yaksha

(feminine *yakshi*) A class of minor **deities** who are essentially nature spirits and are often narrowly associated with particular places. Yakshas are reckoned as the attendants of the **deity Kubera**, who is regarded as the guardian of the northern direction and the lord of wealth. The yakshas are generally regarded as beneficent toward human beings, and because of their associations with the generative power of nature and with Kubera's wealth, they are often regarded as bestowing wealth and fertility. Yakshas have a long history of appearances in Indian sectarian literature, where they are either portrayed as guardian spirits or as examples of depravity. Although it is fairly old, the only extensive monograph on yakshas is Ananda Coomaraswamy, *Yaksas*, 1971.

Yama

God of death and Death personified. Yama is one of the eight **Guardians of the Directions**, associated with the southern direction, and for this reason, the south is considered an inauspicious direction. Yama first appears in the **Vedas**, the oldest Hindu religious texts, where he is described as the first mortal. By virtue of being the first person to suffer death, he was seen as presiding over the **World of the Fathers**, where the virtuous dead feasted and enjoyed themselves (much as they had on **earth**). As the tradition developed, conceptions of Yama shifted in turn, until he was considered the judge of the dead, ruling mainly over the regions of punishment, primarily **hells**, in which people suffered until they were reborn. Yama is often portrayed holding a noose, with which he draws out the person's spirit at the time of death and leads it bound to judgment. Modern poster images of Yama show him seated on a throne as king of the dead, majestic and dark in color; to his left sits the scribe Chitragupta, who keeps a ledger book recording the actions of human beings. Yama's role as the judge of the dead makes him greatly feared in everyday Hindu life. Ideally, this fear can have a pos-

Low fog hovers over the Yamuna River with the Taj Mahal in the distance.

itive outcome—reinforcing people's inclination to abstain from evil—and one of the names for Yama is **Dharmaraja**, the "Lord of Righteous Action." Hindu mythology also has tales of people who somehow manage to outsmart Yama, of whom the best known is **Savitri**, who manages to gain back the life of her husband, **Satyavan**.

Yama

(2) In the **ashtanga** ("eight-part") **yoga** first codified by **Patanjali** (1st c. C.E.?), yama ("restraint") is the first and most basic of the eight constituent elements of yoga practice. Patanjali lists these as five: abstaining from harm to other living things (**ahimsa**), abstaining from theft, truthfulness, **celibacy** (**brahmacharya**), and abstaining from avarice. These can all be characterized as "restraints" because their intent is negative—they do not call for positive actions as much as they entail refraining from certain thoughts or actions deemed especially injurious.

Yamunacharya

(10th c.) According to tradition, a devotee (**bhakta**) of the god **Vishnu**, who is claimed to be the grandson of **Nathamuni**, and the teacher of **Ramanuja**. Nathamuni was the compiler of the *Nalayira Divyaprabandham*, the collected hymns of the **Alvars**, a group of poet-saints who lived in southern India between the seventh and the tenth centuries. All the Alvars were devotees of Vishnu, and they expressed this devotion in passionate hymns sung in the **Tamil language**; among southern Indian **Vaishnavas** (devotees of Vishnu), these hymns are so holy that they are referred to as the "Tamil **Veda**." Ramanuja, on the other hand, was a philosopher who organized and systematized this devotional outpouring into a coherent philosophical position and thus is considered the founder of the **Shrivaishnava** religious community.

It is generally believed that Yamunacharya was Nathamuni's grandson, and thus he was heir to the religious tradition his grandfather had helped create. There is much more doubt about the claim that he was Ramanuja's religious preceptor (**guru**) because it seems more likely that Yamuna's influence on Ramanuja was transmitted by Yamuna's disciples. Still, what is indisputable is that these three are the three main figures in the development of the **Shrivaishnava** tradition, and thus that Yamunacharya occupies a pivotal spot.

Yamuna River

Northern Indian river rising at **Yamunotri** in the **Himalayas**, and flowing west and south of the **Ganges** River, which the Yamuna finally joins at **Allahabad** in the state of **Uttar Pradesh**. The Yamuna is traditionally considered one of the seven sacred rivers of India, along with the Ganges, **Godavari**, **Saraswati**, **Narmada**, **Indus**, and **Cauvery**. The Yamuna flows through the **Braj** region south of Delhi, which is traditionally associated as the homeland of **Krishna**, and his devotees (**bhakta**) revere it even more than the Ganges. For his devotees, places throughout the Braj region carry strong associations with the life of Krishna, but the most important sites are at **Mathura** and **Brindavan**.

Yamunotri

Sacred site (**tirtha**) in the **Himalayas** at the headwaters of the **Yamuna River**. Ritually speaking, Yamunotri is considered to be the source of the Yamuna, although the actual source lies farther upstream, at the foot of the Bandarpunch Mountain. Its high altitude also means that it is only accessible between late April and October, after which it is closed for the winter months—a pattern echoed at **Gangotri**, **Kedarnath**, and **Badrinath**, the other three major Himalayan pilgrim sites. One ritual center in Yamunotri is the river itself, in which pilgrims bathe (**snana**), braving the frigid waters. There are also several temples—the oldest built by one of the kings of **Nepal**—but the temples at Yamunotri are quite modest compared with those at **Gangotri**, and the only large one was built in the 1980s. Aside from the holy river and its temples, Yamunotri is also noted for several hot springs from which **water** emerges almost boiling; some of these hot springs have been channeled into a tank, and many pilgrims take advantage of the hot baths.

Yantra

("instrument") In astrology (**jyotisha**), and in **tantra**, a secret, ritually based religious practice, the word *yantra* most commonly refers to a symbolic diagram, often believed to confer **magic** or spiritual power on those who know how to use it. In some cases such yantras are considered to be an **aniconic** form of a **deity**, as is the case of the most famous yantra, the Shriyantra or **Shrichakra**, which is used in ritual for the **worship** of the **goddess** Tripura Sundari. The most literal meaning of the word is "device for restraining," and in an astrological setting the yantras of the various **planets** are used in rituals to change their effects, usually to restrain or diminish the power of planets judged to be malefic or **inauspicious**.

Yashoda

In Hindu mythology, the god **Krishna's** foster mother, who receives him on the night he is born, and cares for him until he is old enough to return to **Mathura** to claim his throne. Yashoda is a paradigm for selfless devotion, who loves Krishna as if he is her own biological child. Her mythic example of loving, motherly care has provided the model for **vatsalya bhava**, one of the five **modes of devotion** most prominently articulated by **Rupa Goswami**, a devotee (**bhakta**) of the god **Krishna** and a follower of the Bengali saint **Chaitanya**. In the vatsalya mode of devotion, devotees consider themselves as God's parents, lavishing love and care on the **deity** as a **cow** cares for her calf.

Yaska

(5th c. B.C.E.?) Traditionally cited as the author of the *Nirukta*, a text giving etymological explanations for archaic words in the **Veda**. Almost a quarter of the words in the Veda appear only once. Even by Yaska's

A yantra is a symbolic diagram often believed to confer
magic or spiritual power on those who know how to use it.

time, the meanings for many of these words had become either uncertain or completely lost, as the spoken language had changed. Although at times it is clear that Yaska himself is guessing—as when modern linguists can make comparisons to the Iranian *Avesta*, a related sacred text—his work was immeasurably helpful to later readers.

Yathakhyati

("discrimination [of things] as they are") Another name for the **theory of error** known as **satkhyati**. See **satkhyati**.

Yati

(from **Sanskrit** *yam*, "to restrain") From the time of the **Vedas**, the earliest Hindu religious texts, the word *yati* has been one of the terms used to designate an **ascetic**, as someone who had gained control over himself. At the time of the Vedas there seems to be some ambivalence for the yatis, since the storm-god **Indra** is said to have fought with them, but in later times the word takes on an unequivocally positive connotation.

Yatra

("journey") Although in its literal meaning the word *yatra* can refer to any sort of travel, in modern **Hindi** its semantic field is considerably narrower and connotes travel with some serious purpose, rather than a stroll around the block or a sightseeing trip. The word yatra's most important connotation is travel for religious purposes, particularly pilgrimage to the sacred sites (**tirthas**). A yatra is thus a journey, but a particular type of journey.

Yatri

In an **ascetic** context, the word *yatri* denotes a novitiate **Bairagi**, a renunciant ascetic community comprising devotees (**bhakta**) of the god **Vishnu**. As an everyday word it means a person performing a **yatra** ("journey"; more specifically, a trip with the significance of a religious pilgrimage).

Yayati

In Hindu mythology, the son of King **Nahusha** and a king in the lunar dynasty.

Year, Structure of

The Hindu ritual year is determined according to both a solar **calendar** and a lunar calendar. Aside from the Gregorian calendar and the common era, there are two indigenous Hindu calculations of the solar year, both of which have twelve solar months. In northern India these months correspond to the twelve signs of the **zodiac**, and the months change as the **sun** moves through them. As in the Western zodiac, the year begins when the sun enters Aries, although according to Indian astrology this transition takes place around April 14, rather than March 21, as figured in Euro-American astrology. In southern India there is an identical solar calendar, whose names are drawn from the names of certain **nakshatras** or lunar asterisms. Aside from the solar months, the solar year is also divided into halves based on the movement of the sun: the **Uttarayana** for the period when the sun is moving north, and the **Dakshinayana** in the time the sun is moving south. The sun begins its northward journey, considered the more auspicious time, on **Makara Sankranti**, reckoned as falling on January 14; it begins its southward journey six months later on **Karka Sankranti** on July 14.

Far more important for religious purposes is the lunar calendar, which has twelve **lunar months**: Chaitra (March–April), **Baisakh** (April–May), **Jyeshth** (May–June), **Ashadh** (June–July),

Shravan (July–August), **Bhadrapada** (August–September), **Ashvin** (September–October), **Kartik** (October–November), **Margashirsha** (November–December), **Paush** (December–January), **Magh** (January–February), and **Phalgun** (February–March). In northern India, the calendar usually begins in the first day of the bright half of Chaitra, meaning that the last days of the year are those in the dark half of this same month.

Since these lunar months are based on the phases of the **moon** (ending with the **full moon** in northern India and the **new moon** in southern India), the festivals determined by this lunar calendar fall at different times each year with respect to the solar calendar. This is because the twelve lunar months are completed in about 354 solar days, and thus, each lunar year begins eleven days earlier than the last. About every 2½ years this discrepancy is corrected by the addition of an extra lunar month, known as the **intercalary month**, through which the solar and lunar calendars are kept in general correspondence. The intercalary month is added to any lunar month in which the sun does not enter a new sign of the zodiac and can thus fall in any month of the year. In this way, although the solar calendar is less important in everyday life, it helps maintain the general correspondence between the lunar calendar and the seasonal festivals associated with that calendar.

At least in northern India, the three major **seasons** (hot, **monsoon**, and cool) have important links with the **festival calendar**. In general, the most ritually active time is the cool season between October and February; in many places this is also the time following the harvest, when many people have more time and money to spend on religious observances. The hot season has many rites associated with heat, whereas the rainy season, as a time of peril, is often connected with **rites of protection**.

Yellamma

Presiding **goddess** of the shrine on Yellama hill, in the town of Saundatti in the Belgaum district of the state of **Karnataka**. Yellama's temple is infamous for being a traditional center for the dedication of **devadasis** ("[female] servant of the Lord"), a class of **women** kept in temples as singers and dancers in the service of the temple's presiding **deity** and to whom they were usually considered to be "married." In Yellama's temple, however, both boys and girls can be dedicated. Although for the past two centuries the **devadasi** tradition has carried associations with common **prostitution**, in earlier times it was far more common for a devadasi to live with a single man for her entire life, although she could not marry him because she was considered dedicated to the deity.

At times this dedication is done because of a demand by the goddess herself, revealed through **possession**; in other cases the parents do this, hoping to gain some concrete benefit, particularly healing from disease. Yellamma is associated with **fire** and also with causing (and potentially curing) skin diseases, which can be seen as symbolic "burning."

According to the traditional model, devadasis held a definite social position and had special legal rights—they were entitled to family **inheritance** and to perform religious rites, which other women were not. These special rights have disappeared with the outlawing of the devadasi system, done, in part, by the British, and definitively in post-Independence India. Although such dedications still take place, in many cases they are little more than a cover for procurement, with the girls being shipped to brothels in Bombay, Pune, and other central Indian cities. In most cases the girls come from extremely poor families, and the dedication to Yellamma is a way to avoid paying for a wedding, a major expense in contemporary Indian society. The dedications take place on the **full moon** in the **lunar month** of **Magh** (January–February), and are reportedly widespread, but because of secrecy, the laws prohibiting this are rarely enforced. For further consideration of the devadasi system, in this case at the **Jagannath** temple in **Puri**, see Frederique Apffel Marglin, *Wives of the God-King*, 1985.

Yoga

The literal meaning of the word *yoga* is "the act of joining," and it is cognate with the English word "yoke." Just as the latter word can serve as either a verb or a noun—either the act of yoking, or the thing to which animals are yoked—in the same way the word yoga can refer both to the act or process of spiritual development and also to a specific set of teachings fostering this development. Both these meanings can be conveyed by the word "discipline," and this is one of the preferred translations.

There are many specific teachings styling themselves as yogas. The oldest one is laid out in the **Yoga Sutras** attributed to the sage **Patanjali**; this system is known as **ashtanga** ("eight-limbed") **yoga**, because of its eight constituent parts. Other well-known yogas are the three "paths" described by the god **Krishna** in the **Bhagavad Gita**, an important religious text: the yogas of action (**karma**), wisdom (**jnana**), and devotion (**bhakti**). Another well-known yoga is **kundalini yoga**, the practice of which is entirely internal, in the alternate physiological system known as the **subtle body**. Kundalini yoga stresses awakening the kundalini, the latent spiritual power that exists in every person, and through this gaining spiritual benefits. These make up the main categories of teachings, but the members of many particular religious communities will describe their religious practice as yoga: Thus there is the **surat-shabd-yoga** of the **Radha Soamis**, the Raja Yoga of the **Brahma Kumaris**, or the **Siddha** Yoga of the SYDA Foundation. In such cases the word is used to identify a particular religious group's characteristic teaching, which usually includes elements from the classical articulations of yoga.

Yoga Mudra

In Indian **dance**, **sculpture**, and ritual, a particular symbolic hand **gesture** (**mudra**), in which the right hand is placed flat on the left, with both palms pointing up, and the joined hands are laid on the crossed legs. In a sculptural image, this mudra indicates that the figure is adept in **yoga**.

Yogananda, Paramahamsa

(b. Mukunda Lal Ghosh 1893–1952) Modern Hindu teacher and founder of the Self-Realization Fellowship. Yogananda was one of the earliest Hindu missionaries to come to America. He came to Boston in 1920, to address the International Congress of Religious Liberals in Boston and never returned to India. He eventually settled outside Los Angeles, where he established a center and lived for the rest of his life. In his early years in America he was considered something of a curiosity, and there are photos of him taken with President Calvin Coolidge. Yogananda's teachings were largely based in the **ashtanga yoga** of the classical **Yoga Sutras**, but he also stressed the doctrine of kriya ("active") yoga, which is claimed to accelerate spiritual attainment. Most of Yogananda's disciples and both his successors were Americans, and the Self-Realization Fellowship is essentially an American organization with historical roots in India. For further information see Paramahansa Yogananda's *Autobiography of a Yogi*, 1997.

Yoganidra

("sleep of **yoga**") Epithet of the **Goddess** in the first episode of the *Devi-mahatmya*, the earliest and most authoritative text for the mythology of the Goddess. In this episode, the Goddess has lulled **Vishnu** into a stupor through her power of illusion, making him oblivious to **Brahma's** cries for help when he is menaced by the **demons Madhu** and **Kaitabha**. Brahma is saved when he praises the Goddess, after which she withdraws her yogic sleep from Vishnu; he then regains consciousness and rescues Brahma by killing the demons.

Yoga Sutras

("aphorisms on **yoga**") A set of brief sayings traditionally ascribed to the sage **Patanjali**, which are the foundational texts for the Yoga school, one of the **six schools** of traditional Hindu **philosophy**. Patanjali's Yoga Sutras are usually read with a commentary ascribed to the sage **Vyasa**, and this commentary has become accepted as an integral part of the text. The text of the Yoga Sutras is divided into four parts, with each part devoted to a particular theme: The first part focuses on concentration (**samadhi**), the second part on the mechanics of spiritual development (**sadhana**), the third part treats various attainments (**vibhuti**), including **magic** powers (**siddhi**), and the last part describes the state of yogic isolation (**kaivalya**), which the text describes as liberation. The text presupposes the **cosmology** taught by the **Samkhya** school, another of the six schools, and the Yoga school is often considered the "practical" articulation of Samkhya theory.

Yogi

Literally meaning "one possessing **yoga**," in practice the word refers only to a yogic adept—someone who "possesses" yoga in the sense of having mastered it—rather than to anyone simply practicing yoga. True yogis are widely believed to have superhuman powers (**siddhi**) as a by-product of their long spiritual development, which they can and will exercise for the benefit of their disciples—for physical healing of diseases, for psychological help, or for giving guidance on both spiritual and mundane matters. The yogi is seen as a spiritually realized person, and their authority stems completely from this attribution, which paradoxically is not subject to any sort of external verification.

Consequently, there are significant differences of opinion on whether or not any particular person is a yogi.

Yogi Bhajan

(b. Harbhajan Singh Puri, 1927) Modern Hindu missionary and founder of the **3HO/Sikh Dharma Brotherhood**. He first came to the United States in 1969, leaving behind his position as a customs official at the Delhi airport. His initial teachings were the traditional disciplines of **hatha yoga** and **kundalini yoga**, with his followers organized into a group known as the "Happy, Healthy, Holy Organization" (3HO). Hatha yoga is a system of religious discipline (**yoga**) based on a series of bodily postures known as **asanas**; this practice is widely believed to provide various physical benefits, including increased bodily flexibility and the ability to heal chronic ailments. Kundalini yoga is a religious discipline, the primary focus of which is awakening the **kundalini**, the latent spiritual force that exists in every person in the **subtle body**. The kundalini is awakened through a combination of yoga practice and ritual action and is believed to bring further spiritual capacities and ultimately final liberation (**moksha**) of the soul.

These two disciplines remain an important part of Yogi Bhajan's teachings, for he claims to be a master of **tantra**, a secret, ritually based religious practice, but in the 1970s his teaching widened to include traditional Sikh teachings and symbols. The most prominent of these symbols are the "five Ks" that all Sikhs are supposed to wear, so called because each of them begins with the letter *k*: uncut **hair** (kesh), a comb (kangha), a bangle on the right wrist (kara), shorts (kacch), and a ceremonial sword (kirpan). Many of Yogi Bhajan's followers keep the Sikh symbols far more strictly than most people born as Sikhs, but the movement has two important divergences with the traditional Sikh community. One of these is its emphasis on tantra, which has little importance in the Sikh community. The most significant difference, however, is the religious authority that Yogi Bhajan holds over his followers, which is very different from the decentralized, essentially democratic form of the traditional Sikh community.

Yogini Ekadashi

Religious observance falling on the eleventh day (**ekadashi**) of the dark (waning) half of the **lunar month** of **Ashadh** (June–July). As for all the eleventh-day observances, this is dedicated to the **worship** of **Vishnu**, particularly in his form as **Narayana**. Most Hindu festivals have certain prescribed rites, which usually involve fasting (**upavasa**) and worship and often promise specific benefits for faithful performance. On this day the prescribed action is to give gifts to poor brahmins; faithfully observing this festival washes away the sin of cutting down a pipal tree (**ashvattha**) and also brings one **birth** in **heaven**.

Yogmaya

Powerful form of the **Goddess**, particularly noted for her power to bewitch and bewilder people—in other words, her ability to wield **maya**, the power of illusion. In some modern sources Yogmaya is named as the **deity** who takes the form of the infant girl exchanged for the infant god **Krishna** and is later killed by Krishna's wicked uncle, **Kamsa**. According to these sources, it is under her spell the previous night that all the inhabitants of Kamsa's palace fall asleep, and Krishna's father, **Vasudeva**, is able to spirit the infant away. Later in Krishna's career, Yogmaya is believed to facilitate his clandestine meetings with the women of **Braj**—when Krishna plays his flute, the women come to him, but all the others fall into the spell cast by Yogmaya and are unaware of their absence. Because of her ability to wield maya, Yogmaya is a powerful deity; she is worshiped on the fourth day of the fall

Navaratri, the festival of the "nine nights" that are sacred to the Goddess in her varying forms.

Yoni

Although in modern **Hindi** this has become a vulgar word for female genitalia, its most literal meaning is "womb," both in a literal sense as the place of gestation and in a metaphorical sense as any place of origin, source, or generative power.

Yudhishthira

("firm in battle") In the *Mahabharata*, the later of the two great Hindu epics, Yudhishthira is the eldest of the **Pandava** brothers who are the epic's protagonists. Yudhishthira is magically born when his mother, **Kunti**, uses a powerful **mantra** to have a son by **Dharma**, the god of righteousness. Yudhishthira is in all ways his father's son; he is described in the epic as the manifestation of Dharma on earth. He is proverbial for his strict adherence to the truth, is courteous to all, and is committed to righteousness. His only personal flaw is a love of **gambling**, a love matched only by his complete lack of gaming skill, and this flaw has major repercussions.

Because of his virtues, Yudhishthira is selected as heir to the throne by his uncle, **Dhrtarashtra**. This choice raises the jealousy of Dhrtarashtra's son, **Duryodhana**. He first tries to kill the Pandavas by building the flammable **house of lac**. The house is burned, but the Pandavas are able to escape unharmed. Some time later, Duryodhana decides to win Yudhishthira's rights to the kingship in a game of dice. Here Yudhishthira's love for gambling gets the better of his judgment, for he is playing against Duryodhana's maternal uncle, **Shakuni**, who is very skilled. As Yudhishthira begins to lose, he keeps betting bigger and bigger stakes, in an effort to win back what he has lost. After losing their kingdom and all their posses-

sions, Yudhishthira wagers himself and his brothers. After losing this bet, he wagers and loses the Pandava brothers' common wife, **Draupadi**. This loss leads to Draupadi's humiliation, in which she is paraded through the assembly hall by Duryodhana and his brother, **Duhshasana**, her clothes stained with her menstrual **blood**. This event sharpens the already strong enmities between the two groups. Shocked at such treatment, Duryodhana's father, King Dhrtarashtra, gives the Pandavas back their freedom, but because of the loss in the game of dice, the Pandavas agree to go into exile for twelve years and live incognito for the thirteenth, with the condition that if they are discovered in the thirteenth year the cycle will begin anew.

Yudhishthira and his brothers peacefully pass their twelve years in exile. During the thirteenth year, they live in the court of King **Virata**, where they remain undiscovered, despite frantic searching by Duryodhana's spies. When the thirteen years have passed, Yudhishthira and his brothers return to claim their part of the kingdom. Yudhishthira hopes for some sort of peaceful settlement and sends a message to Duryodhana saying that they will be satisfied with a mere five villages, one for each brother. When Duryodhana responds that they will not get as much land as could fit under the point of a needle, Yudhishthira realizes that they will not get their rights without a battle. He reluctantly mobilizes his brothers for war. He fights valiantly in the great war and is crowned the king after their victory.

After ruling for many years, Yudhishthira sets out with his brothers and their wife, Draupadi, for the **Himalayas**, followed by a small **dog**. As they climb the mountains Draupadi and his brothers die one by one, but the dog remains with Yudhishthira. At the top of the Himalayas Yudhishthira finds the god **Indra**, the king of **heaven**, waiting for him in a golden chariot. Indra tells Yudhishthira that he will take him to heaven but that Yudhishthira will have to leave the dog behind. Yudhishthira flatly refuses to abandon his faithful companion, even if it means that he will not go to heaven. The dog then reveals himself to be the god Dharma in disguise. The lesson in this story is that throughout his life Yudhishthira never allows himself to stray far from righteousness; even at the end he refuses to forsake it.

Yuga

A name denoting a unit of **cosmic time**, with two possible meanings. According to traditional belief, time has neither beginning nor end, but alternates between cycles of creation and activity, followed by cessation and quietude. Each of these cycles lasts for 4.32 billion years, with the active phase known as the **Day of Brahma**, and the quiet phase the Night of Brahma. In cosmic time, the Day of Brahma is divided into one thousand **mahayugas** ("great cosmic ages"), each of which lasts for 4.32 million years, and this is one possible meaning of the word *yuga*. The more common use is to refer to a **mahayuga's** four constituent yugas, named the **Krta Yuga**, **Treta Yuga**, **Dvapara Yuga**, and **Kali Yuga**.

Z

are judged to be the winter and the summer solstices but occur in the second weeks of January and July. Given a difference of about three weeks, it is not surprising that there are significant differences in the astrological calculations between these two systems.

Zodiac

The signs of the zodiac in Indian astrology (**jyotisha**) are virtually identical with that of Western astrology, and it is generally accepted that the Greek zodiac was brought to India in the first to third centuries via the Greek kingdoms in modern Afghanistan. There are slight differences in the nomenclature; the Indian zodiac has **Dhanus** ("bow") in place of Sagittarius, Makara (a sea monster sometimes identified as a crocodile) for Capricorn, and Kumbha ("[water] pot") for Aquarius. As with Western astrology, each of the twelve signs has certain characteristics, with which people born in these signs are imbued.

The two systems differ sharply in how they figure the annual starting point, although both begin with the sign of Aries. The zodiac used in Western astrology begins on the vernal equinox, on which the sign of Aries is the beginning. By Indian accounts the starting point of the zodiac comes when the **sun** intersects the midpoint of a group of stars named Ashvini. It is thus based on the position of the sun with regard to the fixed stars, whereas the Western zodiac is based on the position of the sun with regard to the **earth**—that is, when it intersects the equator, and is thus independent of the fixed stars. These differing methods have produced a discrepancy between the two systems, which are now more than three weeks apart—in the Western zodiac Aries begins on March 21, whereas in the Indian zodiac it does not begin until about April 14. This discrepancy can also be seen in the account of **Makara Sankranti** and **Karka Sankranti**, which

I have transliterated Hindi and Sanskrit terms into English to match their original pronunciation as closely as possible. In most cases, the transliteration is a straightforward substitution of Hindi or Sanskrit letters with their counterparts in English. However, discrepancies in the languages create some difficulties in transliteration.

In this book, Hindi and Sanskrit words are made plural by adding the English *s* to the end. This is done to conform the transliterated words to English grammar, even though this is not standard in Hindi or Sanskrit.

For some terms there exist both Sanskritic and Hindi forms, each with different pronunciations. I have transliterated these words from Hindi or Sanskrit depending on the most appropriate context; Sanskritic forms seem fitting when one is discussing Sanskrit texts, but not when reporting a remark by a Hindi speaker.

Transliteration also becomes complicated for words where there is a Hindi or Sanskrit letter that does not directly correspond to a letter in English. For example, single characters in the Hindi alphabet represent sounds that require consonant combinations in English, such as "ch" and "sh." I have used these letter combinations to substitute for the Hindi letters whenever possible. In other cases, transliterating Hindi and Sanskrit pronunciation is not as straightforward. The following list contains Hindi and Sanskrit terms from this book that do not follow standard English pronunciation. They are written here with diacritical marks to indicate the proper pronunciation.

Pronunciation Guide

Vowels

a	as in but
ā	as in father
ai	as in bite
au	as in trout
e	as in pay
i	as in kit
ī	as in feet
o	as in coat
u	as in put
ū	as in boot

Consonants

c	as in check
ḷ	as in lip (with the "l" sound rolled)
ḻ	This is the Tamil "l." To make this sound place the tip of the tongue back in the palate and hold it there while making an "l" sound.
ṁ	This indicates that the previous vowel is nazalized (pronounced through the nose)
ṅ	as in sing or sink
ñ	as pronounced in Spanish (eg. mañana)
ṛ	as in rip (with the "r" sound rolled)
ṟ	This sound is found in Tamil, but not Sanskrit. The "r" sound is pronounced with a trill.
ś	as in shirt

As for ṭ/ṭh, ḍ/ḍh, ṇ, and ṣ, these are pronounced by placing the tip of the tongue at the top of the palate and flexing it forward.

Abhaṅg
Abhāva
Abhīra
Ācamanīya
Ācāra
Adhikamāsa
Adhikāra
Adhvāryum
Adhyāsa
Ādigranth
Āditya
Ādivāsi
Advaita Vedānta
Āgama
Aghorī
Agrahāra
Ahalyā
Aham Brahmāsmi
Ahaṁkār
Ahiṁsa
Ahīr
Airāvata
Aiteraya
 Brāhmaṇa
Ajāmila
Ājīvika
Ājñā Cakra
Ākāśa
Akhaṇḍ Pāṭh
Akhyāti
Akrūra
Akṣaya Tṛtīyā
Alaṁkāra
Ālīḍhāsana
Ālvār
Āmalaka
Ambālika
Amṛta
Ānanda
Ānanda Akhāra
Ānandamaṭh
Ānandawāra
Anaṅga
Anasūyā

Anekāntavāda
Aṅgiras
Aṇimā
Añjali hasta
Añjanā
Annakūṭ
Anṛta
Antaḥpura
Antarāla
Antaryāga
Anumāna
Anyathākhyāti
Apāna
Apūrva
Āraṇyaka
Ārati
Ārdha Kumbha
 Mela
Ārdhamaṇḍapa
Arthāpatti
Arundhatī
Ārya Samāj
Āṣāḍh
Asamañjasa
Āsana
Asatkāryavāda
Aṣṭādhāyī
Atikāya
Atīta
Ātman
Atrī
Avadhī
Avadhūta
Āvāhana
Āvāhana Akhāra
Avatār
Avidyā
Ayamātma Brahman
Āyurveda
Bāba
Bahī
Bahiryāga
Bahūdaka
Bairāgi

Baisākh
Baisākhī
Baiṭhak
Bakāsur
Bālabhadra
Bālajī
Balarāma
Bāṇa
Bāṇa Liṅga
Baniā
Banjāra
Barahmāsa
Bārāt
Barūthānī
 Ekādaśī
Begampūra
Bhadrakālī
Bhādrapada
Bhadrāsana
Bhagavān
Bhāgavata
Bhāgavata Purāṇa
Bhagīrath
Bhagīrathī
Bhāṣya
Bhairava Jayantī
Bhairavī
Bhaiyā Dūj
Bhaktamāl
Bhaktilīlāmṛta
Bhaktimārga
Bhaktirasabodhinī
Bhāmatī Advaita
Bhaṇḍāra
Bhaṇita
Bhāradvaja
Bhārata
Bhāratanāṭyam
Bhārat Mātā
Bharatmilāp
Bhasmāsur
Bhāva
Bhavānī
Bhedābhada

Bhīma
Bhogamaṇḍapa
Bhogawāra
Bholanāth
Bhramargīt
Bhramarī
Bhṛgu
Bhudevī
Bhujaṅgavalaya
Bhūriwāra
Bhuśuṇḍi
Bhūt
Bhūta
Bhūtaliṅgas
Bhūtayajña
Bidhāī Samaroh
Bījak
Brahmā
Brahmahatyā
Brahmā Muhūrta
Brāhmaṇa
Brahmāṇḍa
Brahmā
 Sampradāy
Brahmasūtra
Bhāṣya
Brahma Sūtras
Bhāṣya
Brahmayajña
Brahmī
Brahmo Samāj
Bṛhannala
Bṛhaspati
Buddha Avatār
Buddha Pūrṇima
Caṇḍa
Caṇḍī
Caṇḍikā
Cārvāka
Cāyāgrāhī
Cinnamāsta
Cittirāī
Cuḍākarana
 Saṁskāra
Dābistan-I-Mazahib

789

Dādhupanthī Nāga
Dādupanth
Dakṣiṇa
Dakṣiṇācāra
Dakṣiṇāyana
Ḍamaru
Damayantī
Dāna
Dānava
Daṇḍa
Daṇḍa Hasta
Daṇḍanīti
Daṇḍāsana
Daṇḍavat Praṇām
Daṇḍi Sanyāsi
Dān Līlā
Dāsa Bhāva
Dāsyu
Dāyabhāga
Devadāsī
Devakī
Devanāgarī
Devayajña
Devīmāhātmya
Dhaṅga
Dhangār
Dhanuś
Dhāraṇā
Dharma Sūtras
Dhātuvāda
Dhobī
Dhūnī
Dhūpa
Dhyāna
Dīkṣanāma
Dilīp
Diṇḍi
Dīpa
Dīvya
  Prabandham
Dohā
Draupadī
Drāvida
Droṇa

Durgā
Durvāsas
Dvaitādvaita
  Vedānta
Dvaita Vedānta
Dvāpara Yuga
Dvārapāla
Dvīpas
Dwara Bairāgis
Ekādaśī
Ekmukhī
Ekoddiṣṭha
Four Dhāms
Gadā
Gaṇa
Gaṇapati
Gāndhārī
Gandhi Jayantī
Gaṇḍīva
Gaṅgā
Ganikā
Gānpatya
Garbhādhāna
  Saṁskāra
Gārbhagṛha
Garībdās
Garībdāsī
Garuḍa
Gaurī
Gaurīkuṇḍ
Gayāsura
Gāyatrī Mantra
Gayawāl
Ghaṇṭā
Ghāt
Ghaṭikā
Gītagovinda
Godāna
Gopāla
Gopī
Gorakhnāthī
Govardhan Maṭh
Govardhan Pūjā
Gṛhastha

Gṛhya Sūtras
Gujjār
Guler
Guṇa
Guru Pūrṇimā
Gyān Vāpi
Haladhāra
Hālāhala
Hanumān
Hanumān Cālīsa
Hanumān Jayantī
Hartālika Teej
Harivaṁśa
Haṭha Yoga
Hetvābhāsa
Hindu Mahāsabhā
Hiraṇyagārbha
Hiraṇyakaśipu
Holikā
Hotṛ
Huṇḍī
Iḍā Nāḍī
Indrāṇī
Jābāli
Jaḍa
Jagadambā
Jagadīśa
Jagannāth
Jāhnavī
Jajmān
Jāmbhavān
Jambudvīpa
Jānakī Navamī
Janārdana
Jaṅgama
Jaratkārava
  Artabhāga
Jaratkāru
Jāt
Jaṭa
Jātakarma
  Saṁskāra
Jaṭamakuṭa
Jaṭāyu

Jāti
Jātra
Jhāṅkī
Jīva
Jīvacchrāddha
Jīvānmukta
Jīvānmukti
Jñāna
Jñānakarma-
  samucchāya
Jñānamārga
Jñāna Mudrā
Jñānendriya
Jūṭha
Jyotirliṅga
Jyotir Maṭh
Kabīrpanth
Kādambarī
Kadrū
Kaikeyī
Kailāsanātha
Kāla
Kālāmukha
Kālī
Kālika Devī
Kalīmaṭh
Kalivārjya
Kāliya
Kalki Avatār
Kalpa Sūtras
Kalpavās
Kalyāṇamaṇḍapam
Kāma
Kāmadhenu
Kāmākhya
Kāmakoṭipīṭh
Kamaṇḍalu
Kāmāvasāyitvām
Kāṁsa
Kandarīya
  Mahādev
Kāṅgra
Kānha
Kānphaṭā

790

Kānvar
Kanyādān
Kapāla
Kāpālika
Kapālin
Karaṇa
Karaṇḍamakuṭa
Karka Saṅkrānti
Karmamārga
Karmendriya
Karṇa
Karnāta
Karṇavedha
  Saṁskāra
Karṇī Mātā
Kartigai
Kārtik
Kārtik Pūrṇimā
Kārttikeya
Kaṭaka Hasta
Kathā
Kaṭyavalambita
  Hasta
Katyāyana Smṛti
Kausalyā
Kavitāvalī
Kāvya
Kedārnāth
Khaḍga
Khāṇḍava Forest
Khaṇḍobā
Khaṭvāṅga
Kirīṭamakuṭa
Kīrtan
Kīrtimukha
Kitawāra
Koīl
Koṅkanastha
Kṛpācārya
Kṛta Yuga
Kubjā
Kuladevatā
Kumāra
Kumārasambhava

Kumbhakarṇa
Kumbha Melā
Kumhār
Kuṇḍalinī
Kuṇḍalinī Yoga
Kūrma Avatār
Kurmāsana
Kuṭīcaka
Lāghava
Laghimā
Lāllāvakyāni
Laṅkā
Laṅkālakṣmī
Līlā
Liṅga
Liṅgarāja Temple
Liṅgāyat
Lohār
Loharī
Lokāyata
Lopāmudrā
Loṭa
Mādhava
Mādhurya Bhāva
Mādrī
Māgh
Māgh Melā
Mahābhārata
Mahābhāṣya
Mahābrahman
Mahādeva
Mahākāleśvar
Mahākālī
Mahākāvya
Mahālakṣmi
Mahāmaṇḍaleśvar
Mahāmaṇḍapa
Mahāmantra
Mahāmāyā
Mahānubhav
Mahāpātaka
Mahāpātra
Mahār
Mahāvākya

Mahāvidyās
Mahāyuga
Mahimā
Mahiṣāsura
Mahiṣī
Makarāsana
Makara Saṅkrānti
Mālā
Malamāsa
Mālatīmādhava
Mālī
Mallikārjuna
Mamsa
Manasā
Maṇḍala
Maṇḍapa
Maṇḍodarī
Maṅgalam
Maṇimegalai
Mān Līlā
Maṇipūra Cakra
Mansā Devī
Manthara
Mantrarāja
Manu Smṛti
Maraṇāśauca
Marātha
Mārgaśīrṣa
Mārkaṇḍeya
Mārkaṇḍeya
  Purāṇa
Marwāri
Maṭh
Matsya Avatār
Matsyagandhī
Mauni Amāvasyā
Māyā
Māyā Devī
Meghadūta
Meghanāda
Melā
Menā
Menakā
Mīnākṣi

Mitākṣara
Mithilā
Mohinī
Mohinī Ekādaśī
Mokṣadā Ekādaśī
Mṛcchakatika
Mṛtyunjaya
Mudrā
Muhūrta
Mūlādhāra Cakra
Mūlāmantra
Muṇḍa
Muṇḍan
Muralī
Murārī
Mūrti
Nācciyār Tirumoli
Nāḍī
Nāga
Nāgara
Nāg Pañcamī
Nāī
Nainā Devī
Naiṣṭhika
Nāladiyār
Nalayīra Divya-
  prabandham
Nāmakaraṇa
Nāmarūpa
Namaskāra
Nambūdiri
Nānak Jayanti
Nanda Devi
Nandī
Nandigrāma
Nārada
Nārada Smṛti
Nara-Nārāyaṇa
Narasimha Avatār
Nārāyaṇa
Nasik Melā
Nāstika
Naṭamandira
Naṭarāja

Nāth
Nāṭya
Navarātrī
Navyanyāya
Nāyak Dynasty
Nāyanār
Nāyar
Nīlakaṇṭh
Nimbārki
Nirākara
Nirguṇa
Nirikāri
Nirṛti
Nirvāṇi Ani
Nityasamsārin
Nṛtya
Nṛyajña
Nyāsa
Nyāya
Nyāya Sūtras
Padmāsana
Pāduka
Pān
Pañcāgnitapa
Pañcāmahāyajña
Pancāyat
Pañcāyatana Pūjā
Pañcvānī
Paṇḍa
Pāṇḍava
Paṇḍit
Paṇḍu
Pāṇḍurang
Pāṇigrahaṇa
Pāp
Pāpamocanī Ekādaśī
Pāpāṅkuśa Ekādaśī
Parakīya
Paramātman
Paramparā
Pāraśurām Avatār
Pariṇāmavāda

Parivrājaka
Pārvaṇa
Pārvatī
Paryaṅka
Pāśa
Pātāla
Pattuppāṭṭu
Periya Purāṇam
Pināka
Piṇḍa
Piṇḍadān
Piṅgala Nāḍī
Pippalāda
Pītāmbara
Pītavāsana
Pīṭha
Pitṛ
Pitṛyajña
Poṅgal
Pradakṣiṇa
Pradhāna
Prahlāda
Prajāpatya Marriage
Prajñānam Brahman
Prākāmyam
Prakāśa
Prakāśātman
Prakṛti
Pramāṇa
Prāṇa
Pranava
Prāṇāyāma
Prāpti
Prārthanā Samāj
Prasād
Pratijñā
Pratyabhijñā
Pratyāhāra
Prāyaścitta
Pṛthivī
Pṛthu
Pūjā

Pūjārī
Puṁsavana Saṁskāra
Puṇya
Purāṇa
Purūravas
Pūrva Mīmāṁsā
Pūtanā
Putradā Ekādaśī
Rādhā
Rādhāṣṭamī
Radhavallabh Sampradāy
Rāga
Rāhu
Rājābhiṣeka
Rājādharma
Rājāgṛha
Rājasūya
Rājataraṅginī
Rājput
Raktabīja
Rāmānandī
Ramāvalī
Rāmāyaṇa
Rām Līlā
Rām Navamī
Raṅganātha
Rās Līlā
Rath Yātrā
Ratī
Rātrī
Rāvaṇa
Ravidās Jayantī
Rāwal
Rāwat
Renukā
Ṛg Veda
Rohiṇī
Ṛṣi
Ṛṣyaśṛnga
Ṛta
Ṛtvij
Rudranāth

Rudra Sampradāy
Rukmiṇī
Sadācāra
Sadasatkhyāti
Sādhana
Sādhāraṇa Dharma
Sādhu
Sādhya
Safaī
Sāgar
Saguṇa
Sahajīya
Śakadvīpa
Śākhā
Sakhā Bhāva
Sāla
Salmaladvīpa
Samādhi
Samāna
Samasthāna
Samāvartana Saṁskāra
Samavāya
Sāma Veda
Saṁhārakrama
Samhitā
Saṁkalpa
Sāṁkhya
Sampradāy
Saṁsāra
Saṁskāra
Samvād
Sanakādi
Sanaka Sampradāy
Sanātana
Sanātanadharma
Sanātana Sampradāy
Sanatkumāra
Sandhābhāṣa
Sandhyā
Saṅgam

Sañjaya
Sañjñā
Saṅkaṭ Mocan
Saṅkrānti
Śānta Bhāva
Santāl
Sanyāsī
Sapiṇḍa
Sapiṇḍikaraṇa
Śārada Maṭh
Saramā
Sarvasvāra
Śatākṣī
Satī
Satkāryavāda
Satkhyāti
Ṣaṭṭilā Ekādaśī
Satyabhāma
Satyagrāha
Satyakāma
Satyanārāyan
  Vrat
Satyavān
Satyavatī
Saundāryalaharī
Sāvitrī
Sāvitrī Pūjā
Sevā
Siddhapīṭh
Siddhāsana
Sīmantonnayana
  Saṁskāra
Simhakarṇa
Sinhastha Melā
Śiṣṭācāra
Śiśupāla-vadha
Sītā
Śītalā
Śītalāṣṭamī
Śīvaga-sindāmaṇi
Śivarātrī
Smaraṇa
Smārta
Smṛti

Snāna
Snātaka
Solah Somvār
  Vrat
Somāvatī
  Amāvasyā
Somnāth
Sonār
Sorathā
Sphoṭa
Śrāmaṇa
Śrīnāthjī
Śṛṅgerī Maṭh
Sthala Mūrti
Sthūṇākarṇa
Strīdhan
Strīdharma
Śrīvidyā
Subhadrā
Subodhinī
Subrahmaṇya
Sudāma
Sugrīva
Sulva Sūtras
Sumatī
Sumitrā
Suparṇa
Surapāna
Śūrpanakhā
Sūrsāgar
Sūrya
Suśruta Samhitā
Suṣumṇā
Sūta
Sūtakāśauca
Svādhiṣṭhāna
  Cakra
Svadhyāya
Svakīya
Svarūp
Svāstika
Svastikāsana
Svataḥprāmāṇya
Svayambhū

Svayambhū
  Images
Tagore Jayantī
Tāla
Tāṇḍava
Ṭaṅka
Tanmātras
Tāraka
Tārakeśvar
Tarjinī Hasta
Tarpaṇa
Telī
Thākur
Thaṇḍāī
Ṭīka
Tirruppāvai
Tīrtha
Tīrthayātrā
Tīrukkuṟal
Tirunāvukkaraśu
Tirupati/Tirumāla
  Devasthānam
Tiruttontar
  Purāṇam
Tribhaṅga
Trimūrti
Tripuṇḍra
Tripurāri
Triveṇi
Tṛṇāvarta
Tulsī
Tulsidās Jayantī
Tulsī Vivāh
Tuṅgnāth
Turīya
Tvāṣṭṛ
Tyāg
Udāna
Udāsī
Ūddālaka Aruni
Udgātṛ
Ulaṭbāṁsī
Umā
Upacāra

Upadāna
Upādhi
Upamāna
Upanayana
  Saṁskāra
Upāsaka
Upāsana
Upavāsa
Ūrdhvabāhu
Ūrdhvapuṇḍra
Ūrdhvaretas
Utkuṭikāsana
Utsava Mūrti
Uttara Mīmāṁsā
Uttarāyana
Vaidyanāth
Vaikuṇṭha
Vaitaraṇī
Vājapeya
Vallī
Vālmīki
Vālmīki Jayantī
Vāmācāra
Vāmana Avatār
Vanamālin
Vānaprastha
Varadā Hasta
Varāha Avatār
Varkāri
Varṇa
Varuṇa
Vastradhārī
Vāsudeva
Vāsuki
Vāta
Vātsalya Bhāva
Vāyu
Vedaṅga
Vedānta
Vedānta Sūtras
Vedārambha
  Saṁskāra
Vellāla
Veṇu

Vetāla
Vibhūti
Vidyādhāra
Vidyārambha
  Saṁskāra
Vihāra
Vijñāneśvara
Vimāna
Vīnā
Vinatā
Vindhyavāsinī
Viparītakhyāti
Vīra
Vīrabhadra
Vīragal
Vīrāsana
Virāṭa
Viśiṣṭhādvaita
  Vedānta

Viṭhoba
Viṭṭhala
Viṭṭhalnāth
Vivāha
  Saṁskāra
Vivaraṇa
  Advaita
Vivartavāda
Vivasvān
Vrātya
Vṛtra
Vyākaraṇa
Vyākhyāna
  Mudrā
Vyāna
Vyāpti
Vyās
Vyāsa

Yādava
Yādunandana
Yajamāna
Yajña
Yājñavalkya
Yājñavalkya
  Smṛti
Yajñopavit
Yathākhyāti
Yātrā
Yātri
Yayāti
Yoga Mudrā
Yoganidrā
Yoga Sūtras
Yoginī Ekādaśī
Yogmāyā

Bibliography

Abbott, Justin E., trans. *Bahina Bai: A Translation of Her Autobiography and Verses.* Delhi: Motilal Banarsidass, 1985.

—. *The Life of Eknath.* Delhi: Motilal Banarsidass, 1981.

—. *The Life of Tukaram.* Delhi: Motilal Banarsidass, 1980.

Abbott, Justin E., and Narhar R. Godbole, trans. *Stories of Indian Saints: Translation of Mahipati's Marathi Bhaktavijaya.* Delhi: Motilal Banarsidass, 1982.

Adriel, Jean. *Avatar: The Life Story of the Perfect Master.* Santa Barbara, CA: J.F. Rowny Press, 1947.

Allchin, F. Raymond. *The Archaeology of Early Historic South Asia: The Emergence of Cities and States.* New York: Cambridge University Press, 1995.

—, trans. *Kavitavali.* London: Allen and Unwin, 1964.

Alston, A. J., trans. *The Devotional Poems of Mirabai.* Delhi: Motilal Banarsidass, 1980.

—. *The Naiskarmya Siddhi of Sri Suresvara.* London: Shanti Sadan, 1959.

Andersen, Walter K., and Shridhar D. Damle. *The Brotherhood in Saffron: The Rashtriya Swayamsevak Sangh and Hindu Revivalism.* Boulder, CO: Westview Press, 1987.

Archer, W. G. *Indian Painting.* New York: Oxford University Press, 1957.

—. *Indian Painting in Bundi and Kotah.* London: H. M. Stationery Office, 1959.

—. "Pahari Miniatures: A Concise History." *Marg,* Vol. 28, No. 2, 1975, pp. 3–44.

Avalon, Arthur (Sir John Woodroffe). *Shakti and Shakta.* New York: Dover Publications, 1978.

Babb, Lawrence. *The Divine Hierarchy: Popular Hinduism in Central India.* New York: Columbia University Press, 1975.

—. *Redemptive Encounters: Three Modern Styles in the Hindu Tradition.* Berkeley, CA: University of California Press, 1987.

—. "Sathya Sai Baba's Miracles." *Religion in India.* Ed. T. N. Madan. New York: Oxford University Press, 1991.

—. "Sathya Sai Baba's Saintly Play." *Saints and Virtues.* Ed. John Stratton Hawley. Berkeley, CA: University of California Press, 1987.

Babineau, Edmour J. *Love of God and Social Duty in the Ramcharitmanas.* Delhi: Motilal Banarsidass, 1979.

Baird, Robert D., ed. *Religion in Modern India.* 3rd ed. New Delhi: Manohar, 1998.

Bakker, Hans. *Ayodhya.* Groningen: E. Forsten, 1986

Barz, Richard Keith. *The Bhakti Sect of Vallabhacarya.* Faridabad, India: Thomson Press, 1976.

Basham, Arthur Llewellyn. *History and Doctrines of the Ajivikas, a Vanished Indian Religion.* Delhi: Motilal Banarsidass, 1981.

——. *The Origins and Development of Classical Hinduism.* New York: Oxford University Press, 1991.

——. *The Wonder That Was India: A Survey of the History and Culture of the Indian Sub-Continent Before the Coming of the Muslims.* New York: Taplinger, 1968.

Basu, Tapan, et. al. *Khaki Shorts and Saffron Flags: A Critique of the Hindu Right.* New Delhi: Orient Longman, 1993.

Bayly, Christopher Alan. *Indian Society and the Making of the British Empire.* New York: Cambridge University Press, 1988.

——. *The Raj: India and the British, 1600–1947.* London: National Portrait Gallery, 1990.

——. *Rulers, Townsmen and Bazaars: North Indian Society in the Age of British Expansion, 1770–1870.* New York: Cambridge University Press, 1983.

Bharati, Swami Agehananda. *The Tantric Tradition.* Westport, CT: Greenwood Press, 1977.

Biruni, Abu Rayhan. *Alberuni's India.* Abridged. Trans. Edward C Sachu. Ed. Ainslee Embree. New York: W. W. Norton and Co., 1971.

Björkman, James Warner. *Fundamentalism, Revivalists, and Violence in South Asia.* New Delhi: Manohar, 1988.

Brent, Peter Ludwig. *Godmen of India.* London: Allen Lane, 1972.

Briggs, George Weston. *Gorakhnath and the Kanphata Yogis.* Delhi: Motilal Banarsidass, 1973.

Brooks, Douglas Renfrew. *The Secret of the Three Cities: An Introduction to Hindu Sakta Tantrism.* Chicago: University of Chicago Press, 1990.

Brough, J. "Soma and Amanita Muscaria." *The Bulletin of the School of Oriental and African Studies,* Vol. 34, 1971, pp. 331–362.

Brown, W. Norman. "The Metaphysics of the Truth Act." *Mélanges D'Indianisme à la Mémoire de Louis Renou.* Paris: E. de Boccard, 1968.

Bumiller, Elizabeth. *May You Be the Mother of a Hundred Sons: A Journey Among the Women of India.* New York: Random House, 1990.

Burghart, Richard. "The History of Janakpur." *Kailash,* Vol. 6, No. 4, 1978, pp. 257–284.

Callewaert, Winand, trans. *The Hindi Biography of Dadu Dayal.* Delhi: Motilal Banarsidass, 1988.

——. *The Sarvangi of Gopaldas: A Seventeenth Century Anthology of Bhakti Literature.* New Delhi: Manohar, 1993.

——. *The Sarvangi of the Dadupanthi Rajab.* Leuven: Departement Oriëntalistiek, Katholieke Universiteit, 1978.

Callewaert, Winand, and Peter G. Friedlander, trans. *The Life and Works of Raidas.* New Delhi: Manohar, 1992.

Callewaert, Winand, and Mukund Lath. *The Hindi Padavali of Namdev: A Critical Edition of Namdev's Songs with Translation and Annotation.* Delhi: Motilal Banarsidass, 1989.

Carman, John Braisted. *The Theology of Ramanuja: An Essay in Interreligious Understanding.* New Haven, CT: Yale University Press, 1974.

Chakravarti, Janardana. *Bengal Vaishnavism and Sri Chaitanya.* Calcutta: Asiatic Society, 1975.

Chandra, Pramod. *Elephanta Caves, Gharapuri: A Pictorial Guide.* Bombay: Bhulabhai Memorial Institute, 1970.

Chattopadhyaya, Debiprasad. *Science and Society in Ancient India.* Calcutta: Research India Publications, 1977.

Clothey, Fred. "Pilgrimage Centers in the Tamil Cultus of Murukan." *Journal of the American Academy of Religion,* Vol. 40, No. 1, 1972, pp. 79–85.

Coburn, Thomas B. *Devi Mahatmya: The Crystallization of the Goddess Tradition.* Delhi: Motilal Banarsidass, 1984.

Coomaraswamy, Ananda. *Yaksas.* New Delhi: Munshiram Manoharlal, 1971.

Coulson, Michael, trans. *Three Sanskrit Plays.* New York: Penguin Books, 1981.

Courtright, Paul. *Ganesa: Lord of Obstacles, Lord of Beginnings.* New York: Oxford University Press, 1985.

Coward, Harold, and K. Kunjunni Raja, eds. *The Philosophy of the Grammarians.* Princeton, NJ: Princeton University Press, 1990.

Craven, Roy C. *Indian Art: A Concise History.* London: Thames and Hudson, 1997.

Daniel, E. Valentine. *Fluid Signs: Being a Person on the Tamil Way.* Berkeley, CA: University of California Press, 1984.

Dasgupta, Shashibhushan B. *Obscure Religious Cults.* Calcutta: Firma KLM Private Limited, 1962.

Dass, Nirmal. *Songs of Kabir from the Adi Granth.* Albany, NY: SUNY Press, 1991.

De, Sushil Kumar. *Early History of the Vaishnava Faith and Movement in Bengal, from Sanskrit and Bengali Sources.* Calcutta: Firma K. L. Mukhopadhya, 1961.

Dehejia, Vidya, trans. *Antal and Her Path of Love: Poems of a Woman Saint from South India.* Albany, NY: SUNY Press, 1990.

Deleury, G. A. *The Cult of Vithoba.* Poona, India: Deccan College Postgraduate and Research Institute, 1960.

Dhavamony, M. *Love of God According to Saiva Siddhanta: A Study in the Mysticism and Theology of Saivism.* Oxford, England: Clarendon, 1971.

Dimmitt, Cornelia, and J. A. B. van Buitenen, eds. and trans. *Classical Hindu Mythology: A Reader in the Sanskrit Puranas.* Philadelphia: Temple University Press, 1978.

Dimock, Edward C., Jr. *The Place of the Hidden Moon: Erotic Mysticism in the Vaisnava-Sahajiya Cult of Bengal.* Chicago: University of Chicago Press, 1989.

Dimock, Edward C., Jr., and Denise Levertov, trans. *In Praise of Krishna: Songs from the Bengali.* Chicago: University of Chicago Press, 1981.

Dumont, Louis, "A Folk Deity of Tamil Nad: Aiyanar, the Lord." *Religion in India.* Ed. T. N. Madan. Delhi: Oxford University Press, 1991.

——. *Homo Hierarchicus: The Caste System and Its Implications.* Chicago: University of Chicago Press, 1980.

Eck, Diana. *Banaras: City of Light.* New York: Columbia University Press, 1999.

——. *Darsan: Seeing the Divine in India.* Chambersburg, PA: Anima, 1985.

Egnor, Margaret Thrice. "The Changed Mother, or What the Smallpox Goddess Did When There Was No More Smallpox." *Contributions to Asian Studies XVIII,* 1984, pp. 24–43.

Entwistle, A. W. *Braj: Centre of Krishna Pilgrimage.* Groningen, Netherlands: Egbert Forsten, 1987.

——. "Vaishnava Tilakas—Sectarian Marks Worn by Worshipers of Visnu." *IAVRI,* Bulletin 11 and 12, 1982.

Erndl, Kathleen. *Victory to the Mother: The Hindu Goddess of Northwest India in Myth, Ritual, and Symbol.* New York: Oxford University Press, 1993.

Eschmann, Anncharlott, Hermann Kulke, and Gaya Charan Tripathi. *The Cult of Jagannath and the Regional Tradition of Orissa.* New Delhi: Manohar, 1978.

Fairservis, Walter Ashlin. *The Roots of Ancient India.* Chicago: University of Chicago Press, 1975.

Feldhaus, Anne. "Bahina Bai: Wife and Saint." *Journal of the American Academy of Religion,* Vol. 50, 1982, pp. 591–604.

——. *The Religious System of the Mahanubhav Sect.* New Delhi: Manohar, 1983.

Fischer, Louis. *Gandhi: His Life and Message for the World.* New York: New American Library, 1954.

Frawley, David. *The Myth of the Aryan Invasion of India.* New Delhi: Voice of India, 1994.

Fuller, C. J. "Hindu Temple Priests." *Religion in India.* Ed. T. N. Madan. Delhi: Oxford University Press, 1991.

Gait, E. A. *A History of Assam.* Calcutta: Thacker, Spink, 1963.

Gandhi, Mohandas K. *An Autobiography: The Story of My Experiments with Truth.* Boston: Beacon Press, 1993.

Ghurye, G. S. *Indian Sadhus.* Bombay: Popular Book Depot, 1964.

Gold, Ann Grodzins. *Fruitful Journeys: The Ways of Rajasthani Pilgrims.* New York: Oxford University Press, 1988.

Gold, Daniel. "Organized Hinduisms: From Vedic Truth to Hindu Nation." *Fundamentalisms Observed.* Eds. Martin Marty and R. Scott Appleby. Chicago: University of Chicago Press, 1991.

Goldman, Robert. "Karma, Guilt, and Buried Memories: Public Fantasy and Private Memory in Traditional India." *Journal of the American Oriental Society,* Vol. 105, No. 3, 1985, pp. 413–426

Gopal, Sarvepalli. *Anatomy of a Confrontation: The Babri Masjid-Ramjanmabhumi Issue.* New York: Viking, 1991.

Goswami, Satsvarupdas Dasa. *Prabhupada: He Built a House In Which the Whole World Could Live.* Los Angeles: Bhaktivedanta Book Trust, 1983.

Goswami, Shrivatsa. "Radha: The Play and Perfection of Rasa." *The Divine Consort: Radha and the Goddesses of India.* Eds. John Stratton Hawley and Donna Wulff. Boston: Beacon Press, 1986.

Graham, Bruce Desmond. *Hindu Nationalism and Indian Politics: The Origins and Development of the Bharatiya Jana Sangh.* New York: Cambridge University Press, 1990.

Grierson, Sir George, and Lionel D. Barnett. *Lalla Vakyani, or The Wise Sayings of Lalded, a Mystic Poetess of Ancient Kashmir.* London: Royal Asiatic Society, 1920.

Gross, Robert Lewis. *The Sadhus of India: A Study of Hindu Asceticism.* Jaipur, India: Rawat Publications, 1992.

Hawley, John Stratton. *At Play with Krishna: Pilgrimage Dramas from Brindivan.* Princeton, NJ: Princeton University Press, 1981.

——. *Krishna: The Butter Thief.* Princeton, NJ: Princeton University Press, 1983.

——. "Krishna's Cosmic Victories." *Journal of the American Academy of Religion*, Vol. 47, No. 2, 1979, pp. 201–221.

——. "Morality Beyond Morality in the Lives of Three Hindu Saints." *Saints and Virtues.* Ed. John Stratton Hawley. Berkeley, CA: University of California Press, 1987.

——. *Surdas: Poet, Singer, Saint.* Seattle, WA: University of Washington Press, 1984.

Hawley, John Stratton, and Mark Juergensmeyer, trans. *Songs of the Saints of India.* New York: Oxford University Press, 1988.

Hawley, John Stratton, and Donna Wulff, eds. *Devi: Goddesses of India.* Berkeley, CA: University of California Press, 1996.

——. *The Divine Consort:Radha and the Goddesses of India.* Boston, MA: Beacon Press, 1986.

Hein, Norvin. *The Miracle Plays of Mathura.* New Haven, CT: Yale University Press, 1972.

Hess, Linda, and Shukdev Singh, trans. *The Bijak of Kabir.* San Francisco: North Point Press, 1983.

Hill, W. Douglas P., trans. *The Holy Lake of the Acts of Rama.* Bombay: Oxford University Press, 1971.

Hooper, John Stirling Morley. *Hymns of the Alvars.* New York: Oxford University Press, 1929.

Hsuan Tsang. *Si-yu-ki: Buddhist Records of the Western World.* Trans. Samuel Beal. Delhi: Oriental Books Reprint Corp, 1969.

Hume, Robert Ernest, trans. *Thirteen Principal Upanisads*. New York: Oxford University Press, 1965.

Humes, Cynthia. "The Goddess of the Vindhyas in Banares." *Living Banaras: Hindu Religion in Cultural Context*. Eds. Cynthia Ann Humes and Bradley R. Hertel. Albany, NY: SUNY Press, 1993.

Ingalls, Daniel H. H., trans. *Sanskrit Poetry*. Cambridge, MA: Belknap Press of Harvard University Press, 1968. pp. 281–98.

——."Cynics and Pasupatas: The Seeking of Dishonor," *Harvard Theological Review* 55, 1962.

Isherwood, Christopher. *Ramakrishna and His Disciples*. New York: Simon and Schuster, 1965.

Jacobsen, Doranne. "Golden Handprints and Redpainted Feet: Hindu Childbirth Rituals in Central India." *Unspoken Worlds: Women's Religious Lives*. Eds. Nancy Falk and Rita M. Gross. Belmont, CA: Wadsworth/Thomson Learning, 2000.

Jacobsen, Doranne, and Susan S.Wadley. *Women in India: Two Perspectives*. New Delhi: Manohar, 1992.

Jaffrelot, Christophe. *The Hindu Nationalist Movement in India*. New York: Columbia University Press, 1996.

Jaini, Padmanabh S. "Sramanas: Their Conflict with Brahmanical Society." *Chapters in Indian Civilization: A Handbook of Readings to Accompany Lectures in Indian Civilization*. Rev. ed. Ed. Joseph Elder. Dubuque, IA: Kendall/Hunt, 1970.

Jayakar, Pupul. *Krishnamurti: A Biography*. San Francisco: Harper & Row, 1986

Jayaprasad, K. *The RSS and Hindu Nationalism: Inroads in a Leftist Stronghold*. New Delhi: Deep and Deep Publications, 1991.

Jindel, Rajendra. *Culture of a Sacred Town*. Bombay: Popular Prakashan, 1976.

Jones, Kenneth W., *Arya Dharm: Hindu Consciousness in 19th-Century Punjab*. Berkeley, CA: University of California Press, 1976.

——. "The Arya Samaj in British India, 1875–1947." *Religion in Modern India*. 3rd ed. Ed. Robert D. Baird. New Delhi: Manohar, 1998.

——. "Politicized Hinduism: The Ideology and Program of the Hindu Mahasabha." *Religion in Modern India*. 3rd Ed. Robert D. Baird. New Delhi: Manohar, 1998.

Juergensmeyer, Mark. *Radhasoami Reality: The Logic of a Modern Faith*. Princeton, NJ: Princeton University Press, 1991.

——. "Saint Gandhi." *Saints and Virtues*. Ed. John Stratton Hawley. Berkeley, CA: University of California Press, 1987.

Kakar, Sudhir. "Gandhi and Women." *Intimate Relations: Exploring Indian Sexuality*. Chicago: University of Chicago Press, 1990.

——. *Shamans, Mystics, and Doctors: A Psychological Inquiry into India and Its Healing Traditions*. Chicago: University of Chicago Press, 1991.

Kane, Pandurang Vaman, trans. *A History of Dharmasastra: Ancient and Mediæval Religious and Civil Law in India.* 2nd ed. Poona, India: Bhandarkar Oriental Research Institute, 1968.

Kapur, Anaradha. *Actors, Pilgrims, Kings, and Gods: The Ramlila at Ramnagar.* Calcutta: Seagull Books, 1990.

Kar, Bijayananda. *The Theories of Error in Indian Philosophy: An Analytical Study.* Delhi: Ajanta Publications, 1978.

Karve, I. B. "On the Road." *Journal of Asian Studies*, Vol. 22, No. 1, 1962, pp. 587–602.

Khokar, Mohan. *Traditions of Indian Classical Dance.* New Delhi: Clarion Books, 1984.

Kinsley, David R. *Hindu Goddesses: Visions of the Divine Feminine in the Hindu Religious Tradition.* Berkeley, CA: University of California Press, 1986.

——. *The Sword and the Flute: Kali and Krsna: Dark Visions of the Terrible and the Sublime in Hindu Mythology.* Berkeley, CA: University of California Press, 1975.

Kjaerholm, Lars. "Myth and Fascination in the Aiyappu Cult: A View from Fieldwork in Tamil Nadu." *South Asian Religion and Society.* Ed. Asko Parpola, Bent Smidt Hansen. London: Curzon Press, 1986.

Knipe, David M. "Sapindikarana: The Hindu Rite of Entry into Heaven." *Religious Encounters with Death.* Ed. Frank E. Reynolds and Earle H. Waugh. University Park, PA: Pennsylvania State University Press, 1977.

Kolenda, Pauline. "Purity and Pollution." *Religion in India.* Ed. T. N. Madan. New York: Oxford University Press, 1991.

Kramrisch, Stella. *The Presence of Shiva.* Philadelphia: Philadelphia Museum of Art, 1981.

Kripal, Jeffrey. *Kali's Child: The Mystical and the Erotic in the Life and Teachings of Ramakrishna.* Chicago: University of Chicago Press, 1995.

Kripalani, Krishna. *Rabindranath Tagore: A Biography.* Calcutta: Visva-Bharati, 1980.

Larson, Gerald, and Ram Shankar Bhattacharya, eds. *Samkhya: A Dualist Tradition in Indian Philosophy.* Princeton, NJ: Princeton University Press, 1987.

Lavan, Spencer. "The Brahmo Samaj: India's First Modern Movement for Religious Reform." *Religion in Modern India.* 3rd ed. Ed. Robert D. Baird. New Delhi: Manohar, 1998.

Lochtefeld, James G. "The Vishva Hindu Parishad and the Roots of Hindu Militancy." *Journal of the American Academy of Religion*, Vol. LXII, No. 2, 1994. pp. 587–601.

Lorenzen, David. *Kabir Legends and Ananta-Das's Kabir Parachai.* Albany, NY: SUNY Press, 1991.

——. *The Kapalikas and the Kalamukhas: Two Lost Saivite Sects*. Berkeley, CA:University of California Press, 1972.

——. "Traditions of Non-Caste Hinduism: The Kabir Panth." *Contributions to Indian Sociology*, Vol. 21, No. 2, 1987.

——. "Warrior Ascetics in Indian History." *Journal of the American Oriental Society*, Vol. 98, No. 1, 1978, pp. 61–75.

Lutgendorf, Philip. *The Life of a Text: Performing the Ramcaritmanas of Tulsidas*. Berkeley, CA: University of California Press, 1991.

Madan, T. N., ed. *Religion in India*. New York: Oxford University Press, 1991.

Mahadevan, T. M. P. *Ramana Maharshi: The Sage of Arunachala*. London: Allen and Unwin, 1977.

Marglin, Frederique Apffel. "Time Renewed: Ratha Jatra in Puri." *Religion in India*. Ed. T. N. Madan. New York: Oxford University Press, 1991.

——. *Wives of the God-King: The Rituals of the Devadasis of Puri*. New York: Oxford University Press, 1985.

Marriot, McKim. "The Feast of Love." *Krishna: Myths, Rites, and Attitudes*. Ed. Milton Singer. Chicago: University of Chicago Press, 1966.

——."Hindu Transactions: Diversity Without Dualism." *Transaction and Meaning: Directions in the Anthropology of Exchange and Symbolic Behavior*. Ed. Bruce Kapferer. Philadelphia: Institute for the Study of Human Issues, 1976.

Mathur, K. S. "Hindu Values of Life: Karma and Dharma." *Religion in India*. Ed. T. N. Madan. Delhi: Oxford University Press, 1991.

McGee, Mary. "Desired Fruits: Motive and Intention in the Votive Rites of Hindu Women." *Roles and Rituals for Hindu Women*. Ed. Julia Leslie. Rutherford, NJ: Fairleigh Dickinson University Press, 1991.

McGregor, R. S. *The Love Songs of Vidyapati*. Delhi: Motilal Banarsidass, 1987.

——, ed. and trans. *The Round Dance of Krishna and Uddhav's Message*. London: Luzac and Company, 1973.

McKean, Lise. *Divine Enterprise: Gurus and the Hindu Nationalist Movement*. Chicago: University of Chicago Press, 1996.

Miller, Barbara Stoller, trans. *The Bhagavad-Gita: Krishna's Counsel in Time of War*. New York: Bantam Books, 1991.

——, trans. *The Hermit and the Love-Thief: Sanskrit Poems of Bhartrihari and Bilhana*. New York: Columbia University Press, 1978.

——, ed. and trans. *The Love Song of the Dark Lord: Jayadeva's* Gitagovinda. New York: Columbia University Press, 1977.

Miller, David. "The Divine Life Society Movement." *Religion in Modern India*. 3rd ed. Ed. Robert D. Baird. New Delhi: Manohar, 1998.

Minor, Robert N. "Sarvepalli Radhakrishnan and 'Hinduism' Defined and Defended." *Religion in Modern India*. 3rd ed. Ed. Robert D. Baird. New Delhi: Manohar, 1998.

Mishra, Vibhuti Bhushan. *Religious Beliefs and Practices of North India During the Early Medieval Period.* Leiden, Netherlands: Brill, 1973.

Mitra, Sarat Chandra. *The Cult of the Sun God in Medieval Eastern Bengal.* New Delhi: Northern Book Centre, 1986.

Mitter, Sara. *Dharma's Daughters: Contemporary Indian Women and Hindu Culture.* New Brunswick, NJ: Rutgers University Press, 1991.

Mokashi, Digambar Balkrishna. *Palkhi: An Indian Pilgrimage.* Trans. Philip C. Engblom. Albany, NY: SUNY Press, 1987.

Morinis, E. Alan. *Pilgrimage in the Hindu Tradition: A Case Study of West Bengal.* New York: Oxford University Press, 1984.

Morrison, Judith. *The Book of Ayurveda: A Holistic Approach to Health and Longevity.* New York: Simon and Schuster, 1995.

Muktananda, Swami. *Play of Consciousness: A Spiritual Autobiography.* 3rd ed. South Fallsburg, NY: SYDA Foundation, 2000.

Muller-Ortega, Paul Eduardo. *The Triadic Heart of Siva: Kaula Tantricism of Abhinavagupta in the Non-Dual Shaivism of Kashmir.* Albany, NY: SUNY Press, 1989.

Nanda, Serena. *Neither Man Nor Woman: The Hijras of India.* 2nd ed. Belmont, CA: Wadsworth Publishing Company, 1999.

Nandimath, Sivalingayya Channabasavayya. *A Handbook of Virasaivism.* 2nd ed. Ed. R.N. Nandi. Delhi: Motilal Banarsidass, 1979.

Nivin, Christine, et al. *India.* 8th ed. Oakland, CA: Lonely Planet, 1998.

O'Flaherty, Wendy Doniger. *Siva: The Erotic Ascetic.* New York: Oxford University Press, 1981.

——, ed. *Karma and Rebirth in Classical Indian Traditions.* Berkeley, CA: University of California Press, 1980.

—— and Brian K. Smith, trans. *The Laws of Manu.* New York: Penguin Books, 1991.

Pandey, Raj Bali. *Hindu Samskaras: A Socio-Religious Study of the Hindu Sacraments.* 2nd ed. Delhi: Motilal Banarsidass, 1969.

Parmanand, M. A. *Mahamana Madan Mohan Malviya.* Varanasi, India: Banaras Hindu University, 1985.

Parry, Jonathan. "Ghosts, Greed and Sin: The Occupational Identity of the Benares Funeral Priests." *Man,* Vol. 15, 1980, pp. 88–111.

Pfaffenberger, Bryan. "The Kataragama Pilgrimage." *Journal of Asian Studies,* Vol. 28, No. 2, 1979. pp. 253–70.

Pocock, David F. "The Evil Eye." *Religion in India.* Ed. T. N. Madan. New York: Oxford University Press. 1991.

Potter, Karl H., ed. *Advaita Vedanta up to Samkara and His Pupils.* Princeton, NJ: Princeton University Press, 1981.

——. *Presuppositions of India's Philosophies.* Westport, CT: Greenwood Press, 1972.

Potter, Karl H., and Sibajiban Bhattacharyya, eds. *Indian Philosophical Analysis: Nyaya-Vaisesika from Gangesa to Raghunatha Siromani.* Princeton, NJ: Princeton University Press, 1992.

Radhakrishnan, Sarvepalli. *An Idealist View of Life*. New York: AMS
    Press, 1981.
Radhakrishnan, Sarvepalli, and Charles A. Moore, eds. *A Sourcebook in
    Indian Philosophy*. Princeton, NJ: Princeton University Press, 1957.
Raghavan, A. Shrinivasa. *Nammalvar*. New Delhi: Sahitya Akademi, 1975.
Raghavan, V., ed. *The Ramayana Tradition in Asia*. New Delhi:
    Sahitya Akademi, 1980.
Raheja, Gloria Goodwin. *The Poison in the Gift: Ritual, Presentation, and the
    Dominant Caste in a North Indian Village*. Chicago: University of
    Chicago Press, 1988.
Rajaram, Navaratna S., and David Frawley. *The Vedic Aryans and the Origins
    of Civilization: A Literary and Scientific Perspective*. 2nd ed. New
    Delhi: Voice of India, 1997.
Ramanujan, A. K., trans. *Hymns for the Drowning: Poems for Visnu*.
    Princeton, NJ: Princeton University Press, 1981.
——, trans. *The Interior Landscape: Love Poems from a Classical Tamil
    Anthology*. New York: Oxford University Press, 1994.
——. *Speaking of Siva*. New York: Penguin Books, 1973.
Rangachari, K. *The Sri Vaisnava Brahmans*. Madras, India: Government
    Press, 1931.
Rao, T. A. Gopinatha. *Elements of Hindu Iconography*. New York: Garland
    Publishing, 1981.
Rawson, Philip S. *The Art of Tantra*. Greenwich, CT: New York Graphic
    Society, 1973.
Reynolds, Frank, and Earle Waugh, eds. *Religious Encounters with Death:
    Insights from the History and Anthropology of Religions*. University
    Park, PA: Pennsylvania State University Press, 1977.
Rowland, Benjamin. *The Art and Architecture of India: Buddhist-Hindu-
    Jain*. 3rd ed. New York: Penguin Books, 1971.
Salomon, Richard, trans. *The Bridge to the Three Holy Cities*. Delhi: Motilal
    Banarsidass, 1985.
Saraswati, Dayanand. *Autobiography of Swami Dayanand Saraswati*. 2nd
    ed. Ed. K. C. Yadav. New Delhi: Manohar, 1978.
Sardesai, Govind Sakharam. *A New History of the Marathas*. 2nd ed. Delhi:
    Munshiram Manoharal Publishers, 1986.
Sarkar, Jadunath. *A History of the Dasanami Naga Sanyasis*. Allahabad,
    India: Sri Panchayati Mahanirvani Akhara, 1958.
Sawyer, Dana. "Monastic Structure of Banarsi Dandi Sadhus." *Living
    Banaras: Hindu Religion in Cultural Context*. Eds. Bradley R. Hertel
    and Cynthia Ann Humes. Albany, NY: SUNY Press, 1993.
Sax, William. *Mountain Goddess: Gender and Politics in a Himalayan
    Pilgrimage*. New York: Oxford University Press, 1991.
Schilpp, Paul A. *The Philosophy of Sarvepalli Radhakrishnan*. New York:
    Tudor Publishing Company, 1952.

Schomer, Karine, and W. H. McLeod. *The Sants: Studies in a Devotional Tradition of India.* Berkeley, CA: Berkeley Religious Studies, 1985.

Seely, Clinton, and Leonard Nathan, trans. *Grace and Mercy in Her Wild Hair: Selected Poems to the Mother Goddess.* Prescott, AZ: Hohm Press, 1999.

Sharma, Arvind. "Swami Dayananda Sarasvati." *Religion in Modern India.* 3rd ed. Ed. Robert D. Baird. New Delhi: Manohar, 1998.

Shea, David, and Anthony Troyer, trans. *The Dabistan, or, School Of Manners.* Paris: Allen and Co., 1843.

Shinn, Larry. *The Dark Lord: Cult Images and the Hare Krishnas in America.* Philadelphia: Westminster Press, 1987.

Shulman, David Dean. *Tamil Temple Myths: Sacrifice and Divine Marriage in the South Indian Shaiva Tradition.* Princeton, NJ: Princeton University Press, 1980.

Siegel, Lee. *Fires of Love—Waters of Peace: Passion and Renunciation in Indian Culture.* Honolulu: University of Hawaii Press, 1983.

——. *Net of Magic: Wonders and Deceptions in India.* Chicago: University of Chicago Press, 1991.

Singer, Milton, ed. *Krishna: Myths, Rites, and Attitudes.* Chicago: University of Chicago Press, 1966.

Singh, Jaideva. *Pratyabhijnanahrdayam.* Delhi: Motilal Banarsidass, 1982.

Stanley, John M. "Special Time, Special Power: The Fluidity of Power in a Popular Hindu Festival." *Journal of Asian Studies*, Vol. XXXVII, No. 1, 1977, pp. 27–43.

Temple, R. C. *The Word of Lalla, the Prophetess.* Cambridge, England: Cambridge University Press, 1924.

Thapar, Romila. *Interpreting Early India.* New York: Oxford University Press, 1992.

Tripathi, Bansi Dhar. *Sadhus of India: The Sociological View.* Bombay: Popular Prakashan, 1978

Tuck, Donald R. "Rabindranath Tagore: Religion as a Constant Struggle for Balance." *Religion in Modern India.* 3rd Ed. Robert D. Baird. New Delhi: Manohar, 1998.

Upadhyaya, Ganga Prasad, trans. *Light of Truth: An English Translation of Svami Dayanand's Satyartha Prakasa.* Allahabad, India: Kala Press, 1960.

Vaidyanathan, Kunissery Ramakrishnaier. *Pilgrimage to Sabari.* Bombay: Bharatiya Vidya Bhavan, 1978.

Van Buitenen, J. A. B., and Cornelia Dimmitt, trans. *Classical Hindu Mythology: A Reader in the Sanskrit Puranas.* Philadelphia: Temple University Press, 1978.

Veer, Peter van der, *Gods on Earth: The Management of Religious Experience and Identity in a North Indian Pilgrimage Centre.* Atlantic Highlands, NJ: Athlone Press, 1988.

Vatsayana. *The Complete Kama Sutra: The First Unabridged Modern Translation of the Classic Indian Text by Vatsyayana*. Trans. by Alain Daniélou. Rochester, VT. : Park Street Press, 1994.

Vaudeville, Charlotte. *Barahmasa in Indian Literature: Songs of the Twelve Months in Indo-Aryan Literature*. Delhi: Motilal Banarsidass, 1986.

——, trans. *Kabir*. Oxford, England: Clarendon Press, 1974.

Vivekananda, Swami. *The Complete Works of Swami Vivekananda*. Calcutta: Advaita Ashrama, 1970.

Warrier, Gopi. *The Complete Illustrated Guide to Ayurveda, the Ancient Indian Healing Tradition*. Rockport, MA: Element, 1997.

Wasson, Robert Gordon. *Soma: Divine Mushroom of Immortality*. New York: Harcourt Brace Jovanovich, 1971.

The Wedding of the Goddess. South Asia Center of the University of Wisconsin at Madison, 1976. Film.

Whaling, Frank. *The Rise in the Religious Significance of Rama*. Delhi: Motilal Banarsidass, 1980.

White, Charles S. J., trans. *The Caurasi Pad of Sri Hit Harivams*. Honolulu: University Press of Hawaii, 1977.

White, David Gordon. *The Alchemical Body: Siddha Traditions in Medieval India*. Chicago: University of Chicago Press, 1996.

——. "Alchemy: Indian Alchemy." *Encyclopedia of Religion*. Ed. Mircea Eliade. New York: Macmillan Publishing Company, 1993.

Williams, George M. "The Ramakrishna Movement: A Study in Religious Change." *Religion in Modern India*. 3rd Ed. Robert D. Baird. New Delhi: Manohar, 1998.

——. "Swami Vivekananda." *Religion in Modern India*. 3rd ed. Ed. Robert D. Baird. New Delhi: Manohar, 1998.

Williams, Raymond Brady. *A New Face of Hinduism: The Swaminarayan Religion*. New York: Cambridge University Press, 1984.

Wirz, Paul. *Kataragama: The Holiest Place in Ceylon*. Trans. Doris Berta Pralle. Colombo: Lake House Investments, 1966.

Yocum, Glenn. *Hymns to the Dancing Siva: A Study of Manikkavacakar's Tiruvacakam*. New Delhi: Heritage, 1982.

——. "Shrines, Shamanism, and Love Poetry: Elements in the Emergence of Popular Tamil Bhakti." *Journal of the American Academy of Religion*, Vol. 41, No. 1, 1973, pp. 3–17.

Yogananda, Paramahansa. *Autobiography of a Yogi*. Los Angeles: Self-Realization Fellowship, 1997.

Zelliot, Eleanor. "Chokamela and Eknath: Two Bhakti Modes of Legitimacy for Modern Change." *Journal of Asian and African Studies*, Vol. 15, Nos. 1–2, 1980, pp. 136–156.

Zvelebil, Kamil. *Tamil Literature*. Leiden, Netherlands: Brill, 1975.

A

Aham Brahmasmi, **17**, 113, 408
Ahamkar, **17–18**, 129, 224, 408, 415, 588
Ahimsa, **18**, 41, 63
Ahir, **19**
Aihole, **19**, 51, 751
Aims of Life, **19**, 189, 222, 223, 262, 288, 340, 342, 443, 536, 545. *See also* Life
Aippasi, **19**, 685
Airavata, **19**. *See also* Elephant
Aiteraya Brahmana, **20**, 123, 626
Aiyanar, **20**
Aiyappa, 20, **20–21**, 364, 410, 443, 616
Aja Ekadashi, **21**, 93, 218, 227
Ajamila, **21**
Ajatashatru, **21**, **21–22**, 117
Ajita Keshakambalin, **22**, 430. *See also* Philosophers
Ajivika school, philosophy, **22**, 226, 258, 478, 639
Ajna Chakra, **22**, 137. *See also* Chakras
Akasha, **22–23**, 217, 220
Akbar, **23**, 25, 29, 70, 163, 273, 396, 422, 442
Akhand Path, **23**
Akhara, **23–24**, 26, 35, 69, 97, 140, 474
Akhyati, **24**, 223, 378, 516
Akkadevi, **24**
Akrura, **24**
Akshakumara, **24**, 418
Akshamala, **24–25**
Akshar Purushottam Samstha, **25**, 521, 626
Akshaya Trtiya, **25**, 227, 501
Akshaya Vata, **25–26**, 29
Alakananda River, **26**, 77, 95, 184, 242, 323, 340, 353, 416, 510, 576, 577
Alakhiya Akhara, **26–27**
Alambhusha, **27**
Alamkaras, **27**, 363

Alandi, **27**, 321, 739
Alberuni, 26, **28**
Alberuni's India (Biruni), 28
The Alchemical Body (White), 28, 437, 565, 669
Alchemy, **28**, 153, 564, 668
  Dhatuvada, **192–193**
  mercury, 28, 153, 193, 246, 324, **436**, **436–437**, 486, 564, 669, 771
"Alchemy" (White), 193
Alidhasana, **28**
Allahabad, 25, **29**, 52, 141, 188, 239, 265, 339, 379, 433, 474, 526, 591, 594, 603, 710
  Magh Mela, **398–399**
  Nasik Mela, **463–464**
Allama Prabhu, **29**, 391, 402
Allchin, F. Raymond, 302, 713
Alston, A.J., 440, 673
Alvars, **29–30**, 37, 115, 135, 185, 200, 260, 377, 431, 457, 459, 466, 470, 490, 508, 515, 586, 644, 685, 695, 698, 702, 703, 704, 705, 728, 746. *See also* Poets
Amalaka, **30**
Amalaki Ekadashi, **30**, 219, 227, 509
Amarkantak, **30**, 463
Amarnath, **30–31**
Amarnath cave, 356
Amaru, **31–32**
Amaruka, **32**
Amarushatakam, 31
Amarushatakam, **32**
Amavasya, 394, 659. *See also* Moon
Amba, **32**, 111, 628, 664
Ambakeshvar, **32**
Ambalika, **32**, 33, 111, 194, 210, 496, 610, 749
Ambarisha, **32–33**
Ambedkar, Dr. Bhim Rao, **33**, 236, 407
Ambika, 32, **33**, 111, 139, 194, 449, 496, 610, 749

Bahula Chauth, **79–80**, 93, 227
Baiga, **80**
Baijnath, **80–81**
Bairagi Naga, 24, 59, **81**, 197, 232, 452, 571, 577, 592, 732. *See also* Naga
    Digambara Naga, 40, **197**, 232, 476
    dwaras, 215
    groups, 40, 123–134
        Nirmohi Anis, **476**
        Nirvani Ani, **476**
        Shri Sampraday group, 145, **643–644**
Baird, Robert D., 58, 126, 179, 283, 307, 516, 544, 553, 576, 637, 682, 768
Baisakh, **81**, 87, 128, 613, 729
    festivals, 25, 81, 230, 380, 443, 462, 501, 632, 651
Baisakhi, festival, **81**, 227
Baithak, **81–82**
Bajrang Dal, **82**
Baka, **82**
Bakasur, **82**, 110
Bakker, Hans, 74
Baksheesh, **82**
Balabhadra, **82–83**, 164, 308, 534, 567, 665
Balaji, 51, **83**, 435
Balakrishna, **83**, 149
Balarama, 24, **83–84**, 176, 184, 193, 249, 575
    epithets, 82, 269, 595
Bali, 39, **84**, **84–85**, **85**, 196, 368, 551, 557, 711
Bana, dramatist, **85**, 276, 349, 540
Bana linga, **85**. *See also* Linga
Banaras (Eck), 699
Bana, poet, **85**
Bania, **85–86**
Banjara, **86**
Banking, **86**
    moneylending, 85, 86

Barahmasa, **86**
Barahmasa in Indian Literature (Vaudeville), 86
Barat, **87**
Barnett, Lionel D., 387
Barsana, **87**, 544
Baruthani Ekadashi, 81, **87**, 218, 227
Barz, R. K., 540, 646, 735
Basavanna, poet, **87–88**, 185, 314, 390, 402
Basham, Arthur Llewellyn, 22, 94, 119, 226
Basohli, **88**, 439, 488. *See also* Painting
Basu, Tapan et al., 182, 255, 279, 566, 762
Bath, Mohenjo-Daro, **88**, 298–299
Baudhayana, sage, 48, **88**, 192, 339, 640
Bayly, C. A., 86, 444, 696
Beal, Samuel, 290
Begampura, **88**
Begging, 36, **88–89**, 121, 349, 726, 729
Begram, **89**
Bel, **90**
Belagave, **90**
Bells, 246
Belur, **90**, 269, 289, 353
Belur Math, **90**
Benares, 16, 21, 36, 70, **90–91**, 96, 102, 197, 202, 240, 462, 562, 616
    Kabirpanth, **329**
    Kashi, **356**
    Manikarnika Ghat, 91, 161, **419–420**
    names of, 73
    Varanasi, 90, **739**
Benares Hindu University, **91**, 414
Bengal Vaishnavism and Sri Chaitanya (Chakravarti), 136
Bengali, **91**, 184
Betel, **91–92**
Bhadrakali, **92**, 165, 315, 347, 370, 606, 742

Bhadrapada, 46, **93**, 131, 503, 544, 583, 612, 692
   festivals, 21, 37, 79–80, 218, 227, 237–238, 314, 483, 502, 574
Bhadrasana, **93**
Bhagabhadra, **93**
Bhagavad Gita, 47, 54, 67, **93–94**, 143, 234, 321, 322, 370, 486, 516, 532, 623, 637, 656, 695, 698
The Bhagavad-Gita (Miller), 94
Bhagavan, **94**
Bhagavata, **94**, 493, 731
Bhagavata Purana, 33, **94–95**, 112, 143, 219, 276, 370, 460, 516, 533, 646, 665, 673, 718, 731
Bhagirath, 44, **95**, 198, 238, 310, 350, 365
Bhagirath, King, 239
Bhagirathi, **95–96**
Bhagirathi River, 26, 184, 240, 242, 243
Bhairava, **96**, 108, 119, 121, 201, 221, 252, 323, 349, 413, 719
Bhairava akhara, **96**
Bhairava Jayanti, **96**, 227
Bhairavaprakasha, **96–97**
Bhairavi, **97**, 409, 563
Bhaiya Duj, **97**, 549
Bhajan, **97**
Bhakta, 4, 5, 9, 13, 24, 51, 70, **97–98**, 522, 523, 529, 540, 542, 566, 584, 616
Bhaktamal, **98**, 100, 409, 451, 460, 463
Bhaktavijaya, **98**
Bhaktavijaya, 99, 409
Bhakti, 29, 31, 32, 87, **98–99**, 402, 451, 540, 644
Bhakti poetry, 9, 64, 86, 98, 100, 102, 137, 164, 180, 231, 249, 372, 409, 437, 460, 467, 470, 562–563. *See also* Poetry
   bharud, **107**
   chaupai, **146**, 437

   doha, **202**, 437
   Nanddas, 64, **460**
Bhaktililamrta, 98, 409
Bhaktililamrta, **99**
Bhaktimarga, 93, **100**, 321, 352
Bhaktirasabodhini, **100**, 528
The Bhakti Sect of Vallabhacharya (Barz), 540, 646, 735
Bhamati Advaita, 49, **100–101**
Bhamati school, 487
Bhandara, **101**
Bhandarkar Oriental Research Institute, 101, **101**
Bhandarkar, R. G., **101**
Bhang, **101–102**, 207, 279, 287, 694. *See also* Drugs
Bhanita, **102**
Bharadvaja, 70, **102**, 112, 206, 245, 357
Bharat Mata, **105**
Bharata, **102**, **103**, 151, 174, 329, 460, 467, 555, 621
Bharatanatyam, dance, **103–104**, 126, 146, 147, 170, 420, 443, 466, 484
Bharati Dashanami, 64, **104**, 113, 173, 603
Bharati, Swami Agehananda, 45, 116, 166, 381, 411, 414, 423, 432, 446, 492, 524, 593, 667, 676, 689
Bharatiya Janata Party, 13, 76, **104–105**, 159, 283, 314, 561, 566, 611, 633, 653, 762
Bharatmilap, **105–106**
Bharavi, **106**, 403
Bhartrhari, poet, **106**, 261, 363, 662, 719
Bhartrprapancha, **106–107**, 109. *See also* Philosophers
Bharud, **107**, 220
Bhashya, **107**, 109. *See also* Philosophers
Bhaskara, 106, **107–108**

Chakras, 75, **137**, 231, 257, 278,
    381, 452, 467, 486, 489, 511,
    582, 624, 635, 666, 675, 680,
    703. *See also* Tantra; Yoga
    ajna, **22**, 137, 666
    anahata, **34**, 137, 666
    ida nadi, **293**, 452
    manipura, 137, **420**, 666
    muladhara, 137, 381, **448–449**,
    666
    pingala nadi, 452, **511**, 667, 675
    shrichakra, 117, 587
    sushumna, 381, 452, 667, **675**
    svadhishthana, 137, 666, **677**
    Vishnu's chakra, 622, 624, 667
    vishuddha, 137, 666, **761**
Chakravarti, Janardana, 136
Chakravyuha, **138**
Chakravyuha battle formation, 2
Chalukya Dynasty, 19, 24, **138**,
    289, 306, 377, 409, 462, 490,
    507, 530, 565, 659
Chamar group, 88, **138**, 720
Champaran, **138–139**
Chamunda, **139**, 449, 638
Chanakya, **139**, 142, 446
Chandas, **139**, 187, 339, 403, 449,
    476, 629, 769
Chandella Dynasty, **140**, 188, 266,
    346, 365, 396
Chandi, **140**
Chandidas, poet, **140**
Chandika, **140**, 468
Chandiprakasha, **140–141**
Chandogya Upanishad, **141**, 226,
    253, 525, 609, 649, 691, 717, 722
Chandra Gupta I, **141**, 591
Chandra Gupta II, **141**, 265, 719, 752
Chandra, Pramod, 221
Chandramati, **142**, 275
Chandrayana, **142**, 271, 723
"The Changed Mother" (Egnor), 632
Chapters in Indian Civilization
    (Elder), 61, 639

Charaka, **142**
Charaka Samhita, 75, 142. *See*
    also Ayurveda
Charaka Samhita, **142–143**
Charanadas, **143**, 647
Charanadasi, **143**, 647
Charanamrta, 34, **143**
Charas, **143**, 148, 207, 279, 305, 581
Charity. *See* Dana
Charvaka school, **143**
Chataka, **144**, 162
Chatterjee, Bankim Chandra, 35,
    91, **144**, 599
Chatti, **144–145**
Chattopadhyaya, Debiprasad,
    143, 675
Chatuh-Sampradayi Nagas, 81,
    145, 164, 215. *See also* Nagas
Chaturbhujdas, poet, 64, **145**
Chaturmas, 187, 219
Chaturmas Vrat, 61, **145–146**, 227
Chau dance, 103, **146**, 170
Chaupai, poetry, 116, **146**, 202,
    272, 437
Chaurasi Vaishnavan ki Varta, **146**,
    254, 275, 672
Chauri, **146**
Chayagrahi, **146–147**
Chera Dynasty, **147**, 643
Chidambaram, 115, **147**, 170, 198,
    464, 685
Childhood rites, 44, **147–148**, 591.
    See also Samskaras
Chidvilasananda, Swami, **147**,
    447, 681
Child marriage, 16, 57, **148**, 179.
    See also Marriage
Child widows, **148**
Chillum, **148–149**
    safai, 148, **581**
Chin Mudra, **149**
Chinmayanand, Swami, **149**
Chinmoy, Shri, **149**
Chinnamasta, **149**, 150, 409

Dasgupta, Shashibhushan B., 28, 190, 193, 257, 437, 582, 669

Dashamukha, **173**

Dashanami, **173-174**

Dashanami Sanyasis, 14, 24, 59, 61, 74, 78, 104, 120, 173–174, 216, 232, 258, 458, 499, 519, 534, 570, 623, 625, 691. *See also* Naga

  Dandi Sanyasis, **172**

  Divine Life Society, **199**

  Giri Dashanamis, **247–248**

  Kamakotipith, **341–342**

  Madhusudana Saraswati, **396**

  Parvata Dashanamis, **503**

  Sagara Dashanami, **581–582**

  Shringeri Math, 104, 113, 229, 260, 325, 341, 354, 431, 534, 603, 642, **643**

  subgroups, 15–16, 17, 26–27, 35, 36, 49–50, 64, 171, 325, 452, 534

    Anandawara, **36**, 113

    Bharati, 64, **104**

    Bhogawara, **111–112**, 113

    Bhuriwara, **113**

    Kitawara, 113, **368–369**

    Saraswati, 64, **603**

    Tirtha, 64, **699**

  Tota Puri, **706–707**

  Vana Dashanami, **737–738**

Dashanami Sanyasi akhara, 30

Dasharatha, King, 74, 103, **174–175**, 308, 329, 360, 369, 384, 545, 555, 574, 627

Dashavatar, **175**

Dashavatara Stotra, **175–176**, 249, 308, 542

Dass, Nirmal, 329

Dasya, 67

Dasyus, 56, **176**

Dattatreya, 37, **176**, 209, 249, 323, 405, 726

Datura, **176–177**, 207, 305. *See also* Drugs

Daughters, 80, 165, 166, 168, **177–178**, 302, 614, 661, 664. *See also* Women

in families, 225

as gift, 347–348

for sale, 203

Day. *See also* Calendar; Year

structure of, **178**

Dayabhaga, **178–179**, 303, 319, 440, 664, 751

Dayanand Saraswati, Swami, 57, 158, **179**, 646

Day of Brahma, **180**, 338, 409, 423

De Sushil, Kumar, 5, 136, 243, 258, 259

Death, liberation and, 91

Deathbed rites, **180**

Death rites, *See* Antyeshti Samskara

Debts, 14, 427

  three debts, **695**

Deccan, 24, 51, 117, 138, **180**, 366, 407, 442, 530, 565

Deccan College, 101

Deer, **180–181**, 263, 425. *See also* Animals

Dehejia, Vidya, 38

Dehu, **181**

Deities, **181**. *See also* Village deities

Deleury, G. A., 152, 220, 257, 312, 322, 459, 496, 712, 740, 765

Demons, 14, 20, 34, 38, 63, 73, 82, 108, 139, 139–140, 146–147, 163, 169, 171, 172, 178, **181**, 186, 211, 217, 228, 269, 284, 328, 333, 365, 395, 449, 545, 557, 573, 583, 619, 647, 689, 711, 748. *See also* Rakshasa

  Bali, **84**

  Dhenuka, **193**

  forms, 112

  Kaitabha, 186, 252, **331**

  paishacha marriage, 49, 427, 488

Deogarh, **182**

Naisthika, 135, **456**
Naivedya, **456**, 482, 720
Naiyayika school, 47, 223, **456**
Nakshatra, 130, 151, 327, **456**, 458,
        491, 492, 660, 685
Nakula, 67, 210, 397, 400, **456**,
        495, 582
Nala, King, 6, 168–169, **456–457**, 680
Naladiyar, 218, **457**, 701
Nalayira Divyaprabandham, **457**,
        459, 466, 704, 777
Nalayira Prabandham, 29, 200
Namakarana samskara, 147,
        457–458, 591
Namarupa, **458**
Namaskara, **458**, 720
Nambudiri brahmins, 205, **458**,
        570, 623
Namdev, poet, 9, 36, 98, 164, 312,
        459, 494, 596, 708, 732
Nammalvar, poet, 29, 99, 431,
        459, 704
Nammalvar (Raghavan), 459
Nanak, Guru, 355, 459
Nanak Jayanti, **459**
Nanda, 84, 315, 344, 371, **459**, 742
Nanda Devi, **459–460**
Nanda Dynasty, 142
Nanda, Serena, 132, 281
Nanddas, 64, **460**
Nanddas (McGregor), 718
Nandi, 129, **460**, 640
Nandigrama, 103, **460–461**
Nandimath, Sivalingayya
        Channabasavayya, 391
Nara-Narayana, **461**
Narada, 191, **461**, 577
Narada smrti, **461**
Narak Chaturdashi, 227, 355, **461**
Narasimha avatar. *See* Man-Lion
        avatar
Narasimha Jayanti, 81, **462**
Narasimhavarman, 399, 530
Narasimhavarman I, **462**, 490

Narasimhavarman II, **462**
Narayana, 21, 367, 423, **462**, 542,
        605, 705, 711. *See also* Vishnu
Narayana Bhatta, scholar,
        462–463, 710
Narmada River, 30, 134, 142, 186,
        250, 270, 396, 410, **463**, 482
Narsi Mehta, poet, 98, **463**
Narsingh Jayanti, 227
Nasik, 52, 250, 251, 379, **463**
Nasik district, 32
Nasik Mela, **463–464**
Nastika, **464**, 604
Natal horoscope, 246, 288, 294,
        324, 326, 436, **464**, 513, 574,
        669. *See* Zodiac
Natamandira, architecture, 390,
        454, **464**, 484
Nataraja, 103, 128, 147, 168, 220,
        464–465, 635
    temple, 198
Nath, 70, **466**
Nathamuni, poet, 29, 99, 457, **466**
Nathan, Leonard, 563
Nathdwara, **466**, 540, 641, 646
Nathpanthi, 14, 59, 61, 255,
        257, 278, 322, 328, 347, 432,
        466, **466–467**, 553, 672,
        719, 734
Nationalist Movement in India
        (Jaffrelot), 77
Natya, dance, 171, **467**, 479
Natya shastra, 626
Natyashastra, 103, **467**, 626
Navadurga, 140, 208, **467–468**, 469
Navadvip, 135, 434, **468**
Navaratri, 67, 112, 136, 140, 208,
        212, 227, 336, 455, 467,
        468–469, 550, 562, 613, 620
Navyanyaya school, **469–470**,
        586, 731
Nayachandra Suri, **470**
Nayak, Tirumalai, 398
Nayak Dynasty, 398, **470**, 701

Rock edicts, 63, 125, 366, 510, **575**.
  See also Inscriptions
Rohini, 83, 166, 184, **575**, 595, 660
*Roles and Rituals for Hindu
  Women* (Leslie), 768
The Roots of Ancient India
  (Fairservis), 88, 300
*The Round Dance of Krishna and
  Uddhav's Message*
  (McGregor), 460
Rowland, Benjamin, 366
Roy, Ram Mohan, 125, 148, **575–576**
The RSS and Hindu Nationalism
  (Jayaprasad), 566
Rta, 44, 289, 472, **576**, 741
Rtvij, 536, **576**
Rudra, 188, 301, **576**, 577, 633,
  649, 722
Rudraksha, 25, 244, 412, **576**
  Ekmukhi Rudraksha, **219**
Rudranath, 340, 494, **576–577**
Rudraprayag, 26, 416, **577**
Rudra sampraday, 145, **577**,
  732, 760
Rukmini, 371, 518, **577**
Rulers, Townsmen and Bazaars
  (Bayly), 86, 444
Rupa, 136

S

Sabarmati Ashram, 263, 578
Sabarmati River, **578**
Sacchidananda, 35, **578**, 584, 593,
  604, 645, 706
Sachau, Edward, 28
Sacred ash, **578**
Sacred sites, **578**. *See also* Tirthas
Sacred thread, 120, 187, 263,
  314, 452, **578–579**, 614, 720,
  722, 776
Sacrifice, 7, 15, 20, 29, 33,
  122, 165, 323, 523, 536,
  538, **579**, 629. *See also*
  Animal sacrifice

agnishtoma, **16–17**
bahiryaga, **79**
blood, 341
Brahmayajna, **124**
cult, 535–536
fire, 57
homa, 52, 186, **288**, 526
human, 41, 108, 139, **290–291**,
  335, 413
internal, **305**
pitryajna, **513**
tarpana, 228, 513, **691**
Vedic origins, 16, 50, 60
Sacrificial rites, 722
Sadachara, **579**, 631
Sadasatkhyati, 223, **579**. *See also*
  Theory of error
Sadashiva, **579–580**
Sadhana, **580**
Sadharana dharma, 189, **580**, 593
Sadhu, 60, **580**
Sadhubela, **580–581**
The Sadhus of India (Gross), 61
Sadhya, 47, **581**, 721
Safai, 148, **581**
Sagar Island, 239
Sagar, King, 44, 58, 95, 198, 238,
  296, 365, **581**
Sagar, Ramanand, **554**, 558
Sagara, 173
Sagara Dashanami, **581–582**. *See
  also* Dashanami Sanyasis
Sages. *See also* Philosophers
  Agastya, **13–14**, 231, 296,
    392, 455
  Apastamba, **48**, 88, 192, 339, 640
  Atri, 37, 40, **70**, 102, 112, 245,
    357, 370, 426, 530, 574
  Baudhayana, 48, **88**, 192,
    339, 640
  Bhrgu, 70, 102, **112–113**, 120,
    245, 357, 574, 581
  Brhaspati, **127**, 696
  Dadhichi, 27, **163**

857

Vastradhari, **742**

Vasudeva, 83, 184, 315, 370, **742, 743,** 783

Vasuki, 316, 452, 705, **743**

Vata, 25, 75, 142, 350, 513, 675, **743**

Vatsalya bhava, 83, 442, **743**

Vatsyayana, sage, 342, 481, 528, 529, **743–744**

Vaudeville, Charlotte, 86, 329

Vayu, 42, 83, 109, 262, 271, 495, **744**. *See also* Wind

Veda, 13, 17, 30, 74, **744**

Vedangas, 140, 325, 476, 629, **744–745**, 769

    Kalpa, **339**

Vedanta, 77, 124, 537, 544, 554, 588, 726, **745**. *See also* Advaita Vedanta; Philosophy

    Dvaitadvaita Vedanta, **213**

    Dvaita Vedanta, **213–214**

Vedanta Deshika, **745**

Vedanta school, 456

Vedanta Society, **745–746**

Vedanta Sutras, 77, 623, **746**

Vedarambha samskara, 591, **746**

Vedas, 7, 7–8, 10, **12–13**, 16, 18, 36, 41, 44, 48, 49, 50, 56, 57, 60, 69, 77, 113, 191, 386, 438, 441, 449, 464, 472, 515, 518, 526, 532, 537, 538, 548, 576, 578, 582, 604, 612, 637, 646, 656, 657, 715, 722, 741. *See also* Rg Veda; Upanishads

    Atharva Veda, 36, **69**, 399, 511, 768

    Black Yajur Veda, 48, 88, **118**, 339

    cosmology, 44

    hymns, 159–160

    Sama Veda, 69, 369, **586**, 718

    Samhita, 14–15, 123, **587**

    White Yajur Veda, 118, **771–772**

    Yajur Veda, 7, 69, 113, 123, 573, 626, **776**

Vedic Aryans and the Origins of Civilization (Frawley), 302

Vegetarianism, 149, 163, 164, 198, 199, **746**. *See also* Eating

Vellala, 740, **746**

Velur, 247, **746–747**

Vena, **747**

Venkateshvara, 83, **747**, 753

    temples, 39, 702

Venu, **747**

Venus, 230, 246, 251, 324, 486, **748**, 771. *See also* Goddess; Planets

Veshara style, architecture, 51, **747–748**

Vetala, 181, **748**

Vibhishana, 181, 557, **748**

Vibhuti, 578, 709, 724, **748–749**

Vichitravirya, King, 32, 33, 111, 194, 496, 610, 625, 628, **749**

Vicious circle, 225, **749**. *See also* Philosophy

Victory to the Mother (Erndl), 139, 149, 325, 455, 638, 733

Vidhi, **749**

Vidura, 289, 535, **749**

Vidyadhara, **749**

Vidyapati, poet, 411, **750**

Vidyarambha samskara, 591, 746, **750**

Vighneshvar, **750**

Vihara, 19, **750–751**

Vijaya, 65, 172, 318, **751**

Vijaya Dashami, **751**

Vijaya Ekadashi, 219, 227, 509, **751**

Vijayanagar Dynasty, 353, 373, 470, 497, 643, 684, 701, **751**

Vijnaneshvara, 440, **751–752**

Vikram Era, 130, 719, **752**

Vikramaditya, King, 336, 403, 507, 719, **752**

Vikramorvashiya, 336, **752**

Village deities, 20, 41, 80, 118, 206, 515, 530, **752–753**

Vimana, **753**

Photo Credits

About the Author

James G. Lochtefeld, Ph.D., holds a B.A. from Colgate University, an M.T.S. from the Harvard Divinity School, an M.A. in Asian languages and literature from the University of Washington, and an M.Phil. and Ph.D. from Columbia University. He is an associate professor of religion at Carthage College in Wisconsin, where he has taught since 1992.

Dr. Lochtefeld specializes in Hinduism and is particularly interested in contemporary Hindu religious life. He did fieldwork for his dissertation in the North Indian pilgrimage town of Haridwar under the guidance of the American Institute of Indian Studies and Delhi University. Aside from Hinduism, his areas of teaching have included the Buddhist tradition in India, China, and Japan; Islam; Chinese religion; and Sanskrit. Lochtefeld was three times named a President's Fellow at Columbia University. In 1990, he received the Charlotte W. Newcombe Fellowship, the most prestigious award for dissertations in religion and ethics. In the summer of 1996, he returned to Haridwar to conduct fieldwork. He was awarded a Senior Research Fellowship by the American Institute of Indian Studies, through which he was able to study the Kumbha Mela, the world's largest religious festival, during a sabbatical leave in Haridwar in the spring of 1998.